Twentieth-Century Science | **Chemistry**

Decade by Decade

Arthur Greenberg

Set Editor: William J. Cannon

Facts On File
An imprint of Infobase Publishing

This book is dedicated to my wife, Susan; our children, David and Rachel; to my parents, Murray and Bella; and Susan's parents, Wilbert and Rena.

CHEMISTRY: Decade by Decade

Facts On File, Inc.
An imprint of Infobase Publishing
132 West 31st Street
New York NY 10001

ISBN-10: 0-8160-5531-9
ISBN-13: 978-0-8160-5531-9

Library of Congress Cataloging-in-Publication Data
Greenberg, Arthur.
Chemistry : decade by decade / Arthur Greenberg.
p. cm. — (Twentieth-century science)
Includes bibliographical references and index.
ISBN: 0-8160-5531-9 (acid-free paper)
1. Chemistry—History—20th century. 2. Chemistry—Study and teaching.
I. Title.
QD15.G74 2007
540.9'04—dc22   2006022920

Facts On File books are available at special discounts when purchased in bulk quantities for businesses, associations, institutions, or sales promotions. Please call our Special Sales Department in New York at (212) 967-8800 or (800) 322-8755.

You can find Facts On File on the World Wide Web at
http://www.factsonfile.com

Text design by Dorothy M. Preston and Kerry Casey
Cover design by Dorothy M. Preston and Salvatore Luongo
Illustrations by Bobbi McCutcheon
Photo research by Elizabeth H. Oakes

Printed in the United States of America

VB FOF 10 9 8 7 6 5 4 3 2 1

This book is printed on acid-free paper.

Contents

Preface

The 20th century witnessed an explosive growth in science and technology—more scientists are alive today than have lived during the entire course of earlier human history. New inventions including spaceships, computer chips, lasers, and recombinant deoxyribonucleic acid (DNA) have opened pathways to new fields such as space science, biotechnology, and nanotechnology. Modern seismographs and submarines have given earth and ocean scientists insights into the planet's deepest and darkest secrets. Decades of weather science, aided by satellite observations and computer modeling, now produce long-term, global forecasts with high probabilities (not certainties) of being correct. At the start of the century, science and technology had little impact on the daily lives of most people. This had changed radically by the year 2000.

The purpose of *Twentieth-Century Science*, a new seven-volume book set, is to provide students, teachers, and the general public with an accessible and highly readable source for understanding how science developed, decade by decade, during the century and hints about where it will go during the early decades of the 21st century. Just as an educated and well-informed person should have exposure to great literature, art, and music and an appreciation for history, business, and economics, so too should that person appreciate how science works and how it has become so much a part of our daily lives.

Students are usually taught science from the perspective of what is currently known. In one sense, this is quite understandable—there is a great deal of information to master. However, very often a student (or teacher) may ask questions such as "How did they know that?" or "Why didn't they know that?" This is where some historical perspective makes for fascinating reading. It gives a feeling for the dynamic aspect of science. Some of what students are taught today will change in 20 years. It also provides a sense of humility as one sees how brilliantly scientists coped earlier with less funding, cruder tools, and less sophisticated theories.

Science is distinguished from other equally worthy and challenging human endeavors by its means of investigation—the scientific method—typically described as

a) observations

b) hypothesis

c) experimentation with controls

d) results, and

e) conclusions concerning whether or not the results and data
   from the experiments invalidate or support the hypothesis.

In practice, the scientific process is not quite so "linear." Many related
experiments may also be explored to test the hypothesis. Once a body of
scientific evidence has been collected and checked, the scientist submits
a paper reporting the new work to a peer-reviewed journal. An impartial
editor will send the work to at least two reviewers ("referees") who are
experts in that particular field, and they will recommend to the editor
whether the paper should be accepted, modified, or rejected. Since expert
reviewers are sometimes the author's competitors, high ethical standards
and confidentiality must be the rule during the review process.

If a hypothesis cannot be tested and potentially disproved by experiment
or mathematical equations it is not scientific. While, in principle, one experiment can invalidate a hypothesis, no number of validating experiments can
absolutely prove a hypothesis to be "the truth." However, if repeated testing, using varied and challenging experiments by diverse scientists, continues to validate a hypothesis, it starts to assume the status of a widely accepted
theory. The best friend a theory can have is an outstanding scientist who
doubts it and subjects it to rigorous and honest testing. If it survives these
challenges and makes a convert of the skeptical scientist, then the theory is
strengthened significantly. Such testing also weeds out hypotheses and theories that are weak. Continued validation of an important theory may give
it the stature of a law, even though it is still called a theory. Some theories
when developed can revolutionize a field's entire framework—these are considered "paradigms" (pronounced "paradimes"). Atomic theory is a paradigm. Advanced about 200 years ago, it is fundamental to understanding the
nature of matter. Other such paradigms include evolution; the "big bang"
theory; the modern theory of plate tectonics, which explains the origin of
mountains, volcanoes, and earthquakes; quantum theory; and relativity.

Science is a collective enterprise with the need for free exchange of
information and cooperation. While it is true that scientists have strong
competitive urges, the latter half of the 20th century witnessed science's
becoming increasingly interdisciplinary. Ever more complex problems, with
increasing uncertainty, were tackled and yet often eluded precise solution.

During the 20th century, science found cures for tuberculosis and
polio, and yet fears of the "dark side" of science (e.g., atomic weapons)
began to mount. Skepticism over the benefits of science and its applications started to emerge in the latter part of the 20th century even as its
daily and positive impact upon our lives increased. Many scientists were
sensitive to these issues as well. After atomic bombs devastated Hiroshima
and Nagasaki, some distinguished physicists moved into the life sciences
and others started a magazine, now nearly 60 years old, *The Bulletin of the
Atomic Scientists*, dedicated to eliminating the nuclear threat and promoting

peace. In 1975, shortly after molecular biologists developed recombinant deoxyribonucleic acid (DNA), they held a conference at Asilomar, California, and imposed voluntary limits on certain experiments. They encouraged adoption of regulations in this revolutionary new field. We are in an era when there are repeated and forceful attempts to blur the boundaries between religious faith and science. One argument is that fairness demands equal time for all "theories" (scientific or not). In all times, but especially in these times, scientists must strive to communicate to the public what science is and how it works, what is good science, what is bad science, and what is not science. Only then can we educate future generations of informed citizens and inspire the scientists of the future.

The seven volumes of *Twentieth-Century Science* deal with the following core areas of science: biology, chemistry, Earth science, marine science, physics, space and astronomy, and weather and climate. Each volume contains a glossary. Each chapter within each volume contains the following elements:

- background and perspective for the science it develops, decade by decade, as well as insights about many of the major scientists contributing during each decade
- black-and-white line drawings and photographs
- a chronological "time line" of notable events during each decade
- brief biographical sketches of pioneering individuals, including discussion of their impacts on science and the society at large
- a list of accessible sources for Additional Reading

While all of the scientists profiled are distinguished, we do *not* mean to imply that they are necessarily "the greatest scientists of the decade." They have been chosen to represent the science of the decade because of their outstanding accomplishments. Some of these scientists were born to wealthy and distinguished families, while others were born to middle- and working-class families or into poor families. In a century marked by two world wars, the cold war, countless other wars large and small, and unimaginable genocide, many scientists were forced to flee their countries of birth. Fortunately, the century has also witnessed greater access to the scientific and engineering professions for women and people of color, and ideally all barriers will disappear during the 21st century.

The authors of this set hope that readers appreciate the development of the sciences during the last century and the advancements occurring rapidly now in the 21st century. The history teaches new explorers of the world the benefits of making careful observations, of pursuing paths and ideas that others have neglected or have not ventured to tread, and of always questioning the world around them. Curiosity is one of our most fundamental human instincts. Science, whether done as a career or as a hobby, is after all, an intensely human endeavor.

Acknowledgments

I wish to acknowledge my parents for their love and for the encouragement they gave to me to pursue my passions. My mother, Bella, took me for my first visit to the American Museum of Natural History. At the age of eight it filled me with awe, wonder, and more than a bit of fear. She also encouraged my explorations of the insects in our small Brooklyn backyard. In 1960 she gamely helped to carefully pick hundreds (if not thousands) of newly hatched praying mantises off the wall of the room I shared with my brother, as we solicitously placed them into cans and jars and deposited them in our backyard. Never having had the opportunity to attend college, she still reads voraciously and writes the occasional poem. My father, Murray, could only afford to attend Brooklyn College, very excellent and tuition-free in the late 1930s and early 1940s. He earned a degree in chemistry in 1942 prior to being drafted into the army, serving as an infantryman in World War II. His career as a chemist, first in pharmaceuticals, then in fabricating commercial crayons, clays, children's watercolor and oil paints, commercial inks, and finally artist-quality oil paints, has filled me with admiration for the intellectual challenges met by countless "bench" chemists who produce affordable, safe, high-quality products. My wife, Susan, whom I met when we were chemistry majors in college, is always optimistic, generous in spirit, incredibly patient, and kind.

I also want to acknowledge a friendship of four decades with Joel F. Liebman, a professor at the University of Maryland, Baltimore County, and, like my father, a gifted Brooklyn College graduate. Joel has been teacher, research collaborator, coauthor, coeditor, friend, and "noodge," when needed, throughout our professional careers. He read most of the manuscript and provided numerous insights, suggestions, and corrections. I have also benefited from discussions with my University of New Hampshire chemistry colleagues. I also wish to express my gratitude to Ms. Elizabeth Oakes, photo researcher, and Ms. Bobbi McCutcheon, the person who produced the original artwork for this book. She has been a gracious collaborator in handling many challenging and unanticipated requests. Facts On File's Frank Darmstadt, Kerry Casey, and Sean Fogle have worked hard to align this book with the other books in the set. Their dedication is both acknowledged and appreciated.

Introduction

Chemistry: Decade by Decade provides an outline of the history of 20th century chemistry. It is written to be accessible to a very broad audience of readers who will, hopefully, enjoy it and partake of the "low-lying fruit" as well as the tasty fruit in the higher branches as their backgrounds and desires to climb the tree permit. The coverage is almost completely non-mathematical and the book is best suited for a reader who is taking or has taken (at some time) a high school or college chemistry course. There is useful and accessible material here for the younger student as well as for college students, teachers, nonscientists, and scientists.

Chemistry is the study of matter and its transformations. It has the most colorful history of any of the sciences, with Asian and Arabic roots in mystical and spiritual alchemy, ancient medicine, metallurgy, and crafts. Some 2,500 years ago Greek philosophers developed a framework of four elements (earth, air, fire, and water) composing all matter. It influenced scientific thought for 2,200 years! The Crusades brought Eastern alchemical thought and practice to Europe. Yin and Yang, Sun and Moon, Man and Woman became "Sulfur" and "Mercury." To these two spiritual essences, Renaissance practitioners added "body" or "Salt" and the concept that these three Principles comprise all matter. The 17th century witnessed the true beginnings of experimental science. In England, Robert Boyle (1627–91) demolished the four ancient elements in his 1661 work *The Sceptical Chymist* but could not explain what an element actually is. Boyle and his fellow countryman Isaac Newton (1643–1727) believed that elements could be transmuted into each other ("lead to gold") and both of these giants of science accepted other alchemical beliefs.

The first real unifying theory of chemistry was developed in the late 17th and early 18th centuries, in Germany, by Johann Joachim Becher (1635–82) and Georg Stahl (1660–1734). Fire had mystified humans since the dawn of time. A "principle of fire" was identified and named phlogiston (Φ). According to this theory, any flammable substance such as charcoal contains Φ, which is released and becomes fully visible as fire. Fresh air is required for fires because fresh air lacks Φ. Fires self-extinguish when the surrounding air becomes saturated with Φ. Metals are also full of Φ and lose it to the air when they "rust" (forming a powdery "calx"). If charcoal (full of Φ) is heated with a metal calx such as iron rust (zero Φ), the Φ is simply transferred and the metal (full of Φ) is formed from the calx and only ash remains where there was charcoal. This useful theory held sway for nearly a century until Carl Wilhelm Scheele (1742–86), in Sweden, and Joseph Priestley (1733–1804), in England, independently discovered the gas that the Frenchman Antoine Lavoisier (1743–94) named oxygen. Lavoisier, the father of modern chemistry, explained combustion and calx formation each as a combination with atmospheric oxygen rather than loss of Φ to the atmosphere. His 1789 *Traité Élémentaire de Chimie* is the most important book in the history of chemistry. Fifteen years later, John Dalton (1766–1844), in England, developed atomic theory but it took a century for physicists (and a few famous chemists) to fully accept it.

The 19th century was a period of specialization as chemistry branched into organic, inorganic, physical, analytical, and biological fields. The development of the periodic table by the Russian Dmitri Mendeleev (1834–1907) in 1869 provided an organizing principle of enormous power. Its fundamental basis would only be understood when quantum physics was united with chemistry during the 20th century. The 20th century was a period of explosive scientific growth. Chemistry would furnish materials that make clothing more affordable, medicines that treat tuberculosis and streptococcus infections and control cancer and AIDS, chemicals that increase crop yield, coolants that add convenience and safety to food storage and air-conditioning. In a century darkened by two world wars, numerous other conflicts large and small, and genocides on a scale unprecedented in human history, chemistry had its own dark side: high explosives, poison gas, and napalm. There were also instances in which chemicals that were initially seen as obvious boons to humanity, such as DDT and the chlorofluorocarbons (CFCs), were found decades later to be very harmful to the environment. At the start of the 20th century atoms were not universally accepted and their nature barely understood. By the end of the 20th century the human genome had been decoded and chemists were fabricating nanochips for computers.

There are many excellent books and other sources for learning about 20th-century chemistry. Many of these are listed at the end of this book, while more specific references are listed at the end of each chapter. Perhaps the best single resource for studying 20th-century chemistry is the collection of Nobel Prize acceptance speeches by and biographies of the laureates themselves. These are available from the official Nobel Committee Web site as well as in print versions listed in the Further Resources chapter at the end of this book. These lectures present backgrounds and contexts of discoveries that do not usually appear in journals and books. While many of the biographies are simply outlines of professional lives, others are highly personal, amusing, and dramatic

One of the challenges in writing this book is to bring some balance to the coverage in each chapter as chemistry continues to grow exponentially with the passing of each decade. The Chemical Abstracts Service (CAS) in Columbus, Ohio, began to abstract research journal papers, patents, and books in 1907. The table on the following page summarizes some statistics reported (*CAS Statistical Summary 1907–2004*) for the final year of each decade through the end of the 20th century.

Growth in Chemistry Papers, Patents, and Books during the 20th Century

Year	Volume #	Papers	Patents	Books
1907	1	7,994	3,853	——
1910	4	13,006	3,754	785
1920	14	13,619	4,432	1,275
1930	24	32,731	21,246	1,169
1940	34	40,624	11,635	1,421
1950	44	47,496	10,063	1,539
1960	54	104,484	27,675	2,096
1970	72, 73	230,902	43,044	2,728
1980	92, 93	407,342	61,998	6,399
1990	112, 113	394,945	91,082	3,490
2000	132, 133	573,469	146,590	5,136

(www.cas.org)

Another measure of the explosion of research activity during the 20th century is the growth in the number of reported chemical substances. CAS lists the number of compounds in its Chemical Registry System starting in 1965. These include organic and inorganic compounds, organometallics, metals, alloys, polymers, and mixtures ("small molecules"). Starting in 1994 CAS began to separately register biological sequences of peptides, proteins, polynucleotides, nucleic acids and their derivatives. The table to follow provides an idea of the exponential growth of registered chemical substances.

Growth in the Reported Number of Substances in the CAS Chemical Registry since the Modern Registry Began in 1965

Specific Year	Substances Registered Starting in 1994 "Small Molecules")	Sequences Registered in Each Specific Year	Total Substances Cumulative (Through Specific Year)
1965	211,935	——	211,934
1966	313,763	——	525,697
1970	288,085	——	1,601,933
1980	353,881	——	5,141,872
1990	663,342	——	10,575,961
1994	641,225	135,987	13,407,968
1995	704,535	481,799	14,594,302
2000	900,128	5,131,250	28,499,942
2004	2,380,404	14,945,656	78,289,324

(687,699 substances indexed prior to 1965 were added retroactively during the years 1984–1990)

(www.cas.org)

CAS keeps a constantly updated registry report of the cumulative number of substances registered (www.cas.org/cgi-bin/regreport.pl). At 7:33 A.M. (eastern standard time) on February 17, 2006, there was a cumulative total of 27,345,897 "small molecules" and 57,213,566 biological sequences for a total cumulative substances count of 84,559,463.

The influence of the revolution in biotechnology is most evident in the incredible growth in protein and nucleic acid sequences aided by robotic and information technologies. The growth rate in articles, patents, books, and reported substances toward the end of the 20th century reflects not only increasing technology and number of scientists but also the rise of new scientific powers in Asia, notably Japan, India, China, Taiwan, and South Korea. The table to follow lists relative contributions to the abstracted chemical literature between 1939 and 2004. In 1939, Asia contributed less than 5 percent of the abstracted chemical literature. In 2004 the four nations listed (Japan, China, India, and South Korea) contributed 28.8 percent of the abstracted chemical literature.

Sources (Percent) of Literature Abstracted in Chemical Abstracts

Nation	1939	1947	1951	1956	1962	1972	1982	1993	2000	2004
United States	27.7%	41.8%	36.6%	28.4%	28.4%	28.0%	27.1%	28.1%	23.8%	23.2%
Japan	4.4	4.4	9.1	10.4	6.9	7.9	10.2	13.3	13.4	11.8
China							1.8	4.3	9.5	12.0
Germany	18.7	3.1	7.9	8.4	8.5		6.2[a]	7.5[a]	7.0[b]	6.2[b]
France	9.1	8.4	6.2	6.0	4.8	4.4	4.1	4.7	4.2	3.7
Italy	3.0	3.8	3.3	4.1	1.5	1.9	2.3	2.6	2.8	3.1
U.K.	14.1[c]	15.6[c]	17.4[c]	13.6[c]	8.6	6.4	5.9	5.7	5.0	4.6
Canada	c	c	c	c	1.1	2.8	2.7	3.2	2.5	2.5
India	c	c	c	c	2.5	2.5	3.3	2.6	2.3	2.6
Australia	c	c	c	c		1.2	1.3	1.4	1.4	1.4
USSR	11.1	8.2	6.3	13.5	23.0	24.0	17.6	d	d	d
Russia	d	d	d	d	d	d	d	4.5	4.5	3.7
South Korea								0.3	1.4	2.0	2.4

(www.cas.org)

a. West Germany and East Germany percentages added together.

b. One total value for Germany.

c. British Commonwealth (including U.K., Canada, India, Australia, others) combined.

d. The USSR divided into individual countries after 1989. Only Russian data reported.

One of the joys in writing this book is revisiting the decades of my own education in chemistry (starting in the 1960s). Chemists have a tradition of taking pride in their scientific genealogy, the tradition of laboratories in which their chemical forebears were trained. My "roots" trace back to the great 19th-century German organic chemist, Justus Liebig (1803–73). My 20th-century genealogy begins with Richard Willstätter (1872–1942) in Germany, the 1915 Nobel laureate in chemistry. Willstätter's magnificent contributions to structural organic chemistry culminated with deciphering the structure of chlorophyll. The principled Willstätter quit his secure professor's position in Munich in 1924 to protest rising anti-Semitism in Germany. His student, Richard Kuhn (1900–67), would be awarded the 1938 Nobel Prize in chemistry for separating and solving the structures of the carotenes. Kuhn and his student Edgar Lederer (1908–88), working in Heidelberg, reestablished column chromatography as the premier separation technique for complex mixtures. Hitler and the Nazis assumed power in 1932 and Lederer, a Jew, fled Germany in 1933 just four days ahead of the Gestapo raid on his laboratory. Aided by André Lwoff (1902–94), a fellow Kuhn student (and the future 1965 Nobel Prize winner in physiology or medicine), Lederer would escape the concentration camps and arrive in France. In Germany, Kuhn would have to decline the Nobel Prize in 1938. Willstätter himself was forced to flee Germany in 1939 and settled in Switzerland. My own doctoral mentor at Princeton University, Pierre Laszlo (1938–   ), studied with Lederer at the Sorbonne in Paris.

For those readers who wish to take chemical history field trips, the following opportunities are highly recommended. Visit the Chemical Heritage Foundation in Philadelphia and spend a day looking at historical exhibits, artifacts, rare books, and artwork (the Web site is listed at the end of this book). The foundation publishes a beautiful, highly readable (and inexpensive) quarterly magazine, *Chemical Heritage.* Also, visit the Web site specified at the end of this book, which lists more than 50 American Chemical Society National Historic Landmarks that are open to the public. These include Joseph Priestley's home in Northumberland, Pennsylvania, the Polymer Research Institute in Brooklyn, New York, the George Washington Carver site at Tuskegee Institute in Alabama, and others throughout the United States and internationally.

Chemistry is not intended to be the exhaustive and authoritative history of 20th-century chemistry. I have tried to be balanced and inclusive, discussing in the text all Nobel Prize winners in chemistry through 2006 and many in physics and physiology or medicine. My expertise is in the field of organic chemistry. It is fair to say that an inorganic chemist or a physical chemist, for example, might place their emphases somewhat differently. Although there are hundreds of discoveries and scientists included in this book, there are numerous worthy discoveries and distinguished scientists not mentioned.

I end this introduction with some inspirational words about the culture of science offered by Albert Szent-Györgyi (1893–1986), the discoverer of vitamin C, in his 1937 Nobel Prize address. He was born in Hungary, which would be devastated during World War I and dismembered shortly afterward:

> *One circumstance, however, fills me always with the greatest happiness and gratitude, when I look back on my own struggles. From the moment I seized my staff, a novice in search of knowledge, and left my devastated fatherland to tread the wanderer's path—which has not been without its privations—as an unknown and penniless novice, from that moment to the present one, I always felt myself to belong to a great, international, spiritual family. Always and everywhere I found helping hands, friendship, cooperation and international solidarity. I owe it solely to this spirit of our science that I did not succumb, and that my endeavors are now crowned with the highest human recognition, the award of the Nobel Prize.*

1

1901–1910:
Atoms Are Real but *Not* the Smallest Bits of Matter

Physics Begins to Dramatically Impact Chemistry

During the first decade of the 20th century the application of physics to chemistry once and for all established the reality of atoms. Physicists even "weighed" the *electrons* that are now known to govern chemical properties. The discovery of *radioactive* particles (*alpha* [α] and *beta* [β]) led to the earliest perceptions of "*isotopes.*" The remaining two natural *rare earths* were finally separated and identified, completing the *lanthanide series* of chemical *elements*.

Two great discoveries, one in physics and one in chemistry, would foreshadow the paradox of the 20th century. The mass-energy equivalence law ($E = mc^2$), derived by Albert Einstein (1879–1955), accounts for the forces that bind the atomic nucleus, provides the potential for virtually limitless energy, and is the basis for the atomic and hydrogen bombs. In chemistry Fritz Haber (1868–1934) provided humans with one of the greatest imaginable gifts: fixing nitrogen (80 percent of the Earth's atmosphere) to produce fertilizers such as ammonium nitrate in unlimited quantity. The conversion of nitrogen to ammonia led to the inexpensive production of nitric acid. In turn, nitric acid is a key starting material for numerous explosives such as nitroglycerine and trinitrotoluene (TNT) as well as ammonium nitrate. Haber, a patriotic German Jew, would pioneer and advocate the use of poison gas in the "War to End All Wars" during the following decade. He would have to flee Germany when the Nazis assumed power during the 1930s.

Biochemistry, a new "superorganic chemistry," was in its infancy as the structural elements of *proteins* and *nucleic acids* were deciphered and the nature of enzymes explored. The first decade of the 20th century would also witness synthesis of the first "silver bullet" drug: salvarsan, specifically designed to combat syphilis.

The Periodic Table on the Eve and Early Dawn of the Twentieth Century

A modern periodic table and a brief discussion of its organization appear on pages 431ff. Nine new chemical elements were discovered during the final decade of the 19th century (1891–1900). Starting in 1894, with the discovery of argon by the English scientists Lord Rayleigh (John William Strutt) (1842–1919) and William Ramsay (1852–1916), the *"inert"* gases (also termed "rare" or "noble") helium, krypton, neon, xenon, and even the trace radioactive gas radon were discovered in short order. Ramsay received the 1904 Nobel Prize in chemistry and Rayleigh the 1904 Nobel Prize in physics for this work.

There is nothing "rare" about argon since it comprises almost 1 percent of the earth's atmosphere. An adult inhales and exhales half a pound of argon every day. Argon remained undetected because it is colorless, odorless, tasteless, and completely unreactive (inert), thus invisible in all respects unless one suspects its presence (as Rayleigh and Ramsay did) and searches for it. Argon was isolated by carefully removing all water vapor and carbon dioxide from a large air sample, removing oxygen through reaction with red-hot copper, then consuming the nitrogen that remained by combination with hot magnesium. The "argon" that remained actually included three other noble gases, krypton, neon, and

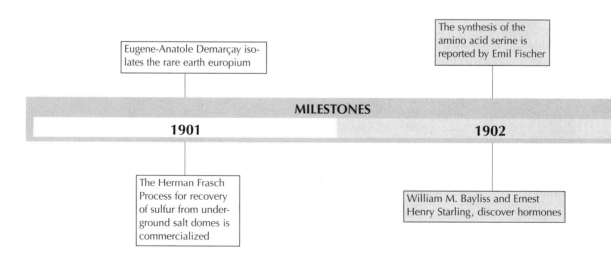

Eugene-Anatole Demarçay isolates the rare earth europium

The synthesis of the amino acid serine is reported by Emil Fischer

MILESTONES

1901

1902

The Herman Frasch Process for recovery of sulfur from underground salt domes is commercialized

William M. Bayliss and Ernest Henry Starling, discover hormones

xenon, which would be isolated during the following four years. An adult inhales and exhales about one ounce of xenon, the least abundant of the rare gases, every four months.

Huge quantities of inert gases in the atmosphere eluded detection because they are physically and chemically "silent." The two radioactive metals, polonium and radium, reported by Marie Curie (1867–1934), Pierre Curie (1859–1906), and Gustave Bémont (1867–1932) in 1898, as well as actinium, discovered by André Debierne (1874–1949) in 1899, had rather "loud voices" for their tiny quantities. One had to use an electroscope to hear these radioactive elements "sing." With the discovery of radioactivity, reported by Henri Becquerel (1852–1908) (Paris) in 1896, the Curies had realized that there was at least one new element in the uranium ore known as pitchblende. First isolating polonium and then radium, they required several tons of pitchblende to obtain 0.0002 pound (0.1 g) of pure radium chloride. Just as Rayleigh and Ramsey "mined" large quantities of atmospheric air for the rare gases, so did the Curies and colleagues effectively mine huge quantities of ore for exceedingly minute quantities of radioactive metals. Becquerel and the Curies shared the 1903 Nobel Prize in physics for their groundbreaking studies on radioactivity. Marie Curie reported elemental radium in 1910 and received the Nobel Prize in chemistry in 1911 for her isolation of radioactive elements. She was the first woman to win a Nobel Prize, the first

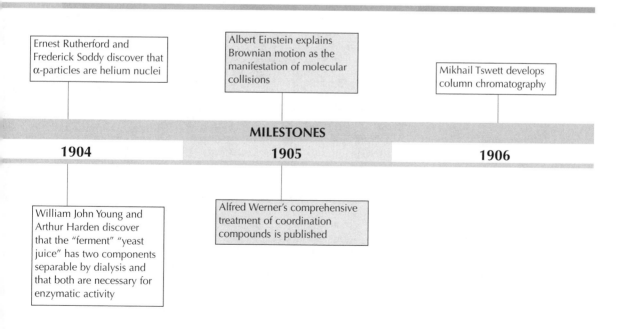

Ernest Rutherford and Frederick Soddy discover that α-particles are helium nuclei

Albert Einstein explains Brownian motion as the manifestation of molecular collisions

Mikhail Tswett develops column chromatography

MILESTONES

1904   **1905**   **1906**

William John Young and Arthur Harden discover that the "ferment" "yeast juice" has two components separable by dialysis and that both are necessary for enzymatic activity

Alfred Werner's comprehensive treatment of coordination compounds is published

scientist to win two Nobel Prizes, and the only scientist to win Nobel Prizes in both chemistry and physics.

On page 6 are two versions of the *periodic table* dating from the mid–1890s, prior to inclusion of the nine elements discovered during the final decade of the 19th century. Missing are the rare gases, the lanthanide series and actinide series, as well as many other elements (see page 434). The first three periods look pretty familiar. But striking is the presence of 12 periods including the zigzag arrangement of elements in each family. This was a very determined (and doomed) attempt to adhere to the rule of octaves first noted some 30 years earlier by William Odling (1829–1921) at Oxford and Dmitri Mendeleev (1834–1907) in St. Petersburg, Russia. The 12-row periodic table attempted to force the transition metals, lanthanides (Ce and so-called Di) and *actinides* (Th and U) into main-group element families to preserve the harmony of the octaves. The second table depicts what was termed the Natural Arrangement of the Elements, advanced by Mendeleev. Di was the abbreviation for the so-called element didymium and chemists would discover that Di was actually a complex mixture of rare earth

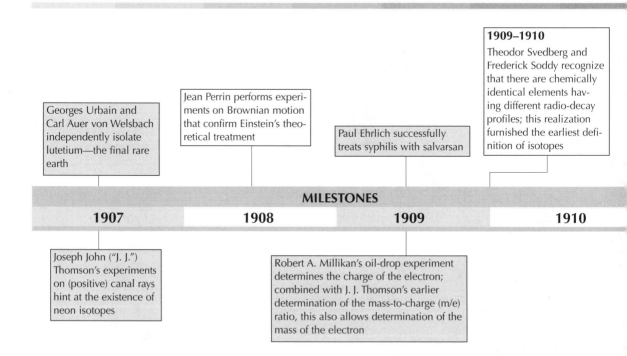

1909–1910
Theodor Svedberg and Frederick Soddy recognize that there are chemically identical elements having different radio-decay profiles; this realization furnished the earliest definition of isotopes

Georges Urbain and Carl Auer von Welsbach independently isolate lutetium—the final rare earth

Jean Perrin performs experiments on Brownian motion that confirm Einstein's theoretical treatment

Paul Ehrlich successfully treats syphilis with salvarsan

MILESTONES

1907 **1908** **1909** **1910**

Joseph John ("J. J.") Thomson's experiments on (positive) canal rays hint at the existence of neon isotopes

Robert A. Millikan's oil-drop experiment determines the charge of the electron; combined with J. J. Thomson's earlier determination of the mass-to-charge (m/e) ratio, this also allows determination of the mass of the electron

elements. Further discussion of the rare earth elements follows in the sidebar below.

The next two figures depict the corresponding periodic table from an edition of the same textbook published early in the first decade of the 20th century. Smaller changes include substitutions of the now-defunct names "glucinum" ("Gl") for beryllium (Be) and "columbium" ("Cb") for niobium (Nb). The most obvious change is the introduction of a new group (Group 0) for the newly discovered inert gases, following Mendeleev's convention for the new family. Since the valences of these gases are zero, placing them at the left-hand side of the periodic table made some sense despite their isolation from the other nonmetals. Radium is included in these tables (although polonium and astatine are not). Redeterminations of atomic masses caused some reversals in order and "Di" was eliminated.

MID-1890s "MENDELEEVIAN" PERIODIC TABLE

Table A

Group	I	II	III	IV	V	VI	VII	VIII
				MH_4	MH_3	MH_2	MH	Hydrogen compounds
Series 1	H							
Series 2	Li 6·98	Be 8·99	B 10·74	C 11·91	N 13·94	O 15·88	F 18·9	
Series 3	Na 22·87	Mg 24·2	Al 26·9	Si 28·2	P 30·8	S 31·82	Cl 35·19	
Series 4	K 38·85	Ca 39·7	Sc 43·8	Ti 47·6	V 50·8	Cr 51·7	Mn 54·6	Fe Ni Co 55·6 58·6 59·4
Series 5	Cu 63·1	Zn 64·9	Ga 69·4	Ge 71·8	As 74·4	Se 78·5	Br 79·36	
Series 6	Rb 84·8	Sr 87·0	Y 88·0	Zr 90·0	Nb 93·5	Mo 95·2	—	Rh Ru Pd 102·0 103·0 104·7
Series 7	Ag 107·13	Cd 111·3	In 112·8	Sn 118·2	Sb 119·4	Te (?) 124·0	I 125·91	
Series 8	Cs 131·9	Ba 136·4	La 137·5	Ce 139·0	Di (?)	—	—	— — —
Series 9	—	—	—	—	—	—	—	
Series 10	—	—	—	—	Ta 181·0	W 182·6	—	Os Ir Pt 189·3 191·7 193·3
Series 11	Au 195·7	Hg 198·9	Tl 202·6	Pb 205·4	Bi 206·4	—	—	
Series 12	—	—	—	Th 230·7	—	U 237·6	—	
	M_2O	MO	M_2O_3	MO_2	M_2O_5	MO_3	M_2O_7	MO_4 Highest salt-forming oxides

MID-1890s "NATURAL ARRANGEMENT" OF THE ELEMENTS

Table B

```
                    H
              (1) Li  Be   B   C   N   O   F  ⎫ Typical periods
              (2) Na  Mg  Al  Si   P   S  Cl  ⎭


              (3) K  Ca  Sc  Ti  V  Cr  Mn Fe  Ni  Co  Cu  Zn  Ga  Ge  As  Se  Br ⎫
              (4) Rb  Sr  Y   Zr  Nb  Mo —  Rh  Ru  Pd  Ag  Cd  In  Sn  Sb  Te  I  ⎪
              (5) Cs  Ba  (La Ce Di) —  —  —  —  —  —  —  —  —  —  —  —  —  ⎬ Double
              (6) —  —  —  —  Ta  W  —  Os  Ir  Pt  Au  Hg  Tl  Pb  Bi  —  —  ⎪ periods
              (7) —  —  —  Th  —  U  —  —  —  —  —  —  —  —  —  —  —  ⎭
```

Even series in table A   Eighth group   Odd series in table A
                          in table A

A) Periodic table in the "Mendeleevian" format dating from mid-1890s; B) same periodic table in more modern "natural order"

Table A

ca. 1907 "MENDELEEVIAN" PERIODIC TABLE

Group	0	I	II	III	IV	V	VI	VII	VIII
					MH_4	MH_3	MH_2	MH	Volatile hydrogen compounds
Series 1		H 1							
Series 2	He 4	Li 6·98	Gl 6·98	B 10·9	C 11·91	N 13·93	O 15·88	F 18·9	
Series 3	Ne 19·9	Na 22·88	Mg 24·18	Al 26·9	Si 28·2	P 30·77	S 31·82	Cl 35·18	
Series 4	A 39·6	K 38·85	Ca 39·7	Sc 43·8	Ti 47·7	V 50·8	Cr 51·7	Mn 54·6	Fe Co Ni 55·5 58·5 58·3
Series 5		Cu 63·1	Zn 64·9	Ga 69·5	Ge 72	As 74·4	Se 78·6	Br 79·36	
Series 6	I 81·2	Rb 84·9	Sr 86·94	Y 88·3	Zr 89·9	Cb 93·3	Mo 95·3	—	Ru Rh Pd 100·9 102·2 105·7
Series 7		Ag 107·11	Cd 111·6	In 114·1	Sn 118·1	Sb 119·3	Te 126·6	I 126·01	
Series 8	Xe 127	Cs 131·9	Ba 136·4	La 137·9	Ce (?) 139·2	—	—	—	— — —
Series 9		—	—	—		—	—	—	
Series 10	—	—	—	—	—	Ta 181·6	W 182·6	—	Os Ir Pt 189·6 191·5 193·3
Series 11		Au 195·7	Hg 198·5	Tl 202·6	Pb 205·35	Bi 206·9	—	—	
Series 12	—	Ra 223·3	—	Th 230·8	—	—	U 236·7	—	— — —
	M_2O	MO	M_2O_3	MO_2	M_2O_5	MO_3	M_2O_7	MO_4 Highest salt-forming oxides	

ca. 1907 "NATURAL ARRANGEMENT" OF THE ELEMENTS

Table B

```
                        H
(1)  He   Li  Gl  B   C   N   O   F  ⎫ Typical periods
(2)  Ne   Na  Mg  Al  Si  P   S   Cl ⎭

(3)  A   K   Ca  Sc  Ti  V   Cr  Mn  Fe  Co  Ni  Cu  Zn  Ga  Ge  As  Se  Br ⎫
(4)  Kr  Rb  Sr  Y   Zr  Cb  Mo  —   Ru  Rh  Pd  Ag  Cd  In  Sn  Sb  Te  I  ⎪
(5)  Xe  Cs  Ba  La  (Ce?)—   —   —   —   —   —   —   —   —   —   —   —   —  ⎬ Double periods
(6)  —   —   —   —   —   Ta  W   —   Os  Ir  Pt  Au  Hg  Tl  Pb  Bi  —   —  ⎪
(7)  —   —   Ra  —   Th  —   U   —   —   —   —   —   —   —   —   —   —      ⎭

        Even series in table A        Eighth group      Odd series in table A
                                       in table A
```

© Infobase Publishing

A) Periodic table in the "Mendeleevian" format dating from middle of the first decade of the 20th century; B) same periodic table in more modern "natural order"

Analysis of Elements by Their Emission Spectra: Enter Quantum Theory

It is true that if one takes a solid object such as a metal and heats it, it will become red hot and eventually white hot. If the white light from the glowing object is focused through a slit and lens and passed through a prism, a continuous *band spectrum*, resembling a rainbow, will be observed on a screen. This is quite similar to the result of collimating sunlight and passing it through a prism onto a screen. However, if a pure metal or its salt is volatilized by heating, there will typically be a glow of a character-istic color in the flame region immediately surrounding the substance.

In 1860, Robert Wilhelm Bunsen (1811–99) and Gustav Robert Kirchhoff (1824–87), working in Heidelberg, published a description of

The Rare Earths Are Really Not So Rare

Two new elements, the rare earths europium (Eu) and lutetium (Lu), were discovered during the first decade of the 20th century. Their discoveries were the final chapters in two mysteries that each lasted more than a century. Throughout the 18th century, the term *earth* was commonly applied to what are now recognized as oxides, as well as carbonates and hydroxides, effectively "earthen materials." The story begins with the discovery in 1787 of a rock by a Swedish army lieutenant in a mine at Ytterby, a location close to Stockholm. He called the mineral "ytterite" and in 1794 Finnish professor Johann Gadolin (1760–1852) analyzed it and identified a new "earth" he named "yttria."

In 1803, the Swedish chemist Johann Jakob Berzelius (1779–1848) and his friend Wilhelm Hisinger (1766–1852) and, independently, the German chemist Martin Heinrich Klaproth (1743–1817) identified a new "earth" which Berzelius and Hisinger named "cerium" after the newly discovered asteroid *Ceres*. In fact, both "yttria" and "ceria" were not pure "earths" but complex mixtures. Generations of chemists spent the 19th century separating them into simpler substances. The two "chemical genealogies" derived from yttria and ceria are shown in the accompanying figure. Ytterite yielded seven lanthanides as well

(continues)

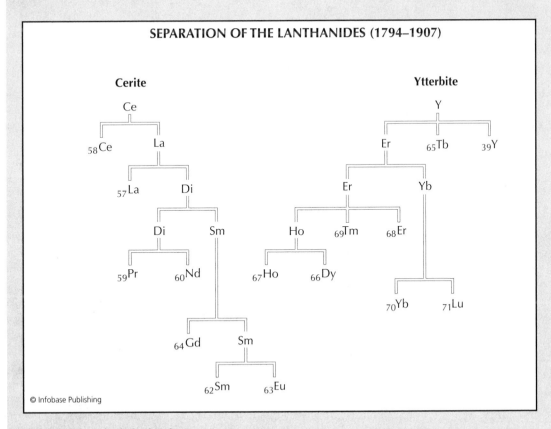

Separation scheme for the lanthanides

(continued)

as yttrium (Y), classified by many (but not always recognized) as a rare earth. Lanthanum (La) is generally considered to be a lanthanide due to its similarity to the rare earths but scandium, which also co-occurs, is not. Cerite provided seven other lanthanides (as well as lanthanum but missing promethium, an artificial element that would be created in the mid-20th century). It was their chemical similarities that made these elements so difficult to isolate. "Didymium" ("Di" in the 1890s periodic table) was found as an impurity in lanthanum (La), itself an impurity in cerium (Ce). However, in its first incarnation "didymium" really included five different rare earths (Pr, Nd, Gd, Sm, and Eu). Even when further purified, its second incarnation included the last three metals of this group. The confusions about which elements were really lanthanides had to await advances in chemical theory more than two decades into the future.

The final isolation from the "cerite tree" occurred in 1901 when Eugene-Anatole Demarçay (1852–1904) reported the separation of europium (Eu). The final isolation from the "ytterbite tree" was reported in 1907 when lutetium (Lu) was separated from the more abundant ytterbium (Yb). The element was discovered by Georges Urbain (1872–1938), at the Sorbonne, and independently by Austrian chemist Carl Auer von Welsbach (1858–1929). Lutetium is named after Lutetia, the ancient name for Paris in Gaul. The abundances (in the earth's crust) of the rare earths make it clear that some are not really so rare. The natural abundance of cerium (Ce), 66.5 parts per million by weight (ppm), is close to that of zinc (70 ppm). The natural abundance of lutetium (Lu) (0.8 ppm), the most elusive of the rare earths, is greater than those of copper (0.6 ppm), silver (0.075 ppm), and gold (0.0043 ppm). It is the difficulty in chemically isolating the individual rare earths, rather than their absolute scarcity, that makes them rare.

When atomic numbers were discovered in 1913 (Chapter 2), it was noted that one element (61) that could fit into the rare earth series was missing. Full understanding of this anomaly would only be achieved in 1945 when the element (named promethium, Pm) was created synthetically and found to be radioactive and short-lived (Chapter 5).

Market prices for metals depend upon demand (rarity, utility, collectibility, and beauty) as well as cost of purification. *Approximate* prices ("pure metals," >99.9 percent; HEFA Rare Earth Canada Co. Ltd, June 2004) indicate that the final two rare earths isolated, Eu ($4,090/lb) and Lu ($2,270/lb), are far more expensive than most of the other rare earths ($13/lb to $48/lb). For comparison's sake, gold costs nearly $10,000/lb as of summer 2006.

their *spectroscope:* an instrument capable of precisely examining the nature of the light produced by substances heated by flames. An early version and a more sophisticated version of their spectroscope are depicted in the accompanying figure. A sample of metal or salt for analysis is suspended into the (nonluminous) flame of a gas-fired Bunsen burner. The intense colored light in the region just above the sample (e.g., green from a sample of nickel) is passed through a collimator tube (entering through a slit and passing through a lens creating parallel light rays), through a hollow glass prism in a box, and then into a telescope through which the viewer sees a colored line (or series of lines) rather than a continuous band spectrum.

The accompanying figure depicts the continuous visible spectrum of the Sun followed by the flame emission spectra of 10 *alkali metals* and *alkaline earth metals* (in black and white rather than color as they appear naturally;

the color ranges are specified at the top of the figure). The alkali metals cesium (Cs) (blue) and rubidium (Rb) (red) were actually discovered by Bunsen and Kirchhoff using their new instrument. The characteristic line spectra for the metals are quite evident from the figure. There is a very singular intense (yellow) band for sodium (Na). It is the reason why a piece

A) Simple version of the ca. 1860 version of the Bunsen-Kirchhoff spectroscope; B) more sophisticated version of the Bunsen-Kirchhoff spectroscope

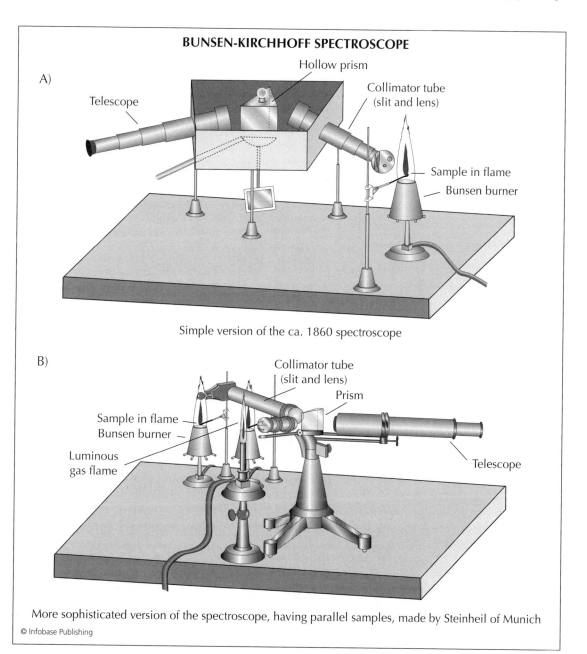

BUNSEN-KIRCHHOFF SPECTROSCOPE

A)

Telescope

Hollow prism

Collimator tube (slit and lens)

Sample in flame

Bunsen burner

Simple version of the ca. 1860 spectroscope

B)

Collimator tube (slit and lens)

Prism

Sample in flame

Bunsen burner

Luminous gas flame

Telescope

More sophisticated version of the spectroscope, having parallel samples, made by Steinheil of Munich

© Infobase Publishing

of glass placed in a flame will produce a strong yellow aura in the flame. Sodium is abundant in glass and a powerful emitter. In the solar spectrum there is a series of dark areas corresponding to lines *missing* from the solar spectrum. These are *Fraunhofer lines* and and the solar spectrum at the top of the figure depicts only the brightest of these. It is now known that lines Fraunhofer labeled "A," "a," and "B" have their origin in the absorption of solar light by O_2 in the Earth's atmosphere. The other Fraunhofer lines depicted in this figure are due to absorption by elements found in the Sun's outer atmosphere (the photosphere). For example, the one strong emission band for sodium corresponds exactly to one of the Fraunhofer lines, mean-

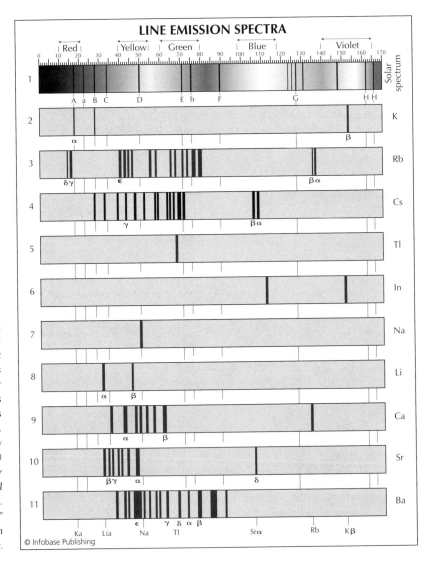

Solar spectrum as well as line emission spectra characteristic of a series of metals (all spectra in black and white rather than color). The lines (bands) of the pure metals are emission lines from each metal. The solar spectrum lines (top) are lines of darkness in the continuous rainbowlike solar spectrum. These Fraunhofer lines (only the most intense are shown) arise from absorption of solar light by the corresponding metal present in the solar photosphere. Fraunhofer lines labeled "A," "a," "B" are due to absorption by O_2 in the Earth's atmosphere.

© Infobase Publishing

ing that sodium occurs in the solar atmosphere. Imagine *that*: chemical analysis of the Sun's atmosphere during the American Civil War!

In 1868, a total solar eclipse provided a unique opportunity to apply the spectroscope to stellar chemistry. At the moment when the Sun was perfectly eclipsed, the solar prominences surrounding the dark disk provided discrete line-emission spectra. Among these was a series of lines that matched no known elements. The discoverer, Joseph Norman Lockyer (1836–1920), postulated the existence of a new chemical element, helium after *Helios* (or Sun). The names of most metals typically end in "ium" or "um" and since most elements are metals helium was first assumed to be a metal and named accordingly. Some 27 years later, helium was identified as a gas emanating from the uranium-containing mineral cleveite by William Ramsay.

The spectroscope was absolutely critical to the separation and analysis of the rare earths described earlier. First, new spectral lines identified new elements. But in situations in which hard-to-separate mixtures were present, the spectroscope also could be used to verify the presence of a mixture and monitor its separation. If a rare earth, initially thought to be pure, was subjected to a purification procedure, the first hints of a mixture might come from seeing specific spectral lines become more intense and others less intense as the mixture is gradually enriched in one metal.

And now a mystery: What is the physical origin of the line spectra that provide unique identities for each of the elements? The first hints were provided by Max Planck (1858–1947), who had to develop an entirely new type of physics to explain a "quiet" paradox in the study of blackbody radiation. A black body is a theoretical construct. In principle, it is an object that absorbs all light (of all wavelengths) impinging upon it and is thus perfectly black. The paradox was treated by Max Planck in 1900 when he suggested that energy is absorbed and emitted in discrete "packets" that he termed "quanta." The "size" of the quantum is:

$$E = h\nu$$

where E is the energy of the quantum, ν is the frequency, and h a constant now called Planck's constant. This fundamentally new idea of "discrete" (or "allowed") quanta would not only explain the origin of atomic spectra, but would also explain the basis of much of the chemistry implicit in the periodic table.

Atoms Are Real: So Say Einstein and Perrin

When chemistry students learn that John Dalton (1766–1844) "discovered" *atoms* in 1803 they leave the lesson happily convinced that the chemistry world was "set right" some two centuries ago and "lived happily ever after." After all, atoms and *molecules* explained a) the law of *conservation of matter*; b) the law of *definite proportions*; c) the law of *multiple proportions*; d) the law of *combining volumes* of gases. Would that things were so simple!

While many chemists accepted atoms and molecules as real entities, many other prominent chemists viewed atomic theory as a useful tool at best but having no firm basis in reality. Here is Wilhelm Ostwald (1853–1932), the most influential chemist of his time, in 1900, almost a century after Dalton's discovery:

> Within the limits here given, the atomic hypothesis has proved to be an exceedingly useful aid to instruction and investigation, since it greatly facilitates the interpretation and the use of the general laws. One must not, however, be led astray by this agreement between picture and reality, and confound the two. So far as we have treated them, the chemical processes occurred in such a way as if the substances were composed of atoms in the sense explained. At best there follows from this the **possibility** that they are in reality so; not, however, the **certainty.** For it is impossible to prove that the laws of chemical combination cannot be deduced with the same completeness by means of quite a different assumption. (emphasis added)

But molecules had provided hints to attentive observers ever since the microscope was invented. In 1808, John Dalton had explained the six-fold symmetries of snow crystals as the result of close packing of spherical water molecules. In 1827, the botanist Robert Brown (1773–1858) noticed the random motion of microscopic particles within pollen grains and studied similar motions in suspensions of fine powders in water. This phenomenon, now known as *Brownian motion*, stimulated scientists in the late 19th century to postulate that its origin was the collision of the invisible molecules of water with the grains visible under magnification. Starting in 1905, Albert Einstein (1880–1952), working in Zurich, derived equations for Brownian motion based upon this assumption. At the Sorbonne in 1908, Jean Perrin (1870–1942) initiated experiments using finely ground powders suspended in water and observed, with the *ultramicroscope*, the motions of individual particles as a function of particle size, temperature, and viscosity. Routine microscopy, involving the transmission of light through a *colloidal* medium, simply shows a clear solution. In the ultramicroscope, a very intense light illuminates the solution perpendicular to the microscope's line of sight and the reflected particles may be viewed. The accompanying figure depicts a schematic of the ultramicroscope as well as Perrin's observed plots of the motion of three grains of mastic suspended in water with positions marked every 30 seconds. Perrin's experimental data closely matched Einstein's theoretical predictions and were, at the time, the most tangible and visible proof of the reality of atoms and molecules. Convinced by this agreement between theory and experiment, Ostwald finally accepted atomic theory in 1909.

Swedish chemist Theodor Svedberg (1884–1971) had also been investigating Brownian motion and, in particular, the vertical motion of suspended particles: a balance of Brownian motion and gravity. His work led to the development of the *ultracentrifuge*, an extraordinarily important instrument for the separation of cell components as well as giant biological molecules. In 1926, Jean Perrin received the Nobel Prize in physics and The Svedberg the Nobel Prize in chemistry.

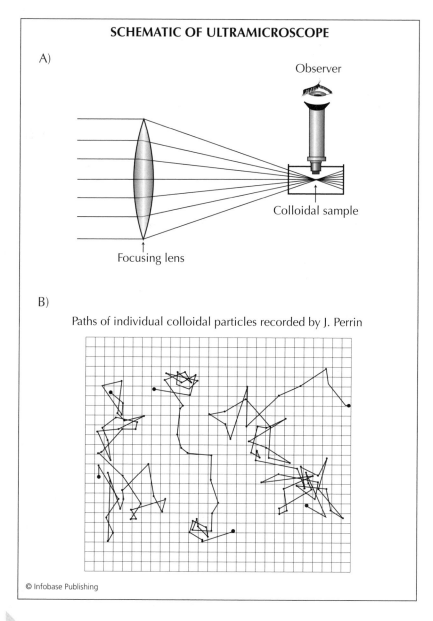

SCHEMATIC OF ULTRAMICROSCOPE

A)

Observer

Colloidal sample

Focusing lens

B)

Paths of individual colloidal particles recorded by J. Perrin

© Infobase Publishing

A) Schematic of the ultramicroscope used by Perrin to observe Brownian motion; B) Perrin's plot of the Brownian motion of three particles of mastic suspended in water

Hints of Subatomic Structure: Mass and Charge of the Electron

Hints of matter even smaller than atoms began to accumulate during the 19th century and included the electrochemical studies of Michael Faraday (1791–1867) and the ionic theory of Svante Arrhenius (1859–1927). However, the most striking experiments were those involving *cathode-ray* tubes developed in Germany during the mid-19th century by Heinrich Geissler (1815–79) and Julius Plücker (1801–68). These scientists and others, notably Eugen Goldstein (1850–1930), discovered that the paths of the cathode rays observed in these tubes could be bent by magnetic fields and could even cast a shadow. The famous experiment by William Crookes (1832–1919), in which he employed a metallic Maltese cross to cast a shadow, is depicted in the accompanying figure. He also demonstrated, using deflections of cathode rays in a magnetic field, that they are negatively charged. In 1897, Joseph John ("J. J.") Thomson (1856–1940), working in Cambridge, carefully compared theory and the experimental

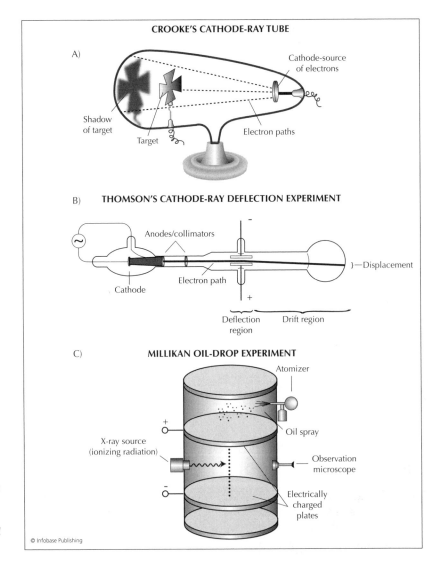

A) Crooke's cathode-ray tube with a Maltese cross target to cast a shadow demonstrating the particle behavior of electrons; B) Thomson's cathode-ray deflection experiment for measuring m/e of the electron; C) Millikan's oil-drop experiment that determined the charge (e) and mass (m) of the electron

deflection pathways of cathode rays in electric fields, and determined the charge-to-mass ratio (e/m) of the electron. The values ranged from 10 million to 31 million electromagnetic units (emu) per gram. The modern value is 17 million emu/g. Thomson found that the e/m for the electron was about one-thousandth that of the hydrogen ion. Thomson's apparatus is depicted in the accompanying figure.

Although the first decade of the 20th century witnessed attempts to determine the charge (e) of the electron and hence its mass, the definitive study was performed by physicist Robert A. Millikan (1868–1953) at the University of Chicago in 1909. The accompanying figure includes a schematic diagram depicting his famous oil drop experiment. An atomizer provides a fine aerosol of oil droplets of roughly 2.5×10^{-8} inch (1 micron or 1×10^{-6} m) in diameter (oil is not volatile and so the droplets do not lose mass through evaporation as water would). The observation chamber below is bounded by two horizontal plates that are charged by a battery. A pinprick hole through the upper plate allows a fraction of the oil drops to fall into the lower chamber. A bright light source is employed to illuminate the chamber and a telescope situated perpendicular to the direction of illumination is employed to observe the motions of individual oil drops. The observational tool is very reminiscent of the ultramicroscope (previous figure) used to detect Brownian motion.

With the voltage off, the few droplets that fall into the lower chamber accelerate due to gravity but reach a constant velocity v (no net force) when the gravitational force (mg) is matched by the frictional force. This allowed Millikan to calculate the mass of the oil droplet. Many of the oil drops acquired a negative charge as they moved through the air. Upon applying and varying voltage to the plates, Millikan provided an electrostatic force EQ (where E is the field strength and Q is the total negative charge on the particle) that opposed the gravitational force (mg). At a specific potential difference, some of the oil droplets are suspended motionless (EQ = mg) and the total charge on the oil droplet can be determined. Millikan discovered that the charges, Q, of the oil droplets differed by multiples of 1.6×10^{-19} coulombs. He understood this to be the smallest common denominator, the charge on an individual electron. The mass of the electron, using e/m, was found to be roughly 1/2000 that of hydrogen, the lightest atom.

In 1886, at an early stage in the studies of cathode-ray tubes, Eugen Goldstein observed that a cathode with a hole ("canal") in it produced rays emitted from this hole in a direction opposite to the cathode rays. In contrast to cathode rays, invisible in the body of the tube and observed only when they hit a luminescent screen, the *"canal rays"* made luminescent tracks through the low-pressure gas in the body of the tube. They produced different colors depending upon the identity of the gas in the tube. Subsequent studies of the deflections, by magnetic or electric fields, of canal rays indicated that the particles producing them were positively charged and thousands of times more massive than the electron. In 1907, J. J. Thomson observed the parabolic paths followed by deflected canal rays. When he employed neon as the gas in the tube he discovered parabolic pathways corresponding to *two* different positive ions: one of mass 20 and one of mass 22. These experiments were precursors to the early mass spectrometer developed by Francis William Aston (1877–1945) in 1919 and provided early hints of isotopes.

Development of the pH Concept

The concepts of acidity and alkalinity are very old ones. Acids tend to be sour and bases slippery. In the 17th century, Otto Tachenius (?–1670?) stated that *acids* and *bases* combined to form salts. In 1675, Robert Boyle (1627–91) defined acids as substances that turn syrup of violets red and *alkalis* as substances that turn this syrup green. However, the true nature of acidity only began to be understood when Arrhenius developed his ionic-dissociation theory in the 1880s. His measurements of *conductivities* and ion transport helped to eventually convince Ostwald of the reality of atoms. Substances that release hydrogen ions (H^+) are acidic and those that release hydroxide ions (OH^-) are basic. In 1909, Soren P. L. Sorenson (1868–1939), working in Carlsberg, studied the influence of hydrogen ion concentration on enzyme activity and developed the *pH* measure ($-\log_{10} [H^+]$) that is employed today, where [H^+] connotes molar concentration of hydrogen ions.

Transformations of Natural Radioelements: "Nature's Alchemy"

One of the early sources of doubt for physicists about the reality of atoms as the smallest elements of matter was the discovery toward the end of the 19th century of subatomic particles. The deflections of cathode rays in magnetic fields indicated that they were composed of negatively charged particles (electrons) lighter than atoms.

Beginning in 1896, Becquerel and the Curies discovered three types of radiation: α-rays (heavy positive particles hardly affected by a magnetic field), β-rays (light negatively charged particles easily deflected by a magnetic field), and *γ-rays* (undeflected by a magnetic field). The γ-rays were found to be similar to the newly discovered *X-rays* but even more penetrating. Four years later, Becquerel measured the deflections of β-particles in electric and magnetic fields and found their e/m ratio to be similar to that of the electron. Rutherford and Soddy published in 1904 their discovery that α-particles are simply helium nuclei. They also confirmed Marie Curie's theory that radiation from radioactive material originates from atomic transformations.

The Earliest Perceptions of Isotopes

During the first decade of the 20th century, the apparent relationships between transformations of radioactive elements became ever more complex until a tentative resolution was reached. In 1907, Professor Bertram B. Boltwood (1870–1927), at Yale, demonstrated that a seemingly new radioactive element he named "ionium," with unique decay characteristics, was generated from the loss of an α-particle during radioactive decay of uranium. In turn, "ionium" lost an α-particle to produce radium. The problem was that "ionium" was chemically identical with (could not be separated from) the known element thorium even though the "two elements" had different radioactive decay patterns.

$$\text{Uranium} \xrightarrow[-\alpha]{} \text{"Ionium"} \xrightarrow[-\alpha]{} \text{Radium}$$

A number of other similar cases were observed in which *seemingly* new radioactive elements with unique decay patterns were chemically identical to known elements. The recognition that there were identical elements with differing radioactive decay properties was made in 1909 and 1910 by Svedberg and Soddy respectively. Soddy coined the term isotope ("same place," i.e., in the periodic table) in 1913.

The modern definition of isotope refers to two or more forms of an element having different atomic masses. The original definition, by Soddy, was derived *not* from comparisons of atomic masses, but from studies of decay of chemically nonseparable, but clearly different, forms of the same radioactive elements. Thomson's 1907 experiment on canal rays passing through neon gas, described earlier, produced two parabolic paths, one corresponding to mass 20 and the other to mass 22. While this was the first evidence for isotopes of light, nonradioactive elements, the data were relatively crude and knowledge of atomic structure was insufficient to fully understand the result.

Thermodynamics, Kinetics, and the Dream of "Fixing" Atmospheric Nitrogen

In his book *The Second Law*, Peter W. Atkins provides an excellent overview of the three laws of thermodynamics:

- First law: Energy is conserved. Alternatively, the change in the internal energy of a system (ΔU) is the sum of the heat (q) absorbed by the system from the surroundings and the work (w) done by the system on the surroundings:

  $\Delta U = q + w$

- Second law: There is a fundamental dissymmetry in nature: While mechanical work can, in principle, be converted completely to heat, the reverse is not true. The second law treats the direction of spontaneous change: mixing two separate gases A and B will (spontaneously) produce a uniform mixture of A and B, but this mixture will not spontaneously re-separate into A and B. Another statement defines a thermodynamic property termed *entropy* (S) and states that total entropy increases (becomes more positive) for any spontaneous process. Entropy is itself a measure of disorder or randomness—thus a system undergoing change in which ΔS is positive ($\Delta S > 0$) becomes more disordered (or random).

These two laws of thermodynamics were developed in the early to middle 19th century. The third law of thermodynamics was postulated in the first decade of the 20th century by the German chemist Walther Hermann Nernst (1864–1941). It treats substances at very low temperature (approaching *absolute zero*, 0 K, -273°C or -459°F). It predicts that absolute zero cannot be reached in a finite number of steps and that, close to absolute zero, the entropy change between two stable states also approaches zero. This allows chemists to calculate absolute entropies for substances at any given temperature. Nernst received the 1920 Nobel Prize in chemistry for this work.

During the first decade of the 20th century, *kinetics* and *thermodynamics* were combined in order to make predictions of chemical behavior. Toward the end of the 19th century Arrhenius had quantitated the dependence of reaction rate on temperature ($k = A\exp[-E/RT]$): Rates increase with increasing temperature (often roughly doubling with every ~20°F [10°C] increase). For a chemical system (e.g., a reaction), the second law can be expressed as follows:

$$\Delta G = \Delta H - T\Delta S; \text{ Spontaneous Change if } \Delta G < 0$$

Here H is the *enthalpy* of a system, very closely related to its internal energy: $H = U + pV$ (where p = pressure; V = volume). The *Gibbs free energy* of a system (defined as $G = H - TS$) is the maximum amount of work the chemical process can produce (other than expansion work). As noted in the equation above, a decrease in Gibbs free energy (ΔG = negative) indicates the direction of spontaneous change in a system. If a chemical system is capable of reaching and maintaining *equilibrium* between reactants and products, then the equilibrium constant, K, is related to the free energy difference as follows:

$$\Delta G = -2.3RT \log K$$

The third law of thermodynamics can now be revisited. In reactions such as:

$$Cl_2 \text{ (g)} + H_2 \text{ (g)} \leftrightharpoons 2 \text{ HCl (g)}$$

$$2 \text{ NO (g)} \leftrightharpoons N_2 \text{ (g)} + O_2 \text{ (g)}$$

the number of gas molecules in reactants and products remain the same. In both examples, very minute changes in equilibrium (ΔG), as the temperature is lowered, parallel the very minute changes in the heat or enthalpy (ΔH) released by the reaction. The reason is that ΔS, the entropy change, is close to zero. In contrast, for a reaction such as:

$$2 H_2 (g) + O_2 (g) \leftrightarrows 2 H_2O (g)$$

the changes in ΔG do not parallel those of ΔH but approach it as absolute zero (0 K) is approached. The reason is that at 0 K the absolute entropies (S) of all substances are zero and hence ΔS disappears for all reactions at 0 K.

One of the most cherished goals of the human race has been to take molecular nitrogen (N_2), which comprises 80 percent of the Earth's atmosphere and is chemically unreactive, and convert it to fertilizer (e.g., ammonium nitrate, NH_4NO_3) for growing crops. That would correspond to converting nitrogen gas into both ammonia (NH_3) and nitric acid (HNO_3) and "fixing" it to form a solid salt. The balanced chemical equation for the difficult step in this process is:

$$N_2 (g) + 3 H_2 (g) \rightarrow 2 NH_3 (g)$$

Dr. Fritz Haber (1868–1934), a German Jew, was both a great scientist and a tragic historical figure. He embraced the challenge of fixing nitrogen during the first decade of the 20th century. By that time chemists, including Haber, were able to calculate, based upon experimental data, the change in enthalpy (ΔH) for this reaction. It was appreciably negative (heat-releasing), thus contributing to the spontaneity of the reaction (ΔG = negative). However, the creation of only two molecules (or *moles*) of gas from four molecules (or moles) of gas corresponds to a large decrease in disorder (ΔS = negative). A glance at the equation above makes it clear that the "- TΔS" term makes a positive contribution to ΔG, tending to oppose spontaneity. At ambient temperature [77°F (25°C) or 298 K], the magnitude of the enthalpy term (ΔH = negative) is much greater than that of the entropy term (TΔS = positive) and the reaction is spontaneous (ΔG = negative). However, at 298 K, the reaction is far too slow to be useful. Increasing the temperature increases the reaction rate but makes the negative entropy contribution greater, thus decreasing the reaction's spontaneity. Increasing the pressure, however, changes the value for ΔG, in this case making it more negative and the reaction more spontaneous. This is a manifestation of *Le Chatelier's principle:* Add stress to the system (e.g., more pressure) and it will adapt by accommodating the stress, in this case driving the reaction to the right where 2 moles of gas occupy less space than 4 moles of gas. Haber had initially miscalculated the thermodynamics for the formation of ammonia from hydrogen and nitrogen. He calculated that, in the presence of an iron *catalyst*, the reaction would run rapidly and produce a high yield of ammonia at about 1,800°F (1,000°C). Haber actually obtained a negligible yield of ammonia. It was Nernst who calculated the effect of increased pressure on increased yield. In the table below, there is a brief summary of values for the equilibrium constant for the Haber process as a function of temperature and pressure. Ultimately, temperatures around

1,020°F (550°C), pressures around 200 Atm (atmospheres) and catalysts, such as iron, were employed to optimize reaction conditions.

Equilibrium constants (K_{eq}) as a function of temperature and pressure (in Atm) for the equilibrium $N_2 + 3\ H_2 \leftrightarrows 2\ NH_3$					
Mole Percent NH_3 in Equilibrium Mixture					
°F	(°C)	K_{eq}: 1 Atm	10 Atm	100 Atm	300 Atm
392	(200)	0.4	51	82	90
572	(300)	4×10^{-3}	15	52	71
932	(500)	2×10^{-5}	1	11	26
1,112	(600)	3×10^{-6}	0.5	5	14

Construction of a plant for manufacture of ammonia and conversion to nitric acid was started by the German firm BASF around 1909. The chemical engineer Carl Bosch (1874–1940) designed a reactor capable of withstanding the high-temperature, high-pressure conditions. The ammonia so produced was employed in the Ostwald Process of conversion to nitric acid. The large industrial facility for making fertilizer and nitrate explosives was completed in 1914, just prior to the start of World War I. This relieved Germany of its dependence on Chile for nitrate, gaining it a strategic (and future economic) advantage and tangibly hurting Chile's economy for decades. The accompanying figure is a schematic diagram of the Bosch-Haber process for synthesis of ammonia from nitrogen. Haber received the Nobel Prize in chemistry in 1918.

Octahedral Coordination Compounds? Stereochemistry to the Rescue!

The concept of valence (literally "value," taken to be the number of bonds), and the critical realization that the valence of carbon is four, was developed in 1858 by Friedrich August Kekulé (1829–96). A decade later valence helped Mendeleev organize the periodic table (monovalent metals such as sodium in Group I, divalent metals such as magnesium in Group II, monovalent nonmetals such as chlorine in Group VII, etc.). In 1874, two young chemists, Jacobus Henricus van't Hoff (1852–1911) and Joseph Achille Le Bel (1847–1930), working quite independently in Paris, took the creative "leap into space" (actually the third dimension) that would inaugurate the field of *stereochemistry*. By postulating that the four atoms or groups bonded to a carbon atom occupy the corners of an imaginary tetrahedron with the carbon atom at its center, they solved questions that had puzzled chemists for decades.

There are two (and only two) distinct three-dimensional representations for lactic acid *enantiomers* (see the figure on page 21): they are

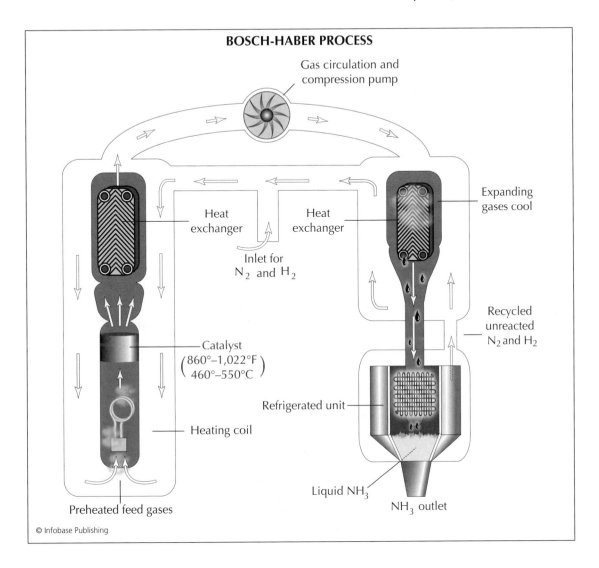

BOSCH-HABER PROCESS

Gas circulation and
compression pump

Heat
exchanger

Heat
exchanger

Expanding
gases cool

Inlet for
N_2 and H_2

Catalyst
$\left(\begin{array}{c} 860°–1,022°F \\ 460°–550°C \end{array}\right)$

Recycled
unreacted
N_2 and H_2

Refrigerated unit

Heating coil

Liquid NH_3

NH_3 outlet

Preheated feed gases

© Infobase Publishing

*Schematic diagram depicting
the Bosch-Haber process for
"fixing" atmospheric nitrogen to
form ammonia*

nonsuperimposable mirror images. Such molecules are termed *"chiral"* ("handed") since left and right hands are nonsuperimposable mirror images. Lactic acid has four different types of groups (H, OH, CH₃, and COOH) attached to a carbon atom. Such a carbon atom, while not common, is not rare either and is termed "asymmetric." The tetrahedral carbon atom explains why naturally occurring lactic acid is optically active while synthetic lactic acid is not. In muscle, only the *S*-(+)-lactic acid [L-(+)- in earlier nomenclature] is present, while in synthetic lactic acid both "enantiomers" [*S*-(+) and *R*-(-)] are present in equal amounts (D,L and *R,S* nomenclature will be explained in chapter 6). The 1:1 mixture is termed the *"racemic modification"* or simply "racemate." In contrast, a molecule such as CH₂FCl (only 3 different groups) is "achiral" ("not chiral").

There was no way to "see" atoms or molecules in 1874 (and not for many future decades). Remember too that many great physicists and chemists, including the famous Ostwald, did not even accept the reality of atoms and molecules at that time. Thus, one need not be shocked by the scorn heaped upon the young van't Hoff, at the time a 26-year-old instructor at the Veterinary College of Utrecht, by the world-famous Herr Doktor Hermann Kolbe (1818–84), professor at Leipzig in 1878:

> *A Dr. J. H. Van't Hoff, of the Veterinary College, Utrecht, appears to have no taste for exact chemical research. He finds it a less arduous task to mount his Pegasus (evidently borrowed from the Veterinary College) and to soar to his own Chemical Parnassus, there to reveal in his "La Chimie dans L'Espace" how he finds the atoms situate in the world's space.*

Stereochemistry had arrived and little over a decade later would contribute mightily toward understanding structure and bonding in *coordination compounds*. In 1891, Alfred Werner (1866–1919), newly appointed to the faculty in Zurich, encountered the following problem: dissolution of $CoCl_2$ in aqueous ammonia followed by air oxidation produces some $CoCl_3$. From this solution, three brightly colored salts that appear to have "absorbed" ammonia (NH_3) molecules may be isolated: $Co(NH_3)_6Cl_3$, $Co(NH_3)_5Cl_3$, and $Co(NH_3)_4Cl_3$. Although ammonia is known to readily react with HCl to form NH_4Cl, the NH_3 units in these three cobalt complexes are unreactive with HCl. Reaction of one mole of $Co(NH_3)_6Cl_3$ with excess silver nitrate ($AgNO_3$) immediately precipitates three moles of AgCl. Reaction of one mole of $Co(NH_3)_5Cl_3$ with silver nitrate precipitates two moles of AgCl. Reaction of one mole of $Co(NH_3)_4Cl_3$ with silver nitrate precipitates only one mole of AgCl. What is the nature of these cobalt complexes?

In modern terms it is recognized that the cobalt ion is in the Co^{3+} oxidation state in all three complexes. One would expect tight binding with the three Cl^- ions that neutralize the charge on cobalt ("primary valences") and much looser association, if any, with the neutral ammonia molecules ("secondary valences"). The fact that the ammonia molecules in $Co(NH_3)_6Cl_3$ are unreactive while all three Cl- ions are readily pre-

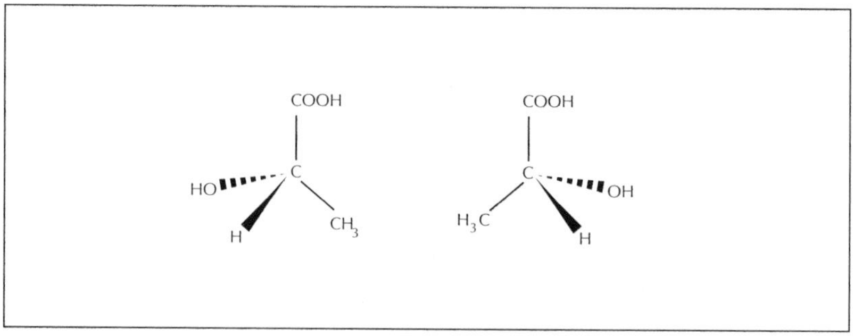

(-)- and (+)- lactic acid enantiomers

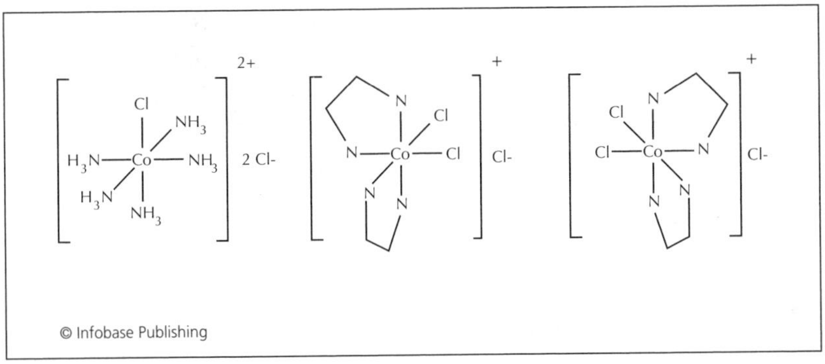

© Infobase Publishing

Werner complexes of cobalt

cipitated by Ag^+ (as they would be from aqueous Na^+Cl^-) suggests that the NH_3 molecules are tightly bound to Co^{3+} while the three Cl^-s are free in solution. Even more fascinating are the observations that in $Co(NH_3)_5Cl_3$ one Cl^- is tightly bound while in $Co(NH_3)_4Cl_3$ two of the three Cl^-s are tightly bound. Werner concluded that in all three salts six NH_3 *"ligands"* are tightly bound to the central metal ion. His seminal work (English translation: "Newer Views of the Field of Inorganic Chemistry") was published in 1905.

When six ligands are attached to a central metal ion, Werner predicted an octahedral structure. Thus, for $Co(NH_3)_5Cl_3$, he postulated a structure in which the five ammonia molecules and only one of the three chloride ions are ligands tightly bound to cobalt. The other two chloride ions are free in aqueous solution and readily precipitate with Ag^+. He termed such chemical species "coordination compounds" and identified six as the *coordination number* for Co^{3+}. Further proof came from Werner's identification of *cis*-(Cl-Co-Cl angle 90°) and *trans*- (Cl-Co-Cl angle 180°) isomers for $Co(NH_3)_4Cl_3$, and the actual isolation of enantiomers (see the structures depicted) in 1911. For this work, Werner received the Nobel Prize in chemistry in 1913.

Column Chromatography: The Beginnings of Modern Separation Science

Any 21st-century chemist would recognize the column *chromatography* apparatus depicted in the accompanying figure since it differs little from what is often employed in the laboratory today. The figure was published in 1906 by Mikhail Tswett (1872–1919), who conducted his research in Poland and Russia and developed the new technique around 1903. Tswett knew that colored solutions could often be clarified by adding solid powder (chalk, sugar), insoluble in the specific organic extract, to adsorb the colored substances. He successfully exploited the differing affinities for solid adsorbent that permitted separation of individual compounds in complex mixtures.

Depiction of Tswett's 1906 column chromatography apparatus as separate components (top) and assembled manifold apparatus (bottom) (Adapted from H. H. Strain and J. Sherma, *Journal of Chemical Education* 44 (1967): 238–42)

Tswett discovered that leaves contained two distinct green chlorophyll pigments and three or four yellow (xanthophylls) pigments. The accompanying figure depicts the separation of pigments achieved by Tswett using carbon disulfide as solvent. Once the experiment was completed, these layers were removed individually from the column with a spatula and washed with solvent or eluted selectively with solvents.

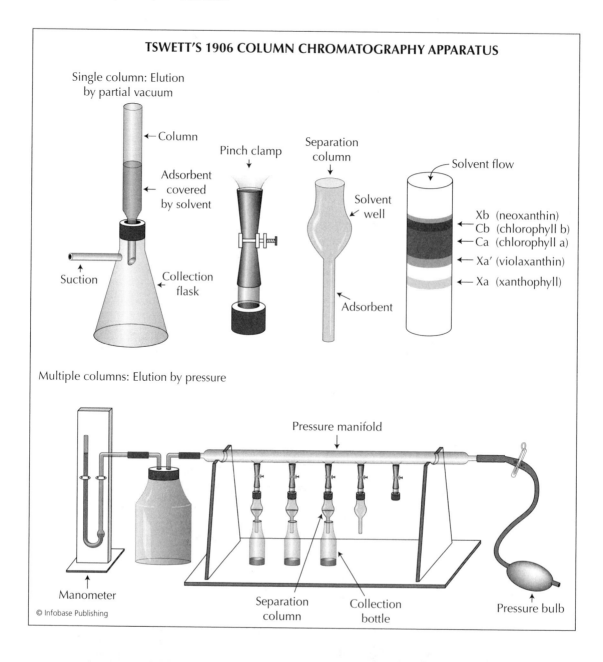

TSWETT'S 1906 COLUMN CHROMATOGRAPHY APPARATUS

Single column: Elution by partial vacuum

Column

Adsorbent covered by solvent

Suction

Collection flask

Pinch clamp

Separation column

Solvent well

Adsorbent

Solvent flow

Xb (neoxanthin)
Cb (chlorophyll b)
Ca (chlorophyll a)
Xa' (violaxanthin)
Xa (xanthophyll)

Multiple columns: Elution by pressure

Pressure manifold

Manometer

Separation column

Collection bottle

Pressure bulb

Another vital advance during this period was the development of microanalysis, notably by Friedrich Emich (1860–1940) and Fritz Pregl (1869–1930), in Graz (Austria). Starting in the early 1830s, Bunsen and Jean Baptiste Andre Dumas (1800–84) and others developed techniques for extremely accurate analysis of grams of organic compounds. However, the search for natural products coupled with increasingly complex, multistep syntheses that provided much smaller amounts of material made the development of more sensitive techniques necessary. Emich and Pregl developed sensitive techniques that employed newly designed microbalances and microware for analyses of milligrams (rather than grams) of substances. Pregl developed and systemized spot tests for different chemical groups. Pregl received the 1923 Nobel Prize in chemistry.

Advances in Organic Synthesis

Organic chemistry, the chemistry of carbon compounds, emerged as a distinct field in the early 19th century. Carbon is distinguished by the following features: a) a valence of four capable of deployment in various combinations of single, double, and triple bonds; b) the ability to form very stable single, double, and triple bonds with other carbon atoms in an almost innumerable array of chains and rings; c) formation of stable bonds with most of the chemical elements. For these reasons, the number of known organic compounds is enormous and increasing rapidly. There are almost 25 million known chemical substances ("small molecules") of which well over 95 percent are organic. Some 4,000 new substances are reported each day.

A very important task for organic chemists is to form new carbon-carbon bonds in order to design new molecular networks or to reproduce rare and valuable compounds that occur in nature. One very powerful family of organic synthesis techniques employs organometallic compounds. The carbon atom in a carbon-metal bond is at least partially if not almost fully negative in charge. Such carbons are typically highly reactive, tending to ferociously pull H^+ from H_2O, and to attack a variety of electron-poor sites such as carbonyl (C=O) groups in other molecules. The task is to "domesticate" these "chemical tigers" for practical synthetic purposes.

In 1900, François-Auguste-Victor Grignard (1871–1935) made one of the greatest, if not *the* greatest, discoveries in the history of organic synthesis. He pioneered a new class of organomagnesium reagents that are stable, safe, adaptable, and more effective than the organozinc reagents of the late 19th century. A Grignard reagent is synthesized from an organic halide (RX; X is usually Br or I) and magnesium in dry diethyl ether (or tetrahydrofuran). Although it is not a "chemical tiger," neither is it a "pussycat" and it must be protected from moisture. There is a huge inventory of synthetic reactions utilizing Grignard reagents. For now,

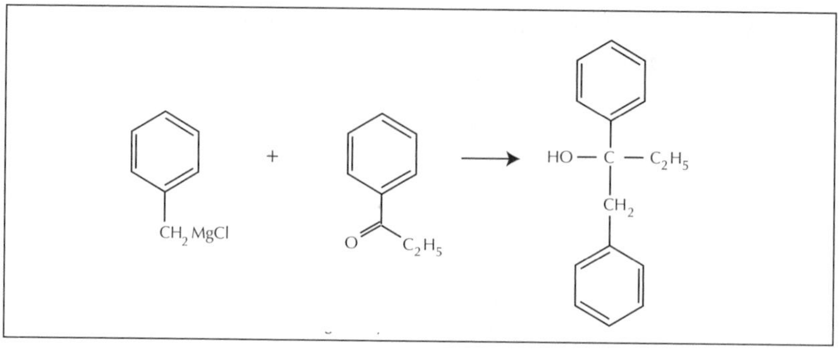

Grignard synthesis of alcohols

only one is displayed below: the reaction of a Grignard reagent with a carbonyl compound to synthesize an alcohol having a much more complex molecular framework.

During the 1820s, Johann Wolfgang Döbereiner (1780–1849) discovered that if a jet of hydrogen gas is passed over spongy platinum in open air, the hydrogen burns. He realized that platinum was somehow increasing the reactivity of hydrogen and coined the term "metallic action" for what we now recognize as catalysis. Beginning in 1897, Paul Sabatier (1854–1941) began decades of study on catalysis including applications to organic chemistry. His most important work, completed during the first decade of the 20th century, was the catalytic hydrogenation of organic compounds using platinum and related metals. For their major contributions to organic synthesis, Grignard and Sabatier shared the 1912 Nobel Prize in chemistry.

A Surprise and a Hint of a New Century of Adventure in Mechanism

During the 19th century organic chemists observed that conversions such as ethyl alcohol (C_2H_5OH) to ethyl chloride (C_2H_5Cl) to triethylamine [$(C_2H_5)_3N$] suggested that the C_2H_5 unit remained together as an ethyl "*radical*" (Latin *radicis*, "a root"). Many 19th-century organic chemists tried unsuccessfully to intercept "*free radicals*" as they changed chemical partners. In 1900, Moses Gomberg (1866–1947), at the University of Michigan, attempted to synthesize hexaphenylethane [$(C_6H_5)_3C-C(C_6H_5)_3$], a hitherto (and still) unknown compound. To his surprise, and that of the chemical community, Gomberg obtained a yellow solution that was reasonably stable but reacted with atmospheric oxygen to yield a peroxide, and decolorized iodine to yield an iodide. Gomberg had made triphenylmethyl (see structure below), the first isolable free radical, a species in which one carbon atom forms only three bonds, not four. Identification of triphenylmethyl radical was one of the earliest steps in

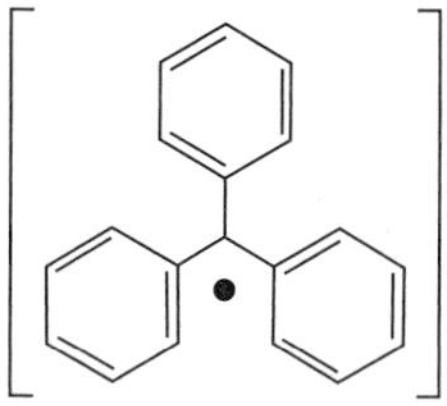

Gomberg's triphenylmethyl radical

the study of organic chemistry reaction mechanisms that would come to dominate the 20th century.

Beginnings of Biochemistry as "Super-Organic Chemistry:" Sugars and Proteins

By the start of the 20th century "the table had been set" to explore the seeming "superorganic chemistry" that we call biochemistry. In Berlin, the brilliant structure proof of (+)-glucose, by Emil Fischer (1852–1919), was published in 1891. Fischer received the 1902 Nobel Prize in chemistry. By the end of the 19th century, most of the common amino acids had been isolated as well as synthesized. Fischer reported the synthesis of serine in 1902 and isolated valine, proline, and hydroxyproline. However, his major contribution to modern protein chemistry was the condensation of *amino acids* to form what he termed polypeptides, connected by -CO-NH- (*peptide*) linkages. In 1907, Fischer synthesized an octadecapeptide, of molecular weight 1,212, containing 15 glycine and 3 leucine residues.

"Ferments" and Enzymes

During the first half of the 19th century a substance called diastase, capable of digesting starch to form sugar, was isolated from malt; pepsin was isolated from stomach juice; and trypsin from pancreatic juice.

From the mid-19th century onward, it had become obvious that whole yeast, a unicellular fungus, catalyzes the fermentation of sugar to ethyl alcohol, a very dramatic chemical change. Fermentation was defined as metabolism that produced gas as a by-product, for example, in the rising of bread during leavening. Gas production (CO_2, CH_4, H_2S) appeared to be associated with living cells only. During this period, Louis Pasteur (1822–95) demonstrated that formation of lactic acid during fermentation is catalyzed by bacteria. The concept of "ferments" as active chemical components *organized within living cells* was generally adopted during at this period. Although the term *enzyme*, literally "in-leaven," had been coined in 1878 by Willy Kühne (1837–1900), his concept was meant to define the *unorganized* biological catalysts found *free* from living cells. In 1894, Fischer demonstrated the amazing specificities of different enzymes in choosing one or the other stereoisomer of a glucose derivative, which differ only very slightly in shape, and proposed the "lock-and-key" concept.

The critical investigation was that of Eduard Buchner (1860–1917) who, in 1897, isolated cell-free yeast extract and demonstrated its full activity in fermenting sugar to alcohol. The distinction between ferments and enzymes became meaningless: Enzymes were simply understood to be chemical substances, although not simple ones. Buchner won the 1907 Nobel Prize in chemistry. In 1904 William John Young (1878–1942) and Arthur Harden (1865–1940), at the Lister Institute in London, further investigated this yeast extract and determined that *dialysis* (which employs a semipermeable membrane to separate colloids from soluble substances) separated the active "juice" into two components, neither of which could catalyze fermentation on its own. Once reconstituted, the mixture was fully active and the soluble (dialyzable) fraction was termed the coenzyme. While enzymes were suspected to be proteins, the complexities of the mixtures and the tiny number of known enzymes made such a generalized conclusion a tentative one at that time.

Nucleic Acids

Nucleic acids were first obtained (accompanied by proteins) by Fritz Miescher (1844–95), who in 1869 isolated a substance he called "nuclein" from the nuclei of pus-producing bacteria. In a few short years Miescher succeeded in extracting the nucleic acids free of proteins. The next stage was the chemical understanding of nucleic acids. Physiologist Albrecht Kossel (1853–1927), who won the 1910 Nobel Prize in medicine or physiology, and organic chemist Phoebus Aaron Levene (1869–1940), working at the Rockefeller Institute, New York, led the study with Emil Fischer contributing indirectly. Kossel discovered that boiling water releases phosphate and yields an organic base, hypoxanthine, and in 1885 he isolated adenine from pancreatic cells. It was Fischer who ultimately worked out the structural complexities of the purines (including xanthines, adenine, and guanine) and synthesized purine itself in 1898. As part of his groundbreaking stereochemical studies, Fischer had deciphered the structure of ribose in 1891. Some of the confusion in the early studies of nucleic acids was due to difficulties in differentiating DNA from RNA. The sugar portion of DNA, 2-deoxyribose, was only firmly characterized by Levene in 1929.

In 1909, Levene and his colleague Walter A. Jacobs (1883–1967) correctly concluded that the building blocks for nucleic acids were nucleotides in which the organic base is attached to ribose, itself attached by an

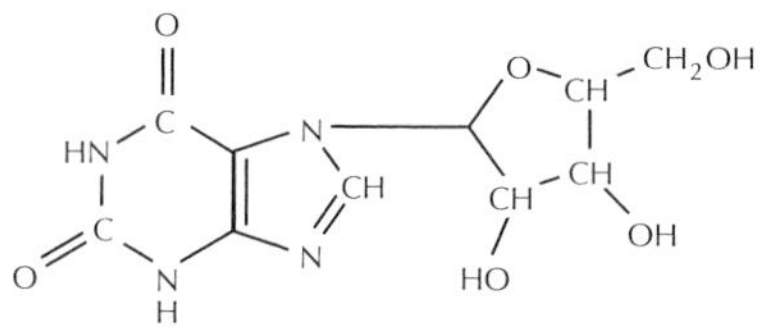

Levene's initial (incorrect) structure for inosine

ester linkage to phosphate. The corresponding nucleoside structure lacks phosphate. The first (essentially) correct structures proposed were for the nucleoside inosine (the structure shown and published in 1911 incorrectly attaches the base at N7 instead of N9) and the nucleotide inosine phosphate. It is ironic that, despite Levene's groundbreaking work in nucleic acid chemistry, he is perhaps most often remembered the father of the tetranucleotide hypothesis of nucleic acid structure (see chapter 5). This hypothesis misled chemists from any reasonable notions that nucleic acids, despite their presence in chromosomes, could be genetic material. That role appeared to be reserved for proteins, with 20 different building blocks instead of only four. The critical missing piece in the DNA puzzle was a firm understanding of super-large molecules (macromolecules).

Macromolecules and Colloids: Insights and Confusions

The conceptual groundwork for understanding giant molecules (*macromolecules*) was laid by August Kekulé (1829–96) in 1858 when he postulated that carbon forms four bonds and can form chains and rings containing C-C bonds with no obvious limitation. The reality of such macromolecules became clouded when chemists encountered colloids. Today colloidal dispersions (or simply colloids) are considered to comprise particles that are roughly 4×10^{-8} to 8×10^{-6} inch (10–2,000 *angstroms* [Å], i.e., 1–200 *nanometers* [nm] or billionths of a meter) in diameter. Milk is a familiar example of a colloid. It is a dispersion of microscopic fat droplets in aqueous solution. Colloids scatter intense focused light beams so that the beam path is clearly visible in the dispersion (Tyndall effect) and that is one reason why high-beam lights are of limited use in fog. Colloidal dispersions can also consist of giant molecules such as hemoglobin (molecular weight or MW = 64,500; dimensions on the order of 2.0×10^{-7} to 2.6×10^{-7} inch [50–65 Å or 5-6.5 nm]) dispersed in aqueous media. Richard Zsigmondy (1865–1929), who coinvented the ultramicroscope in 1902 in Jena, went on to win the 1925 Nobel Prize in chemistry for his studies of the coagulation of colloids.

Confusion arises since molecules of soap (e.g., sodium stearate, MW only 306) can form colloidal dispersions consisting of *micelles:* huge aggregates of hundreds of small molecules. It seemed reasonable that proteinaceous materials such as albumin or hemoglobin were likely to be made of smaller molecules combining to form colloidal particles. This was given some theoretical grounding by Werner's concept, discussed earlier, of primary and secondary bonding. Presumably the primary bonds were those connecting the C-C bonds in sodium stearate (or proteins) and the secondary bonds were the weaker ones holding micelles or other complexes together. Emil Fischer himself had proposed that proteins needed to be no more than 30 residues in length to account for a virtually limitless number (20^{30}) of possibilities based upon 20 different amino acids. The other difficulty was the determination of molecular weights for proteins, using measurements of freezing point depression or osmotic pressure of solutions, as well as light scattering. These techniques frequently provided very different values in different laboratories.

Hormones and Synthetic Drugs

In 1902, William M. Bayliss (1860–1924) and Ernest Henry Starling (1866–1927) discovered a secretion, termed "secretin," from the duodenal mucosa that entered the bloodstream and stimulated secretions at a distant organ: the pancreas. The discovery of this controlling effect from one organ to a distant organ in the same body was a new finding. They coined the term *hormone* (German "to stimulate") to describe the new class of biological agent. It required another 50 years to separate and fully identify the active agent, a polypeptide containing 27 amino acid residues.

Toward the end of the 19th century, scientists began to explore rational theories of drug design. Paul Ehrlich (1854–1915), in Frankfurt, had been experimenting with dyes capable of selectively staining bacteria. If such dyes had toxic effects they could function as "magic bullets." During the first decade of the 20th century the causative agent for syphilis was discovered. Based upon experiences with drugs containing arsenic against organisms similar to this agent, Ehrlich explored a large number of arsenicals. The 606th candidate was salvarsan (see the structure). This substance, used successfully against syphilis in 1909, was the first molecular therapeutic agent created to fight a specific disease. It was succeeded by sulfa drugs (chapter 4), the first broad-spectrum antibacterials in the 1930s, and penicillins and tetracyclines during the 1940s (chapter 5).

Industrial Processes: Sulfur and Sulfuric Acid

Sulfuric acid (H_2SO_4) is today of immense importance in the chemical industry and a greater quantity of this chemical (more than 40 million tons annually) is produced than any other manufactured chemical. It is used to manufacture fertilizers, other chemical reagents including nitric and hydrochloric acids, for batteries in cars and for cleaning ("pickling") metals among numerous other uses. Although demand for sulfuric acid

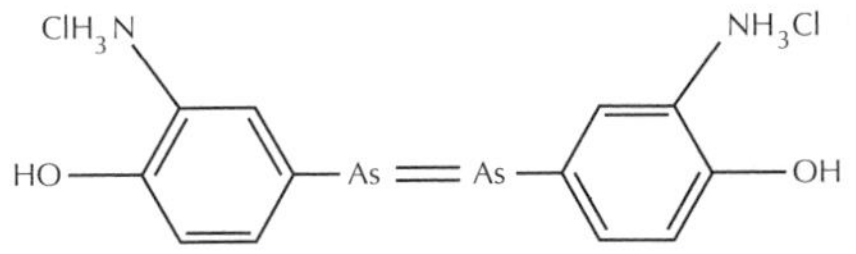

Salvarsan

was relatively modest through the early 19th century, it increased dramatically when the Leblanc process for manufacture of alkalis (sodium carbonate and sodium hydroxide) became commercially feasible in England starting in 1823. Such alkalis were of critical importance in soap and glass manufacture. An important step in the Leblanc process is the reaction of sulfuric acid and sodium chloride to form sodium sulfate. In the 1890s, Herman Frasch (1851–1914), a German-born immigrant to the United States, developed a process for recovering elemental sulfur from deep underground deposits of the element. The process was first applied commercially in 1901 to salt domes loaded with elemental sulfur deposits. Sulfur's low melting point and low density were the keys to the success of the Frasch Process, depicted in the accompanying figure. A high-pressure tube blowing hot water and air melts the sulfur and brings the liquid to the surface where it is deposited as a solid.

Industrial Processes: Artificial Rubber

Rubber is made from sap tapped from rubber trees, notably from South America. Although useful in bicycle tires and other special applications, the need for rubber exploded during the early 20th century with the introduction of the automobile. Not surprisingly, during World War I it became a strategic material and Germany was seriously disadvantaged by the need to cross the Atlantic Ocean to obtain this substance and was forced to use its talented chemical community to find substitutes.

Natural rubber polymerizes upon standing, but the soft material so obtained had limited utility until Charles Goodyear (1800–60) discovered in 1839 that addition of sulfur (vulcanization) produces a hard, inert, and robust material. Hints of its chemical nature emerged from mid-19th-century studies, demonstrating that distillation of rubber provides isoprene (C_5H_8). In 1909, Fritz Hofmann (1866–1956), of Baeyer in Germany, successfully polymerized isoprene (2-methyl-1,3-butadiene) to form artificial rubber, albeit expensively and in an inferior form. German scientists of this period also polymerized methyl isoprene (2,3–dimethyl-1,3-butadiene). During World War I, the Germans used this methyl rubber substitute because the starting materials were relative inexpensive. It was, however, markedly inferior to natural rubber. After the war, they

FRASCH PROCESS

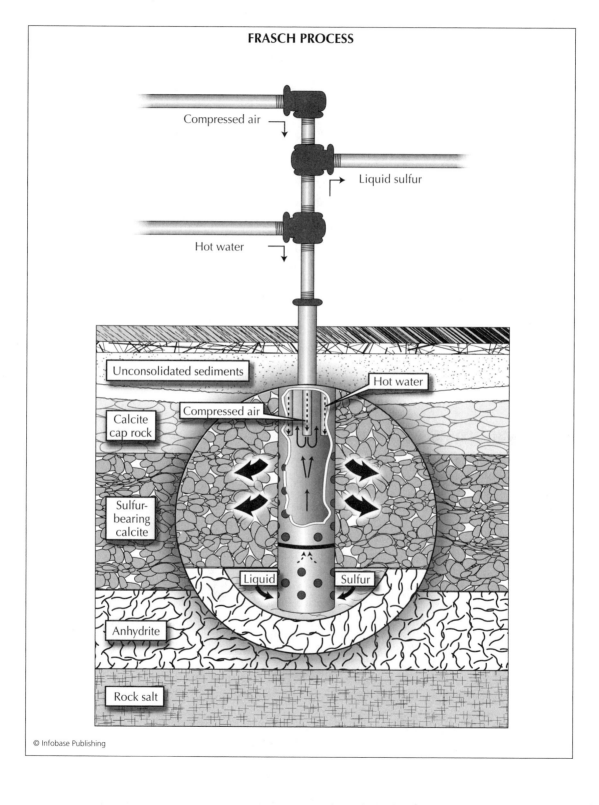

Compressed air

Liquid sulfur

Hot water

Unconsolidated sediments

Compressed air

Hot water

Calcite
cap rock

Sulfur-
bearing
calcite

Liquid

Sulfur

Anhydrite

Rock salt

(Opposite page) Schematic diagram depicting Frasch Process for recovering molten sulfur from underground deposits

developed a type of rubber synthesized from 1,3-butadiene and polymerized using sodium. "Buna," the rubber derived from butadiene (Bu) and Sodium (Na), became a reasonably successful rubber substitute for many years. As the knowledge of polymer chemistry advanced during the first 30 years or so of the 20th century, chemists came to understand that natural rubber is composed of high-molecular-weight polyisoprene.

Bakelite: The Age of Plastics Begins

The Plastics Revolution began during the first decade of the 20th century with the invention of Bakelite. It was a true "wonder material" that allowed one to literally pour out of a flask objects of virtually any shape: combs, brushes, mirrors, coffee pots, radio cases, telephones, kitchen counter tops, and toys of dazzling variety. The success of plastics—they are inexpensive, water resistant and virtually indestructible—proved to be a double-edged sword. By the final decades of the 20th century, wealthy industrial nations had developed "throwaway" economies based upon products such as disposable pens and cups, which both fed and created demand for petroleum-based raw materials.

The first plastics were actually developed during the last half of the 19th century. Paper is composed to a significant extent of the natural polymer cellulose and closely related substances. Treatment of paper with nitric acid produced the first (semi-) artificial polymer, nitrocellulose. Dissolution of nitrocellulose in alcohol/ether gave a viscous solution (collodion) which forms a hard film upon solvent evaporation. The polymer thus formed was quite flammable. An improved product based on nitrocellulose, termed celluloid, was molded into

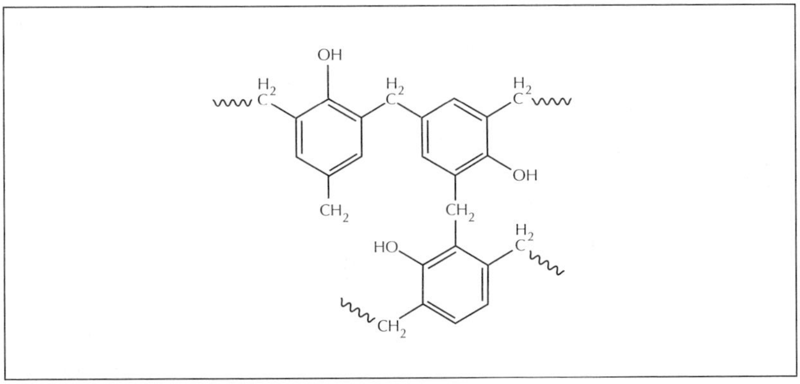

Bakelite

General Electric Bakelite radio
(Microphonerentals.com)

useful objects such as combs during the last quarter of the 19th century. Another approach was the reaction of the natural polymer casein, a protein in milk, with formaldehyde. Molding commercial products started in 1897.

A breakthrough was made by a Belgian, Leo H. Baekeland (1863–1944), who had emigrated to the United States. In 1907, he combined formaldehyde and phenol and discovered a polymer that could be poured into a mold and heated to produce a tough plastic material he called Bakelite. Although, as noted earlier, the true nature of polymers was not understood during the first two decades of the 20th century, subsequent work demonstrated the structure of Bakelite to be polymeric. Among its earliest uses were as molding in the electrical industry and for fabricating the diverse and often lovely art deco cases for radios that came to dominate the 1920s. In 1910 Baekeland formed the General Baekelite Company, which decades later became Union Carbide. While Bakelite has been long surpassed by other plastics, Bakelite "antiques" remain highly sought after and collectible today (see the photograph of a Bakelite radio).

Conclusion

One hundred years after Dalton's atomic theory, physicists finally accepted the reality of atoms. Nonetheless, many mysteries remained including the structure of the atom, since it clearly consisted of positive and negative subparticles. The underlying logic of the periodic table remained mysterious, especially since there were some anomalies in the order of elements based upon their atomic weights. The next decade

Scientist of the Decade: Marie Curie (1867–1934)

Marie Curie was the first woman to win a Nobel Prize and the first scientist to win the prestigious prize twice. She is depicted here with her husband, Pierre Curie, with whom she shared the 1903 Nobel Prize in physics. (AIP Emilio Segrè Visual Archives)

Marya Sklowdowska was born in Poland and came to Paris in 1891 to study physics and mathematics. Overcoming privation, she obtained the equivalent of a master's degree in physics from the Sorbonne in 1893, graduating at the top of her class. In 1894, she obtained an advanced degree in mathematics and met Pierre Curie, a professor at the Municipal School of Industrial Physics and Chemistry. Following their marriage in 1895, they began joint research projects at the Municipal School. Marie Sklowdowska Curie, using Pierre's electrometer, discovered that thorium, like uranium, manifested the newly discovered prop-

erty of radioactivity. In 1898, she discovered that pitchblende, a uranium ore, was much more radioactive than its uranium content would predict and she suspected the presence of a hitherto unknown element. Her incredibly laborious physical exertions and ingenious chemical separations ultimately provided about 0.0002 pound (0.1 g) of pure radium chloride from tons of lower grade (cheaper) pitchblende. She also discovered polonium in a different fraction derived from her pitchblende extract. Madame Curie described the physical travail of her labors: "Sometimes I had to spend a whole day mixing a boiling mass with a heavy iron rod nearly as large as myself. I would be broken with fatigue at the end of the day." Marie Curie, Pierre Curie, and Henri Becquerel shared the 1903 Nobel Prize in physics for their fundamental studies on radioactivity. Pierre Curie was killed in a street accident in 1906 and Marie replaced him and became the first woman to be appointed to the faculty of the Sorbonne in its 650-year history. In 1911 she failed to be elected to the French Academy of Sciences but shortly afterward won the 1911 Nobel Prize in chemistry for her discoveries of radium and polonium, becoming the first person (and one of the very few in history) to win two Nobel Prizes.

Incredibly, at the outbreak of World War I, Marie Curie abandoned her research and, along with her daughter Irène, enlisted as an X-ray technician on mobile units serving France and its allies. Daughter Irène Joliot-Curie (1897–1956) shared the 1935 Nobel Prize in chemistry with her husband Frédéric Joliot-Curie (1900–58) for their discovery of artificial radioactive elements. Marie Curie was strangely oblivious to the mounting evidence of radiation-induced cancer for workers and technicians handling these materials. She died of leukemia at age 67 and Irène Joliot-Curie died of leukemia at age 59. In 1962 the French Academy of Sciences finally elected a woman to its membership, Marguerite Catherine Perey (1909–75), discoverer of element 87 (francium).

would witness solutions to both of these riddles. The start of the 20th century also marked the dawn of biochemistry with meaningful explorations of the structures of carbohydrates, proteins, and nucleic acids. Real understanding of these classes of biological molecules could only come after the natures of colloids and macromolecules (giant molecules) were understood. The first tentative steps in macromolecule chemistry would occur shortly after the end of the First World War.

Further Reading

Atkins, Peter W. *The Second Law.* New York: W. H. Freeman and Company, 1984. This book, in the *Scientific American Library* series, provides a very readable and pictorial introduction to the second law of thermodynamics.

Brock, William H. *The Norton History of Chemistry,* chapter 9. New York: W. W. Norton & Co., 1993. This is a discussion of the discoveries of rare gases and rare earths.

Curie, Eva. *Madame Curie: A Biography.* Garden City, N.Y.: Literary Guild, 1937. This is a popular biography of Marie Curie authored by her daughter.

Electric Prism, Inc., Woodstock, New York. Available online. URL: www.periodicspiral.com. Accessed on March 1, 2007. This site provides access to an interactive periodic table arranged in a spiral motif and designed by Jeff Moran of Woodstock, New York.

Ihde, Aaron J. *The Development of Modern Chemistry.* New York: Harper and Row, 1964. This book provides succinct discussions of microanalysis (577–81), early-20th-century biochemistry (643–70), the cathode-ray tube (478–83), and late-19th-century and early-20th-century industrial chemistry (695–724).

Olby, Robert. *The Path to the Double Helix,* chapters 1–3. Seattle: University of Washington Press, 1974. This book provides a superb discussion of the understandings and confusions associated with biological macromolecules in the early 20th century.

Ramberg, Peter J. *Chemical Structure, Spatial Arrangement: The Early History of Stereochemistry, 1874–1914.* Aldershot (UK): Ashgate Publishing Ltd., 2003. This book provides an accessible discussion of the first 40 years of stereochemical research.

Rayner-Canham, Marelene, and Geoffrey Rayner-Canham. *Women in Chemistry: Their Changing Roles from Alchemical Times to the Mid-Twentieth Century,* 97–107. Washington, D.C. and Philadelphia: American Chemical Society and Chemical Heritage Foundation, 1998. This book provides is an excellent discussion of Marie Curie including the quotation cited in this chapter.

Read, John. *Humour and Humanism in Chemistry,* 262–82. London: G. Bell and Sons Ltd, 1947. This reading includes a wonderfully personal account of working with Alfred Werner by his Ph.D. student John Read, a renowned chemical historian.

2 1911–1920:
Discovering the Atomic Nucleus and Understanding the Octet Rule

Insights into the Periodic Table

By the end of the second decade of the 20th century, a recognizably modern picture of the atom, its substructure, and rules for chemical bonding would begin to emerge. In the middle of the decade *X-ray crystallography* would allow chemists to make accurate determinations of the distances between atoms and ions. The discovery of the atomic number would explain the "roll call" of elements in the periodic table. It left some tantalizing gaps, challenging chemists to search for as-yet-undiscovered elements. The development of the mass spectrometer led to the modern definition of isotopes but opened up another mystery: What was the nature of the difference between the nuclei of the isotopes ^{20}Ne and ^{22}Ne? The *neutron* would not be discovered until 1932.

Although one could never credit chemistry with innocence (consider gunpowder and a variety of poisons well known to the ancients), the second decade of the 20th century would witness some of the most horrific uses of its technology, in the manufacture of explosives and in new poisonous gases that were used to terrible effect against soldiers. Biochemistry started to emerge from organic chemistry as structures of complex natural products were deciphered and synthesized. The first firm concepts of macromolecules developed. These would ultimately set the basis for understanding the structures of polysaccharides such as cellulose, proteins, and nucleic acids, as well as the synthesis and fabrication of synthetic materials so commonly in use today.

The Atomic Nucleus: "The Fly in the Cathedral"

Not long after radioactivity was discovered by Becquerel, scientists began investigating its nature. In 1899, Ernest Rutherford, who had studied with J. J. Thomson in Cambridge, discovered that uranium emits two types of radiation: one stopped by a thin sheet of aluminum foil that he termed α-rays, and another stopped by a thick sheet of aluminum foil that he termed β-rays. During the following year, γ-rays, about 160 times as penetrating as β-rays, were discovered in the emanations from radium. Not long afterward, β-rays were shown to be identical to electrons. Rutherford's fundamental studies of the origin and nature of radioactivity earned him the Nobel Prize in chemistry in 1908, but his most memorable discovery still lay in the future.

By 1908, Rutherford concluded that the α-particle is a doubly charged cation of helium (He^{2+}), a dense, highly charged particle of matter. In Rutherford's Manchester laboratory, Hans Geiger (1882–1945) and Ernest Marsden (1889–1970) conducted experiments in which they observed the fluorescence scintillations produced by individual α-particles as they collided with a zinc sulfide screen. In 1909, they conducted the famous experiment, diagrammed schematically on page 39. A source of α-particles (polonium) was placed near a thin (0.000016 inch or 0.00004 cm thick) sheet of gold foil and the radiation passing through the sheet captured through various angles onto the screen. The remarkable result was that the overwhelming majority of α-particles passed through

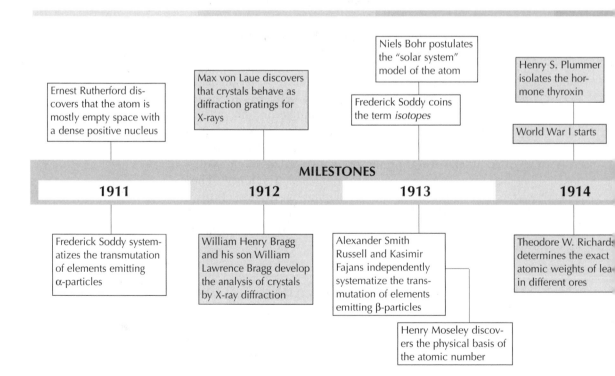

Niels Bohr postulates the "solar system" model of the atom

Henry S. Plummer isolates the hormone thyroxin

Ernest Rutherford discovers that the atom is mostly empty space with a dense positive nucleus

Max von Laue discovers that crystals behave as diffraction gratings for X-rays

Frederick Soddy coins the term *isotopes*

World War I starts

MILESTONES

| 1911 | 1912 | 1913 | 1914 |

Frederick Soddy systematizes the transmutation of elements emitting α-particles

William Henry Bragg and his son William Lawrence Bragg develop the analysis of crystals by X-ray diffraction

Alexander Smith Russell and Kasimir Fajans independently systematize the transmutation of elements emitting β-particles

Theodore W. Richards determines the exact atomic weights of lead in different ores

Henry Moseley discovers the physical basis of the atomic number

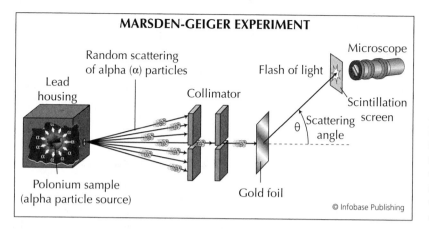

MARSDEN-GEIGER EXPERIMENT

Random scattering of alpha (α) particles

Microscope

Flash of light

Lead housing

Collimator

Scintillation screen

θ Scattering angle

Polonium sample (alpha particle source)

Gold foil

© Infobase Publishing

Schematic diagram of the Marsden-Geiger experiment, using α-particles aimed at a thin sheet of gold foil, which demonstrated that matter was overwhelmingly empty space with dense nuclei at the centers of the atoms.

the gold foil with virtually no deflection. A very minute fraction was deflected strongly (even backwards). For example, only one α-particle in 20,000 was scattered through a deflection angle of 90°. In 1911, Rutherford analyzed the data of Marsden and Geiger, using classical Newtonian physics and statistics, and drew the conclusion that such large deflections were due to single encounters with superdense, positively charged nuclei and

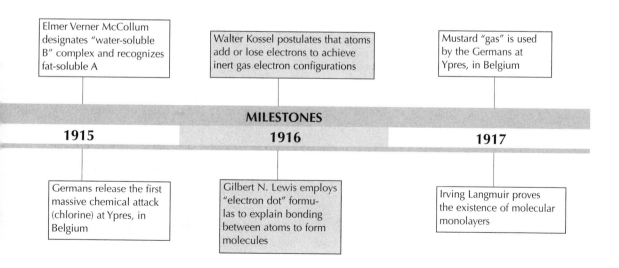

Elmer Verner McCollum designates "water-soluble B" complex and recognizes fat-soluble A

Walter Kossel postulates that atoms add or lose electrons to achieve inert gas electron configurations

Mustard "gas" is used by the Germans at Ypres, in Belgium

MILESTONES

1915

1916

1917

Germans release the first massive chemical attack (chlorine) at Ypres, in Belgium

Gilbert N. Lewis employs "electron dot" formulas to explain bonding between atoms to form molecules

Irving Langmuir proves the existence of molecular monolayers

that atoms are mostly empty space. Another confirmation derived from observing α-particles emitted in the Wilson cloud chamber. The straight tracks caused by α-particles typically ran several centimeters before showing a sudden strong deflection. Each helium *nucleus* passed through thousands of atoms before colliding with the nucleus of a single atom. A book titled *The Fly in the Cathedral*, quotes Rutherford referring to the atomic nucleus in the atom as "the gnat in the Albert Hall."

Measuring Accurate Distances between Atoms or Ions

Nature demands much from her mortal, but inquisitive, subjects before yielding her secrets. However, every once in a while she provides a gift. One such gift, first discovered by Max von Laue (1879–1960) in Zurich in 1912, is that the wavelengths of X-rays (typically 10^{-8} or 10^{-9} cm; same orders of magnitude in inches) are very similar to the separations between atoms or *ions* in crystalline substances. Atomic separations are typically provided in units of angstroms (1 Å = 10^{-8} cm = 10^{-10} m = ~ 4 × 10^{-9} inch) or nanometers (1 nm = 10 Å = 10^{-7} cm = 10^{-9} m = ~ 4 × 10^{-8} inch).

By the end of the 19th century, the wave nature of light and its *diffraction* was understood. A strip of transparent film, uniformly scored

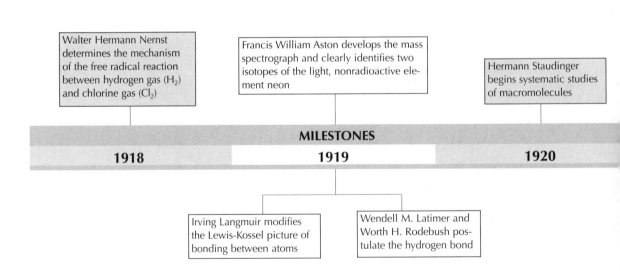

Walter Hermann Nernst determines the mechanism of the free radical reaction between hydrogen gas (H_2) and chlorine gas (Cl_2)

Francis William Aston develops the mass spectrograph and clearly identifies two isotopes of the light, nonradioactive element neon

Hermann Staudinger begins systematic studies of macromolecules

MILESTONES

1918

1919

1920

Irving Langmuir modifies the Lewis-Kossel picture of bonding between atoms

Wendell M. Latimer and Worth H. Rodebush postulate the hydrogen bond

to 7,000 lines per centimeter (0.0000563 inch or 0.000143 cm spacing between lines), provides a grating capable of diffracting light much as a prism diffracts light. This is so because the separation between the lines

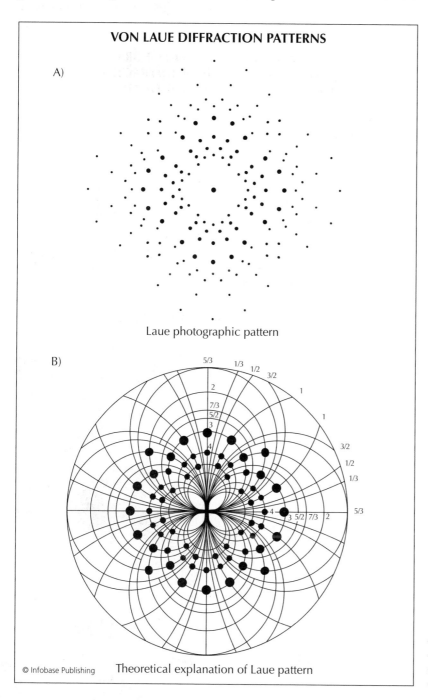

VON LAUE DIFFRACTION PATTERNS

A)

Laue photographic pattern

B)

Theoretical explanation of Laue pattern

© Infobase Publishing

A) An experimental Laue X-ray diffraction pattern on exposed film; B) analysis of the experimental pattern

on the grating is very similar to the wavelengths of light. Yellow light has a wavelength of 589 nm (0.0000589 cm or 0.0000232 inch). Layers of identical atoms rather than lines etched on a film serve as the diffraction grating for X-rays. X-rays are invisible and their diffraction is observed

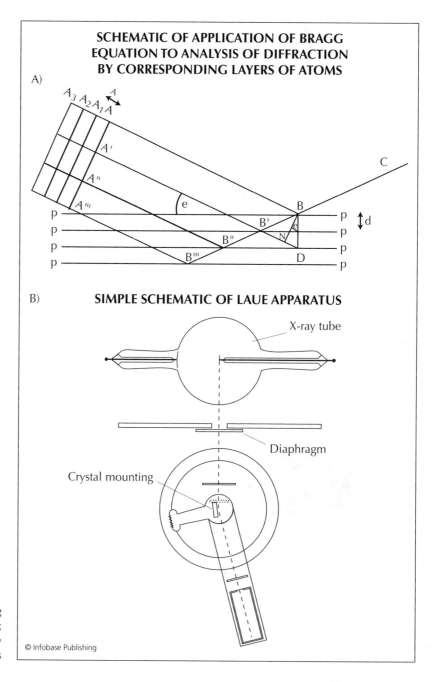

SCHEMATIC OF APPLICATION OF BRAGG EQUATION TO ANALYSIS OF DIFFRACTION BY CORRESPONDING LAYERS OF ATOMS

A)

SIMPLE SCHEMATIC OF LAUE APPARATUS

B)

X-ray tube

Diaphragm

Crystal mounting

A) Derivation of the Bragg equation for X-ray diffraction; B) schematic diagram of X-ray diffraction apparatus

© Infobase Publishing

through exposure of photographic film (a Von Laue pattern on a photographic plate along with the corresponding Bragg analysis is shown in the accompanying figure).

It remained for William Henry Bragg (1862–1942) and his son William Lawrence Bragg (1890–1971), in England, to develop in 1912 the mathematical analysis for determining interatomic (or interionic) distances. The figure on page 42 depicts the distances between layers of atoms and the re-enforcement of reflections of X-rays giving rise to diffraction. In its simplest form, the Bragg equation is written:

$$n\lambda = 2d \sin \theta$$

Here θ is the angle of incidence of X-rays to the surface, d is the distance between layers of atoms or ions, λ is the wavelength of the X-rays and n is an integer (n = 1,2,3, . . .). In practice, λ is known for a given experiment, θ is measured experimentally, assumed values for n are employed and d is determined from these results. The figure depicts the "measurables" in Braggs' law (top) and a schematic of the X-ray apparatus (bottom). Laue received the 1914 Nobel Prize in physics and the two Braggs shared the 1915 Nobel Prize in physics. Young William Lawrence Bragg was only 25 years old at the time; he was, nonetheless, a full co-equal in the scientific discovery.

The Bohr Atom: The Quantum Makes Its Chemical Debut

Chapter 1 includes a brief description of the development of the spectroscope and its application to obtaining line spectra so characteristic of individual elements. But what is the origin of these line spectra? The earliest quantum mechanics of Planck (see chapter 1) treats different sized packets of energy or "quanta" corresponding to each wavelength of light. In 1885 the Swiss schoolmaster Johann Jacob Balmer (1825–98), using the experimental data published by Swedish physicist Anders Jonas Ångström (1814–74), published an incredibly simple equation that accurately accounted for the wavelengths (λ) of the bright colored lines in the visible spectrum of hydrogen (1 nm = 4×10^{-8} inch): Red (656.28 nm); Green (486.13 nm); Blue (434.05 nm); and Violet (410.18 nm). A more general equation was later derived by the Swedish physicist Johannes Robert Rydberg (1854–1919), where R is now known as the Rydberg constant. It can be written:

$$1/\lambda = R \{1/n_f^2 - 1/n_i^2\}$$

For the *Balmer series*, n_f is simply 2 and n_i takes the values 3, 4, 5, or 6. In 1908 the German physicist Friedrich Paschen (1865–1947) discovered new spectral lines fitting the above equation if $n_f = 3$ and $n_i = 4$ and $n_i = 5$. In 1906, Harvard physicist Theodore Lyman (1874–1954) discovered an ultraviolet series of spectral lines from hydrogen corresponding to $n_f = 1$ and some 16 years later infrared spectral lines were discovered corresponding to $n_f = 4$ and $n_f = 5$.

BOHR MODEL OF THE ATOM

A)   Depicted as two-dimensional orbits

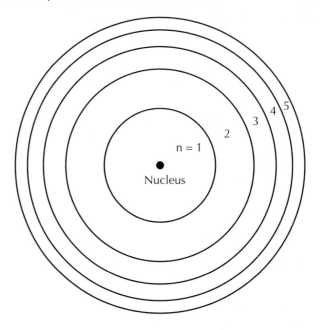

B)   Depicted as three-dimensional shells

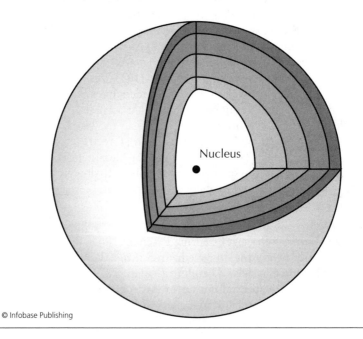

A) Two-dimensional Bohr solar system model of the atom depicting the first five orbits (n = 1 - 5); B) three-dimensional equivalent of the Bohr model of the atom

© Infobase Publishing

In 1913, the Danish physicist Niels Bohr (1885–1962) combined Planck's early quantum theory ($\Delta E = h\nu$) with the modified Balmer equation and some classical physics to derive a physical picture often referred to as the "solar system model" of the atom (see figure page 44). Atoms are three-dimensional and the analog to the *Bohr model* would consist of spherical concentric shells (bottom of figure). In the Bohr model, the lowest energy state for an electron corresponds to its occupancy of the orbit (or shell) closest to the nucleus. When sufficient energy is applied (via heat, light, or electricity) the electron will be "promoted" to an orbit further from the nucleus and instantaneously "relax back" to an inner orbit. The physical explanation for the Balmer series rests upon the idea that the electron in hydrogen may be promoted to an initial orbit (n_i = 6,5,4, or 3) and relax back to the final orbit (n_f = 2) giving off violet, blue, green, or red light respectively. The λ values noted above correspond to these four spectral lines. The energy values ($\Delta E = h\nu$) correspond to the differences in energy of an electron moving from an outer orbit to n = 2. The *Paschen series* corresponds to electrons relaxing back to the third orbit (n_f = 3), the ultraviolet *Lyman series* corresponds to relaxation back to the first orbit (n_f = 1), and the infrared series corresponds to relaxations from higher orbits to n_f = 4 and n_f = 5. For higher and higher values of n, the orbits squeeze closer and closer together. For n_f = ∞, λ = 364.56 nm and the energy change (ΔE) equals 13.6 *electron volts* (313.6 Kcal/mol or 1,312.2 KJ/mol). This is the *ionization potential* (IP), the energy required to completely remove the electron ("to infinity") from the hydrogen atom. Bohr received the 1922 Nobel Prize in physics for his atomic model.

The Bohr model looks comfortably familiar: it suggests the solar system. However, the literal meaning of the Bohr model is that an electron can occupy orbits n = 1,2,3,4,5,6,7. . . . but can *never* be found between orbits. This raises the question of just how an electron moves from, for example, n_i = 4 to n_f = 2. As scientists learned during the 1920s, electrons are not simply particles, like green peas, and humans are not capable of drawing a meaningful mental picture of this process.

The "Roll Call" of Elements: The Atomic Number

In the α-particle scattering experiment performed in 1908 by Marsden and Geiger in Rutherford's laboratory, only a very minute fraction of α-particles experienced significant deflection by the thin gold-foil target. When targets were made from different metal foils, Marsden and Geiger observed that the count of large deflections per minute increased with increasing atomic weight of the metal. That made sense if the number of positive particles in the nucleus increased with increasing atomic weight. If the positive charge in the nucleus is assumed to be roughly numerically equal to half the atomic mass, then these values (e.g., 27/2 for aluminum; 64/2 for copper) are *close*

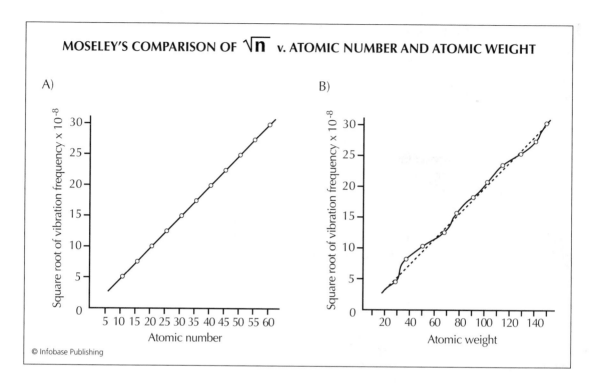

MOSELEY'S COMPARISON OF $\sqrt{n}$ v. ATOMIC NUMBER AND ATOMIC WEIGHT

A)

Square root of vibration frequency x 10^{-8}

Atomic number

B)

Square root of vibration frequency x 10^{-8}

Atomic weight

© Infobase Publishing

A) Moseley's linear relationship between atomic number and the square root of the K_α X-ray frequency of the corresponding element; B) the inferior relationship between atomic mass and the square root of the K_α X-ray frequency of the element

to their positions in the periodic table (13 and 29 respectively). In Utrecht in 1911, Anton Van den Broek (1856–1917) postulated that the total nuclear charge for each type of atom is actually a simple ordinal number (1,2,3 …) corresponding to the element's sequential position in the periodic table (assuming H = 1). He termed the total nuclear charge the *atomic number.*

For some years, it was known that when cathode rays hit various elements (acting in effect as "anti-cathodes"), characteristic X-rays were produced. In 1913, Henry Moseley (1887–1915) began an investigation to determine whether the properties of the X-rays were related to atomic mass or to atomic number. Using a crystal as a tool to provide a diffraction grating for the emitted X-rays, he observed certain X-rays, called K-rays, which were split into two sets: K_α and K_β. In studying a series of metal targets, Moseley noted a simple linear relationship between the square root of the frequency ($[v]^{1/2}$) of the K_α X-ray emission and N, the simple ordinal atomic number (see the accompanying figure) The relationship between $(v)^{1/2}$ and *atomic weight* (accompanying figure) was inferior.

This powerful observation once and for all provided real physical meaning to the atomic number. The atomic number (N, often called Z from the German *zu zahlen*, "to count") is more than just a "roll-call" assignment; it has physical reality. Moseley's discovery settled some knotty problems in the periodic table and made powerful new predictions. The pairs of consecutive elements argon-potassium, nickel-cobalt, and tellurium-iodine had seemed to be anomalies in the periodic table. In each case the order in the periodic table made chemical sense only if the heavier element came *before* the lighter element. Moseley's method established that placement according to chemical properties, not atomic weight, is correct. Much as Mendeleev had left gaps in his periodic table, Moseley's discovery predicted that atomic numbers 43, 61, 72, 85, and 87 were missing elements, all later discovered. Moseley, a draftee during World War I, was killed in 1915 at the age of 28 in the battle of Gallipoli.

Valence Electrons: The Octet Rule and Lewis Structures

Valence was a concept developed during the mid-19th century at a time when many prominent chemists and physicists did not accept the reality of atoms and certainly had no thoughts about subatomic structure. The periodic table classified the known elements according to their common valences, but provided no hint of the basis for valence. And yet, ever since Luigi Galvani (1737–98) demonstrated in 1780 that two different metals connected by the muscle of a frog pass an electric current, and Alessandro Volta's (1745–1827) development in 1800 of the first battery, it was clear that electricity is intimately connected with matter. Electrolysis of water produces hydrogen and oxygen. In 1807, Humphry Davy (1778–1829) decomposed solid potash (KOH) electrolytically and discovered silvery beads of liquid potassium that exploded and burned with a bright flame. His brother Edmund writes that Davy "actually bounded about the room in ecstatic delight." But the most important discovery, relating electricity to chemistry, was made by Michael Faraday (1791–1867) in the 1830s: The quantity of electricity (current x time) required to produce 1 gram (0.0022 lb) of hydrogen gas (1 chemical equivalent) equals the quantity of electricity that produces 8 grams (0.018 lb) of oxygen gas (1 chemical equivalent), or plates out 31.8 grams (0.070 lb) of copper (1 chemical equivalent) in various *electrolysis* experiments.

Ideas about the "octet" were really intrinsic to the periodic table and the "law of octaves," the periodic repetition of chemical properties every eighth element (noble gases were unknown in the 1860s). Mendeleev observed that the highest known valence of any element was 8 [for example, osmium tetroxide (OsO_4), the valence of oxygen is 2]. He found that if one summed the (periodic table) column number and multiplied by the number of equivalents, the total was commonly 8: HCl (1 + 7); H_2O ([1 times 2] + 6); AsH_3 (5 + [1 times 3]).

A major insight came from the discovery of the noble gases during the 1890s and the realization that chemical stability (inertness) is associated with an octet of electrons in the outermost shell of the (Bohr) atom (helium fills its outermost shell with only two electrons). The counting of electrons was, of course, based upon the assumption that the number of positive charges in the nucleus equals 1 for hydrogen, 2 for helium, etc.

Kossel depiction of the octet rule demonstrating completion of the octet at each noble gas (Ne, Ar, Kr, Xe) (Adapted from Max Born's The Constitution of Matter. London: Methuen & Co. Ltd., 1923, p. 22)

and that the number of electrons in an atom match these nuclear charges. This led Walter Kossel (1888–1956), son of Albrecht Kossel (see chapter 1), to propose in 1916 that atoms react through their outermost (valence) electrons to achieve the electronic structure of the nearest inert gas. This was most easily understood for "highly polar" (i.e., ionic) compounds. It was clear that an alkali metal such as sodium easily lost one electron,

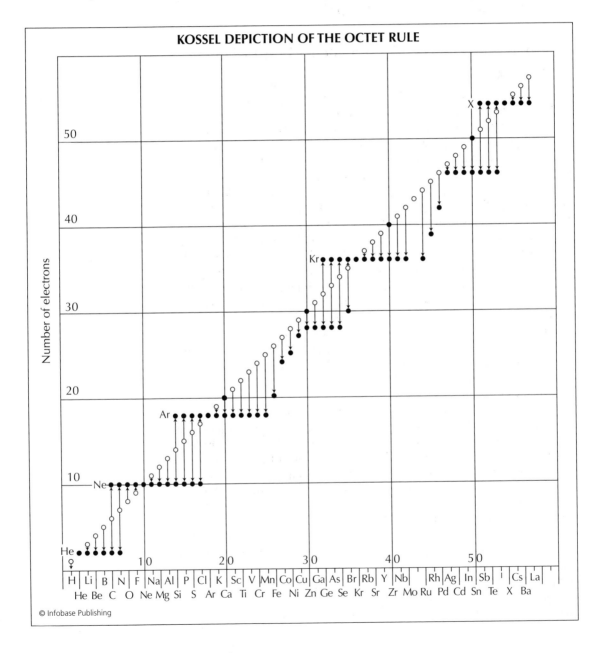

KOSSEL DEPICTION OF THE OCTET RULE

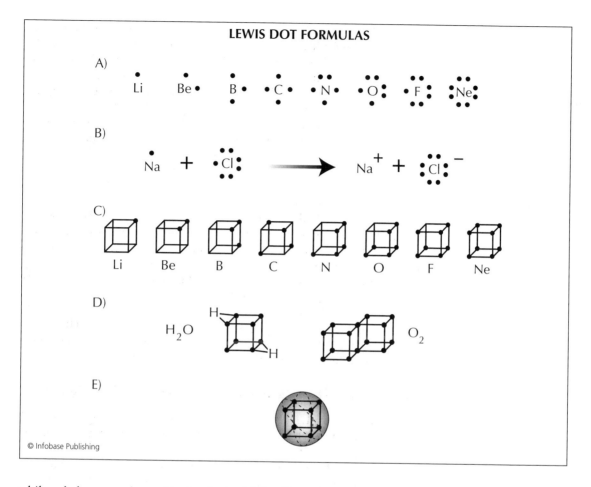

LEWIS DOT FORMULAS

A) Lewis dot structures for Li, Be, B, C, N, O, F, Ne; B) Lewis dot structures depicting $Na + Cl \rightarrow Na^+ + Cl^-$; C) cubic atom structures for Li, Be, B, C, N, O, F, Ne; D) cubic atoms bonded in H_2O and O_2 with corresponding Lewis dot structures; E) a spherical Bohr electron shell inscribed around a Lewis "cubical atom" of neon

while a halogen such as chlorine had a high affinity for capturing one electron to form an ionic salt. Magnesium has a strong tendency to lose two electrons and oxygen a high affinity for gaining two electrons. The figure on page 48 graphically represents this concept, the *octet rule*.

In 1916, Gilbert N. Lewis (1875–1946), at Berkeley, moved even further with this concept and provided the notation commonly employed today: *Lewis dot structures.* His concepts were modified in 1919 by Irving Langmuir (1881–1957), who coined the term *covalence.* Chemical bonding is recognized to arise from transfer or sharing of the outermost (valence) electrons. Examples of Lewis dot structures are provided for the atoms in the second row of the periodic table (see figure above). The dots represent electrons in the outermost or valence shell. Effectively, the symbol of the element represents a "core" consisting of the nucleus and the remaining sub-valence ("inner shell") electrons. Of the 17 electrons in the chlorine atom, only the 7 in the third ("M-shell") are depicted. For a "highly polar" (ionic) substance such as table salt, the depiction in this figure represents the neon core (Na^+) and the argon valence shell (Cl^-) of the ions formed by transfer of one electron from the sodium atom to the chlorine atom. Atoms also achieve completed octets by sharing electrons. Lewis found it useful to represent atoms as cubes in which the electrons in the outermost shell, the valence shell, occupy the corners (accompanying figure). Single bonds are formed when edges contributing one valence electron each are shared. Sharing of a face (4 electrons total) gives a double bond (accompanying figure). Lewis noted (as the reader may have) that the simple cube model cannot be used to represent triple bonds, such as those in acetylene (H-C≡C-H) or nitrogen (:N≡N:). This was a weakness in his theory. For acetylene and other organic molecules, he fell back to the van't Hoff view (see chapter 1) that a C-C bond forms at a shared point (vertex) of two tetrahedra, a C=C bond is formed when two tetrahedra share an edge in common, and a C≡C bond is formed by two tetrahedra sharing a triangular base in common. Electrons were unknown in 1874, but van't Hoff was well aware of valence and carbon's ability to form single, double, and triple bonds. In the accompanying figure, Lewis dot structures are shown for H_2O and O_2. Inscribing a sphere onto a cubic neon atom (accompanying figure) conveys a simplistic connection between the Lewis and Bohr atoms. Although the modern quantum theory, developed during the 1920s (see chapter 3), would render pictures such as these obsolete, Lewis dot structures remain useful "counting tools" and are today still a staple of instruction in the introductory chemistry course.

Hydrogen Bonds between Polar Molecules

The Kossel-Lewis-Langmuir model for chemical bonding recognized *covalent bonds* in which electrons are shared to form complete octets for each of two bonded atoms. The model classified highly polar compounds as those in which electrons are transferred from one atom to another to form ions. It was obvious even then that there are gradations of polarity with resulting chemical and physical consequences.

It is worthwhile spending a moment to illustrate how the new technique of X-ray crystallography contributed to the understanding of *ionic bonding*. As noted in chapter 1, Arrhenius's studies of conductivity of electrolytes during the 1880s established that salts such as NaCl form ions in aqueous solution. Sodium chloride is also known to conduct electricity in its molten state, since its ions diffuse. Crystalline NaCl does not conduct electricity. Could the crystal be composed of an arrangement of individual Na-Cl molecules? Crystallographic studies performed during this period established that each sodium "atom" is surrounded by six symmetrically placed chlorines and each chlorine "atom" is surrounded by six symmetrically placed sodium "atoms" (see small figure on page 51). These were not Na-Cl units but Na^+ ions surrounded by the maximum number of Cl^- *anions* that can fit around each *cation*.

With the advent of Lewis structures, chemists began to test them with ever more subtle questions. It was recognized that covalent bonds between different atoms (e.g., HCl) involved unequal sharing and this,

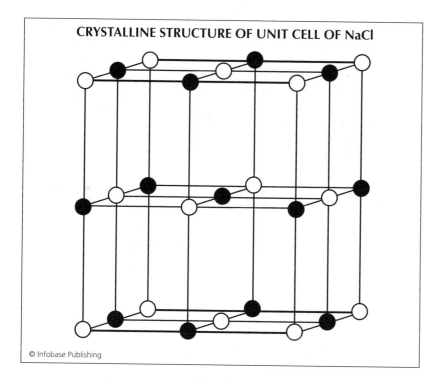

CRYSTALLINE STRUCTURE OF UNIT CELL OF NaCl

© Infobase Publishing

Unit cell for the sodium chloride (NaCl) crystal. Each of the 12 sodium ions (•) on an edge of the unit cell is shared by four unit cells including the one shown; the sodium ion in the center belongs totally to the unit cell shown; each of the six chloride ions (○) on a face of the unit cell is shared by one adjacent unit cell; the eight chloride ions on the corners of the unit cell are each shared by eight unit cells, including the one shown. In the NaCl unit cell there are 12/4 + 1 = 4 sodium ions and 6/2 + 8/8 = 4 chloride ions.

in turn, gave rise to molecular *dipoles* and *dipole moments*. The dipoles produce attractions between different molecules changing the physical properties of the compounds to varying extents.

Wendell M. Latimer (1893–1955) and Worth H. Rodebush (1887–1959), Lewis's colleagues at Berkeley, were intrigued with anomalies in the properties of compounds in which hydrogen is covalently attached to the electronegative elements fluorine, oxygen, and nitrogen. For example, the boiling point of water (212°F or 100°C) is amazingly high for its low molecular weight. Latimer and Rodebush realized that hydrogen is unique because its valence shell is also the innermost shell. If hydrogen is attached to an atom of high *electronegativity* (especially F, O, and N), the electrons it shares will be pulled toward its partner leaving its core, the hydrogen nucleus, "exposed." This would explain the anomalously strong associations between molecules manifested in high boiling points. Latimer and Rodebush employed the accompanying structure to represent what is today termed the *hydrogen-bonding* association between water molecules.

$$H:\ddot{O}:H:\ddot{O}: \quad \begin{matrix} H \\ \\ H \end{matrix}$$

Hydrogen-bonded water dimer

Family Relationships between Radioactive Isotopes

Chapter 1 describes the bewildering discoveries of radioactive elements having identical chemical properties but different radioactive emissions. In

1913, Soddy termed these elements "isotopes." Two years earlier, he realized that when a radioactive element emits an α-particle, it transmutes to an element 2 atomic number units lower with a loss of 4.0 units of atomic weight. In 1913, Alexander Smith Russell (1888–1972) and Kasimir Fajans (1887–1975) independently published the finding that emission of a β-particle transmutes an element to another element one atomic number unit higher with no change in atomic weight. In the same year, Fajans consolidated these findings and recognized the three distinct radioactive series depicted in the figure below. He also identified the isotopes as "inserts" in

Fajans's three radioactive series published in 1913

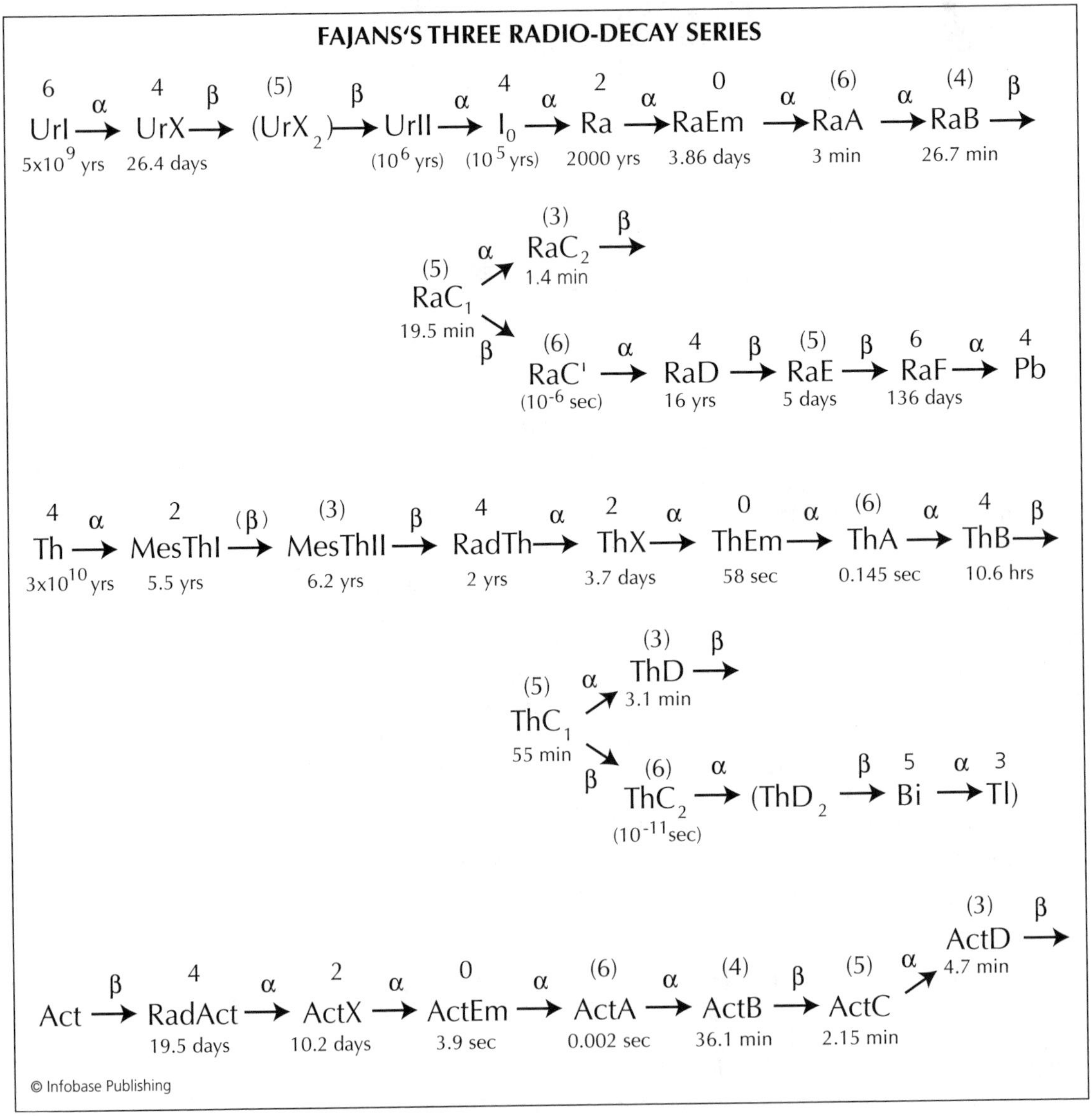

FAJANS'S THREE RADIO-DECAY SERIES

FAJANS'S PERIODIC TABLE–STYLE LISTING OF ISOTOPES						
0	**I**	**II**	**III**	**IV**	**V**	**VI**
	Au 197.2	Hg 200.6	**Tl 204.4**			
			ActD 206.5	**Pb 206.5**		
			ThD 208.4	**ThD$_2$ 208.4**	**Bi 208.4**	
			RaC$_2$ 210.5	(RaD 210.5	**RaE 210.5**	
				(ActB 210.5)	ActC 210.5	**RaF 210.5**
				(ThB 212.4)	**ThC$_1$ 212.4**	**ThC$_2$ 212.4**
				(RaB 214.5)	**RaC 214.5**	**RaC 214.5**
						ActA 214.5
						ThA 216.4
						RaA 218.4
ActEm 218.5	(ActX$_2$) 218.5					
ThEm 220.4	**(ThX$_2$) 218.5**					
RaEm 222.5	**(RaX) 222.5**					
		ActX 222.5		RadAct 226.5		
		ThX 224.4	Act 226.5	**RadTh 228.4**		
		Ra 226.5				
		MesThI 228.4	**MesThII 228.4**	**Io 230.5**		
				Th 232.4		
				UrX 234.5	**(UrX$_2$) 234.5**	**UrII 234.5**
						UrI 238.5

the periodic table (see figure above). For example, in column IV stable lead (Pb) is listed along with four distinct isotopes with short half-lives: "ThD2", $t_{1/2}$ = not provided; "RaD", $t_{1/2}$ = 16 years; "ThB", $t_{1/2}$ = 10.6 hours; "RaB", $t_{1/2}$ = 26.7 min. (Today, the atomic weight of lead is taken as 207.19; there are four stable lead isotopes and at least 20 short-lived isotopes).

In 1914, Theodore W. Richards (1868–1928) at Harvard experimentally verified the principle advanced by Fajans. He investigated lead from a nonradioactive ore ("common lead") and compared its atomic weight with lead obtained from five other types of ore samples. The amazing results are shown in the table on page 54: lead from North Carolina uraninite ore is 0.75 *atomic mass units* (almost one full unit!) lighter than "common lead." The various ore samples had different radioactive elements in different proportions and produced their own unique series of lead isotopes. In contrast, Richards found that copper obtained from ore

Fajans's periodic table–style listing of isotopes in 1913 (see the figure on page 52)

samples collected from different parts of the earth had identical atomic weights. For this work and related studies of precise atomic weights Richards became, in 1914, the first American to win the Nobel Prize in chemistry.

Atomic Weights of Lead Obtained from Various Radioactive Ores and Published in 1914 by Theodore W. Richards and Max E. Lembert

Sample	Atomic Weight (amu)
Lead from North Carolina uraninite	206.40
Lead from Joachimsthal pitchblende	206.57
Lead from Colorado carnotite	206.59
Lead from Ceylonese thorianite	206.82
Lead from English pitchblende	206.86
Common Lead	207.15

Isotopes of Light, Nonradioactive Elements: The Mass Spectrometer

In 1907, J. J. Thomson observed that when a vacuum tube is filled with neon gas under low pressure, the introduction of magnetic and electric fields produces two parabolic luminescent paths of canal rays (see chapter 1), corresponding to two different masses (20 and 22) for charged particles. The potentially revolutionary results were treated cautiously since impurities could be the cause. In 1909, Francis William Aston (1877–1945) became Thomson's assistant at Cambridge. Aston and Thomson attempted to apply Graham's law of diffusion to separate the two different components of neon gas and, after thousands of cycles of diffusion operations, obtained in 1913 a mass difference of 0.7 between the lighter and heavier fractions. World War I delayed continuation of this groundbreaking project for a few years.

After the war ended, Aston continued his studies on the "positive rays." By 1919, he improved their resolutions, allowing all particles of a given e/m ratio to focus at a given point and collecting images on film. Aston's positive ray spectrograph (or mass spectrograph) is shown schematically in the accompanying figure. He used it to demonstrate that neon consists of two components, one of mass 20 and one of mass 22. This was the first definitive demonstration of isotopes for a light, nonradioactive element and led to the modern definition of isotopes (atoms having the same atomic number and different atomic mass). Soddy's earlier definition of isotopes (chemically identical atoms having different radioactive decays) was relevant only to isotopes of radioactive elements. These are only a subset of all possible isotopes. With the advantage of a new instru-

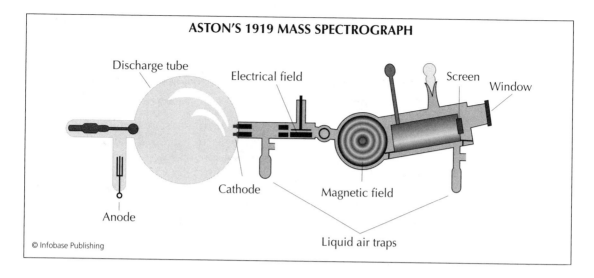

ASTON'S 1919 MASS SPECTROGRAPH

Discharge tube

Electrical field

Screen

Window

Cathode

Magnetic field

Anode

Liquid air traps

© Infobase Publishing

ment, Aston succeeded in identifying 212 of the 287 naturally occurring nuclides. He was awarded the Nobel Prize for chemistry in 1922.

Aston mass spectrograph of 1919 that demonstrated that there are two distinct isotopes (by the modern definition) of neon

Manipulating Volatile Compounds That React Violently with Air or Water

In 1912 Alfred Stock (1876–1946) developed techniques to explore two new series of exotic compounds: silicon hydrides and boron hydrides. The latter were synthesized as a mixture through reaction of magnesium boride with hydrogen chloride as shown below (not balanced).

$$MgB_2(s) + HCl(g) \rightarrow B_4H_{10}(g) + B_5H_9(l) + B_5H_{11}(l) + B_6H_{10}(l) + B_{10}H_{14}(s)$$

These compounds are flammable in the presence of oxygen or water. In order to separate the mixture, characterize compounds individually, and test their reactivities, Stock pioneered high-vacuum technologies. In these systems, water and oxygen are rigorously pumped out and the apparatus thoroughly dried by heating under vacuum. Volatile hydrides, freshly synthesized, are rapidly transferred using vacuum lines from one part of the apparatus to a cooled vessel in another part of the apparatus. Such vacuum techniques are now commonly used by chemists to manipulate volatile, air-sensitive compounds (see chapter 6).

Stock continued these studies between 1912 and 1936 and succeeded in isolating diborane (B_2H_6). The formulas of diborane and the higher boron hydrides do not fit the comfortable Lewis-Langmuir electron pair structures. For example, BH_3 (the monomer of diborane) has a total of only 6 valence shell electrons. Diborane is electron deficient by two electrons with no "nice" Lewis structure. It would be some decades before the structures and bonding in these curious and highly reactive compounds would be understood.

Rates of Reaction and the Basis for Reaction Mechanisms

Ever since chemistry became a science of atoms, ions, and molecules, one of its holy grails was to gain the ability to witness chemical change step-by-step, atom-by-atom. This is one way of describing a *reaction mechanism*. In the 20th century, measurements of rates of chemical reactions (chemical kinetics), their dependence upon concentrations of reactants, and their temperature dependence would provide (and continues to provide) critical information about reaction mechanisms.

During the 1880s, Jacobus van't Hoff recognized the relationships between concentrations of reactants and reaction rates. They were not necessarily self-evident from the chemical equation. He originally used the term *molecularity* to describe what is today termed the order of a reaction. Decomposition of arsine (AsH_3) to arsenic and hydrogen is a first-order reaction and the decomposition of hydrogen iodide into hydrogen and iodine is second-order in HI (see below). Doubling the concentration of arsine doubles the rate of reaction. Doubling the concentration of HI quadruples the rate.

$$AsH_3 \rightarrow As + 3/2\ H_2;\ Rate = k[AsH_3]\ (First\text{-}Order)$$

$$2\ HI \rightarrow H_2 + I_2;\ Rate = k[HI]^2\ (Second\text{-}Order)$$

The above relationships appear deceptively simple since they would seem to be predictable from a glance at the chemical equation. This is not, however, the case. The decomposition of arsine could have just as well been found to quadruple in rate were arsine's concentration doubled. In this hypothetical case, the reaction rate would be proportional to $[AsH_3]^2$. Van't Hoff noted that first-order and second-order reactions are relatively common, and third-order reactions are uncommon. He provided the example of the oxidation of hydriodic acid by hydrogen peroxide:

$$2\ HI + H_2O_2 \rightarrow I_2 + 2\ H_2O;\ Rate = k[HI][H_2O_2]\ (Second\text{-}Order)$$

Experimentally, it is a second-order reaction despite three molecules of reactant in the overall reaction. Van't Hoff indicated that the reaction probably takes place in two steps, as shown below, with the first step involving two molecules and constituting the slow, or rate-determining step, hence it is bimolecular. This is an early example of kinetics eliminating one mechanism (a one-step collision of two HI molecules with one H_2O_2 molecule) and supporting (although not proving) a two-step mechanism. In this mechanism, HOI is a short-lived reaction intermediate:

$$Step\ 1:\ HI + H_2O_2 \rightarrow HOI + H_2O$$

$$Step\ 2:\ HOI + HI \rightarrow H_2O + I_2$$

In 1913, David L. Chapman (1869–1958) and his student L. K. Underhill at Oxford developed the *steady-state approximation*. The rate of formation of a short-lived intermediate, such as HOI, is treated mathematically as virtually equal to its rate of decomposition. Therefore, the actual (steady-state) concentration of the intermediate is vanishingly small (virtually zero).

Van't Hoff, as well as some other scientists, studied the increase in rate constants with increasing temperature. An earlier equation was modified by the Swedish chemist Svante Arrhenius to the form noted below. The Arrhenius equation is more than a semi-empirical equation to account for the usual doubling or tripling of reaction rate for every 18°F (10°C) increase. The "E" denotes the energy needed to induce reaction and "A" represents a "frequency factor" related to the probability of reaction. These parameters would be better understood during the 1930s with the development of transition-state theory. Wilhelm Ostwald's contributions to kinetics were many and included the application of thermodynamics to kinetics and mechanism as well as the explanation of catalysis. This magnificent triumvirate of physical chemists would all win Nobel Prizes in chemistry: van't Hoff (1901); Arrhenius (1903); Ostwald (1909).

$$k = Ae^{-E/RT} \text{ (Arrhenius equation)}$$

During the second decade of the 20th century a new general mechanism was discovered that would dramatically impact thermal chemistry, especially combustion, and photochemistry. Hydrogen gas (H_2) and chlorine gas (Cl_2) do not react with each other in the dark at moderate temperatures. However, in the presence of ultraviolet light they react explosively. In 1913, Max Bodenstein (1871–1942) noted that photochemical reaction of chlorine gas with hydrogen gas yields about 1 million (10^6) molecules of HCl per photon of ultraviolet light absorbed. This yield of 10^6 molecules per photon, now termed the quantum yield (Φ), remains the "world's record." Bodenstein's original interpretation involved ions. The correct explanation was provided by Nernst in 1918. He postulated the critical presence of a free radical (in this case a chlorine atom) that is consumed and regenerated in the *chain reaction* steps depicted in the equations below. Bodenstein verified Chapman's steady state theory and applied it to the short-lived free radicals he postulated. The "chain reaction" steps convey the predominant chemical reaction occurring in this transformation (that is, ca. 10^6 complete chain-propagating steps before chain-terminating steps such as $2\ Cl \rightarrow Cl_2$ and $H + Cl \rightarrow HCl$).

$$Cl + H_2 \rightarrow HCl + H$$

$$H + Cl_2 \rightarrow HCl + Cl$$

$$\text{NET: } H_2 + Cl_2 \rightarrow 2\ HCl$$

Free radicals had been of interest since the middle of the 19th century. Gomberg's observation of the persistent triphenylmethyl radical (see chapter 1) added support to the case for the intermediacy of free radicals. In the case of Cl radical (or atom), only a minute steady-state concentration needs to be generated by the photochemical chain-initiating step: $Cl_2 + h\nu \rightarrow 2\ Cl$. Free radicals are generally extremely reactive and short-lived, like Cl, rather than persistent, like Gomberg's triphenylmethyl radical. That is why even a minor impurity giving rise to free radicals can substantially change the outcome of a reaction.

Chemical Kinetics of Enzyme-Catalyzed Reactions

Not long after Buchner and others isolated enzymes (see chapter 1), chemists began to explore the kinetics of these amazing natural catalysts. In 1913, the German biochemist Leonor Michaelis (1875–1949), collaborating with Canadian Maud Lenora Menten (1879–1960), observed that plots of reaction rate versus substrate concentration for enzyme-catalyzed reactions typically yield curves like that in the figure on page 59. If the reaction were simply one step, first-order in substrate and first-order in catalyst, (i.e., Substrate + catalyst $\rightarrow$ Product + catalyst), rate should increase linearly with substrate concentration. Instead, the observed curves demonstrate a limit to the rate that can not be exceeded by adding more substrate. Michaelis and Menten ascribed this limiting rate to saturation of the enzyme by substrate. Specifically, they postulated the general enzyme mechanism provided below: rapid reversible enzyme-substrate complex (ES) formation followed by rate-determining dissociation of the complex to yield product plus free enzyme. A "cartoon" depicting this mechanism is shown in the figure on page 59:

$$E + S \underset{k_{-1}}{\overset{k_1}{\leftrightarrows}} ES$$

$$ES \overset{k_2}{\rightarrow} E + P$$

The derived equation for the rate of this reaction as a function of the substrate concentration ([S]), when [S] is very small, is given below (where $[E]_o$ is the total concentration of enzyme [unbound plus bound]). When [S] is high and the enzyme is saturated, the resulting rate equation is independent of [S]. In that case the velocity curve is horizontal as depicted in the accompanying figure.

$$v = k_2[E]_o[S]/K_m \text{ (when [S] is very low)}$$

$$v = k_2[E]_o \text{ (when [S] is high)}$$

Thin Films, Monolayers, and a Foretaste of Modern Nanotechnology

In 1774, Benjamin Franklin reported this observation to the Royal Society:

At length at Clapman where there is, on the common, a large pond, which I observed to be one day very rough with the wind, I fetched

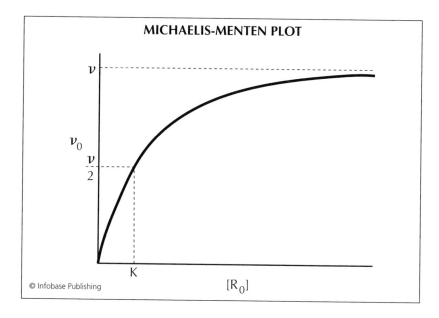

MICHAELIS-MENTEN PLOT

© Infobase Publishing

A generalized Michaelis-Menten plot depicting the rate (v_o) versus concentration of substrate or reactant ($[R_o]$). At higher concentrations, the rate approaches a maximum value (v) due to saturation of the enzyme. At $v/2$, $[R_o] = K$, the binding constant of enzyme for substrate.

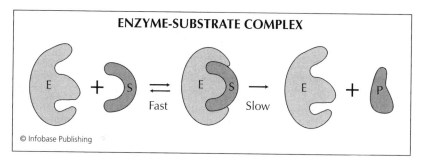

ENZYME-SUBSTRATE COMPLEX

© Infobase Publishing

Cartoon depicting the rapid, reversible binding of substrate S by enzyme E to form enzyme-substrate complex ES that dissociates in a slow step to product P

> *out a cruet of oil, and dropped a little of it on the water. I saw it spread itself with surprising swiftness upon the surface . . . the oil, though not more than a teaspoonful, produced an instant calm over a space several yards square, which spread amazingly and extended itself gradually until it reached the leeside, making all that quarter of a pond, perhaps half an acre, as smooth as a looking glass.*

Modern calculations suggest that this half-acre film was about 2 nm (0.00000008 inches) thick.

In 1891, Agnes Pockels (1862–1935), a German woman of modest education, wrote to Lord Rayleigh describing her rather "homely" experiments on surface tension in her kitchen. Rayleigh communicated her letter to the journal *Nature*, which published it in the same year. Miss Pockels measured the difference between the high surface tension of pure water and reduced surface tensions of various types and concentrations of impure water. She employed a simple tin trough (27.5 in long, 2.0 in wide, 0.8 in

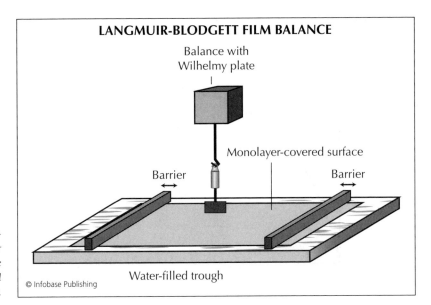

LANGMUIR-BLODGETT FILM BALANCE

Balance with Wilhelmy plate

Monolayer-covered surface

Barrier

Barrier

© Infobase Publishing

Water-filled trough

Schematic diagram of Langmuir-Blodgett film balance for measuring surface pressure. The barriers are moved outward until a thin continuous film is made.

deep) filled to the brim with water. Her apparatus included a movable 0.6-inch-wide strip of tin that divided the trough into two compartments. Miss Pockels measured the surface tension of the compartment in question by using a 0.24-in disk attached to a simple balance and determining the force needed to pull it from the surface of the liquid. If she started with a solution of a salt, sugar, or a wax in one chamber and then compressed it gradually by moving the position of the tin strip, the surface tension in that chamber decreased. Rayleigh, whose work in this area attracted the communication from Miss Pockels, postulated in 1899 that when oil reaches its maximum

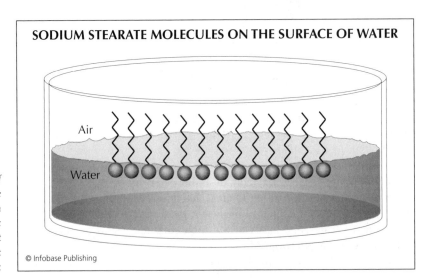

SODIUM STEARATE MOLECULES ON THE SURFACE OF WATER

Air

Water

© Infobase Publishing

Figure depicting alignment of closely packed sodium stearate molecules as a monolayer on the surface of water. Hydrophilic (ionic) "heads" are in contact with water and hydrophobic "tails" stick up into the air.

degree of spreading on such a surface, it has formed a *monolayer*; a thickness of one molecule. This assumption was subsequently demonstrated to be correct and the sidebar below describes how Avogadro's number can be derived from such a monolayer.

Related investigations were undertaken over a decade later by Irving Langmuir (1881–1957) and Katherine Burr Blodgett (1898–1979) at General Electric in Schenectady, New York. Together they developed a refined version of the Pockels apparatus. A schematic drawing of this apparatus is depicted below. Dr. Blodgett was a remarkable trailblazer: the first woman to obtain a Ph.D. in physics at Cambridge (1928) and the first female research scientist at General Electric. Langmuir's studies of carefully formed monolayers, using fatty acids (>12 carbons) and related molecules, established in 1917 that such *amphiphilic* molecules ("water-loving" or *hydrophilic* at one end and "water-hating" or *hydrophobic* at the other) cover the surface of an aqueous solution. The accompanying figure depicts sodium stearate ("soap") molecules whose ionic, hydrophilic heads closely pack the surface and whose nonpolar, hydrophobic hydrocarbon tails are aligned perpendicular to and above the surface. By manipulating the size of the surface so that it is completely covered, a closely packed "pile carpet" of hydrocarbon tails can be assembled. For this work and related studies on colloids, Langmuir received the Nobel Prize in chemistry in 1932.

Very dilute solutions of surfactants such as sodium stearate $[CH_3(CH_2)_{16}CO2^-Na^+]$ or sodium lauryl sulfate $[CH_3(CH_2)_{10}CH_2OSO_3^- Na^+]$ act simply as dilute solutions of strong *electrolytes* like Na^+Cl^-. As concentrations are increased, there is a smooth change in properties until a concentration is reached where an abrupt change is observed. This behavior is depicted in the accompanying figure that graphs surface tension and osmotic pressure of aqueous solutions of sodium lauryl sulfate. At 0.2 percent concentration, aggregates of 50–100 surfactant molecules form globular structures termed *micelles*. The discontinuity in the plot corresponds to the *critical micelle concentration* (cmc).

Organic Chemistry Spawns Biochemistry

Until the middle of the 19th century, organic chemistry was synonymous with "animal chemistry" and "plant chemistry." The theory of "vitalism" was based upon the belief that organic compounds could only be made by animals and plants. The synthesis of "organic" urea from "inorganic" compounds by Friedrich Wöhler (1800–82) in 1828 was the first nail in vitalism's coffin. At the start of the 20th century organic chemistry began to spawn a new discipline: biochemistry. Chapter 1 described early contributions of organic chemistry toward understanding of protein and DNA structures.

Starting in 1906 Richard Willstätter (1872–1942), professor at Zurich, began to investigate the pigments in green plants. While the original studies of these compounds began in the mid-19th century, the substances were simply too complex for analysis. Willstätter's studies, summarized

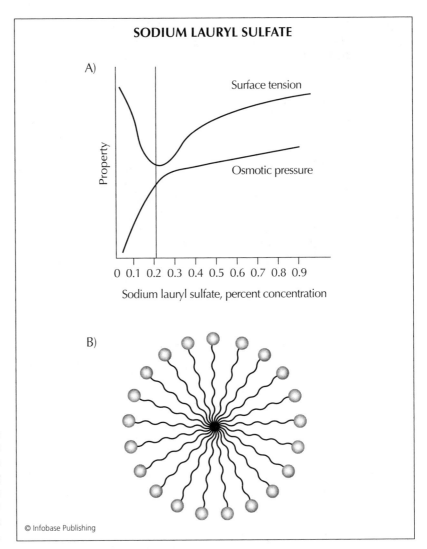

SODIUM LAURYL SULFATE

A)

Property

Surface tension

Osmotic pressure

0 0.1 0.2 0.3 0.4 0.5 0.6 0.7 0.8 0.9

Sodium lauryl sulfate, percent concentration

B)

© Infobase Publishing

A) Graphs of surface tension as well as osmotic pressure plotted versus concentration of sodium lauryl sulfate, demonstrating critical micelle concentration at about 0.21 percent. B) Representation of a sodium lauryl sulfate micelle.

in 1913, established that there were two chlorophylls in green plants: chlorophyll-a ($C_{55}H_{72}O_5N_4Mg$) and chlorophyll-b ($C_{55}H_{70}O_6N_4Mg$). He found that the chlorophylls contain 5-membered pyrrole rings. The full structure determinations awaited Hans Fischer more than a decade later. The structures of chlorophyll-a and chlorophyll-b are provided below. Mikhail Tswett's column chromatographic studies (chapter 1) confirmed the fact that there were precisely two chlorophylls. Both Willstätter and Tswett studied the other pigments in green plants: xanthophylls and carotenes. For his studies of plant pigments, and in particular the chlorophylls, Willstätter won the 1915 Nobel Prize in chemistry. Willstätter, a close friend of Fritz Haber who was also Jewish, quit his professorship

The Origins of the Mole and Avogadro's Number

In introductory chemistry courses teachers introduce the mole (the atomic or molecular mass of a substance in grams) and *Avogadro's number* (6.022×10^{23} particles per mole of a substance). Rarely is it confessed that the mole and Avogadro's number have a somewhat arbitrary aspect. Both terms were introduced in the first decade of the 20th century. Amadeo Avogadro (1776–1856) did not "discover" the number that bears his name. In 1811, shortly after Dalton published atomic theory, Avogadro postulated that equal volumes of gases (same pressure and temperature) consist of equal numbers of the units composing those gases. It would take almost 50 years for the import of this hypothesis to be fully appreciated by Stanislao Cannizzaro (1826–1910) in 1858. In 1865 Johann Joseph Loschmidt (1821–95), an Austrian, employed the new kinetic molecular theory to calculate the number of molecules in one cm^3 of gas under standard temperature and pressure (2.6×10^{19} molecules/cm^3). This became known as Loschmidt's constant (n_0) and today the National Institute of Standards and Technology (NIST) lists the value at standard temperature and pressure (STP) as 2.68678×10^{25} molecules/m^3. It was the predecessor of Avogadro's number (and equally valid).

The term *mole* was introduced by Wilhelm Ostwald in 1901. He derived it from the Latin for a "mass" or "clump" (the term *molecule* dated from the 17th century). In Ostwald's time, atomic and molecular weights (relative to oxygen = precisely 16) were known reasonably accurately. To define the mole as atomic or molecular weight in grams was as simple and reasonable as it was arbitrary.

Jean Perrin's studies of Brownian motion led him to determine that the number of molecules in the recently defined mole was roughly between 6.5×10^{23} and 6.9×10^{23}. In 1908 he first termed this Avogadro's number in honor of the hypothesis advanced almost a century earlier. The first accurate determination of Avogadro's number came from Robert A. Millikan's accurate determination of the charge on one electron (modern value 1.602×10^{-19} coulombs; see chapter 1) combined with Faraday's laws, developed almost 80 years earlier. It requires 96,485 coulombs (1 mole of electrons) to deposit 1 equivalent (in this case, also 1 mole) of silver metal from a solution containing Ag^+ ions. Dividing 96,485 by 1.602×10^{-19} yields Avogadro's number. The studies by Rutherford, Geiger, and colleagues that established that α-particles are helium nuclei furnished another method for obtaining Avogadro's number. The half-life of radium is 1,620 years. Simple calculations show that 0.1 percent of the mass of a sample of radium is lost through emission of α-particles over the course of 2.3 years. Statistical sampling of radium decay using a Geiger counter indicated that in one year, 11.6×10^{17} emitted α-particles produced 0.043 mL (milliliters) of helium gas (at STP [standard temperature and pressure] or 0°C and 1 atmosphere). One mole of an ideal gas at STP occupies 22.4 liters (L). Thus,

$$22.4 \text{ L/mol} \div 0.000043 \text{ L} \times 11.6 \times 10^{17}$$
$$\alpha\text{-particles} = 6.04 \times 10^{23} \ \alpha\text{-particles/mol}$$

X-ray crystallography furnished yet another method, regarded today as the most accurate, for determining this value. The accompanying figure helps to demonstrate this method using X-ray data derived from crystalline metallic nickel. The metal atoms pack in a face-centered cubic *unit cell*. Two neighboring cubes share each face, four share each edge, and eight share each corner. Therefore, of the nickel atoms occupying the center of each face, only 6/2 = 3 "belong to" the unit cell. Of the nickel atoms at the corners, only 8/8 = 1 "belong to" the unit cell. The unit cell thus has 4 nickel atoms. X-ray crystallography supplies the distance between nickel atoms along the edge of the cube = 4.07 Å (4.07×10^{-8} cm or 1.60×10^{-8} in). The density is 10.6 g/cm^3 and the atomic mass of nickel is 58.69. Avogadro's number is easily calculated from these data. Perrin refined his work and by 1914, his studies of Brownian motion

(continues)

FACE-CENTERED CUBIC STRUCTURE

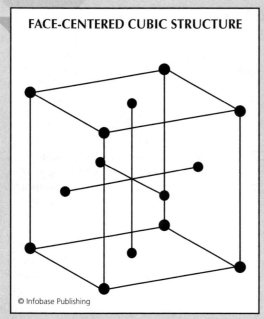

© Infobase Publishing

A face-centered cubic unit cell for a pure metal. The distance along a face diagonal is four times the atomic radius of the metal.

(continued)

provided a value of 6.2×10^{23}. In 1924, the French philosopher-scientist Pierre Lecomte du Nouy (1883–1947) assembled a monolayer of sodium stearate (see the earlier figure) and used the data to calculate a value of 6.004×10^{23}. Variations of his experiment are commonly used today in the introductory chemistry laboratory.

at the University of Munich in 1924 to protest rising anti-Semitism. In 1938 he was forced to flee Germany to save his own life.

Willstätter made numerous important contributions to organic chemistry and biochemistry during his productive life. Among these were contributions toward understanding the structure of tropane alkaloids. Organic bases (*alkaloids*), derived from plants, were first isolated during the mid-19th century. The alkaloids include atropine and cocaine (structure below). Renaissance ladies used eyedrops of belladonna extract (from *Atropa belladonna*) to dilate their pupils to make themselves more attractive. The properties of coca leaves had been known for centuries. In the early years of the 20th century, Willstätter synthesized cocaine.

In 1917, Robert Robinson (1886–1975) published a "one-pot" synthesis of tropinone, a precursor of some tropane alkaloids, from addition of relatively simple molecules in aqueous solution. This synthesis made the tropane alkaloids much more accessible. Robinson came to suspect that the reaction he employed suggested the actual natural biosynthetic pathway for tropane syntheses. Nearly a century later, many chemists feel that Robinson's hypothesis was correct.

Bile is a complex aqueous solution including electrolytes, cholesterol, bile acids, bilirubin, phospholipids, and other surfactant molecules such

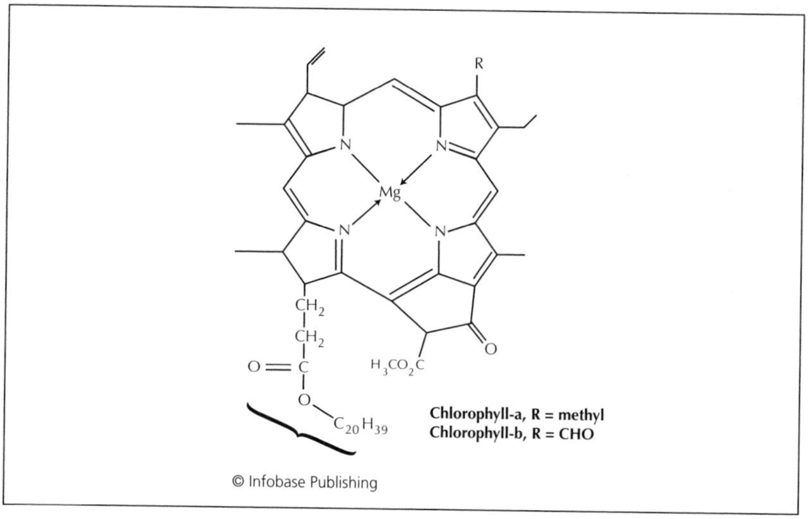

Chlorophyll structures determined by Willstätter in 1913

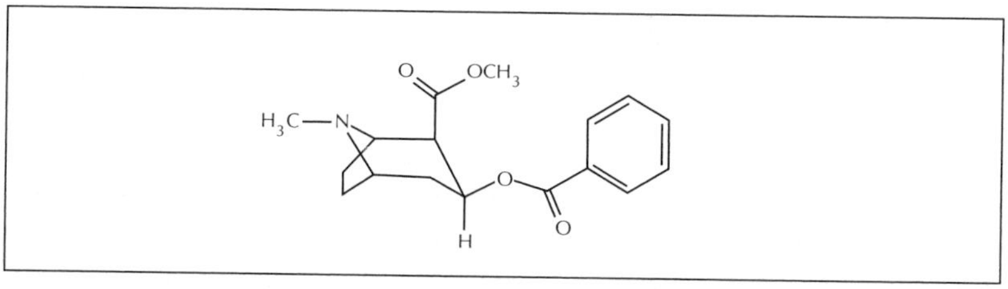

Chlorophyll-a, R = methyl
Chlorophyll-b, R = CHO

© Infobase Publishing

Cocaine

as lecithin. It is produced in the liver, secreted through bile ducts and then through the gallbladder. The function is to aid digestion and absorption of fats and fat-soluble vitamins (A, D, E, and K) through the small intestine and the elimination of organic by-products (especially cholesterol) via the feces. Gallstones are mostly composed of solid cholesterol.

While separation and characterization of bile acids began in the mid-19th century, it was Heinrich Otto Wieland (1877–1957), starting studies in Germany in 1912, who would decipher the structures of the major bile acids. His work provided the structure of cholic acid ($C_{24}H_{40}O_5$), the major acid in bile as well as other closely related bile acids, and Wieland received the 1927 Nobel Prize in chemistry. The structure he presented in his acceptance speech in 1928 was actually incorrect. The correct structure was deduced in 1932 (both structures are shown on page 66). One of the related bile acids deciphered by Wieland, glycocholic acid (see structure), clearly shows its structural aptitude as a surfactant: an amphiphilic molecule with a hydrophobic section (derived from cholic acid) and a hydrophilic section (derived from glycine). Glycocholic acid forms micelles that emulsify by "burying" cholesterol molecules in their hydrophobic interiors.

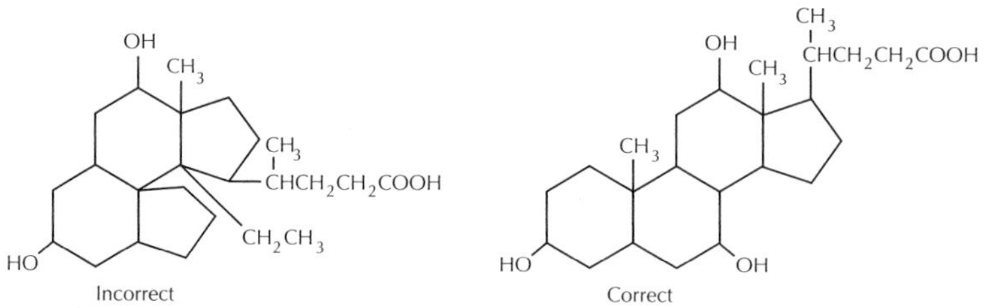

Incorrect (1928) and correct (1932) structures of cholic acid

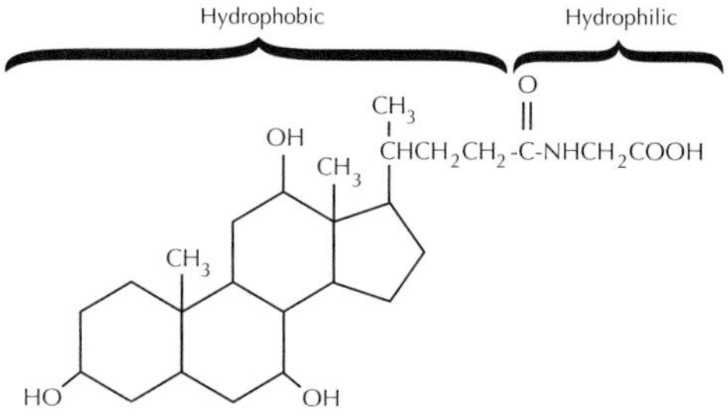

Glycocholic acid (a bile acid)

It is difficult to discuss Wieland's work without including the research of his contemporary and fellow German Adolph Windaus (1876–1959). It was clear that bile acids such as cholic acid not only were found jointly with cholesterol ($C_{27}H_{46}O$) but that, in addition to the similarities in formula, they shared some color reactions in common. It was also known that some oxidations of cholesterol produce acetone, while acetone is not formed in oxidations of cholic acid. Loss of a three-carbon acetone unit leaves a C24 unit, the same carbon number as in cholic acid. Windaus received the 1928 Nobel Prize in chemistry for clarifying the relationships between cholesterol and other *steroids*. His initial structure for cholesterol, consistent with the early incorrect representation of cholic acid, was also incorrect. The correct structure (below) was published in 1932.

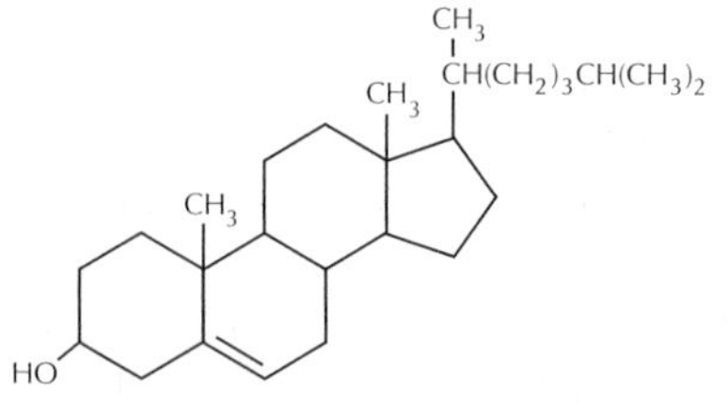

Correct (1932) structure of cholesterol

In 1914, the major hormone of the thyroid gland, thyroxine, was isolated by Henry S. Plummer (1874–1936) of the Mayo Clinic. This was the second hormone to be isolated pure (adrenalin or epinephrine was isolated in 1901). Thyroxin-containing extracts, as well as the crystalline material, were successful in treatments of Graves' disease ("goiter"). The chemical structure of thyroxin would be reported in 1926.

The Vitamin Concept

Scientific discoveries often occur when an unusual occurrence amplifies an otherwise-unnoticed effect. Scurvy, a debilitating disease characterized by swollen gums, loosened teeth, joint pain, subcutaneous bleeding, and anemia, was described in accounts during the late Crusades. In the 15th century, it was recognized as a disease endemic to sailors on long journeys. Sailors on such voyages passed long periods of time dependent upon extremely limited diets. This was, in effect, an unintended scientific experiment on human subjects. In 1753, Scottish naval doctor James Lind (1716–94) recognized that inclusion of fruits and vegetables, especially citrus fruits, could cure and prevent scurvy. Similarly beriberi, a potentially fatal disease that has severe neurological and cardiac symptoms, afflicted as many as half of Japanese sailors, many of whom died, during the 19th century. White rice (rice polished of its hulls) was a major staple in the sailors' very limited diet. The Japanese navy discovered that it could treat and prevent beriberi with a diversified diet and later learned that unpolished rice also prevents beriberi.

But what are the elusive ingredients in citrus fruits and rice hulls that prevent these "deficiency diseases?" The late 19th century witnessed trendy attempts to produce synthetic animal feed using pure proteins, carbohydrates, fats, and minerals. The results were vastly inferior compared to animals raised on natural food. In 1906, British biochemist Frederick Gowland Hopkins (1861–1947) (1929 Nobel Prize in physiology or medicine) recognized the existence in natural foods of "accessory factors," beyond the major components, that are required for a healthy diet.

Polish-born Casimir Funk (1884–1967), at the Lister Institute in London, began working with extracts of rice polishings, known to be a cure for beriberi. Recognizing the importance of these compounds to life ("vita") and their relationship to nitrogenous organic bases (amines), Funk termed the bioactive substances *vitamens*, later shortened to *vitamins*. In 1915, Elmer Verner McCollum (1879–1967) introduced the term *water-soluble B* to describe what is now understood to be a highly complex mixture. McCollum and Marguerite Davis (1887–1967), who helped establish Rutgers University School of Pharmacy, recognized a "fat-soluble A" present in kidney, liver, and plant leaves. In 1919, Harry Steenbock (1886–1967) associated vitamin A activity with colored foods containing carotene. These early studies were hindered by the trace levels of vitamins, and the complexity of their mixtures and chemical structures. The next two decades would witness the transformation of vitamins from concept to hard science.

World War I and Aftermath: Explosives, Chemical Warfare, and the Flu Pandemic

The First World War began in 1914 and was a human catastrophe almost beyond imagination; its roots were Serbian wars during 1912–13 and a tangled series of alliances, missed communications, miscalculations, and sheer arrogance. After five years and numerous false starts at peace, the armistice ending World War I was signed on November 11, 1918 (Veteran's Day in the United States). The Treaty of Versailles, signed on June 28, 1919, laid out the terms of peace. The Allies suffered 5 million killed (60 percent French and Russians) and the Central Powers some 3.4 million killed (90 percent from Germany and Austria-Hungary). The total wounded numbered at least 21 million.

Gunpowder (black powder) may have been invented as early as 1150 C.E. (or A.D. 1150) by the Chinese, and its use spread quickly throughout the world. It is a mixture of *saltpeter* (KNO_3), charcoal, and sulfur. Its explosive properties originate in the *exothermicity* of its combustion reaction and rapid expansion of the resulting gases. The idealized chemical reaction for the explosion of gunpowder is:

$$2\ KNO_3 + 3\ C \rightarrow N_2(g) + 3\ CO_2\ (g) + K_2S$$

Gunpowder is actually classified as a "low explosive" since it deflagrates (burns rapidly with intense heat and light) when ignited in a confined container. The first high explosive, nitroglycerine [$O_2NOCH_2CH(ONO_2)CH_2ONO_2$], was synthesized accidentally by an Italian chemist, Ascanio Sobrero (1812–88), in 1846. It is incredibly sensitive and Sobrero was injured by the surprise explosion of his discovery. It was also around this time that Christian Friedrich Schönbein (1799–1868) accidentally discovered nitrocellulose ("guncotton"). During the 1880s it would be powderized for use as an explosive. (Schönbein also discovered ozone, in 1844).

In 1866 Alfred Nobel (1833–96) developed a stabilized form of nitroglycerin by mixing it with kieselguhr, a kind of clay. He called his invention dynamite and, while it was primarily used for detonation for mining and other clearing purposes, he very well understood its potential as a weapon. Three years earlier, Joseph Wilbrand had discovered the explosive that would dominate the First World War: 2,4,6-trinitrotoluene [TNT, $C_7H_5(NO_2)_3$]. TNT had many ideal properties for a high explosive. It was quite stable to shock and needed a strong detonator [e.g., lead azide, $Pb(N_3)_2$]. The low melting point of TNT allowed it to be poured as a liquid into artillery shells, grenades, or bombs. Frequently, TNT would be packed in combination with ammonium nitrate (NH_4NO_3).

World War I did not advance the technology of explosives very much. It was the means of delivery (tanks, artillery, and aircraft) that provided the new technology of warfare.

During World War I the British made use of a propellant called cordite, a mixture of nitroglycerin and nitrocellulose. Its manufacture required acetone and the British were faced with shortages of this critical solvent. Coincidentally, Chaim Weizmann (1874–1952), University of Manchester, had adapted a fermentation process that converted starch to acetone and butyl alcohol in a ratio of 1:2. The British government brought this process into commercial production during the war. Weizmann was a dedicated Zionist and, rather than accept monetary rewards for his contribution to the war effort, succeeded in obtaining the Balfour Declaration, issued on November 2, 1917, supporting "the establishment in Palestine of a national home for the Jewish people." The declaration, whose provisions were included in the British mandate for Palestine, was approved in 1922 by the League of Nations. It also included the provision that "nothing shall be done which may prejudice the civil and religious rights of existing non-Jewish communities in Palestine." Israel achieved nationhood in 1948 and Chaim Weizmann, the organic chemist, became its first president. The ambiguities in the declaration and the subsequent history of the Middle East continue to haunt the 21st century.

During The Great War, Germany encountered great difficulty procuring oil, but it had huge stockpiles of brown coal (lignite). While oil could be distilled from lignite, the yields were low. During this period, Frederick Bergius (1884–1949) of BASF (*Badische Anilin und Soda Fabrik*) developed the first practical process for liquefaction of coal to form oil. The Bergius process involved grinding coal into powder and heating it in the presence of an iron oxide catalyst under hydrogen at 200–700 atmospheres of pressure at 800–900°F (425–480°C). It remained an inefficient and expensive process during the war but by the early 1930s was an important and economical process. Bergius would share the 1931 Nobel Prize in chemistry with Carl Bosch.

The phrase "war is hell" is used so commonly that it has become almost trite. However, the true meaning of "hell" was horribly real to the millions of soldiers who occupied trenches filled with mud, filthy water, and rats, as they tried to survive artillery shells, grenades, bombs, bayonets, and a new horror: poison gas. In 1899 major European nations and the United States signed a declaration from the Hague Convention swearing not to employ "poison or poisoned weapons." Nonetheless, some of the countries fighting the war had earlier investigated gas technology and were prepared to use it.

On April 15, 1915, the Germans conducted the first massive attack using chemical weapons. It was relatively crude, but effective. Along a four-mile front in the vicinity of Ypres, Belgium, were arrayed 6,000 pressurized cylinders that delivered a total of 160 to 180 tons of deadly chlorine gas. Two attacks within two days killed 10,000 British soldiers and wounded 15,000. In many ways the wounded were worse off than the dead, enduring weeks, months, or years of debilitation from damaged lungs. By 1916 gas was being employed by both sides. Deadly phosgene ($COCl_2$), another compound discovered decades earlier, was employed in late 1915 and hydrogen cyanide gas (HCN) was used at the Battle of the Somme in 1916. Mustard "gas" [$(ClCH_2CH_2)_2S$] was first employed by the Germans in July 1917, again at Ypres. Mustard is an oily liquid that was packed into shells and is dispersed as aerosol upon explosion. It is a vesicant, meaning that it raises painful blisters. Although eye irritation was felt immediately, the worst effects from mustard came from blistering, which began to appear some 12 hours after exposure. Many soldiers attacked with mustard must have felt like the "walking dead" as they awaited the full development of symptoms. After the war ended, the newly formed League of Nations took up the subject of chemical warfare and, in 1925, developed the protocols of the Geneva Convention banning chemical weapons.

The hell of the First World War was even further compounded by the dearth of medicines to prevent or treat disease. Vaccinations protecting individuals from rabies, diphtheria, tuberculosis, and tetanus were developed and deployed in the late 19th and early 20th centuries. In the absence of broad-spectrum antibiotics, a deep wound or even just a deep cut or puncture could lead to fatal tetanus or gangrene. The treatments were very limited. Wounds, cuts, and punctures could be dressed with tincture of iodine, hydrogen peroxide, or potassium permanganate to disinfect surfaces. But broad-spectrum antibiotics like penicillin were still decades in the future (see chapter 5). One bright note, if it can be called that, was the use of salvarsan, invented a decade earlier to treat syphilis, the deadly venereal disease that threatened countless lives. Amputations and other operations were performed with anesthetics dating from the mid-19th century (nitrous oxide, ether, and chloroform) but the risk of infection was huge.

For the most part, the roles of medications were as treatments of symptoms. Pharmaceuticals were largely derived from plants or simple derivatives of these botanical substances. Chemistry provided the science for identification, synthesis and purification, and chemical engineering the technology for manufacture of these natural medicines. The poppy yielded morphine from which codeine and heroin could be made, all three potent painkillers. The barks of white willow trees contain saligenin, a substance that is metabolized to salicylic acid, which has the physiological effect of reducing pain and swelling (see chapter 8). Aspirin (acetylsalicylic acid, see the accompanying figure, left) may be considered a semisynthetic substance. It is readily

Acetylsalicylic acid (aspirin)

transformed into salicylic acid in the body. The Baeyer Company in Germany first developed an effective commercial synthesis of aspirin in 1897 and started producing it on an industrial scale in 1899. Aspirin was widely used to control fever and pain during World War I. The discoveries of hormones, discussed in chapter 1, included the isolation of pure epinephrine (adrenalin) by Japanese chemist Jokichi Takamine (1854–1922) in 1901.

This feeble arsenal of drugs, essentially devoid of antibiotics, was no match for the catastrophe that followed on the heels of World War I: a flu pandemic (sometimes called the "Spanish flu"), arguably the greatest natural catastrophe of the 20th century. It ravaged a world weakened by war with millions of soldiers in transit. The flu killed more than 20 million, while medical science had to humbly recommend rest, "lots of fluid," and aspirin as the disease ran its course between 1918 and 1920.

Rubber Is a Macromolecule: Understanding Plastics, Proteins, and DNA

Chapter 1 described some of the early efforts of chemists beginning to grapple with proteins and nucleic acids, substances now understood to be macromolecular, composed of giant molecules. This was a difficult concept in the early years of the 20th century due to confusions between macromolecules and colloids composed of micelles, aggregates of smaller molecules held together by molecular association. As noted in chapter 1, thermal decomposition of rubber yields isoprene (C_5H_8). But the early suspicion was that rubber consisted of small chains of chemically bonded isoprene units held together in much larger colloidal particles by weaker association forces.

In 1920, Hermann Staudinger (1881–1965), in Zurich, started to make sense of an array of chemical and physical observations and reasoned that substances like rubber were actually huge molecules with backbones of covalent bonds. He hydrogenated rubber and did not find the degradation into smaller, volatile hydrocarbons that would have come from a micelle-like aggregate. Instead, he found "hydrorubber," still colloidal in nature. This makes sense if natural rubber is a huge molecule with an enormous backbone of covalent carbon-carbon bonds. Staudinger coined the term *macromolecule* for a molecule such as rubber (and hydrorubber). Few scientists were ready in the early 1920s to accept the reality of macromolecules. By the end of the decade, Staudinger's revolutionary view would become the paradigm of the new field of *polymer* chemistry. The rapid development of this field during the 1920s will be described in chapter 3. Staudinger would win the 1953 Nobel Prize in chemistry, by which time his work formed the fundamental basis for understanding synthetic and natural polymers.

Scientist of the Decade: Niels Bohr (1885–1962)

Niels Bohr was a physicist and not a chemist. Nevertheless, his contributions to the understanding of chemistry were so profound that it would be inappropriate to not celebrate them here. Born in Denmark, he received his Ph.D. at the University of Copenhagen in 1911, having studied the properties of electrons in metals. Bohr moved to England and studied with J. J. Thomson at Cambridge and then Rutherford in Manchester, probing the structure of the atom. His major contribution to chemistry during this period was the application of Planck's quantum theory to the explanation of atomic structure. In 1911, Rutherford discovered that the atom is mostly empty space with its mass concentrated in a minute, positively charged nucleus at its center. In 1913, Bohr developed the "planetary atom" to depict the "orbits" occupied by electrons that surround the nucleus. The model was revolutionary in its concept, placing electrons in specific shells with no physical presence at all between shells. It fully explained the emission spectra of the hydrogen atom, although Bohr understood that it did not work for helium and other multi-electron systems. Although it would be superseded by the modern quantum theory developed during the 1920s, this first crucial application of quantum physics to chemical structure laid the basis for modern views of matter. This illustrates an important point about scientific theories: A theory may be excellent and fundamentally important even if eventually corrected or replaced, because it explains the data of the day and suggests the questions that permit its testing.

Jacob Bronowski, the renowned mathematician and philosopher of science, cited Bohr's theory as an example of human creativity in developing scientific theories. If there is, in reality, no "planetary structure" of the atom, how did Bohr derive his "picture"? Bronowski speculated that, much as an artist or an author composes metaphors based upon life experiences and world views, perhaps Bohr's innate desire to imagine a unified pattern in nature led him to postulate a structure for the smallest chemically significant bits of matter reflecting one of the largest structures, the solar system. Bohr was awarded the Nobel Prize in physics in 1922.

Although the story is not a simple one, during the early 1920s Bohr used theory to aid in the discovery of a "missing" chemical element, number 72. This element was first assumed to be a lanthanide and was sought, unsuccessfully, in ores containing the mixtures of rare earths whose separation challenged chemists for more than a century. Bohr employed theory to conclude that element 72 should closely resemble zirconium. Much like Mendeleev 50 years earlier, Bohr's prediction led to the separation and isolation of the new element, hafnium, from zirconium ores by his young colleague George Hevesy in 1923.

Conclusion

Although a modern-looking model of the atom and its substructure had emerged during the decade, huge changes would occur during the 1920s. The modern quantum theory of Heisenberg, de Broglie, Schrödinger, Hund, and Pauli would drastically change the understanding and treatment of chemical bonding. Linus Pauling and Robert Mulliken, exposed to the new quantum theory in Germany, would adapt it to the needs of chemists in the coming decades. Macromolecular chemistry, barely

Niels Bohr, who was awarded the 1922 Nobel Prize in physics for his work in the quantum mechanics of atomic structure, shown here with his mother (Niels Bohr Archive, courtesy AIP Emilio Segrè Archives)

In the 1920s Bohr became a close friend of the brilliant German scientist Werner Heisenberg. During World War II Heisenberg was named to direct the Nazi effort to develop an atomic bomb. Heisenberg's visit to Bohr's home in occupied Denmark in 1941 formed the basis for the play *Copenhagen,* by Michael Frayn, which debuted in 1998 and won the 2000 Tony Award. It explored Heisenberg's role in the German bomb project and the termination of the two-decade friendship between these two towering physicists. Bohr escaped to Sweden by fishing boat in 1943.

understood in 1920, would join chemistry with materials science by 1930, and new synthetic materials would soon be on the horizon.

Further Reading

American Chemical Society. *The Pharmaceutical Century: Ten Decades of Drug Discovery.* Washington, D.C.: American Chemical Society, 2000. This is a presentation of advances in the pharmaceutical industry during each decade of the 20th century.

Bohr, Niels. *Atomic Physics and Human Knowledge.* New York: John Wiley & Sons, 1958. These are Bohr's autobiographical reflections on science.

Cathcart, Brian. *The Fly in the Cathedral: How a Group of Cambridge Scientists Won the International Race to Split the Atom.* Gordonsville, Va.: Farrar, Straus and Giroux, 2005. This book describes the early history of the exploration of subatomic structure.

Frayn, Michael. *Copenhagen.* New York: Anchor Books (Random House), 2000. A play that dramatizes the famous meeting between Niels Bohr and Werner Heisenberg in Copenhagen during World War II.

Giunta, Carmen. "Selected Classic Papers from the History of Chemistry," Le Moyne College, 2006. Available online. URL: http://web.lemoyne. edu~giunta/index.html. Accessed February 11, 2006. This site provides English translations of many significant historical papers, including Fajans's 1913 paper in *Berichte der Deutschen Chemischen Gesellschaft* from which the two related figures in this chapter are derived.

Hoffmann, Roald, and Pierre Laszlo. "Coping with Fritz Haber's Somber Literary Shadow." *Angewandte Chemie International Edition* 40 (2001): 4,599–4,604. This essay examines the paradox of Fritz Haber's life: development of nitrogen fixation as a means to increase crop production and the invention of means to produce weapons of war.

Laidler, Keith J. *The World of Physical Chemistry.* Oxford: Oxford University Press, 1993. This book provides highly readable and stimulating coverage of the history of physical chemistry including coverage of the chemical kinetics described in this chapter.

Mülhaupt, Rolf. "Hermann Staudinger and the Origin of Macromolecular Chemistry." *Angewandte Chemie International Edition* 43 (2004): 1,054–1,063. This is a presentation about the German father of polymer chemistry by a renowned historian of science.

Partington, James R. *A History of Chemistry*, Vol. 4, 929–953. London: MacMillan & Co. Ltd., 1964. This section provides an excellent discussion of the early history of studies of radioactivity and its relation to atomic structure and transmutation.

Rayner-Canham, Marelene, and Geoffrey Rayner-Canham. *Women in Chemistry: Their Changing Roles from Alchemical Times to the Mid-Twentieth Century.* Washington, D.C. and Philadelphia: American Chemical Society and the Chemical Heritage Foundation, 1998. This book includes brief discussions of Agnes Pockels, Katherine Burr Blodgett, and Maud Lenora Menten.

Tucker, Jonathan B. *War of Nerves: Chemical Warfare from World War I to Al-Qaeda.* New York: Pantheon Books, 2006. This book provides both a scientific and political perspective tracing the historical development of chemical weapons and examining the threats they pose during the 21st century.

3

1921–1930:
The New Quantum Theory and the Rise of Polymer Chemistry

New Theories of Chemical Bonding and Early Mechanistic Chemistry

The 1920s witnessed the discovery of the final two naturally occurring chemical elements, hafnium and rhenium, and the development of modern *quantum theory*. Quantum mechanics would dramatically alter views of the atom, introducing probability and uncertainty and wave-particle duality and the basis for atomic and molecular orbital theory. The accumulation of X-ray crystallographic data that started in the previous decade would provide the basis for understanding structure and bonding in the solid state. Definitions of acids and bases would emerge that were tied to advances in understanding solution chemistry as well as structural chemistry.

The explosive reaction of hydrogen and oxygen to produce water (and similar reactions) would be explained by branched free radical chain reactions. The first direct chemical evidence for the finite existence of a short-lived organic free radical (recall that triphenylmethyl radical is persistent) would contribute to the new mechanistic organic chemistry. This field would advance even further thanks to evidence supporting the intermediacy of short-lived *carbocations* in solution. *Conjugated olefins* become a "playground" for chemists interested in mechanisms, natural products, and macromolecules. A revolution in understanding of macromolecules will dominate the 1920s and presage the development of commercial products such as nylon during the 1930s.

Advances in organic chemistry, including cyclic structures for glucose and related molecules, and in macromolecular chemistry, including the structures for starch and cellulose, will open the field of structural biochemistry. Isolation and structure proofs of steroid hormones, vitamin C, alkaloids, and *macrocyclic* sex attractants such as civetone begin to reveal the incredible diversity of nature's smaller molecules. Advances in synthetic organic chemistry, especially the Diels-Alder reaction, will enable syntheses of numerous biomolecules. Intermediary metabolism starts to emerge as a distinct field of biochemistry. Alexander Fleming's accidental discovery of penicillin will eventually place the first truly potent antibacterial into the well-worn "doctor's bag" of the 1940s.

Discovery of the Final Two Natural Chemical Elements

Henry Moseley's discovery, in 1913, of the atomic number exposed gaps in the periodic table including those for "missing" elements 72 and 75. It is important to remember that lutetium, element number 71, the last rare earth element to be isolated, was reported only six years earlier. There were no guarantees that the lanthanides (elements 57–71) would not conceal yet one more surprise. And here the history of science also tantalizes: Did theory predict experiment or did theory merely rationalize experiment?

Hafnium (element 72) was discovered in 1923 by George Karl von Hevesy (1885–1966), a Hungarian, and Dirk Coster (1889–1950), from Holland, at the Institute of Theoretical Physics in Copenhagen ("Hafnia" in Latin), directed by Niels Bohr. The most widely held view of hafnium's

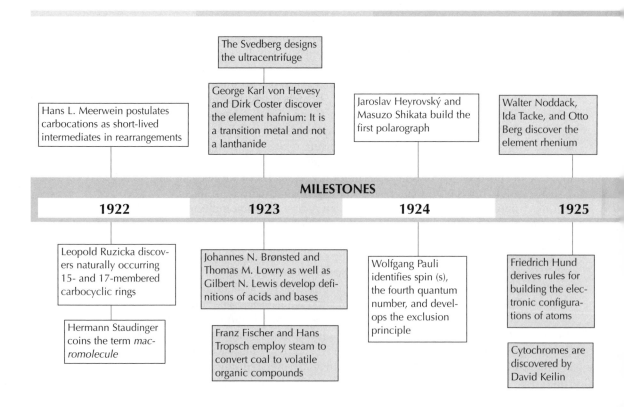

The Svedberg designs the ultracentrifuge

George Karl von Hevesy and Dirk Coster discover the element hafnium: It is a transition metal and not a lanthanide

Jaroslav Heyrovský and Masuzo Shikata build the first polarograph

Walter Noddack, Ida Tacke, and Otto Berg discover the element rhenium

Hans L. Meerwein postulates carbocations as short-lived intermediates in rearrangements

MILESTONES

| 1922 | 1923 | 1924 | 1925 |

Leopold Ruzicka discovers naturally occurring 15- and 17-membered carbocyclic rings

Johannes N. Brønsted and Thomas M. Lowry as well as Gilbert N. Lewis develop definitions of acids and bases

Wolfgang Pauli identifies spin (s), the fourth quantum number, and develops the exclusion principle

Friedrich Hund derives rules for building the electronic configurations of atoms

Hermann Staudinger coins the term *macromolecule*

Franz Fischer and Hans Tropsch employ steam to convert coal to volatile organic compounds

Cytochromes are discovered by David Keilin

discovery is that it provides a spectacular example of the power of theory to make a risky prediction and be validated by experiment. Bohr is said to have concluded that hafnium's electronic structure suggested its resemblance to zirconium and that hafnium should be tetravalent (MX_4) rather than trivalent (MX_3) like lanthanides such as lutetium. Much in the manner of Mendeleev, he then advised institute colleagues Hevesy and Coster to search for the new element in zirconium ores. Their success was a powerful validation of theory, although the history does appear to be a bit more complex.

Now that hafnium (element 72) was known to be a *transition metal* and not a rare earth (lanthanide), the "missing elements" 43 and 75 were both understood to belong to the same family as manganese and were referred to as *eka*-manganese and *dwi*-manganese. Three German scientists, Walter Noddack (1893–1960), Ida Tacke (1896–1978) (later Tacke-Noddack), and Otto Berg (1873–1939) investigated manganese and iron ores and ultimately discovered, in 1925, traces of element 75, confirmed by spectroscopy, in gadolinite ore. They named the metal rhenium (Re) after the Rhine River.

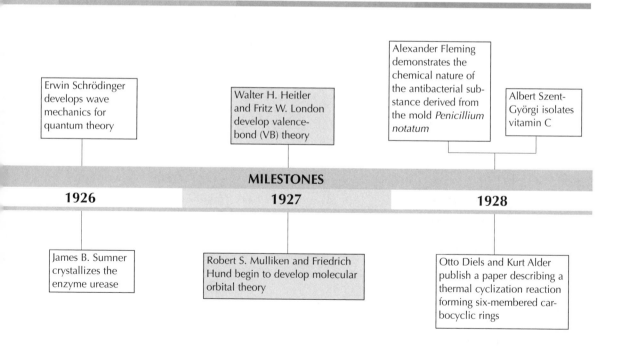

Erwin Schrödinger develops wave mechanics for quantum theory

Walter H. Heitler and Fritz W. London develop valence-bond (VB) theory

Alexander Fleming demonstrates the chemical nature of the antibacterial substance derived from the mold *Penicillium notatum*

Albert Szent-Györgi isolates vitamin C

MILESTONES

1926

1927

1928

James B. Sumner crystallizes the enzyme urease

Robert S. Mulliken and Friedrich Hund begin to develop molecular orbital theory

Otto Diels and Kurt Alder publish a paper describing a thermal cyclization reaction forming six-membered carbocyclic rings

Why Do Electrons Behave As Particles on Mondays but As Waves on Tuesdays?

In 1905, Einstein's explanation of the photoelectric effect (the threshold light frequency needed to cause a metal to lose an electron) relied upon the particle nature of light as its foundation. However, it was still difficult for physicists to take photons seriously as particles until the Compton effect was demonstrated in 1922 (Arthur H. Compton [1892–1962]; independently by Peter J. Debye [1884–1966] in 1923). In this experiment, X-rays of a given wavelength collide with electrons in matter, lose some energy and are deflected with a longer wavelength. Compton won the 1927 Nobel Prize in physics for this work.

In 1924, Louis de Broglie (1892–1987), studying at the Sorbonne, published his doctoral thesis in which he proposed an essential symmetry in nature: Just as electromagnetic radiation (e.g., visible light, X-rays), commonly analyzed as waves, exhibits particle-like properties, matter may exhibit wavelike properties. The wavelength of such "de Broglie waves" is:

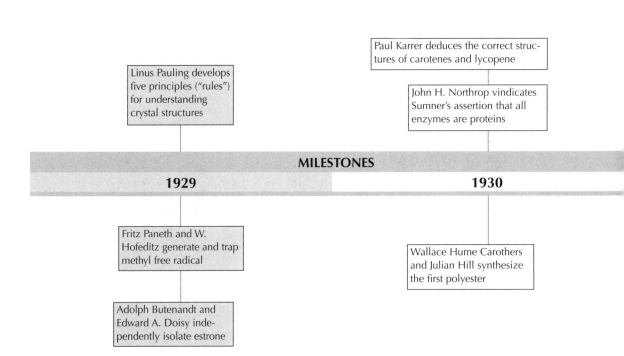

Paul Karrer deduces the correct structures of carotenes and lycopene

Linus Pauling develops five principles ("rules") for understanding crystal structures

John H. Northrop vindicates Sumner's assertion that all enzymes are proteins

MILESTONES

1929   **1930**

Fritz Paneth and W. Hofeditz generate and trap methyl free radical

Wallace Hume Carothers and Julian Hill synthesize the first polyester

Adolph Butenandt and Edward A. Doisy independently isolate estrone

$$\lambda = h/mv$$

where λ is the wavelength, h is Planck's constant, and m the mass of the particle, and v its velocity (mv = p, momentum of the particle).

Diffraction is a characteristic wave property. It is useful to recall that the mass of the electron was determined accurately by Millikan in 1909. A precise mass is very much a particle-type property. Geiger counters monitor β-particles (electrons) one by one ("click-click-click"): another particle property. The de Broglie equation suggests that wavelengths (λ) are associated with electrons and that these should be on the order of 10^{-11} m. In principle, electrons should be diffracted by crystals, a prediction confirmed in 1927 by Clinton Joseph Davisson (1881–1958) and Lester Halbert Germer (1896–1971), at Bell Telephone Laboratories. De Broglie was awarded the 1929 Nobel Prize in physics and Davisson won a share of the 1937 Nobel Prize in physics.

While electrons are now commonly said to be "both particles and waves or neither" people live in a macroscopic, slow-moving world and lack the ability to truly imagine a "particle-wave." This difficulty was nicely stated by Jacob Bronowski: "On Mondays, Wednesdays and Fridays, the electron would behave like a particle; on Tuesdays, Thursdays and Saturdays it would behave as a wave."

Atoms and Molecules in the Roaring Twenties: Transition to Quantum Mechanics

In 1924, Wolfgang Pauli (1900–58) added to the earlier work of Bohr and Arnold Sommerfeld (1868–1951) and identified the fourth quantum number, spin or s, confined to two (noninteger) values +½ and -½. This was followed by the *Pauli exclusion principle*: no two electrons in the same atom can have four identical *quantum numbers*: n, l, m, and s, and these are subject to the following rules:

$$n = 1, 2, 3, 4, \ldots$$

$$l = 0, 1, 2, \ldots (n-1)$$

$$m = 0, \pm1, \pm2, \pm3, \ldots \pm l$$

$$s = \pm\tfrac{1}{2}$$

Pauli's research would lead to his receipt of the 1945 Nobel Prize in physics. In 1925, physicist Friedrich Hund (1896–1997) explained atomic spectroscopic data with a "rule of maximum multiplicity": Electrons are added to build up an atom so that the maximum number of energy levels (of equal energy) is filled with one electron each before electrons are paired. In 1926, Erwin Schrödinger (1887–1961), then at the University of Zurich, extended de Broglie's concept and treated electrons in atoms (and molecules) as standing waves and derived the new quantum mechanics. Electronic properties are determined by solving for the wave function, Ψ, and energy for an atom or molecule.

Schrödinger shared the 1933 Nobel Prize in physics with Paul A. M. Dirac (1902–1984), who developed many of the techniques required to solve the quantum mechanics.

Although the four quantum numbers n, l, m, and s, the Pauli Exclusion Principle, and Hund's rules were developed in the context of the Bohr-Sommerfeld model, they all found immediate application to Schrödinger's new quantum mechanics. The first three numbers specified atomic *orbitals* (replacing Bohr's orbits). Physicist Max Born (1882–1970) equated the square of the wave functions, Ψ^2, to regions of probability for finding electrons in each orbital. Werner Heisenberg (1901–76), whose mathematics provide the foundation of quantum mechanics, developed the uncertainty principle: the product of the uncertainty in position (Δx) of a tiny particle such as an atom (or an electron) and the uncertainty in its momentum (Δp) is larger than the quantum ($h/4\pi$):

$$\Delta x\ \Delta p > h/4\pi$$

Newer Views on Chemical Bonding

The Lewis-Langmuir theory of electron donation (ionic compounds) and electron sharing (covalent compounds), formulated between 1916 and 1919, still left many questions unanswered. For example, what is the nature of the chemical bonding in Werner complexes such as $Co(NH_3)_6Cl_3$ (chapter 1)? The six ammonia molecules have an intimate and strong association with cobalt(III), yet each NH_3 fully satisfies the octet rule. In 1923, Nevil V. Sidgwick (1873–1952) postulated the *coordinate covalent* (*dative*) bond, commonly depicted A→B, to account for molecules in which one atom, ion, or group donates a nonbonded electron pair to an acceptor. In his 1923 book *Valence and the Structure of Atoms and Molecules*, Gilbert N. Lewis developed a broad definition of bases as electron-pair donors (e.g., H_3N:) and acids as electron pair acceptors (e.g., BCl_3). The salt formed from NH_3 and BCl_3 could simply be depicted as the structure shown here (left). If one considers the proton (H^+) as an electron-pair acceptor, then *Lewis acid-base* theory is seen to be a broader generalization of the acid-base theory published independently in 1923 by Johannes Nicolaus Brønsted (1879–1947), in Copenhagen, and Thomas Martin Lowry (1874–1936), in Cambridge, where acids are proton donors and bases proton acceptors.

X-ray crystallography advanced rapidly throughout the 1920s as its practitioners, including the Braggs, started to accumulate enough data to begin to search for patterns and generalizations. The powder diffraction technique, introduced in 1916 by Peter Debye, in Göttingen, and Paul Scherrer (1890–1969), in Zurich, and (independently) by Albert W. Hull (1880–1966), at General Electric, aided exploration of a broad array of substances, since relatively few compounds of simple formula

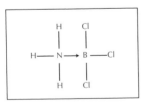

Coordinate covalent (dative) bond between NH_3 and BCl_3

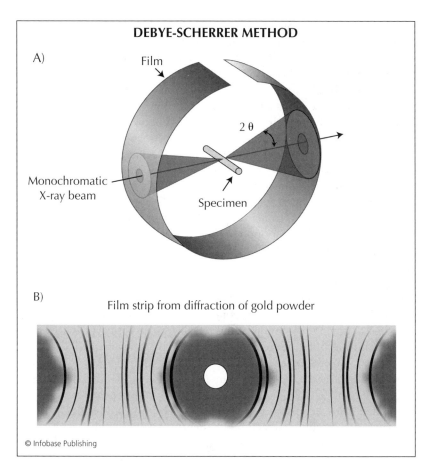

DEBYE-SCHERRER METHOD

A)

Film

2 θ

Monochromatic
X-ray beam

Specimen

B)

Film strip from diffraction of gold powder

© Infobase Publishing

A) Schematic of the Debye-Scherrer method, developed in 1916, for X-ray diffraction of powders (polycrystalline samples). Each characteristic interplanar spacing in the crystal gives rise to a cone of diffracted X-rays, segments of which are captured on the film strip placed inside the camera. B) The powder diffraction pattern obtained for gold.

form large enough crystals for single-crystal crystallography. The figure above includes a schematic of the Debye-Scherrer-Hull method in which a powdered crystalline specimen in a rotating glass capillary tube is exposed to a monochromatic beam of X-rays. A film lying on the interior surface of the X-ray camera records segments of the concentric rings diffracted from each unique plane. The figure also depicts a photographic plate obtained using the X-ray camera. An early investigator was Linus Pauling (1901–94) who, in 1922, began graduate studies at California Institute of Technology, a young university with lofty aspirations.

The accumulation of lattice constants gave rise to a growing library of interatomic (and interionic) distances, providing atomic and ionic radii. In 1929 Pauling published five principles (rules) that formed the first rational basis for understanding crystal structures. For example, the ratio of the ionic radii of cations to anions determines coordination number in crystals: coordination number 6 for each chlorine and sodium ion in NaCl; coordination number 8 for each ion in CsCl.

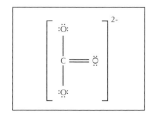

Lewis structure for carbonate ion

X-ray crystallography also provided some tantalizing surprises. For example, the figure below depicts the arrangement of ions in calcite (Iceland spar), $CaCO_3$. The structure was surprising in that the three oxygen atoms in each carbonate (CO_3^{2-}) ion are at the corners of an equilateral triangle with carbon at its center; the three carbon-oxygen bond distances are equal (see the carbonate structure, left). That contradicts the Lewis-Langmuir structure for this ion which implies two single (long) bonds and one double (short) bond.

Pauling completed his Ph.D. at Caltech and spent the next two years at the great quantum theory centers of Europe during 1926 and 1927. Upon his return to Caltech as a faculty member, he began to apply quantum mechanics to chemical problems and make the abstract physics intelligible to and useful for chemists. In 1927 physicists Walter H. Heitler (1904–81) and Fritz W. London (1900–54), at the University of Zurich, developed *valence-bond (VB) theory*. The next year, Pauling interpreted the Heitler-London concept of *resonance*, the exchange of equivalent electrons between bound atoms (e.g., in the H_2 molecule) providing the driving force for bonding, and demonstrated that it was equivalent to the Lewis-Langmuir electron-pair concept. In that same paper he hinted at his theory-based explanation of the tetrahedral structure of four-coordinate carbon. A fuller discussion of this concept, today termed "*hybridization theory*," would appear in 1931. Robert S. Mulliken (1896–1986) also traveled to Europe to learn quantum physics. He befriended the physicist Hund and, in 1927–28, they developed a theory of *molecular* orbitals that explained many details of the spectroscopy of simple molecules. A rivalry between the Pauling valence-bond theory and the Mulliken *molecular-orbital theory* would begin in the 1930s and is still active today.

In 1912, Peter Debye developed the concept of the permanent dipole moment (μ), a measure of the charge separation in an unsymmetrical molecule (e.g., H_2O, whose geometry is nonlinear). In contrast, CO_2 is a symmetrical, linear molecule lacking a permanent dipole moment. In 1921, Debye explained the underlying basis of the 19th-century van der Waals equation which treats the departures of the pressure-volume properties of real gases from ideality, particularly at high pressures:

$$(P + a/b^2)(V - b) = RT$$

Debye postulated that close approach of molecules mutually distorts their charge distributions, creating induced dipoles that reduce repulsion and increase attraction between them. The result is the apparent slight reduction in pressure due to "stickiness" (*van der Waals attractions*) of these brief molecular collisions.

The work of Debye and Erich Hückel (1896–1880), published in 1923, led to a theory of ionic solutions that explained a number of anomalies concerning conductivities of electrolytic solutions. In 1926, Lars Onsager (1903–76) added the treatment of Brownian motion toward understanding the transport properties of ions in melts, aqueous, and

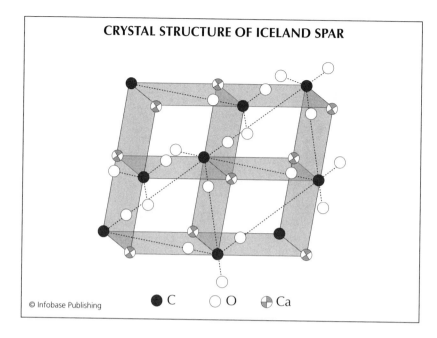

CRYSTAL STRUCTURE OF ICELAND SPAR

● C   ○ O   ◕ Ca

© Infobase Publishing

Crystalline structure of calcite (Iceland spar, $CaCO_3$). Contrary to simple Lewis structures, all three C-O bond lengths in CO_3^{2-} are equal. (Adapted from J. R. Partington, *Everyday Chemistry.* London: Macmillan and Co. Ltd., 1929, p. 190)

nonaqueous solutions. More than 40 years after Arrhenius first proposed it, solution ion theory finally rested on a firm foundation. For his work on X-ray powder diffraction, dipole moments, and theories of solution, Peter Debye received the 1936 Nobel Prize in chemistry. Onsager would win the 1968 Nobel Prize in chemistry.

Radioactive "Tags": Following Trace Amounts of Metals in Their Travels

Following a brief period with Haber, Georg Hevesy began work with Rutherford at Manchester in 1910. In 1913, he began work with Fritz Paneth in Vienna and conducted the first radiotracer experiments. At that time, it was known that one of the products of radium decay was a substance, having its own unique decay signature, called radium-D. Hevesy tried unsuccessfully to separate radium-D from lead. In 1913, Alexander Fleck (1889–1968), working with Soddy, found that radium-D, radium-B, thorium-B, and actinium-B were chemically inseparable from lead and were, therefore, isotopes of lead.

Although Hevesy and Paneth were not absolutely certain of the chemical identity of radium-D at the time, the fact that it was radioactive and inseparable from lead suggested an idea. Tiny amounts of this radioactive tracer, even of unknown purity, could be added to samples having minute quantities of lead and this "doped" sample separated chemically from other metals in mixtures and analyzed. If 50 percent of the radioactivity due to radium-D remained in the final sample, the final quantity would simply be multiplied by two. Hevesy and Paneth applied their new technique, today called "isotopic dilution," to the analysis of solubilities of sparingly soluble salts. They made an aqueous solution of lead nitrate containing 10 mg (2.2×10^{-5} lb) lead. To this was added a solution containing a minute quantity of the lead isotope thorium-B having 100,000 relative units of radioactivity. Soluble chromate was added, a precipitate of lead chromate formed, the solution equilibrated at a set temperature, and a few milliliters of the supernatant solution evaporated to dryness. The quantity of thorium-B radiation in this nearly invisible residue was measured and the solubility of $PbCrO_4$ was found to be 2×10^{-7} mol/L.

One of Hevesy's most far-reaching studies involved mixing plumbous acetate [$Pb(OAc)_2$, where OAc = CH_3CO_2] and labeled plumbic acetate [$*Pb(OAc)_4$] in acetic acid and then separating the two salts by fractional crystallization. The reverse mixture [$*Pb(OAc)_2$ and $Pb(OAc)_4$] was also investigated. Both experiments gave the same result: rapid equilibration of labeled and unlabeled lead demonstrating the rapid self-exchange between Pb^{2+} and Pb^{4+} ions. Such a reaction is among the most fundamental in all of chemistry and Hevesy's farsighted study would anticipate the research of two Nobel laureates three and four decades later.

In 1923, Hevesy applied his radioactive tracer studies to the absorption of minerals by plants. It had long been assumed that plants, in contrast to animals, do not excrete the minerals they absorb. Hevesy demonstrated that solutions containing the lead isotope then termed thorium-B were absorbed by plants and caused them to retain some radioactivity. When unlabelled lead solution was subsequently used as nutrient, Hevesy found that the radioactive isotope gradually returned to the nutrient solution. Clearly, there was active metal exchange occurring at all times.

Hevesy was drafted into the Austrian-Hungarian army in 1915, survived World War I, and settled in Copenhagen in 1920 to work in Bohr's new institute. There he discovered element 72, hafnium, as described earlier. Following periods at Freiburg and Cornell, Hevesy returned to Copenhagen in 1934. He received the 1943 Nobel Prize in chemistry for his radiotracer studies.

Understanding the Explosive Reaction: $H_2 + \frac{1}{2} O_2 \rightarrow H_2O$

During the 1920s, one of the mysteries of the reaction between hydrogen and oxygen was its peculiar behavior as a function of the temperature and pressure of the gas mixture. The figure on page 85 depicts a graph of the explosive properties of a precise stoichiometric mixture (two moles: one mole) of H_2 gas and O_2 gas in the absence of a flame or a spark. The shaded area marks temperature-pressure conditions that cause this gas mixture to explode. From this graph, it is clear that at temperatures lower than 860°F (460°C), no explosion (absent a spark or flame) will occur, while at temperatures above ca. 1,110°F (ca. 600°C), explosions occur at virtually all pressures. At very low pressure at ca. 930°F (500°C) (for example, point *a* in the figure), no explosion occurs. Once the pressure is increased to ca. 2 mm (point *b*) at this temperature, an explosion occurs. Similarly, at 500°C, pressure corresponding to point *c* causes an explosion but the higher pressure at point *e* does not. Curiously enough, if the pressure on the gas mixture at *e* is reduced to ca. 100 mm (point *d*) an explosion occurs. An explosion also occurs if this mixture remains at 500°C (point *e*) while the pressure increases to that at point *f*. What is the source of these three separate "explosion limits"?

This challenge was met by Russian chemist Nikolai Nikolaevich Semenov (1896–1986), working in St. Petersburg, and, independently, English chemist Cyril Norman Hinshelwood (1897–1967) at Oxford. In 1928 they each developed the concept of a "branched chain reaction" to account for the kinetics of these explosions and their strange dependence on pressure and temperature.

It is important to recall from chapter 2 the observation by Bodenstein that absorption of a single photon can provide up to 10^6 molecules of product HCl in the photochemically initiated combination of H_2 and

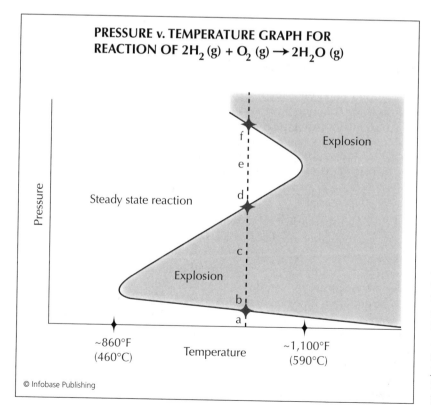

PRESSURE v. TEMPERATURE GRAPH FOR REACTION OF $2H_2$ (g) + O_2 (g) → $2H_2O$ (g)

Pressure

Steady state reaction

Explosion

Explosion

f

e

d

c

b

a

~860°F (460°C)   Temperature   ~1,100°F (590°C)

© Infobase Publishing

Regions (pressure v. temperature) of steady-steady and explosive reaction of stoichiometric quantities of hydrogen and oxygen gas to yield water. The dotted line connotes the behavior (steady reaction or explosion) of this mixture at a temperature between 932°F (500°C) and 1,112°F (600°C) as a function of pressure. (Adapted from K. J. Laidler, Chemical Kinetics. New York: 3d ed., Harper & Row, 1987, p. 324)

Cl_2. The free radical mechanism was clarified by Nernst: It is initiated by chlorine free radical (Cl). Each cycle of the mechanism starts with one Cl and regenerates one Cl. The chain-propagating steps for the reaction of hydrogen and oxygen include the following:

$$H + O_2 \rightarrow OH + O$$

$$O + H_2 \rightarrow OH + H$$

$$2\ OH + 2\ H_2 \rightarrow 2\ H_2O + 2\ H$$

The sum of the reaction for these three steps (the last employed twice) is:

$$H + 3\ H_2 + O_2 \rightarrow 2\ H_2O + 3\ H$$

The result is that one reactive particle (H) generates three. It is this chain-branching mechanism that generates the explosive potential in the formation of water.

At pressures below the first threshold (see the figure), the radical intermediates are more likely to react with the container surface than with the very dilute gas-phase reactants, and there is no explosion. At pressures between the second and third explosion thresholds, the concentration of gas molecules is enough to lower the concentration of radicals sufficiently to slow the rate of reaction, hence no explosion. For these studies, Semenov and Hinshelwood shared the 1956 Nobel Prize in chemistry.

Releasing and Recapturing Short-Lived Free Radicals in a Glass Tube

The notion of a "radical," a group of atoms that remains together as a unit, is a very old one. In observing reactions such as the transformation of CH_3CH_2-Cl to CH_3CH_2-OH, chemists wondered whether a "radical" or alkyl group, commonly abbreviated "R," such as CH_3CH_2 (C_2H_5) is ever completely free, even for an instant. Is it ever a "free radical"? When Edward Frankland (1825–99) first exposed gaseous ethyl chloride (C_2H_5Cl) to heated zinc metal in 1848, he obtained $ZnCl_2$ and a gas whose empirical formula was C_2H_5. At first, Frankland thought that he had captured the elusive ethyl radical. Further study indicated that the gas was actually butane (C_4H_{10} or $CH_3CH_2CH_2CH_3$), the dimer (R-R) of ethyl radical. When Gomberg isolated the persistent triphenylmethyl radical in 1900 (see chapter 1), some 50 years later, there was considerable excitement in the worldwide chemical community.

The question, however, remained: Is there direct evidence for the types of simple, transient (very short-lived) free radicals postulated as reaction intermediates and present in very minute ("steady-state") concentrations? To this question, Paneth and his coworker Wilhelm Hofeditz provided, in 1929, a graphic answer. The weak carbon-lead (Pb-C) single bond in tetramethyllead allows ready dissociation at elevated temperatures. This was a factor in the antiknock properties of tetraethyllead, introduced as a gasoline additive in 1921. Paneth and Hofeditz passed nitrogen gas containing tetramethyllead, $(CH_3)_4Pb$, through a tube heated near its outlet. In the region of heating near the outlet, a "mirror" of metallic lead was formed and the gas collected from the tube was found to be ethane (CH_3CH_3). The exposed tube was then heated closer to the inlet, a lead "mirror" formed near the inlet, the lead near the outlet disappeared, and $(CH_3)_4Pb$ and ethane emerged from the tube. In the first stage, heating had released methyl free radicals (CH_3) and deposited lead. The radicals immediately dimerized to CH_3CH_3 before exiting the tube. In the second stage of the experiment, methyl radicals were released near the inlet as lead was deposited, some radicals immediately dimerized while others reacted with the lead "mirror" near the outlet to reform tetramethyllead. With careful control experiments, this study established the independent existence of transient, gas-phase methyl free radicals (CH_3). Further studies of the flow kinetics indicated that CH_3 lived for about 0.008 second under these conditions.

Carbocation Intermediates: Their Formation and Rearrangements

If the "radical" is truly the "root" or "foundation" underlying inter-conversion of, for example, CH_3CH_2-Cl to CH_3CH_2-OH, then what happens to that foundation if the "radical" (i.e., alkyl group R) alters its structure during the process? For example, if $(CH_3)_3C$-$CH(CH_3)$-Cl forms $(CH_3)_2CH$-$C(CH_3)_2$-OH, the carbon skeleton has rearranged from C_3C-CC to C_2C-CC_2. That would appear to place the ability to predict products derived from reactants on somewhat shaky ground. When organic chemistry began to emerge as a recognizable field during the 19th century, chemists recorded reactions in which the alkyl group (R) suffers totally unanticipated rearrangements.

The first breakthrough in understanding carbon-centered rearrangements was achieved by Hans L. Meerwein (1879–1965) in 1922 and is described in the figure on page 89. He observed a rearrangement of camphene hydrochloride to isonorbornyl chloride catalyzed by $AlCl_3$. Meerwein carefully investigated the rate of the reaction in different solvents and discovered that it increases with increasing dielectric constant of the solvent. Solvents, such as water, that have high dielectric constants ease the separation of oppositely charged ions. The solubilities of ionic salts generally increase in solvents of increasing dielectric constant. Meerwein proposed that a carbocation salt is formed as an initial intermediate and that it rearranges to another carbocation prior to product formation. There was precedent for this idea. Following the discovery of triphenylmethyl radical in 1900, Gomberg and other chemists demonstrated that some triphenylmethyl derivatives form carbocation salts $[(C_6H_5)_3C^+X^-]$ in high-dielectric constant solvents. These stable carbocation salts increase solution conductivities just as Na^+X^- and other simple inorganic salts do.

The Ultracentrifuge: Separating and Measuring Masses of Colloidal Particles

During the previous decade, Theodor Svedberg made important contributions to the science of colloids along with Perrin, Zsigmondy, and others (see chapter 2). Svedberg realized that only a centrifuge capable of enormous rotational velocity and very high centrifugal force could potentially separate colloidal particles and thus continue to advance colloid science.

Svedberg conducted his investigations at the University of Uppsala in Sweden. In 1923, he designed the ultracentrifuge and built an apparatus in 1924 that was capable of 12,000 rpm (revolutions per minute) with the generation of a net force of 7,000g (7,000 times the force of gravity). During 1925–26, he built an apparatus capable of 42,000 rpm and 100,000g. The accompanying figure depicts a single cell from Svedberg's ultracentrifuge in longitudinal section and in cross section. The colloidal suspension to be studied is placed in the wedge-shaped space between two transparent glass or quartz plates. Five such cells are placed in a rotor (see the figure on page 90, which also includes a schematic of the entire apparatus). As the rotor spins, the colloidal particles move from the center of the wedge-shaped space toward its outer edge. The movement is tracked by impinging filtered light (e.g., ultraviolet) through transparent ultramicroscope cells and recording the positions and velocities on film. Actually, a mechanical stroboscope, a rotating disk with slits in it and coordinated with the rotor, is employed so that the individual cells appear to be motionless, thus allowing sensitive photographs.

The movement of colloidal particles is governed by the centrifugal force of the ultracentrifuge which is opposed by the frictional force of the suspended particles. At equilibrium, the two forces are equal. Molecular weights can be derived both kinetically (from the velocity of sedimentation) and thermodynamically (from the final positions at equilibrium). Svedberg and his coworkers used their ultramicroscope to determine the masses of some proteins during 1925 and 1926. The molecular weight of hemoglobin was determined to be 68,350 using sedimentation velocity and 67,870 based upon the equilibrium method. Although the value is 5 percent higher than the (modern) value (ca. 64,500), the technique was still much more accurate than freezing point depression and osmotic pressure techniques. Its primary strength is the ability to separate colloidal particles based upon both mass and shape. Svedberg received the 1926 Nobel Prize in chemistry in the same year Perrin received the Nobel Prize in physics. In 1925, Zsigmondy won the Nobel Prize in chemistry. Clearly, colloids furnished one of the great research areas of the day. In 1925, one of Svedberg's students, Arne Tiselius (1902–71),

MEERWEIN REARRANGEMENT
OF CAMPHENE HYDROCHLORIDE

3

Equivalent to

3   **3+**

4   **4+**

Equivalent to

4

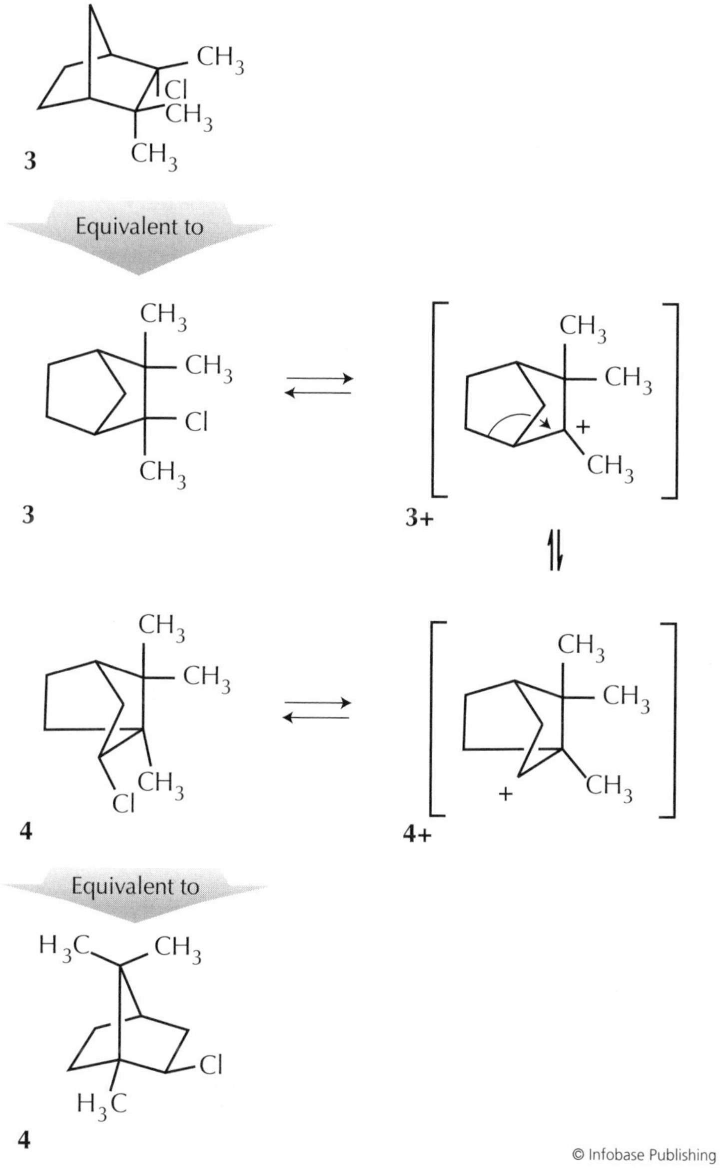

© Infobase Publishing

Depiction of Meerwein's interpretation, in 1922, of the rearrangement of camphene hydrochloride to isonorbornyl chloride, involving the intermediacy of camphene cation, which rearranges to isonorbornyl cation

started to study the motion of colloidal suspensions of charged particles in solution in electrical forces. His discovery of electrophoresis would lead to his receipt of the 1948 Nobel Prize in chemistry.

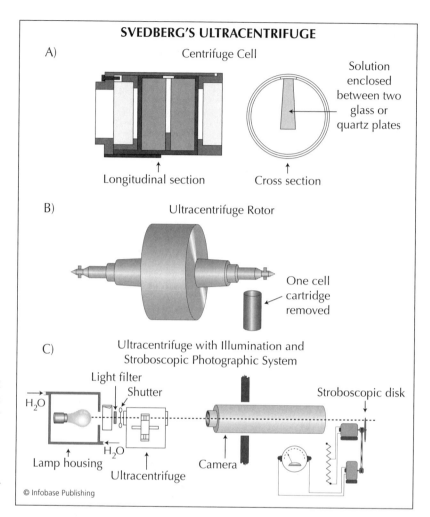

SVEDBERG'S ULTRACENTRIFUGE

A) Centrifuge Cell

Solution enclosed between two glass or quartz plates

Longitudinal section   Cross section

B) Ultracentrifuge Rotor

One cell cartridge removed

C) Ultracentrifuge with Illumination and Stroboscopic Photographic System

Light filter
Shutter
H_2O
Stroboscopic disk
Lamp housing
H_2O
Ultracentrifuge
Camera

© Infobase Publishing

A) Depiction of longitudinal section (left) and cross section (right) of a single ultracentrifuge cell from Svedberg's 1926 apparatus; B) ultracentrifuge rotor that contains five ultracentrifuge cells; C) schematic depiction of the ultracentrifuge

Other New Instrumental Techniques: Raman Spectroscopy and Polarography

The Compton effect, discovered in 1922, was treated earlier in this chapter. This nonelastic scattering of X-rays established the particle nature of radiation. In an extension of this work, a young Indian physicist, Chrandrasekhara Venkata ("C. V.") Raman (1888–1970), working in Calcutta, investigated the scattering of visible light.

The effects of *elastic* (no change in wavelength) scattering of sunlight by molecules in the Earth's atmosphere are well established. This is Rayleigh scattering and depends upon many factors including the wavelength (λ) of light (intensity proportional to $1/\lambda^4$). The consequence of this relationship to wavelength is that the intensity of scattering is by far greatest for the shortest wavelengths of visible light (i.e., blue light). The daytime sky appears to be blue. Raman and his colleague K. S. Krishnan (1898–1961) published his work in *Nature* in 1928 reporting their investigation of nonelastic scattering of visible light. The effect was a very weak one (it is known now that only 1 in 10^7 photons experience such scattering) but they did observe scattering of longer-wavelength light. For this work, Raman received the 1930 Nobel Prize in physics. Although the Raman effect is observed using visible light (nowadays one might employ the intense 488-nm line from an argon laser), the wavelength lengthening observed actually reflects vibrational effects in the substances of interest. There is a very interesting complementarity with IR spectroscopy, which also provides vibrational frequencies. In IR spectroscopy, a vibration is "infrared-active" if it causes a change in the molecular dipole moment. Carbon dioxide (O=C=O) is a linear molecule. Symmetrical stretching of the two C=O bonds in carbon dioxide does not change the dipole moment from zero. While this symmetrical stretching vibration does occur, no corresponding IR absorption band is observed. In contrast, unsymmetrical stretching (as well as symmetrical bending) in CO_2 does produce changes in dipole moment and characteristic IR absorption bands. In contrast, "selection rules" for Raman spectroscopy reflect changes in polarizability rather than in dipole moment. The symmetric stretch in CO_2 causes changes in polarizability while the unsymmetrical stretch does not. The first vibration is "Raman-active," the second is not.

In the early 1920s Jaroslav Heyrovský (1890–1967), in Prague, started a project in which he investigated the behavior of mercury in glass capillary tubes by monitoring the drops as they left the bottom of the vertical tube and formed a puddle below. Seeking a convenient means to monitor the flow, he set up a potential difference, through an electrolytic solution, between mercury in the capillary tube and mercury in the puddle. It became apparent that this caused chemical reduction of various ionic species in solutions at characteristic voltage differences. This offered possibilities for selective analysis. In collaboration with a colleague, Masuzo Shikata (1895–1964), Heyrovský assembled, in 1924, the first polarograph. Each tiny mercury droplet furnishes a surface for reduction of various species in solution. Rather than accumulate impurities on the surface, as a platinum electrode might, each droplet lasts a few seconds, falls into the mercury pool, and is replaced by a fresh droplet. The voltage potential drop is varied continuously throughout the experiment and "steps" occur corresponding to each different reduction potential. The heights of each step measure the relative concentration of each reducible species. The technique was a sensitive and highly selective one for determining concentrations of metal impurities. Applications were also found for organic molecules capable of *reduction-oxidation* (*REDOX*) chemistry. Heyrovský received the Nobel Prize in chemistry in 1959 for the discovery and development of polarography. Today polarography is little used but its close relative, cyclic voltammetry, is very widely employed to determine the electrochemistry of organic and inorganic substances.

Synthesizing Nature's Favorite Ring System

In 1906 Walter Albrecht discovered that cyclopentadiene and *p*-quinone react rapidly to provide a new product, although the structure was initially unknown. In the 1920s, Otto Diels (1876–1954) and his student Kurt Alder (1902–58) investigated this reaction and numerous related ones. The result was the discovery, published in 1928, of a major new thermally induced synthetic reaction between a conjugated diene, such as cyclopentadiene, and a dienophile, such as *p*-quinone, to form a new six-membered ring (see the reaction below). Any carbon-carbon bond-forming reaction is very important. The Nobel Prize awarded to Grignard in 1912 (see chapter 1) recognized this point quite explicitly. The Diels-Alder reaction forms *two* new C-C bonds simultaneously and in a highly specific manner.

It is striking that Diels and Alder finally received the Nobel Prize in chemistry in 1950, more than two decades after their initial publication. The science of total synthesis of natural products was slow to advance and was hindered by World War II. These factors perhaps explain the delay in fully appreciating the impact of the Diels-Alder reaction. The modern era of total organic synthesis is generally considered to have started during the 1940s. In 1952, Robert Burns ("R. B.") Woodward (1917–79) at Harvard would employ the Diels-Alder reaction to brilliant effect en route to total syntheses of the steroids cortisone and cholesterol.

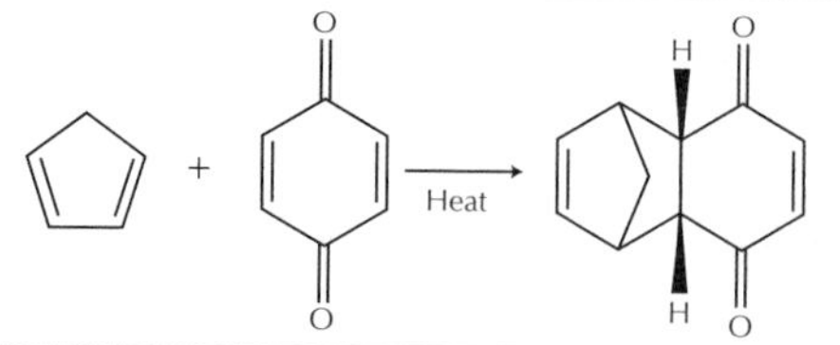

Diels-Alder reaction between cyclopentadiene and para-quinone

Highly Colored Natural Products: Conjugated Polyenes

When Mikhail Tswett invented column chromatography and applied it to the separation of plant pigments in 1907 (see chapter 1), he had no clue about the structure of these compounds. In fact, he had chemically separated two distinct classes of molecules, polycyclic magnesium-containing chlorophylls as well as carotenes (including the related oxygen-containing xanthophylls). The key advances in structure determination of these pigments were made during the late 1920s.

In 1930, Paul Karrer (1889–1971), working in Zurich, deduced the correct structures of the carotenes and lycopene (corroborated by Richard Kuhn [1900–67]). The methods he employed involved hydrogenation, to

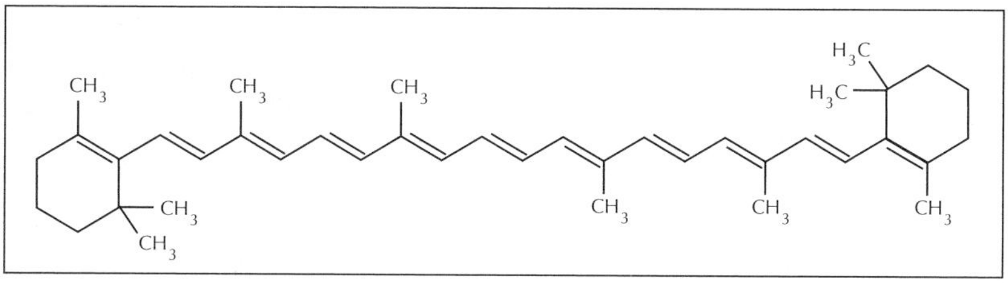

β-carotene; vitamin A

assess the degrees of *unsaturation* of these substances, as well as ozonolysis, a degradation technique that enabled his research group to "reassemble" the structure in the manner of a puzzle. Lycopene is the primary pigment in tomatoes (as well as red rose hips). Its formula is $C_{40}H_{56}$ and it is an isomer of β-carotene. Each molecule of lycopene absorbs 13 molecules of H_2; however, β-carotene absorbs only 11 molecules of H_2. This suggested two rings replacing two double bonds, and Karrer demonstrated that β-carotene has the structure shown above. It was later demonstrated that lycopene is a metabolic precursor to carotene. Much as the conjugated double bonds in 1,3-butadiene provide enhanced reactivity and unusual chemistry (e.g., 1,4-addition), those in lycopene, β-carotene, and related compounds react upon prolonged exposure to air. It is the extended conjugation of double bonds that is also a source for the colors of these pigments. A chemical relationship between carotenes and vitamin A had been deduced a decade earlier. In 1931, Karrer established the structure of vitamin A (below) and formally demonstrated that it is essentially one-half of a β-carotene molecule. Karrer shared the 1937 Nobel Prize in chemistry with Haworth (who established the cyclic structure for glucose that is discussed in the next section).

Chemical studies of hemoglobin and chlorophyll commenced during the first decades of the 20th century. As noted earlier, Richard Willstätter played the key role in establishing that heme units are composed of substituted pyrroles. The formula for hemin, the nonprotein pigment part of hemoglobin, was known to be $C_{34}H_{32}O_4N_4$ FeCl. In 1912 Wilhelm Z. Küster (1863–1929) presented a fairly complete structure for this pure compound. However, it was Hans Fischer (1881–1945), working in Germany, who deduced the complete structure of hemin and for this work received the 1930 Nobel Prize in chemistry.

There are a variety of pathways for removing iron from hemin and generating what is now termed protoporphyrin IX. This is, in turn,

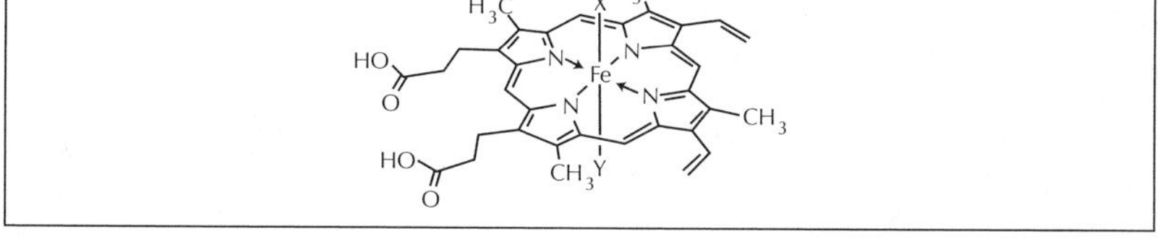

Protoporphyrin IX unit in myoglobin and hemoglobin

"Curly Arrows": Hieroglyphics of the Organic Chemist

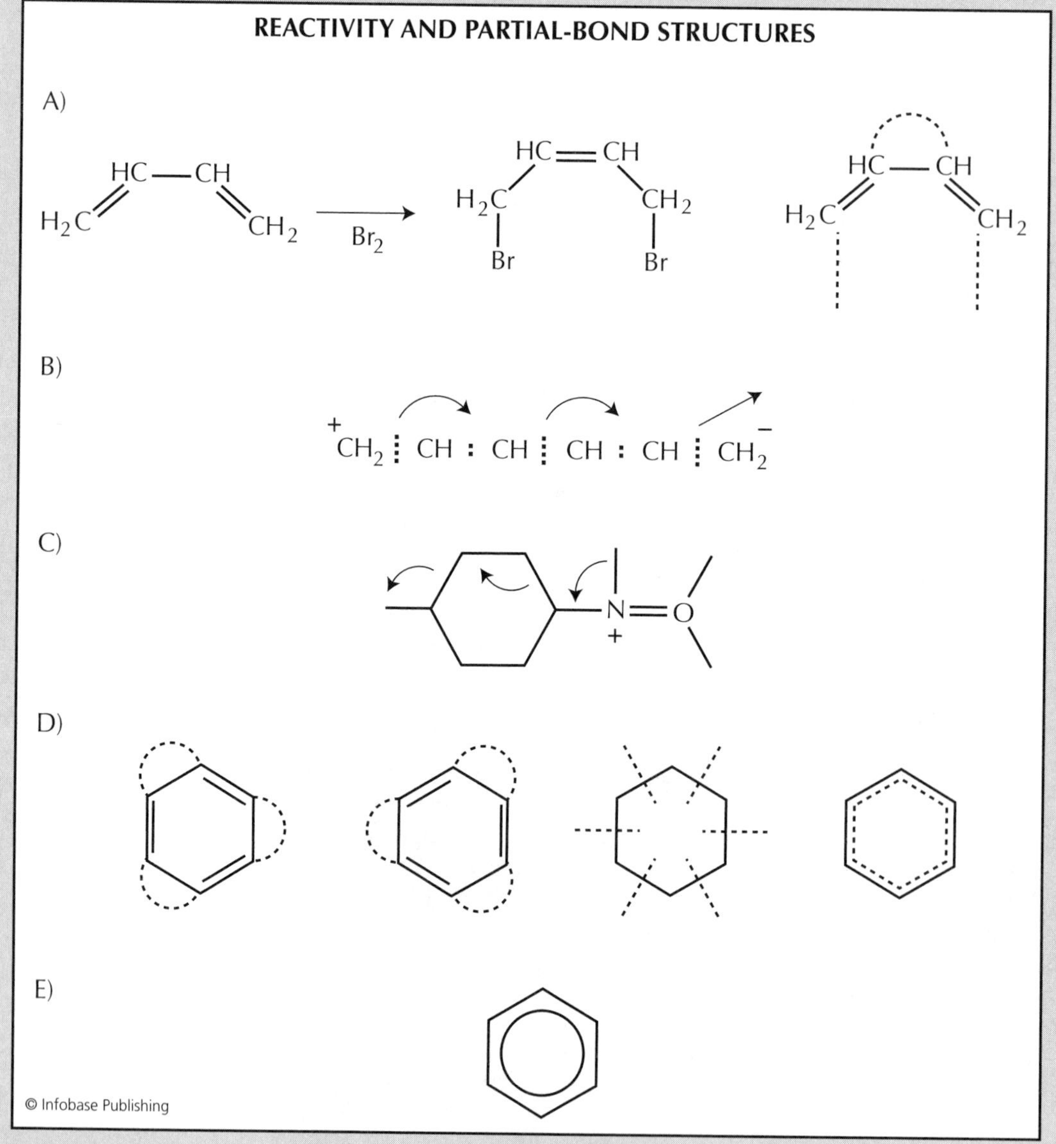

REACTIVITY AND PARTIAL-BOND STRUCTURES

A)

B)

C)

D)

E)

Early depictions relevant to the development of the electronic theory of organic chemistry: A) representation of the reaction between 1,3-butadiene and Br₂, in the manner of Robinson, depicting partial bonds and polarities; B) the "birth" of the Robinson-Kernack "curly arrows" representing partial valences in 1,3-butadiene; C) application by Robinson of "curly arrows" toward the explanation of meta substitution in nitroso benzene; D) early representations by Thiele and others of the equivalence of all bonds in benzene; E) Robinson's 1925 representation of benzene

From alchemical times onward, chemistry has been known for its symbols and emblems (its own unique "hieroglyphics"). Organic chemists, in particular, seem to have evolved their own special hieroglyphics. Why is this so? The answer, in part, is that carbon forms stable single, double, and triple bonds with other carbons (and many other elements) in a seemingly infinite array of chains and cycles. Moreover, when double bonds are conjugated (C=C-C=C, C=C-C=C-C=C, C=C-C=O, etc.), they strongly influence each other and produce a chemistry different from the "simple sum" of individual double bonds. Almost unique to organic chemists is the art of the "curly arrow." Introductory courses teach young students to skillfully wield this conceptual "weapon." Its use was honed during the 1920s.

Just prior to the 20th century Johannes Thiele (1865–1918) studied additions to conjugated dienes and discovered a tendency toward 1,4-addition, for example, the bromination of 1,3-butadiene to form 1,4-dibromo-2-butene (part A in the accompanying figure). There were apparently unsatisfied "residual valences" on carbons 1 and 4 of 1,3-butadiene that rendered these positions reactive. On the other hand, the "residual valences" on carbons 2 and 3 of 1,3-butadiene were adjacent and "saturated each other" rendering these positions unreactive. The Lewis-Langmuir electron-pair structures, developed during the period 1916–19 (see chapter 2), had begun by this time to influence the organic chemistry community. Robert Robinson, and his coauthor William O. Kernack (1898–1970), are credited with being the first to use "curly arrows" (Part B in the figure) to account for chemical reactivity in conjugated and simpler systems.

During the 1920s the growing application of the new electronic theory to organic chemistry attracted many brilliant contributors. It also became a field for a growing, and bitter, decades-long rivalry between Robinson and the younger Englishman Christopher Kelk Ingold (1893–1970). The chemistry of benzene and related aromatic compounds became an important testing field for theory. Robinson explained *meta* substitution in nitrosobenzene using the "curly arrow" model in Part C of the accompanying figure (the vertical line above nitrogen represents a non-bonded electron pair in the Lewis-Langmuir tradition). Although this explanation differs somewhat from the manner in which *meta* substitution is explained today, the method of this diagram and the accompanying explanation are quite similar to the modern ones. Thiele and others postulated a variety of partial-valence structures to account for benzene's reactivity (Part D in the figure). In 1925 Robinson suggested the benzene representation in common use today (Part E in the accompanying figure).

derived from a fundamental unit, porphin, a planar, highly conjugated system of double bonds. It is now understood that the iron in hemin is actually Fe(III) while that in heme, as it occurs in hemoglobin (and myoglobin), is Fe(II). In protoporphyrin IX, four of the six coordination sites of Fe(II) are bonded to the four porphin nitrogens. In hemoglobin or myoglobin, the fifth site is attached to protein and the sixth is typically attached to O_2 (or other molecules such as CO) (see the figure on page 93).

Cytochromes were discovered and their role in oxidation explored by David Keilin (1887–1963) in England in 1925. Most cytochromes contain the protoporphyrin IX unit found in hemoglobin and myoglobin. However, in cytochromes both the fifth and sixth coordination sites are occupied by proteins. In contrast to hemoglobin and myoglobin, which always function in the Fe(II) state, the cytochromes interconvert between Fe(II) and Fe(III) as they perform electron transfer.

At the time that he received his Nobel Prize in 1930, Fischer was investigating the structure of the pigments chlorophyll *a* and *b*, magnesium complexes of a close relative of protoporphyrin IX. Willstätter's early work had demonstrated a long-chain ester in chlorophyll and, around 1930, James B. Conant (1893–1978) at Harvard deduced its structure (phytol). Structures for the chlorophylls were finally solved by Fischer around 1940 and he also published the structure of bilirubin in 1942. Fischer worked in Munich before and throughout World War II. Following an Allied bombing raid that destroyed his laboratory, Fischer committed suicide on March 31, 1945, five weeks before the war in Europe ended.

The Cyclic Structure of Glucose: The Most Abundant Organic Unit in Nature

Emil Fischer's brilliant determination of the stereochemistry of glucose during the 1880s remains today a classical example of elegant scientific investigation and was the major contribution leading to his Nobel Prize in chemistry (1902). D-glucose is the most abundant organic unit in nature. It comprises starch as well as cellulose. The Fischer structure for D-glucose (top left structure in the figure on page 97) was an open chain containing an aldehyde group as C1 while C2, C3, C4, and C5 are asymmetric carbons. It is worth noting here that Pasteur knew that either this structure, or its mirror image, was equally likely to represent the naturally occurring (*dextrorotatory*) D-(+)-glucose. It was not until 1951 that Fischer's arbitrary (50:50) candidate was found to have the correct absolute configuration. There would have been no problem had Fischer chosen the mirror image to represent D-(+)-glucose. He simply would have had to take the mirror image of all the related molecules he had assigned as the correct configurations.

There remained some nagging problems about Fischer's original open-chain structure. One of these was the discovery of two distinct methyl glycosides derived from D-(+)-glucose. Fischer adroitly dealt with this problem (i.e., two distinct glycosides termed α and β), which could not be explained using his open structure, by invoking five-membered-ring structures (two top right structures in the figure). Each is a chemically distinct diastereomer having five asymmetric carbons. Pasteur's choice of a five-membered ring to solve the methyl glycoside problem was based upon his full acceptance of *ring-strain* theory as originally proposed by Adolph von Baeyer (1835–1917).

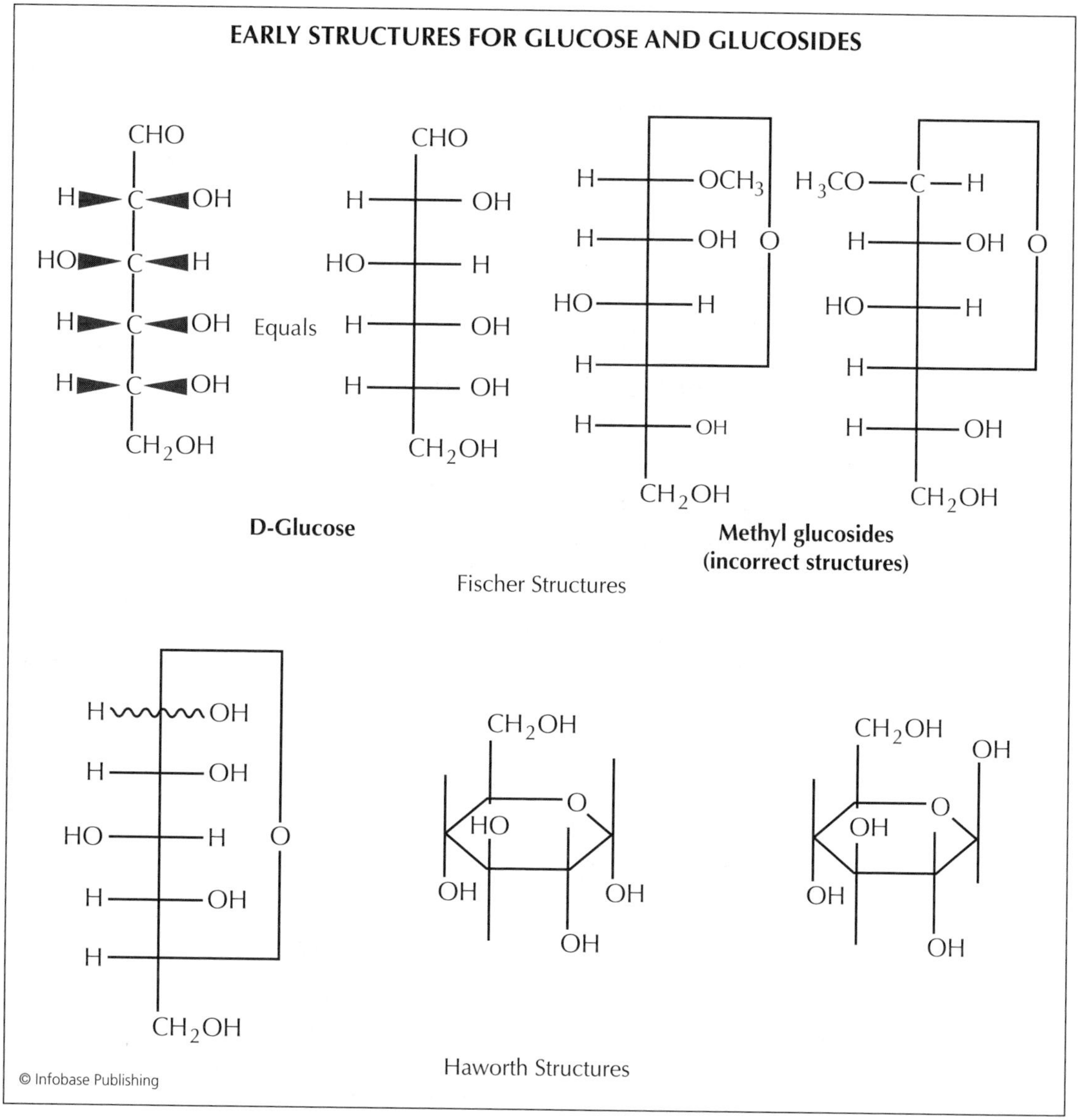

EARLY STRUCTURES FOR GLUCOSE AND GLUCOSIDES

D-Glucose

Methyl glucosides
(incorrect structures)

Fischer Structures

© Infobase Publishing

Haworth Structures

In late 1925, W. Norman Haworth (1883–1950), at the University of Durham (U.K.), made a compelling case that glucose is a six-membered ring (bottom left of figure). He developed a useful (and still frequently employed) representation of the stereochemistry of saccharides including α-(+)-glucose and β-(+)-glucose (bottom middle and right structures in accompanying figure). Haworth's work on glucose and related stereochemical studies earned him the 1937 Nobel Prize in chemistry, shared with Paul Karrer, who was recognized for his work on plant pigments.

Fischer's open-chain structure for (+)-glucose with its Fischer projection and two (incorrect) cyclic structures for its methyl glucosides (top). Haworth's correct assignment of a six-membered ring for glucose and Haworth structures for the two anomers of (+)-glucose (bottom)

Six-Membered Rings

It is worthwhile to visit early views about naturally occurring organic ring compounds. The first cyclic molecule to have its structure established was benzene in 1865 and, for a brief period, six-membered rings were thought to be the only possibility. During the 1880s William H. Perkin, Jr. (1860–1929), the son of William H. Perkin (1838–1907) who discovered the dye mauve, and a student of Baeyer, established the existence of three-, four-, and five-membered carbocycles. Baeyer strain in cyclopropane causes it to react with HCl as if it were an alkene rather than an alkane.

In 1904, Richard Willstätter synthesized cyclooctatetraene, an eight-membered ring. His attempts at synthesizing a nine-membered ring were unsuccessful and, by the 1920s, there was general acceptance that ring systems larger than eight had large C-C-C bond angles, high Baeyer strain and were highly unlikely to exist.

During the early 1920s, Leopold Ruzicka (1887–1976), born in Austria–Hungary, accepted a position in Zurich at the Eidgenössische Technische Hochschule (ETH, the Swiss Federal Institute of Technology). Continuing earlier studies of terpenes, many of which are essential perfume oils, he developed partnerships with German and later Swiss perfume manufacturers. In 1922 he commenced an investigation of two essential oils, civetone ($C_{17}H_{30}O$) and muscone ($C_{16}H_{30}O$), derived from the scent glands of the male civet cat and the male musk deer, both of interest to the perfume industry.

In performing his investigations, Ruzicka extensively oxidized civetone (using hot potassium permanganate or ozone) and then further oxidized the degradation products. This classical technique provides a series of small, well-known pieces that permitted Ruzicka to "reconstruct" civetone. When he used milder oxidation, he was surprised to find a single long-chain product. Following additional detective work, Ruzicka's conclusion was unavoidable: Civetone has a 17-membered ring (see left). Muscone has a very similar odor to civetone and Ruzicka suspected another large ring system. He deduced a structure with a 15-membered ring, including a single asymmetric carbon, fully consistent with the observed optical activity of muscone.

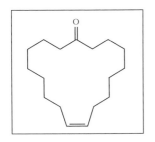

Civetone

Cyclohexane rings and cyclopentane rings are structural features of the steroids investigated by Wieland, Windaus, Diels, and others during the previous decade (chapter 2). In 1929, Adolph Butenandt (1903–95), working in Göttingen, isolated from the urines of pregnant women a new substance that he obtained in crystalline form. Independently and virtually simultaneously, Edward A. Doisy (1893–1980) also isolated this substance. Initially named "folliculine" by Butenandt, it is now known as estrone, the first female hormone to be isolated. Butenandt determined its formula as $C_{18}H_{22}O_2$ and demonstrated that it is a steroid. Ruzicka and Butenandt would share the 1939 Nobel Prize in chemistry. Doisy would share the 1943 Nobel Prize in physiology or medicine.

Alkaloids are naturally occurring carbocyclic compounds that owe their alkaline properties to the presence of nitrogen atoms. Chapter 2 included discussion of the early structural elucidation of tropane alkaloids and the synthesis of one of these, cocaine, by Willstätter, as well as Robinson's synthesis of tropinone. Robinson had speculated that his synthesis of tropinone might shed some light on natural biosynthetic pathways. He was one of the first scientists to seriously ponder biosynthetic pathways. These insights led him to imagine a biosynthetic pathway to morphine from a much simpler molecule, papaverine, which, like morphine, is extracted from the juice of the poppy. Robinson virtually solved the structure of morphine by applying this brilliant bit of intuition. He also correctly predicted that papaverine has its biosynthetic origins in two molecules of the amino acid tyrosine. The intellectual range displayed throughout Robinson's career was evidenced by his development of new reactions, total syntheses of natural products, virtually starting the field of biosynthesis and, as noted earlier, fundamental contributions to the theory of organic chemistry.

In 1928, Alexander Fleming (1881–1955), a Scottish bacteriologist working in London, observed that spores of blue mold (*Penicillium notatum*), that had accidentally contaminated a culture of *staphylococcus* he was studying, were surrounded by a ring within which there were no bacteria. He realized that diffusion from the mold through the medium implied the action of specific chemical substances. His early studies demonstrated anti-*staphylococcus* activity at dilutions of almost one-thousandfold. Fleming named the substance penicillin but it would not be until 1940 that it would be isolated in pure form. Fleming would share the 1945 Nobel Prize in physiology or medicine.

Intermediary Metabolism: Fermentation and Respiration

When cell-free yeast extract ("juice") was shown to be a fully active ferment by Buchner in 1897, it clearly implied that intermediary metabolism is based on rational chemistry (see chapter 1). Of particular interest is the metabolism of carbohydrates. Aerobic organisms, including mammals, derive energy by combining oxygen with food to produce carbon dioxide and water. They draw their energy from *respiration*. Strictly anaerobic organisms do not employ oxygen during metabolism; oxygen may even be deadly to the organism. They draw their energy from *fermentation*. Facultative anaerobes live by fermentation in oxygen-free conditions and oxidize their products of fermentation when oxygen is present.

In 1929, the Nobel Prize in chemistry was shared by Arthur Harden and Hans von Euler-Chelpin (1873–1964) for their work, culminating in the 1920s, establishing the role of phosphate in the fermentation of sugars such as glucose. Their studies explicitly connected the formation of lactic acid in muscle with the formation of ethanol in the fermentation of sugar by yeast. A key intermediate is fructose-1,6-diphosphate, the final six-carbon intermediate before breakdown into two three-carbon chains. Historically, the route from glucose-6-phosphate to lactate has been known as *glycolysis* although this is now taken to represent the pathway down to pyruvate. Studies in bacterial fermentation were conducted during the 1920s by the Finnish scientist Arturi I. Virtanen (1895–1973), recipient of the 1945 Nobel Prize in chemistry.

One of the major contributors to discoveries during the 1930s of the biological electron transfer pathways was Hungarian biochemist Albert Szent-Györgyi (pronounced "saint georgie") (1893–1986). During the 1920s, his interest in biological oxidations led him to make a connection between the brown pigmentation occurring when a sliced apple is allowed to sit and the brown pigmentation that stains an adrenal cortex that ceases to function. Enzymes known as peroxidases had been discovered in plants and in animal tissues. Their function is to activate hydrogen peroxide toward oxidation. Szent-Györgyi discovered an unstable reducing agent, in trace levels in fruit juices, capable of returning peroxidase to its active state. Much to his delight, he discovered that the adrenal cortex is a rich source of this reducing agent. Szent-Györgyi managed to isolate about 25 grams of this unstable substance, obtained from the adrenal cortices of oxen, in crystalline form. Its formula was determined to be $C_6H_8O_6$. However, its chemical structure would not be deciphered until much larger quantities were made available and Szent-Györgyi partnered with organic chemists Haworth and Karrer during the early 1930s to solve the structure. He named the substance hexuronic acid and, based upon its occurrence and biological properties, identified it as the long-sought vitamin C. It was later renamed ascorbic acid by Szent-Györgyi and Haworth. Szent-Györgyi would win the 1937 Nobel Prize in physiology or medicine.

During the 1920s, German biochemist Otto Warburg (1883–1970) introduced a technique for monitoring intermediary metabolism in vitro ("in glass"), improving the manometric methods of Joseph Bancroft (1872–1947). The "surviving-slice method" employed the Warburg-Bancroft apparatus depicted schematically in the figure on page 101. It includes a modified Erlenmeyer flask containing a buffered reaction medium into which thin (less than 0.016 inch or 0.4 mm) slices of tissue or minced tissue are suspended. The center well contains filter paper and KOH to absorb the CO_2 generated. The side arm of the flask contains a solution of the substrate to be metabolized by the tissue. The flask is connected to a manometer. Oxygen uptake is monitored continuously and the entire system allows variation of many parameters (e.g., temperature, substrate, and inhibitor concentrations).

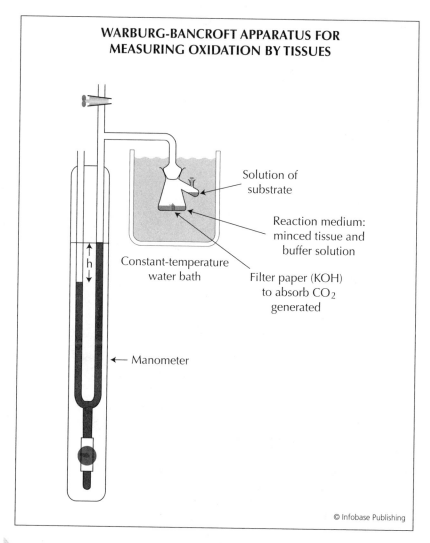

WARBURG-BANCROFT APPARATUS FOR
MEASURING OXIDATION BY TISSUES

Solution of substrate

Reaction medium: minced tissue and buffer solution

Constant-temperature water bath

Filter paper (KOH) to absorb CO_2 generated

Manometer

h

© Infobase Publishing

Schematic diagram depicting the Warburg-Bancroft apparatus for measuring the uptake of oxygen gas by a buffered suspension of minced or thinly sliced tissue. See the text for discussion of the use of this apparatus.

All Enzymes Are Proteins

The first cell-free "ferments" were derived from yeast by Buchner in 1897 and studies by Harden and Young in 1904 using dialysis led to further understanding of their general nature (see chapter 1). Although ferments were suspected to be proteinaceous, proteins themselves were not understood and neither chemical theory nor the experiments of the period could characterize them as the complex macromolecules known today.

In 1926, James B. Sumner (1887–1955), working at Cornell University, managed to extract the enzyme urease (which catalyzes the decomposition of urea into CO_2 and NH_3) and crystallize it. This was the first time that an enzyme had been crystallized, an unassailable measure of its purity. The difficulties in this challenging isolation included the variability of enzyme samples received, uncertainties in their chemical analyses, their chemical sensitivities and ready degradation, and conceptual problems in understanding the macromolecular nature of proteins, as opposed to viewing them as micelles (see the next section of this chapter).

Sumner's analytical studies convinced him that urease was a protein. This conclusion was resisted by the chemical community but John H. Northrop's (1891–1987) crystallization of pepsin in 1930 at the Rockefeller Institute in New York City and its unambiguous decomposition into amino acids fully vindicated Sumner. Sumner and Northrop were able to make use of the ultracentrifuge developed by Svedberg and the electrophoresis technique developed by his student Tiselius to fully establish purities and molecular weights of their enzymes. Sumner and his coworkers then crystallized trypsin and chymotrypsin. Sumner and Northrop shared the 1946 Nobel Prize in chemistry with Wendell M. Stanley (1904–71), who in 1935 crystallized the tobacco mosaic virus in his laboratory at the Rockefeller Institute.

Understanding and Exploiting Giant Molecules

Hermann Staudinger (1881–1965) began his distinguished scientific career in Karlsruhe, Germany, studying small molecules. He was the first to synthesize and explore the chemistry of ketenes ($R_2C=C=O$), made important contributions to the chemistry of divalent carbon (*"carbenes"*), organophosphorus chemistry, autooxidation, insecticides, *terpenes*, isoprene, and various pharmaceuticals, and developed synthetic pepper for the pepper-starved Germans during World War I.

In 1912, Staudinger moved to Zurich and within a few years commenced the study of macromolecules that would eventually earn him the 1953 Nobel Prize in chemistry. Staudinger's colleagues in Europe were rather mystified to watch his research move from fruitful investigations of small molecules to *"schmierenchemie"* ("grease chemistry"). However, he brilliantly recognized the potential of an entirely new field of chemistry founded in the tarry residues at the bottoms of flasks. One of the greatest chemical problems of the age related to understanding the nature of colloids (see chapters 1 and 2). During the early 20th century, most chemists thought it unlikely that extremely large molecules could even exist. Thanks to Staudinger, the reality of giant molecules would be accepted and the role of polymers in colloid chemistry largely understood by the beginning of the 1930s.

Staudinger published an important study of the catalytic hydrogenation of polyisoprene (rubber) in 1922. If the high experimental molecular weight of this substance arose from micelles composed of numerous smaller molecules, then hydrogenation should destroy the micellar structure and produce much lower molecular weight substances. In fact, the molecular weight and the other physical properties of the hydrogenated product were very similar to those of polyisoprene itself. In that paper Staudinger coined the term *"makromolekule."*

Among Staudinger's early projects was the study of polyoxymethylene, a polymer formed from liquid formaldehyde in a reaction occasionally prone to explode. He applied the relatively new technique of X-ray crystallography to his powdered samples of polyoxymethylene. Much to his delight, the substance exhibited crystalline properties that provided data on the size of the unit cell. By the 1920s, a great deal was already known about unit cells and interatomic (or interionic) distances. Typically, a unit cell included more than one molecular unit of the substance in question. It was understood at the time that unit cells had to be larger than the molecules that occupied them. Study of polyoxymethylene powder diffraction patterns indicated the presence of only four monomeric -CH_2O- units per unit cell. Staudinger and his colleagues established, during the 1920s, that polymeric substances have unit cells that contain only sections of the giant macromolecules. Similar studies on cellulose helped to establish its polymeric character. Staudinger returned to Germany in 1926, accepting an appointment at Freiburg.

Staudinger and his colleagues pioneered "end-group analysis" as another technique for determining molecular weight (effectively average molecular weight). For example, polyoxyethylene has free hydroxyl groups at the two chain termini. If it reacts with acetic anhydride, acetyl derivatives are formed at each end. Analysis of the acetyl content of the polymer provides its molecular weight. A diacetylated molecule consisting of five CH_2CH_2O units (degree of polymerization = 5) has an acetyl content of 26.7 percent. If the acetyl content of a different sample is 8.4 percent, the degree of polymerization is 20 and the molecular weight of the polyoxyethylene sample is 940. An acetyl content of 0.92 percent in polyethoxyethylene corresponds to a degree of polymerization of 210 and a molecular weight of 9,300. Staudinger found excellent agreement between these molecular weight values and those obtained using cryoscopic techniques such as freezing point depression. His fundamental studies of the *viscosity* of polymer solutions as a function of molecular weight (viscometry) also began in the 1920s.

Wallace Hume Carothers (1896–1937) would achieve an incredible amount in a life tragically shortened by his suicide at the age of 41. Obtaining his Ph.D. in chemistry from the University of Illinois at Urbana-Champaign in 1924, Carothers joined the Harvard faculty but was lured away by DuPont de Nemours in 1928 to direct basic research at this venerable "powerhouse" in Wilmington, Delaware. DuPont made an almost unique commitment at the time by investing in fundamental research. The rewards reaped by the company over the years have repaid the investment manyfold.

One of the challenges to chemists of this period was the creation of artificial rubber, hopefully better than natural rubber, which is easily dissolved by oils. Following World War I, German chemists developed a rubber based on 1,3-butadiene, termed Buna rubber, which was useful but inferior to the natural product (see chapter 1). Carothers's DuPont colleagues synthesized 2-chloro-1,3-butadiene and polymerized it to form neoprene, the first commercially successful synthetic rubber. The new polymer was superior to rubber in oil and chemical resistance as well as resistance to abrasion, sunlight, and extreme temperatures. It was a "natural" for gaskets and today finds particular application in the manufacture of wet suits.

Carothers was a strong supporter of Staudinger's theory of macromolecules and sought ways to demonstrate its veracity. He and his colleague Julian Hill (1904–96) developed a new form of polymer synthesis: step–wise polymerization. They reasoned that since a carboxylic acid (RCOOH) and an alcohol (R'OH) "condense" to form an ester (RCOOR'), a dicarboxylic acid and a difunctional diol should form a macromolecular polyester. In 1930 they reacted a dicarboxylic acid and a diol and obtained a polyester (see the accompanying figure). The molecular weight (actually an average) determined for this polyester was about 12,000 (roughly three times the existing "world's record" for a synthetic substance). Moreover, polyester could be spun into fibers. Although Carothers succeeded in verifying Staudinger's theory, the first polyesters synthesized had low melting points and were dissolved by common cleaning solvents. However, they laid the groundwork for the discovery of polyamides such as nylon during the 1930s. DuPont and other companies would develop economically valuable polyesters in future years.

Formation of an early polyester from a dicarboxylic acid and a diol

EARLY FORMATION OF POLYESTER

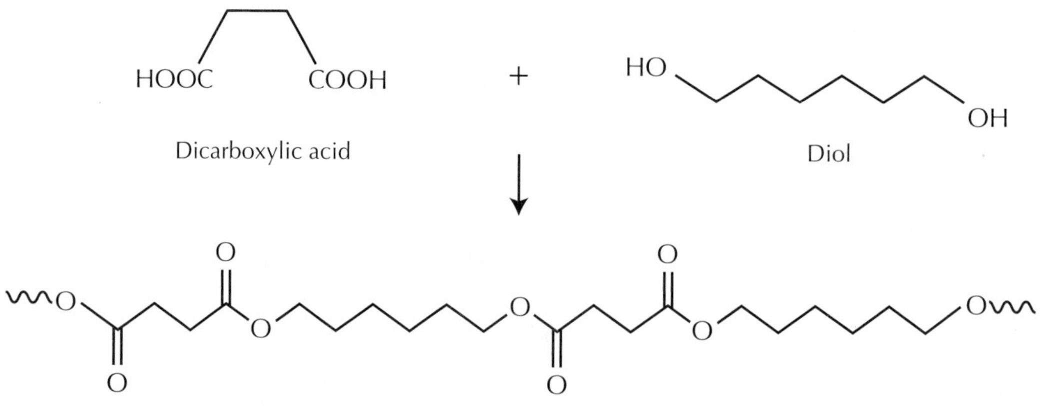

Dicarboxylic acid   +   Diol

Polyester

© Infobase Publishing

Making the Most of Coal

Coal is the final product of the decomposition of plant material during millions of years. The compositions and "structures" of coals are both highly complex and highly variable. Typically, dry bituminous coal consists of about 75 percent carbon, 7 percent oxygen, 5 percent hydrogen, 3 percent nitrogen and sulfur, and 10 percent ash. There are enormous reserves of coal in the world and, in the United States, coal reserves are vastly greater than petroleum reserves. Typically, most coal is burned as fuel. It normally presents many problems as a fuel, particularly when employed on a small scale (in residential furnaces for example). Lumps of coal burn inefficiently and produce less energy and more carbon monoxide than petroleum. The presence of sulfur is the source of corrosive oxides of sulfur. On larger scales, pulverized coal can flow and burn more efficiently and methods for removing sulfur from coal coupled with trapping unwanted pollutants can make commercial power plants both efficient and clean. However, transportation of coal is clumsy and costly. Moreover, it is a pity to simply burn such unimaginable quantities of carbon building blocks. Dry distillation of coal (2,000–2,375°F [1,100–1,300°C]) produces coal gas (mostly CH_4 and H_2), an ammoniacal aqueous solution, viscous coal tar, and a solid residue of coke. Fractional distillation of tar provides of a variety of aromatic compounds, including benzene, and formed the basis for the 19th-century dye industry.

   If steam is passed over coke, a flammable gas (termed "water gas") is produced:

   Coke + H_2O (steam) = CO + H_2 ("water gas")

In 1923 two German scientists, Franz Fischer (1877–1947) and Hans Tropsch (1889–1935) developed a process whereby coke exposed to steam in the presence of catalysts forms a variety of organic compounds (hydrocarbons, aldehydes, ketones, alcohols) depending upon the catalyst and other specific conditions. Around this time, Alwin Mittasch (1869–1953), who developed the catalyst for the Haber-Bosch Process (chapter 1), introduced a related reaction in which carbon monoxide and hydrogen are combined in the presence of chromium oxide and zinc oxide (and similar combinations) to form methanol. The Fischer-Tropsch process played an important role in the synthesis of fuels

   CO + 2 H_2 → CH_3OH

by Germany during World War II and its manufacturing plants were important targets for Allied bombers. Specific mixtures of pure CO and H_2, generated from a variety of sources, are collectively called "synthesis gas." The ability to convert coal into light hydrocarbons and derivatives, such as alcohols and aldehydes, remains an area of very active interest as natural petroleum reserves dwindle.

Scientist of the Decade: Hermann Staudinger (1881–1965)

Hermann Staudinger was born in Worms, Germany, and was interested at an early age in pursuing a career in botany. His father, Franz Staudinger, a well-known philosopher, after speaking with professors of botany, advised his son to learn chemistry as an aid to studying botany. The younger Staudinger found himself more intrigued with chemistry. He learned analytical chemistry, spent time with Baeyer in Munich, and completed a doctoral thesis with Daniel Vörlander at the University of Halle in 1903. Vörlander studied 1,4-additions to conjugated dienes and was an early contributor to the electronic theory of organic chemistry. Not surprisingly, he interested Staudinger in this new area. Staudinger moved on to the Thiele Institute in Strasbourg where he made his mark by creating a new class of organic molecules, the ketenes. In 1907 he moved to Karlsruhe where he continued ketene research and other areas of investigation including 1,3-butadiene and its 2-methyl derivative isoprene.

In 1912, Staudinger moved from his native Germany to Zurich to succeed Willstätter at the ETH. (Willstätter had accepted an appointment at the Kaiser-Wilhelm Institute in Berlin). Staudinger remained at the ETH until 1926. During World War I, he was openly critical of the aggressive militaristic policy of his homeland Germany. He returned to accept a chair at Freiburg in 1926 where he remained until retirement in 1951.

Staudinger began his groundbreaking studies of macromolecules in the ETH around 1920. At the time, many prominent chemists were convinced that the existence of molecules with molecular weights significantly exceeding 4,000 was impossible. The explanation for colloids of apparent high molecular weight was based upon micelles. Staudinger's firm grounding in organic chemistry led him to suspect the

Hermann Staudinger, who pioneered polymer chemistry and won the 1953 Nobel Prize in chemistry (Chemical Heritage Foundation)

existence of huge macromolecules held together by nothing more mysterious than covalent bonds. His triumph involved using numerous techniques in organic chemistry and physical chemistry to make an uncontestable case for macromolecules by the end of 1930 and he created an entirely new field of chemistry. Without the macromolecular paradigm it is impossible to make any sense of proteins, polysaccharides such as starch and cellulose, or nucleic acids such as DNA and RNA. Staudinger received the 1953 Nobel Prize in chemistry. He died in Germany in 1965.

Conclusion

The X-ray structural data collected during the 1920s and the new quantum mechanics developed in Germany would lead to consolidation of theory and structure during the 1930s. Linus Pauling developed axioms based on crystallography at the end of the 1920s and he would pioneer valence bond theory during the following decade. Robert Mulliken pioneered molecular orbital theory during this period. During the 1920s, Hermann Staudinger started the field of macromolecular chemistry and it would have major commercial successes in the following decade. Discoveries of free radical, branched-chain, and carbocation mechanisms would be further clarified by transition-state theory and the application of stereochemistry to mechanistic theory in the 1930s. The first important discoveries in intermediary metabolism were made in the 1920s, including the complete mechanism for glycolysis. If glycolysis is likened to a "small propeller plane," then respiration is a "jet airliner" and the associated Krebs cycle and electron transport chain to oxygen will be significantly clarified in the next decade. The Roaring Twenties was a period of relief from a horrible war and a flu pandemic and was full of music and dancing to accompany a wild, speculative stock market. The following decade would be one of enormous financial pain during the Great Depression and a march toward world war.

Further Reading

Brock, William H. *The Norton History of Chemistry*, 506–537. New York: W.W. Norton & Co., 1993. This is a superb discussion of the early electronic theory of organic chemistry including the Lapworth-Robinson collaboration and Robinson-Ingold rivalry.

Chemical Heritage Foundation. *Spinning the Elements: Wallace Carothers and the Nylon Legacy.* Available online. URL: www.chemheritage.org/ EducationalServices/nylon/nylon.html, 2000. Accessed February 12, 2006. This Web site offers an excellent tour through the history of polymer chemistry.

Hager, Thomas. *Force of Nature: The Life of Linus Pauling.* New York: Simon & Schuster, 1995. This is a balanced biography of Pauling that includes an accessible discussion of his scientific work.

Laidler, Keith J. *Chemical Kinetics.* 3rd ed., 322–328. New York: Harper & Row, 1987. This section provides an excellent discussion with historical context of the kinetics of the reaction between hydrogen and oxygen.

Olah, George. "My Search for Carbocations and Their Role in Chemistry." In *Nobel Lectures 1991–1995.* Edited by B. G. Malmström. Singapore: World Scientific Publishing Co., 1997. Available online. URL: http:// nobelprize.org/chemistry/laureates/1994/olah-lecture.html. Accessed

February 12, 2006. This is the December 8, 1994, Nobel Prize lecture by George A. Olah.

Partington, James R. *A History of Chemistry.* Vol. 4, 955–959; 963–966. London: MacMillan & Co. Ltd., 1964. These two sections provide very succinct discussions of the development of quantum numbers.

Scerri, Eric R. "It's Elemental: The Periodic Table." *Chemical & Engineering News* 81 (September 8, 2003): 138. This brief essay, in a special issue of *C & E News,* is devoted to hafnium, especially the history of its discovery as interpreted by the author.

Staudinger, Hermann. *From Organic Chemistry to Macromolecules.* New York: Wiley-Interscience, 1970. This is the English translation of Staudinger's autobiography.

4

1931–1940:
Nuclear Physics, Natural Products, and the Nature of the Chemical Bond

Artificial Isotopes and the Structures of Important Biological Molecules

During the 1930s, the United States along with the rest of the world found itself mired in the Great Depression, a tragedy that only really ended with the start of World War II. The discovery of the neutron once and for all explained the nature of isotopes. The neutron would become the "philosopher's stone" of the 20th century, initiating real transmutations between elements. The new quantum theory, developed during the 1920s, enhanced understanding of chemical structure and reactivity. The separation of deuterium from light hydrogen provided a subtle probe of incalculable value for exploring reaction mechanisms and metabolic pathways. During this decade, great strides would be made in the identification and synthesis of natural products: terpenes, steroids, vitamins, and hormones. The first fully synthetic antibiotics, *sulfa drugs*, would aid in fighting *streptococcus* and other deadly bacteria. The decade would witness the elucidation of some major intermediary metabolic pathways, the light reaction of photosynthesis, and connections between protein and carbohydrate metabolism. The decade would end with mass production of nylon stockings, the discovery of nuclear fission, the start of World War II, and the decision to fund the Manhattan Project and build an atomic bomb.

Discovery of the Neutron

James Chadwick (1891–1974) had been held in Germany as a prisoner of war for four years when World War I ended. He resumed his career as a physicist, joining Ernest Rutherford in Cambridge and obtaining a Ph.D. in 1921. Rutherford was interested in a problem that had puzzled chemists for more than a decade. The "canal rays" (chapter 1), discovered by Goldstein in 1886, were later understood to be the positively charged nuclei of atoms. In the case of the hydrogen atom, both the relative mass and the charge of the nucleus were equal to one, corresponding to a nucleus of one proton. However, the nucleus of helium (and all other elements) have masses that are double the nuclear charge or more (He nucleus: charge = 2; mass = 4). Where do the extra mass units in the nuclei come from? In 1920, Rutherford postulated the existence of "neutral doublets" consisting of a proton and an electron that he dubbed the "neutron." Chadwick spent more than a decade searching for this elusive subatomic neutral particle before he found his quarry.

In 1930, Walther Bothe (1891–1957) and his student Herbert Becker discovered that bombarding beryllium with α-particles produces a highly penetrating radiation. Shortly afterward, Irène Joliot-Curie (1897–1956), the daughter of Marie and Pierre Curie, and her husband Frédéric Joliot-Curie (1900–58) fired this high-energy radiation at paraffin wax (carbon and hydrogen) and produced protons having very high velocities. Although the newly discovered radiation was thought to be composed of γ-rays, Chadwick found that light atoms such as nitrogen were seen (in *cloud chambers*) to recoil when hit by these emissions. Chadwick calculated a mass close to 1, consistent with a neutral subatomic particle roughly

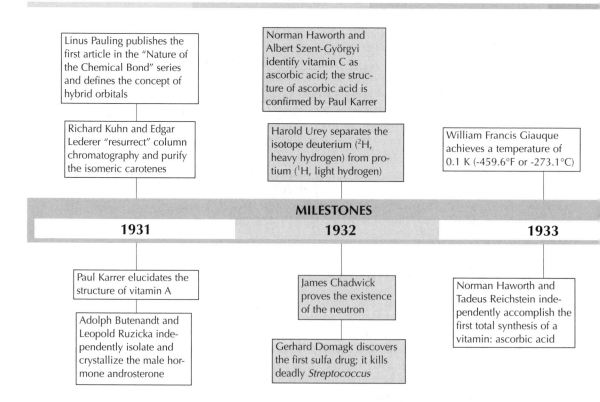

Linus Pauling publishes the first article in the "Nature of the Chemical Bond" series and defines the concept of hybrid orbitals

Norman Haworth and Albert Szent-Györgyi identify vitamin C as ascorbic acid; the structure of ascorbic acid is confirmed by Paul Karrer

Richard Kuhn and Edgar Lederer "resurrect" column chromatography and purify the isomeric carotenes

Harold Urey separates the isotope deuterium (^2H, heavy hydrogen) from protium (^1H, light hydrogen)

William Francis Giauque achieves a temperature of 0.1 K (-459.6°F or -273.1°C)

MILESTONES

1931   **1932**   **1933**

Paul Karrer elucidates the structure of vitamin A

Adolph Butenandt and Leopold Ruzicka independently isolate and crystallize the male hormone androsterone

James Chadwick proves the existence of the neutron

Gerhard Domagk discovers the first sulfa drug; it kills deadly *Streptococcus*

Norman Haworth and Tadeus Reichstein independently accomplish the first total synthesis of a vitamin: ascorbic acid

the mass of a proton. Although this could well have been Rutherford's "neutral doublet," Werner Heisenberg demonstrated that the "neutral doublet" is not consistent with quantum theory. Chadwick published his discovery in 1932 and received the 1935 Nobel Prize in physics. Isotopes would henceforth be understood as atoms of the same element differing only in the number of neutrons in the nucleus.

Artificial Radioisotopes: A New World of Tracers

When George Karl von Hevesy developed the technique of isotope dilution analysis (chapter 3), his source of lead isotopes was the natural decay of radioactive substances. In his 1944 Nobel lecture, Hevesy related his "utopian" wish from that period, some two decades earlier: "[Imagine] the great progress which might be expected if radioactive indicators of the common elements were made available to chemical and biological research." This was the discovery of the Joliot-Curies made in 1934, a

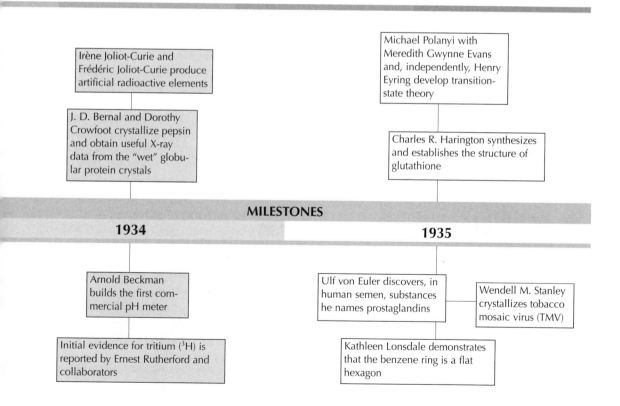

Irène Joliot-Curie and Frédéric Joliot-Curie produce artificial radioactive elements

J. D. Bernal and Dorothy Crowfoot crystallize pepsin and obtain useful X-ray data from the "wet" globular protein crystals

Michael Polanyi with Meredith Gwynne Evans and, independently, Henry Eyring develop transition-state theory

Charles R. Harington synthesizes and establishes the structure of glutathione

MILESTONES

1934

1935

Arnold Beckman builds the first commercial pH meter

Initial evidence for tritium (^{3}H) is reported by Ernest Rutherford and collaborators

Ulf von Euler discovers, in human semen, substances he names prostaglandins

Wendell M. Stanley crystallizes tobacco mosaic virus (TMV)

Kathleen Lonsdale demonstrates that the benzene ring is a flat hexagon

decade after Hevesy started work with naturally occurring isotopes. The Joliot-Curies discovered that bombarding aluminum with neutrons produces a radioactive phosphorus isotope (^{30}P) that decays to silicon (^{30}Si). The Joliot-Curies shared the 1935 Nobel Prize in chemistry for their discovery of artificial radioactivity.

Shortly after the Joliot-Curies' discovery, Hevesy irradiated 10 liters of carbon disulfide (CS_2) with neutrons and produced radio-phosphorus (^{32}P), in a form readily extracted with dilute nitric acid or water (the remainder of the CS_2 is recycled). Radio-phosphorus was administered to rats and its uptake in bones and tissues analyzed. Hevesy's later research involved studying the formation and decomposition of glucose-6-phosphate, ATP, and other compounds vital for understanding intermediary metabolism.

Discovery and Separation of Deuterium

The atomic weight of hydrogen became a particularly vexing problem in the late 19th century as these measurements became more accurate. Accurate determination of the composition of water gave the ratio of

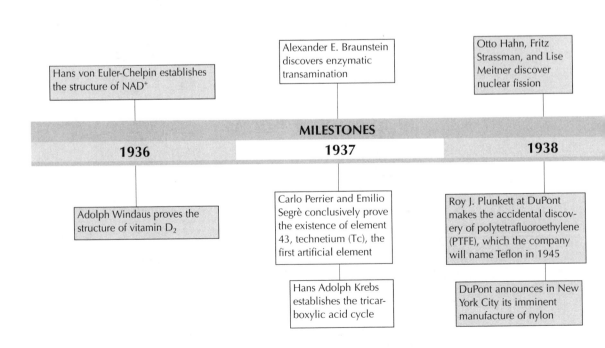

Hans von Euler-Chelpin establishes the structure of NAD$^+$

Alexander E. Braunstein discovers enzymatic transamination

Otto Hahn, Fritz Strassman, and Lise Meitner discover nuclear fission

MILESTONES

1936   **1937**   **1938**

Adolph Windaus proves the structure of vitamin D_2

Carlo Perrier and Emilio Segrè conclusively prove the existence of element 43, technetium (Tc), the first artificial element

Roy J. Plunkett at DuPont makes the accidental discovery of polytetrafluoroethylene (PTFE), which the company will name Teflon in 1945

Hans Adolph Krebs establishes the tricarboxylic acid cycle

DuPont announces in New York City its imminent manufacture of nylon

masses of O/H as 16.00/1.008. Mass spectroscopic studies by Francis Aston during the 1920s and related studies suggested the presence of an exceedingly minute amount of a heavy isotope of hydrogen, ^{2}H or deuterium. The huge 2:1 ratio in masses between *deuterium* and ^{1}H (*protium*) would aid their separation and be the key factor in future research employing the heavier isotope. At Columbia University, Harold C. Urey (1893–1981) calculated the ratio of vapor pressures of HD to H_2 and found it to be sufficient to allow fractional distillation as part of an enrichment process to unequivocally prove the existence of deuterium and separate it. Urey published his discovery in 1932 and received the 1934 Nobel Prize in chemistry. Almost immediately, deuterium nuclei (deuterons) were investigated as substitutes for protons in probing nuclear structure since they have twice the mass. High-speed deuterons were found to be 10 times as effective as protons in disintegrating atomic nuclei.

Ernest Rutherford and colleagues started employing deuterons in 1933 to hit protium-containing and deuterium-containing substances. In the latter cases, they actually succeeded in 1934 in generating *tritium* (^{3}H)

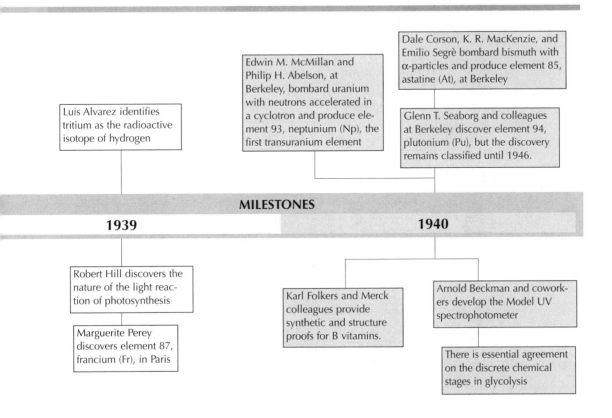

but thought they made radioactive ^{3}He. In 1939, Luis W. Alvarez (1911–88) proved conclusively that the observed radioactivity was due to ^{3}H since ^{3}He is not radioactive. Alvarez would win the 1968 Nobel Prize in physics. Starting in 1935, deuterium labeling was employed at Columbia University to investigate *lipid* metabolism. In the long term, deuterium has proved to be of simply incalculable value for probing chemical reaction mechanisms, metabolism, and countless other phenomena involving hydrogen atoms.

New Elements

In 1925, when Ida Noddack-Tacke, Walter Noddack, and Otto Berg first claimed the discovery of element 75, rhenium (see chapter 3), their work was dismissed because of the extremely minute quantity reported. Their case was solidly proven in 1928 when they were able to accumulate a gram of the metal. In 1925, they had also claimed discovery of the missing element 43 in samples of uranium-rich ores. However, this was also dismissed because of the extremely minute quantity evident from the weak X-ray emission line. In contrast to their subsequent success with rhenium, they could never isolate a quantity to support their claim for element 43. In recent years, evidence does appear to suggest that they probably were correct. Definitive proof was produced by Carlo Perrier (1886–1948) and Emilio Segrè (1905–89), who bombarded molybdenum with neutrons. This was the first new element to be produced artificially.

In 1939, while Marguerite Perey (1909–75) was studying the radioactive decay products of element 89, actinium (Ac), known since 1899, she discovered element 87, later named francium. Its longest-lived isotope has a half-life of only about 20 minutes. She demonstrated that its chemistry is similar to that of other alkali metals. Perey was the first woman admitted to the French Academy of Sciences (Madame Curie had been rejected decades earlier). In 1940, Dale R. Corson (1914–), K. R. MacKenzie (1907–76), and Emilio Segrè synthesized the missing element 85, astatine (At), by bombarding bismuth with α-particles. (Incredibly tiny amounts of At are now known to occur in the Earth's crust). A solid element below iodine in the periodic table, when astatine is injected into guinea pigs it is sequestered in the thyroid gland, the normal location for sequestering iodine. Corson would eventually become president of Cornell University (1969–77).

In 1940, Edwin M. McMillan (1907–91) and Philip H. Abelson (1913–2004), working in Berkeley, bombarded uranium with cyclotron-produced neutrons, producing element 93, neptunium (Np). Neptunium was the first *transuranium element* to be reported. It is one beyond uranium in atomic number, hence the name, after the planet Neptune which is the one beyond Uranus. In the same year Glenn T. Seaborg (1912–99) and others in the Berkeley group discovered element 94, plutonium (Pu). Its potential for *nuclear fission* was soon apparent and the discovery was only made public in 1946. Seaborg and McMillan would share the 1951 Nobel Prize in chemistry. Segrè would share the 1959 Nobel Prize in physics.

Applications of Quantum Theory to Common Chemical Problems

Starting around 1930 and lasting throughout the rest of the 20th century and beyond, two schools of theory competed for widespread adoption by chemists. One of these is the valence bond/resonance theory: Its foremost chemistry proponent was Linus Pauling at the California Institute of Technology. The other is molecular orbital theory: Its foremost proponent was Robert S. Mulliken at the University of Chicago. Both Pauling and Mulliken visited Germany during the mid-1920s and witnessed the revolutionary work of Hund, Pauli, Schrödinger, Heisenberg, and the other great physicists who developed the new quantum theory. Mulliken and Hund collaborated on molecular orbital theory. The triumph of the two American chemists was their ability to make the highly mathematical and abstract quantum mechanics accessible to and useful for chemists.

During the years 1931 through 1933, Pauling published seven papers on chemical structure and bonding in a series titled "The Nature of the Chemical Bond." In 1939, Pauling's book *The Nature of the Chemical Bond* was published and became the most important chemistry book of the 20th century (its third edition appeared in 1960, with a shortened, modified version in 1967). Aside from his enormous success in explaining a broad spectrum of chemical phenomena, Pauling was successful at "selling" his ideas by using deceptively simple, extremely appealing models and vocabulary. For example, the tetrahedral symmetry in methane (CH_4) was explained in terms of "hybridizing" the 2s and the three 2p orbitals in carbon to form four localized equivalent sp^3 "hybrid" orbitals. Pauling's early and deep experience in crystallography and structural chemistry suggested to him the need to explain structural anomalies that were inconsistent with Lewis-Langmuir structures. For example, benzene behaves as if it has hexagonal symmetry despite having three C-C and three C=C bonds in alternating sequence (see chapter 3). In London, starting in 1929 Kathleen Lonsdale (1903–71) determined that the benzene ring system is, physically speaking, a flat hexagon. Lonsdale learned her crystallography from William Henry Bragg, whose laboratory welcomed female scientists, and she became the first in a line of famous female crystallographers, the first woman elected a Fellow of the Royal Society and the first female professor at University College in London.

The top panel in the accompanying figure depicts valence bond structures for the two major resonance contributors of benzene. Contrary to earlier notions of two rapidly fluctuating structures, Pauling's resonance theory, developed with his student George W. Wheland (1907–74), viewed benzene as represented by two idealized but fictional resonance contributors (all atoms in the same positions in each structure; the relationship represented by ⟷ [*not* by ⇆]). The "reality" is best represented by the resonance "hybrid" shown in this panel. Pauling's "resonance" terminology evokes two identical tuning forks mounted together on a box: strike one and eventually the other will pick up its vibration and total transfer will move back and forth between the two.

Resonance theory not only explained structure, but stability as well. If a molecule (or ion) is represented by two (as in benzene) or more equivalent resonance contributors, extra stability is the result. Pauling rationalized benzene's amazing resistance to addition reactions to its C=C bonds by invoking resonance stabilization. The carbonate ion (CO_3^{2-}) is commonly found in minerals. Despite a Lewis structure that suggests one short double bond and two longer single bonds, the ion has threefold symmetry

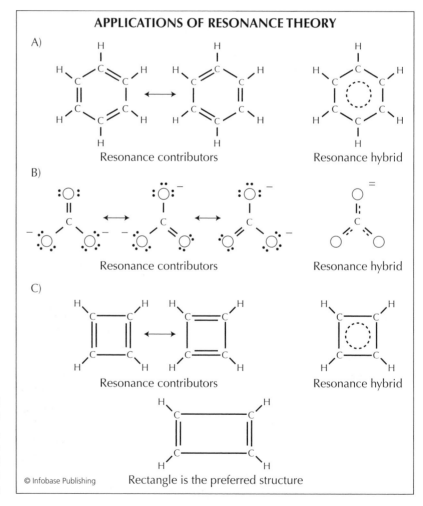

APPLICATIONS OF RESONANCE THEORY

Resonance contributors and resonance hybrids for benzene (top), carbonate ion (middle), and cyclobutadiene (bottom), which actually adopts a rectangular structure due to Jahn-Teller distortion

© Infobase Publishing

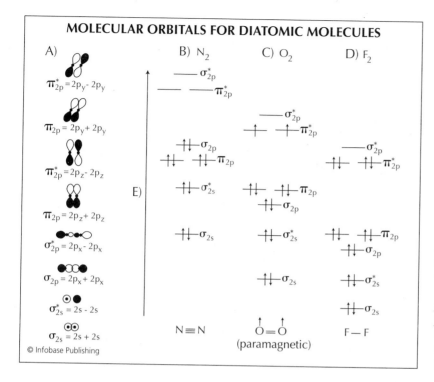

MOLECULAR ORBITALS FOR DIATOMIC MOLECULES

A) Description of valence-shell molecular orbitals for second-row homo-diatomic molecules (X_2); B) molecular orbitals for N_2; C) molecular orbitals for O_2 (note that there are two unpaired spins and this molecule is a triplet diradical; D) molecular orbitals for F_2

(see chapter 3). The explanation of the symmetric structure and stability is provided by the three equivalent resonance contributors and the resonance hybrid in the second panel in the accompanying figure.

According to resonance theory, cyclobutadiene should have stability reminiscent of benzene: it has two equivalent resonance contributors and a resonance hybrid (third panel in accompanying figure). However, it had eluded attempts at synthesis for decades (August Kekulé, in 1872, William H. Perkin, Jr. [1860–1927], in 1894, and Richard Willstätter, in 1905, all tried and failed). The four-membered ring suggests significant angle (Baeyer) strain (see chapter 3), yet cyclopropanes and cyclobutanes were known since the late 19th century. The inability to isolate cyclobutadiene suggested a weakness in resonance theory.

The molecular orbital (MO) theory developed by Hund and Mulliken can simply be regarded as an extension of atomic orbital theory, applied to structures having more than one nucleus. Mulliken lacked Pauling's charisma and did not immediately publish a chemical "best seller." The MO methodology was not nearly as familiar to chemists as the valence bond (Lewis-Langmuir) structures employed by Pauling, yet, starting in the 1940s, MO theory began to overtake valence bond theory in its use by chemists.

Some simple illustrations are provided in the figure above. Part A depicts in-phase and out-of-phase combinations of 2s and 2p atomic orbitals (from the valence "shell" of second-row atoms) to produce diatomic molecular orbitals (bonding and anti-bonding respectively). Overlap of s atomic orbitals yields sigma (σ) bonding and anti-bonding (σ^*) molecular orbitals (MOs); end-on overlap of p-orbitals also produces σ (and σ^*) orbitals; sideways overlap of p atomic orbitals produces π (and π^*) molecular orbitals. Parts B-D in this figure depict relative energies of these molecular orbitals in the homonuclear-diatomic molecules N_2, O_2, and F_2 respectively. Molecular orbitals are filled like atomic orbitals (*Hund's rules*): lowest-energy orbitals are filled (two spin-paired electrons each) first; two or more orbitals that are equal in energy (*degenerate*) are half-filled first with electrons having parallel spins.

The electronic configuration of the N_2 molecule (Part B in the figure) shows full occupation of four bonding MOs and one antibonding MO. The net, three bonding MOs, roughly equates to the triple bond in N_2. The electronic configuration in F_2 (Part D in the figure) shows full occupation of four bonding and three antibonding MOs. The net, one bonding MO, roughly equates to the single bond in F_2. All electrons in N_2 and F_2 (and the vast majority of molecules) are spin-paired (no net spin, $S = 0$), and the molecules are said to be in the singlet state ($2S + 1 = 1$), thus *diamagnetic* (repelled by magnets).

Molecular oxygen (O_2) represents a singular triumph for simple MO theory. The most striking prediction is that the highest occupied molecular orbitals (HOMOs), the two π^* MOs, are each singly occupied and the two electrons have parallel spins (net spin, $S = \frac{1}{2} + \frac{1}{2} = 1$) and the molecule is a triplet ($2S + 1 = 3$) *diradical* (2 unpaired electrons). Such a molecule shows *paramagnetic* properties: it was known since the 19th century that oxygen is attracted by a magnetic field. There are eight bonding and four antibonding electrons in O_2: the net of four bonding electrons roughly equates to a double bond. Valence bond theory does not make such a straightforward prediction for O_2 and its explanation for the ground-state (lowest energy) triplet for this molecule is much more complex than the simple MO explanation.

Since oxygen is such an important molecule, it is worth dwelling on its reactivity for a moment. The discussions of radicals in chapters 1 and 3 indicate that such molecules, having a single unpaired electron, are normally highly reactive and short-lived. Molecular oxygen is a diradical and, one would anticipate, extraordinarily reactive and short-lived. Its stability is rather amazing. It is due in part to a principle titled conservation of spin that is best explained elsewhere and in some detail. Nonetheless, oxygen is far from inert and will react spontaneously with numerous substances at ambient temperature (or lower). It is interesting that both water and oxygen, fundamental life substances, are each very unusual in their physical and chemical properties.

In 1931, Erich Hückel (1896–1980) recognized that the 6 p_z orbitals perpendicular to the (xy) plane of the hexagonal ring in benzene can be treated separately from the remaining s and p orbitals in the molecule. Using this extremely simplified approach to MOs, he demonstrated that benzene's symmetrical structure and chemical stability are the result of the low-energy configuration of the extended π-type MOs in this molecule. He generalized his discovery to what is now called the 4n + 2 rule. The benzene ring has three double bonds, thus, 6 π electrons. It satisfies the 4n + 2 rule where n = 1 (n can be 0, 1, 2, 3, etc). In contrast, cyclobutadiene does not obey Hückel's rule (n = ½ is not valid). It does not have the special stability (*aromaticity*) of benzene. Square cyclobutadiene is predicted by simple MO theory to be a triplet, although (second-order *Jahn-Teller*) distortion to a rectangular structure (see the previous figure) would provide a singlet, albeit a very reactive molecule. As noted earlier in this section, straightforward application of simple valence bond/resonance theory does not account for the extraordinary reactivity of this molecule, while exceedingly simple MO theory does.

Electronegativity

Although the concept of electronegative elements (elements readily accommodating negative charge) dates back to the early 19th century, Linus Pauling introduced a quantitative definition of *electronegativity* in 1932. It was known that the energies of polar bonds are greater than those of comparable nonpolar bonds. For example, below are the heats of formation of the four hydrogen halides (all substances in gaseous state):

$$\tfrac{1}{2} H_2 + \tfrac{1}{2} F_2 \rightarrow HF \qquad \Delta H = -64 \text{ kcal/mol}$$

$$\tfrac{1}{2} H_2 + \tfrac{1}{2} Cl_2 \rightarrow HCl \qquad \Delta H = -22 \text{ kcal/mol}$$

$$\tfrac{1}{2} H_2 + \tfrac{1}{2} Br_2 \rightarrow HBr \qquad \Delta H = -12.5 \text{ kcal/mol}$$

$$\tfrac{1}{2} H_2 + \tfrac{1}{2} I_2 \rightarrow HI \qquad \Delta H = -1.5 \text{ kcal/mol}$$

The idea is that the strength of the H-F bond is due to H-X $\leftrightarrow$ H$^+$X$^-$ type resonance, which is most significant for the most electronegative element (F). Pauling scaled his electronegativity (χ) scale to F (most electronegative, 4.0). On this scale, the least electronegative element is Cs (0.7) and the values for some other important elements were: H (2.1); I (2.4); C (2.5); Br (2.8); N (3.0); Cl (3.0); O (3.5). Pauling assumed that a $\Delta\chi$ value = 3.3 (i.e. CsF) denotes pure ionic character; $\Delta\chi$ = 0 denotes pure covalence and $\Delta\chi$ = 1.6 denotes 50 percent ionic character in the bond.

In 1934, Mulliken proposed a different electronegativity scale based upon the average of the ionization potential in volts (IP: X $\rightarrow$ X$^+$ + e$^-$) and the *electron affinity* (EA: X + e$^-$ $\rightarrow$ X$^-$) of the gas-phase atoms. This approach is more in character with Mulliken's MO approach since IP reflects the energy of the *highest occupied molecular orbital* (*HOMO*) while the EA has a relationship to the energy of the *lowest unoccupied molecular orbital* (*LUMO*). Not surprisingly, there has been continued debate ever since over the superiority of these two and numerous later electronegativity scales.

Approaching Absolute Zero

William Thomson (Lord Kelvin) (1824–1907) taught natural philosophy at Glasgow. In 1854 he proposed the absolute scale of temperature that bears his name. The zero point on such a scale corresponds to zero molecular motion: that is to say, zero volume occupied by the gases except for the combined volume of the gas molecules themselves. By experimentally studying decreases in volumes of various gases with decreasing temperatures using the gas laws, by the early 20th century absolute zero (0 K) was found to be -459.69°F (-273.15°C). But how does one actually attain such temperatures and what surprises await the first scientists to reach "regions" colder than Pluto?

In 1852 Thomson and James Prescott Joule (1818–1889) demonstrated that expansion of a gas into a vacuum causes the gas to cool. (It is now understood that this is due to the work expended to overcome attractions between the gas molecules). Joule-Thomson expansion (compression of a gas at the coldest possible temperature followed by expansion into a vacuum) was employed over the next few decades to achieve record temperatures: 90 K (liquid oxygen, 1883); 54 K (solid oxygen, 1886); 21 K (liquid hydrogen, 1898); 14 K (solid hydrogen, 1899). In 1908, the Dutch scientist Heike Kamerlingh Onnes (1853–1926) liquefied helium (4.2 K), using the cooling "cascade" chloromethane, ethylene, oxygen, liquid air, hydrogen, and helium. He discovered that at such low temperatures certain substances have zero electrical resistance and are therefore *superconductors*. (This will subsequently become a field of great interest some 75 years later, see chapter 9.)

At Berkeley, Canadian-born William F. Giauque (1895–1982) studied entropy and wished to experimentally test the third law of thermodynamics (see chapter 1). One statement of this law is that all disorder in a crystalline substance disappears at 0 K (thus absolute entropy S = 0). Giauque employed an entirely new technique to approach absolute zero. A disordered paramagnetic crystalline solid can be perfectly aligned by a magnetic field with loss of heat. *Adiabatic* (zero heat exchange) demagnetization can realign the molecules in the crystal and (indirectly) remove heat from the substance of interest. Giauque achieved a temperature of about 0.1 K in 1933. No thermometers were calibrated for this region and the volume of a gas (helium) could not be used to calibrate temperature because its vapor pressure is virtually nil at this temperature. Giauque employed diamagnetic susceptibility measurements, demonstrated to be very temperature sensitive. He received the 1949 Nobel Prize in chemistry. Today scientists have achieved temperatures lower than one-billionth of 1 Kelvin.

Step-by-Step Transformations of Molecules: Mechanism and Theory

If a chemist were to be granted one wish, it might be to actually witness, in all of its discrete steps, the transformation of reactant molecules into product molecules. Aside from the sheer enjoyment of watching their subjects perform, the observations would lead to a more profound understanding of chemical science. Even large molecules are typically less than one-thousandth the size of a submicroscopic virus particle and collide with other molecules billions of times per second. Thus, "observations" of chemical reactions must be indirect and deductive, since scientists live in a slow-moving, macroscopic world.

Fascinating hints about reaction mechanisms had been gleaned during the previous two decades. Chemical kinetics disclosed whether reactions occurred in one step or more (see chapters 2 and 3). Meerwein's observation of rearrangements suggested the existence of short-lived (transient) intermediate carbocations. The generation and trapping of the transient methyl radical CH_3 (see chapter 3) also contributed to a growing body of evidence that stimulated mechanistic chemistry during the 1930s. Lacking were coherent pictures of the transitions between interconverting molecules. Unobservable on both practical and theoretical grounds, this was an opportunity for chemical theory to play a powerful role.

In 1931, Michael Polanyi (1891–1976) and Henry Eyring (1901–81), working together in Berlin, applied quantum theory (aided by experiment) to study the *reaction surface* for one of the simplest reactions imaginable: H + H-H → H-H + H. There were three geometric dimensions to track: the distances between each pair of hydrogens ($H_a–H_b$; $H_a–H_c$; $H_b–H_c$) or equivalently two such distances and the H–H–H angle. The fourth dimension is the total energy of the system. As a four-dimensional plot cannot be visualized, so three three-dimensional plots of energy versus geometry were generated. If one assumes a constant H–H–H angle, then a three-dimensional surface can be plotted where the peaks and valleys correspond to potential energy maxima and minima. In three dimensions, such plots typically produce a "saddle-point" region. The saddle point represents the *transition state* region on the reaction surface. The actual species present at this point is the *activated complex*. It disappears upon bond vibration in the direction of products (H---H—H) or reactants (H—H---H).

A theory of reaction rates based on this picture, transition-state theory, was published in 1935 independently and almost simultaneously by Eyring as well as Polanyi working with Meredith Gwynne Evans (1904–52). It treats the activated complex (denoted by ‡) as if it is in equilibrium with the reactants and handles motion of the molecular system over the "saddle-point" separately from its other motions. A much simplified representation is depicted in the figure on page 122. Part A is a two-dimensional profile depicting the lowest-energy pathway from reactants to products and includes the transition-state as a maximum. The species at the transition state is the activated complex. The energy of activation is roughly equivalent to the Arrhenius activation energy (see chapter 2).

Mechanisms Applied to Organic Chemistry

In 1930, Welshman Edward D. Hughes (1906–63) joined the research group of Christopher K. Ingold at University College, London. (Ingold's

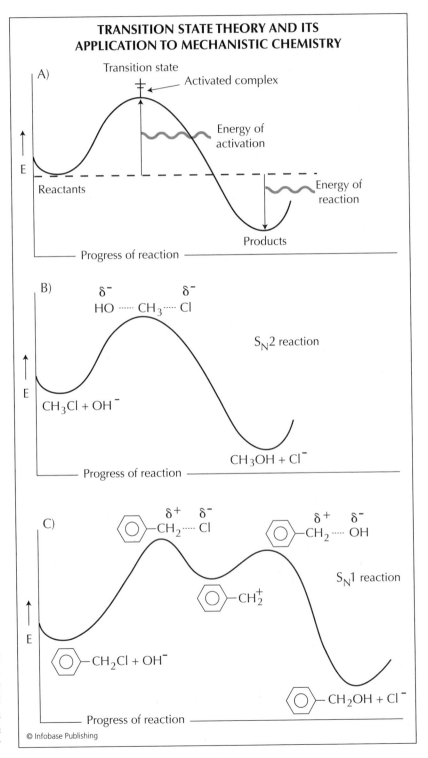

**TRANSITION STATE THEORY AND ITS
APPLICATION TO MECHANISTIC CHEMISTRY**

A) A simplified reaction coordinate diagram depicting the concept of the transition state; B) reaction coordinate for the S_N2 reaction of methyl chloride with OH⁻; C) reaction coordinate for the S_{N1} reaction of benzyl choride with OH⁻

© Infobase Publishing

bitter decades-long rivalry with Robert Robinson was mentioned in chapter 3.) Their partnership, between a gifted organic chemist and a gifted physical chemist, is now legendary and represented the application of chemical kinetics to organic chemistry that has evolved into physical organic chemistry. Their kinetic studies led them to conclude that there are two competing mechanisms for nucleophilic substitution reactions of the general type $RX + Z^- \rightarrow RZ + X^-$ (Z^- is the nucleophile; X^- is the *leaving group*). They termed the reactions S_N1 (substitution nucleophilic unimolecular) and S_N2 (bimolecular). There was also a competing bimolecular order elimination reaction (E2) and two years later, a competing E1 reaction was also identified. The kinetic treatment of short-lived carbocations in the S_N1 reaction successfully applied the steady-state assumption developed two decades earlier by Chapman and Underhill and applied by Bodenstein (see chapter 2).

In 1937, Hughes and Ingold examined the stereochemistry of the two nucleophilic substitution reactions and compared them with kinetic data. Paul Walden (1863–1957) had discovered in 1896 that substitution reactions of some optically active compounds occur with complete inversion of configuration (the "Walden inversion"). Hughes and Ingold established that these are S_N2 reactions. Their studies led them to postulate that S_N2 reaction involves attack, in a single step, of the *nucleophile* (Z^-) at the rear of the molecule with the leaving group (X^-) departing from the front. In contrast kinetics, solvent effects, and stereochemistry suggested that the S_N1 reaction proceeds in two steps with formation of an intermediate carbocation. Part B in the last figure is a reaction coordinate diagram for S_N2 reaction between chloromethane (CH_3Cl) and hydroxide ion. It occurs in one step: The activated complex depicts the back-side attack by the incoming nucleophile OH^-. Part C of this figure depicts S_N1 substitution of benzyl chloride by hydroxide. This reaction occurs in two steps, forming a discrete carbocation intermediate. The first step has the higher-energy transition state, an activated complex starting to resemble the incipient carbocation, and is the slow (rate-determining) step in the mechanism.

Even more subtle probes of transition-state structure were developed around this period. At Columbia University, Louis P. Hammett (1894–1987) used substituents (atoms or groups of atoms) attached to benzene rings to probe structures of transition states. For example, the transition state depicted in Part C of the accompanying figure has carbocation-like character. If an electronegative substituent (e.g., NO_2) is attached to the benzene ring, this transition state does not stabilize charge well, its energy is relatively high, and thus the energy of activation is high and the reaction rate low. A series of related substituted compounds may well give a straight line if plotted as:

Log k/k_o = $\sigma\rho$ Hammett equation

Here, k_o is the specific rate constant for the unsubstituted compound (substituent = H; substituent constant $\sigma = 0$); k refers to rate constants corresponding to specific substituents (each with a unique value for σ).

Plotting Log k versus σ may well provide a straight line; values of σ for electron-withdrawing substituents (e.g. NO_2) are positive and those for electron-releasing substituents (e.g. CH_3) are negative. A straight line with a negative slope (ρ = -) is consistent with a reaction involving a carbocation-like transition state as depicted in Part C of the figure. A steep negative slope implies a great deal of C–Cl bond breaking and charge buildup in the activated complex. A mild negative slope implies slight C–Cl bond breakage and slight charge buildup in the activated complex.

Another famous application of mechanistic chemistry was contributed by Morris Kharasch (1895–1957) at the University of Chicago. It was well known since the mid-19th century that addition reactions of HX (HCl, H-OH, etc) to unsymmetrical alkenes occur in a manner that places hydrogen on the olefinic carbon attached to more hydrogen atoms than the other olefinic carbon (Markovnikov's rule). However, when HX is hydrogen bromide (HBr), addition is typically anti-Markovnikov. Kharasch found that traces of peroxides (commonly present on glassware surfaces) initiate a free radical chain reaction for HBr (not for other HX). Careful removal of peroxides from glassware prior to reaction removes the potential free radical mechanism and HBr adds in a normal Markovnikov mode (intermediacy of carbocation, rather than free radical, intermediates).

Enzyme Kinetics Simplified: Probing How Enzymes Work

The Michaelis-Menten equation developed in 1913 ushered in the era of enzyme kinetics and mechanism (chapter 2). Experimentally, its application involves graphing rates (velocities) of reaction (v) against trial concentrations of substrate ([S]). A "saturation" curve is usually observed in which there is a leveling off of v, so as to approach the maximum rate (V_{max}) as [S] reaches saturation concentration. In practice, it is difficult to accurately determine the onset of saturation and this led to considerable uncertainty in the values of V_{max} as well as the enzyme-substrate binding constants (K_m in chapter 2).

In 1934, Dean Burk (1904–88) and Hans Lineweaver (1907–), at the United States Department of Agriculture, proposed an extremely simple mathematical solution to this experimental problem. By simply plotting the reciprocals of the experimental rates (1/v) versus the reciprocals of the substrate concentrations (1/[S]), a straight line should be the result of simple saturation (Michaelis-Menten) kinetics:

$$1/v = (K_m/V_{max})(1/[S]) + 1/V_{max}$$

Use of the Lineweaver-Burk equation no longer required attempts to accurately discern the onset of saturation. Instead, a judicious number and range of measurements typically provides excellent straight lines of slope K_m/V_{max} and intercept $1/V_{max}$.

Burk and Lineweaver submitted their paper to the *Journal of the American Chemical Society* (*JACS*). Although the opinion of the reviewers was to reject the paper as too trivial a contribution, the *JACS* editor understood its potential impact. It has become ". . . by far the most highly cited paper to ever appear in *JACS*," according to a 2003 remark in *Chemical & Engineering News*.

The 1930s were a period of fruitful application of chemical kinetics to organic reaction mechanisms. In addition, the application of kinetics to enzyme mechanisms also began to flourish during this decade as described in the next sidebar.

Let a Thousand Natural Products Bloom: Terpenes, Steroids, and Vitamins

Although many derivatives of benzene including benzaldehyde (almond oil) are "aromatic," late-19th-century chemists began to realize that nature's true scent molecules were not benzene derivatives. The volatile essential oils present in pine needles, orange peels, caraway seeds, peppermint, eucalyptus, and countless other plants often share a common formula: $C_{10}H_{16}$. Since this formula corresponds to three units of unsaturation (rings and/or double bonds), these oils could not possibly contain a benzene ring since it has four units of unsaturation (a ring and three double bonds). During the 19th century, such natural oils were crudely classified as "terpenes" (liquids) and "camphors" (solids).

Otto Wallach (1847–1930) entered this chemical "jungle" in the latter part of the 19th century. He worked briefly with August Kekulé in Bonn in 1870 before conscription into the Franco-Prussian War. Kekulé, the "father of benzene chemistry," had himself become interested in the terpenes and postulated their relationship to the substituted benzene "cymol" ($C_{10}H_{14}$, cymene or p-isopropyltoluene). Without fully understanding the structures, Wallach demonstrated simple chemical interconversions between various $C_{10}H_{16}$ isomers (pinene, limonene, terpinene) and their conversions to simple derivatives (carvone, eucalyptole). Wallach's studies of terpenes of formula $C_{15}H_{24}$ made clear that the C_{10} compounds (termed monoterpenes) and the C_{15} compounds (sesquiterpenes) were, in a formal sense, dimers and trimers, respectively, of isoprene (C_5H_8). He formulated the "isoprene rule" in 1887. Baeyer "synthesized" natural rubber in 1908 by polymerization of isoprene (see chapter 1). In addition to the scientific importance of Wallach's work, it helped to transform the essential oils (e.g., perfumes) industry in Germany. For these fundamental contributions, Wallach received the Nobel Prize in chemistry in 1910. He is a direct personal link between August Kekulé and the chemists who would solve the structures of natural products during the 1930s.

Leopold Ruzicka's structural studies of hydrocarbons, also in collaboration with the perfume industry (see chapter 3), took Wallach's terpene studies to a new level. He studied the dehydrogenation of monoterpenes (to form p-cymene) as well as the dehydrogenation, using selenium (Diels reaction), of sesquiterpenes (C_{15}), diterpenes (C_{20}), and triterpenes (C_{30}), and dehydrogenated them (via the Diels reaction, to form aromatics derivatives of naphthalene, anthracene, chrysene, and others). During the 1920s Ruzicka postulated that steroids are derived from terpenes and, in

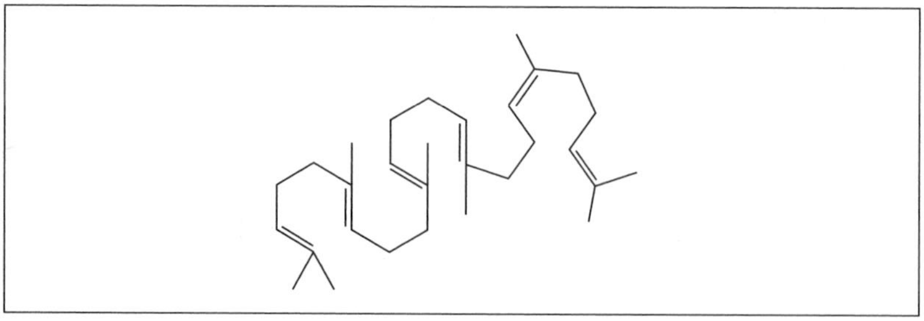

Squalene, a triterpene

1934, Robert Robinson postulated that cholesterol is derived from the triterpene squalene (see the structure above). The correct structure of cholesterol (see chapter 2) was finally proven in 1932 by independent chemical studies by Wieland and Windaus and crystallographic studies by John Desmond ("J. D.") Bernal (1901–70), Dorothy Crowfoot (1910–94; after 1937 Dorothy Crowfoot Hodgkin) and Otto Rosenheim (1871–1955).

Ruzicka would eventually enunciate a "biogenic isoprene rule": all terpenes have a common biological origin. Studies that would eventually explain the true basis of the biogenic isoprene rule started during the 1930s. In 1935, Rudolph Schoenheimer (1898–1941) and David Rittenberg (1906–70) applied the isotope deuterium, recently discovered by their Columbia University colleague Harold Urey, to studies of lipids. Unlike other chemical labels, which change the properties of the substances studied, substitution of deuterium for hydrogen induces almost no significant chemical change. Exploration of the biosyntheses of terpenes, steroids, and other lipids, aided by deuterium-labelling, would become a great success story during the following two decades.

Before natural-products chemistry could advance, there had to be breakthroughs in purification of complex mixtures. Mikhail Tswett's column chromatography method (chapter 1) was not widely employed during the two decades that followed its introduction. The renowned Richard Willstätter had raised doubts about its efficacy and chromatography was largely forgotten. It became apparent years later that the conditions used by Willstätter, in his failed attempt to purify the chlorophylls, were too harsh and actually decomposed them. However, in 1931, Edgar Lederer (1908–88) and his mentor Richard Kuhn (1900–67), a former student of Willstätter, improved Tswett's chromatography technique and firmly established it as a formidable and effective purification technique.

Kuhn and Lederer isolated and purified α-carotene and β-carotene and two years later, a third isomer, γ-carotene. This work would be critical to Karrer's success in 1931 in elucidating the structure of vitamin A and its relationship to that of β-carotene (see chapter 3), providing the first insight into the chemical structure of a vitamin. Numerous other insights were derived by Karrer and others studying the carotenes. While β-carotene is effectively a symmetric dimer of vitamin A, half of the α-carotene and γ-carotene structures are also essentially vitamin A. Hence, these two also behave as "provitamins," metabolic precursors to vitamin A. Karrer provided another far-reaching insight into the role of vitamins. Although a family of 16 potential *cis-trans* isomers, including vitamin A, were possible, only one is truly effective. Since the chemistries of the 16 isomers are very similar, the fact that only one is effective clearly implied a profound and intimate relationship with enzymes, agents known for their profound specificities. Karrer's 1937 Nobel speech removed some of the veil of mystery from vitamins:

> *We may perhaps remember that scarcely ten years have elapsed since the time when many research scientists doubted the material specificity of the vitamins, and were of the opinion that a special state of matter, a special colloidal character, was the cause of the peculiar vitamin effects which had been observed.*

In 1932, a young New Yorker named George Wald (1906–1997) spent a postdoctoral year in Germany in the laboratories of three Nobel laureates: Otto Warburg, Paul Karrer and Otto Meyerhof (1884–1951). In Warburg's laboratory, Wald discovered that the retina is rich in vitamin A. He then journeyed to visit Karrer, who had recently proved the structure of vitamin A. Returning to the United States in 1934, Wald joined the Harvard faculty and discovered in the late 1930s that the visual pigment rhodopsin contains a simple derivative of vitamin A. This was the start of decades of research that would eventually earn Wald the 1967 Nobel Prize in physiology or medicine for discovering the mechanism of vision.

Rational chemical studies of human sex hormones began in 1929 with Adolph Butenandt's isolation of pure crystalline estrone, the follicular hormone, from the urine of pregnant women. In 1931 Butenandt as well as Ruzicka isolated androsterone from male urine. Androsterone was found to be capable of producing male characteristics in castrated animals. In 1934, Butenandt obtained pure progesterone from the *corpus luteum* of female ovaries and in 1935 Ernst Laqueur (1880–1947) isolated testosterone from testes, finding it to be considerably more bioactive than androsterone. The relationships between the structures of these hormones and cholesterol became explicit in 1934 when Ruzicka chemically converted epi-dihydrocholesterol (readily obtained from cholesterol) into androsterone by oxidizing its side-chain completely with CrO_3. This was the first synthesis of a sex hormone and it connected the relative stereochemistries of the two compounds. In 1939, Butenandt as well as Ruzicka converted androsterone to testosterone and Butenandt also converted cholesterol to progesterone. A large family of sex hormones, including estrone, is directly related to cholesterol. The structures of these four steroid hormones are presented below. Butenandt and Ruzicka shared the 1939 Nobel Prize in chemistry. Ruzicka, working in Switzerland, had to delay receipt of his medal until the end of World War II. Like Kuhn, Butenandt was prohibited by the Nazi government from accepting his Nobel Prize and finally accepted his medal in 1949. Twelve years later Butenandt paid homage to his old mentor Windaus, who had written to his young student in 1933:

> To have to look at injustice and not be able to help is difficult to bear . . . at this moment people are carrying past placards on which stands the most unbelievable and hellish slander against Jews.

Windaus had refused to perform research on poison gas during World War I and saved a Jewish graduate student from dismissal at Göttingen during the early 1930s. Not wishing to contribute to Nazi science, he halted research in 1938, at the still-productive age of 62.

The 1930s and 1940s have been termed the "golden age of steroids." Vitamin D_2 (calciferol), whose correct structure was determined by Windaus in 1936, is formed photochemically from ergosterol, a steroid. Vitamin D (in its various forms) prevents (and cures) rickets. A mere 1×10^{-8} gram (10 nanograms) of Vitamin D_2 fed daily to rats suffering from rickets cures them in two months. Actually, Δ^7-dehydrocholesterol (a C=C bond between C_7 and C_8), derived from cholesterol, is present in the epidermis of human skin. Sunlight converts it to vitamin D_3. "Vitamin D" is a misnomer since the provitamin is biosynthesized by humans. However, deficiencies do occur and may be treated through administration of foods rich in D or its provitamin. In the late 1930s, steroidal hormones from the adrenal cortex were identified. (Adrenaline [epinephrine] was isolated three decades earlier and synthesized in 1904 [see chapter 1]. It is not a steroid.) Tadeus Reichstein (1897–1996) isolated cortisone among related hormones and, much to his surprise, found that these water-soluble, oxygen-rich compounds were steroidal in nature.

Closely related steroids

In 1932, Norman Haworth collaborated with Szent-Györgyi and demonstrated that ascorbic acid and vitamin C (see chapter 3) are the same substance. Karrer also confirmed the structure of vitamin C (see the structure below). Haworth demonstrated reversible oxidation and reduction of ascorbic acid and also proved that its unique 1,2-enediol structure is also responsible for its acidity. In 1933, both Haworth and Reichstein synthesized ascorbic acid, the first vitamin to be prepared by total artificial synthesis, demonstrating the simple chemical character of a vitamin.

The 1930s were a golden age for the discoveries of structures and functions of other vitamins. In 1935, the laboratories of both Kuhn and Karrer reported synthesis of vitamin B_2 (riboflavin, see the structure below). Two years earlier Warburg found a yellow oxidative enzyme in bottom yeasts and Kuhn identified it as vitamin B_2. Its REDOX role in the metabolism of carbohydrates, fats, and proteins would soon be under-

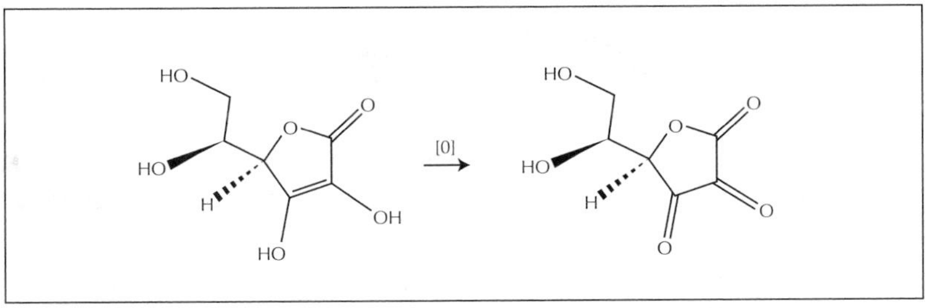

Ascorbic acid (vitamin C) reduced and oxidized

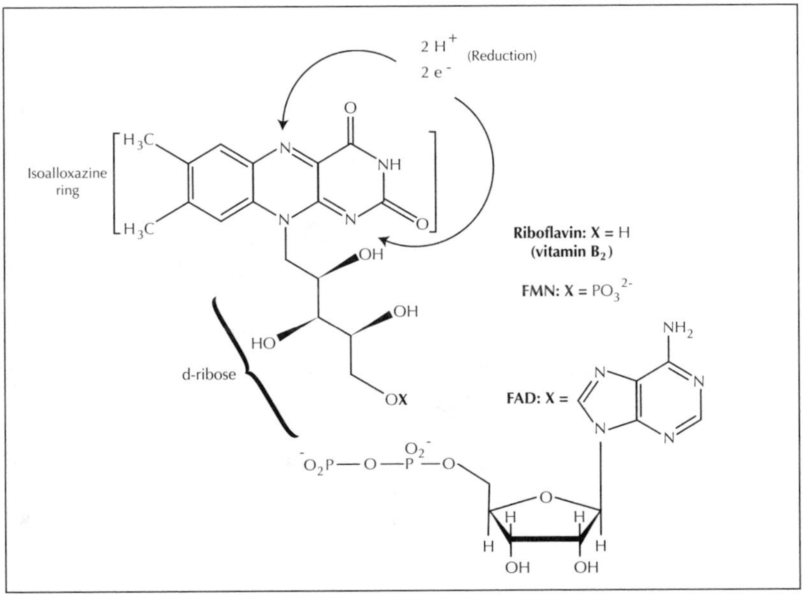

Riboflavin (Vitamin B_2) and its derivatives FMN and FAD

stood. Riboflavin is incorporated in the hydrogen transfer coenzymes flavin mononucleotide (FMN) and flavin adenine dinucleotide (FAD) (see the structure). Both are capable of transferring either one electron (H^+ + e^-) or two electrons ($2H^+$ + $2e^-$) at a time (see the structure).

Arthur Harden and William J. Young (see chapter 1) showed three decades earlier that the fermentation enzyme in yeast is separable into a colloidal fraction ("zymase") and a heat-stable, water-soluble fraction ("cozymase"). The two fractions separately show no enzymatic activity. Warburg later demonstrated the activity of cozymase and, in 1936, nicotinic acid (niacin or vitamin B_3) was found to be its hydrolysis by-product. In that year, Hans von Euler-Chelpin published the structure of nicotinamide adenosine dinucleotide (NAD^+) and its phosphate derivative ($NADP^+$) (see the structure below). Euler-Chelpin shared the 1929 Nobel Prize in chemistry with Arthur Harden for their independent studies on cozymase, seven years before publication of the NAD^+ structure. In contrast to FMN and FAD, NAD^+, and $NADP^+$ only transfer two electrons (H^+ + $2e^-$) at a time (see the structure below).

Other members of the B-complex vitamins isolated during the 1930s included pyridoxine (vitamin B_6), pantothenic acid, and biotin. Among a distinguished group of researchers, Karl Folkers (1906–97) and his group at Merck Laboratories in Rahway, New Jersey, furnished syntheses and structure proofs in 1940 and Merck began to dominate the emerging field of vitamin production. Structures of α- and β-tocopherols, active components of vitamin E found in wheat germ, were determined unambiguously by Karrer. Vitamin K, a factor involved in blood coagulation, was isolated in 1929 and its composition and structure determined by four distinguished laboratories.

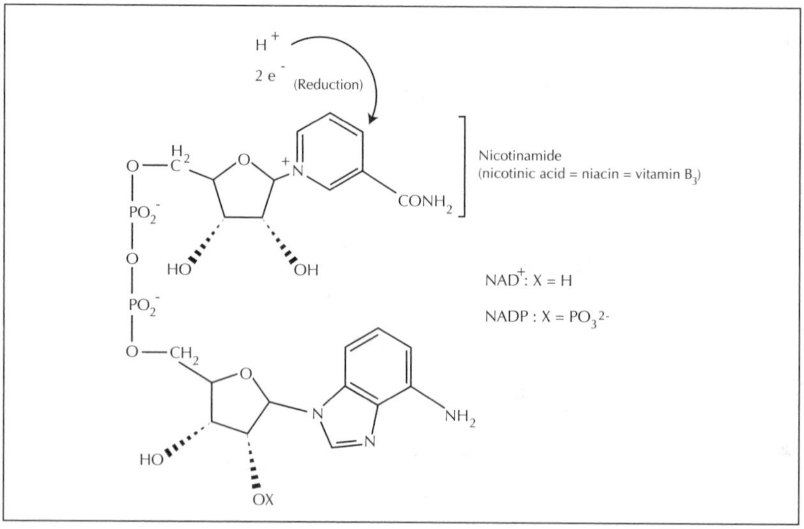

Nicotinamide adenosine dinucleotide (NAD⁺)

In 1935, Ulf von Euler (1905–83), the Karolinska Institute in Stockholm, isolated a component from human semen that was found to dramatically lower blood pressure and induce contractions of uterine tissue. Erroneously assuming that the compounds came from prostate glands, he called them prostaglandins. Although the minute concentrations of the compounds precluded their identification for decades, Euler had discovered an entirely new natural regulatory system. This line of research led to Euler's receipt of the 1970 Nobel Prize in physiology or medicine. (Euler's father was Hans von Euler-Chelpin, 1929 Nobel laureate in chemistry; his mother Astrid was a renowned botanist; her father, Per Teodor Cleve, discovered the rare earths thulium and holmium; for good measure, Ulf Euler's godfather was Svante Arrhenius).

Early Hints about the Structures of Proteins

When one thinks of sulfur, the aroma of rotten eggs comes to mind. However, sulfur is present in living organisms and two of the common 20 amino acids, methionine and cysteine, contain sulfur. Cysteine has a reactive ($-CH_2SH$) group that readily oxidizes to form the dimeric cystine, held together by a disulfide linkage ($-CH_2S-SCH_2-$). During 1925–27, Vincent du Vigneaud (1901–78) began studies of the hormone insulin, isolated only two years earlier, and established the presence of cystine and disulfide linkages in this protein. The synthesis of peptides and proteins containing cysteine was a challenge because of the reactivity of the thiol linkage. Yet rational synthesis was the most effective way at the time of proving peptide structure through comparison of the biological activities of the synthetic and natural products. Du Vigneaud studied glutathione, an important and abundant peptide, and suspected that it was a tripeptide of glutamic acid, cysteine, and glycine (i.e., γ-glu.cys.gly), having the unusual feature of the γ-COOH on glutamic acid, rather than its α-COOH, forming the peptide linkage. He reported the synthesis of glutathione in 1936. The honor of the synthetic structure proof went to Charles R. Harington (1897–1972), who published his work in late 1935. (In 1926, Harington had proved the structure of thyroxine, a vital metabolic regulator containing four iodine atoms).

Glutathione is a gentle reagent, reducing disulfide bonds to thiol linkages at room temperature and neutral pH. Du Vigneaud found that when glutathione reduces insulin and the sample is subsequently reoxidized, it does not regain insulin activity. In a far-reaching conclusion, du Vigneaud realized that complex protein folding was involved and that insulin could not spontaneously refold into its active form. Protein folding remains today, in the 21st century, one of the most important and complex problems in biochemistry. During the early 1930s, du Vigneaud started to study two hormones, oxytocin and vasopressin, each containing nine amino acids and one disulfide linkage. His synthesis and structure proof of these two hormones in 1953 would gain him the 1955 Nobel Prize in chemistry.

Proteins comprise more than 50 percent of the dry weight of animals. Humans are estimated to have more than 30,000 different proteins. Study of the structures of proteins is vital to understanding their functions. In 1934, Dorothy Crowfoot (1910–94), studying pepsin with J. D. Bernal (1901–71) in Cambridge, made the surprising discovery that "wet" crystals of globular proteins provide better X-ray crystallographic data than dried crystals. Moving to Oxford later that year, she would also obtain crystallographic data for insulin.

In 1935, Wendell M. Stanley (1904–1971), working at Rockefeller University, crystallized tobacco mosaic virus (TMV) and conducted its chemical analysis just like any other pure crystalline chemical substance. He demonstrated that crystalline TMV becomes fully active as a virus when bioassayed. For this work, Stanley shared the 1946 Nobel Prize in chemistry with James B. Sumner and John H. Northrop, who had established in the 1920s that all enzymes are proteins (see chapter 3).

Intermediary Metabolism of Carbohydrates

The early studies of Harden and Young on the fermentation of glucose to ethanol and carbon dioxide (see chapter 1) dealt with anaerobic metabolism. Although Otto Meyerhof clarified many of the details of the fermentation of glucose, sharing the 1922 Nobel Prize in physiology or medicine with Archibald V. Hill (1886–1977), important details were provided by Gustav G. Embden (1874–1933), in 1932, as well as later studies by Carl Neuberg (1877–1956), Jacob Parnas (1884–1949), Otto Warburg, Gerty Cori (1896–1957), and Carl Cori (1896–1984). By 1940, a complete picture of glycolysis (sometimes termed the Embden-Meyerhof pathway), the anaerobic metabolism of glucose to pyruvate, had emerged (see figure on page 133). Pyruvate is the conjugate base of pyruvic acid just as citrate, malate, succinate, fumarate, and oxaloacetate are conjugate bases of the corresponding acids. A six-carbon unit is broken down into two three-carbon units with net generation of stored energy in the form of two molecules of ATP (adenosine triphosphate) and two molecules of NADH. Pyruvate has two alternative anaerobic pathways: conversion to ethanol and CO_2 (fermentation) or conversion to lactate. These pathways are not shown in the figure, nor is the Cori cycle which accounts for glycogen mobilization. (The Coris shared half of the 1947 Nobel Prize in physiology or medicine for their work).

For the sake of simplicity, the accompanying figure also shows the tricarboxylic acid (citric acid or Krebs) cycle as it is understood today. Although Hans Adolph Krebs (1900–81) arrived at this famous catalytic cycle in 1937, he was not certain about the connection between pyruvate

(Opposite page) *Glycolysis of glucose and the associated Krebs (citric acid or tricarboxylic acid) cycle. The role of acetyl CoA was not understood until 1948.*

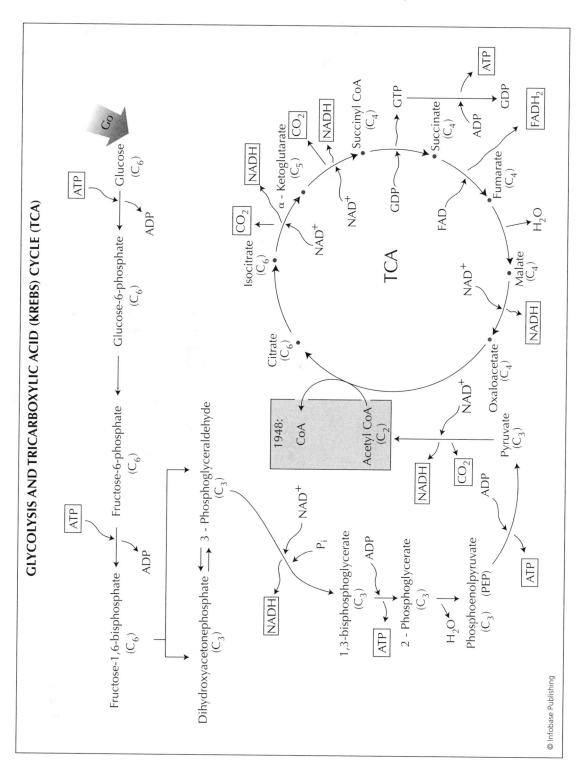

GLYCOLYSIS AND TRICARBOXYLIC ACID (KREBS) CYCLE (TCA)

and the cycle. It was not until 1948 that acetyl CoA would furnish the missing "entry point." Krebs shared the 1953 Nobel Prize in physiology or medicine. In contrast to glycolysis, the tricarboxylic acid cycle requires oxygen. It is not a direct "combustion," but involves loss of electrons and their transfer via a series of steps that will be described later. Each turn through the cycle attaches a C_2 (acetyl) to a C_4 (oxaloacetate) to form a C_6 (citrate) and cycles back to the original C_4 with stepwise loss of two molecules of CO_2. Each turn produces three molecules of NADH, one $FADH_2$, and one ATP. As shown in the figure, conversion of pyruvate to acetyl-CoA produces one molecule each of CO_2 and NADH.

In 1935, Albert Szent-Györgyi demonstrated the steps that connected the four four-carbon dicarboxylic acids succinate, fumarate, malate, and oxaloacetate, and he discovered that these compounds are catalytic (not consumed). However, in 1937 it was Krebs who made the critical finding that citric acid is also catalytic, added four more compounds (C_6 and C_5 species), and finally "closed the loop" on the "citric acid" cycle.

Starting with Keilin's discovery of *cytochromes* a, b, and c in 1925 (see page 93, where X and Y are proteins), the 1930s would witness exploration of how O_2 "connects" with glycolysis and the tricarboxylic acid cycle to form water. This complex problem sparked a controversy between Wieland, who favored the concept that the fundamental metabolic process involves activation of hydrogen atoms to react with O_2, and Warburg, who favored the process as one in which activation of O_2 is the primary driver. As more evidence emerged during the 1930s, it would become clear that they were both correct.

The discoveries of the structures of FMN and FAD as well as NAD^+ during the 1930s provided insights into coenzymes associated with dehydrogenases, such as succinate dehydrogenase (FAD) and malate dehydrogenase (NAD^+). By 1939, studies in many laboratories led to consensus for an electron-transport pathway involving four distinct cytochrome (cyt) species:

$$dehydrogenase \rightarrow cyt\ b \rightarrow cyt\ c \rightarrow cyt\ a \rightarrow cyt\ a_3 \rightarrow O_2$$

These energy-producing reactions occur in the mitochondria of all cells. Cytochrome c is a globular, water-soluble protein, while the other cytochromes are associated with membranes. Further refinement of the electron-transfer pathway would continue decades into the future and will be treated later in this book.

During 1939 and 1940, Vladimir A. Belitzer in Russia, Herman M. Kalckar (1908–91) in Copenhagen, and Severa Ochoa (1905–93) in England demonstrated that the oxidation of glucose is not so much a release of energy in forming CO_2 and H_2O, as storage of energy in the form of ATP through coupling with the electron-transfer chain. Further studies demonstrated that each NADH may produce 3 ATPs and each $FADH_2$ may produce 2 ATPs. Born in Spain, Ochoa's odyssey would take him from the Civil War in Spain during the 1930s to England. He would eventually share the 1959 Nobel Prize in physiology or medicine.

With the aid of the previous figure, a "biochemical accountant" obtains a balance sheet for the oxidation of one molecule of glucose to water and oxygen. Here is the balanced equation:

$$C_6H_{12}O_6 \text{ (glucose)} + 6\,O_2 \rightarrow 6\,CO_2 + 6\,H_2O$$

In effect, 12 oxygen atoms (present in six O_2 molecules) are gaining two electrons each to become 12 "O^{2-}" atoms in CO_2 and H_2O in addition to the six "O^{2-}" atoms already present in glucose. The figure demonstrates that each of the two C_3 units derived from glucose (C_6) provide two NADH prior to the tricarboxylic acid cycle and three NADH molecules through a full turn of the cycle. Similarly, one $FADH_2$ is produced from each C_3 unit. Oxidation of one glucose molecule yields 10 NADH and two $FADH_2$. These can, in principle, provide $(10 \times 3) + (2 \times 2) = 34$ ATPs. In addition, the *net* ATP production during glycolysis is two ATPs per glucose and two ATPs are produced through the tricarboxylic acid cycle per glucose. The total, 38 ATPs, is actually an upper limit, but a ratio of nearly 3 ATPs per oxygen atom (in O_2) consumed is realistic.

In 1937, Alexander E. Braunstein (1902–86), working in Moscow, was studying the metabolism of glutamate in muscles and made the interesting observation that when glutamate levels decrease so do lactate (anaerobic conditions) or pyruvate (aerobic conditions). In each case the concentrations of alanine increase. He had discovered the reversible transamination reactions that connect the intermediary metabolisms of proteins and carbohydrates.

During this period, Robert Hill (1899–1991), an English plant biologist, was investigating electron transport in photosynthesis and began to study chloroplasts in 1932. In 1939, Hill discovered that during the light-requiring stage of photosynthesis, water furnishes electrons to $NADP^+$ and light effectively pumps them through an electron-transport chain. He demonstrated that it is the light-requiring stage that produces oxygen, and it is fully decoupled from the reduction of CO_2:

$$\text{Hill Reaction: } H_2O + 2\,NADP^+ + \text{light} \rightarrow 2\,NADPH + \tfrac{1}{2}\,O_2$$

The Beckman pH Meter and DU Spectrometer

During the early 1930s, accurate measurements of pH (see chapter 1) required custom-built apparatuses occupying entire bench tops in the laboratories of physical chemists. Arnold O. Beckman (1900–2004) was raised in modest circumstances in rural Illinois. To cover his tuition and expenses at the University of Illinois, the exuberant young Beckman played piano to accompany silent films. He later went on to earn his Ph.D. at California Institute of Technology and then joined its faculty.

In 1934, a former fellow graduate student employed in the California citrus fruit industry described to Professor Beckman the importance of

Early Beckmann DU model pH meter ("acidometer") that was the start of Beckman Instruments (Beckmann Coulter, Inc.)

having fast and accurate measurements of pH to assess the quality of lemons and other fruit. Beckman designed and built a new self-contained pH meter-in-a-box that married glass electrode technology to the newly available vacuum tube (see the photograph). Measurements of pH of 99.9 percent accuracy could now be made by a novice in minutes. In 1935, Beckman started his company, National Technical Laboratories, and sold pH meters at $230 each (today roughly equivalent to $5,000). The Coleman Company broke Beckman's monopoly in 1940 with an instrument that also measured ultraviolet spectra. In 1940, Beckman designed an improved spectrometer, the Model D, and in 1941 marketed the Beckman Model DU ($723 each), which dominated the market for more than 20 years. Decades after the invention of the DU, Nobel laureate Bruce Merrifield called it "probably the most important instrument ever developed to the advancement of bioscience."

Sulfa Drugs: Antibacterials Discovered in the Nick of Time

Gerhard Domagk (1895–1964), born in Germany, was wounded in 1914, the first year of World War I. Scientifically trained and assigned to work in hospitals thereafter, he witnessed the helpless state of the treatment of bacterial infections such as gangrene. At I.G. Farben years later, Domagk dedicated himself to the discovery of antibacterials, testing the activities of thousands of compounds. In 1932, he was given a sample of a red dye called Prontosil rubrum. When he treated mice and rabbits infected with deadly *staphylococcus*, he cured the treated animals while the untreated controls died. Most dramatically during this period, Domagk's daughter developed a serious case of deadly strep infection. He quietly treated her with Prontosil and she recovered. Domagk only made this known in 1935 after clinical trials demonstrated the drug's efficacy. Prontosil (see the structure) is a derivative of sulfanilamide (p-aminobenzenesulfonamide), a compound first synthesized in 1908. The discovery of prontisil led to syntheses of numerous related derivatives. During World War II, GIs were equipped with individual packets of sulfa drugs that they were instructed to sprinkle liberally on wounds to prevent infection. Domagk won the 1939 Nobel Prize in physiology or medicine but was prevented by the Nazis from accepting his award. He finally received his medal in 1947.

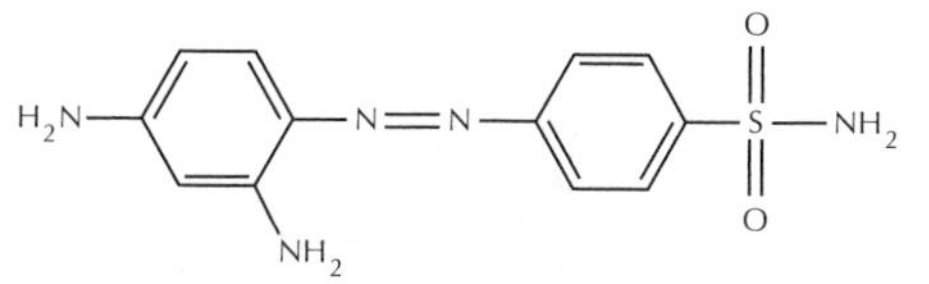

Prontosil, the first sulfa drug

The Discovery of Nylon

The DuPont Company's investment in polymer chemistry in the late 1920s and 1930s soon paid a handsome dividend. Acetate and rayon fibers, popular in the 1920s, were derived from naturally occurring cellulose (e.g., wood pulp). In 1930, Wallace Hume Carothers and Julian Hill produced the first fully synthetic condensation polymer, a polyester (see chapter 3). However, in the following years the search for a synthetic substitute for silk led them to experiment with polyamides. Silk, a protein, consists of chains linked by peptide (amide) bonds. The polymer chains bind to each other through hydrogen bonding of these linkages. While the silkworm moth (*Bombyx*) is native to China, it has long been cultivated throughout the world. Thus, strategic access was never a problem but the process is an expensive one.

Many different formulations to mimic silk were tried with various degrees of success. The combination of adipic acid ($HOOC\text{-}(CH_2)_4\text{-}COOH$) and hexamethylene diamine ($H_2N\text{-}(CH_2)_6\text{-}NH_2$) produced nylon-66 (see figure on page 139), which was found to provide the best combination of fiber properties and cost. DuPont scientists worked to optimize an average molecular weight of 10,000, the best range for fiber spinning. This was done by initially forming the salt between the component diacid and diamine and then heating this "nylon salt" to 545°F (285°C).

On October 27, 1938, at the site of the 1939 World's Fair in New York City, DuPont formally announced production of the first totally synthetic fiber. The factory, located in Seaford, Del., started producing stockings in late 1939. The new fiber was employed in sewing thread, fishing line, parachute fiber, and (especially) hosiery. During the first year of production some 64 million pairs of nylon stockings were sold. However, when the United States entered World War II in 1941, nylon became a stra-

Wallace Hume Carothers, demonstrating the elastic properties of neoprene (Hagley Museum and Library)

- NH-(CH$_2$)$_6$-NH-CO-(CH$_2$)$_4$-CO-NH-(CH$_2$)$_6$-NH-CO-(CH$_2$)$_4$-CO-

Nylon-66

tegic material (parachutes, tires, tents, ponchos) and stockings that were selling for $1.25 per pair jumped to $10 on the black market.

A company such as DuPont that aspires to reach and maintain world leadership must be a leader in research and development. In 1934 DuPont hired Paul J. Flory (1910–85) to work in the Carothers group. The concept of giant molecules had only achieved wide acceptance a few years earlier. Flory's task was to develop the immensely complex reaction dynamics and kinetics for these molecular giants as they twisted, coiled, "swam," and collided with each other in solution. Carothers died in 1937 and Flory would join Esso (now Exxon Mobil) in 1940, Goodyear in 1943, and he eventually entered academe (Cornell in 1948 and Stanford in 1961 where he completed his career). Flory was awarded the 1974 Nobel Prize in chemistry. Academic polymer science also took a giant step forward when the eminent Austrian chemist Herman F. Mark (1895–1992) fled the holocaust, landing in Canada in 1938, and arriving at Brooklyn Polytechnic Institute in 1940. The Polymer Research Institute he established during the 1940s continues to train generations of distinguished polymer scientists.

In 1938 Roy J. Plunkett (1910–94), at DuPont, made the accidental discovery of polytetrafluoroethylene (PTFE), which DuPont would call Teflon in 1945. Working with fluorocarbon refrigerants, he discovered that a seemingly empty tank of tetrafluoroethylene (C$_2$F$_4$) gas weighed more than it should have if empty. Cutting the tank open Plunkett discovered a slippery white solid with better lubricant properties than graphite and virtual chemical inertness. Teflon would become one of the major commercial materials of modern society starting in the 1950s.

Discovery of Nuclear Fission

Reading a paper by Rutherford, Leo Szilard (1898–1964), born in Hungary and living in England, developed the concept of a nuclear chain reaction even though nuclear fission had not yet been discovered. He patented his idea in 1936 and assigned it to the British Admiralty (U.K. Patent 630726). Only two years later, chemist Otto Hahn (1879–1968) and physicist Lise Meitner (1878–1968), in Berlin, as well as the Joliot-Curies, in Paris, observed behavior suggesting nuclear fission. Meitner, a Jew, had received protection from colleagues but, in July 1938, she was forced to flee to Sweden. In late 1938 Hahn and Fritz Strassman (1902–80) witnessed nuclear fission with certainty; their paper was published in Germany in early 1939. Hahn would win the 1944 Nobel Prize in chemistry for this work. In 1939, Leo Szilard and Albert Einstein,

Scientist of the Decade: Linus Pauling (1901–1994)

Linus C. Pauling picketing the White House as part of a mass demonstration opposing the resumption of atmospheric nuclear tests. Pauling won the 1954 Nobel Prize in chemistry and the 1963 Nobel Peace Prize. (NARA; AIP Emilio Segrè Visual Archives)

Linus Carl Pauling was born in Portland, Oregon. In 1917 he entered Oregon State Agricultural College (now part of Oregon State University), graduated in 1922, and married Ava Helen, a fellow student, in 1923. Pauling entered California Institute of Technology to pursue his graduate studies with Roscoe Dickerson, the X-ray crystallographer, who literally led the young Pauling by the hand into the realm of structural chemistry. At that time Arthur Amos Noyes had just been recruited to direct the Gates Chemical Laboratory at this new university of high aspirations. Noyes recognized a future star and, with increasing trepidation, watched Pauling's growing friendship with Gilbert N. Lewis, director of the chemistry laboratory at Berkeley. Before Lewis could entice Caltech's future "franchise player" to Berkeley, Noyes arranged a Guggenheim Fellowship for Pauling and sent his young star to Germany.

In Germany, during the 1920s, Pauling witnessed the development and earliest applications of quantum theory to chemistry. Returning to a faculty appointment at Caltech, he translated the abstract physics into comfortable concepts and models for chemists. Much of what is taught in freshman chemistry today (electronegativity, bond polarity, resonance, orbital hybridization) is due to Pauling and was included in his 1939 book, *The Nature of the Chemical Bond,* the most important chemistry book of the 20th century. He pioneered the use of molecular models in biochemistry and developed *alpha*-helix and *beta*-sheet structures for proteins during the 1940s. For these contributions, Pauling received the 1954 Nobel Prize in chemistry. During the 1950s, he would also explain the basis of sickle-cell anemia, the first disease understood at the molecular level.

Pauling's fear of nuclear war and atmospheric contamination from above-ground nuclear testing led to political activism that made him an object for the attention of the McCarthy-era House Un-American Activities Committee. Pauling was harassed in manners both petty and significant throughout the 1950s. Amusingly, the Communist Party of the USSR found his resonance theory to be "revisionist" and openly reviled it. (One must truly admire somebody who simultaneously offends hard-line Communists *and* hard-line anti-Communists). Invited with other Nobel laureates in April 1962 to join President John F. Kennedy and Jacqueline Kennedy for a formal dinner, Pauling arrived in Washington and joined a demonstration against the United States' decision to resume atmospheric testing of nuclear weapons (accompanying photograph). The following day, he attended the black tie dinner at the White House. Pauling's activism played an important role in moving the 1963 Partial Test-Ban Treaty and earned him the 1963 Nobel Peace Prize. He left Caltech in 1964, taking positions at the Center for the Study of Democratic Institutions, then the University of California, San Diego (1968), and finally Stanford University in 1969. Upon his compulsory retirement in 1974, Pauling formed the Institute of Orthomolecular Medicine in Palo Alto. He is now perhaps best known popularly for his advocacy of the use of high doses of vitamin C to treat colds and prevent cancer. He died in 1994 following a long, vigorous, and incredibly creative life. The Linus Pauling Archives can be visited at Oregon State University.

now at Columbia and Princeton respectively, wrote their famous letter to President Franklin D. Roosevelt urging that the United States immediately move to develop an atomic bomb. The result was the Manhattan Project and the destruction of Hiroshima and Nagasaki in August 1945, followed by the end of World War II.

Conclusion

The breakthroughs in structural biology and in understanding the mechanisms of intermediary metabolism during the 1930s would provide the underpinnings for the designs of specific "antimetabolites" (drugs) during the 1940s. The potent class of sulfa drugs developed during the thirties, and widely deployed in the field kits of soldiers during World War II, would soon be eclipsed by penicillin and other broad-spectrum antibiotics. Chemical theories that came to fruition during the 1930s would be applied during the 1940s to explain many subtle details of chemical mechanisms and begin to shed some light on the activities of biological molecules. The Second World War would not witness the use of chemical warfare, even by the Nazis, who were promised massive retaliation in kind. However, the discovery of nuclear fission in Germany in 1938 would have its denouement in the two atomic bombs dropped on Japan that ended the war.

Further Reading

American Chemical Society. "It's Elemental: The Periodic Table." *Chemical & Engineering News (Special Issue)* 81 (September 8, 2003). The essays are devoted to the history and properties of each element in order of atomic number.

———. "The Top Pharmaceuticals That Changed the World." *Chemical & Engineering News (Special Issue)* 83 (June 20, 2005). This magazine presents essays on top pharmaceuticals listed in alphabetical order.

Kimball, John W. Online Biology Textbook. Available online. URL: http://users.rcn.com/jkimball.ma.ultranet/BiologyPages/C/CellularRespiration.html. 2006. Accessed February 12, 2006. This is an excellent illustrated presentation on cellular respiration.

Pauling, Linus. *The Nature of the Chemical Bond and the Structure of Molecules and Crystals: An Introduction to Modern Structural Chemistry.* 3rd ed. Ithaca: Cornell University Press, 1960. The first edition of this book, the most important chemistry book of the 20th century, appeared in 1939.

Rife, Patricia. *Lise Meitner and the Dawn of the Nuclear Age.* New York: Springer-Verlag, 1999. This is a biography of a codiscoverer of nuclear fission forced to leave Germany just prior to World War II.

Slater, Edward C. "Keilin, Cytochrome, and the Respiratory Chain." *Journal of Biological Chemistry* 278 (2003): 16455–61. This is an accessible presentation about the scientist who first discovered the cytochrome electron-transfer pathway.

Staudinger, Hermann, *From Organic Chemistry to Macromolecules: A Scientific Autobiography.* New York: John Wiley & Sons, 1970. This autobiography is written by the father of polymer chemistry.

Willstätter, Richard, *From My Life, The Memoirs of Richard Willstätter.* Translated by Lilli S. Hornig. New York: W.A. Benjamin, 1965. This is the English translation of the autobiography of the famous German organic chemist.

5

1941–1950:
Triumph and Tragedy:
Antibiotics and Atom Bombs

Nuclear Chemistry Provides New Elements and a Clock for Archaeologists

The chemistry breakthroughs of the 1940s would be dominated by radiochemistry and the Manhattan Project and a growing revolution in pharmaceutical chemistry and rational drug design. The pharmaceutical industry would also help stimulate the early total syntheses of complex natural products aided by advances in the separation of complex mixtures using chromatography, and the new generation of commercial spectrometers. Fluorine chemistry played a major role in the Manhattan Project and would accelerate the development of Teflon and chlorofluorocarbons (CFCs). The newly created carbon 14 isotope will play a major role in the exploration of the complex pathways of intermediary metabolism and in understanding the function of vitamins. The role of acetyl coenzyme A in delivering two-carbon units to the Krebs cycle will be established. The metabolism of glucose generates energy that is not usable as heat, since animal bodies are essentially at constant temperature. The energy is stored chemically as ATP (adenosine triphosphate) rather than given off as heat. *Carbon 14* dating will emerge as a vital tool for archaeologists, anthropologists, and paleontologists.

New Elements and a New Series in the Periodic Table

The developments in nuclear chemistry during the 1930s, the observation of nuclear fission in 1938, and the urgency of the Manhattan Project will launch this discipline into a decade of breakthroughs. Uranium 235, rather than its more abundant isotope U-238, is rapidly fissionable by neutrons. In 1941, Glenn Seaborg and coworkers discovered that their newly discovered element, plutonium (specifically Pu-239), has fission properties comparable to U-235. The Berkeley 60-inch *cyclotron*, employed between the years 1939 and 1941, is displayed in the accompa-

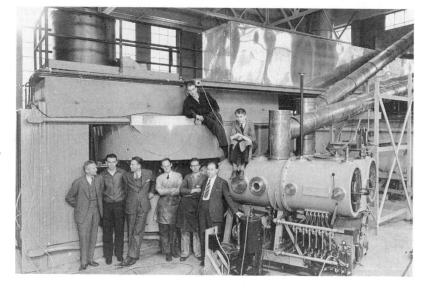

The 60-inch cyclotron group at Berkeley: Donald Cooksey, Dale R. Corson, Ernest O. Lawrence, Robert L. Thornton, John Backus, Winfield W. ("W. W.") Salisbury, Luis W. Alvarez, and Edwin M. McMillan, 1939 (Lawrence Berkeley National Laboratory)

Glenn Seaborg and his colleagues at Berkeley discover that plutonium 239 has nuclear fission properties comparable to those of uranium 235

Gerhard Herzberg establishes that the spectrum observed by astronomer Walter S. Adams is due to interstellar CH^+

The Manhattan Project to develop an atomic bomb is initiated in August

E. L. Robert Stockstad and coworkers at Lederle Laboratory isolate crystalline folic acid, a biosynthesis product of PABA: the resemblance of sulfa drugs to PABA explains their effectiveness as antimetabolite antibiotics

MILESTONES

1941   **1942**   **1943**

Archer J. P. Martin and Richard L. M. Synge invent partition chromatography

Fritz A. Lipmann postulates that metabolic energy is stored in ATP

Howard W. Florey, Ernst B. Chain, and Edward P. Abraham demonstrate that purified penicillin is an effective antibiotic in humans

Louis F. Fieser at Harvard invents napalm

nying photograph. The race was on to isolate large quantities of U-235 and Pu-239.

Henry Moseley's discovery (chapter 2) of the atomic number, the "roll call" of the periodic table, stimulated searches for new (missing) elements. During the 1920s, elements 72 (hafnium) and 75 (rhenium) were found in naturally occurring minerals (chapter 3). In 1939 and 1940, five new elements were reported, all created synthetically (chapter 4). Three of these, 43 (technetium), 85 (astatine), and 87 (francium) were suburanium elements. While ultratraces of astatine and francium exist in the Earth's crust (a few grams on the entire planet), technetium is totally synthetic. The artificial elements neptunium and plutonium were not anticipated by Moseley since they exceed the atomic number of the highest naturally occurring element known by him (uranium).

There remained one last "truant": element 61, a member of the lanthanides ("rare earths") that had confused great chemists for more than a century (chapter 1). In 1945, Jacob Marinsky (1918–   ) and Larry Glendenin (1918–   ), working with Charles D. Coryell (1912–71) at Oak

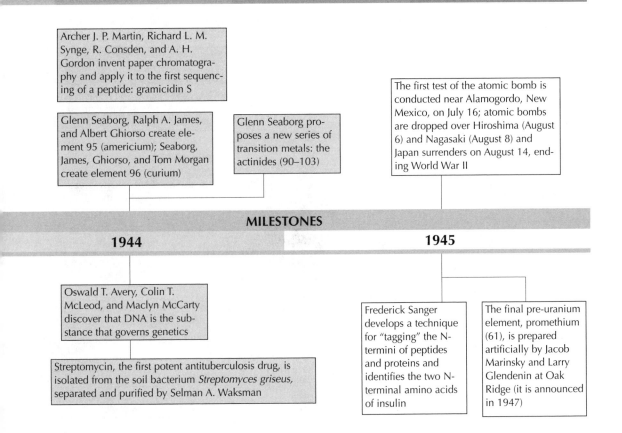

Archer J. P. Martin, Richard L. M. Synge, R. Consden, and A. H. Gordon invent paper chromatography and apply it to the first sequencing of a peptide: gramicidin S

The first test of the atomic bomb is conducted near Alamogordo, New Mexico, on July 16; atomic bombs are dropped over Hiroshima (August 6) and Nagasaki (August 8) and Japan surrenders on August 14, ending World War II

Glenn Seaborg, Ralph A. James, and Albert Ghiorso create element 95 (americium); Seaborg, James, Ghiorso, and Tom Morgan create element 96 (curium)

Glenn Seaborg proposes a new series of transition metals: the actinides (90–103)

MILESTONES

1944

1945

Oswald T. Avery, Colin T. McLeod, and Maclyn McCarty discover that DNA is the substance that governs genetics

Streptomycin, the first potent antituberculosis drug, is isolated from the soil bacterium *Streptomyces griseus*, separated and purified by Selman A. Waksman

Frederick Sanger develops a technique for "tagging" the N-termini of peptides and proteins and identifies the two N-terminal amino acids of insulin

The final pre-uranium element, promethium (61), is prepared artificially by Jacob Marinsky and Larry Glendenin at Oak Ridge (it is announced in 1947)

Ridge National Laboratory, discovered element 61 as a by-product of uranium fission and also by bombarding neodymium 146 with neutrons. The discovery was announced in 1947 and the name promethium suggested, after the Greek Titan who took pity on mankind and presented the gift of fire stolen from the gods. Its most stable isotope, Pm-145, has a *half-life* of only 17.7 years. As predicted, promethium displays typical lanthanide chemistry although its rarity, price, and high radioactivity allow very few labs the luxury of chemical studies.

In July 1944, working in Berkeley, Seaborg, Ralph A. James (1920–), and Albert Ghiorso (1915–) bombarded Pu-239 with high-energy α-particles, transported the exposed Pu-239 sample to Chicago (now Argonne National Laboratory) for chemical separation and element 95 (atomic mass 243) was separated. Later that year, similar studies by Seaborg, James, Ghiorso, and Leon O. (Tom) Morgan (1919–) led to the discovery of element 96. While exploring the chemistry of the two new elements, Seaborg found that they readily form the +3 oxidation state and resemble the lanthanides 63 (europium) and 64 (gadolinium). Although uranium's most stable oxidation state is +6 (e.g., UF_6), this element as well

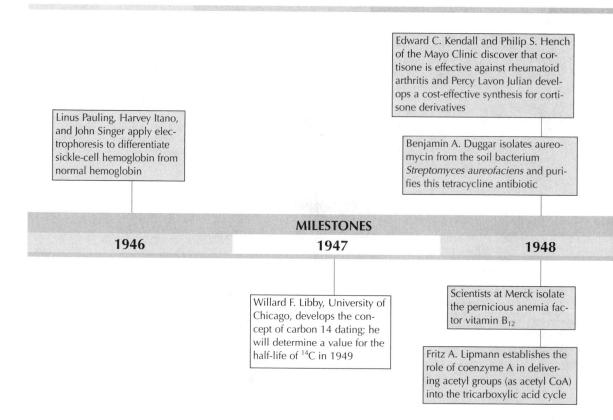

Edward C. Kendall and Philip S. Hench of the Mayo Clinic discover that cortisone is effective against rheumatoid arthritis and Percy Lavon Julian develops a cost-effective synthesis for cortisone derivatives

Linus Pauling, Harvey Itano, and John Singer apply electrophoresis to differentiate sickle-cell hemoglobin from normal hemoglobin

Benjamin A. Duggar isolates aureomycin from the soil bacterium *Streptomyces aureofaciens* and purifies this tetracycline antibiotic

MILESTONES

1946

1947

1948

Willard F. Libby, University of Chicago, develops the concept of carbon 14 dating; he will determine a value for the half-life of ^{14}C in 1949

Scientists at Merck isolate the pernicious anemia factor vitamin B_{12}

Fritz A. Lipmann establishes the role of coenzyme A in delivering acetyl groups (as acetyl CoA) into the tricarboxylic acid cycle

as thorium, protactinium, neptunium, and plutonium also have accessible +3 oxidation states. Based on these observations, Seaborg proposed in 1944 an entirely new series of transition elements, the *actinides*, analogous to the lanthanides. This is the present form of the periodic table (see page 422). By 1944, it was understood that the 14 lanthanides correspond to stepwise filling of the seven 4f atomic orbitals. Analogously, the actinides would correspond to filling the seven 5f orbitals. Although only seven actinides were known in 1944 (90–96), the series was predicted to end with 103, an element that should also be lanthanide-like. This was not at all self-evident. The first edition of Linus Pauling's *General Chemistry* (1947) "hedges its bets": the elements thorium-curium are shown in the main table (below transition metals 72–78) *and* in their own horizontal series ("Uranium Metals") below the "Rare Earth Metals" series.

The first public announcement of elements 95 and 96 did not occur, as scheduled, on November 16, 1945, at the National Meeting of the American Chemical Society but five days earlier on the popular radio program *Quiz Kids*. The famous Dr. Seaborg made a guest appearance on November 11 and one of the precocious contestants asked him if any

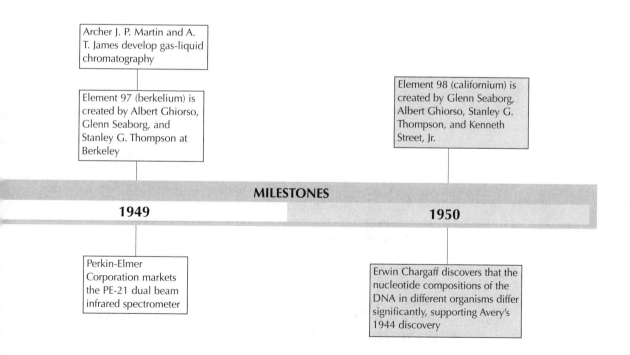

Archer J. P. Martin and A. T. James develop gas-liquid chromatography

Element 97 (berkelium) is created by Albert Ghiorso, Glenn Seaborg, and Stanley G. Thompson at Berkeley

Element 98 (californium) is created by Glenn Seaborg, Albert Ghiorso, Stanley G. Thompson, and Kenneth Street, Jr.

MILESTONES

1949

1950

Perkin-Elmer Corporation markets the PE-21 dual beam infrared spectrometer

Erwin Chargaff discovers that the nucleotide compositions of the DNA in different organisms differ significantly, supporting Avery's 1944 discovery

new chemical elements had been made recently. Seaborg spontaneously disclosed the news about elements 95 and 96. Later he would suggest the names americium for 95 and curium for 96.

The 1940s would witness syntheses of two more actinides: 97, produced by Ghiorso, Seaborg, and Stanley G. Thompson (1912–76) in 1949, later named berkelium, and 98, produced by Seaborg, Ghiorso, Thompson, and Kenneth Street, Jr. in 1950, and later named californium. As Seaborg had predicted six years earlier, 97 and 98 (as well as 99–101 and 103, discovered in 1961), as actinides, were most stable in the +3 oxidation state. (For element 102, the penultimate actinide, +2 is most stable although +3 is accessible; for ytterbium, the penultimate lanthanide, +3 is most stable but +2 is very accessible). Seaborg and his colleague Edwin M. McMillan, who in 1940 discovered neptunium, the first transuranium element, would share the 1951 Nobel Prize in chemistry.

A Philosopher-Scientist Applies Thermodynamics to Life Processes

Ilya Prigogine (1917–2003) was born in Moscow a few months before the Russian Revolution. His family would migrate to Germany in 1921 and to Belgium in 1929 where he conducted his greatest work at the Free University in Brussels, becoming a Belgian citizen in 1949. Early in his career, Prigogine was struck by the fact that the laws of thermodynamics (chapter 1) apply rigorously only to systems at equilibrium (completely reversible systems) while all *real* processes are not perfectly at equilibrium (irreversible). Spontaneous processes always lose ("dissipate") some chemical or mechanical energy in the form of heat. Prigogine realized that such dissipation processes, operating far from equilibrium, can create ordered states of matter called "dissipative structures." The creation of such "dissipative structures" is related to random fluctuations and highly undeterministic, even chaotic events.

Prigogine attacked the daunting problem of irreversible processes and non-equilibrium thermodynamics, especially systems in states far from equilibrium, starting in 1945. With wry humor, he dubbed classical thermodynamics "thermostatics" and applied his non-equilibrium thermodynamics to problems of biological organization and even to broader societal and philosophical questions. In 1977 Ilya Prigogine received the Nobel Prize in chemistry for his applications of thermodynamics to irreversible processes.

Short-Lived Free Radicals in the Laboratory and in Interstellar Space

When excited by light or electricity, isolated gas-phase atoms emit sharp line spectra (see chapter 1) because their quantized electronic levels are widely separated in energy. A diatomic "A-B" molecule such as H_2 has a bond between two atoms and bond vibrations that are also quantized, but much closer in energy than the electronic levels. In addition, rotations of diatomic molecules also influence these vibration-rotation energy sublevels. That is why even simple electronically excited molecules emit (broad) band spectra rather than (sharp) line spectra. For a triatomic "A-B-C" molecule, such as N_2O, there are two bond distances and a bond angle that can "flex" and the spectra are much more complex. For a linear "A-B-C-D" tetratomic molecule, such as H_2O_2, there are three bond distances, two bond angles, and one torsional angle (the projection of one A-B bond over the C-D bond viewed down the B-C axis). For a tetratomic molecule like CH_2O, where B, C, and D are each attached to A, there are three bond distances and three bond angles. The spectra of tetratomics are considerably more complex than those of triatomics.

During the late 1930s, experimental observations of molecular spectra began to "partner" with Mulliken's molecular orbital theory. The most successful spectroscopist to emerge and employ experiment and theory during this period was Gerhard Herzberg (1904–99). Born in Germany, Herzberg was forced to flee in 1935 to Canada (his wife was Jewish), where he spent all but three years of his later life. Herzberg demonstrated that careful analysis of the visible and ultraviolet absorption and emission spectra of small molecules can provide information on the symmetry, geometry, electronic state (*singlet, doublet, triplet*), and ionization potential (e.g., $H_2 \rightarrow H_2^+$) of the species studied. Starting around 1940, he and his collaborators would study scores of small molecules, short-lived radicals and ions, and their electronic excited states.

When Paneth and Hofeditz heated a sample of tetramethyl lead [$Pb(CH_3)_4$] in 1929, they generated and trapped methyl radicals (CH_3) with lifetimes (under laboratory conditions) of 0.008 seconds (see chapter 3). Extremely low steady-state concentrations of free radicals are known to be generated in flames (the emission bands from a Bunsen burner centered at 3889 and 4314 Å were known to come from unstable CH radicals in the burning hydrocarbon gas). In 1937, the Belgian astronomer Polydore ("Pol") Swings (1906–83) discovered the emission from CH in space, the first report of an interstellar radical. Why should there be discernible concentrations of normally transient species such as CH in interstellar space? The reason becomes clearer if one imagines heating an individual $Pb(CH_3)_4$ molecule in interstellar space to form a lead atom and four methyl radicals that fly off into the ultrahigh vacuum. Unless CH_3 falls apart on its own, it may take decades before it encounters a molecule, radical, or atom with which to react (and very likely a dust particle needed, as a third body, to disperse some of the collision energy).

In 1941, astronomer Walter S. Adams (1876–1956) discovered another new chemical species in interstellar space. Herzberg generated the same species in the laboratory by burning methane. Comparison of experiment and theory confirmed that it was CH^+. In 1942, Herzberg investigated a set of emission bands observed earlier in a comet (comet 1940c) and centered

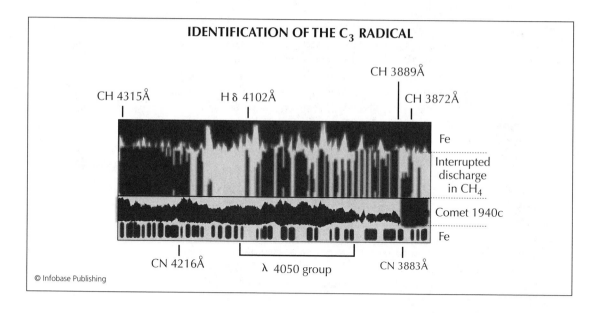

IDENTIFICATION OF THE C_3 RADICAL

CH 4315Å　　H δ 4102Å　　　　CH 3889Å　　CH 3872Å

Fe

Interrupted discharge in CH_4

Comet 1940c

Fe

CN 4216Å　　λ 4050 group　　CN 3883Å

© Infobase Publishing

Spectrum recorded for the discharge of Comet 1940c and its comparison with the spectrum emitted from a discharge in CH_4 that established the presence of C_3 in the comet

around 4050 Å (the "λ 4050 group"; see the accompanying figure). He was able to generate the same emission spectrum in the laboratory starting with methane CH_4. The arrangement of the bands, coupled with earlier theoretical calculations, led Herzberg to conclude that they were due to a bent singlet (all electrons paired) methylene molecule (CH_2). Seven years later, two Belgian scientists, André Monfils and Boris Rosen, discovered that emission from CD_4 yielded precisely the same λ 4050 group. Since CH_2 and CD_2 *must* provide slightly different spectra, it was immediately clear that Herzberg's CH_2 hypothesis was incorrect. Herzberg's colleague Alexander E. Douglas (1913–) reinvestigated this reaction in 1954 using a 1:1 mixture of CH_4 and $^{13}CH_4$ (*CH_4). He correctly concluded that the comet's "mystery molecule" was C_3 (accompanying figure) since the spectra of all six distinct isotopic combinations of this molecule were observed: CCC, *CCC, C*CC, *C*CC, *CC*C, and *C*C*C. It is now known that C_3 is a major component in carbon vapor (as is C_2).

Herzberg's interest in the tiny, fundamental, and highly reactive CH_2 persisted. Hermann Staudinger had demonstrated in 1912 that heating diazomethane (CH_2N_2), in the presence of alkenes or carbon monoxide releases CH_2, which is instantaneously trapped by these compounds. Diazomethane also produces CH_2 photochemically and Herzberg used the new flash photolysis technique developed by Ronald G. W. Norrish (1897–1978) and George Porter (1920–2002) in 1949: An intense light flash, milliseconds in duration, impinges upon a sample and transient spectra are recorded (Norrish and Porter would soon shorten the timescale from milliseconds to microseconds). In 1950 they flash-photolyzed Cl_2 to 2 Cl and monitored the reappearance of Cl_2 molecules. Herzberg's flash-photolysis study of CH_2 was successful and he determined its geometry and electronic state. Herzberg went on to win the 1971 Nobel Prize in chemistry. Norrish and Porter shared the 1967 Nobel Prize in chemistry with Manfred Eigen (see chapter 6).

The First Modern Spectrometers: Accurate Analysis in a "Box"

The development in 1940 of the first commercial *ultraviolet-visible spectrometer*, the Beckman DU, and its marketing in 1941 (see chapter 4) revolutionized analytical chemistry and had significant impact on biology. During the early years of World War II another laboratory workhouse, the *infrared spectrometer* was developed in order to help solve a strategic national problem: rubber.

The United States had always obtained its strategic reserves of natural rubber from Malaysia and the Dutch East Indies. When the Japanese occupied these Asian lands early in World War II, American industry raced to produce butadiene-based synthetic rubber (buna [see chapter 1] and improved buna-S [S= styrene]) and the Federal Office of Rubber Reserve was formed. A significant difficulty in rubber manufacture was the degree of polymerization of butadiene and styrene, best monitored by infrared (IR) spectroscopy. Although the U.S. National Bureau of Standards had collected IR spectra since 1905, IR analysis was not a routine operation. The Office of Rubber Reserve hurriedly called together a small group of instrumentation manufacturers and provided support to develop a simple and robust instrument to monitor rubber synthesis. The first instrument marketed was the Beckman IR-1, shipped in September 1942. However, another new company founded by two amateur astronomers, Richard S. Perkin (1906–69) and Charles Elmer (1872–1954), had a marked advantage over Beckman in the design of optics mirrors and lenses. Their first commercial instrument, the Perkin-Elmer 12A, was marketed in 1944. Both the IR-1 and the P-E 12A were single-beam instruments and required considerable calibration to obtain useful spectra. In 1949, Perkin-Elmer began to market the P-E 21, a dual-beam instrument, far superior in its ability to obtain spectra. The Beckman DU and the P-E 21 would become the laboratory workhorses of the 1950s and early 1960s.

Today the most useful chemical instrument is probably the *nuclear magnetic resonance (NMR) spectrometer*. Magnetic resonance imaging (MRI), vital in modern medicine, is derived from NMR. In late 1945, a physics group at Stanford, led by Felix Bloch (1905–83) (with William W. Hanson [1909–49] and Martin W. Packard), and one at Harvard, led by Edward M. Purcell (1912–97) (with Henry C. Torrey [1911–99] and Robert V. Pound [1919–   ]), independently discovered the phenomenon of nuclear magnetic resonance. In order to manifest NMR an atomic nucleus must have nonzero nuclear spin. Of the roughly 100 stable isotopes that have nonzero nuclear spin, ^1H, present in the vast majority of organic compounds, received immediate attention. Unfortunately, the common isotopes of carbon (^{12}C) and oxygen (^{16}O) lack nuclear spin. Bloch and Purcell had been investigating the influence of magnetic fields on nuclear spin. Confounding their studies was the unexpected finding that the *chemical* environment of the ^{1}H nucleus (e.g., H_2O versus CH_4) produced tiny but significant effects termed "chemical shifts." This "confounding" effect for physicists would soon become a gold mine for chemists. NMR technology benefited from the development, during World War II, of the klystron (invented by Hanson in 1937): a generator of microwave power and a critical component of radar. In 1948, the Varian brothers, Russell (1898–1959) and Sigurd (1901–61), friends and collaborators of Hanson for more than a decade, formed the Varian Corporation in Palo Alto that would dominate NMR spectrometry for decades. Bloch and Purcell shared the 1952 Nobel Prize in physics.

A New Day in Chromatography and the Dawn of Protein Sequencing

Not only did the 1940s witness the beginning of modern instrumental analysis; it was also a decade of enormous advances in chemical separation and purification. The technique published in 1906 by Mikhail Tswett (see chapter 1) was adsorption chromatography: the separation of a chlorophyll pigment mixture adsorbed on a solid (e.g., sugar, chalk) and developed by a solvent such as carbon disulfide. During the early 1930s Richard Kuhn and Edgar Lederer exploited this technique to separate and identify the carotenoids (see chapter 4). In 1941, an even more powerful technique, based upon partition chromatography, was announced by two Englishmen, Archer J. P. Martin (1910–2002) and Richard L. M. Synge (1914–94), at the Wool Industries Research Association. The analysis of proteins, including wool, was an important challenge during that period. Arne Tiselius (1902–71), investigating electrophoresis during the 1920s, established it as a protein purification technique by 1937 and received the Nobel Prize in chemistry in 1948. Martin and Synge shared the 1952 Nobel Prize in chemistry for discovering partition chromatography and employing it to obtain the first complete amino acid sequence for a naturally occurring peptide: gramicidin S.

Liquid-partition chromatography was a hybrid of Tswett's column-adsorption chromatography and a technique widely employed in industry called countercurrent extraction. The latter involved passing two immiscible liquids moving in opposite directions in contact with each other to separate components differing in their relative solubilities (partition coefficients) in the two solvents. Martin and Synge discovered that a solid support such as silica gel can be wetted by water to form, in essence, a stationary aqueous phase. The surface of the wetted silica gel has, surprisingly, the same solvent properties as pure water. When the stationary phase is packed in a tube and eluted with an immiscible solvent such as chloroform, solutes undergo numerous equilibrations between the adsorbed aqueous and mobile chloroform phases.

At the age of 12, Martin had constructed distillation columns from soldered coffee cans. During the late 1930s, he constructed what Synge would refer to as the "bizarre-looking apparatus" that successfully purified vitamin E using countercurrent extraction. While Martin's interests focused on apparatus, Synge was interested in biochemical applications. Liquid-partition column chromatography proved to be effective in the separation of acetylated amino acids. It offered considerable potential in solving one of the great problems of the day: amino acid sequencing in peptides and proteins. In 1944, Martin, Synge, R. Consden, and A. H. Gordon discovered that cellulose (filter paper), thoroughly wetted with water, is an excellent medium for separating amino acids and found ninhydrin to be an ideal reagent for locating them following separation. In addition, they developed two-dimensional paper chromatography: partial

The Analysis of Peptide and Protein Sequences

The development of liquid-partition chromatography, paper chromatography, and two-dimensional paper chromatography provided the means to separate and identify amino acids and very simple peptides. These techniques allowed Synge to analyze the amino acid sequence of gramicidin S. While human proteins, for example, are for the most part limited to 20 common amino acids having the L- absolute configuration (see chapter 6), bacterial peptides contain a high frequency of unusual amino acids. Gramicidin S contains two unusual amino acids: L-ornithine and D-phenylalanine (rather than the L-phenylalanine). The cyclic decapeptide is actually a dimer: two D-phenylalanine-L-proline-L-valine-L-ornithine-L-leucine units linked head-to-tail. Nature provides numerous small- and medium-sized peptides as "training grounds" for the analysis of proteins. The two nonapeptide hormones, oxytocin and vasopressin, that Vincent DuVigneaud sequenced in the early 1950s, would be "practice" molecules for more complex analyses and syntheses.

In 1945, Frederick Sanger (1918–) developed a technique for N-terminus amino acid analysis of proteins: reaction with 2,4-dinitro-fluorobenzene at the terminal amino group. Following total hydrolysis, the N-terminal amino acid retains the 2,4-dinitrophenyl tag. Sanger immediately identified the N-termini of the two peptide chains that comprise insulin with the aid of Martin and Synge's chromatographic techniques. The complexity of this 51-amino-acid protein would challenge chemists for one more decade. In 1953, Sanger identified the amino acid sequences of the two insulin chains, and two years later he identified the locations of the three disulfide linkages (one intra-chain and two inter-chain). Sanger's breakthroughs in protein sequencing were recognized by his receipt of the Nobel Prize in chemistry in 1958. Starting in 1960, Sanger began his attack on the problem of nucleic acid sequencing. Major discoveries during the 1970s led to a second Nobel Prize in chemistry in 1980, shared with Paul Berg and Walter Gilbert (see chapter 8). Sanger is the only person to receive two Nobel Prizes in chemistry. Others receiving two Nobel Prizes include Marie Curie (physics; chemistry), Linus Pauling (chemistry; Peace) and John Bardeen (twice in physics).

separation of an amino acid mixture in the "x-direction" of a square filter paper and sub-fractionation in the "y-direction." These techniques were applied to the problem of sequencing small peptides. For example, if a pentapeptide, A-B-C-D-E, is totally hydrolyzed in acid, the amino acid content (A, B, C, D, E) is useful but provides no information on sequence. Partial acidic hydrolysis provides fragments (A-B, B-C, C-D, D-E) that disclose the original sequence. Coupling partial hydrolysis with paper chromatography, Synge determined the sequence of the antibiotic gramicidin S, a cyclic decapeptide isolated from the soil bacterium *Bacillus brevis*. This was the first sequencing of a naturally occurring peptide. Further advances in protein sequencing developed during this decade are described in the sidebar below.

When partition chromatography was disclosed by Martin and Synge in 1941, they also proposed the possibility of chromatography based upon partitioning of volatile solutes between liquid and vapor phases. With Anthony T. James, Martin developed this technique, gas-liquid chromatography (GLC) in 1949. Almost a decade earlier, Erika Cremer (1900–96), working in Austria, had developed the concept of gas chromatography. Her laboratory was bombed during World War II. After the war, Cremer, then director of physical chemistry at the University of Innsbrück, and her student Fritz Prior, built the apparatus, and their work was finally published in 1951. In contrast to Martin and Synge, Cremer's apparatus was based upon differential adsorption of gases (e.g., acetylene and ethylene) on a solid substance (e.g., activated charcoal), rather than on gas-liquid partition chromatography.

Linus Pauling, the *Alpha*-Helix, "Complementarity," and Sickle-Cell Anemia

Linus Pauling's studies of crystal structures during the 1920s led to his formulation of a set of crystallographic rules (see chapter 3) and laid the basis for his 1939 masterwork *The Nature of the Chemical Bond* (see chapter 4). In the 1930s Pauling and his research group began their systematic ("bottom-up") studies of amino acids and dipeptides in order to understand protein structure. They established the planarity (and dimensions) of the peptide linkage. In the 1940s a formidable group of English crystallographers, William T. Astbury (1898–1961), Dorothy Hodgkin, J. D. Bernal, Max F. Perutz (1914–2002), and John C. Kendrew (1917–97), focused their efforts on protein structure and sometimes employed a "top-down" approach (i.e., overall shape, structure, and function). Visions of spirals and helices danced in the minds of these scientists and Pauling's collaborator, Maurice L. Huggins (1897–1981), encouraged him to consider this approach and the role of hydrogen bonding.

Visiting Oxford in spring 1948, Pauling developed a severe sinus infection and was forced to bed:

The first day I read detective stories and just tried to keep from feeling miserable, and the second day too. But I got bored with that, so I thought, "Why don't I think about the structure of proteins?"

Specifically, Pauling drew a polypeptide chain, with correct structural dimensions, on a sheet of paper. Playing with the sheet he rolled it into a cylindrical structure that placed every fifth amino acid residue above its corresponding residue (1-5-9; 2-6-10, etc). These "top-down" predictions were consistent with X-ray data. Pauling was cautious about his conclusions and only in 1950 did he publish a note with his colleague Robert B. Corey (1897–1971). In early 1951, Pauling, Corey, and Herman R. Branson (1914–95) published the full first paper on this topic in the *Proceedings of the National Academy of Sciences* (*USA*) (*PNAS*). Bransom, an African-American physics professor on leave from Howard University, had briefly joined Pauling's group to apply his mathematical talents to chemical problems. He would become president of Central State University in Ohio (1968–70) and then Lincoln University in Pennsylvania (1970–85).

One month later, Pauling and Corey published seven consecutive papers in the *PNAS* disclosing their structures for the *alpha*-helix (see the figure on page 156), the *beta*-sheet, and their conclusions on the structures of keratins, fibrous proteins, and some globular proteins including hemoglobin. Although the *beta*-structure has been somewhat modified since, Pauling's *alpha*-helical structure remains as a triumph of structural biochemistry. His "top-down" model-building approach set the stage for the race to the DNA double helix that started almost immediately.

During the 1940s, Linus Pauling applied his formidable intuitive intellect to problems in biology and medicine and developed a fundamental concept of "complementarity." Complementarity explained the interactions between antigens and antibodies, shapes of taste and odor molecules and their receptors and, most significantly, the binding of substrates by enzymes. While Emil Fischer's lock-and-key model seemed to explain the specificity of enzymes, it had a major paradox in light of the new transition-state theory (see chapter 4). If an enzyme forms a lock-and-key enzyme-substrate complex, it should *stabilize* the substrate rather than increasing its reactivity. Pauling postulated that the enzyme actually binds the activated complex more tightly than either the substrate or the product, lowering the activation energy and thus increasing reaction rate.

Attending a dinner of medical doctors in spring 1945, Pauling learned about sickle-cell anemia, a disease largely limited in the United States to African Americans. Sickling (i.e., folding) of red blood cells causes blockages and blood clots in the lungs, kidneys, and brain. Most of the sickled cells are found in oxygen-poor venous blood rather than in oxygen-rich arterial blood. Realizing that red blood cells are essentially sacks containing hemoglobin and water, Pauling's intuition suggested that the origin of

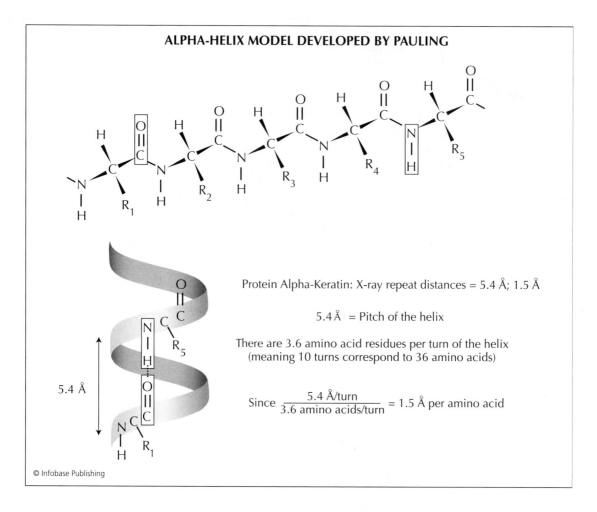

ALPHA-HELIX MODEL DEVELOPED BY PAULING

Protein Alpha-Keratin: X-ray repeat distances = 5.4 Å; 1.5 Å

5.4 Å = Pitch of the helix

There are 3.6 amino acid residues per turn of the helix
(meaning 10 turns correspond to 36 amino acids)

Since $\dfrac{5.4 \text{ Å/turn}}{3.6 \text{ amino acids/turn}} = 1.5$ Å per amino acid

© Infobase Publishing

A linear segment of protein (top) and its relationship to the structure of the α-helix deduced by Linus Pauling

sickle-cell anemia might be understandable at the molecular level. In fall 1946, Harvey A. Itano (1920–   ), a young physician and research associate with Pauling, began to investigate the chemical properties of sickle-cell hemoglobin. The anomaly seemed to rest in the globin (protein) rather than the heme part. Joined by a young physical chemist, John Singer, the Pauling group built a Tiselius electrophoresis apparatus. The results were exquisitely sensitive: Sickle-cell hemoglobin migrated to the cathode of the apparatus more rapidly than normal hemoglobin. The sickle-cell variant carries on its surface more positive charges than normal hemoglobin. Years later the effect would be traced to replacement of a single valine residue by glutamic acid in each of hemoglobin's two β-chains. A human disease was seen, for the first time, to have a clear molecular origin.

Harvey Akio Itano did not receive his medal as the outstanding student of the Berkeley Class of 1942 at the commencement ceremony because three weeks earlier he had been moved with his family to an internment camp for Japanese Americans. (Linus Pauling took a very public stance against internment of Japanese Americans following the attack on Pearl Harbor, was publicly criticized and his house vandalized). Itano was released July 4, 1942, and permitted to enter medical school. When Itano joined Pauling's group in 1946, he was working for the U.S. Public Health Service. In 1979, he would be elected to the National Academy of Sciences.

A Revolution in Pharmaceuticals: Making the Old Doctor's Bag Truly Potent

The discoveries of the antibiotic penicillin by Fleming in 1928 (see chapter 3) and Prontosil, the first sulfa drug, by Gerhardt Domagk during the 1930s (see chapter 4) each involved a considerable degree of serendipity. The 1940s would witness a revolution in rational drug design based upon the concept of "antimetabolites." It was a new theme on a familiar idea. The notion of specific enzyme-substrate (or more generally protein-substrate) complexes had been accepted for decades. If a chemical was found effective, closely related derivatives would be synthesized and scrutinized for activity since they might fit the active site and produce the same chemistry, perhaps more effectively with fewer side effects. A rational drug design strategy could be based upon the concept of the "antimetabolite," a substance that competes for the active site with the natural metabolite and blocks the next metabolic stage.

Sulfa drugs are perhaps the earliest examples of antimetabolites. During 1935, Daniele Bovet (1907–92), a Swiss-born scientist working at the Pasteur Institute in Paris, demonstrated that the medicinally active part of Prontosil (see chapter 4) is *para*-aminobenzenesulfonamide (see the figure below). Following this lead, some 5,000 different sulfa drugs were synthesized over the next few years, of which 15–20 were found to be useful. Subsequent research demonstrated that the sulfa drugs worked, not by actually killing bacteria, but by inhibiting bacterial conversion of *para*-aminobenzoic acid ("PABA") into folic acid (see figure), vital to their growth and multiplication. E. L. Robert Stockstad (1913–95) and coworkers at Lederle Laboratories isolated crystalline folic acid and

Para-aminobenzenesulfonamide; para-aminobenzoic acid (PABA)

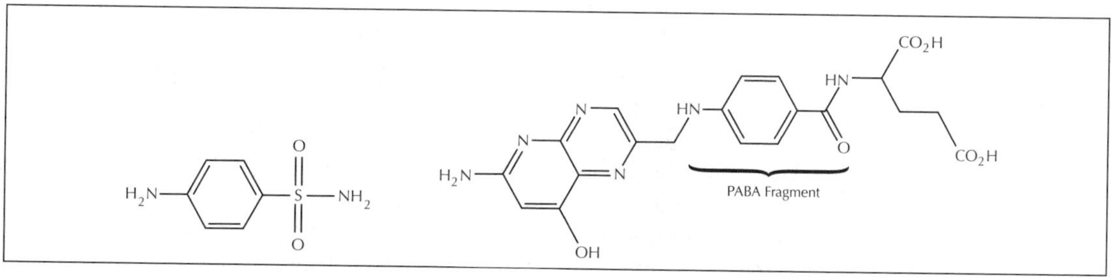

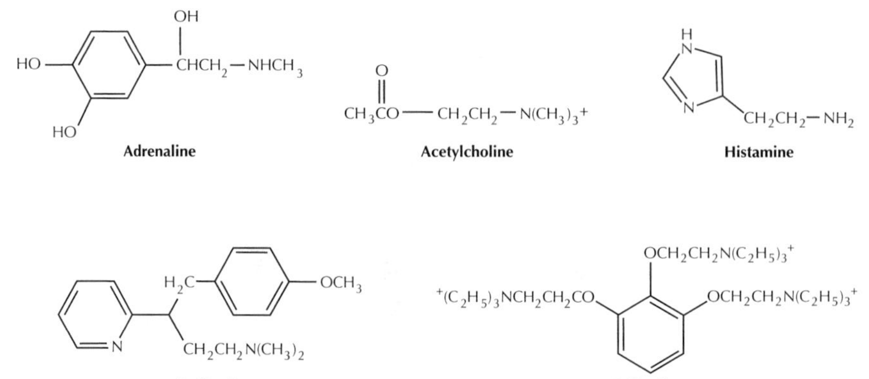

Neurotransmitters and their antagonists old 3-"adrenaline," "acetylcholine," "histamine," "pyrilamine," "gallamine"

proved its structure in 1943. The similarity of *para*-aminobenzenesulfon-amide to PABA made it clear that it acts as an antimetabolite, inhibiting conversion of PABA to folic acid. Since humans obtain folic acid from foods (it is one of the B-complex vitamins) inhibition of folic acid synthesis by a sulfa drug is not harmful.

Bovet soon applied the antimetabolite paradigm to design drugs active on the autonomous nervous system. The three neurotransmitters adrenaline, acetylcholine, and histamine (see above) share some structural similarities. During the 1940s, Bovet and coworkers synthesized a series of antimetabolites that acted as antagonists to these neurotransmitters, thus relieving undesirable symptoms. For example, in 1944, the group synthesized the antihistamine pyrilamine (see figure above). In 1947, Bovet moved to Rome and began work on synthetic analogues of the curare alkaloids. Crude curare, used by native South American peoples to tip poison arrows, is a mixture of substances that act as deadly antagonists to acetylcholine. Bovet synthesized a series of antagonists, such as gallamine (see figure above), whose activities could be "fine-tuned," and some were effective as muscle relaxants. Bovet would be awarded the 1957 Nobel Prize in physiology or medicine.

In 1940, 12 years after Alexander Fleming discovered penicillin, Howard W. Florey (1898–1968) and Ernst B. Chain (1906–79), at the Dunn School of Pathology in Oxford, extracted the *Penicillium* fungus and obtained the substance in a fairly pure state. Edward P. Abraham (1913–99), working with Chain, then injected eight mice with deadly *Streptococci*, treated four with penicillin, and left four untreated. In August 1940, the exciting results were published: the four mice treated with penicillin lived and the other four died. In 1941 the Oxford group used paper chromatography to purify penicillin, began human trials, and obtained positive results. Five patients seriously ill with *Staphyloccus* and *Streptococcus* infections resistant to sulfa drugs responded positively to penicillin. With Great Britain already at war and ominous events unfolding in the Pacific, both Britain and the United States began an urgent effort to produce penicillin in massive quantity using fermentation. In the United States, Merck, Pfizer, and Squibb collaborated on penicillin development. The first production plant was Pfizer's fermentation plant in Brooklyn, New York. Ominously, in 1940 Chain and Abraham identified a strain of *Staphylococcus aureus* that developed resistance to penicillin. This was a foreshadowing of the frightening race between the development of new drugs and the development of bacterial resistance that threatens the health of humankind during the 21st century.

The empirical formula of penicillin was obtained in the next two years, but its molecular structure would remain a challenge. The Oxford group was producing a slightly different penicillin ("Penicillin F") compared to that produced in the USDA Northern Regional Research Laboratory in Peoria ("Penicillin G"). The latter was more stable and, by good fortune, the two had virtually identical antibiotic activities. At the start of 1943, penicillin research was classified, although the "invisible college" of scientists on both sides of the Atlantic communicated with each other on this topic. Ultimately, two structures remained as possibilities for the penicillins: the β-lactam structure (see below), advocated by Robert Burns ("R. B.") Woodward (1917–79) at Harvard, and a structure with a five-membered instead of a four-membered ring, supported by Robert Robinson at Oxford. The organic chemist Woodward employed the physical chemistry technique of combustion calorimetry to demonstrate ring strain (see chapter 3) consistent with a four-membered ring. The decisive experiment was the crystallographic study in 1945 by Dorothy Crowfoot Hodgkin that firmly established the β-lactam structure for penicillin. This was too late to establish a synthetic effort for the war. Several American pharmaceutical companies were mass-producing penicillin G using fermentation and were able to meet demand for the mass casualties of the June 6, 1944, D-day invasion. Florey and Chain would share the 1945 Nobel Prize in physiology or medicine with Fleming for their work with penicillin. Hodgkin, whose work during the previous decade contributed to elucidating the structure of cholesterol, would later solve the structures of insulin and vitamin B_{12} and receive the 1964 Nobel Prize in chemistry. Total synthesis of penicillin would be accomplished by John C. Sheehan (1915–92), at MIT, in 1957.

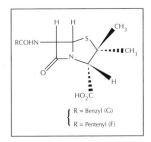

Penicillins G and F

The fact that 20–50 percent of the bacteria in soil are effective in destroying a variety of microorganisms, including other bacteria, has been known for many decades. In 1939 this prompted René Dubos (1901–82), at the Rockefeller Institute for Medical Research, to examine one such bacterium, *Bacillus brevis*, from which he isolated a chemical component, tyrothricin, capable of destroying bacteria. The cyclic decapeptide gramicidin S, sequenced by Martin and Synge, is derived from tyrothricin.

Selman A. Waksman (1888–1973), working at Rutgers University, made the critical breakthrough in this research field. Stimulated by

Fleming's work on *Penicillium* fungus and the broad spectrum of penicillin efficacies, Waksman studied soil bacteria in the *Actinomycetes* group. These unusual bacteria, which have filaments reminiscent of fungi, contribute to decomposition of animal and plant matter and the formation of soil humus, and are effective in destroying other microorganisms including bacteria. The species studied, *Streptomyces griseus*, was isolated in September 1943, its active antibiotic (streptomycin) separated and purified in January 1944, and, with the urgency of the war, tested clinically before the end of the year. Streptomycin (see the structure below) was found to be a broad-spectrum antibiotic, with the ability to treat many species of bacteria that were resistant to penicillin. Its greatest success was its effectiveness in treating *Mycobacterium tuberculis*, the cause of the highly communicable and deadly disease tuberculosis (TB). Virtually overnight, this changed TB from the scourge of the tenements to a treatable and controllable disease. Merck started mass production of streptomycin during World War II. In his acceptance speech for the 1952 Nobel Prize in physiology or medicine, Waksman commenced with a biblical quote from *Ecclesiastes*:

The Lord hath created medicines out of the earth; and he that is wise will not abhor them.

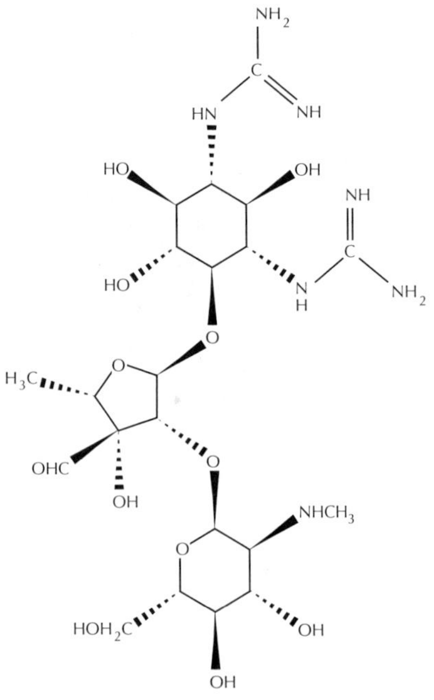

"Streptomycin," "Chlortetracycline (Aureomycin)"

In 1948, Benjamin M. Duggar (1872–1956), University of Wisconsin, isolated chlortetracycline (see below) from *Sterptomyces aureofaciens*. It

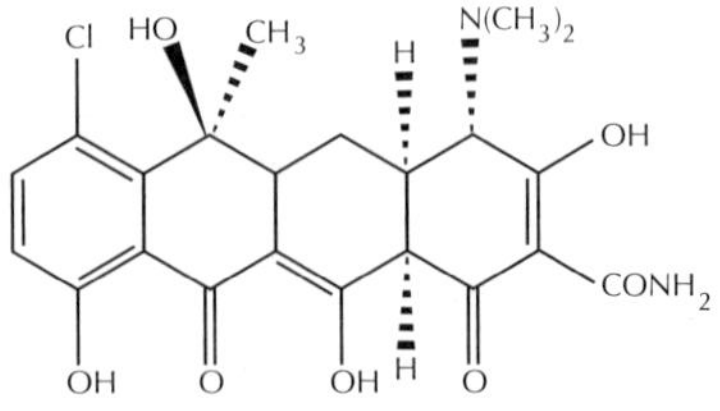

Chlortetracycline (Aureomycin)

Streptomycin

was the first in a series of tetracycline antibiotics developed over the next decades. Aureomycin is considered to be the first broad-spectrum antibiotic, capable of treating a wide variety of *Gram-positive* and *Gram-negative* bacteria, protozoans, and *Rickettsias* (present in fleas and ticks: typhus, Rocky Mountain fever). The structures of chlortetracycline and the related oxytetracycline (Terramycin) were determined by R. B. Woodward and coworkers in 1952.

Although malaria is thought of as a tropical disease, a mild form (ague) afflicted residents of England for centuries; soldiers fighting in the South died from malaria during the American Civil War. The largest impact is in tropical countries where it kills millions each year even in the early 21st century (see chapter 7). The disease is caused by a protozoan, *Plasmodium*, which enters the bloodstream; its vector is the *Anopheles* mosquito. The best means of combating malaria is prevention and in 1939, Paul Müller (1899–1965) and coworkers at J.R. Geigy in Switzerland discovered the efficacy of DDT as an insecticide (mosquitos, flies, lice, and others). For his discovery of DDT and other pesticides, Müller received the 1948 Nobel Prize in physiology or medicine. This may surprise most readers today since DDT was later shown to be an ecological hazard, particularly to birds of prey, and has long been banned in the United States and other developed countries. However, DDT has saved literally millions of lives and continues to do so today in hot and tropical lands. During World War II, malaria was widely encountered in the South Pacific (by the end of 1942, 8,500 American troops had contracted this deadly disease after only six months of occupation in the Philippines). The U.S. Army was successful in halting outbreaks of malaria in Casablanca and typhus in Naples through its use of DDT.

A natural cure for malaria was discovered by Europeans during 17th-century explorations of South American forests. The cinchona tree produces a substance called quinine. It is bitter and English colonials would temper it with alcohol to make its imbibing more tolerable. This became a national habit and quinine water ("bitters") and gin is a favored British export. However, a glass of quinine water contains only 10–20 milligrams (0.0003 - 0.0006 oz) of quinine while treatment of malaria typically requires pills containing a total of 500–750 milligrams (0.015 - 0.018 oz) per day.

During the 1930s, the German company I.G. Farben developed an effective, if unpleasant, synthetic antimalarial called atabrine. It was the preventative treatment of choice for the Allies during World War II, since they had not stocked sufficient stores of quinine before the war. The war stimulated interest in synthetic antimalarials. Louis F. Fieser (1899–1977) and Mary Peters Fieser (1909–97) at Harvard synthesized lapinone which had antimalarial activity but required injections.

The chemical synthesis of quinine remained a major goal and therein lies an interesting story. A German chemist named Paul Rabe (1869–1952) had claimed, in 1918, to have chemically converted a degradation product of quinine, called quinotoxine, back into quinine. His notes were very sketchy

Quinine

and today his success is considered dubious at best. In 1943, the laboratory of Vladimir Prelog (1906–98), in Zurich, demonstrated the decomposition of quinotoxine into homomeroquinene and the conversion of this compound back into quinotoxine. Encouraged by this discovery, R. B. Woodward and his associate William E. Doering (1917–   ) accomplished total synthesis of homomeroquinene. In effect, they felt they had completed the entire pathway to quinine and, in 1944, "total synthesis of quinine" was announced. Due to the problems of the Rabe study, it has been subjected to careful scrutiny and clarified. The structure of quinine (left) includes four chiral centers (asymmetric carbons [*], see chapter 1). There are 2^4, or 16 stereoisomers, only one of which is quinine, and even a successful approach during the 1940s would have been doomed to very low yields. In 2001, Gilbert Stork (1921–   ) announced the total synthesis of quinine with the correct stereochemical configurations depicted left.

During the 1930s, German scientists had synthesized another antimalarial called chloroquine and studied it intensively during World War II. Today, it is the most widely used treatment for malaria. Following the war, other major discoveries included the isolation of the "pernicious anemia factor," vitamin B_{12}, at Merck in 1948. The structure of this amazing molecule would be solved by Dorothy Crowfoot Hodgkin during the next decade. Its total synthesis would begin in 1961, be completed in 1972, and involve two brilliant research groups and over 100 chemists. Under the leadership of Max Tischler (1906–89), the director of research, Merck produced vitamins on an industrial scale during the 1940s. The antimetabolite paradigm would be employed by George Hitchings (1905–98) and Gertrude Elion (1918–99), at Burroughs Wellcome in England, to synthesize the anticancer drugs 2,6-diaminopurine and thioguanine in 1948. These drugs mimic DNA bases and inhibit the DNA synthesis which occurs in all cells, but much more rapidly in cancer cells. Hitchings and Elion shared the 1988 Nobel Prize in physiology or medicine with James W. Black (1924–   ).

In 1948, Edward C. Kendall, who clarified steroid structures during the 1930s (see chapter 4), and Philip S. Hench (1896–1965), at the Mayo Clinic, demonstrated that the steroid hormone cortisone relieves symptoms of rheumatoid arthritis. Kendall, Hench, and Tadeus Reichstein would share the 1950 Nobel Prize in physiology or medicine. Although Lewis Sarett (1917–99) at Merck had accomplished a total synthesis of cortisone in 1944 (Woodward published a more elegant one in 1951), cortisone and its close derivatives would have remained extremely expensive were it not for the efforts of Percy L. Julian (1899–1975). As soon as he learned of the Mayo Clinic discovery, Julian developed a rapid, inexpensive synthesis of Reichstein's Substance S, also isolated from the adrenal cortex. This steroid is easily converted to dihydrocortisone and Julian's pathway remains today the major commercial route to this over-the-counter topical remedy for sunburn, mosquito bites, and other uncomfortable skin irritations.

Percy Lavon Julian was born in Montgomery, Alabama, in 1899, the grandson of slaves. Despite the limited opportunities for education available to African Americans, Julian obtained a bachelor's degree (class valedictorian) at DePauw University in 1920, a master's degree from Harvard (1923), and a doctorate from the University of Vienna, where he met Josef Pikl. Julian and Pikl joined the Howard University faculty, succeeding St. Elmo Brady [1884–1966], the first African-American Ph.D. in chemistry, and then moved to DePauw University in 1933. In 1935 Julian, assisted by Pikl, synthesized physostigmine, a potent antiglaucoma drug. In 1936, he became the director of research of the soya products of the Glidden Company, the first African-American research director of a major corporation. Julian obtained more than 100 patents during his illustrious career and was elected a member of the National Academy of Sciences in 1973.

Intermediary Metabolism: Connecting Glycolysis to the Krebs Cycle

By 1940 details of glycolysis, fermentation, and the tricarboxylic acid (citric or Krebs) cycle (see chapter 4) were generally well understood. The manner in which pyruvate and the tricarboxylic acid cycle were connected was not clear. It was also not clear how chemical energy generated during glycolysis, and especially from the Krebs cycle and electron transfer to oxygen, was exploited. Heat performs work if it is transferred from a higher-temperature to a lower-temperature environment. In living organisms temperature is essentially uniform.

Both of these puzzles would be solved by Fritz A. Lipmann (1899–1986) and his colleagues. Born in Germany, Lipmann was at the Cornell University School of Medicine in 1939 when he began studies of bioenergetics that continued after he moved to Massachusetts General Hospital in 1941 (he was appointed professor of medicine at Harvard Medical School in 1949). Lipmann postulated in 1941 that energies from biochemical reactions are stored by coupling these reactions with phosphorylation of adenosine diphosphate (ADP) to form adenosine triphosphate (ATP). Such reactions are catalyzed by enzymes that couple an energy-producing reaction with formation of ATP. The energy available in the metabolic "combustion" of a single molecule of glucose (to CO_2 and H_2O) is equivalent, in principle, to energy stored in 38 ATP molecules (see chapter 4). Energy-requiring reactions are coupled to conversion of ATP to ADP. Lipmann coined the term "energy-rich phosphate bonds" in the context of ATP energy storage.

In 1948, Lipmann and his coworkers established the structure and the role of coenzyme A in its conversion to acetyl CoA (see the structure below), noting that the thioacetate linkage ($-S-COCH_3$) is a high-energy linkage like the pyrophosphate linkage in ATP. The presence of pantothenic acid, one of the B vitamins, in the structure of coenzyme A (see the structure) explains its vital role in intermediary metabolism. For these major contributions to biochemistry, Lipmann shared the 1953 Nobel Prize in physiology or medicine with Hans A. Krebs. Total synthesis of ATP (see the structure below) was reported in 1948 by Alexander R. Todd (1907–97). Todd had been appointed at Manchester in 1938, began studying nucleosides in 1939, and moved to Cambridge in 1944. As he later commented, the reason why chemists were relatively late in exploring the structures of nucleosides (ATP, NAD, FMN, FAD, the four ribonucleotides, and the four deoxyribonucleotides) was that they were difficult to purify. The development of paper and ion chromatographies, electrophoresis, and countercurrent extraction made purification of these compounds feasible. Todd's work established the structures and stereo-chemistries of the ribonucleotides, deoxyribonucleotides, and ATP. He would receive the 1957 Nobel Prize in chemistry.

The Genetic Material Is DNA?! . . . Not *Proteins?*

Although deoxyribonucleic acid (DNA) had been known since 1869 (see chapter 1), its biological role remained a mystery until the 1940s. By 1940, the general constitutions of DNA and RNA were known: deoxyribose or ribose; purine or pyrimidine base and phosphate. Alexander Todd and others were working actively to understand the specific structural chemistry of the nucleotides. While DNA was known to be a high-molecular-weight polymer, the presence of only four different building blocks (guanine [G], adenine [A], thymine [T], and cytosine [C]) suggested a "monotonous" oligomev lacking much information (Levene hypothesis). Chromosomes are composed of both DNA and proteins. With 20 amino acid building blocks (comparable to letters in the alphabet), proteins were widely believed to be the archives for genetic information. But, at the Rockefeller Institute in New York City, experiments upon bacteria were providing surprises that would eventually shake the world of biology to its roots and launch modern genetics.

During the 1920s, British bacteriologists began studies of the interconversions of two strains of *pneumococcal* bacteria, the nonvirulent R type and the virulent S type (R = colonies with rough surfaces; S = smooth surfaces). Transformations of the R-type to S-type *pneumococci* were observed in animals and in vitro. In 1930, a cellfree extract of "transforming principle" was isolated. At the Rockefeller Institute, bacteriologist Oswald T. Avery (1877–1955) and his colleague Colin M. MacLeod (1909–72) and later Maclyn McCarty (1911–2005) studied the nature of this "transforming principle."

The accompanying figure depicts aspects of their classic study. Injection of heat-killed virulent S strain was not fatal to the laboratory mice studied. However, coinjection of heat-killed S strain and live nonvirulent R strain killed the mice. The newly created strain continued to be virulent in succeeding generations. Clearly, the genetic factor in the S strain was heat stable and transferred to the R strain. Avery and colleagues purified

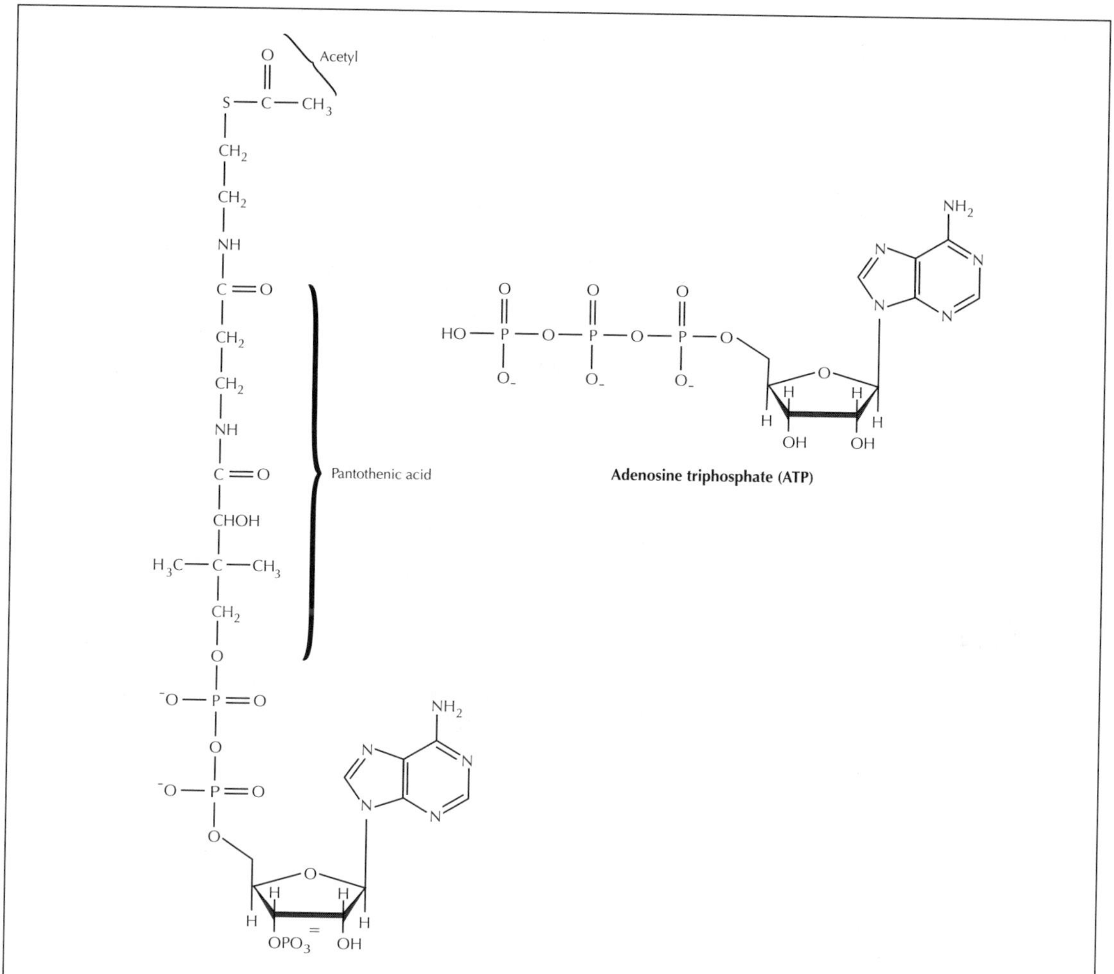

Acetyl

Pantothenic acid

Adenosine triphosphate (ATP)

Acetyl CoA

the "transforming principle" and found that treatment with proteases and lipases did not destroy its activity, thus it was neither protein nor lipid. Chemical studies indicated that it was not a saccharide. Highly purified "transforming principle" was rich in nucleic acids but ribonuclease did not alter its activity, hence RNA was not the active agent. The conclusion was almost inescapable: the genetic material is DNA. As Avery commented in May 1943, "Who could have guessed it?"

Avery, MacLeod, and McCarty submitted a paper in late 1943, and it was published in the *Journal of Experimental Medicine* in 1944. Although Avery was a highly respected scientist, and bacteriologists and other researchers took note of his paper, his findings remained highly controversial. Many argued that the DNA was, in all likelihood, contaminated with chromosomal protein. Those who have analyzed the slow acceptance

"Acetyl CoA"; "Adenosine triphosphate (ATP)"

1944 EXPERIMENT SUPPORTING DNA AS THE GENETIC SUBSTANCE

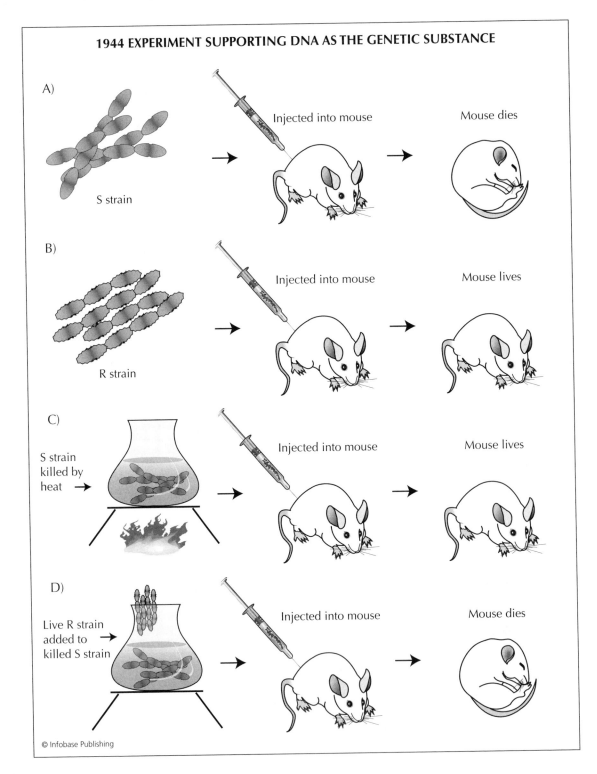

A)

S strain

Injected into mouse

Mouse dies

B)

R strain

Injected into mouse

Mouse lives

C)

S strain killed by heat →

Injected into mouse

Mouse lives

D)

Live R strain added to killed S strain →

Injected into mouse

Mouse dies

© Infobase Publishing

(Opposite page) *Schematic diagram of the Avery experiment in 1944 that established DNA as the genetic material: A) Injection of virulent S (smooth) strain of pneumonococcal bacteria into mice killing them. B) Mice survive injection of the nonvirulent R (rough) strain of pneumococci. C) When the virulent S strain is heat killed and injected into mice, they survive. D) When killed S strain is combined with live nonvirulent R strain, the mice die due to transfer of genetic material from killed S to live R.*

of Avery's groundbreaking result focus on his quiet, self-effacing nature. In addition, the journal selected for publication was not as prestigious as *Science, Nature,* or the *Proceedings of the National Academy of Sciences.* But the best argument seems to be that without understanding the structure of DNA there was no logical basis for knowing how this seemingly "monotonous" and information-poor compound could function as the genetic material. However, at Columbia University, Erwin Chargaff (1905–2002) read the paper and made DNA the top priority of his research laboratory. By 1950, he would establish that the G, A, T, C compositions, constant in a given species, vary considerably from species to species. Even more important, the percent of C = the percent of G; the percent of T = the percent of A ("Chargaff's rule"). It was becoming apparent that DNA is rich in information.

Making Benzenes: From Acetylenes and via Zeolites

When Richard Willstätter reported the first synthesis of cyclooctatetraene (COT, C_8H_8) in 1904, he employed a multistep, rational synthesis to obtain a low yield of his target molecule. Starting in 1940 and culminating in 1948, Walter J. Reppe (1892–1969) at the German firm BASF discovered a "one-pot" route to COT: reaction of acetylene (C_2H_2) at elevated temperature and pressure in the presence of a catalyst [$Ni(CO)_4$]. There are a number of simple pathways that convert COT into ethylbenzene and related species. A slight change in catalyst [$Ni(CO)_4$ to which $P(C_6H_5)_3$ is added] converts acetylene into benzene (C_6H_6). Although it offered great potential for synthesis of some valuable substituted benzenes, modified multistep "Reppe-style" syntheses prevail today. Reppe has been called the "father of acetylene chemistry" because of his success during the 1920s in using acetylene, produced from coal or petroleum cracking, as a vinyl (C_2) "add-on" in a number of syntheses of useful chemical intermediates.

Zeolites are complex inorganic minerals whose crystals contain pores that are regular and molecule-sized. The first natural zeolite was discovered in 1756 by the Swedish chemist Axel Frederic Cronstedt (1703–68). Heating a sample of the mineral using a blowpipe he watched it literally boil off water ("zeolite" is derived from the Greek "boiling stone"). In 1932, James W. McBain (1882–1953), at Bristol, discovered that zeolites have the ability to separate ("sieve") molecules on the basis of size and shape and coined the term "molecular sieve." In 1948, Richard M. Barrer (1910–96), in London and then Aberdeen, made the first artificial zeolite, mordenite, by mixing colloidal silica, sodium aluminate, potassium hydroxide, and sodium hydroxide and heating in an autoclave. The solid formed had a formula of roughly $[Na(AlSi_5O_{12}).3H_2O]$ and consists of five-membered rings (counting the SiO_4 and AlO_4 tetrahedra) in regular arrangements. Starting in 1949, Robert M. Milton (1920–80) and Donald W. Breck, in the Linde Air Products Division of Union Carbide, began to perfect zeolites as agents for purifying gases. In 1953, Linde Type A molecular sieves were employed commercially to remove oxygen (O_2) from argon. During the late 1950s, Hungarian-born Jule A. Rabo (1923–   ), working at Linde, pioneered the discovery of zeolites as catalysts for the cracking of heavy crude petroleum to gasoline. Molecular sieves would eventually save hundreds of millions of barrels of oil in later decades.

Chemistry and World War II

During World War II chemists contributed to the Allied effort by developing and producing antibacterials (sulfa drugs, penicillin), antimalarials, and synthetic buna-S (GR-S) rubber. They contributed to the purification of uranium 235 and plutonium 239 as well as the development of conventional explosives needed for the Manhattan Project.

It is a human tragedy that once wars start they develop their own momentum and logic. World War I began with hints of civility and degenerated into poison gas warfare. The character of World War II, on the other hand, was established early: the rape of Nanking by the Japanese during 1937–38 and a genocidal holocaust in Europe by technologically proficient Nazis and their allies. On November 8, 1940, in retaliation for an air attack by the Royal Air Force on Munich, the headquarters of the Nazi party, 500 German bombers massed and dropped incendiary bombs (white phosphorus) and high explosives, virtually destroying the city of Coventry in England. Indiscriminate bombing of civilian populations became the rule for the Allies as well as the Axis powers.

In this frightening and desperate environment new, more effective weapons of war were sought. The discovery that thickeners, added to gasoline, produce a "jelly" that flows smoothly under pressure and sticks to its target led to the development of napalm. This ghastly agent of war was developed in 1942–43 in the laboratory of Louis F. Fieser at Harvard. Naphthenate and palmitate (hence na-palm) "soaps" of aluminum were added, with charcoal and wood fillers, to thicken gasoline. Napalm was used in flamethrowers (particularly against troops in caves and bunkers) as well as in fire bombs and land mines. It burns at a temperature greater than 3,700°F (2,040°C), sufficient to melt steel, and kills by asphyxiation if the victims escape incineration. Napalm was used by the Allies in the firebombing of Tokyo in March 1945 and in two attacks in February 1945 that destroyed Dresden in Germany. Novelist Kurt Vonnegut, an

American prisoner of war (POW), was in Dresden and survived the fire-bombing of the city as he hid deep in the cellar of a slaughterhouse. In his 1963 novel *Cat's Cradle*, Vonnegut ruminates over the evil that may emerge from the noble intentions of technology. His 1968 novel *Slaughterhouse Five* was, in a sense, a catharsis for his Dresden experience.

Although considerable research was performed to discover new high explosives, innovation in this area actually involved the discovery in 1940 at McGill University of a safe and effective means of manufacturing RDX ("royal demolition explosive" and sometimes "research department explosive," hexahydro-1,3,5-trinitro-1,3,5-triazene). The explosive properties of this compound, first synthesized during the 1890s by German chemist Hans Henning and marketed as a medicine, were discovered around 1920. Bombs commonly included mixtures of TNT and RDX. In 1941 Werner E. Bachmann (1901–51), at the University of Michigan and John C. Sheehan (1915–92), who had just completed his Ph.D. with Bachmann, developed a process for RDX manufacture and also discovered the closely related high explosive HMX ("high melting explosive," octanitro-1,3,5,7-tetranitro-1,3,5,7-tetrazocine). Sheehan would move on to Merck, a company very much involved in penicillin study and manufacture, and then to MIT where he would complete the first penicillin synthesis in 1957. Research on poison gases during World War II focused on organophosphorus nerve agents such as tabun and sarin. Although these agents were never used against soldiers during the war, Mussolini had employed mustard agent (see chapter 2) during his 1935–36 invasion of Ethiopia. Hydrogen cyanide was used to kill millions of victims in the gas chambers of World War II concentration camps.

Chemistry and the Manhattan Project

In 1938, nuclear fission was discovered in Germany, the cradle of modern physics. Einstein's mass-energy law ($E = mc^2$) demonstrated that the energies of nuclear explosions are millions of times greater than those obtainable from chemical explosives such as TNT. Although many great physicists and chemists fled Germany during the 1930s, a significant number of the world's most brilliant scientists and engineers remained. The possibility of atomic bombs in the hands of Hitler was so frightening that President Franklin D. Roosevelt, heeding an urgent 1939 letter from Albert Einstein and Leo Szilard (1898–1964), would authorize the top-secret Manhattan Project. In 1941 the Federal Office of Science Research and Development (OSRD) was established under the supervision of Vannevar Bush (1890–1974), a professor of electrical engineering at Massachusetts Institute of Technology (MIT). (Later, a chemistry effort [Division B] would be headed by Harvard chemist James B. Conant [1893–1978]). Although related work had begun earlier, the Manhattan Project would start in August 1942. The director of the Manhattan Project, General Leslie Groves (1896–1970), an engineer who had supervised construction of the Pentagon, was appointed in September 1942. In Oak Ridge, Tennessee there would be a massive effort to isolate the fissionable isotope of uranium, U 235, that comprises only 0.72 percent of naturally occurring uranium (U 238 comprises 99.27 percent). In Hanford, Washington, another massive effort would focus on the nuclear synthesis and chemical separation of the fissionable isotope of the newly discovered element plutonium, Pu 239. The third major site of the Manhattan Project was Los Alamos, New Mexico, where the nuclear fuels were sent and the bombs assembled. Its supervision was the responsibility of Berkeley physicist J. Robert Oppenheimer (1904–67), "the father of the atomic bomb."

The Brookings Institution estimates the entire cost of the Manhattan Project at $21.57 billion (in 1996 dollars). It employed 125,000 people, sworn to secrecy, and was larger than the nation's entire automobile industry. Its team of American, Canadian, British, and European refugee scientists included the greatest minds in chemistry, physics, and engineering and a vast array of superb scientists and engineers working under their direction. Four atomic bombs were fabricated. The first was tested in the desert at the Trinity test site some 60 miles northwest of Alamogordo, New Mexico, on July 16, 1945. The second, a U 235 bomb dubbed Little Boy, was dropped on Hiroshima, Japan on August 6, 1945. It was estimated to be equivalent to 20,000 tons or 40 million pounds of TNT. The Avalon Project of Yale Law School estimates the pre-bomb population of Hiroshima at 255,000, of whom 66,000 died and 69,000 were injured. The third, a Pu 239 bomb dubbed Fat Man, was dropped on August 8, 1945. Nagasaki's pre-bomb population was about 195,000, of whom 39,000 died and 25,000 were wounded. Sixty percent of the immediate deaths at Hiroshima were caused by burns and this was estimated to be more than 90 percent at Nagasaki. Those who died instantaneously were more fortunate than the "walking dead" who eventually succumbed to intense radiation poisoning. Japan surrendered on August 14, 1945, bringing an end to World War II. The fourth bomb was never used.

The technical challenge at Oak Ridge was to provide a large quantity (more than 100 pounds) of over 90 percent purity in U 235. The abundant U 238 isotope and its rare U 235 "contaminant" (the natural ratio is 138:1) have virtually identical chemical properties. The only hope for separation of the minor isotope hinged upon exploitation of the atomic mass difference. Today, purification of U 235 (usually employed at a purity of about 3–4 percent in civilian nuclear reactors) relies upon chemical conversion of metallic uranium into gaseous UF_6. Physical separation then relies upon Graham's law of gaseous effusion (developed in the mid-19th century):

$$\text{Rate}_{Eff}\ (A)/\text{Rate}_{Eff}\ (B) = MW\ (B)/MW\ (A)$$

Since the molecular weight ratio of $^{235}UF_6$ compared to $^{238}UF_6$ is 349/352, the effusion rate of the lighter isotope is only 1.004 times that of the heavier one. The design of the porous membrane to affect the separation was an immense challenge and the K-25 unit at Oak Ridge accomplished a significant degree of separation by repeating this separation stage 4,000 times.

The other major purification technique in Oak Ridge, Electromagnetic Isotope Separation (EMIS), involved the creation of a huge mass spectrometer covering acres. Magnetic fields bend the tracks of ions with higher fields required for higher masses (see chapters 1 and 2). UF_4 was heated and, under the conditions employed, produced $^{235}U^+$ and $^{238}U^+$ ions that could be separated to a considerable extent, although half of the metal was apparently "lost" to the separation unit.

In practice, Oak Ridge employed the following sequence: Natural uranium (0.7 percent U 235) was purified in Building S-50, by a process termed thermal diffusion, to a level of 0.86 percent U 235 (this step would be deleted following completion of the first bomb). This material was purified to a level of about 7 percent U 235 via gaseous diffusion in Building K-25. The product was transferred to Building Y-12 where two separate units, termed α and β, performed sequential separations using the EMIS technique. After completion of the α-stage, the material was enriched to about 15 percent U 235 and upon completion of the β-stage, purification exceeded 90 percent U 235.

While the separations at Oak Ridge were mostly of a physical nature, dependent upon differences in atomic or molecular masses, separations at the Hanford site were mostly chemical in nature. Bombardment of uranium with neutrons produced Pu 239, a mixture of lighter metals, notably rare earths, created as nuclear fission by-products, and unchanged uranium. One consequence of the Hanford operation was the development of ion-exchange chromatography as a major purification and analytical method to separate the rare earths. It would become a general technique for separating ionic substances.

In Los Alamos, it was understood that the way to achieve a nuclear detonation using U 235 was to instantaneously assemble a *critical mass* of fuel. In the U 235 bomb this was achieved by firing part of the critical mass at the remainder, using a gun-type detonator. The problem of achieving critical mass for the Pu 239 bomb was more complex and was ultimately solved by George Kistiakowsky (1900–82), Harvard University, who recommended surrounding the fuel with high explosive, arranged in a "shaped" beehive-like arrangement, in the bomb casing. This "explosion lens" would compress the fuel in order to cause the explosion. Both bombs were ignited in the atmosphere using an altimeter mechanism.

Einstein would later declare "The unleashed power of the atom has changed everything save our modes of thinking, and thus we will drift toward unparalleled catastrophe." In 1945 a group of nuclear scientists began a magazine that continues today titled *Bulletin of the Atomic Scientists*. Its goal is to reduce the threat of nuclear war. Starting in 1947 each cover included the "doomsday clock," changed 17 times over the next six decades to reflect the current state of danger (in 1952 it read two minutes to midnight after the first test of the hydrogen bomb).

Carbon 14: Probing Photosynthesis and Measuring Archaeological Time

On the day the Japanese surrendered, Ernest Lawrence, director of the Berkeley Radiation Laboratory, told his young faculty colleague Melvin Calvin (1911–97) that it was "time to do something useful with carbon 14." Carbon 14 was first prepared at Berkeley in 1940 by the Russia-born American chemist Martin D. Kamen (1913–2002). Kamen wished to probe the mechanism of CO_2 incorporation in photosynthesis using radioactive carbon, but only carbon 11 was accessible and its short half-life (21 minutes) made it impractical. Firing deuterons (^2H) at graphite (^{12}C) he made radioactive ^{14}C that was, by comparison, very long-lived. Before Kamen could further pursue investigation of photosynthesis he became immersed in the Manhattan Project effort.

Schematic depiction of Calvin's use of carbon 14 to label intermediates and discover the carbon pathway in photosynthesis

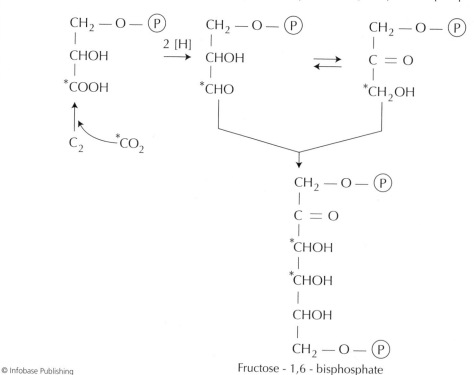

CALVIN'S USE OF RADIO-LABELED (^{14}C) CARBON DIOXIDE TO DEDUCE THE MECHANISM OF PHOTOSYNTHESIS

He would later have political difficulties during the McCarthy era of the early 1950s.

Calvin began his studies in 1945 and would succeed during the following decade in tracing the photosynthetic pathway from carbon dioxide to glucose. This pathway was distinct from the Hill reaction (see chapter 4) that employed light to convert water to oxygen. Calvin would infuse live algae cells with $^{14}CO_2$ ($^*CO_2$), stop the reaction at various time intervals

Scientist of the Decade: Dorothy Crowfoot Hodgkin (1910–1994)

Dorothy Crowfoot was born in Cairo where her father administered schools for the British government. Her interests in science and crystals were evident at an early age and she read a children's book, *Concerning the Nature of Things,* by William Henry Bragg, one of the fathers of crystallography. She

entered Oxford in 1926, graduated in 1931 and, in 1932, joined the crystallography research group of J. D. Bernal at Cambridge. Bernal had studied crystallography with William H. Bragg who, unlike most of

(continues)

Dorothy Crowfoot Hodgkin, winner of the 1964 Nobel Prize in chemistry (AIP Emilio Segrè Visual Archives, Physics Today Collection)

(continued)

his contemporaries, was very welcoming to female scientists and Bernal maintained this tradition.

In Cambridge, Crowfoot studied steroids and helped contribute to solving the correct structure of cholesterol and other steroids in 1932. She was recruited as tutor to Somerville College, Oxford in 1934 and left the convivial Bernal group. It was here that she began her crystallographic study of insulin that would, some three decades hence, become one of her greatest triumphs. In 1937, she married historian Thomas Hodgkin and they would raise three children. Hodgkin was completely supportive of his wife's career, sharing child-rearing responsibilities, as she began a distinguished career. In 1942, now Dorothy Crowfoot Hodgkin, she took on the very challenging and important task of determining the structure of penicillin. She solved this structure in 1945, too late for the war effort, but set the stage for future syntheses of literally tens of thousands of penicillin derivatives. She was admitted to the Royal Society in 1947, only the third woman in its nearly three-century-old history. In 1948, Dr. Hodgkin audaciously tackled the structure of vitamin B_{12}, only recently recognized as the active anti-pernicious anemia substance. The empirical formula of the red crystals supplied to her was known at the time to be approximately: $C_{61-64}H_{84-90}N_{14}O_{13-14}PCo$. Hodgkin completed structural determination of this enormously complex compound in 1956. In turn, her work set the stage for the joint effort, by more than 100 researchers in the R. B. Woodward (Harvard) and Albert Eschenmoser (1925–) (ETH in Zurich) research groups, that achieved the molecule's total synthesis in 1972 after 11 years of brilliant chemistry.

Her pacifist activism during the 1930s and membership in the Science for Peace organization following World War II attracted the attention of the U.S. Department of State during the 1950s. Dr. Hodgkin was denied a visa to attend a scientific meeting in 1953, and encountered political obstacles in the USA for nearly three more decades. She advanced only slowly through the faculty ranks in Oxford and when she finally did achieve the rank of a professorial chair, the Wolfson Research Professorship of the Royal Society, it was funded by the society and not the university. Four years later Professor Dorothy Crowfoot Hodgkin received the 1964 Nobel Prize in chemistry. She would retire formally in 1977 but remained scientifically active until she died in 1994.

The welcoming laboratory of William H. Bragg and his students, including J. D. Bernal, started a multigeneration network of famous female crystallographers: Kathleen Yardley Lonsdale (see chapter 4) studied with Bragg; Crowfoot with Bernal. During the 1940s, Rosalind Franklin (1920–58), whose X-ray results furnished the critical data for solving the structure of DNA, learned crystallography from Marcel Mathieu, another W. H. Bragg student, in Paris. One of Dorothy Crowfoot Hodgkin's research students was a certain Margaret Hilda Roberts (later Thatcher; 1925–), elected decades later, as a member of the Conservative Party, prime minister of the United Kingdom: the first and only woman to serve as prime minister and the longest service as PM (1979–90) in 150 years. One can only try to imagine the animated dinner discussions involving the future Conservative prime minister and the left-leaning Hodgkin household.

by plunging the sample into alcohol, work up the products by paper chromatography, and check the distribution of the radiolabel among the products. The accompanying figure on page 172 depicts the application of carbon 14 labeling to one photosynthesis reaction. Calvin's work would gain him the 1961 Nobel Prize in chemistry.

In 1947, Willard F. Libby (1908–80), at the University of Chicago, proposed the concept of carbon dating using carbon 14. It was then understood that cosmic rays enter Earth's atmosphere generating high-energy neutrons that collide with atmospheric nitrogen (^{14}N in N_2) and convert it to ^{14}C with emission of a proton. The newly created ^{14}C reacts with atmospheric oxygen to generate $^{14}CO_2$. If the cosmic ray bombardment is constant (not strictly true over thousands of years), then there is a minuscule but constant (steady-state) ratio of $^{14}CO_2/^{12}CO2$ in the atmosphere. Living organisms incorporate CO_2 (into plants; animals eat plants; animals are eaten by other animals; microorganisms provide cleanup of dead plants and animals) and "fix" this $^{14}C/^{12}C$ ratio in their bodies. Once a living organism dies, incorporation of CO_2 stops, the ^{14}C continues radioactive decay, and the $^{14}C/^{12}C$ ratio decreases with time.

In 1949, Libby and coworkers determined the half-life ($t_{1/2}$) of carbon 14 to be 5,568 ± 40 years. Researchers at Cambridge University later refined this value to 5,730 ± 40 years. Carbon 14 dating is generally employed for objects of less than 50,000 years in age. Its value, particularly to archaeologists and anthropologists, simply cannot be overstated. For developing carbon 14 dating Libby received the 1960 Nobel Prize in chemistry.

Conclusion

The end of World War II would witness the birth of an optimistic and energetic society that would rebuild war-torn Europe and help Japan establish a stable democracy. The late 1940s and the 1950s would witness a huge increase in the consumption of petroleum products in cars, larger houses, and more throwaway plastics. The atomic bomb, developed by the Manhattan Project, would become a specter haunting the remainder of the century and beyond and would prompt unprecedented political activism by scientists on education, nuclear disarmament, and the environment. The revolution in the design and synthesis of pharmaceuticals based upon the ever-increasing knowledge concerning metabolic pathways, started during the 1940s, would blossom into a broad spectrum of effective drugs to fight infections. The 1940s witnessed the true beginnings of structural biology and the science that would lead to the discovery of the structure of DNA in 1953.

Further Reading

American Chemical Society. *The Pharmaceutical Century: Ten Decades of Drug Discovery*. Washington, D.C.: American Chemical Society, 2000. This book provides an accessible coverage of the decade-by-decade developments in pharmaceutical chemistry.

Bird, Kai, and Martin J. Sherwin. "Building the Bomb." *Smithsonian* 36 (August 2005): 88–96. This article is adapted from the book by these authors on the history of the atomic bomb: *American Prometheus*. New York: Alfred A. Knopf, 2005.

Bowden, Mary Ellen, Amy Beth Crow, and Tracy Sullivan. *Pharmaceutical Achievers: The Human Face of Pharmaceutical Research*. Philadelphia: Chemical Heritage Press, 2003. This book provides brief biographies of notable chemists in the pharmaceutical industry.

Chemical Heritage Foundation, Philadelphia. *The Life and Science of Percy Lavon Julian*. Available online. URL: www.chemheritage.org/scialive. Accessed February 12, 2006. This site describes the life and scientific contributions of the African-American chemist Percy L. Julian.

Dewel, Guy, Dilip Kondepudi, and Ilya Prigogine. "Chemistry Far from Equilibrium: Thermodynamics, Order, and Chaos." In *The New Chemistry*, edited by Nona Hall, 440–446. Cambridge: Cambridge University Press (2000). This chapter describes the mathematics of systems far removed from equilibrium and the chemical consequences.

Hodgkin, Dorothy Crowfoot. *Birkbeck, Science and History. The First Bernal Lecture Delivered at Birkbeck College London, 23rd October, 1969*. London: Birkbech College, 1970. This brief presentation was made in honor of Dorothy Hodgkin's early mentor J. D. Bernal.

Hughes, Jeff. *The Manhattan Project: Big Science and the Atom Bomb*. New York: Columbia University Press, 2003. This book provides historical coverage of the Manhattan Project emphasizing organization of big science.

National Academy Press, Washington, D.C. "Biographical Members: Percy Lavon Julian," Available online. URL: www.nap.edu/html/biomems/pjulian.html. Accessed February 12, 2006. This is a brief biography of the African-American pioneer Percy L. Julian.

Remers, William A. *Chemists at War: Accounts of Chemical Research in the United States During World War II*. Tucson: Clarice Publications, 2000. This book summarizes the wide-ranging contributions of chemistry in World War II, arranged in chapters according to area (e.g., medicines, explosives).

Settle, Frank. "Nuclear Chemistry Uranium Enrichment," Available online. URL: http://chemcases.com/nuclear/nc-07.htm. 2005. Accessed February 12, 2006. This site provides coverage of the purification of uranium during the Manhattan Project.

Snow, C. P. *Science and Government*. Cambridge: Harvard University Press, 1961. This brief book provides a cautionary case study about how a narrow range of scientific advice to Prime Minister Winston Churchill had potentially disastrous results.

WGBH. *NOVA: Forgotten Genius*. Boston: WGBH, 2007. This two-hour television program highlights the autobiography of the African-American chemist Percy L. Julian.

6

1951–1960:
Unveiling the Structures of
Fabulous Biological Molecules

Discoveries of Biosynthetic Pathways and the Structures of DNA and Proteins

The 1950s would witness a revolution in structural biology, a renaissance in inorganic chemistry, and new frontiers in the applications of chemical theory, chemical structure proof, and total organic synthesis. Solution of the double helix structure of DNA came rapidly on the heels of the solution of the protein α-helix structure. Determinations of the amino acid sequences of insulin and ribonuclease-A were accomplished even as the three-dimensional structures of myoglobin and hemoglobin were solved. Total syntheses of cortisone, cholesterol, penicillin-G, and chlorophyll whetted the appetites of synthetic chemists for targets such as vitamin B_{12} recently determined by X-ray. Carbon 14 labeling would clarify the pathway for photosynthesis as well as biosyntheses of terpenes and steroids. New types of inorganic compounds, such as organometallic "sandwich" compounds and electron-deficient boron compounds, challenged theorists who would also begin to make major contributions to organic chemistry.

A Man-Made Supernova on the Surface of Our Planet

Although the United States and Russia (Union of Soviet Socialist Republics [USSR]) were, formally speaking, allies during World War II, the postwar occupation of Eastern Europe by the USSR behind an "iron curtain," its mercurial and murderous Communist leader Joseph Stalin (1879–1953), and the pervasive fear of nuclear weapons contributed to the start of the cold war. The USSR detonated its first atomic bomb in 1949 and the ensuing arms race would dominate the second half of the 20th century.

On November 1, 1952, the United States detonated the world's first hydrogen bomb ("Ivy Mike") over Enewetak Island in the Pacific Ocean. The H-bomb relies upon *nuclear fusion* rather than nuclear fission and produces vastly greater energy than the atomic bomb. It requires an atomic bomb to create temperatures exceeding the 100 million °F necessary to fuse small nuclei, hence the term *thermonuclear* for the H-bomb. The fuel inside the first H-bomb was lithium deuteride (LiD or Li^2H) and the enormous temperatures and neutron flux created helium and tritium nuclei, fusing deuterium with tritium and tritium with tritium. The first H-bomb was estimated to be equivalent to 10.4 million tons of TNT—nearly 1,000 times more powerful than the atomic bomb dropped over Hiroshima. In 1953, the USSR tested its first H-bomb.

Following the 1952 atmospheric test, Albert Ghiorso and his Berkeley colleagues learned that plutonium 244 was formed in the explosion and realized this could occur if uranium 238 had absorbed six neutrons. Such conditions had never been witnessed in nuclear accelerators and caused great excitement among the scientists. Initially they obtained a sample of filter paper covered with fallout (radioactive dust), collected by an airplane sampling the dust cloud. Upon discovering emissions of *alpha*-particles of unprecedented energy they requested and received barrels of fallout dust from a neighboring Pacific Island. Employing ion

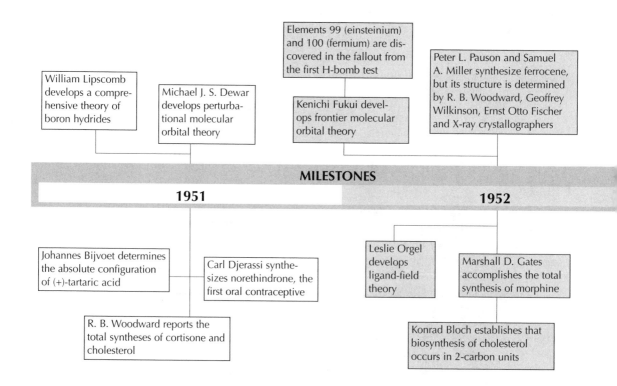

William Lipscomb develops a comprehensive theory of boron hydrides

Michael J. S. Dewar develops perturbational molecular orbital theory

Elements 99 (einsteinium) and 100 (fermium) are discovered in the fallout from the first H-bomb test

Kenichi Fukui develops frontier molecular orbital theory

Peter L. Pauson and Samuel A. Miller synthesize ferrocene, but its structure is determined by R. B. Woodward, Geoffrey Wilkinson, Ernst Otto Fischer and X-ray crystallographers

MILESTONES

1951

1952

Johannes Bijvoet determines the absolute configuration of (+)-tartaric acid

Carl Djerassi synthesizes norethindrone, the first oral contraceptive

R. B. Woodward reports the total syntheses of cortisone and cholesterol

Leslie Orgel develops ligand-field theory

Marshall D. Gates accomplishes the total synthesis of morphine

Konrad Bloch establishes that biosynthesis of cholesterol occurs in 2-carbon units

chromatography, Ghiorso and his colleagues discovered two new actinide elements: 99 (einsteinium) and 100 (fermium).

According to modern theory the universe began some 15 billion years ago. In the first three minutes of the big bang, fusion reactions formed deuterium, helium, and some lithium. Synthesis of nuclei, as heavy as iron (26), is a continuing process in stars larger than the Sun (e.g., red giants). Iron 56 has the greatest binding energy per nucleon of any nucleus. Such synthesis is termed the "slow" or "s-process" since it takes place over thousands of years. The surface temperature of the Sun (roughly 11,000°F) is too low for fusion of hydrogen to helium; this occurs in the sun's interior (ca. 27 million °F). Supernovas exceed temperatures of 100 million °F and that is where synthesis of elements higher in atomic number than iron takes place. Elements 99 and 100 were created in a manmade supernova in the atmosphere of our own planet!

The original einsteinium isotope discovered in Enewetak fallout was ^{252}Es with a half-life of 20 days. Eventually other einsteinium isotopes were created under controlled conditions. The longest-lived is ^{254}Es, $t_{1/2}$ = 275 days. The longest-lived isotope of fermium is ^{257}Fm, $t_{1/2}$ = 100.5 days. Chemically speaking, einsteinium and fermium are

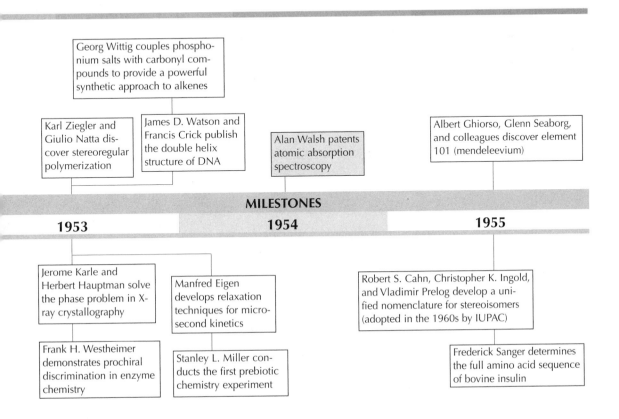

Georg Wittig couples phosphonium salts with carbonyl compounds to provide a powerful synthetic approach to alkenes

Karl Ziegler and Giulio Natta discover stereoregular polymerization

James D. Watson and Francis Crick publish the double helix structure of DNA

Alan Walsh patents atomic absorption spectroscopy

Albert Ghiorso, Glenn Seaborg, and colleagues discover element 101 (mendeleevium)

MILESTONES

1953   **1954**   **1955**

Jerome Karle and Herbert Hauptman solve the phase problem in X-ray crystallography

Manfred Eigen develops relaxation techniques for microsecond kinetics

Robert S. Cahn, Christopher K. Ingold, and Vladimir Prelog develop a unified nomenclature for stereoisomers (adopted in the 1960s by IUPAC)

Frank H. Westheimer demonstrates prochiral discrimination in enzyme chemistry

Stanley L. Miller conducts the first prebiotic chemistry experiment

Frederick Sanger determines the full amino acid sequence of bovine insulin

most stable in the +3 oxidation state as expected for actinides, as Seaborg predicted.

Two other new artificial elements were created at Berkeley during the 1950s by Ghiorso, Seaborg, and their colleagues. In early 1955, bombarding einsteinium 253 with helium ions produced the 256 isotope of element 101 (mendelevium), $t_{1/2}$ = 76 minutes. The most stable isotope of mendelevium is ^{258}Md, $t_{1/2}$ = 2 months. In early 1957, American, British, and Swedish scientists claimed synthesis of element 102, tentatively named nobelium. Studies during the 1960s demonstrated that the 1957 claim was incorrect. Unambiguous creation of 102 was reported in 1958; the name nobelium was retained. Its most stable isotope is ^{255}No, $t_{1/2}$ = 3 minutes. Mendelevium and nobelium behave chemically as actinides.

Serendipity and "The Renaissance of Inorganic Chemistry"

During the first half of the 20th century it was understood that bonds between carbon and transition metals are weak and very reactive. For

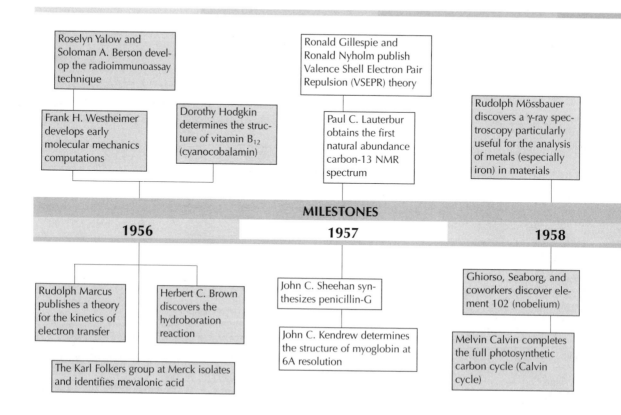

example, diethylzinc, made by Edward Frankland (1825–99) in 1849, is pyrophoric (spontaneously flammable in air). Although a stable salt of platinum and ethylene, $KPtCl_3(C_2H_4)$, was prepared by William C. Zeise (1789–1847) in 1827, its nature would remain a mystery for well over a century. It was thus a great surprise when Peter L. Pauson (1925–   ) and his graduate student Thomas J. Kealy (1927–   ) at Duquesne University disclosed their work in *Nature* in late 1951 describing a stable yellow crystalline compound of formula $C_{10}H_{10}Fe$ that does not decompose at 750°F (400°C). Samuel A. Miller (1912–70) and coworkers at the British Oxygen Company had earlier heated cyclopentadiene over iron filings under N_2 obtaining the same substance; their paper was published in early 1952. Both research groups postulated an open linear structure with a central C-Fe-C linkage.

Reports of a "rock-stable" organo-iron compound provoked considerable interest in the chemical community. At Harvard, R. B. Woodward and a junior faculty colleague, Geoffrey Wilkinson (1921–96), agreed that the compound's structure was likely to be the unprecedented "sandwich" represented by the figure to the right. With two young

Ferrocene

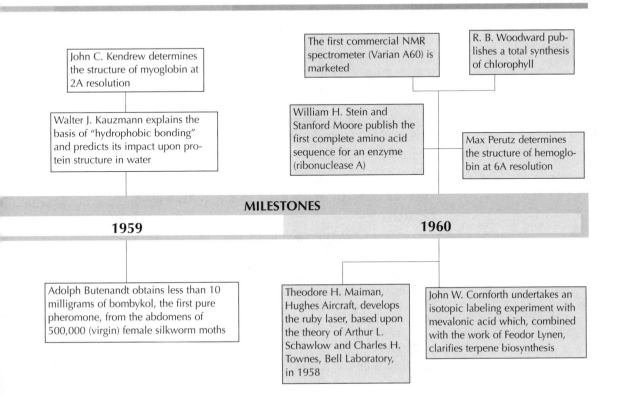

John C. Kendrew determines the structure of myoglobin at 2A resolution

Walter J. Kauzmann explains the basis of "hydrophobic bonding" and predicts its impact upon protein structure in water

The first commercial NMR spectrometer (Varian A60) is marketed

William H. Stein and Stanford Moore publish the first complete amino acid sequence for an enzyme (ribonuclease A)

R. B. Woodward publishes a total synthesis of chlorophyll

Max Perutz determines the structure of hemoglobin at 6A resolution

MILESTONES

1959

1960

Adolph Butenandt obtains less than 10 milligrams of bombykol, the first pure pheromone, from the abdomens of 500,000 (virgin) female silkworm moths

Theodore H. Maiman, Hughes Aircraft, develops the ruby laser, based upon the theory of Arthur L. Schawlow and Charles H. Townes, Bell Laboratory, in 1958

John W. Cornforth undertakes an isotopic labeling experiment with mevalonic acid which, combined with the work of Feodor Lynen, clarifies terpene biosynthesis

coworkers, they conducted experiments that eliminated the open C-Fe-C structure and jointly published their structure in 1952. Ernest Otto Fischer (1918–), at the Technical University of Munich, had also read the initial papers on $C_{10}H_{10}Fe$ and independently proposed the same structure. Each of the two 5-membered rings are cyclopentadienide ($C_5H_5^-$), a stable anion "obeying" the Hückel 4n +2 rule (see chapter 4). Two other research groups soon obtained positive proof, using X-ray crystallography, for this "sandwich" structure: Philip F. Eiland and Ray Pepinsky at Penn State and Jack D. Dunitz (1923–) and Leslie E. Orgel (1927–) at Oxford. Woodward postulated that the amazing stability of the new compound made it a kind of three-dimensional benzene and his laboratory confirmed its ability to undergo a characteristic benzene substitution reaction, hence the name "ferrocene" to evoke its similarity to benzene.

Woodward would author two more papers on ferrocene and then return to his first love, syntheses of complex natural products that would eventually earn him the 1965 Nobel Prize in chemistry. In 1955, Fischer synthesized dibenzenechromium [$(C_6H_6)_2Cr$]. He and Wilkinson would continue to independently pioneer organometallic chemistry. In 1973, they would share the Nobel Prize in chemistry. It is ironic that the two groups that discovered ferrocene did not share the Nobel Prize, rather they were beaten to the structure proof by other research groups. Woodward himself protested that he should have shared this Nobel Prize. Presumably, the Nobel Committee chose to recognize ferrocene as part of a lifetime of achievement in organometallic chemistry by both Wilkinson and Fischer. And yet another irony: Prior to these discoveries, Union Carbide Corporation encountered problems caused by a yellow sludge clogging iron pipes pumping cyclopentadiene. It was ferrocene, but the realization occurred after the fundamental discoveries were published.

Novel Structures and New Theories of Bonding

The amazing stability of ferrocene demanded a fresh look at chemical theory. When Dunitz and Orgel published their X-ray structure of ferrocene, they also provided a theoretical explanation of the chemical bonding using *ligand field theory*. Crystal-field theory had been developed around 1930 by physicists Hans A. Bethe (1906–2005) and John H. Van Vleck (1899–1980). It treated a transition metal (M) in a compound such as MX_6 by considering M and the X groups to be ions whose only influence is electrostatic. It was, however, clear from the properties of ferrocene and metal carbonyls like $Fe(CO)_5$ that these were covalent compounds and covalent bonding needed to be part of any theoretical treatment of these compounds. Gas-phase electron diffraction studies of metal carbonyls, published during the 1930s by Lawrence O. Brockway (1907–79), provided useful structural data for the later molecular orbital studies of organometallic compounds.

In 1951, Michael J. S. Dewar (1918–97) published a molecular orbital (MO) theory of bonding between unsaturated compounds and transition metals later augmented by Joseph Chatt (1914–94) and Leonard A. Duncanson. It recognized σ-type overlap of an occupied π-orbital on the ligand (e.g., ethylene, benzene, cyclopentadienide) with a vacant d-orbital of appropriate symmetry on the transition metal, coupled with "back-donation" through π-type overlap of an occupied d-orbital on the metal with a vacant (antibonding) π*-type orbital on the ligand.

Alfred Stock's pioneering studies of air-sensitive boron hydrides (see chapter 2) made these novel compounds accessible for structure determination starting in the 1940s. Boron hydrides are commonly termed "electron deficient" since they contain fewer valence electrons than valence orbitals. In 1941, spectroscopic analysis of diborane by Fred Stitt provided the first evidence of a hydrogen-bridged structure (see the figure on page 184; the geometric parameters were later determined using electron diffraction). In 1949, Hugh Christopher Longuet-Higgins (1923–2004) provided the first description of a new type of covalent bond, the three-center two-electron BHB bond (Part B of the figure on page 184); an MO description is depicted in Part C of the figure. In 1950, a breakthrough in crystallographic analysis by David Harker (1906–91) and John S. Kasper (1915–) at General Electric provided the means to solve the first structure of a higher-order boron hydride, decaborane ($B_{10}H_{11}$, see the structure, right), demonstrating electron-deficient B-B-B bonding. During the following two years William N. Lipscomb (1919–) and William J. Dalmage, University of Minnesota, and Kenneth W. Hedberg (1920–), Morton E. Jones (1928–), and Verner Schomaker (1914–97), at Caltech, solved structures for B_5H_9 and then B_4H_{10}. Lipscomb developed a set of rules useful in predicting new members of the boron hydride class. Many of these were subsequently synthesized, demonstrating the power of his theory. For his pioneering studies in structural inorganic chemistry, Lipscomb received the 1976 Nobel Prize in chemistry.

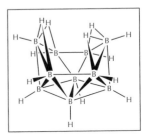

Decaborane ($B_{10}H_{11}$)

Lewis-Langmuir electron-dot formulas (see chapter 2) account for bonding and nonbonding ("lone") pairs of electrons in molecules. Lone pairs were employed by Nevil J. Sidgwick (see chapter 3) to account for dative bonds and the bonding in the coordination compounds explored by Alfred Werner (see chapter 1). In 1927, Sidgwick predicted special stability for transition metal compounds that attain the closed-shell configuration of the nearest rare gas: 18 valence-shell electrons. Structural studies of metal carbonyls during the 1930s largely supported the *18-electron rule*. For example, carbon monoxide binds at carbon to transition metals; each CO ligand donates 2 electrons. Since iron is in Group 8 of the periodic table (see page 422), has 8 valence electrons, and requires

STRUCTURE AND BONDING IN DIBORANE (B_2H_6): AN ELECTRON-DEFICIENT MOLECULE

A) Structure (gas-phase electron diffraction)

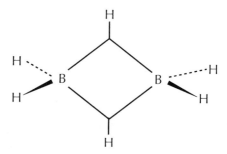

B - H_t 1.19 Å

B - H_b 1.33 Å

B - B   1.77 Å

B) Represent as a pair of three-centered, two-electron bonds

C) Molecular orbital description of B ⬦ B bonding

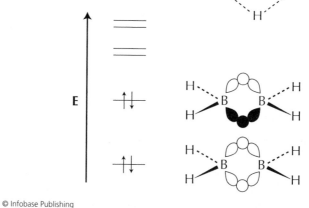

A) Gas-phase structure of diborane (B_2H_6) with structural parameters determined by electron diffraction; B) representation by Longuet-Higgins and Lipscomb of three-center, two-electron bonds; C) molecular orbital description of three-center, two-electron bonding

10 more electrons to satisfy the 18-electron rule, it forms $Fe(CO)_5$. Nickel, in Group 10, requires 8 electrons and forms $Ni(CO)_4$. Ferrocene also obeys the 18-electron rule since it combines Fe^{2+} (6 valence elec-

trons) with two $C_5H_5^-$ ligands, each donating 6 π-electrons. $Cr(C_6H_6)_2$ combines a chromium atom (Group 6) with two benzene molecules, each supplying 6 π-electrons. Decades of research have shown that the eighteen-electron "rule" is very useful but not universal and is really more of a guideline than an absolute rule.

In 1940, Sidgwick and his Oxford colleague Herbert M. Powell (1906–91) published an important paper concerning the relationship between electron pairs and molecular geometry. Seventeen years later, Ronald J. Gillespie (1924–) and Ronald S. Nyholm (1917–72), colleagues at University College in London, extended the Sidgwick-Powell theory with a model that most high school and college chemistry student are taught today. While Gillespie and Nyholm respected Pauling's hybridization theory (see chapter 4), they felt it was abstract and better in explaining known structures than predicting new ones. The theory they developed, *valence shell electron repulsion theory* (*VSEPR*), is as simple as it is useful. An atom's bonded and nonbonded electron pairs are treated as spheres on the spherical surface of that atom. The electron pairs move as far apart from each other as possible. In applying VSEPR to molecular geometry, single bonds, double bonds, and triple bonds are treated as if they are single bonds (one bonded electron pair). Lone pairs are equivalent to bonded pairs, although VSEPR treats them as slightly larger.

VSEPR predicts that an XY_2 molecule with two (bonding) pairs of electrons on the central atom (e.g., $BeCl_2$) will be linear; three bonding pairs (e.g., BCl_3) will assume trigonal planar geometry, and four bonding pairs produce a tetrahedral structure (e.g., CH_4). Werner had, fifty years earlier, entertained a similar idea concerning the geometry of ligands in coordination complexes (six ligands correspond to octahedral geometry). Ammonia (NH_3) is not trigonal planar like BCl_3 because the extra lone pair on nitrogen occupies space and makes the molecule a trigonal pyramid. Similarly, H_2O is not linear like $BeCl_2$ or CO_2 but bent since the oxygen in water has two lone pairs as well as two bonded pairs.

VSEPR theory offers a very simple framework (accessible to the high school student) for making predictions. The most convincing early successes for VSEPR were predictions of the geometries of noble gas compounds (see chapter 7), unknown in 1957, the year Nyholm published "The Renaissance of Inorganic Chemistry."

Three New Spectroscopies for Chemical Elements

Atomic emission spectroscopy, born in the mid-19th century, was immediately applied to analyses of minute quantities of chemical elements (see chapter 1). Almost a century later, Alan Walsh (1916–98), Council for Scientific Research in Melbourne, Australia, posed a fundamental question: Why were chemical elements analyzed by emission spectroscopy while compounds were analyzed by absorption spectroscopy (IR, UV-visible)? When an element is introduced into a flame, only a tiny fraction of its atoms are electronically excited and emit light, limiting the technique's sensitivity. Emission spectroscopy is also plagued by interferences that reduce its sensitivity. Why not explore *atomic* absorption spectroscopy? Walsh demonstrated that light from a sodium vapor lamp is completely absorbed when passed through vaporized saltwater. While he initially used continuum wavelength lamps to analyze other metals, Walsh quickly realized that the best results would be obtained by making an emission lamp of a given metal to produce the spectral sharp line that excites that same metal selectively and sensitively. In 1954, he patented the new technique and started fabricating cathode lamps for different metals. In 1995, he published a landmark paper on atomic absorption spectroscopy. This sensitive and selective technique is widely applied in 21st-century analytical laboratories.

The 1950s witnessed development of two spectroscopies that would provide new insights into chemical bonding, especially for inorganic materials. In Stockholm in 1950, physicist Kai M. Siegbahn (1918–) invented a technique, electron spectroscopy for chemical analysis (ESCA), to measure the kinetic energies of photoelectrons released by substances impacted by X-rays (Einstein's photoelectric effect). In 1954, he moved to Uppsala and continued to improve this X-ray photoelectron spectroscopy technique. ESCA can measure the energies of "K-shell" or core electrons including 1s electrons. Since 1s electrons are not involved in chemical bonding (except for hydrogen atoms), subtle changes in chemical shifts for elements in different environments are related to their charges. The core (1s) energies of metal atoms are higher in their oxides than in the free metals, since metals are positively charged in the oxides. Another illustration is thiosulfate ($S_2O_3^{2-}$): ESCA finds two distinct sulfur 1s peaks corresponding to two distinct sulfur atoms ($[S-SO_3]^{2-}$) having formal charges of -1 and +2 respectively. Kai Siegbahn was awarded a share of the 1981 Nobel Prize in physics for this work. His father Manne Siegbahn (1886–1978) won the Nobel Prize in physics in 1924.

In 1957, Rudolph L. Mössbauer (1929–), working on his doctoral thesis in Heidelberg, discovered that ^{191}Ir nuclei in a solid emit and absorb gamma radiation without recoil. This is quite different from individual atoms, where recoil from γ-ray emission is quite significant. The Mössbauer effect, published in 1958, is the source of Mössbauer spectroscopy, useful for many metal isotopes, but most often applied to ^{57}Fe in solids (including biological substances). In operation, γ-rays from cobalt 57 impact iron 57 to form excited-state nuclei that emit 14.4 KeV γ-rays. Since there is no recoil, the energy resolution (10^{-8} eV) is exceedingly fine and allows measurement of exceedingly subtle chemical differences "sensed" by the ^{57}Fe nucleus in different samples. In operation, the ^{57}Fe γ-ray source is moved toward and away from a stationary solid sample providing a Doppler shift that senses very minute changes in the iron atom environments in various materials. For this discovery Mössbauer shared the 1961 Nobel Prize in physics.

New Theories of Reactivity in Organic Chemistry

During the late 1940s and the 1950s, "arrow-pushing" electronic theories (see chapter 3) rooted in valence-bond structures, started losing ground to molecular orbital theories of organic chemistry. In England Michael J. S. Dewar, Robert Robinson's most brilliant protégé, influenced by Robert Mulliken as well as Charles A. Coulson (1910–74) at Oxford, pioneered the application of quantum mechanics to organic chemistry. Dewar, like Robinson, was an amazing polymath, theorist and experimentalist with wide-ranging interests outside of science and a tough argumentation style. Using techniques pioneered a decade earlier by Erich Hückel (see chapter 4), Dewar's theoretical and experimental study of stipitatic acid in 1945 solved its structure (see the first tropolone structure), attributing to it stability similar to that of benzene. During the period 1944–47 the Japanese chemist, Tetsuo Nozoe (1902–96), deduced the structure of the related compound hinokitiol (see the second tropolone structure), but the work was not widely known until 1950. Dewar named the parent compound "tropolone" (third structure) and predicted its chemical and spectroscopic properties. This was the beginning of nonbenzenoid aromatic chemistry, a field that would take off during the 1950s and 1960s: William von Eggers Doering would report the tropylium cation in 1954; Ronald Breslow (1931–) reported cyclopropenium ion in 1959.

Dewar explained attack of *electrophiles*, such as NO_2^+ on the 1-position (not 2-position of naphthalene, see below) using MO calculations of the nitrated intermediates. In 1951, he published a series of six articles on perturbational molecular orbital (PMO) theory, the start of four decades of computational techniques provided to organic chemists by the Dewar group. After leaving England in 1959 to settle in the United States, Dewar moved to the University of Texas at Austin in 1964 and helped grow one of the country's premier chemistry departments. Kenichi Fukui (1918–98) was born in Japan and educated as a chemical engineer. During World War II he worked in the Army Fuel Laboratory before accepting a faculty position at Kyoto Imperial University in 1943 where he performed experimental studies on a wide range of pure and applied scientific and engineering problems. In 1952, Fukui published a theory of great utility. Reasoning that valence-shell atomic orbitals govern the reactivities of atoms to form molecules, he postulated that valence-level molecular orbitals govern reactions of molecules. Fukui focused on the highest occupied molecular orbital (HOMO) of the electron-donor molecule and the lowest unoccupied molecular orbital (LUMO) of the electron-acceptor molecule as the dominant interaction in their bimolecular reaction. In understanding the preference for attack of NO_2^+ at the 1-position (rather

$X = CO_2H; Y = OH$
$X = CH(CH_3)_2; Y = H$
$X = Y = H$

Tropolones

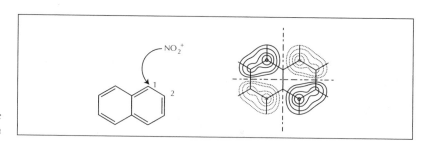

Attack at the 1-naphthalene position

than the 2-position) of naphthalene, Fukui observed that the LUMO of the acceptor (NO_2^+) has a more favorable bonding interaction at the 1-position (because it has more electron density in the HOMO, see the structure above) than at the 2-position. This *frontier orbital* concept would have wide application in chemistry. During the early 1960s a complementary orbital-symmetry model would be developed by R. B. Woodward and Roald Hoffmann (1937–) (see chapter 7). Fukui and Hoffmann would share the 1981 Nobel Prize in chemistry.

Predicting Reactivities of Organic Molecules

It is a major tenet of quantum mechanics that absolutely rigorous calculations can be made only for one-electron systems such as H, He^+, and H_2^+. Approximations must be introduced when two or more electrons are present; the larger the system, the cruder the approximations. The success of Hückel molecular orbital (HMO) theory (see chapter 4) derived from its ability to separate out the π-orbital system in flat molecules like benzene. The π molecular orbitals in benzene are treated as linear combinations of six p_z atomic orbitals, while the 30 other occupied atomic orbitals (1s on each hydrogen; 1s, 2s, $2p_x$, and $2p_y$ on each carbon) are ignored. As crude as this approach is, it provides very useful results for molecules like benzene, naphthalene, anthracene, cyclobutadiene, tropolone, and heterocycles including compounds, such as pyridine that includes nitrogen. Large symmetrical molecules (e.g., coronene, $C_{24}H_{12}$, with sixfold symmetry) can be calculated by hand. HMO theory made useful predictions for reactions between flat π-systems (e.g., the Diels-Alder reaction) since the HOMOs and LUMOs are so easily obtained.

In the 1950s applications of molecular orbital theory, computers (hardware) and computer programs (hardware) were all in their infancies. While in principle quantum theory could provide decent predictions of structures, physical properties, and reactivities for large three-dimensional molecules with full arrays of atoms and bond types, these were intractable problems at the time. However, inventive organic chemists were not going to be denied opportunities to make useful quantitative predictions even if rigorous (or even slightly rigorous) theory was lacking. The linear free energy (LFE) approach taken by Hammett in the 1930s (see chapter 4) was of great use but its limitations were all too apparent two decades later. Among many researchers mining the LFE field, Robert W. Taft (1922–96) was particularly successful. He recognized that Hammett's substituent constants (σ) held within them polarity (inductive) as well as electronic (e.g., resonance) effects. While Hammett explicitly avoided *steric effects* (repulsions between nonbonded groups), they are so common that Taft treated them explicitly. Many other research groups developed related theories and this approach morphed in the second half of the 20th century into quantitative structure-activity relationships (QSARs) useful in designing drugs.

In 1956, Frank H. Westheimer (1912–2007), at Harvard, developed a method for calculating steric effects. For decades spectroscopists had successfully treated chemical bonds as if they were springs. Modest amounts of bond stretching and angle bending obey a Hooke's Law relationship: $V = k(\Delta x)^2$, where V is the distortion energy, Δx is the distortion in bond length or bond angle and k the force constant. Chemical bonds are "stiff," therefore $k_{stretch}$ is large, and even small changes in bond length are "costly" in energy. In contrast, bond angles are opened or compressed easily (k_{bend} is small). Thus, distortions of bond angles are the most effective means of minimizing steric effects. Since V is proportional to $(\Delta x)^2$, steric effects are best minimized through small distortions of many bond angles rather than large distortions of one or two bond angles. Westheimer's calculated structures balanced distortion energy with relief of nonbonded repulsions.

Westheimer's method gave quite good agreement with data for strain energies of molecules with small angle distortions but overestimated Baeyer strain (see chapter 3) in cyclobutane and cyclopropane. He even applied it to the analysis of strain in short-lived (unobservable) carbocations (see chapters 3 and 4). In 1939, Paul D. Bartlett (1907–97) and Lawrence Knox, at Harvard, demonstrated that 1-bromonorbornane, whose derived bridgehead carbocation must be highly nonplanar, is totally unreactive to S_N1 chemistry. Bartlett concluded that carbocations must be planar or very nearly so. Westheimer estimated the angle strain in 1-norbornyl cation to be about 20 kcal/mol, high enough to make it unattainable. During the 1960s, this methodology would be widely adopted and modified by other researchers who refer to it as "molecular mechanics," a mainstay of the pharmaceutical industry throughout the remainder of the 20th century and beyond.

The Absolute Positions in Space of Atoms in Molecules

When Van't Hoff and Le Bel proposed tetrahedral carbon in 1874 they understood that enantiomers (see page 20) are opposite in their *relative* configurations (nonsuperimposable mirror images) but they could not assign an *absolute* configuration to either (dextrorotatory or levorotatory) enantiomer. During the 1880s, Emil Fischer developed projection formulas ("Fischer projections") to demonstrate chemical relationships between monosaccharides. Dextrorotatory (+)-glucose was depicted as a Fischer structure (see page 97). Fischer knew that this projection could just as likely represent the other (unnatural) enantiomer of glucose, (-)-glucose. It was impossible, until 1951, to determine the absolute configurations of these and other molecules. What Fischer did know was that (+)-glucose converts to (-)-fructose and that if one knows the absolute configuration of one, the other is known. In 1906, Martin A. Rosanoff (1874–1951), New York University, modified Fischer's nomenclature slightly, introducing D and L for the absolute configurations of monosaccharides (later extended to amino acids). Using Rosanoff's nomenclature, the original Fischer structure is D-glucose, or more completely, D-(+)-glucose. This means that the chemically-derived fructose, directly related to D-(+)-glucose, is D-(-)-fructose. Like Fischer, Rosanoff did not know if the D-structure was (+)-glucose or (-)-glucose. There was a fifty-fifty chance that the arbitrary Fischer-Rosanoff assignment was correct. The "coin-flip" would not be decided until 1951.

The reason was that, powerful as X-ray crystallography is, for the first four decades of its application, it could not differentiate enantiomers. In 1951, Johannes M. Bijvoet (1892–1980), employing a treatment of "anomalous" dispersion of X-rays developed in 1930, was able to assign the absolute configuration of (+)-tartaric acid. Bijvoet was aware that (+)-tartaric acid is chemically related to (+)-glyceraldehyde, whose absolute configuration must therefore be the D-form (see the figure below). In turn, it was known since Fischer's time that (+)-glyceraldehyde is a member of a series that can be built up from its CHO unit to provide (+)-glucose. Fischer's original structure was indeed D-(+)-glucose; Fischer had correctly "called heads." Had he "called tails," the problem would have been solved easily by simply reversing all assignments (D to L).

Specification of absolute configurations using the D,L convention for sugars such as glucose and for amino acids is useful but very limited. One must memorize the specific rules for these two classes but they are not applicable to countless other chiral molecules. In 1950, Christopher K. Ingold and Robert S. Cahn (1899–1981) invented a universal stereochemical nomenclature, further generalized by Vladimir Prelog (1906–98) in his

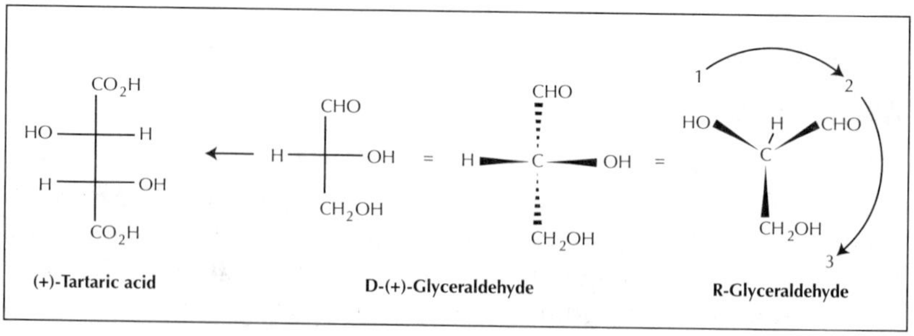

Relationship between absolute configurations of tartaric acid and glyceraldehydes

(+)-Tartaric acid   D-(+)-Glyceraldehyde   R-Glyceraldehyde

collaboration with them in 1955. The *Cahn-Ingold-Prelog (CIP) rules* were officially adopted a decade later by IUPAC. The nomenclature is illustrated very briefly for D-glyceraldehyde (see the previous structures). Detailed rules are found in IUPAC publications and in introductory organic chemistry texts. The four atoms bonded to an asymmetric carbon atom are placed in priority order according to atomic number. For glyceraldehyde the highest (#1) priority is oxygen (OH) and the lowest priority (#4) is hydrogen. The remaining substituents, CHO and CH_2OH, both bond to the asymmetric center with carbon, so the next bond is considered. CHO and CH_2OH appear at first to remain "tied" for second priority since oxygen is the highest atomic number attachment in each. However, CHO has two C-O bonds while CH_2OH has but one, hence CHO has priority #2 and CH_2OH priority #3. The next step is to view the molecule outward down the axis extending from the central carbon toward the lowest priority atom/group (H in the glyceraldehydes enantiomer depicted above). If the connection of the other three groups (#1 → #2 → #3) is clockwise when the molecule is viewed this way, it is termed "*R*" ("*rectus*"); if the connection is counterclockwise, the molecule is termed "*S*" ("*sinister*"). In CIP nomenclature *R*-glyceraldehyde is equivalent to D-glyceraldehyde.

Prelog was born in Sarajevo (referred to as the capital of Bosnia today). He had a faculty appointment at the University of Zagreb in 1941 when the Nazis occupied the city. Shortly afterward, Leopold Ruzicka managed to arrange his move to the ETH in Zurich and decades later Prelog would succeed Ruzicka as Director of Chemistry. His studies of medium-size rings, natural products, and systematic investigations in stereochemistry would earn him the 1975 Nobel Prize in chemistry (shared with John Cornforth, whose work will be described later in this chapter). In his Nobel Prize acceptance speech, Prelog paid homage to "my 'imaginary' teachers" Ruzicka, Robinson, and Ingold.

The identification of absolute configurations and other complex structural problems received an enormous boost from the highly mathematical and experimental studies of Herbert Hauptman (1917–), Jerome Karle (1918–), and Isabella L. Karle (1921–). Hauptman and Jerome Karle both attended City College of New York (CCNY) during the 1930s. It was tuition-free; students paid a one-dollar library fee and purchased their own books and supplies. Their studies at the Naval Research Laboratory (NRL) led, in 1953, to mathematical solution of the "phase problem," demonstrating to crystallographers that it is possible to go directly from diffraction patterns to structures without needing to assume the identities of the component atoms. The Karles met as Ph.D. students at the University of Michigan and both worked on the Manhattan Project. Isabella L. Karle integrated theory and experiment and made numerous fundamental contributions to electron diffraction and crystallography. In addition to determining absolute configurations of molecules such as the drug reserpine, the Karles investigated the crystal structures of 11-*cis* and all-*trans* retinal, critical isomers in the mechanism of vision pioneered by George Wald (see chapter 4). For developing direct methods in crystal structure determination, Herbert Hauptman and Jerome Karle shared the 1985 Nobel Prize in chemistry.

Measuring Rates of Reactions That Last Microseconds

To measure the rate of a chemical reaction, one might simply mix reactants A and B and use a timer to measure their disappearance and the formation of product C until there is no further change. Although it takes a few moments to add A to B and thoroughly mix them, if the reaction is sufficiently slow, the mixing time is negligible and does not affect the results. But what is the consequence of mixing A and B in one second if the reaction is complete in five seconds? How does one mix reactants and then time the reaction if it is complete in milliseconds (or microseconds or less)?

In 1923, Hamilton Hartridge (1886–1976) and Francis J. W. Roughton (1899–1972), studying the extremely rapid uptake of oxygen by hemoglobin, developed the flow method of chemical kinetics. It involved high-velocity flow of reagent streams, "instantaneous" (10^{-3} sec) mixing, and determining the distance traveled in the observation tube as the measure of chemical reaction time. This method was modified in 1940 by Britton Chance (1913–   ) using a stopped-flow technique. Flash photolysis was developed in 1949 by Norrish and Porter (see chapter 5). At the Max Planck Institute in Göttingen, Manfred Eigen (1927–   ) realized that there was a huge unknown region of reaction times between those measurable by flash-photolysis (originally 10^{-3} sec or milliseconds) and those that were diffusion-controlled ($10^{-10} - 10^{-11}$ sec), instantaneous reactions in solution with no significant activation energies. Since a reaction at equilibrium is really a dynamic balance between the rates of forward and reverse reactions, Eigen realized that an instantaneous (pulsed) disturbance, by a sudden jump in temperature or pressure, could reveal the rates of these reactions as the equilibrium is immediately reestablished. This strategy totally avoids any reactant mixing step! During 1953–54, Eigen used pulsed changes in electrical conductivity to monitor the microsecond (10^{-6} sec) rates of dissociation and association in aqueous ammonium hydroxide and in aqueous acetic acid. He had reduced the timescale for observing chemical reactions by at least three orders of magnitude. The technique found application in biological as well as chemical systems. Manfred Eigen would share the 1967 Nobel Prize in chemistry for developing these relaxation methods.

Exchanging Electrons between Fe^{2+} and Fe^{3+}: What Could Be Simpler?

Rudolph A. Marcus (1923–   ) had already made major contributions to chemical kinetics when, in 1955 at Brooklyn Polytechnic Institute, he encountered a surprising riddle. Using radiolabeled atoms and new stopped-flow techniques, chemists discovered that simple electron-transfer reactions differ enormously in their rates. Electron transfer, with no bond-breaking or bond-making, is about the simplest chemical reaction possible. Its detailed examination should provide fundamental information about reaction dynamics. Specifically, electron transfer between simple ions in aqueous solution, such as Fe^{2+} and Fe^{3+}, was found to be relatively slow while that between complex ions, such as $Fe(CN)_6^{3-}$ and $Fe(CN)_6^{4-}$ was many orders of magnitude faster:

$$Fe^{2+}(aq) + Fe^{3+}(aq) \rightarrow Fe^{3+}(aq) + Fe^{2+}(aq) \quad \text{Relatively Slow}$$

$$Fe(CN)_6^{-}(aq) + Fe(CN)_6^{3-}(aq) \rightarrow Fe(CN)_6^{3-}(aq) + Fe(CN)_6^{4-}(aq) \text{ Relatively Fast}$$

Marcus realized that electron transfer occured more rapidly than a newly formed ion could re-optimize its geometry or realign solvent molecules (Franck-Condon Principle). The picture is further complicated by the countless arrangements of ion and solvent geometries existing at any specific instant. In 1956, he developed a theory invoking a "reorganization energy" (λ) and demonstrated its simple relationship with the free energy of reaction and the free energy of activation (rate). Although the only change on Fe^{2+} as it becomes Fe^{3+} is some shrinkage of the ion, the changes in its tightly bound solvent shells are more dramatic and slow the reaction. In contrast, complex ions of the $Fe(CN)_6$ type are less tightly solvated, thus the Fe(II) and Fe(III) complexes (in this case) are very similar in geometry, hence λ is small and the rate is rapid. However, sometimes the exception proves the rule and electron transfer between $Co(NH_3)_6^{2+}$ and $Co(NH_3)_6^{3+}$ occurs slowly, despite light solvation, because the geometries of these two complex ions themselves (minus the solvent shell) differ considerably.

For most electron-transfer reactions of the type $A^- + B \rightarrow A + B^-$, where there is a change in free energy, Marcus' predictions match intuition and experience: the more *exergonic* (the more free energy released), the faster the reaction. However, his truly amazing prediction, published in 1960, was that in some very highly exergonic electron transfers, there should be an "inversion region" in which rates actually decrease. The best test of a theory is a demanding prediction. Experimental confirmation of the "inversion region" was published some 25 years later (see chapter 9). The electron-transfer theory derived by Marcus would find enormous application in photosynthesis and other biological processes, more complex reaction mechanisms involving bond-making and breaking, and countless fascinating problems in materials science. Marcus received the 1992 Nobel Prize in chemistry.

NMR Takes the Field

Applications of the newly discovered property of nuclear magnetic resonance (NMR, see chapter 5) came very quickly. The Physics Department at Stanford University built an NMR instrument and in 1951 obtained the first low resolution ^{1}H-nmr spectrum of a liquid: ethanol. A schematic of a proton NMR spectrometer is depicted in the accompanying figure. A liquid sample is placed in a glass tube that spins rapidly to provide a homogeneous field. The sample tube is housed in a probe that consists of a radio frequency transmitter and a radio frequency receiver between the poles of a large magnet. At a given radio frequency very slight changes (ca. 0.01 parts per million or ppm) in magnetic field sense hydrogen nuclei in different chemical environments.

The accompanying figure also depicts a moderate resolution spectrum of pure ethanol with a trace of tetramethylsilane [TMS, $Si(CH_3)_4$] added to adjust chemical shift to a scale where the 12 equivalent hydrogen nuclei in TMS are set to zero ppm (this is called the δ-scale). The ^{1}H-NMR spectrum of ethanol exhibits the following features:

1) Three discrete peaks "downfield" from TMS for the three distinct types of hydrogen in ethanol: methyl, methylene and hydroxyl.
2) The chemical shifts reflect the environment: H attached to electronegative oxygen is most "deshielded" (δ 4.8 ppm); the methyl group (δ 1.1 ppm) is furthest from oxygen and least deshielded; methylene is centered at δ 3.6 ppm.
3) The methyl peak is split into a characteristic triplet (three peaks of 1:2:1 relative intensities) because it has *two* equivalent neighboring CH_2 hydrogens.
4) The methylene peak is split into a characteristic quartet (four peaks of 1:3:3:1 relative intensities) because it has *three* equivalent neighboring CH_3 hydrogens.
5) The separation between the three peaks in the methyl triplet is identical to that between the four peaks of the methylene quartet. This is so because the methyl and methylene hydrogens are "coupled" to each other. The separation is the coupling constant. Higher magnetic fields increase chemical shift differences between different types of hydrogen but do not affect coupling constants.
6) The hydroxyl (OH) hydrogen is a singlet (in this spectrum), a typical observation for alcohols with a trace of moisture in the sample.
7) The total (integrated) areas under the three peaks (relative 3:2:1) reflect the relative numbers of each type of hydrogen in the molecule.

Among the early pioneers of NMR spectroscopy, Herbert S. Gutowsky (1919–2000) and John D. Roberts (1918–   ) are particularly noteworthy. At the University of Illinois, Gutowsky pioneered the use of spin-spin coupling for structure determination as well as dynamic processes that exchange hydrogen nuclei. At MIT and later Caltech, Roberts pioneered studies of relationships between ^{1}H-NMR data and chemical structure. He was one of the very first researchers to exploit ^{19}F-NMR spectroscopy, of interest due to the greater range in chemical shifts when compared to ^{1}H-NMR.

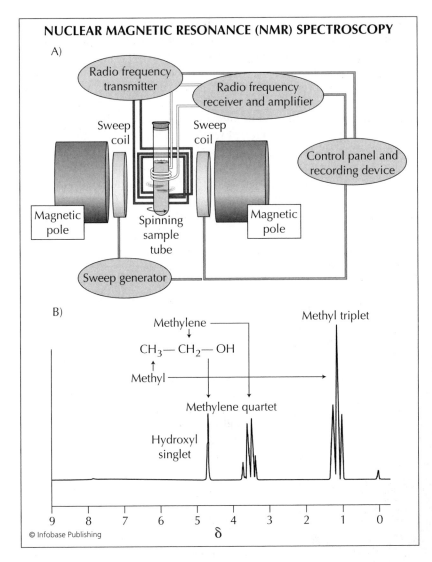

NUCLEAR MAGNETIC RESONANCE (NMR) SPECTROSCOPY

A)

Radio frequency transmitter

Radio frequency receiver and amplifier

Sweep coil

Sweep coil

Control panel and recording device

Magnetic pole

Spinning sample tube

Magnetic pole

Sweep generator

B)

Methyl triplet

Methylene

$CH_3 — CH_2 — OH$

Methyl

Methylene quartet

Hydroxyl singlet

9 8 7 6 5 4 3 2 1 0

© Infobase Publishing

δ

A) Schematic diagram of a simple nuclear magnetic resonance (NMR) spectrometer. The sample is placed in solution in a long, thin tube and spins in a probe sitting in a magnetic and surrounded by radio-frequency (RF) coils; B) proton NMR spectrum of ethanol (C_2H_6O) with tetramethylsilane (TMS) added as internal standard. On the δ-scale of chemical shifts, 0 ppm is upfield and 9 ppm downfield.

During this exploratory period in magnetic resonance spectroscopy, Harden M. McConnell (1927–), at Caltech, helped launch electron paramagnetic resonance (EPR) spectroscopy. Like the proton, the electron has two values for spin, $+\frac{1}{2}$ and $-\frac{1}{2}$. Instead of radio frequencies, microwave frequencies are employed but the principle is similar to NMR. EPR was initially applied to studies of molecules containing an unpaired electron. By studying the coupling of hydrogen atoms with the unpaired electron, McConnell was able to directly determine regions of high and low spin density. For example, if 1,3-butadiene is reduced to form the radical anion $[CH_2=CH-CH=CH_2]^-$, larger coupling constants between the unpaired electron and the equivalent terminal CH_2 groups indicate that the spin density is higher (the unpaired electron is most likely to be "localized") at these carbons. This is consistent with the prediction of simple Hückel π molecular orbital theory (see chapter 4) when the extra electron is placed in the LUMO of 1,3-butadiene. EPR would blossom into an extremely powerful tool for exploring materials and investigating the activities of metalloenzymes. McConnell also derived the modified Bloch equations that allowed monitoring of dynamic molecular processes. For example, at typical ambient temperatures the ^{1}H-NMR spectrum of cyclohexane (C_6H_{12}) has a single peak since the six equatorial and six axial hydrogens are rapidly exchanging as the chair conformation "flips" more than 100,000 times per second. Cooling the sample broadens the peak and at low enough temperatures (ca. -75°F or -60°C), separate peaks are observed for the axial and equatorial hydrogens because ring flipping has slowed considerably (perhaps 10 per second). McConnell's equations allowed the calculations of rates for a variety of such dynamic processes including the restricted rotation of the planar peptide bond. In 1957, Paul C. Lauterbur (1929–2007) took the first natural abundance carbon-13 NMR spectra of organic compounds. (Varian built a C13-NMR spectrometer for him.) Widespread application of this promising technique would have to wait until the 1970s, when computers would become an integral part of NMR spectrometers.

Varian A-60 NMR, the first commercial NMR spectrometer (Varian, Inc)

In 1960, Varian Corporation built and marketed the first commercial NMR spectrometer, the 60 MHz A-60 model (see the photograph). It was a workhorse that brought NMR spectroscopy to chemistry departments industrial and academic, large and small during the 1960s. Not long afterward, Varian marketed the HA-100 (100 MHz provides separations of peaks 67 percent better than 60 MHz), and by the end of the decade, some elite corporations and universities were acquiring 220 MHz instruments. The most powerful analytical tool in the chemist's laboratory had arrived and yet its fabulous future potential was only dimly perceived.

"Nonclassical" Carbocations: Real or Are Our "Chemical Clocks" Too Slow?

Among the distinguishing hallmarks of carbocation ("carbonium ion") chemistry are rearrangements of the type attributed to them by Hans Meerwein (see chapter 3). Beginning in the late 1930s, stereochemical observations suggested that "neighboring groups" (e.g., bromine in a Br-

C-C⁺-type intermediate) could form a bridge with the electron-deficient carbon in carbocations. This was not too difficult to accept since a lone pair of electrons on bromine can be shared with the electron-deficient carbon to form a three-membered ring. The same stereochemical results could also be explained by assuming that bromine rapidly shifts back and forth, to and from its neighbor (like a windshield wiper), with the three-membered, bridged ion characterizing the transition state for this 1,2-shift.

In the late 1940s and throughout the fifties, a related problem would emerge that would roil the waters of organic chemistry for three decades. It is important to remember that carbocations generated as intermediates in chemical reactions are present only in miniscule amounts since they disappear as rapidly as they are created (the steady-state assumption described in chapter 2). The lure of chemical research includes the quest to deduce the structures of such transient intermediates: thousands of times too small to be viewed in the best optical microscopes, moving at velocities of hundreds of miles per hour, and having lifetimes of perhaps a millionth of a second.

The figure on page 198 depicts S_N1 reactions (see chapter 4) for *endo*-2-norbornyl and *exo*-2-norbornyl compounds. Saul Winstein (1912–69) and Daniel S. Trifan (1919–2002), at UCLA, observed that along with the rearrangements so characteristic of the carbocation intermediates, there were surprising rate effects. The exo isomer reacts hundreds of times more rapidly than the *endo* isomer. Their hypothesis was "neighboring-group" participation accelerating the *exo* reaction (only) and forming a bridged ("nonclassical") carbonium ion intermediate. In this figure, the structure of such an intermediate is depicted; it contains a carbon atom bound to five atoms. While penta-coordinate carbon was fully accepted in the transition states (energy maxima) of S_N2 reactions (see chapter 4), the possibility of penta-coordinate carbon as a stable (if short-lived) ground state (energy minimum) was hard to accept since it violates the octet rule. Another perspective is that a C-C bonding pair of electrons (rather than a lone pair as in Br) is shared with the electron-deficient carbon. Skepticism is a healthy scientific habit and among those who felt that a more classical explanation was sufficient was Herbert C. Brown (1912–2004) at Purdue. He argued that it was not that the *exo* S_N1 reaction was unusually fast, but that the *endo* reaction was slow due to steric repulsion of the incoming nucleophile Y⁻. Brown argued that the carbocation derived from the *exo* compound is a classical one and that pentacoordinate carbon is only viable in the transition state. John D. Roberts observed rearrangements and rate accelerations in the reactions of cyclopropyl-CH_2X molecules and calculated, using Hückel molecular orbital theory, that nonclassical carbocations are true intermediates. Ultimately, NMR, computational chemistry, and ESCA would settle this stormy debate . . . three decades hence.

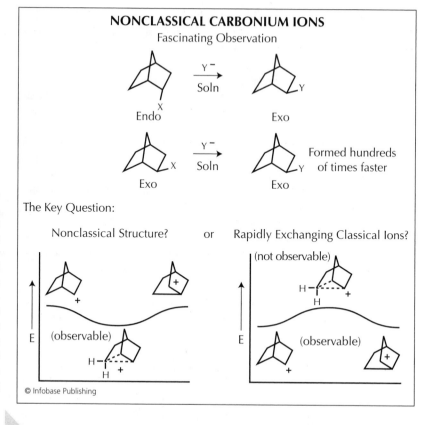

The nonclassical carbocation problem simply summarized. The exo stereoisomer reacts hundreds of times faster than the endo. This is explained by the exo forming a stabilized nonclassical carbocation in the rate-determining step. A nonclassical ion (note the 5-coordinate carbon) is a potential-energy minimum (lower left) rather than a transition state between two rapidly interconverting classical ions (lower right).

Clarifying the Biosynthesis of Steroids

While the 1930s and 1940s were a "Golden Age of Steroids" (see chapters 3 and 4), research during the 1950s established their surprising origins, firmly established the connection to terpenes, produced brilliant syntheses mimicking Nature's own pathways, and opened a new field of stereochemistry, conformational analysis.

Isotopic labeling would play an absolutely critical role in elucidating the biological origins of steroids and terpenes. Konrad Bloch (1912–2000), a Jew born in Germany, fled to the United States in 1936 where he obtained his Ph.D. with Hans T. Clarke at Columbia University in 1938. Joining the research group of Rudolf Schoenheimer (1898–1941), a colleague of Harold Urey's at Columbia, he was one of the first chemists to apply deuterium labeling to studies of problems in biosynthesis. Following Schoenheimer's death, Bloch started to exploit the recently discovered radioactive isotope carbon 14. When he began these studies, the "isoprene rule" for terpenes was already well accepted. Leopold Ruzicka had earlier postulated a relationship between terpenes and steroids; Robert Robinson had envisioned a structural relationship between

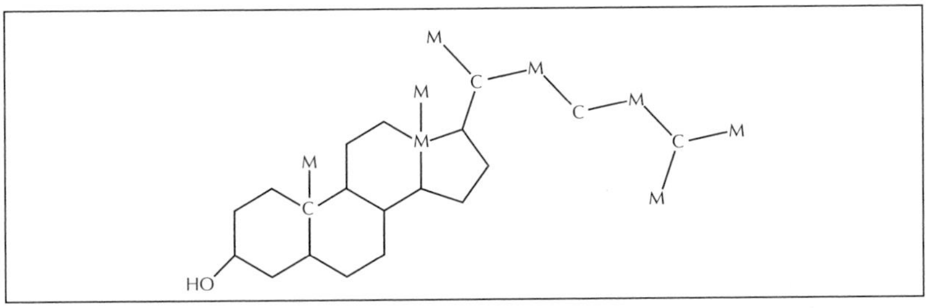

Biosynthesis route to cholesterol

the steroid cholesterol and the triterpene squalene. Working with acetic acid labeled at the methyl group ($*CH_3CO_2H$) or the carboxyl group (CH_3*CO_2H), Bloch established that cholesterol is built from two-carbon units rather than directly from the five-carbon isoprene unit (see the figure above representing the structure deduced in 1952, where M = methyl carbon; C = carboxyl carbon).

In Munich, Feodor Lynen (1911–79) learned that another former Wieland student, Robert Sonderhoff, had demonstrated that deuterated acetic acid is incorporated into fatty acids and steroids and not directly into carbohydrates. This stimulated Lynen to search for "activated acetic acid" but he was narrowly beaten to the discovery of acetyl Co-A by Fritz Lipmann in 1948 (see chapter 5). These studies led Lynen and his colleagues to explore pathways for fatty acid and terpene biosynthesis. They elucidated the role of acetyl Co-A and searched for "activated isoprene," the critical unit in terpene synthesis. The missing link was supplied, unsuspectingly, by the Karl Folkers group at Merck, Sharpe & Dohme in 1956. Certain strains of *Lactobacillus acidophilus* depend upon acetate for nutrition. However, in *Lactobacillus* deprived of acetate, Folkers discovered a substance, mevalonic acid (see the figure on page 200), which substitutes for acetate. It was logical to explore the relationship between acetate and mevalonic acid and Lynen established that stepwise combination of three acetyl-CoA (two-carbon) units provide the six-carbon mevalonic acid. Lynen's subsequent work established that mevalonic acid is elaborated to the high-energy five-carbon 3-isopentenyl pyrophosphate (3-IPP, see the figure), "activated isoprene," through cleavage of three high-energy ATPs and loss of CO_2. Subsequently, 3-IPP isomerizes to 3,3-dimethylallyl pyrophosphate (also a C_5) which combines with another molecule of 3-IPP to form geranyl phosphate (C_{10}) which adds another molecule of 3-IPP to form farnesyl pyrophosphate (C_{15}). This last molecule is dimerized to squalene (C_{30}). While Lynen pioneered the pathway from acetic acid (C_2) to squalene (C_{30}), R. B. Woodward was reconsidering Robinson's early suggestion of a direct relationship between squalene and cholesterol. In 1953, Woodward and Bloch suggested a new "folding" mechanism for transforming squalene into lanosterol (see figure), itself a direct precursor of cholesterol. This was soon verified as the correct pathway. Konrad E. Bloch and Feodor

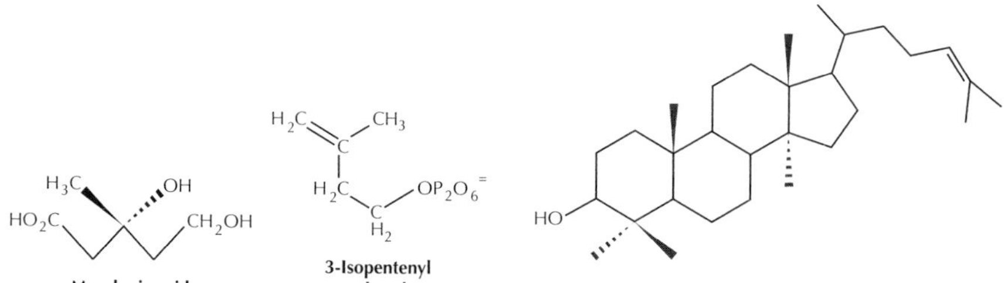

"Mevalonic acid"; "3-Isopentenyl pyrophosphate"; "lanosterol"

Lynen would share the 1964 Nobel Prize in chemistry for their achievements in elucidating steroid and terpene biosynthesis and related studies. During the 1950s, Luis Leloir (1906–87), an Argentinean biochemist, made enormous breakthroughs in the biosynthesis of sugars and sugar nucleotides for which he would win the 1970 Nobel Prize in chemistry.

Throughout the 1950s, Melvin Calvin continued to employ carbon-14 labeling in his studies of the fate of carbon in photosynthesis (see chapter 5). He completed the photosynthetic carbon cycle ("Calvin cycle") in 1958 and received the Nobel Prize in chemistry in 1961.

The first total synthesis (from simple starting materials) of a steroid was achieved in 1939 by Werner E. Bachmann (1901–51) at the University of Michigan. His target, the estrogen equilenin, has a flat naphthalene system and only two asymmetric carbons. Even more challenging are more saturated steroids such as cholesterol that lack aromatic rings and have more chiral centers. R. B. Woodward had entered MIT at 16, was suspended for a semester for not taking his nonchemistry courses seriously enough, graduated at 19, then directed his own Ph.D. thesis at MIT which he completed at 20. If the world-famous Bachmann could synthesize equilenin (2 chiral centers), why could not the precocious Woodward, then 22 and an instructor at Harvard, synthesize estrone (4 chiral centers)? While other chemists would synthesize estrone, in 1951 Woodward employed the Diels-Alder reaction to synthesize cortisone (7 chiral centers) as well as cholesterol. In 1954, he synthesized lanosterol. Other triumphs during this decade included strychnine (1954), reserpine (1956), and chlorophyll (1960). Woodward's characteristically brilliant syntheses gained him the Nobel Prize in chemistry in 1965. During this decade, William S. Johnson (1913–95) at Wisconsin discovered a biosynthetic-style "zipper reaction" that uses carbocation chemistry to close squalene to lanosterol with simultaneous creation of chiral centers having correct relative configurations. Another triumph of the period was the total synthesis of morphine in 1952 by Marshall D. Gates (1915–2003), University of Rochester.

While total synthesis of a complex molecule is like a "hero's climb up a tall mountain," the development of new reactions of synthetic importance plays an equally critical role in organic chemistry. In 1953, Georg Wittig (1897–1987) at Heidelberg discovered an amazingly useful reaction that couples phosphorus ylides, such as $(C_6H_5)_3P=CHR$ (readily available from alkyl halides like RCH_2Br), with carbonyl compounds, such as O=CHR', to form larger molecules like R'CH=CHR. This is a robust and widely applicable transformation and the Wittig reaction was later employed to synthesize terpenoids including vitamin A and β-carotene. In 1956, Herbert C. Brown discovered the addition of diborane across C=C bonds to generate trialkyl boranes (R_3B) which could in turn be transformed into alcohols. The reactions are anti-Markovnikov in orientation (see chapter 4) and involve no unwanted rearrangements. Variations on the hydroboration theme now comprise an entire symphony of synthetic possibilities. Brown and Wittig shared the 1979 Nobel Prize in chemistry. In 1958, Howard E. Simmons, Jr. (1929–71), at DuPont, "tamed" the short-lived methylene (CH_2) by reacting CH_2I_2 with zinc/copper and forming a stable metal-carbene-like substance ("ICH_2ZnI"). The Simmons-Smith reaction provides a method to insert CH_2 into a carbon chain. Eight years earlier, Simmons as a graduate student of John D. Roberts famously applied carbon-14 labeling to establish the true intermediacy of the symmetrical transient 1,2-benzyne (*ortho*-benzyne, C_6H_4).

The rigid skeletons of steroids would teach their own lessons much as monoterpenes had taught lessons about carbocations to Wagner (1920s), Bartlett (1930s), and Winstein (1940s). The steroid nucleus has three rigid fused cyclohexane rings. Starting with X-ray crystallography in 1930 and then electron diffraction in the 1940s, Odd Hassel (1897–1981), University of Oslo, established the reality of the chair conformation of the cyclohexane ring and that attached substituents such as methyl (CH_3) prefer the equatorial position to the more crowded axial position. (Shortly after Hassel published this work in 1943 he was arrested by Norwegian Nazis but released in November 1944). In 1950 Derek H. R. Barton (1918–98), Imperial College, published studies in which he explained a great deal of steroid chemistry based upon whether substituents in cyclohexane rings are equatorial or axial. For example, the C5-C6 double bond in cholesterol is readily brominated to form diaxial derivative (see the figure below). This dibromide easily rearranges to the isomer in which the two bromines on C5 and C6 are equatorial

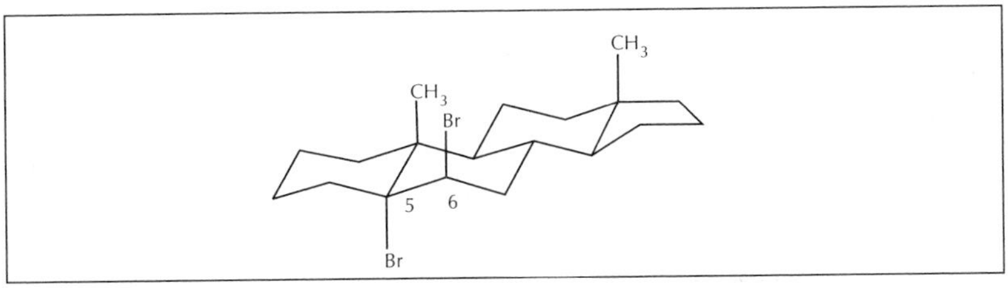

Trans-dibromo-derivative of a steroid

since it is less crowded. Since it was known that elimination of adjacent bromine atoms is fastest when these atoms are *anti* (one straight up, the other straight down), it became obvious why the diaxial isomer rapidly eliminates Br_2 to reform cholesterol while the diequatorial isomer is much less reactive. This was the start of a stereochemical subspecialty termed *conformational analysis*, and Barton and Hassel would share the 1969 Nobel Prize in chemistry.

Development of the Birth Control Pill

Birth control has been a major and emotional issue for individuals, families, societies, and religions for centuries. What is beyond controversy is the profound impact "the pill" has had in societies where it has been widely available starting in the 1960s.

During the 1930s, Russell Marker (1902–95), at Pennsylvania State College, learned that Mexican women had for centuries been eating a species of wild yam that helped them avoid pregnancy. He analyzed the yams and discovered a substance (diosgenin), similar to progesterone, a steroid hormone known to stop ovulation in rabbits. Marker succeeded in converting diosgenin to progesterone and, in 1944, helped start a company, Syntex, based in Mexico City. Progesterone decomposes in the stomach and is not suitable as an oral contraceptive. In 1949 Carl Djerassi (1923–   ) joined Syntex (Marker had departed earlier in a dispute with his partners) and, in 1951, synthesized the steroid norethindrone, the first oral contraceptive. Shortly afterward, Frank Colton (1923–2003), at G.D. Searle, synthesized norethynodrel, a compound differing from norethindrone only in the position of one double bond.

Margaret Sanger (1879–1966) grew up in an Irish working-class family. Her beloved mother had 11 children in 18 pregnancies and Sanger was convinced that her death from tuberculosis at 50 was the result of her weakened state. Sanger's work as a nurse in the poorest sections of pre–World War I New York City convinced her of the need for family planning. In 1916 she opened in Brooklyn the first birth-control clinic in the United States, was promptly arrested, and the clinic was closed. Sanger later founded the organization that would become the Planned Parenthood Federation of America. During the 1950s, Sanger partnered with wealthy heiress and activist Katherine Dexter McCormick (1875–1967), one of the first female graduates of MIT, to promote and fund birth control research. They contacted Gregory G. Pincus (1903–67), a biologist in Worcester, Massachusetts, who was studying both norethindrone and norethynodrel. McCormick provided most of the funding for the early clinical trials. Although Djerassi at Syntex was the first to synthesize an oral contraceptive (he is often called "the father of the pill"), Searle was first to market it ("Enovid"). The Food and Drug Administration approved these drugs during the early 1960s. The risks from side effects soon became another factor in the decision by women to take or not take the pill. Modern birth-control pills have less than 20 percent of the steroid content of 1960s pills.

Vitamin B$_{12}$: "The 'Sound Barrier' Was Broken"

Every aspect of vitamin B$_{12}$ amazes! It is the active component in the liver that reverses pernicious anemia and it has multiple functions in DNA synthesis and intermediary metabolism. Vitamin B$_{12}$ is synthesized by bacteria (and fungi), is present in soil, and is commonly obtained from meat, milk, eggs, and fish; calf liver is a particularly rich source. Bacteria in the human colon synthesize this substance but, ironically, humans cannot absorb "their own" B$_{12}$. Ingested vitamin B$_{12}$ requires adequate "intrinsic factor" (IF) in gastric juice in order to be absorbed and IF levels tend to decrease with aging.

Unlike other coenzymes that mediate reactions known to organic chemistry, vitamin B$_{12}$ is a cofactor in enzymatic reactions that simply have no counterpart in nonbiological chemistry! It was first isolated in crystalline form in 1948 by the Folkers group at Merck using column chromatography (see chapter 4). E. Lester Smith, at Glaxo in England, also isolated crystalline vitamin B$_{12}$ and sent a sample of the deep-red crystals to Oxford to see if the crystal morphology (the external structure) was identical to that of the Merck crystals. Dorothy Hodgkin performed some preliminary X-ray work and found that vitamin B$_{12}$ was a candidate for crystallographic study. By 1951, all she knew was that the formula of the compound was C$_{63}$H$_{88}$O$_{14}$N$_{14}$PCo and she was aware of the identities of some of the fragments but knew little about how they were connected. The complexity of the problem dwarfed that of penicillin (see chapter 5), which thanks to Hodgkin's structural work finally succumbed to total synthesis by John C. Sheehan at MIT in 1957.

In collecting their crystallographic data, Hodgkin and her talented colleagues employed the heavy atom cobalt to orient their data in conjunction with mapping techniques developed two decades earlier. Kenneth N. Trueblood (1920–98), at UCLA, had programmed the National Bureau of Standards Western Automatic Computer (SWAC) to solve crystallography problems and his offer of collaboration was happily accepted by the Hodgkin group. Eight years after she first examined the crystals, Dorothy Hodgkin solved the structure of vitamin B$_{12}$ (cyanocobalamin, see *A* in figure on next page). It was an amazing structure, with a central corrin ring system, that includes 13 chiral centers. But then a surprise! In 1958, Horace A. Barker (1907–2000), at Berkeley, discovered that the true natural coenzyme was not cyanocobalamin but rather the 5'-deoxyadenosine compound (adenosylcobalamin, see *B* below). Another derivative, methylcobalamine (see *C* below), was also found to be a natural coenzyme.

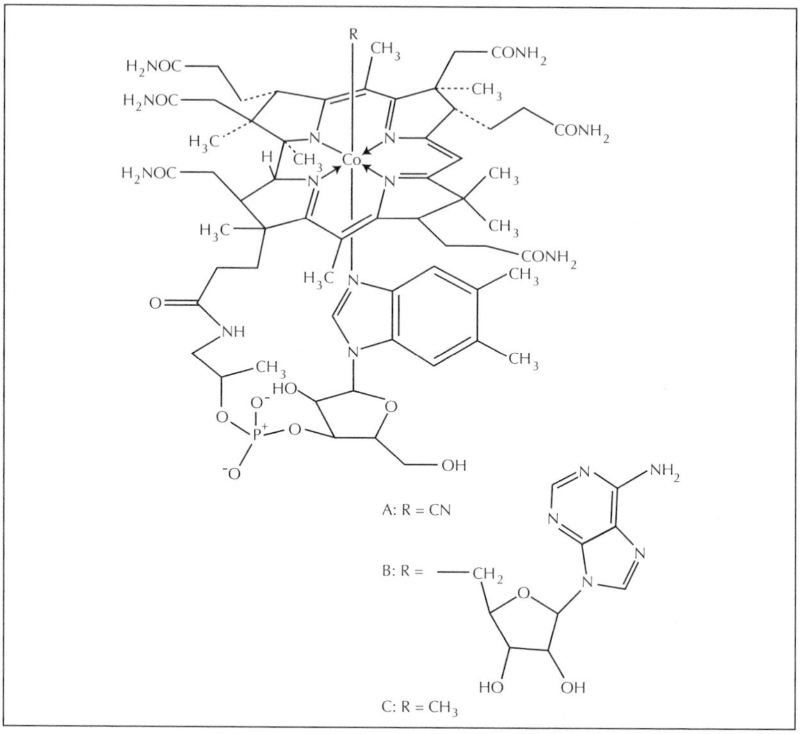

Vitamin B₁₂ family

The initial isolation of crystalline cyanocobalamin was simply an artifact of the purification procedure. Nevertheless, although not fully "organic" (i.e., "natural"), cyanocobalamin is the oral form sold over the counter and, by general adoption, is called vitamin B_{12}.

In 1961, Hodgkin and coworkers reported the structure of the true coenzyme, adenosylcobalamin. It was the first biological compound known to have a carbon bond to a transition metal (CN and CO ligands are considered inorganic). Sir Lawrence Bragg, in characterizing this amazing achievement in crystallography, said: "the 'sound barrier' was broken." What a fitting end to the 1950s, the decade that ushered in the "renaissance in inorganic chemistry"! The structure of adenosylcobalamin provides clear clues to its function. Steric repulsions flex the corrin ring and lengthen (weaken) its Co-C bond. This bond breaks to form an adenosyl radical that attacks the substrate molecule sharing the enzyme cavity; the substrate radical produced rapidly rearranges, retakes a hydrogen atom from its neighbor, restoring the adenosyl radical which then reforms the Co-C bond. In 1985, Jenny Pickworth Glusker (1931–), one of Hodgkin's students and a coauthor on the original vitamin B_{12} work, her postdoctoral associate Miriam Rossi (1952–), and other collaborators published the crystal structure of methylcobalamin.

Chromatography and Crystallography Converge: Protein Structures Emerge

During the 1940s, the separation of amino acids by paper chromatography, the beginnings of peptide sequencing, and advances in crystallography and structural chemistry set the table for the true start of structural biology in the 1950s. William H. Stein (1911–80) and Stanford Moore (1913–82), at the Rockefeller Institute, pioneered the application of ion chromatography to separate amino acids for purposes of sequencing. By 1958 they had developed an automated analyzer for this purpose. A major advance in peptide and protein sequencing was perfected around 1956 by Pehr V. Edman (1916–77) following a stay at the Rockefeller Institute. The "Edman degradation" employs phenylisothiocyanate (PITC, C_6H_5-N=C=S) to react at the N-terminal amino acid residue and gentle hydrolysis to cleave that residue as its phenylthiohydantoin (PTH) derivative while leaving the remainder of the peptide or protein chain intact. (Recall that Sanger's analysis requires hydrolysis of the entire N-labeled peptide chain with great loss of information). The PTH-amino acid derivatives are easy to separate and analyze and the technique permits complete analysis of a peptide chain one amino acid at a time in sequence starting from the N-terminal.

In 1955, Frederick Sanger published the full amino acid sequence of bovine insulin. It was the first complete amino acid sequence determined for a protein and, in 1958, he would receive the first of two Nobel Prizes in chemistry. Insulin comprises two peptide chains containing 21 and 30 amino acids respectively and joined by two disulfide (-S-S-) linkages. The actual three-dimensional structure of insulin was finally determined in 1969 by Dorothy Hodgkin some 35 years after she first engaged the problem in the "*ur*-period" of protein crystallography. In 1960, Stein and Moore reported the complete amino acid sequence (*primary structure*) of a second protein (the first enzyme sequence): ribonuclease A, a single chain but, with 124 amino acid residues (MW = 13,683), more than twice the size of insulin. The active protein's chain holds four disulfide linkages. At the National Institutes of Health (NIH), Christian B. Anfinsen (1916–95), whose work contributed to the ribonuclease success, made a fundamental discovery concerning protein activity. He employed mercaptoethanol to reduce and break the disulfide linkages along with urea to fully denature the protein. When the inactive, denatured protein was separated from these denaturants it spontaneously reassembled and resumed 100 percent activity. This profound observation led Anfinsen to conclude that the primary structure (amino acid sequence) of a protein contains all the information needed to establish its active (lowest-energy) three-dimensional structure. It is useful at this point to recall DuVigneaud's study of insulin denaturation during the early 1930s (see chapter 4). Just as Anfinsen employed mercaptoethanol to reduce disulfide linkages in ribonuclease A, DuVigneaud employed glutathione to reduce the disulfide linkages in insulin. When he reoxidized the two separated chains they did not reassemble into active insulin.

A quick calculation suggests that spontaneous refolding (renaturation) of a single protein chain the size of ribonuclease should take at least 10 billion years if every possible conformation is "tried." This is termed the "Levinthal paradox," after molecular biologist Cyrus Levinthal (1922– 90) who proposed it in 1968. Anfinsen discovered that renaturation of ribonuclease A in vitro (in glassware) occurs in hours. There must be a specific folding pathway. In vivo (in living organism) renaturation of ribonuclease A takes only minutes! This was the beginning of a search for "chaperones" that somehow aid folding of proteins. While ribonuclease A spontaneously renatures to the fully active protein, such simple behavior is not universal. Protein folding remains today a critical research area in structural biology. In 1972 Christian B. Anfinsen, Stanford Moore, and William H. Stein shared the Nobel Prize in chemistry.

During this period of great interest in insulin and the treatment of diabetes with animal insulin, Roselyn Yalow (1921–) and Solomon A. Berson (1918–72), working at the Veterans Administration Hospital in the Bronx, made an unexpected and far-reaching discovery. Yalow's Ph.D. in nuclear physics helped her move into nuclear medicine and she and Berson discovered that radiolabeled (^{131}I) insulin is eliminated more slowly from the blood serum of diabetics than from serums of nondiabetics. Their hypothesis, controversial at the time, was that humans produce ultratrace levels of antibodies to these animal insulins. By 1956 they had fully developed the principles for a technique called radioimmunoassay (RIA). An extraordinarily minute sample of radiolabeled foreign substance (antigen), such as animal insulin, is added to the serum sample and competes with the same antigen already in the serum for binding to the antibody in question: the higher the blood insulin, the lower the binding of added ^{131}I-insulin. The technique allowed sensitivities of less than 0.1 pg (1 pg or picogram = 10^{-12} gram) of antigen. It was successfully applied to assay insulin levels in human blood serum in 1959 and extended to hundreds of biological compounds since. In 1977 Roselyn Yalow shared the Nobel Prize in physiology or medicine for her discovery of the RIA technique.

Max F. Perutz (1914–2002) was born in Vienna to Jewish parents who had developed a prosperous textile business. Upon completing his undergraduate degree at the University of Vienna, Perutz knew that he wanted to pursue his Ph.D. at Cambridge and, helped financially by his parents, he joined J. D. Bernal's crystallography group at the Cavendish Laboratory in 1936. On March 12, 1938, German troops, accompanied by Hitler, marched into Austria and demanded union with Germany (*Anschluss*); the Nazi-backed government complied the next day. The family business was expropriated and Perutz's parents became refugees. Short on financial support, Perutz's scientific career was saved by funding from the Rockefeller Foundation and he joined William Lawrence Bragg's research group at the Cavendish in January 1939.

Perutz had started crystallographic studies on hemoglobin while in the Bernal group at the Cavendish. Biological preparation and purification was soon done in collaboration with Keilin's group at a different location in Cambridge. John C. Kendrew (1917–97) joined the Bragg group in 1946 and started a long and happy collaboration with Perutz on protein structure. Their three-dimensional studies of the oxygen-transport proteins myoglobin and hemoglobin began around 1955. The amino acid sequences (primary structures) of these proteins were not known at the time. Myoglobin consists of one protein chain (153 amino acids) and a single heme group. In contrast, hemoglobin has four protein chains (two *alpha*, 141 amino acids each; two *beta*, 146 amino acids each), four hemes, and has a molecular weight of about 64,500. The ability to obtain well-formed crystalline proteins was, of course, critical to any successful study. While Perutz was able to obtain suitable crystals of "reduced" (really oxygen-free) human hemoglobin, human oxyhemoglobin did not crystallize well. In its place, he used crystals of reduced horse hemoglobin. Perutz was obviously interested in comparing oxygenated and oxygen-free hemoglobin and the close similarity in the primary structures of human and horse hemoglobin provided confidence in this comparison. After searching numerous candidates for his project, Kendrew found that sperm whale myoglobin formed the most satisfactory crystals.

Kendrew and Perutz benefited from improvements in crystallographic analysis techniques and, in particular from a technique termed "isomorphous heavy atom replacement" developed a few years earlier by Dorothy Hodgkin. Kendrew also made use of an EDSAC I electronic computer in his analysis. In 1957, Kendrew succeeded in determining the structure of myoglobin at 6 A (0.6 nm) resolution (for comparison, a carbon-carbon bond is typically 1.2-1.5 A or 0.12-0.15 nm in length). This is sufficient to describe the overall shape of the protein chain and the placement of the heme "disk," but insufficient to resolve the amino acid residues. In 1959, he succeeded in solving myoglobin at 2 A, resolving amino acid residues but not individual atoms and in the early 1960s refined this to 1.4 A. While Kendrew was working on the crystallographic structure of myoglobin, Allen B. Edmundson (1932–) and his doctoral mentor C. H. Werner Hirs (1923–2000), in the Stein and Moore unit at Rockefeller, were deciphering the amino acid sequence of myoglobin. To Kendrew's surprise, his 2 A study was helpful in the chemical sequencing and the two groups published consecutive papers in *Nature* in 1961. Kendrew solved the *secondary structure* of myoglobin: Its eight straight sections were *alpha*-helices. The *tertiary structure* of myoglobin indicated an overall globular shape governed by the bends connecting the eight *alpha*-helices.

Perutz was studying a much bigger molecule. In 1960, he solved the hemoglobin structure at 6 A resolution. While the primary structure was not yet established, the secondary and tertiary structures bore similarities to myoglobin. Since hemoglobin has four protein chains (two α, two β) associated but not formally bonded to each other, it has a *quaternary struc-*

ture: a nearly tetrahedral arrangement of these four individual protein chains. In turn, studies of oxyhemoglobin and oxygen-free hemoglobin helped to explain the Bohr effect (rapid uptake of four oxygen molecules in oxygen-rich environments; rapid loss of four oxygen molecules in oxygen-poor environments; Christian Bohr [1855–1911] was the father of Niels Bohr). A change in shape in one α-chain induces a change in its β-chain neighbor which rapidly induces changes in the remaining α- and β- chains. Such cooperativity is called allosterism. Max F. Perutz and John C. Kendrew shared the 1962 Nobel Prize in chemistry for the first solutions of protein structures by crystallography. One can only try to imagine the joy this brought to Sir Lawrence Bragg, their director, and the codiscoverer (with his father) of X-ray crystallography 50 years earlier! The globular structures of myoglobin and hemoglobin tend to place hydrophilic amino acid residues on the surface of the protein molecules and hydrophobic amino acid residues in the interior. The sidebar below describes the nature of hydrophobic interactions.

The renaissance in inorganic chemistry joined the new age of protein crystallography in the late 1950s. It had long been known that oxygen-free ("deoxy") hemoglobin is paramagnetic while oxygenated hemoglobin is diamagnetic. In the language of ligand-field theory, deoxyhemoglobin surrounds its central Fe(II) iron with a weak electrostatic field.

The application of ligand-field theory to the properties of deoxyhemoglobin and oxyhemoglobin. Deoxyhemoglobin is paramagnetic (four unpaired electrons) because the ligands attached to iron (II) set up a weak crystal field placing the triply degenerate set of d orbitals close in energy to the doubly degenerate set. Oxyhemoglobin is diamagnetic because the ligand field is stronger, the split larger and all six electrons occupy the lower-energy triply degenerate set with spins paired. (An alternative view is that iron is in the III state, not the II state, and interacts with O$_2$).

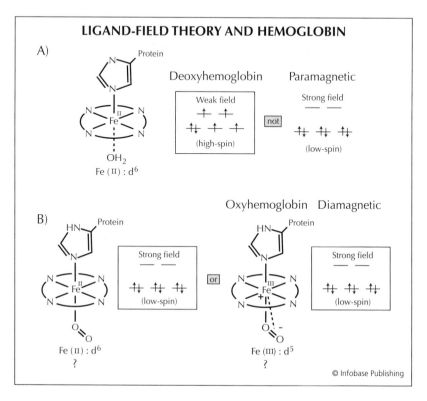

LIGAND-FIELD THEORY AND HEMOGLOBIN

A)

Deoxyhemoglobin   Paramagnetic

Fe (II) : d^6

B)

Oxyhemoglobin   Diamagnetic

Fe (II) : d^6
?

Fe (III) : d^5
?

© Infobase Publishing

Hydrophobic Molecules Do Not "Fear" Water

When two people do not like each other they are said to "mix about as well as oil and water." One of the most familiar classifications in chemistry is one that differentiates hydrophilic ("water-loving") molecules (and parts of molecules) from "hydrophobic" ("water-fearing") molecules (and parts of molecules). The structures of Langmuir monolayer micelles, described in chapter 2, and cell membrane bilayers are often said to result from "hydrophobic bonding" of long hydrophobic hydrocarbon chains.

In 1959, Walter J. Kauzmann (1916–) at Princeton clarified the notions of "hydrophobic bonding" when he noted that water is actually attracted to hydrophobic molecules with a very small amount of heat *released* upon association. This is the result of nonbonding (van der Waals) attraction and in some cases (e.g., benzene) some

very weak hydrogen bonding. In creating "holes" in the solvent water, some stronger hydrogen bonds between the solvent molecules must be lost compensating in part for the energy gain in solvating the nonpolar hydrocarbon. The most significant effect is an increased ordering of the solvent molecules around and near the nonpolar solute. While the exothermic association with water is favorable (ΔH = negative), increased organization of solvent structure is larger in magnitude and unfavorable (ΔS = negative). The overall effect on free energy ($\Delta G = \Delta H - T\Delta S$) is unfavorable ($\Delta G$ = positive) and "hydrophobic bonding" results in insolubility, monolayers, or micelles. Kauzmann used this concept to correctly predict that globular proteins fold so as to expose hydrophilic amino acids to water while placing hydrophobic amino acids in the interior shielded from water.

This causes weak energy separation between two sets of d-orbitals on iron and permits a high-spin state (Part A in the figure on page 208). If the electrostatic field were stronger, the separation between the two sets of orbitals would be greater, the six d-electrons would occupy only the three lower-energy orbitals (Part B in the figure), be spin-paired, and the protein would be diamagnetic, contrary to experiment. The substitution of O_2 for H_2O causes a stronger field at Fe(II), greater separation of energy levels, pairing of the six d-electrons (Part B in the figure) and diamagnetism. (Speculation about the possibility of a fully spin-paired Fe(III)–O_2^- structure is also included in Part B of the figure).

Stereochemical Subtleties of Enzymes: Surprises and New Insights

The ordered structures of proteins (*alpha*-helices, *beta*-sheets) readily explain the fact that all protein molecules (on Earth at least) are comprised of L-α-amino acids (since an occasional D-amino acid would disrupt the ordered structure of L-enantiomers). The configurations of L-amino acids are described by the structure below; they are consistent with carbohydrate nomenclature as seen by comparison with the D-glyceraldehyde structure shown earlier in this chapter. In both classes,

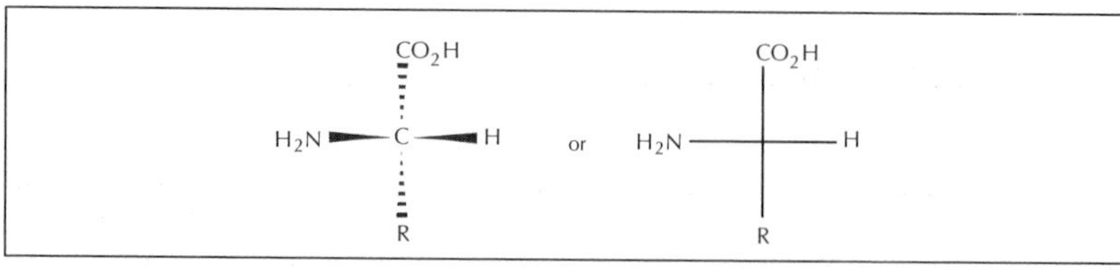

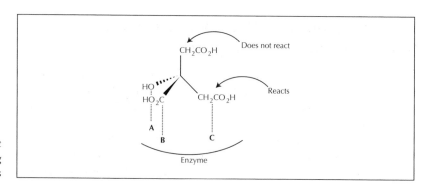

Three-dimensional and Fischer projection of L-amino acids

placing the most oxidized carbons (CHO or CO_2H), least oxidized carbons (CH_3, CH_2OH, most R), hydrogen (H), and the functional groups (OH or NH_2) congruently leads to the same D- or L-designation. Of the 20 common amino acids, one (glycine, R = H) is achiral, 18 are *S* in the CIP nomenclature and one L-amino acid is *R* (cysteine, R = CH_2SH: due to its reversal in priority with CO_2H). D-Amino acids are very rare in higher organisms but much more common in lower organisms such as bacteria. For example, two of the 10 amino acids in the cyclic peptide gramicidin-S, sequenced by Synge (see chapter 5), are D-phenylalanines. Higher organisms have evolved D-amino acid oxidases to destroy these unusual amino acids while bacteria have evolved amino acid racemases to "customize" some of the L-amino acids they ingest.

Not long after Hans Krebs solved the tricarboxylic acid cycle and carbon 14 became available, an awkward surprise emerged. Incubation of pyruvic acid with labeled CO_2 ($*CO_2$) would be expected to form $[(HO_2{}^{\frac{1}{2}*}CCH_2)C(OH)(CO_2H)(CH_2{}^{1/2}*CO_2H)]$, citric acid in which the label is equally distributed between the two identical CH_2CO_2H substituents. Subsequent conversion to succinic acid ($HO_2CCH_2CH_2CO_2H$) and CO_2 should distribute the label equally between these two molecules. However, all *C label is found in the emitted carbon dioxide and none is found in succinic acid! This was worrisome indeed because it seemed to be incompatible with the intermediacy of the symmetrical citric acid molecule. In 1948, Alexander G. Ogston (1911–96), in Oxford, developed an ingenious hypothesis to explain this paradox. If an enzyme (always chiral) presents three points of attachment, then the two seemingly identical groups can be differentiated (see the structure below).

Three-point attachment schematic of enzyme binding of substrates

In 1953, Frank Westheimer presented another illustration of this phenomenon in which he furnished an elegant proof. He demonstrated that alcohol dehydrogenase reduces deuterated acetaldehyde (CH_3CDO) to ethanol (CH_3CHDOH) and that reoxidation of this specific molecule yields only CH_3CDO (no CH_3CHO). The enzyme is able to differentiate between the two seemingly identical methylene hydrogens in CH_3CH_2OH, always removing the same one. There is no enzyme "magic" here since it was soon realized that other (non-enzyme) chiral reagents also differentiate two such *prochiral* atoms or groups. Starting in 1960, John W. Cornforth (1917–), an Australian, conducted an extensive isotopic labeling study of the three pairs of methylene hydrogens in mevalonic acid (see the structure earlier in this chapter). The results helped clarify the biosynthesis of terpenes (and steroids) and Cornforth shared the 1975 Nobel Prize in chemistry with Vladimir Prelog.

The Beginnings of Exobiology

Nineteenth-century spectroscopes allowed astronomers to record emission spectra of stars, comets, and planets, and even to discover a new element (helium) on the Sun. In Germany, Hermann Vogel (1842–1907) discovered that the major components of Jupiter's atmosphere are hydrogen and helium, very similar to the Sun. In the earlier years of the 20th century, Vesto M. Slipher (1875–1969), at the Lowell Observatory, recorded spectra from Jupiter, Saturn, Uranus, and Neptune and in the early 1930s German astronomer Rupert Wildt (1905–76) analyzed them and discovered traces of methane (CH_4) and ammonia (NH_3) in the atmospheres of these frigid outer planets.

In 1924, with discoveries of traces of hydrocarbons in dim red stars, comets, and some meteorites, the Russian biochemist Alexandr I. Oparin (1894–1980) postulated that the prebiotic Earth's atmosphere was devoid of oxygen and likely to be "reducing" in nature. In such an environment, bursts of high energy (e.g., lightning, ultraviolet light) could transform the reduced forms of hydrogen (H_2), oxygen (H_2O), carbon (CH_4 and other hydrocarbons) and nitrogen (NH_3), into biologically significant precursors such as amino acids. Over eons, these precursors could build into complex biomolecules. At a certain level of complexity life would emerge. Oparin's work started to reach western scientists during the 1930s. In 1951, Harold C. Urey, the 1934 Nobel Laureate then at the University of Chicago, concluded independently that the prebiotic Earth's atmosphere was reducing and suggested an experiment to his graduate student Stanley L. Miller (1930–). Miller set up an apparatus that circulated H_2, NH_3, H_2O, and CH_4 through an electric arc for a period of 30 days (see the accompanying photograph). The stunning and gratifying result was the generation of significant quantities of amino acids in the dark "soup" that developed. In 1969, a carbon-rich meteorite crashed into Murchison, Australia. Amino acids were found at significant

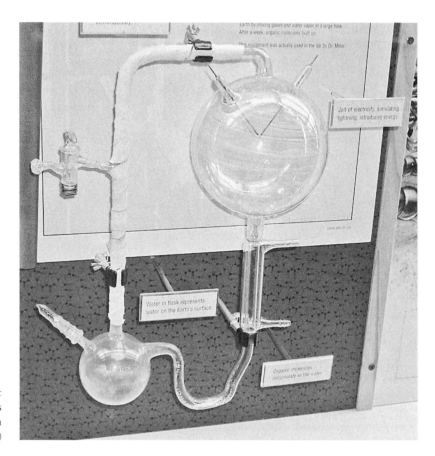

Stanley Miller's 1953 prebiotic soup experiment apparatus (University of California, San Diego)

levels (ca. 100 ppm) in this meteorite. How did the investigating scientists know the amino acids on the meteorite were extraterrestrial and not the result of terrestrial contamination? The Murchison meteorite amino acids were racemic (optically inactive), rather than rich in the L-amino acids anticipated if earthly contamination was the source (control experiments supported this conclusion). In addition, some of the meteorite's amino acids were uncommon ones not found in proteins. Exobiology was off to a hot start and, while there remains considerable debate over Miller's specific conditions, similar experiments and much more sophisticated ones over the next decades strongly support an abiotic origin for the complex molecules of life.

Controlling the Stereochemistry of Polymers

In 1953, Karl Ziegler (1898–1973), at the Max Planck Institute for Coal Research, discovered that a mixture of catalysts, triethylaluminum [$(C_2H_5)_3Al$] and titanium tetrachloride ($TiCl_4$), drastically lowers the pressure and temperature required to polymerize ethylene ($CH_2=CH_2$).

The white, powdery polyethylene formed was easily isolated from the reaction vessel for further processing. This "low-pressure" (high-density) polyethylene was a tougher polymer and its molded products held up better to force. Ziegler also discovered that polymers, like polypropylene or polystyrene, in which the "head" and "tail" of the monomer are different (e.g., propylene [$CH_2=CHCH_3$]), are specifically head-to-tail (H-T) in structure and not a mixture of H-H, T-T, and H-T.

Giulio Natta (1903–75) was trained in X-ray crystallography before turning his attention to polymers prior to the Second World War. Working at the Institute of Technology in Milan, Natta investigated methods for synthesizing artificial rubber, a problem of great concern to all nations as war clouds began to gather. In 1953, Natta attended a lecture by Ziegler and became excited about the structures of polypropylene and related polymers. His crystallographic studies helped to establish that polymers, such as polyethylene and polypropylene, tend to adopt helical conformations, much as Pauling found for α-keratin. Furthermore, depending upon the specific catalysts and conditions

Stereoregular polymers synthesized with (A and B) and without (C) the Ziegler-Natta catalyst: A) isotactic polypropylene; B) syndiotactic polypropylene; C) atactic polypropylene

STEREOISOMERS OF POLYPROPYLENE

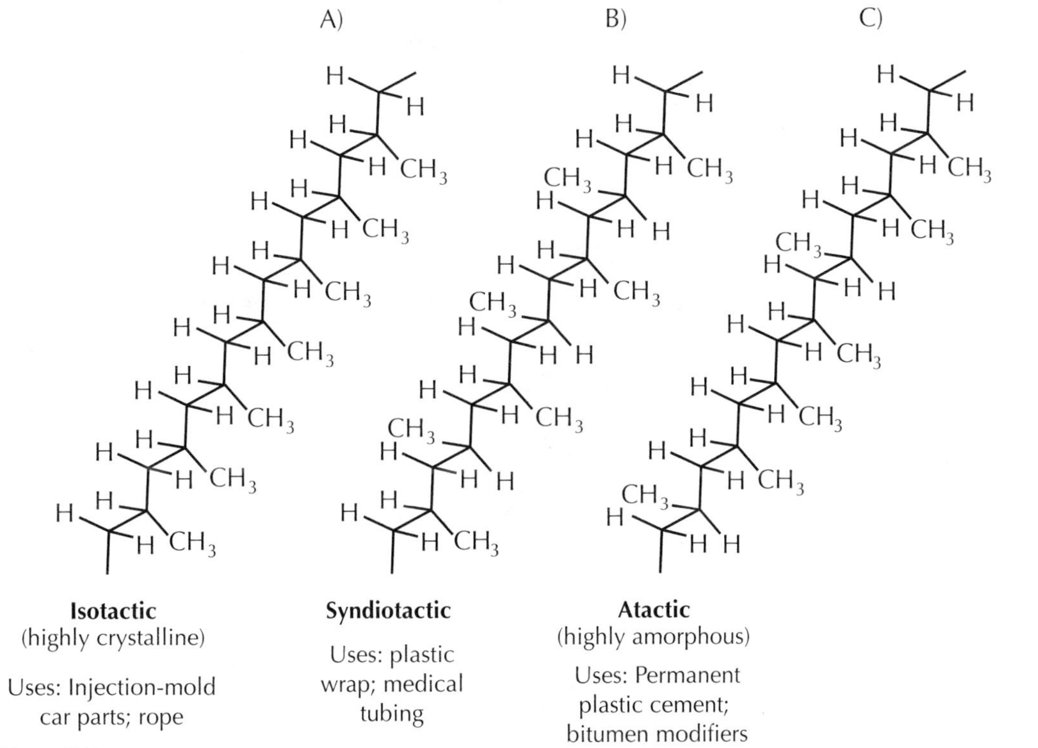

Isotactic (highly crystalline)

Uses: Injection-mold car parts; rope

Syndiotactic

Uses: plastic wrap; medical tubing

Atactic (highly amorphous)

Uses: Permanent plastic cement; bitumen modifiers

chosen, polypropylene and related compounds are polymerized head-to-tail with all asymmetric carbons in the chain having the same configuration, opposite configurations, or random configurations. Mrs. Natta suggested the terms *isotactic*, *syndiotactic*, and *atactic* for these three limiting cases (see the figure on page 213). Isotactic polypropylene is the most crystalline and the atactic polymer is least crystalline. The applications of these two polymers differ on this account. Not long after these discoveries were made the organometallic mechanistic chemistry of the polymerization was solved, providing yet another triumph in the renaissance of inorganic chemistry. Ziegler-Natta polymerization remains one of the greatest advances in the molecular design of materials and the codiscoverers shared the 1963 Nobel Prize in chemistry.

The 1950s were a period of commercialization of polymers including those that hit the market in the 1930s (polystyrene, polyamides including nylon, polyvinyl chloride [PVC], and polyethylene), the 1940s (polyurethanes, polyesters, silicones, and epoxies) and the newly marketed (Teflon, polypropylene, polyacetal, and polycarbonate). During the 1950s W. Lincoln Hawkins (1911–92) developed an antioxidant system compatible with the carbon black in the polyethylene telephone wire and cable coatings that enabled them to remain stable and flexible under conditions of heat and physical stress. Following his Ph.D. at McGill University and postdoctoral study at Columbia University, in 1942 "Linc" Hawkins became the first African-American scientist to join the staff at Bell Laboratories. More than 140 patents later he would become the first African American elected to the National Academy of Engineering and would receive the National Medal of Technology in 1992.

The DNA Double Helix: Function Follows Form and Form Follows Function

One of the greatest discoveries in human history appeared in *Nature* in 1953. The authors James D. Watson (1928–   ) and Francis Crick (1916–2004) (see the photograph), at the Cavendish Laboratory in Cambridge, begin their note simply:

> We wish to suggest a structure for the salt of deoxyribose nucleic acid (D.N.A.). This structure has novel features which are of considerable biological interest.

Then, in a masterpiece of British understatement, their penultimate sentence reads:

> It has not escaped our notice that the specific pairing we have postulated suggests a possible copying mechanism for the genetic material.

The march toward the solution of the structure of DNA began with Phoebus Levene's chemical studies in the early 20th century, the development of X-ray crystallography by the Braggs, and the fundamental understanding of polymers by Staudinger. Lord Todd's successes in solving the structures of nucleotides in the 1940s became even more significant after Oswald Avery, with little notice at first in 1944, established that DNA is the genetic material. The discovery by Erwin Chargaff that nucleotide composition is uniform within a species, but differs between species played a critical role in gaining support for DNA as the genetic material. Chargaff's discovery that thymine (T) and adenine (A) bases are found in equal quantities as are guanine (G) and cytosine (C) was critical in helping Watson and Crick to understand that the bases are stacked within the helix and not on its outside. Linus Pauling's systematization of structural chemistry in the 1930s and his audacious use of "top-down" concepts and modeling, that earlier produced the protein alpha-helix, provided the strategy that helped Watson and Crick "beat him at his own game." In the end, it was the crystallographic photograph ("Photograph 51"; see the photograph below) of the B-form of DNA, obtained by Rosalind Franklin (1920–1958), working in an uneasy and ambiguous collaboration with Maurice Wilkins (1916–2004) at Kings College in London, that

Francis Crick and James D. Watson with their successful model of DNA (A. Barrington Brown/Science Photo Library)

Rosalind Franklin and the Double Helix

In 1968, James D. Watson published a groundbreaking book titled *The Double Helix*. In it he presents his recollection of what he regarded (with considerable justice) as a race to discover the structure of DNA. His book presented great scientists as people, albeit gifted ones, with motivations, passions, obsessions, quirks, and warts common to creative people in all walks of life. It was a revelation to nonscientists weaned on idealized films about Madame Curie and Louis Pasteur. Furthermore, with a little "investment" in the science, the reader was treated to a page-turning thriller and genuine insights into the ways in which science is done.

The book was controversial before it went to press, and Harvard University Press declined to publish it as originally planned. Nonetheless it

enjoyed huge commercial success and is a worthwhile read. (Some books on the history of DNA are listed at the end of this chapter). The book's most controversial aspect is Watson's depiction of Rosalind Franklin, whose X-ray data were shared with Crick and himself, by her Kings College colleague Maurice Wilkins, without her knowledge and permission. A critical issue is the misunderstanding by Wilkins and Franklin of their formal relationship at Kings.

Franklin left the Cavendish Laboratory in 1953 for J. D. Bernal's group at Birkbeck in London. There she commenced crystallographic study of the tobacco mosaic virus (TMV). She clarified the structural roles of RNA and the protein coat in TMV, and her hypothesis that RNA in TMV was single-stranded was subsequently validated. In 1956, Rosalind Franklin was diagnosed with ovarian cancer. In 1957, she commenced a study of the polio virus that others would complete following her death in 1958. Aaron Klug (1926–   ) joined the Birkbeck group in 1954 and began work with Franklin on TMV. He and other colleagues completed the work and published the structure in 1959. It was dedicated to the memory and work of Rosalind Franklin. When Klug won the 1982 Nobel Prize in chemistry for his subsequent studies of the associations between biopolymers he had this to say in his acceptance speech in Stockholm:

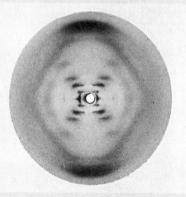

This was Linus Pauling's personal copy of this photo and he annotated it to the right of the figure. This furnished the critical clue that solved the double-helix structure of DNA. (The Valley Library, Oregon State University)

> It was Rosalind Franklin who set me the example of tackling large and difficult problems. Had her life not been cut tragically short, she might well have stood in this place on an earlier occasion.

would provide the critical data. Franklin died of ovarian cancer. Watson, Crick, and Wilkins shared the Nobel Prize in physiology or medicine in 1962, just four years before the genetic code was deciphered.

The beauty of the double helix is that its function was immediately apparent. Its form (twofold symmetry) perfectly fit one of its critical func-

Scientist of the Decade: Glenn T. Seaborg (1912–1999)

Glenn T. Seaborg in old plutonium laboratory; he recognized the actinide series in the periodic table and was awarded the 1951 Nobel Prize in chemistry. (Lawrence Berkeley National Laboratory)

Glenn Theodore Seaborg was born in 1912 in Ishpeming, Michigan. Following his family's move to Los Angeles, Seaborg worked his way through UCLA, graduated in 1934, and obtained his Ph.D. in 1937 at Berkeley where he studied chemistry with Gilbert N. Lewis and physics with Ernest O. Lawrence. For the next two years, Seaborg worked with physicist John J. Livingood (1903–86) at Berkeley and together they isolated new radioisotopes of iron (^{59}Fe), cobalt (^{60}Co), and iodine (^{131}I). These last two became the most important isotopes for radiation treatment of disease. The life of Seaborg's mother was extended by several years through treatment with ^{131}I. With Emilio Segrè, Seaborg discovered technetium-99m—an important radioisotope for diagnosis. The "m" stands for metastable. Technetium-99m is a *nuclear isomer* of technetium 99 in which either a proton or a neutron is in an excited spin state. Most nuclear isomers very rapidly change spin states, hence the metastable designation. Seaborg was appointed an instructor at Berkeley in 1939 and assistant professor in 1941.

Seaborg's codiscovery of plutonium in 1940 made him a person of strategic importance and in 1942 he was "drafted" to work in the metallurgical laboratory at the University of Chicago as part of the Manhattan Project. About one month after V-day, Seaborg joined with six other prominent scientists (including Leo Szilard, who cosigned with Einstein the 1939 letter to President Roosevelt) in signing the Franck Report (June 11, 1945) to President Truman. It advocated demonstration of the atomic bomb before the world's nations rather than its use against civilian populations. Seaborg would eventually become a prominent activist for nuclear disarmament.

Starting in 1940, Seaborg was the principal investigator or a coinvestigator in the syntheses of all transuranium elements up to and including 102 (nobelium). In 1944 he suggested a reformulation of the periodic table to include a new series, the actinide metals, and his Mendeleev-like predictions of the chemistry of the actinides have been overwhelmingly validated. In 1946, Seaborg assumed directorship of Nuclear Chemistry Research at the Lawrence Radiation Laboratory. In 1951, Seaborg shared the Nobel Prize in chemistry with his colleague Edwin M. McMillan. In 1958, Seaborg was appointed Chancellor of the University of California at Berkeley, but he stepped down to accept President Kennedy's appointment in 1961 as chairman of the Atomic Energy Commission. Seaborg served as chair for 10 years under Presidents Kennedy, Johnson, and Nixon. In 1971, Seaborg returned to a professorship at Berkeley. He subsequently served on President Reagan's 1983 National Commission on Excellence in Education and in 1991 received the National Medal of Science from President George H. W. Bush.

In 1997, element 106 was officially named seaborgium by IUPAC, the only element named after a person still living. While at the National ACS Meeting in Boston in 1998, where he was to be honored, Seaborg suffered a stroke. He died on February 25, 1999, at his home near Berkeley, the embodiment of a great scientist committed to public service and a more humane society.

tions: replication. Crick had earlier noted that replication ("two-ness") is the "perfect biological principle" and this function helped Watson and Crick to deduce the form of the molecule. In 1959 Arthur Kornberg (1918–   ), Stanford University, and Severo Ochoa (1905–93), New York University School of Medicine, shared the Nobel Prize in physiology or medicine for their discoveries, respectively, of the biosyntheses of DNA and RNA.

Conclusion

The 1950s were a period of advancements in the applications of theory (molecular orbital approaches to bonding and structure), developments of new instrumentation such as NMR spectrometers, and new applications of theory and computation techniques in crystallography. The next decade would witness the emergence of the computer in all of these applications, vastly increasing the size and complexity of research problems tackled. While the primary structures (amino acid sequences) of proteins were deduced during the 1950s, advances in structural techniques would provide second, tertiary, and (where relevant) quarternary structures in the following decade. The discovery of the structure of DNA in 1953 would be followed by discoveries of the mechanisms for replication and transcription and deciphering of the genetic code during the 1960s. That decade will also witness the beginnings of the modern environmental movement, aided in part by new analytical techniques. Dissent over the Vietnam War and growing concerns about the environment would raise doubts about the 1950s' fervent faith in technology.

Further Reading

British Broadcasting Corporation (BBC). *The Race for the Double Helix.* London: British Broadcasting Corporation, 1987. This movie features actor Jeff Goldblum as J. D. Watson and is a faithful adaptation of Watson's book but with a more nuanced portrait of Rosalind Franklin.

Berson, Jerome A. *Chemical Creativity: Ideas from the Work of Woodward, Hückel, Meerwein and Others.* Weinheim: Wiley-VCH, 1999. This book has historical and philosophical reflections on selected topics in organic chemistry, including Erich Hückel's emotional conflict during the Nazi era and the creative genius of Robert Burns Woodward.

Brock, William H. *The Norton History of Chemistry,* New York: W. W. Norton & Co., 1993. Chapter 14 includes discussion of the bitter Robinson-Ingold rivalry and chapter 15 describes the renaissance in inorganic chemistry that began in the 1950s.

Djerassi, Carl. *This Man's Pill: Reflections on the 50th Birthday of the Pill.* New York: Oxford University Press, 2001. This is a highly personalized history of the development of the birth control pill by the person often termed "the father of the birth control pill."

Gillespie, Ronald J., and Ronald S. Nyholm. "Inorganic Stereochemistry." *Quarterly Reviews of the Chemical Society (London)* 11 (1957): 339–80. This essay introduced Valence Shell Electron Pair Repulsion (VSEPR) theory to the chemical community.

Hoffmann, Roald, and Pierre Laszlo. "Ferrocene: Ironclad History or *Rashomon* Tale?" *Angewandte Chemie International Edition* 39 (2000): 123–4. This brief essay attempts to sort out the claims for priority in the discovery of ferrocene.

Jensen, William B. "The Origin of the 18-Electron Rule" *Journal of Chemical Education* 82 (2005): 28. This is a summary of the history and utility of the bonding rule that has been useful in transition metal chemistry.

Maddox, Brenda. *Rosalind Franklin: The Dark Lady of DNA.* New York: HarperCollins, 2003. This is a biography of the scientist whose X-ray data furnished the definitive proof of the structure of DNA but who did not share the Nobel Prize.

Nyholm, Ronald S. "The Renaissance of Inorganic Chemistry." *Journal of Chemical Education* 34 (1957): 166–69. This accessible article reviews the rebirth of inorganic chemistry that occurred during the 1950s.

Olby, Robert. *The Path to the Double Helix.* Seattle: University of Washington Press, 1974. This is a very thorough history of the discovery of the structure of DNA in a broad scientific and historical perspective.

Sayre, Ann. *Rosalind Franklin and DNA.* New York: W. W. Norton & Co., 1975. This book takes J. D. Watson's book *The Double Helix* to task for its treatment of Rosalind Franklin.

Seaborg, Glenn Theodore. *The Actinide Elements.* New York: McGraw-Hill, 1954. This is Seaborg's popularized presentation on the actinide series that he was the first to formally recognize.

Watson, James D., and Francis H. C. Crick. "Molecular Structure of Nucleic Acids. A Structure for Deoxyribose Nucleic Acid." *Nature* 171 (1953): 737–78. This is the epochal paper disclosing the double-helix structure of DNA.

———. *The Double Helix.* New York: Atheneum, 1968. This best-selling book by a Nobel Laureate discusses his very personal history of the discovery of the structure of DNA.

WGBH, Boston. *NOVA* Program: *Secret of Photo 51,* 2003. This one-hour program discusses the uses of Rosalind Franklin's photo 51 (X-ray of the B-form of DNA).

Wilkins, Maurice. *The Third Man of the Double Helix: The Autobiography of Maurice Wilkins.* New York: Oxford University Press, 2003. This is the autobiography of one of the scientists who shared the Nobel Prize for discovering the structure of DNA.

7

1961–1970:
Chemicals in the Environment:
Hidden Messages

Instrumentation Coupled with Computers
Enables Exploration of New Frontiers

The 1960s would witness extension of the periodic table to the first elements beyond the actinides. True to Glenn Seaborg's predictions, these *transactinides* behaved as main-group elements rather than actinides. At the start of the decade, computers were barely a part of the lives of chemists. The development of ever more sophisticated techniques to calculate the properties of molecules as well as new techniques, such as Fourier transform nuclear magnetic resonance (FT NMR) and infrared (FTIR), brought the computer into the chemist's laboratory. New techniques such as capillary gas chromatography/mass spectrometry (GC/MS) and high performance liquid chromatography (HPLC) vastly improved the separation and identification of complex mixtures. These methods were applied to detect trace levels of environmental *carcinogens*, chemicals in human tissue, as well as to determine the structures of long-known mysterious substances such as *prostaglandins* and *pheromones*.

The renaissance in inorganic chemistry continued with the synthesis of the first noble gas compounds, the discovery of the quadruple bond in some transition metal compounds, and advances in homogeneous catalysis. Organic chemists would observe using NMR normally short-lived carbocations in superacids and test the limits of bonding theory by constructing highly strained molecules. The *Woodward-Hoffmann rules* would rationalize concerted reactions including the Diels-Alder reaction.

During the 1960s, syntheses of peptides, proteins, and nucleic acids were developed where growing chains were attached to polymer supports (beads) allowing their purification in high yields. X-ray crystallographic studies of enzymes would provide insights on their structures as well as mechanisms of catalysis and would also aid in understanding the structures and functions of antibodies.

The 1960s witnessed the start of the environmental movement. Advances in analytical separations and detection allowed scientists to investigate exceedingly low levels of pollutants. The decade culminated with the creation of the United States Environmental Protection Agency in 1970.

Three New Chemical Elements: Uncertainties When Yields Are but a Few Atoms

Three new transuranium elements (elements 103-105) were created during the 1960s, each carrying its own scientific questions. Element 103 is the final actinide. Does it really behave like one? Elements 104 and 105 are the first transactinides: are they similar to the 5d transition metals hafnium (72) and tantalum (73)? The uncertainties about these heavy elements result from the incredible difficulty in making them, the miniscule amounts (a few atoms) obtained in experiments, and their very short lifetimes. Experiments on single atoms or small groups of atoms challenge our most fundamental concepts of equilibrium, usually limited to collections of billions of billions of atoms.

The lanthanide series in most modern periodic tables (e.g., the Periodic Table Appendix) includes elements 57 to 70. Chemically speaking, the series

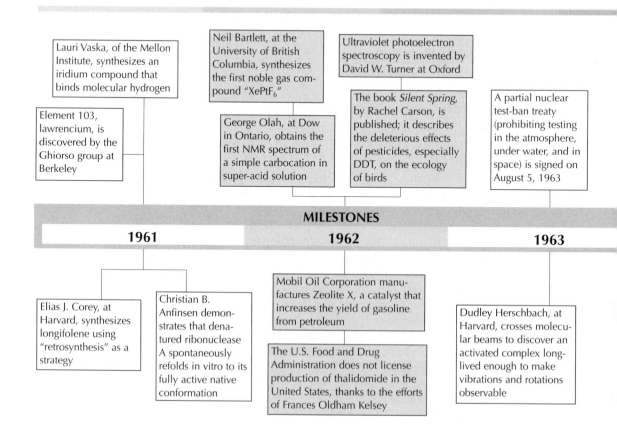

Lauri Vaska, of the Mellon Institute, synthesizes an iridium compound that binds molecular hydrogen

Neil Bartlett, at the University of British Columbia, synthesizes the first noble gas compound "XePtF₆"

Ultraviolet photoelectron spectroscopy is invented by David W. Turner at Oxford

Element 103, lawrencium, is discovered by the Ghiorso group at Berkeley

George Olah, at Dow in Ontario, obtains the first NMR spectrum of a simple carbocation in super-acid solution

The book *Silent Spring*, by Rachel Carson, is published; it describes the deleterious effects of pesticides, especially DDT, on the ecology of birds

A partial nuclear test-ban treaty (prohibiting testing in the atmosphere, under water, and in space) is signed on August 5, 1963

MILESTONES

1961　　　**1962**　　　**1963**

Elias J. Corey, at Harvard, synthesizes longifolene using "retrosynthesis" as a strategy

Christian B. Anfinsen demonstrates that denatured ribonuclease A spontaneously refolds in vitro to its fully active native conformation

Mobil Oil Corporation manufactures Zeolite X, a catalyst that increases the yield of gasoline from petroleum

The U.S. Food and Drug Administration does not license production of thalidomide in the United States, thanks to the efforts of Frances Oldham Kelsey

Dudley Herschbach, at Harvard, crosses molecular beams to discover an activated complex long-lived enough to make vibrations and rotations observable

really includes elements 58 (cerium)–71(lutetium). One simple illustration of this dichotomy is that the electronic configuration of 57 (lanthanum) is actually $4f^0 5d^1 6s^2$ *not* $4f^1 5d^0 6s^2$ as the simplest rules predict. The actinide Series, presented as 89-102 in most periodic tables (see page 422), chemically corresponds to 90 (thorium)–103 (lawrencium).

In 1961, the Ghiorso group at Berkeley bombarded 3 micrograms of californium 251 with ^{11}B ions and obtained element 103 with an apparent atomic mass of 257 and $t_{1/2}$ of 8 seconds (later corrected to mass 258, $t_{1/2}$, 3.9 seconds). In 1965, the Joint Institute for Nuclear Reactions (JINR) in Dubna reported an isotope of mass 256 with $t_{1/2}$ of 35 seconds. In 1968, Ghiorso's group demonstrated that element 103 is in the +3 oxidation state as predicted by Seaborg, unlike its predecessor nobelium (which favors +2) but consistent with most of the other actinides. The new element was eventually named lawrencium (Lr) after Ernest O. Lawrence (1901–58), the inventor of the cyclotron. The most stable isotope is now known to be ^{262}Lr ($t_{1/2}$, 3.6 hrs).

In 1964, the Dubna group reported element 104 (the 260 isotope) derived from bombarding ^{242}Pu with ^{22}Ne ions. While the Berkeley group

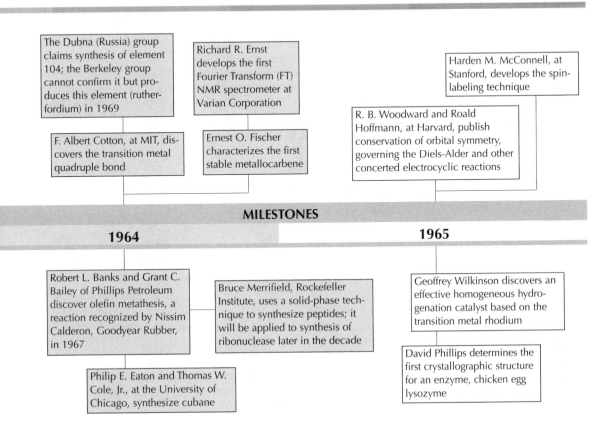

The Dubna (Russia) group claims synthesis of element 104; the Berkeley group cannot confirm it but produces this element (rutherfordium) in 1969

Richard R. Ernst develops the first Fourier Transform (FT) NMR spectrometer at Varian Corporation

Harden M. McConnell, at Stanford, develops the spin-labeling technique

R. B. Woodward and Roald Hoffmann, at Harvard, publish conservation of orbital symmetry, governing the Diels-Alder and other concerted electrocyclic reactions

F. Albert Cotton, at MIT, discovers the transition metal quadruple bond

Ernest O. Fischer characterizes the first stable metallocarbene

MILESTONES

1964

1965

Robert L. Banks and Grant C. Bailey of Phillips Petroleum discover olefin metathesis, a reaction recognized by Nissim Calderon, Goodyear Rubber, in 1967

Bruce Merrifield, Rockefeller Institute, uses a solid-phase technique to synthesize peptides; it will be applied to synthesis of ribonuclease later in the decade

Geoffrey Wilkinson discovers an effective homogeneous hydrogenation catalyst based on the transition metal rhodium

Philip E. Eaton and Thomas W. Cole, Jr., at the University of Chicago, synthesize cubane

David Phillips determines the first crystallographic structure for an enzyme, chicken egg lysozyme

could not duplicate the Russian experiment, in 1969 it accelerated ^{12}C and ^{13}C ions into ^{248}Cf and ^{249}Cf and observed four other isotopes of element 104. The most stable isotope of this element, later named rutherfordium, is ^{263}Rf, $t_{1/2}$ of 10 minutes. Rutherfordium is the first transactinide. Ion chromatography established that Rf favors the +4 oxidation state (it forms $RfCl_6^{2-}$ ions) since it co-elutes with its "family members" zirconium and hafnium rather than with the actinides, which are retained on the column.

In 1967, the JINR reported creation of a few atoms of element 105 with mass 261 and a lifetime of 1.8 seconds and reported other isotopes three years later. In 1970, the Berkeley group synthesized element 105 with mass 260 and $t_{1/2}$ of 1.52 seconds but could not reproduce the 1967 Russian data. While the Berkeley group promoted "hahnium" as the name for element 105, IUPAC adopted the name dubnium (Db) in 1977. The most stable isotope (discovered in 2004 in Dubna) is ^{268}Db, $t_{1/2}$, 16 hours.

Not All Rare Gases Are "Noble"

The inert gases, also termed rare or noble, remained hidden until the 1890s precisely because of their inertness. Since argon comprises almost

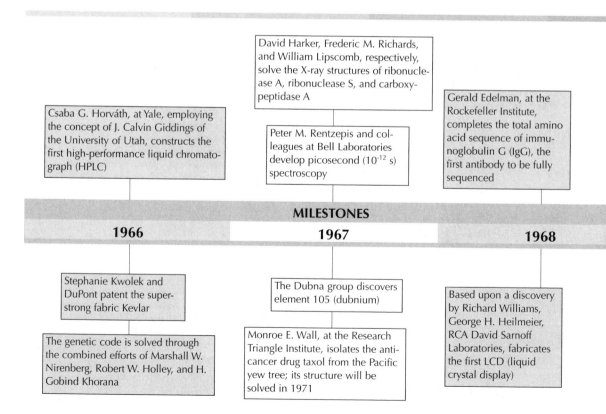

David Harker, Frederic M. Richards, and William Lipscomb, respectively, solve the X-ray structures of ribonuclease A, ribonuclease S, and carboxypeptidase A

Csaba G. Horváth, at Yale, employing the concept of J. Calvin Giddings of the University of Utah, constructs the first high-performance liquid chromatograph (HPLC)

Peter M. Rentzepis and colleagues at Bell Laboratories develop picosecond (10^{-12} s) spectroscopy

Gerald Edelman, at the Rockefeller Institute, completes the total amino acid sequence of immunoglobulin G (IgG), the first antibody to be fully sequenced

MILESTONES

1966   **1967**   **1968**

Stephanie Kwolek and DuPont patent the super-strong fabric Kevlar

The Dubna group discovers element 105 (dubnium)

Based upon a discovery by Richard Williams, George H. Heilmeier, RCA David Sarnoff Laboratories, fabricates the first LCD (liquid crystal display)

The genetic code is solved through the combined efforts of Marshall W. Nirenberg, Robert W. Holley, and H. Gobind Khorana

Monroe E. Wall, at the Research Triangle Institute, isolates the anti-cancer drug taxol from the Pacific yew tree; its structure will be solved in 1971

1 percent of the atmosphere (see chapter 1), it could hardly be called rare. Over a century ago, Henri Moissan obtained a sample of argon from William Ramsay, placed it in a vessel with his ferociously reactive fluorine gas, and sparked the mixture but observed no reaction between the two gases. Twenty years later, when Lewis developed his electron-dot formulas, he relied upon the completed valence shells of the noble gases as a basis for explaining the octet rule. Their chemistry is consistent with full occupancy of valence atomic orbitals: He ($1s^2$); Ne ($2s^22p^6$); Ar ($3s^23p^6$); Kr ($4s^24p^6$); Xe ($5s^25p^6$). In the early 1930s, Linus Pauling realized that since xenon has the lowest ionization potential (IP, the energy required to remove an electron from an atom or molecule) of the rare gases it might lose an electron to fluorine, the most electronegative element. However, his colleague Donald M. Yost (1893–1977) was not successful in inducing reaction between F_2, "the irresistible force," and Xe, "the immovable object."

In 1961, Neil Bartlett (1932–   ), at the University of British Columbia in Canada, had his graduate student Derek Lohmann investigate an ionic salt he had made earlier. They discovered it has the formula $O_2^+PtF_6^-$; the oxygen molecule had been oxidized by PtF_6. The idea that an oxidizing

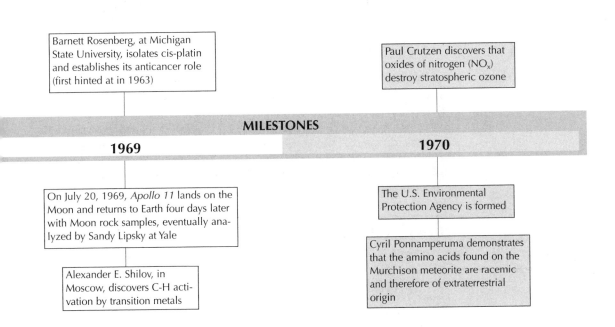

Barnett Rosenberg, at Michigan State University, isolates cis-platin and establishes its anticancer role (first hinted at in 1963)

Paul Crutzen discovers that oxides of nitrogen (NO_x) destroy stratospheric ozone

MILESTONES

1969

1970

On July 20, 1969, *Apollo 11* lands on the Moon and returns to Earth four days later with Moon rock samples, eventually analyzed by Sandy Lipsky at Yale

Alexander E. Shilov, in Moscow, discovers C-H activation by transition metals

The U.S. Environmental Protection Agency is formed

Cyril Ponnamperuma demonstrates that the amino acids found on the Murchison meteorite are racemic and therefore of extraterrestrial origin

agent, even as strong as PtF_6, could turn oxygen into a reducing agent was met with skepticism. Looking for confirming evidence, Bartlett noted that the IP of xenon (12.1 electron volts or eV, roughly the energy required to break an N_2 molecule into atoms) is actually slightly lower than that of O_2 (12.2 eV). If PtF_6 can oxidize O_2 to O_2^+, it should also oxidize Xe to Xe^+. In March 1962, Bartlett brought deep red PtF_6 into contact with colorless xenon and observed formation of a yellow substance. Although initially thought to be $Xe^+PtF_6^-$, it is really $XeF^+PtF_5^-$, where the PtF_5 units form long chains with each other.

The psychological barrier had been broken. Later in 1962, researchers at Argonne National Laboratory formed XeF_4, by heating Xe and F_2 to 750°F (400°C), succeeding where Pauling and Yost failed. Not long afterward, XeF_2, XeF_6, the explosive oxides XeO_3 and XeO_4, as well as other covalent compounds and salts were reported. Compared to xenon, the IPs of helium (24.6 eV) and neon (21.6 eV) are incredibly high and there are no known compounds of these two elements. The IP of krypton (14.0 eV) is only 1.9 eV greater than that of xenon and KrF_2 was reported in 1963. The IP of radioactive radon (Rn) is 10.7 eV, 1.4 eV *lower* than xenon. Researchers at Argonne apparently made tiny quantities of RnF_2 in 1962, but radon's short lifetime limits such studies. There continue today very active searches for compounds of argon (IP = 15.8 eV); although Bartlett predicts that ArF_2 cannot be made, the first true argon compound, argon fluorohydride (HArF), which is stable up to 27 K (-411°F or -246°C), would be discovered in 2000 (see chapter 10).

The new xenon compounds, unimagined by Gillespie and Nyholm when they formulated VSEPR theory during the 1950s, were excellent candidates to test their theory (the fifth-row element xenon can "expand its octet"). As predicted, XeO_3 is a trigonal pyramid, reflecting a lone pair on xenon, and XeO_4 is tetrahedral. In remarkable agreement with VSEPR theory, XeF_4 is square planar, reflecting four bonded pairs of electrons and two lone pairs on Xe; the larger lone pairs are on opposite sides of the XeF_4 molecular plane. The geometry of XeF_6 is, as predicted, not octahedral due to the extra lone pair on Xe. There is no totally symmetrical three-dimensional structure for seven electron pairs and XeF_6 rapidly fluctuates between different structures. A similar situation exists for many five-coordinate structures: Compounds such as PF_5 and $Fe(CO)_5$ are also "fluxional" and rapidly "pseudorotate" between trigonal bipyramid structures by the so-called Berry mechanism discovered by R. Stephen Berry (1932–   ) in 1960.

Quadruple Bonds between Transition Metal Atoms

Molecules with more than one transition metal atom have been known since 1850, but even Alfred Werner (see chapter 1) did not consider the possibility that they contained direct metal-metal bonding. It is noteworthy that the mercurous ion has been known to be Hg_2^{2+} since the late-19th century and the covalent bond holding the two atoms together is a strong one. X-ray crystallography changed this situation when, in 1938, it disclosed that while the two iron atoms in $Fe_2(CO)_9$ are bridged by carbonyls (CO), they are close enough to suggest bonding between them. Almost 20 years later, the structure of $Mn_2(CO)_{10}$ [i.e. $(CO)_5Mn-Mn(CO)_5$] demonstrated direct bonding between the two metal atoms, since there are no bridging carbonyls. This was the start of transition metal cluster chemistry and soon hundreds of compounds containing three, four, and more metal atoms directly bonded to each other were reported. In the early 1960s, metal-metal double and triple bonds were discovered and F. Albert Cotton (1930–2007), at MIT, pioneered the use of theory and experiment to understand these structures.

In 1964, Cotton made a major breakthrough investigating the $(Re_2Cl_8^{2-})$ ion in salts such as $K_2Re_2Cl_8$. The ion (see the figure below, right) has a rhenium-rhenium distance of only 2.24 Å. This is much shorter than the Re-Re distance (2.75 Å) in rhenium metal and the 2.48 Å distance in the Re_3Cl_9 cluster. But there is another curious aspect: The two sets of chlorines on the two rhenium atoms are eclipsed. This was surprising since the nonbonded chlorine atoms seemed too close for "comfort." Cotton developed a novel and now well-accepted explanation, the quadruple bond between transition metals. A d-orbital on one rhenium overlaps all four lobes with a d-orbital on the other rhenium creating a bonding combination and an antibonding combination. Just as s-atomic orbitals form sigma (σ) molecular orbitals and p-orbitals form π-orbitals (as well as σ) (see chapter 4), d-orbitals form δ-molecular orbitals (as well as π and σ). This overlap between d-orbitals is fairly small so that the bonding MO (δ) is not too much lower in energy than the antibonding δ^* MO. Thus, the additional ("fourth") bond is not very strong. In $Re_2Cl_8^{2-}$, one σ, two π, and one δ molecular orbital are filled, providing eight shared bonding electrons: a quadruple bond. The small energy gap between the HOMO (δ) and the LUMO (δ^*) is the origin of the deep color in $K_2Re_2Cl_8$.

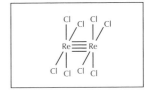

A quadruple bond

The Roles of Simple Numbers and Symmetry in Chemical Reactivity

Simple numbers play a huge role in understanding chemical reactivity. For example, the periodic table has 18 columns (families) of chemical elements and (for now) 7 rows or periods. The periods correspond to Bohr's orbits (n = 1,2,3, . . .) which are simple integers. When the new quantum mechanics appeared during the 1920s, simple integers for quantum numbers n, l, and m_l specified atomic orbitals.

The 4n + 2 rule, developed by Hückel in the 1930s, is another example. Allowed values for n are integers only (n = 0, 1, 2, 3, . . .). Benzene, the stable aromatic compound, has 6 π electrons satisfying the 4n + 2 rule (n = 1). Cyclobutadiene (see chapter 4) has 4 π electrons, does not satisfy the

4n + 2 rule, and is extremely reactive and short-lived. The 1960s witnessed widespread testing of concepts of aromaticity with NMR furnishing a sensitive probe. Particularly striking is [18]-annulene (see structure below), prepared by Franz Sondheimer (1926–81) in London. This planar 18-membered ring satisfies the 4n + 2 rule (n = 4), is stable and displays aromatic chemical and NMR properties. In 1964, Rowland Pettit (1927–81), University of Texas, prepared a stable iron complex containing square cyclobutadiene (see structure below). The complex satisfies the 18-electron rule and releases its short-lived "captive" upon oxidation by Ce^{4+}.

The type of pictorial, "back-of-the-envelope," application of theory exemplified by the 4n + 2 rule would soon be applied toward understanding a wide range of "no-mechanism" reactions. The Diels-Alder reaction (see chapter 3) is one example. The reverse reaction ("retro-Diels-Alder") also occurs readily. In one step (one transition state), three π bonds are broken and two new σ bonds and one π bond are created. The simultaneous cleavage and formation of all bonds in one step is referred to as "concerted" and such reactions often occur under mild conditions and form specific stereoisomers. Since the bonds made and broken form a continuous cycle in the transition state, the Diels-Alder is an example of an "electrocyclic" reaction. In contrast to the Diels-Alder reaction, dimerizations of two alkene molecules ($R_2C=CR_2$) to cyclobutanes typically fail (as do the reverse thermal decompositions of cyclobutanes). These reactions often succeed when ultraviolet light (photochemistry) is used in place of heat (thermal chemistry).

R. B. Woodward, challenged by the structure of adenosylcobalamin (vitamin B_{12}) determined by Dorothy Hodgkin in 1961, embarked on the total synthesis of this extraordinarily complex molecule. So did Albert Eschenmoser (1925–   ) at the ETH in Zurich. The two groups would join forces in a project lasting more than a decade. During this project Woodward confronted a curiosity that can be illustrated with a simple example. When heated, the 1,3,5-triene (shown on page 229), having *trans*- (or *E*-) geometry at both terminal double bonds, closes to form the *cis*-1,3-cyclohexadiene isomer shown. This is a bit curious since steric repulsion between the two methyl groups should make this *cis*-isomer less stable than the *trans*-isomer. In this *isomerization*, the two terminal carbon groups of the triene rotate simultaneously, one clockwise and one counterclockwise, maintaining a plane of symmetry as the triene isomerizes to the trans-cyclohexadiene shown. This type of rotation is referred to

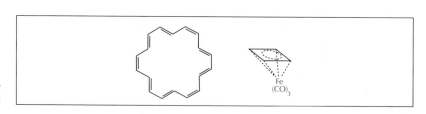

[18]-Annulene; cyclobutadiene iron tricarbonyl

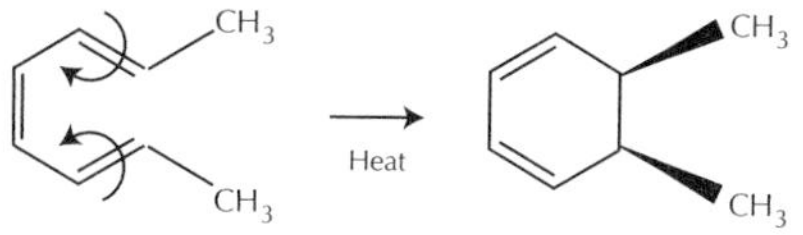

Disrotatory ring closure of a 1,3,5-hexatriene to a 1,3-cyclohexadiene

as "disrotatory." When the related 1,3,5-triene having a *cis*-double bond at one terminus and a *trans*-double bond at the other is heated, it forms the *trans*-1,3-cyclohexadiene isomer. This is also disrotatory ring closure. In contrast, when 1,3-butadienes (4 π systems) are heated they close to cyclobutenes, but in a "conrotatory" manner: Both terminal groups rotate clockwise (or counter-clockwise) maintaining a twofold axis of symmetry, not a plane. This dichotomy has echoes of the difference between 4n + 2 π-systems like benzene and 4n π-systems like cyclobutadiene (i.e., the Hückel 4n + 2 rule). In contrast to the thermal chemistry, photochemical ring closure of a 1,3,5-triene is conrotatory, while photochemical closure of a 1,3-butadienes is disrotatory.

This alternation of chemical behavior, 6π-system versus 4π-system, thermal versus photochemical, has at its core the quantum effects that dictate the symmetries of molecular orbitals. In 1964, Roald Hoffmann (1937–) was 27, had completed his Ph.D. at Harvard two years earlier, and was in the second year of an appointment as a Harvard junior fellow. The renowned Woodward (who would win the Nobel Prize in chemistry in 1965) discussed his observations on electrocyclic reactions with Hoffmann. Although Kenichi Fukui had developed frontier molecular orbital theory more than a decade earlier and many related theoretical ideas were "percolating" in the chemical community, it was Woodward and Hoffmann who published, in 1965, their intellectual synthesis as a book titled *The Conservation of Orbital Symmetry*. Their theory explained a broad spectrum of concerted reactions and made bold predictions that were later verified.

The figure on page 230 illustrates the theory for the "thermally allowed" ("photochemically forbidden") Diels-Alder reaction. 1,3-Butadiene (4π) and ethylene (2π) come together in a manner that maintains a plane of symmetry from reactants through transition state to products. Thermal reactions involve molecules in their ground states (lowest-energy orbitals occupied). The key molecular orbitals of the reactant molecules are the π-orbital in ethylene, which is symmetric (S) with respect to the plane, and two combined π-orbitals in butadiene that are, respectively, symmetric (S) and anti-symmetric (A). The key molecular orbitals of the product, cyclohexene, are its symmetric (S) π-orbital and two "extended" σ-orbitals that are symmetric (S) and antisymmetric (A) respectively. The figure shows that bonding MOs in the reactants "correlate" with bonding MOs in the product implying a low energy of activation for this "allowed" reaction.

EXPLANATIONS OF DIELS-ALDER REACTION BASED ON ORBITAL SYMMETRY

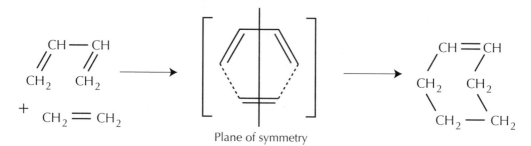

Plane of symmetry

A) Conservation of Orbital Symmetry

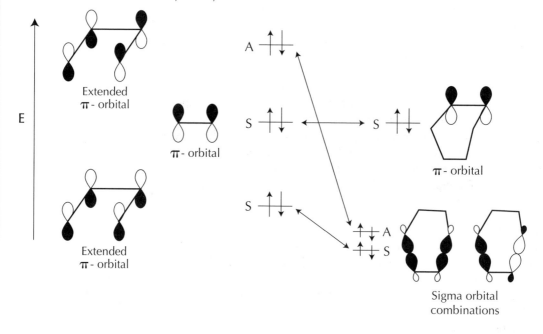

Extended
π- orbital

π- orbital

Extended
π- orbital

π- orbital

Sigma orbital
combinations

B) Frontier Molecular Orbital Theory

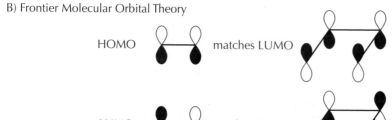

HOMO   matches LUMO

LUMO   matches HOMO

(Opposite page) Molecular orbital picture diagrams rationalizing the Diels-Alder reaction between 1,3-butadiene and ethylene (top) using A) the conservation of orbital symmetry (Woodward and Hoffmann); B) frontier molecular orbital theory (Fukui).

In contrast, the thermal reaction of two ethylenes (not shown) correlates one of the bonding MOs of the reactants with an antibonding MO of the product. The result is a very high energy of activation and a "forbidden" reaction. Actually, such a "forbidden" reaction may well occur, but it is slower and perhaps nonconcerted (forming one new bond at a time). Photochemical reactions involve exciting an electron from HOMO to LUMO in a reactant. Correlation of occupied orbitals in the reactants with orbitals of similar or lower energy in the products, corresponds to an "allowed" reaction. If the correlation is with orbitals of higher energy in the products it is "forbidden." This simple but powerful theory explains the alternation between 6 π systems and 4 π systems as well as the alternation between thermal and photochemical behavior for a given system.

The lower part of the figure demonstrates that Fukui frontier molecular orbital theory also provides a good rationalization of the Diels-Alder (and other) concerted reactions. In 1981, Roald Hoffmann and Kenichi Fukui shared the Nobel Prize in chemistry (Woodward had died in 1979).

Computational Chemistry

Conservation of orbital symmetry and frontier molecular orbital theory are qualitative, "back-of-the-envelope" approaches that are highly valuable but lack numerical power. During the late 1950s and throughout the 1960s huge mainframe computers became fixtures at research institutions and could perform high-level quantum calculations on very small molecules (H_2O, CO, C_2H_4). Larger molecules required major approximations. Hückel MO theory (see chapter 4) treats only p_z-orbitals and the π-systems they form. The next, more complex, step is to consider all valence-level atomic orbitals while neglecting "core" orbitals (e.g., 1s in carbon; 1s, 2s, 2p in sulfur) so as to mix σ and π bonding. These semiempirical calculations were an important step and produced many successes as well as failures during the 1960s.

Ab initio ("from the beginning") calculations employ all atomic orbitals including the core. Even with relatively simple atomic orbital "basis sets," these were still limited to relatively small (<10-carbon) organic molecules by the end of the 1960s. The early ab initio calculations had numerous successes and some notable failures. Experimentalists cast a wary eye at calculations that often appeared to be much better at explanation after the experiment than prediction before the experiment. John A. Pople (1925–2004) began to develop programs for ab initio calculations during the mid-1960s at Carnegie Mellon University. His programs placed ab initio calculations into the hands of less computationally skilled chemists who would begin decades of applications. Pople's ab initio calculations were based upon approximate solutions to the Schrödinger wave function Ψ (see chapter 3). The complexity of these calculations increase rapidly as molecules get larger: Complexity is proportional to ~N^4, where N = number of orbitals. This fixed the fundamental limits on both the size of molecules that could be computed as well as the sophistication of the mathematical descriptions of the orbitals (basis sets) employed. The net result was to limit ab initio to fairly small molecules. For example, in going from a single fixed geometry of a molecule of water, H_2O (1 core and 6 valence-level atomic orbitals), to a single fixed geometry of water dimer ($[H_2O]_2$) (2 core and 12 valence-level orbitals), the increase in the complexity of a given level of *ab initio* calculation increases by a factor of roughly 16 (2^4). This does not even take into account the added complexity of calculating the best (lowest-energy) geometry for the bigger system. In 1964, Walter Kohn (1923–   ), at the University of California at San Diego, started to develop Density Functional Theory (DFT). DFT was based upon the electron density distribution [$n(r)$] rather than on Ψ. The complexity of the calculation rose much less rapidly with the size of the molecule and DFT theory would ultimately enable complex ab initio MO calculations on very large molecules. DFT calculations would really enter common use starting in 1993. John A. Pople and Walter Kohn would share the 1998 Nobel Prize in chemistry.

An exciting development during this period was the ultraviolet photoelectron spectrometer invented by David W. Turner (1927–   ) at Oxford in 1962. While X-ray photoelectron spectroscopy (ESCA) (see chapter 6) provides energies of core (e.g., 1s) orbitals, UV photoelectron spectroscopy (UV PES) yields energies of valence-level MOs from the HOMO downward. The shapes of the UV PES bands also provide information about the nature of the orbitals. UV PES helped to improve computational theory and as computations improved they helped chemists pull more detail from UV PES data.

Here is one illustration of the interplay between computational MO theory and UV PES. DABCO (see structure below) is an amine and thus a base. A classical prediction would suggest that there are two separate, fully equivalent nitrogen lone pairs in this molecule. The second nitrogen in DABCO, since it is electronegative, should make DABCO a weaker base than model amines with a single nitrogen. DABCO is actually a much stronger base than its models. Why? Quantum computations predict that the lone pairs on the two nitrogen atoms occupy orbitals (n) that interact through space to form two new molecular orbitals: a high-energy combination ($n + n$) and a low-energy combination ($n - n$), each filled with two electrons. The high energy MO is the source of the high basicity in DABCO and the molecule's low ionization potential. Experimentally, the UV PE spectrum shows two separate peaks corresponding to these two MOs.

Molecular mechanics methods, based on Westheimer's approach (see chapter 6), were refined into software packages by a number of groups. Molecular mechanics calculations depend heavily on input data from known

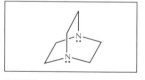

DABCO

molecules. Unlike early quantum calculations that, while weak on accuracy, provided unanticipated insights into bonding, molecular mechanics gave accurate results but little insight into bonding. One early and very beautiful application of molecular mechanics was the study by Paul von Ragué Schleyer (1930–), Princeton University, of rearrangement pathways to adamantane ($C_{10}H_{16}$, see the accompanying figure). He discovered, starting in 1957, that any $C_{10}H_{16}$ isomer, in the presence of Lewis acid "sludge catalysts," rearranges to the stable adamantane. Schleyer had discovered a fundamental natural process, since adamantane is found in petroleum.

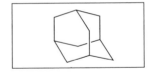

Adamantane

Computers "Hook Up" with Instrumentation

During the 1960s computers evolved into more powerful, smaller units and became major components of spectroscopic and spectrometric instruments. Computers did not merely aid in the collection, storage and treatment of data, they sometimes fundamentally changed the very nature of the measurement.

Richard R. Ernst (1933–), born and educated in Switzerland, joined the Varian Corporation in 1962 and pioneered the development in 1964 of the Fourier transform (FT NMR) spectrometer. Instead of slowly sweeping through a range of radiofrequencies (RF) in a constant magnetic field (see chapter 6), the sample is exposed to a very short RF pulse with a range of frequencies. RF absorption data is collected in a very short time period in the form of absorption versus time ("time domain"). The *Fourier transform* is a mathematical technique that allows dissection of any complex curve into individual sine and cosine curves of specific frequencies and amplitudes: the "frequency domain" curve that is the normal NMR spectrum. FT NMR introduced vast improvements in signal-to-noise allowing the new spectrometers to analyze much smaller samples and opened the way to studies of proteins and nucleic acids. Ernst returned to Switzerland at the end of 1968 to accept a position at the ETH. His FT NMR work continued with the development of ^{13}C NMR and two-dimensional NMR starting in the early 1970s. Ernst received the Nobel Prize in chemistry in 1991.

Fourier transform infrared spectroscopy (FTIR) had its origins in the interferometer developed by Michelson in 1880 and experiments by astrophysicists some seventy years later. A commercial FTIR instrument required development of the laser (1960, by Theodore H. Maiman [1927–], Hughes Aircraft), refined optics, and computer hardware and software. The Fourier transform takes data collected in "time domain" and converts them to "frequency domain," the normal infrared (IR) spectrum. FTIR provided vastly improved signal-to-noise ratios allowing routine analyses of microgram samples.

The mid-1960s witnessed the "marriage" between gas chromatography (GC) and mass spectrometry (MS) (see the figure on page 234). Marcel J. E. Golay (1902–89) developed the idea of the capillary (or open-tubular) GC column in 1957. Capillary GC, capable of extremely high resolution, became an important analytical technique during the 1960s. The mass spectrometer is extremely sensitive and provides fragmentation "fingerprints" for each individual compound exiting the GC column. The first GC/MS is considered to be the one assembled in 1958 by Fred McLafferty (1923–   ) and Roland S. Gohlke (1929–   ) at Dow Chemical, with another around the same time assembled by Ragnar Ryhage in Stockholm. Among the earliest to explore GC/MS was Seymour (Sandy) Lipsky (1924–86) at Yale Medical School. In 1960, Lipsky and James E. Lovelock (1919–   ) published their invention of the highly sensitive and selective electron capture detector (ECD) for GC. Lipsky would use GC/MS to analyze Moon rock samples from *Apollo 11*, which landed on the Moon on July 20, 1969, and returned July 24.

Mass spectrometry data are readily digitized and "libraries" of mass spectral data for individual substances could be stored on computer tapes. Klaus Biemann (1926–   ), at MIT, had accumulated a library of 8,000 mass

A schematic diagram of a gas chromatograph/mass spectrometer (GC/MS) interfaced with a computer library of mass spectra for identification of compounds

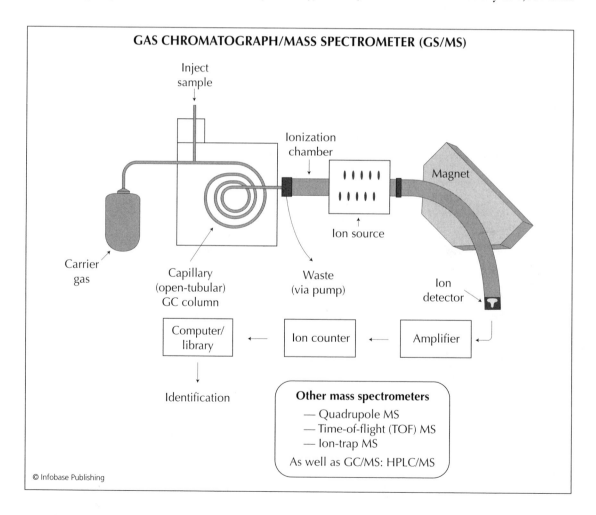

GAS CHROMATOGRAPH/MASS SPECTROMETER (GS/MS)

Inject sample

Ionization chamber

Magnet

Ion source

Carrier gas

Capillary (open-tubular) GC column

Waste (via pump)

Ion detector

Computer/ library ← Ion counter ← Amplifier

Identification

Other mass spectrometers
— Quadrupole MS
— Time-of-flight (TOF) MS
— Ion-trap MS
As well as GC/MS: HPLC/MS

spectra. What if the mass spectrum of an unknown compound could be compared with a computerized library? The new computer science of artificial intelligence played an important early role, and chemists, such as Fred McLafferty now at Cornell, helped design "quality indexes" for data matching. In the early 1970s, the National Institute of Standards and Technology (NIST) started an MS database that today forms the core of computer libraries that are supplied on CDs with commercial GC/MS instruments that aid environmental and forensic scientists as well as chemists.

Another powerful analytical instrument joined the chemist's arsenal during the 1960s. Classical column chromatography uses relatively large particles in the stationary phase allowing solvent to pass through the column at atmospheric pressure. In 1964 J. Calvin Giddings (1930–96), at the University of Utah, conceptualized high-performance liquid chromatography (HPLC), in which uniform microscopic particles are employed as the stationary phase, requiring high pressure to force solvent through the column. The result would be a vast increase in resolution, comparable to or better than capillary GC. In 1966, Csaba G. Horváth (1930–2004), at Yale, built the first HPLC instrument. HPLC would become the workhorse for separating nonvolatile compounds during the coming decades with a computer controlling the elution solvent as well as data analysis.

What Happens When Individual Atoms and Molecules Collide?

Classical reaction-rate (chemical kinetics) studies rely on varying the concentrations and temperatures of collections of billions of billions of molecules. The data are extremely useful *and* limited. Concentration data provide strong hints about reaction mechanisms: chain reactions (see chapter 2), explosions due to branched-chain reactions (see chapter 3), and S_N1 and S_N2 reactions (see chapter 4). The Arrhenius equation yields the activation energy (E_a) and the frequency factor (A) when rate constants (k) are plotted against the reciprocal of absolute temperature (1/T). Reaction coordinate energy surfaces developed by Henry Eyring and Michael Polanyi during the 1930s gave more precise meaning to the energy of activation. Chemists were eager to discover how individual collisions between atoms and/or molecules occurred. How are the kinetic energies of collisions distributed in the speeds and directions (translations), rotations, and vibrations of product molecules?

Dudley R. Herschbach (1932–) began a series of molecular beam experiments at Berkeley starting in 1960. He employed two small ovens with slits producing crossed beams of molecules or atoms under very low pressure that collide in a vacuum reaction chamber. The early apparatus was built upon a turntable directing the stream of products toward a surface ionization detector sensitive to alkali metals and their salts. His first successful experiment crossed beams of potassium atoms and CH_3I molecules:

$$K + CH_3I \rightarrow K^+I^- + CH_3$$

An atom-molecule reaction of this type has a very minute activation barrier. His analysis indicated that the lifetime of the activated complex formed $(K \ldots I \ldots CH_3)$ was $\sim 10^{-13}$ seconds, shorter than the lifetime of rotation or vibration of the complex. In 1963, Herschbach moved to Harvard and built a more sophisticated apparatus. He calculated that a reaction that breaks an ionic bond, rather than a covalent bond, to form an ionic bond should have a longer-lived (more "persistent") activated complex (A, B = alkali metals; X = halogen):

$$A + X^-B^+ \rightarrow A^+X^- + B$$

This reaction did provide, as predicted, a longer-lived activated complex $(>10^{-12}$ seconds) that rotates and vibrates several times before falling apart. The number of collisions that provided products was smaller than expected. Herschbach and his coworkers realized that this was due to attack by A at the "wrong end" of X^-B^+ to form some $(A \ldots B \ldots X)$ complexes, not so well suited to "falling apart" to A^+X^- and B.

In 1967, Yuan T. Lee (1936–   ) joined Herschbach as a researcher after completing his Ph.D. at Berkeley. Lee designed and built an apparatus with supersonic beam nozzles and an electron bombardment ionizer that functioned as a universal detector. Supersonic beams propel species in the same direction at nearly the same speed and allow very few collisions. For this reason, chlorine atoms, much more reactive than potassium atoms, could be employed in the new and even more sensitive apparatus:

$$Cl + Br_2 \rightarrow BrCl + Br$$

Lee joined the University of Chicago faculty in 1968, moving to Berkeley in 1974. His analyses of reactants, products, and complexes, including excited vibrational and rotational states, provided new mechanistic insights. For example, concerted reaction of F_2 and I_2 to form IF molecules is symmetry-forbidden, but occurs easily. Lee discovered that I_2F, a radical species, is an intermediate and explains the rapid rate of this reaction.

John C. Polanyi (1929–   ) was born in Berlin to parents of Hungarian descent. His father, Michael Polanyi, developed transition state theory (see chapter 4) and also studied collisions between alkali metals and halogen molecules. The Polanyi family left Germany in 1933 for England where John received his education. He joined the University of Toronto in 1956 and used IR chemiluminescence, pioneered by his father, to study molecular collisions. In 1986, Dudley R. Herschbach, Yuan T. Lee, and John C. Polanyi shared the 1986 Nobel Prize in chemistry for the contributions to reaction dynamics.

Transition Metals: New Compounds, New Reactions, and New Insights

One of the simplest possible reactions is the transfer of electrons from one ion to another. George Hevesy pioneered this field in the 1920s when he employed radioactive lead to study electron transfers between

Pb^{2+} and Pb^{4+}. This reaction is termed "self-exchange" since there is no *net* chemical reaction. Electron transfer between two different metals such as Co^{3+} and Cr^{2+} is termed oxidation-reduction (REDOX). Rudolph Marcus analyzed the rates of these reactions in terms of their driving force and the dynamics of their reorganizations of structure (see chapter 6). During the 1950s and the 1960s, Canadian-born Henry Taube (1915–2005), first at the University of Chicago and then at Stanford, made the links between the kinetics of these reactions and the electronic structures of the transition metal reactants and products.

In solution, electron transfer usually occurs when the Donor (D) and Acceptor (A) species come into close contact to form a "precursor complex" (D/A) having significant overlap between their outermost orbitals. Electron transfer to the "successor complex" (D^+/A^-) precedes dissociation into products. Since electron transfer occurs much more rapidly than movement of nuclei (Franck-Condon Principle), efficient (lowest-energy) electron transfer occurs when vibrations of the D/A complex allow it to adopt geometry similar to D^+/A^-. This type of transfer is termed "outer-sphere" where electron transfer occurs much more rapidly than ligand exchange. There are also reactions in which electron transfer is very slow and accompanies ligand exchange. Taube and coworkers established one such case, termed an "inner-sphere" reaction, when they observed chloride (ligand) transfer accompanying electron transfer:

$$[(NH_3)_5CoCl]^{2+} (aq) + Cr^{2+}(aq) \rightarrow [(NH_3)_5Co-Cl-Cr(H_2O)_5]^{4++} (aq)$$
$$\rightarrow [ClCr(H_2O)_5]^{2+} (aq) + Co^{2+}(aq)$$

Taube received the 1990 Nobel Prize in chemistry for his studies of electron-transfer.

Paul Sabatier had shared the 1912 Nobel Prize in chemistry for application of platinum metal and other transition metals as hydrogenation catalysts. In order to be a catalyst, any Pt-H bonds on the surface of the metal (M) must be weak and easily broken. No stable compounds containing M-H bonds were known until 1957, when Joseph Chatt and colleagues synthesized *trans*-Pt(H)Cl(PEt$_3$)$_2$ (where Et = ethyl or C_2H_5). It is a square planar complex with platinum in the center, the two PEt$_3$ groups on opposite corners of the square, and the H^- and Cl^- ligands occupying the other two corners. This complex reacts with dry HCl to produce a crystalline compound of formula Pt(H)$_2$(Cl)$_2$(PEt$_3$)$_2$. Subsequent studies between 1958 and 1961 provided other examples of this new class of chemical reaction termed "oxidative addition."

The count of valence-shell electrons in Pt(H)Cl(PEt$_3$)$_2$ is as follows: 2 electrons each for the 4 ligands (H^-, Cl^-, and the 2 PEt$_3$); 8 electrons for Pt^{2+} (Pt^0 has 10 valence-shell electrons [$5d^9 6s^1$]). The 16 valence electrons are 2 short of the stable 18-electron configuration. There is room above and below the square planar structure for 2 more ligands to form an octahedral complex. When HCl adds to the square planar complex, the H and

Cl atoms are reduced to form H^- and Cl^- and the metal is oxidized to Pt^{4+}. The valence electron count following oxidative addition is 18.

In 1961, Lauri Vaska (1925–), at the Mellon Institute, reported the synthesis of another square planar transition metal complex: $IrCl(CO)(PPh_3)_2$ (where Ph = phenyl or C_6H_5). Ir^0 has 9 valence-shell electrons ($5d^7 6s^2$). The square planar iridium complex has 16 valence-shell electrons and two vacant coordination sites. "Vaska's compound" had two interesting surprises for the chemists who discovered it. It reacts with hydrogen gas to produce a very stable crystalline compound, $Ir(H)_2Cl(CO)(PPh_3)_2$, the product of oxidative addition of H_2, having two Ir-H bonds. Vaska's compound opened the door for a new series of soluble hydrogenation catalysts, although the stability of its H_2 adduct precluded its application as a catalyst since it cannot turn over hydrogen rapidly. The second surprise was that it binds oxygen (O_2) reversibly making Vaska's compound a model for myoglobin and hemoglobin.

In 1965, Geoffrey Wilkinson, at Imperial College in London, synthesized $RhCl(PPh_3)_3$ and discovered that it catalyzes alkene hydrogenation at room temperature and only 1 atmosphere pressure. Wilkinson's catalyst reacts by oxidative addition, like Vaska's compound, but the H_2 adduct is much less stable and its rapid turnover of H_2 allows it to be a catalyst. This was a major advance since homogeneous catalysis requires mild conditions and is highly selective: It may allow hydrogenation of only one of two or more different types of C=C bond in the same molecule. In contrast, heterogeneous catalysis, using catalysts such as platinum metal, often requires high pressures and temperatures and is often not very selective.

The ability of a transition metal to break the H-H bond and form two M-H bonds by oxidative addition suggested a fascinating possibility. One of chemistry's "holy grails" is chemical activation of C-H bonds in alkanes such as methane (CH_4), ethane (C_2H_6), and propane (C_3H_8). Alkanes, the major components of natural gas, are very unreactive except in combustion and in reactions with free radicals. Methane, a greenhouse gas, is a by-product of anaerobic bacteria and is produced in prodigious quantities by cows as well as landfills. If methane could be converted to methanol, or ethane to ethanol, the alcohols could be transported efficiently and safely over long distances and used as fuel and as feedstock for fine chemicals. The C-H bond in methane is almost as nonpolar as the H-H bond and the bond energies are virtually identical. Therefore, transition metal complexes that add H_2 might activate alkane C-H bonds. In 1969, Alexander E. Shilov (1930–), in Moscow, observed transition metal-catalyzed exchange of methane hydrogen with deuterium atoms in D_2O under mild conditions. This indicated activation of methane's C-H bonds. Although another decade would pass before real progress was made in this area, the door was opened to C-H activation under mild conditions.

In 1964, Robert L. Banks and Grant C. Bailey, at Phillips Petroleum, discovered that $Mo(CO)_6$ catalyzes conversion of propene ($CH_3CH=CH_2$) to ethene ($CH_2=CH_2$) and butenes ($CH_3CH=CHCH_3$). Three years later

Nissim Calderon (1933–), at Goodyear Tire & Rubber, concluded that catalytic conversion of a mixture of $A_2C=CA_2$ and $B_2C=CB_2$ to form $A_2C=CB_2$ is a general reaction he termed "olefin metathesis." It immediately became a very important industrial reaction. Its mechanism would be solved during the 1970s and would lead to a Nobel Prize in 2005.

Carbenes ($:CR_2$) are the most reactive organic intermediates. The Simmons-Smith reaction (see chapter 6) "tamed" the extraordinarily reactive methylene ($:CH_2$) in the form of a metal-carbenoid ("ICH_2ZnI"). In 1964, Ernest Otto Fischer made the first metallocarbenes [e.g., $(CO)_5W=CCH_3(OCH_3)$] and they were stable enough for X-ray diffraction studies on crystalline samples. Although unsuspected at the time, metallocarbenes would hold the secret to the "magic" of olefin metathesis.

Simple Carbocations Are Stable in Magic Acid

Chemists feel that they understand a reaction when they know its mechanism. In a two-step mechanism such as S_N1, kinetics and stereochemistry imply short-lived carbocations as intermediates (see chapter 4). In accordance with the steady-state approximation in chemical kinetics, the rate of formation of carbocations is virtually equal to their rate of disappearance under S_N1 reaction conditions, and their steady-state concentrations are too low to observe directly. Is it ever possible to find conditions allowing one to "see" these transient species using spectroscopy? Carbocations such as t-butyl [$(CH_3)_3C^+$] violate the octet rule and vigorously seek a pair of electrons: They are very strong electrophiles and Lewis acids. It is not surprising that they are exceedingly reactive and short-lived under typical conditions. The question, however, that should come to mind is "Reactive with what?" When t-butyl bromide is placed in polar solutions, it forms a miniscule steady-state concentration of $(CH_3)_3C^+$ since the "leaving group" (Br^-) and the solvent (alcohol for example) are reactive enough nucleophiles to attack any carbocation just formed. It is true that stable solutions of triphenylmethyl carbocations [$(C_6H_5)_3C^+$] were known since 1901 (see chapter 1). However, these highly resonance-stabilized, sterically hindered carbocations are not at all typical. They are vastly more stable than the simple carbocations, such as t-butyl, that are intermediates in S_N1 and related reactions.

George Olah (1927–) developed systems in which the nucleophilic reactivities of both the leaving group and the solvent are so weak that even simple carbocations, like t-butyl, can exist in high concentrations over the course of hours. Olah was born and educated in Budapest. Hungary, which had been devastated by World War II and occupied by the USSR. In 1956, a rebellion was ruthlessly crushed, and shortly thereafter Olah and his family migrated to Canada. In Ontario, he continued an earlier interest in fluorine chemistry and began to exploit SbF_5 (antimony pentafluoride). In 1962, Olah published the first spectroscopic observation

(NMR) of a simple alkyl carbocation, the *t*-butyl carbocation. In this reaction, SbF_5 is both Lewis acid acceptor of F^- and solvent:

$$(CH_3)_3C\text{-}COF + SbF_5 \rightarrow SbF_6^- + [(CH_3)_3C\text{-}CO^+] \rightarrow$$
$$(CH_3)_3C^+ \text{ (}observed\text{)} + CO$$

The SbF_6^- anion was one of the first examples of a weakly coordinating anion (WCA) or "superweak anion," an anion so unreactive as to coexist in a salt with a simple, highly reactive carbocation. Chemists could scarcely believe this feat had been accomplished. Olah realized that carbocations such as *t*-butyl may also reversibly eliminate H^+ to form alkenes:

$$(CH_3)_3C^+ \rightleftarrows (CH_3)_2C\text{=}CH_2 + H^+$$

This elimination reaction is suppressed by using exceedingly powerful protic acids in an application of Le Chatelier's principle. As the 1960s moved forward (Olah joined Western Reserve University, later Case Western Reserve, in 1965), he would employ a series of super-acids which were billions of times stronger than concentrated sulfuric acid. One of these was a mixture of the Lewis acid SbF_5 and the Brønsted acid FSO_3H, called magic acid. Diluted with SO_2, magic acid solutions of simple carbocations were observed by NMR for indefinitely long periods at low temperatures. In this way, a large number of carbocations were made, monitored, and their Meerwein rearrangements (see chapter 3) observed in "slow motion."

The nonclassical carbonium ion controversy proved an attractive target for Olah's studies. In 1969 an NMR spectrum of the norbornyl cation at $-254°F$ ($-159°C$) showed a single structure rather than two rapidly equilibrating structures. As described in chapter 6, this could be explained by a single nonclassical carbocation or two rapidly exchanging classical carbocations with a very low energy barrier separating them. The controversy ended in the early 1980s when other researchers demonstrated that solid-state NMR (^1H and ^{13}C) showed a single structure at temperatures as low as $-450°F$ ($-268°C$ or 5 K). At such low temperatures, any barrier separating two classical structures is so small as to be meaningless. ESCA (see chapter 6) also fully supported the nonclassical structure. Olah's work in carbocationic chemistry led him to clarify the nomenclature in this field. Carbocations of the type CR_3^+ are now termed "carbenium ions" while those of type CR_5^+ are "carbonium ions." For his studies of carbocation chemistry in superacid media, George Olah received the 1994 Nobel Prize in chemistry.

Stretching, Bending, and Twisting the Rules of Bonding

The rarity and reactivity of three- and four-membered rings led Adolph von Baeyer to enunciate his theory of ring strain in 1885. Alkanes normally favor tetrahedral geometry with bond angles close to 109.5°. In

1924, Julius Bredt (1855–1937) observed that molecules containing twisted carbon-carbon double bonds are "prohibited" because alkenes favor planar double bonds with bond angles near 120°. Alkynes, such as acetylene (HC≡CH), favor linear geometry (180°) about their triply bonded carbons. The benzene ring was shown in the 1930s to be flat.

Starting in the 1950s, accelerating through the 1960s, and perhaps reaching a zenith in the 1970s, organic chemists tested the limits of these rules. Cyclopropane, cyclobutane, and spiropentane had been synthesized during the 19th century (see the accompanying figure for these and the other molecules described here). The bicyclobutane system (two fused cyclopropanes) was first reported by Kenneth B. Wiberg (1927–   ) at Yale in 1959. It has 10 kcal/mol more strain energy than two separate cyclopropane rings (28 kcal/mol each). Breaking the central bond in bicyclobutane forms a cyclobutane (27 kcal/mol of strain energy), releasing

Some representative strained organic molecules in different classes: A) simple, spiro, and fused cycloalkanes; B) distorted and twisted alkenes; C) strained polycyclic compounds

STRAINED ORGANIC MOLECULES: BENDING AND STRETCHING THE RULES OF BONDING AND STRUCTURE

A) Compounds with significant departures from 109° C-C-C angle

Cyclopropane
(19th century)

Cyclobutane
(19th century)

Spiropentane
(19th century)

1950s

B) Alkenes distorted from 120° angles and/or planarity

Cyclopropenes
(1950s)

(1970s)

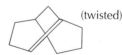

(twisted)

(1960s)

C) Strained polyhedral molecules

"Prismanes"
(1960-70s)

"Cubanes"
(1960s)

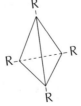

Substituted
tetrahedranes
(1970-80s)

"Dodecahedranes"
(1980s)

almost 40 kcal/mol of extra strain. This large driving force is one reason for the high reactivity of bicyclobutane at this bond.

Polycyclic molecules comprised of strained rings were particularly interesting synthetic targets. In 1964, Philip E. Eaton (1936–) and Thomas W. Cole, Jr. (1941–), at the University of Chicago, synthesized "cubane" (C_8H_8), the first of three possible "platonic" hydrocarbons. (Cole, an African American, would become the first president of Clark-Atlanta University in 1989.) The total strain energy in cubane (ca. 157 kcal/mol) is huge and equals the sum of its six cyclobutane faces. The first "prismanes" were reported in 1964 and 1965. Prismane is a valence isomer of benzene: they are both $(CH)_6$ so that a relatively simple "flattening and unfolding" of prismane could provide benzene. Prismane is more than 90 kcal/mol higher in energy than benzene, an enormous driving force for this rearrangement. Yet prismanes are surprisingly stable. Why? The reaction is symmetry-forbidden according to the Woodward-Hoffmann rules described earlier in this chapter. Roald Hoffmann called prismane "an angry tiger unable to break out of a paper cage." Two remaining platonic hydrocarbons, tetrahedrane and dodecahedrane, awaited synthesis. Each posed daunting challenges to the chemists that dared dream of them. The strain energy in tetrahedrane (C_4H_4) is about 130 kcal/mol. If one carbon-carbon bond is broken, a bicyclobutane system is formed with release of strain energy almost equal to the energy of a typical unstrained C-C bond. It was not surprising that every attempt to date to make tetrahedrane failed. Dodecahedrane posed a very different challenge. While it is also strained, the real problem is entropy: How does one induce 20 CH units to merge together into this one improbable, highly ordered array when so many other arrangements are possible?

If two C-C bonds on opposite sides of one square face are broken, cubane loses half of its strain energy. Despite this huge driving force, heating cubane does not induce this reaction because it is "thermally forbidden" according to the Woodward-Hoffmann rules. The reverse reaction is, of course, also thermally forbidden and "photochemically allowed." This offers a pathway to store ultraviolet light energy. How can stored light energy be rapidly released if ring opening is "thermally forbidden"? Transition metals catalyze the ring opening reaction by oxidative addition, offering a promising pathway for storage of light energy: photochemical closure to store energy in strained molecules like cubane and rapid ring opening using transition metals to release heat when needed.

Computer-Aided Design of Organic Syntheses

Elias J. ("E.J.") Corey (1928–) was educated as an engineer and later applied his mathematical training to look at organic synthesis in a new way. Organic chemists had typically viewed a complex target molecule from the perspective of a promising starting molecule. At Harvard, Corey

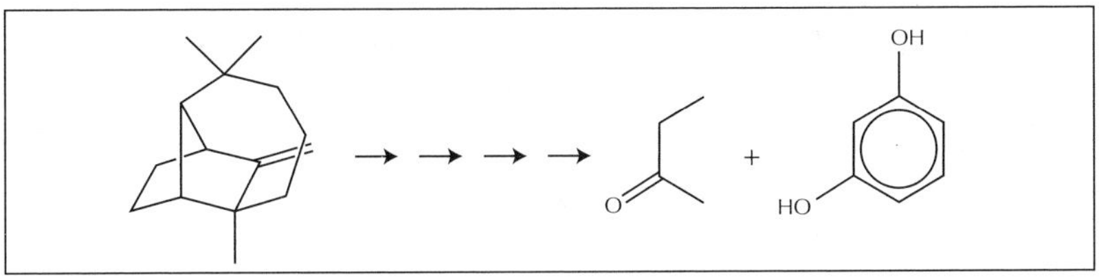

Retrosynthesis of longifolene

pioneered an approach termed "retrosynthesis" (each retrosynthetic step designated by "⇨") whereby the target is "deconstructed" step-by-step into "branches," the best pathways determined and simple starting materials identified. An example is the 1961 "retrosynthesis" of longifolene depicted above, through four conceptual stages, to simple starting compounds. This approach is now the way most organic chemists plan complex syntheses. Corey used this approach to synthesize very challenging natural products, inventing as many as 50 new synthetic methods in the process. One of his most exceptional contributions was the application of retrosynthetic design to the first syntheses (in 1969) of prostaglandins. The structures of these chemical messengers, first isolated by Ulf von Euler in 1935 (see chapter 4) in trace levels, were deciphered during the 1950s and 1960s by Sune K. Bergström (1916–2004) and Bengt I. Samuelsson (1934–) at Lund (see chapter 8 for further discussion of the prostaglandins). Starting in the late 1960s Corey and his colleagues developed computer programs that evaluate and "grade" all potential retrosynthetic pathways for a given target molecule in order to attempt to predict the best synthetic pathway. E. J. Corey received the 1990 Nobel Prize in chemistry for his numerous contributions to synthetic organic chemistry.

Synthesizing Proteins in Solid Beads

Any chemist knows that the more steps there are in a chemical synthesis, the lower the final yield. For example, if each step in a 10-step synthesis furnishes a 90 percent yield of product, the yield of the final product will be only about 35 percent. That is why it is not possible to extend Du Vigneaud's masterful syntheses (see chapter 6) of the hormones oxytocin and vasopressin (9 amino acid residues each) to proteins, even small ones such as ribonuclease A (124 amino acid residues). In order to pursue this daunting challenge Robert Bruce Merrifield (1921–2006), at Rockefeller University, devised a new concept: solid-phase synthesis. The idea is disarmingly simple: covalently attach an amino acid to a macroscopic particle that can be exposed to the reaction, washed, and then separated by simple filtration. Each reaction step requires no chromatography and no crystallization, just washing and filtering. At the end, completed peptide chains are chemically released from the particles.

The diagram on page 244 depicts the Merrifield synthesis. The resin ("R") is composed of beads of styrene, copolymerized with 1

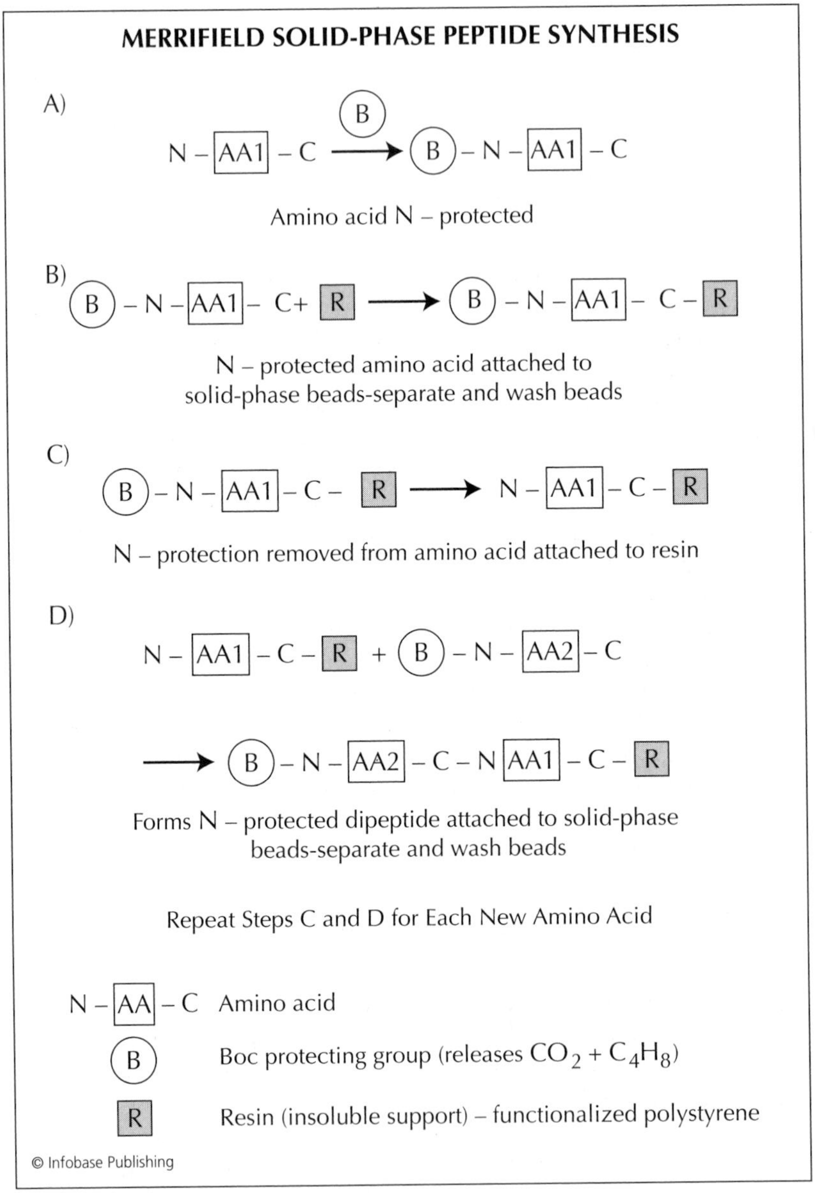

MERRIFIELD SOLID-PHASE PEPTIDE SYNTHESIS

A)

N – AA1 – C ⟶(B) (B) – N – AA1 – C

Amino acid N – protected

B)

(B) – N – AA1 – C + R ⟶ (B) – N – AA1 – C – R

N – protected amino acid attached to
solid-phase beads-separate and wash beads

C)

(B) – N – AA1 – C – R ⟶ N – AA1 – C – R

N – protection removed from amino acid attached to resin

D)

N – AA1 – C – R + (B) – N – AA2 – C

⟶ (B) – N – AA2 – C – N AA1 – C – R

Forms N – protected dipeptide attached to solid-phase
beads-separate and wash beads

Repeat Steps C and D for Each New Amino Acid

N – AA – C   Amino acid

(B)   Boc protecting group (releases $CO_2 + C_4H_8$)

R   Resin (insoluble support) – functionalized polystyrene

The steps in the Merrifield solid-phase peptide and protein synthesis: attachment of an amino acid to a polymer bead followed by cycles of attachment of other amino acids allows extremely high yield syntheses at each step and acceptable yields for syntheses that exceed 100 amino acid condensations.

percent divinylbenzene for cross-linking, which have been functionalized to react with the carboxyl group of the C-terminal amino acid (AA1). While some growing chains are attached to the surface of the beads, most of the reactions occur in the interior. Merrifield showed that the interior of the beads expand as the chain grows and always leave plenty of room for solvent and reagent molecules. The first amino acid (AA1) is chemically protected, to avoid unwanted chemistry on the amino (N) end, by a "Boc" group [*t*-butyloxycarbonyl $(CH_3)_3C-O(CO)-$] group. The N-protected AA1 is then chemically attached to the resin at the C-end. Mild hydrolysis cleaves the "Boc" group which departs the solution in the form of two gases, CO_2 and isobutylene. The free amino group on AA1 reacts with the carboxyl group on Boc-N-protected amino acid 2 (AA2), losing water aided by a dehydrating agent, to form a dipeptide attached to the bead by AA1 and N-protected on AA2. Cleanup and filtration separates the beads and the cycle is repeated. At the end, the protein chains are chemically released from the resin particles. During 1964–65, Merrifield and his group synthesized three "practice" peptides including oxytocin and built a manually operated protein synthesizer. In 1966 they constructed a fully automated synthesizer (see photograph below).

Bruce Merrifield ca. 1969
with his protein synthesizer
(Rockefeller University
Archives)

In the synthesis of ribonuclease A, attachment of the C-terminal amino acid (valine) to the resin is followed by stepwise addition of 123 individual amino acids to form a 124-residue chain attached to the beads. The total yield of bead-attached protein chain was only 17 percent. This seems pretty modest at first. It corresponds, however, to an average 98.6 percent yield for each of the 123 steps [i.e. $(0.986)^{123}$]. Solid-phase synthesis had enabled nearly 100 percent yield for each amino acid step. Following cleavage from the resin, the 124-unit chain was recovered in very good yield. However, it was not yet ribonuclease A; the eight cysteine residues were in the reduced ($-CH_2SH$) state. Christian B. Anfinsen had demonstrated a few years earlier that when natural ribonuclease A is reduced and denatured it spontaneously reforms the native structure with full activity upon oxidation. Merrifield found that when his totally synthetic 124-amino acid chain was exposed to air oxidation it spontaneously formed ribonuclease A, fully validating Anfinsen's earlier discovery. For his virtuoso combination of polymer chemistry, organic chemistry, enzyme chemistry, and new instrumentation, Merrifield received the 1984 Nobel Prize in chemistry.

Three-Dimensional Views of Enzymes and How They Work

All globular proteins have three levels of structure and many have four. The amino acid sequence is the *primary structure*; arrangements such as the α-helix or β-sheet specify *secondary structure*. Successful analyses of primary and secondary structures of proteins began during the 1950s. *Tertiary structure* refers to the three-dimensional folding of the chains in globular proteins. The first successes in determining tertiary structures derived from the analyses of myoglobin and hemoglobin at the end of that decade. The three-dimensional structure of insulin was finally determined by Dorothy Hodgkin in 1969, nearly 35 years after she first started to study this protein. Hemoglobin has four separate protein chains, two α and two β, and its *quaternary structure* refers to spatial arrangements of these and other multi-chain proteins.

While tertiary structures are of interest for all proteins, of particular interest are the three-dimensional structures, including the structures of the active sites, of enzymes. The "lock-and-key" picture formulated by Emil Fischer (see chapter 1) postulated that substrate fits enzyme like a key in a lock. Linus Pauling modified this view by noting that the activated complex rather than the substrate should be the "key" in the "lock." In 1958, Daniel E. Koshland, Jr. (1920–   ), then at Brookhaven National Laboratory and Rockefeller Institute, postulated the "induced fit" model to explain anomalies in enzyme activities. He postulated that binding a good substrate induces proper fit by causing a change in the enzyme's shape that brings its reactive groups to the active site. Koshland termed this "hand in glove" instead of "lock and key." His 1965 study of phosphoglucomutase provided support for the "induced fit" model.

In order to understand mechanisms of enzyme catalysis not only are the tertiary structures of enzymes of interest but so too are the tertiary structures of enzyme-substrate complexes. There was, however, a problem: As incredibly efficient catalysts, enzymes "turn over" substrate molecules in fractions of a second, while (40 years ago) collection of crystallographic data took days. The answer to the problem was to study complexes of exceedingly sluggish substrates, unreactive model substrates, as well as strongly bound inhibitors that compete for the active site.

The first tertiary structure for an enzyme, chicken egg lysozyme, was published in 1965 by David C. Phillips (1924–99) in London. Lysozyme is an enzyme that attacks bacteria by cleaving polysaccharide chains in their cell walls. Examination of the lysozyme complex, using a sluggish substrate, indicated key roles for two amino acid residues, glutamic acid 35 and aspartic acid 52, in breaking a linkage in the polysaccharide. In 1967, two research groups, David Harker at Roswell Park Cancer Institute in Buffalo and Frederic M. Richards at Yale, independently published crystallographic structures for ribonuclease A and ribonuclease S. Their active sites have histidine residues 12 and 119 in close proximity consistent with earlier chemical studies by William Stein and Stanford Moore. While the changes in shape induced in lysozyme and in ribonuclease by substrates are fairly small, those in the enzyme carboxypeptidase are much larger. In 1967, William Lipscomb's group at Harvard demonstrated that in carboxypeptidase A, model substrates and inhibitors bind close to the zinc atom, suggesting a mechanistic role for the metal. They also observed a large structural change between the enzyme-substrate model and the enzyme that was consistent with Koshland's "induced-fit" model.

At Stanford, Harden M. McConnell developed a new technique, called spin labelling, based upon EPR spectroscopy. While carbon-centered free radicals are extremely reactive and short-lived, radical oxides of nitrogen, such as NO and NO_2, are moderately stable. McConnell noted that nitroxyl radicals (RR'N-O) are extremely stable if R and R' are tertiary and can be chemically attached to biological molecules of interest. In 1965, he published the concept of spin labeling and, in 1966, demonstrated that a spin-labelled substrate added to α-chymotrypsin forms a covalent enzyme-substrate complex. The EPR signal was quite broad suggesting restricted motion consistent with Koshland's induced-fit model. In 1971, McConnell published a study in which spin labelling indicated flip-flop motions of lipids in cell membranes. This was the start of dynamic studies of cell membranes.

This first decade of crystallographic study of enzymes helped to create two new fields: bio-inorganic chemistry and mechanistic bio-organic chemistry. Harry B. Gray (1935–), at Caltech, began to make fundamental contributions to the chemistry and chemical physics of metalloproteins. Unlike reactions between transition metal ions and their complexes, which involve intimate contact and electron-transfer upon collision, electron transfer between metals on different proteins is not so intimate and may require several collisions and may proceed through quantum-mechanical *tunneling*. One of Gray's early studies demonstrated that Co(II) or Ni(II) could be substituted for Zn(II) in carboxypeptidase A with full retention of activity.

One of the most fascinating catalytic systems is the serine 195/histidine 57/aspartic acid 102 "triad" in the proteolytic enzyme chymotrypsin. It was discovered in 1969 by David M. Blow (1931–2004) at Cambridge. The presence of ionic groups in a hydrophobic reaction site enormously increases the basicities and reactivities of these catalytic groups.

During the late 1960s, Ronald Breslow at Columbia founded the field of biomimetic chemistry. Among his early studies, he observed catalytic activities and different specificities for three cyclic oligomers of glucose: α-, β- and γ-cyclodextrins (cyclo-[D-glucose]$_n$, where n = 6, 7, and 8 respectively). These are large donut-shaped molecules with a hydrophobic interior and reactive hydroxyl groups on the edge of one rim. Breslow was able to mimic some aspects of enzyme catalysis wherein a nonpolar substrate in an aqueous solution finds the cyclodextrin's hydrophobic cavity. The hydroxyl groups play the role of catalytic groups selectively functionalizing only the exposed part of the aligned substrate.

The Structures and Functions of Antibodies

Smallpox is a disfiguring and often deadly disease. In 18th-century England a widespread practice was to take tissue from a person with a mild smallpox infection and inoculate a healthy person. While this often protected the person from a severe case of the disease, it did on occasion lead to severe cases and sometimes death. It also created new cases that could infect others. The breakthrough discovery was made in 1796 by English surgeon Edward Jenner (1749–1823) when he successfully inoculated an eight-year-old boy against smallpox by using tissue from a young woman infected by cowpox, a much milder disease. During the early 20th century it became clear that immunity arises from substances, termed *antibodies*, in the blood serum of vertebrates.

In 1937, Arne Tiselius discovered, using electrophoresis, that antibodies are proteins. The mixture of antibodies was very complex but their molecular weights were quite uniform. Cells called B lymphocytes, a class of leukocytes (white blood cells), are the sources of antibodies. Specific antibodies bind foreign substances called antigens. An antigen can be a macromolecule, like a protein or polysaccharide, or a small molecule, termed a hapten, attached to a large biomolecule. For example, poison ivy exudes oily substances composed of small molecules called urushiols. Once absorbed into the body they are converted to quinones, the haptens, which react with proteins. It is this hapten part of the "tagged" protein that is recognized by the antibody. One can imagine an almost infinite number of antigens. How does the immune response cover all of these possibilities? Each unique B lymphocyte produces one specific antibody. When an antigen is introduced, it binds to a specific site on the B lymphocyte inducing these cells to divide and produce clones in a cascade that yields sufficient antibody to combine with antigen and leave a residue of protection. What are the structures of proteins that provide such a seemingly infinite array of chemical structures "on command"?

Serious structural investigations of antibody structures began in the late 1950s. Among numerous investigators Rodney R. Porter (1917–85), a former student of Frederick Sanger's working in London and then Oxford, and Gerald M. Edelman (1929–), working at the Rockefeller Institute, were most prominent. There were five recognized subclasses of antibodies, termed immunoglobulins, and both research groups focused on examples of immunoglobulin G (IgG), the most abundant and lightest (molecular weights ~143,000–149,000). Their initial chemical approaches were complementary. Porter's group employed the enzyme papain to digest rabbit IgG into two different fractions: F_{ab}, the antigen-binding fraction, and F_c, the crystallizable fraction. He initially perceived the antibody to be a single protein chain. Edelman chemically reduced the disulfide linkages in IgG, denaturing the protein in urea solution, and discovered that IgG has a multichain structure. There were two major problems in obtaining detailed amino acid sequencing and other structural information. One was the sheer size of the IgG molecules; the other was the heterogeneity (complexity of the mixture) in IgGs isolated from serum. Some unanticipated help with these problems was supplied by Nature. Tumors of lymph cells, called myelomas, stimulate production of homogeneous IgG, called Bence-Jones proteins, found in the urines of those afflicted with this disease. They were soon found to be the lighter components (MW ~23,000) of the IgGs. The overall structural nature of antibodies was deduced during the 1960s and Edelman completely sequenced an IgG between 1965 and 1968.

The figure on page 250 depicts the two-dimensional view of antibodies derived from studies of Porter, Edelman, and others. It is Y-shaped, has twofold symmetry, and is bifunctional with two heavy chains and two light chains. The two "arms" correspond to identical F_{ab} units and the remainder to the F_c unit. Connections between the light chains and heavy chains as well as between the heavy chains are due to disulfide linkages. At the ends of the two arms of the Y section are CDRs (complementary determining regions) that bind the antigens. Near the CDRs are sections that are highly variable (V) in their amino acid composition on both the light and heavy chains (VL and VH). The remaining section on each light chain (CL) has constant amino acid composition and there are three such sections on each heavy chain (CH1, CH2, and CH3). The difunctional antibodies form cross-linked insoluble complexes with antigens, including bacteria and viruses, which precipitate from blood serum. Porter and Edelman shared the 1972 Nobel Prize in physiology or medicine for their discoveries of the structures and function of antibodies. In 1977, a crystallographic structure was published for a complete human IgG. It clearly demonstrated twofold symmetry as well as sites for antigen binding in the F_{ab} "arms."

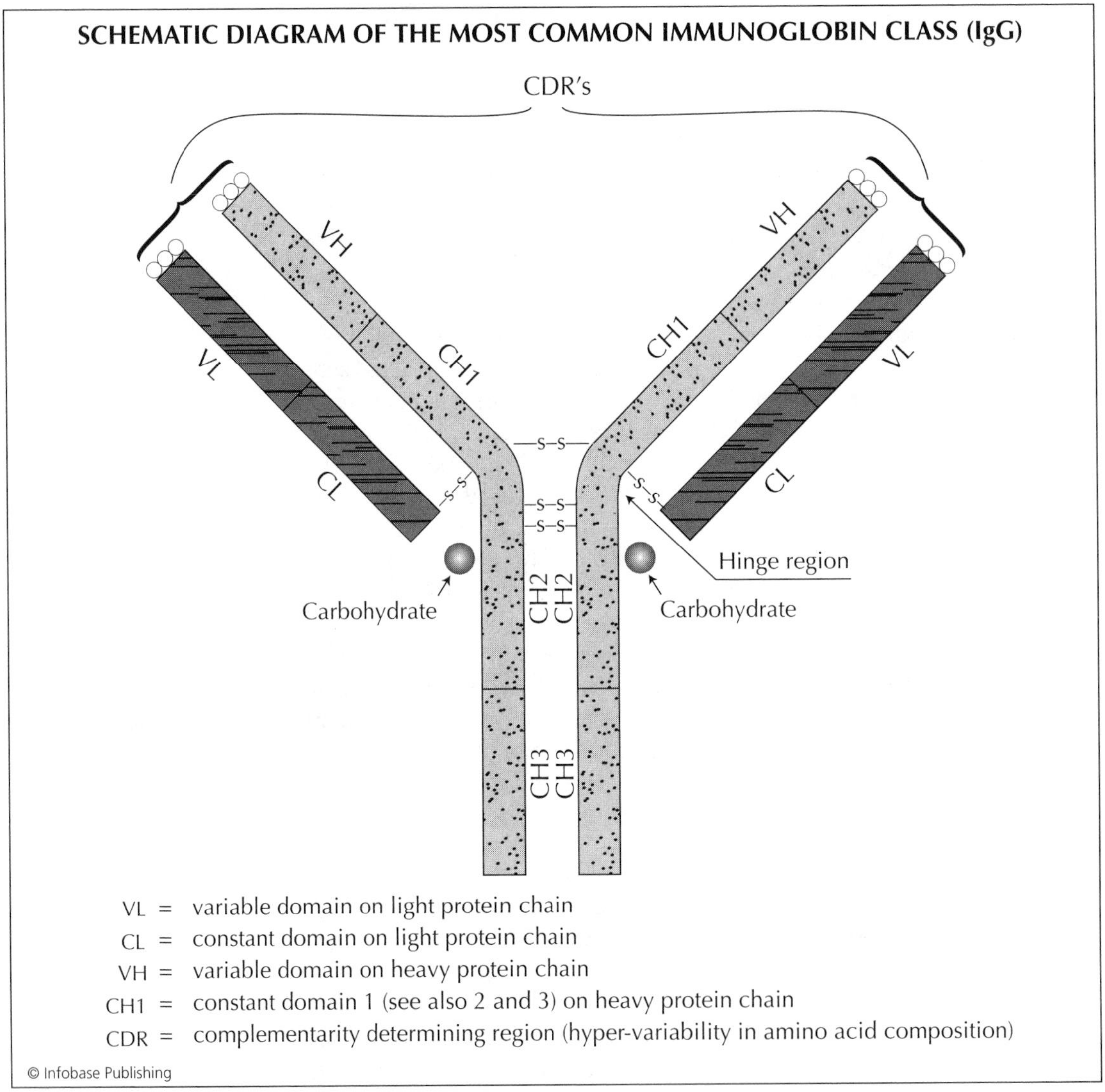

SCHEMATIC DIAGRAM OF THE MOST COMMON IMMUNOGLOBIN CLASS (IgG)

CDR's

VH

VH

CH1

CH1

VL

VL

CL

CL

—S—S—

—S—S—

—S—S—
—S—S—

Hinge region

CH2
CH2

CH3
CH3

Carbohydrate

Carbohydrate

VL = variable domain on light protein chain
CL = constant domain on light protein chain
VH = variable domain on heavy protein chain
CH1 = constant domain 1 (see also 2 and 3) on heavy protein chain
CDR = complementarity determining region (hyper-variability in amino acid composition)

© Infobase Publishing

The general twofold symmetrical structure of an immunoglobulin G. There are three constant sections on the heavy chains (CH1, CH2, CH3) and one variable section (VH). Each light chain has a constant (CL) and a variable (VL) section. Antigens are bound by the hypervariable CDRs (complementary determining regions).

The Road to the Genetic Code and Chemical Synthesis of a Working Gene

In 1941, George W. Beadle (1903–89) and Edward L. Tatum (1909–75), working at Stanford University, discovered that specific mutations of a bread mold, induced by X-rays or UV light, cause the mold to lose its ability to synthesize specific molecules such as pyridoxine (vitamin B_6). This led them to propose the "one gene-one enzyme" theory. At that time, the chemical nature of the gene was unknown, although proteins were the prime suspects. Beadle and Tatum would later share the

1959 Nobel Prize in physiology or medicine with Joshua Lederberg (1925–).

After Watson and Crick discovered the structure of DNA in 1953, the next major question was how its composition translates into coding for proteins and what role ribonucleic acid (RNA) plays. In 1954, the year he moved to Berkeley, Russian-born physicist George Gamow (1904–68) formed the "RNA Tie Club." It had 20 members, one for each amino acid, and four honorary members, one for each nucleotide, and he presented to each member a tie decorated with an embroidered helix. The club's goal was to solve the RNA problem. Crick and Watson, "Tyrosine" and "Proline" respectively, were among the member amino acids. Gamow reasoned that while a dinucleotide offers only 4 × 4 or 16 combinations, insufficient for coding 20 amino acids, a trinucleotide has 64 combinations and is probably the coding unit. Crick named this unit the "codon." In 1955, he postulated the "adapter hypothesis" in which some unknown substance carries amino acids and places them in order on a nucleic acid molecule. Two years later, Mathew Meselson (1930–) and Franklin W. Stahl (1929–), at Caltech, demonstrated the replication pathway for DNA. In 1960, Crick and Sydney Brenner (1927–), in Cambridge, and François Jacob (1920–) and Jacques Monod (1910–76), at the Pasteur Institute in Paris, discovered messenger RNA (mRNA) in ribosomes. Much as Watson was Crick's partner in solving the structure of DNA, Brenner formed a powerful intellectual collaboration with Crick in helping solve the genetic code. Sol Spiegelman (1914–83), at the University of Illinois, demonstrated that only one strand of DNA transmits genetic information. Alexander Rich (1924–), then at the NIH, formed the first DNA/RNA hybrids, and demonstrated that mRNA only forms hybrids with the coding strand of DNA. Monod and Jacob also amplified on the triplet nature of the genetic code, including the initiation and termination code on genes. Crick, the theoretician, in a rare foray into experimentation, demonstrated that insertion of an extra foreign nucleotide (causing a "phase shift") introduces inactive viral RNA. Insertion of two foreign nucleotides also produced inactive RNA. However, insertion of three foreign nucleotides produced active RNA. Thus, the coding units were in threes since "phase" was reestablished. Monod and Jacob would share the 1965 Nobel Prize in physiology or medicine with André Lwoff (1902–94). Brenner would share the Nobel Prize physiology or medicine in 2002.

The years 1961–65 witnessed a cascade of discoveries in the relationship between information stored in DNA and the structure and biosynthesis of proteins. In 1961, Marshall W. Nirenberg (1927–), National Institutes of Health (NIH) in Bethesda, added polyuridylic acid (a synthetic pseudo-RNA) to cell-free preparations of mRNA-depleted *E. coli* ribosomes, mixed with enzymes and 18 different amino acids. The ribosomes used polyuridylic acid in place of their own mRNA and synthesized the polypeptide polyphenylalanine. The first entry into the genetic code was therefore UUU in RNA coding for phenylalanine in protein.

Starting in 1956, Robert W. Holley (1922–93), on leave from Cornell, began a study of the soluble RNA in yeast. He discovered that these relatively small nucleic acids, termed transfer RNAs (tRNAs), are the molecules that remove activated amino acids from enzymes and transport them to ribosomes. The tRNAs are the "adapters" postulated earlier by Crick. By 1962, Holley had concentrated roughly 300 pounds (140 kg) of baker's yeast to about 0.4 pounds (200 g) of transfer RNAs. Countercurrent separation provided 1 gram of highly purified yeast alanine transfer RNA. In 1965, Holley fully sequenced yeast alanine tRNA (tRNA$_{ala}$), using techniques resembling Sanger's protein sequencing. It was the first sequence for any nucleic acid and consisted of 77 nucleotides. Some of the bases in tRNAs are unusual and it was later learned that they are enzymatic modifications of the original four bases (adenine, guanine, cytosine, and uracil) following biosynthesis of the original tRNA chain. In 1965, Frederick Sanger turned his attention to nucleic acid sequencing and developed a ^{32}P-labelling technique which, in conjunction with two-dimensional chromatography, was rapid and sensitive. In 1967, he published the sequence for *E. coli* 5S RNA (120 nucleotides). During the next decade Sanger would develop related techniques for DNA sequencing that would gain him a share of the 1980 Nobel Prize in chemistry. He is the only person to win two Nobel Prizes in chemistry.

Rational chemical synthesis of nucleic acids would soon become the domain of Har Gobind Khorana (1922–   ). Khorana was born to an Indian Hindu family in a tiny village in Punjab (now part of Pakistan). His parents persevered in obtaining a first-rate education for him, and Khorana obtained his Ph.D. in England. Following research appointments with two future Nobel laureates, Vladimir Prelog in Zurich and Alexander R. Todd in Cambridge, Khorana came to the University of British Columbia in 1952. He joined the faculty of the University of Wisconsin in 1960, and moved to MIT in 1970.

Just as syntheses of peptides and proteins require protecting groups, so too do syntheses of nucleic acids. Khorana employed derivatives of the triphenylmethyl ("trityl") group at the 5' end (start) of the nucleic acid. For his nucleic acid syntheses, Khorana employed solid-phase techniques similar to Merrifield's and for the same reasons: to simplify separation and cleanup so that each step in a 100-step procedure occurs in extremely high yield. The trityl protecting group can be covalently bound to polymer (polystyrene) beads, binding the growing nucleic acid chain (see the figure on page 253). One of Khorana's first experiments involved directed synthesis of the alternating synthetic RNA polymer UCUCUCUCUCUCY. . . . Cell-free ribosomal preparations produced the repeating peptide serine-leucine-serine-leucine. . . . His research group then synthesized all 64 trinucleotide codons. The work of Nirenberg, Holley, and Khorana led, in 1966, to the "cracking" of the genetic code. They shared the 1968 Nobel Prize in physiology or medicine.

In 1967, Martin F. Gellert (1929–   ) and coworkers at the NIH isolated DNA ligase, an enzyme capable of "gluing together" duplex seg-

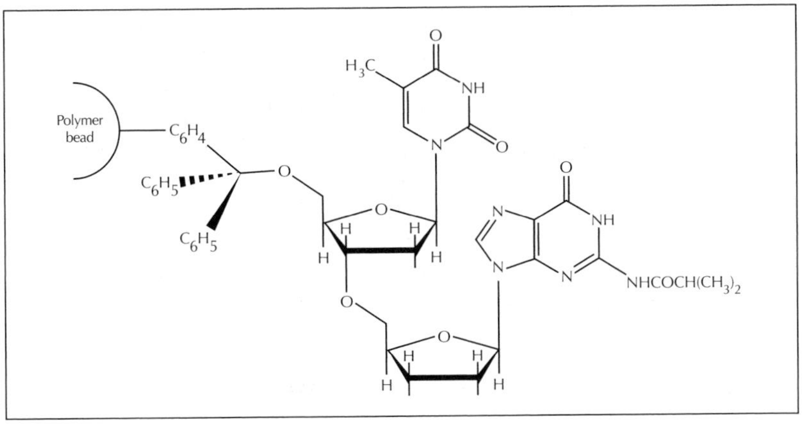

Growing synthetic DNA chain attached to polymer bead

ments of DNA having protruding single chain sequences ("sticky ends"). This enzyme provided a critical tool for Khorana to pursue an amazing goal: total synthesis of a gene. Since the complete sequence of the 77-nucleotide yeast tRNA$_{ala}$ was known from Holley's work, knowledge of the genetic code made the identity of its corresponding gene obvious. Khorana completed the synthesis of this gene and published it in 1972. However, without the initiation and termination codes, it was not a working gene. In 1976, Khorana published the first total synthesis of a fully functioning gene: the *E. coli* tyrosine suppressor tRNA gene (126 nucleotides). Khorana and his colleagues had chemically synthesized 26 DNA segments, used DNA ligase to join segments to form 4 DNA duplexes, and joined these to form a functioning gene. It is surely one of the greatest achievements in the history of science.

Cisplatin: Luck Leads to a Simple and Powerful Anticancer Drug

In 1963, Barnett Rosenberg and his colleagues at Michigan State University found that an electric current (between platinum electrodes) limits cell division in *E. coli*. They soon learned that it was not the physical influence of the electrical current as expected, but the chemicals in solution that caused the effect. Since cancer cells multiply more rapidly than noncancer cells, chemicals that limit cell division are potential anticancer agents. After trying various combinations of dissolved platinum, chloride, and ammonia, Rosenberg discovered that a very simple compound ["cisplatin", *cis*-PtCl$_2$(NH$_3$)$_2$] was responsible for this behavior and exhibited antitumor properties and published this finding in 1969.

The stereochemistry of cisplatin and its *trans*-isomer had been solved by Alfred Werner (see chapter 1) in 1893. The *trans*-isomer, unlike cisplatin, is not active against tumors. Subsequent studies of the mechanism of the cisplatin activity by many groups demonstrated that it binds to DNA by forming a compound between adjacent purine-bearing nucleotides on the same chain, thus preventing replication and transcription. The *trans*-isomer is incapable of forming such complexes. Cisplatin was approved by the U.S. Food and Drug Administration (FDA) in 1978. It remains today a potent drug against ovarian tumors and especially testicular tumors although it has significant toxicity and tumor cells tend to develop some resistance to it. A new generation of cisplatin relatives, including oxaliplatin, is now in use as scientists continue to investigate the mechanism of action. Surprises have been a recurring theme in drug discovery and the sidebar on page 255 presents two examples: a disastrous surprise and a pleasant one.

Pheromones: Chemical Communication between Individuals of the Same Species

How do female butterflies attract males of the same species over long distances? How do ants follow pathways to food and back to the colony (see the accompanying figure)? Is it really true that once stung by a bee, other bees swarm and inflict more stings? How do fish in a school sense dominance? How does a jungle cat mark territory? Do people "fall in love at first sight"? If so, what roles do hidden chemical signals play?

Adolph Butenandt, who shared the 1939 Nobel Prize in chemistry for isolation and structure proofs of human sex hormones, was intrigued by the highly specific attraction of female moths for male moths at great

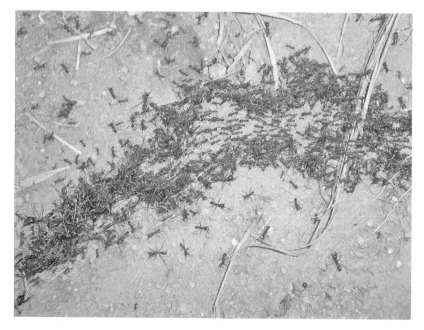

Column of Matabele army ants (Dorylus [Anomma] wilverthi) en route to raiding a ground termite mound in South Luangwu National Park, Zambia, Africa. The column moves as a unit following ant trail pheromones laid by the scout worker ants. (Bruce G. Marcot)

Thalidomide and Taxol: Lessons Learned from Two Drugs

Thalidomide (see the structure below) was synthesized and marketed by a German company in 1957 as an anti-nausea agent for pregnant women as well as a sedative. It was sold in more than 20 countries by 1960, the year before the German company discovered that it was associated with seriously deformed babies and pulled it from the market. In 1960, an American company applied to market thalidomide. The case was reviewed by Frances Oldham Kelsey (1914–) of the FDA. Despite pressure from the company, Kelsey did not feel that the safety of the drug had been fully established. When news of "thalidomide babies" started to appear in 1961, it became clear that Kelsey's principled stand had saved the United States from a disaster. The company's U.S. application was withdrawn in 1962.

One positive result of the thalidomide disaster is that drugs are now tested for teratogenic (birth defect-inducing) properties. Another interesting issue surfaced in connection with thalidomide. It has one asymmetric carbon atom (labeled by * in the structure). Evidence was cited suggesting that one enantiomer had the desired antinausea effect while the other enantiomer was associated with birth defects. This was a new issue for the pharmaceutical industry which routinely provided synthetic drugs in their racemic (optically inactive) form. Pharmaceutical companies now carefully test the activities of each enantiomer of a drug and have developed innovative synthetic and manufacturing techniques to provide only one enantiomer where appropriate. Ironically, recent studies demonstrated that, under physiological conditions, each of the thalidomide enantiomers racemizes spontaneously: The "good enantiomer" spontaneously forms the "bad enantiomer" under any circumstance. Another irony is that, in recent years, thalidomide has been found to be effective and safe as an anti-inflammatory drug. It is now marketed as thalomid and not prescribed for women who are or may become pregnant.

During the period 1961–80, the National Cancer Institute funded a massive "drug mining" program for natural products from plants and animals. In 1967, Monroe E. Wall (1916–2002), at the Research Triangle Institute, isolated a substance with potential anticancer properties from the poisonous bark of the Pacific yew tree. He published its extremely complex structure in 1971. The quantities were minute: the bark from 2,000 to 3,000 yew trees yields 2.2 pounds (1 kg) of the active substance, Taxol (paclitaxel). Robert A. Holton (1944–), at Florida State University, later discovered that needles of English yew shrubs, much more common than Pacific yew trees, yield much larger amounts of a closely related compound that is readily converted to Taxol. Bristol-Myers Squibb marketed Taxol starting in 1993 and it is today an effective treatment for ovarian cancer, breast cancer, and some forms of lung cancer.

When a new and totally unexpected structure, such as that of Taxol, is discovered in nature, drug companies view it as a *lead compound* that might lead to development of even more effective related drugs. This provides a very compelling argument for maintaining the Earth's biodiversity. There was yet one more bonus in the Taxol discovery. In the late 1970s Susan Band Horwitz (1937–) at Albert Einstein College of Medicine in New York City discovered that the pharmacological action of Taxol as an anticancer agent occurs by a new mechanism: stabilization of the microtubules formed during cell division to an extent that limits cell division. This fundamental discovery opened a new front in the war against cancer.

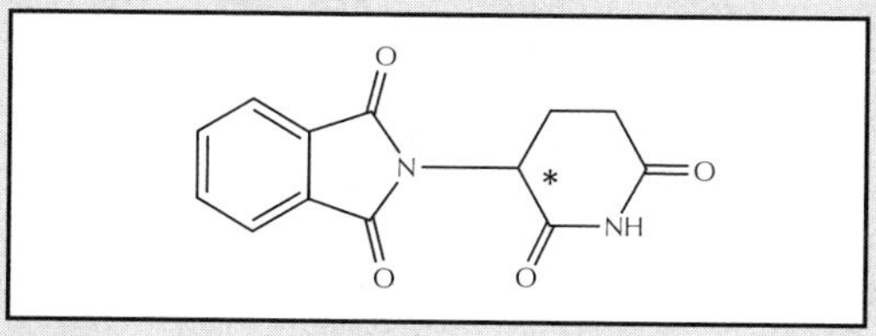

Thalidomide

distances. Over the course of three decades he carefully cut the abdomen tips from 500,000 (virgin) female silk moths (*Bombyx mori*), ground them up, extracted them, and separated the extracts into fractions. By exposing male silk moths to each fraction and monitoring their wing flutters he was able to isolate fractions and subfractions containing the active substance. In 1959, Butenandt reported the isolation and structure proof of less than 10 mg of the sexual attractant, which he called "bombykol" (see the structure below). His colleagues Peter Karlson and Martin Lüscher coined the term *pheromone* ("carrier of excitement") for a chemical that communicates between two or more animals of the same species. Karlson too had a long-standing interest in communication between insects. Some years earlier he consulted his neighbor, biologist Dietrich Schneider, about a sensitive, species-specific way to sense unimaginably small quantities of such chemical signals. In 1957, Schneider developed a process in which the antenna of a freshly killed insect is cut off at the base, the tip also cut, and electrodes attached to the two ends of the antenna which is soaked in brine. Air containing the chemical candidate is gently blown past the antenna which responds with a signal pattern termed an electroantennogram (EAG). Current studies suggest that a female moth can attract a male from distances on the order of five miles. In principle, the total sex attractant from a single female moth (perhaps 1 µg [microgram]) could attract over a trillion males if conditions were right and it may well be that a single molecule is sufficient to elicit a response.

The development of pheromone chemistry exploded during the 1960s as interdisciplinary research became more common and chemical instrumentation, particularly capillary column GC/MS and FT NMR, advanced. Most of the earliest studies were performed upon insects: They are inexpensive, easier to study, and simple in their behavior when compared to mammals. In the U.S., chemist Jerrold Meinwald (1927–) partnered with Cornell colleague entomologist Thomas Eisner (1929–) to pioneer a new field called chemical ecology. Edward O. Wilson (1929–), at Harvard, has been a leader in studying the chemical "vocabularies" of social insects, particularly ants. The field of chemical ecology goes far beyond pheromones since it is not limited to chemical interactions between individuals of the same species. It poses some fascinating ecological questions as scientists learn about extremely subtle, complex chemical communications in the nexus of life and ponder what influence people exert as they introduce tens of thousands of new chemicals into the environment.

Bombykol, a moth sexual attractant pheromone

The Environmental Movement Is Born

Documented concerns over the effects of chemical pollution on human health date back more than eight centuries, well before chemistry became a science. Until the 12th century, citizens of England burned wood for heating and cooking, but as the forests became depleted started using soft bituminous coal ("sea coal") obtained off the coast. The air in London became so bad that, in 1272, king Edward I banned the burning and selling of sea coal under punishment of torture or death. That law was unenforceable and, in 1306, the king banned coal burning whenever Parliament was in session. In December 1930 a "killer smog" in the Meuse valley of Belgium, a densely populated coal-mining and steelmaking region, caused 63 deaths and widespread illness. The primary causes were sulfur dioxide (SO_2) and particulates from the sulfur-rich coal. A similar incident in Donora, Pennsylvania, in October 1948 killed 20 citizens and made over 7,000 ill.

Concerns about human health gave rise to the environmental movement. The atmospheric testing of nuclear weapons during the 1950s also became a major health concern. Aside from the simple fact that testing increased the risk of nuclear war, radioactivity from fallout was known to be dangerous. In particular, radioactive strontium 90, a fission by-product chemically similar to calcium, was found to accumulate in young bones and teeth. Linus Pauling became a leading advocate for a ban on nuclear bomb tests. In 1957 he obtained the signatures of more than 11,000 scientists from 49 countries on a letter that he submitted to Dag Hammerskjöld, secretary-general of the United Nations. The second paragraph of the letter read as follows:

> *Each nuclear bomb test spreads an added burden of radioactive elements over every part of the world. Each added amount of radiation causes damage to the health of human beings all over the world and causes damage to the pool of human germ plasm such as to lead to an increase in the number of seriously defective children that will be born in future generations.*

Pauling won the 1962 Nobel Peace Prize for his activism and on August 5, 1963, a ban on testing nuclear weapons in the atmosphere, space, and underwater was signed in Moscow.

In 1958, Rachel Carson (1907–64), a marine biologist and writer, learned of a large number of bird kills following systematic application of DDT in Cape Cod. This launched a four-year journalistic study culminating in one of the most important books of the century, *Silent Spring*, published in 1962. In her book Carson documented disastrous ecological effects of DDT as it moves up the food chain and renders the eggs of birds of prey too fragile to bear young. The impact of *Silent Spring* was to make the world aware of the ecological impact of pesticides, especially DDT, and expand interest beyond human health alone. DDT had been synthesized and developed into a pesticide just prior to World War II and it saved countless lives of soldiers and civilians in Northern Africa, the Middle East, and Asia during the war. Carson's book initiated a successful and valued movement that virtually eliminated DDT in developed countries.

Although DDT is considered throughout the developed world to be a "bad" chemical, it is worthwhile balancing this view with some perspective from the world's poorest nations. The Johns Hopkins Bloomberg School of Public Health states that each year worldwide there are 300-500 million clinical cases of malaria, a debilitating disease, causing approximately 1.5-3 million deaths per year. Since DDT is inexpensive and long-lived (persistence in the environment is a double-edged sword), it remains today the chemical of choice for poorer countries that cannot afford more expensive pesticides. The malaria microorganism that infects blood, *Plasmodia*, has in the 21st century developed resistance to most drugs. Thus, killing mosquitoes, the first line of defense, assumes even greater urgency. The point here is not to decide right or wrong but to understand that the cost-benefit analysis for DDT is different in wealthy Western countries than in subtropical Africa or southern Asia.

Ernest L. Wynder (1922–99), Sloan-Kettering, and Dietrich Hoffmann (1924–   ), American Health Foundation, decisively connected smoking to cancer. In 1964 the surgeon general released the report "Smoking and Health: Report of the Advisory Committee to the Surgeon General of the Public Health Service." During this period, Irving J. Selikoff (1915–92), Mount Sinai Medical School, studied cases of a rare cancer called mesothelioma and linked it to the exposure of shipyard workers who had years earlier coated ship interiors with asbestos. The sad irony here is that asbestos was widely used in industrial and residential venues to prevent fires. It is hard to calculate the number of lives saved by asbestos. Selikoff's work demonstrated the need for occupational safety. From a "good" chemical, asbestos became a "bad" chemical and is no longer used in fire-protective insulation or coatings. Tetraethyllead, discovered in 1921 and marketed as a gasoline additive, improves engine performance by reducing knocking, the inefficient "microexplosions" of gasoline inside the engine. Typically, a gallon of leaded gasoline contained about 2 grams of lead. Although the toxicity of lead was known for centuries, there appeared to have been no really serious objection for nearly four decades to automobile lead emissions. Throughout the 1960s there were no standards for lead content in gasoline or lead emissions from cars. In December 1970 the United States Environmental Protection Agency was inaugurated, the Clean Air Act passed in that same year, the Clean Water Act passed in 1972, and in 1973 the United States started phasing out leaded gasoline.

Ozone (O_3) plays a critical protective role in the Earth's upper stratosphere. The lower atmosphere (troposphere) is separated from the upper atmosphere (stratosphere) by a region called the tropopause which varies in altitude from 5 miles (8 km) at the Earth's poles to 11 miles (18 km) at the equator. At an altitude of roughly 20 miles (33 km) there exists an ozone layer that absorbs 99 percent of the high-energy, damaging ultraviolet light with wavelengths below 320 nm. The energy of absorbed UV light cleaves ozone into O_2 molecules and extremely reactive oxygen atoms. However, these reactions are normally matched by other reactions that recombine these chemical species to reform ozone and maintain equilibrium.

During the late 1960s companies in the United States, Europe, and Russia explored the attractive-sounding idea of supersonic transport aircraft ("SSTs," see the photograph). Since SSTs would fly near the altitude of the ozone layer, there was concern about their impact on this vital protective shield. Initially, the concern was that water vapor from fuel combustion by SSTs would be split into reactive species that could decompose ozone and disrupt the balance. Paul Crutzen (1933–), a Dutch citizen studying at Oxford, discovered that the major ozone decomposition mechanism would, in fact, involve oxides of nitrogen ("NO_x") rather than water. Specifically, he discovered that species such as nitric oxide (NO) could play a catalytic role:

$$NO + O_3 \rightarrow NO_2 + O_2$$

$$NO_2 + O \rightarrow NO + O_2$$

Net: $O_3 + O \rightarrow 2\,O_2$

Boeing 2707 supersonic transport (SST) prototype
(Boeing)

The young Crutzen published this vital study in 1970. At this time Harold Johnston (1920–), a renowned chemistry professor at Berkeley, also came to realize the critical role of NO_x in destroying stratospheric ozone and published, in 1971, his studies of the potential impact of SSTs. In the final analysis, the United States did not build an SST largely for business reasons. The British and French entered a joint venture and built the Concorde, certainly one of the most beautiful planes ever flown. After 30 years of travel for the elite, the early 21st century witnessed the "mothballing" of the Concorde fleet in favor of increasingly large subsonic airbuses. Crutzen would share the 1995 Nobel Prize in chemistry with two other chemists for studies of stratospheric ozone, a topic that will be discussed in chapter 8. Atmospheric ozone is a global problem. So is the *greenhouse effect* associated with molecules such as CO_2 and CH_4 that absorb heat reflected from the Earth and trap it, causing global warming (see chapter 8).

While ozone is a "good molecule" high in the stratosphere, its "reviews" in the lower troposphere are decidedly "mixed." It is the source of minuscule concentrations of hydroxyl radical (OH, 10^6 molecules/cm^3). Hydroxyl is so extraordinarily active that it reacts with hydrocarbons (methane, benzene, etc) and most atmospheric compounds. Some extremely stable molecules, including chlorofluorocarbons like $CFCl_3$ and CF_2Cl_2 and N_2O (nitrous oxide from fertilizers, a source of stratospheric NO), do not react with OH and migrate to the upper stratosphere (see chapter 8 for the consequences).

More and Higher Octane Gasoline from Petroleum: New Zeolites

Zeolites (see chapter 5) consist of silica and alumina tetrahedra and have extensive pore structures (see the figure below) allowing selective entrainment of molecules based on size and shape. In 1962, Mobil Oil Corporation developed a process to manufacture Zeolite X. It proved to be an effective catalyst in cracking petroleum to "squeeze" 40 percent more gasoline out of each barrel of crude oil. At Union Carbide, Edith M. Flanigen (1929–   ) began research on zeolites in 1956 and a few years later developed a means to make Zeolite Y, another catalyst effective for converting crude petroleum to gasoline. Edith Flanigen was awarded the

The structure of Linde Zeolite A consists of silicate and aluminate tetrahedra with accompanying cations.

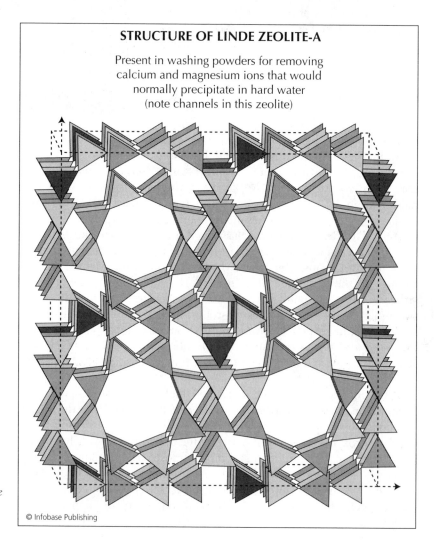

STRUCTURE OF LINDE ZEOLITE-A

Present in washing powders for removing calcium and magnesium ions that would normally precipitate in hard water (note channels in this zeolite)

© Infobase Publishing

Perkin Medal by the American Chemical Society in 1992. She was the first woman to win this award. Tradition dictated that the winner wear a mauve-colored tie (in honor of William H. Perkin, who synthesized mauve, the first dye derived from coal tar). In keeping with the spirit, if not the letter, of this tradition, Flanigen purchased a spectacular mauve-colored dress for the occasion of her award.

During the early 1970s, Clarence D. Chang, Anthony J. Silvestri, and William Lang, at Mobil Research and Development, discovered Zeolite ZSM-5, one of the most important catalysts ever produced. Zeolite ZSM-5 is a superacidic substance that catalyzes isomerization of *ortho-* and *meta*-xylenes to *para*-xylene; the latter's cylindrical shape helps it to diffuse much more rapidly through the zeolite matrix. Quite by accident, they discovered that ZSM-5 catalyzes the conversion of methanol to

Scientist of the Decade: Robert Burns Woodward (1917–1979)

Robert Burns ("R. B.") Woodward was, if not the greatest chemist of the 20th century as many would argue, almost certainly the greatest organic chemist. He was born in Boston, Massachusetts, attended public schools in nearby Quincy, and performed his first chemistry experiment in his home lab at age 12. Woodward entered MIT at 16, was not very interested in courses outside of chemistry, achieved poor grades, and was placed on probation for one semester. Readmitted, he registered for classes in the first term of his junior year and scheduled 186 hours per week of class meetings (Note: 7 days × 24 hours/day = 168 hours). All told, Woodward finished his B.S. and Ph.D. degrees in four years (by the age of 20).

Woodward began his career as instructor at Harvard in autumn 1937 and remained there until he died. He is renowned for brilliant syntheses of natural products. With his first student, William von Eggers Doering, Woodward published in 1944 what was considered at the time the first total synthesis of quinine. He was an early advocate of instrumentation, developing useful rules for ultraviolet spectroscopy. The 28-year-old Woodward employed combustion calorimetry to successfully argue against Sir Robert Robinson's

proposed structure for penicillin. As brilliant and all-encompassing as Robinson was as an organic chemist, Woodward would eclipse him by mid-century in ingenious syntheses of cholesterol, cortisone, strychnine, and chlorophyll among natural products leading to the 1965 Nobel Prize in chemistry. Upon learning of the structure of vitamin B_{12} (adenosylcobalamin), Woodward set out to synthesize this amazing molecule, later joining forces with Albert Eschenmoser and achieving success in 1973. Woodward described his motivation to synthesize complex molecules thusly:

> The structure known, but not yet accessible by synthesis, is to the chemist what the unclimbed mountain, the uncharted sea, the untilled field, the unreached planet, are to other men.

Early in his quest for vitamin B_{12}, Woodward noted the curious stereochemistries of some rearrangements and consulted a gifted young theoretician, Roald Hoffmann, a Harvard Junior Fellow. The Woodward-Hoffmann rules were published in 1965 and started a revolution in the way chemists treated concerted reactions such as the Diels-Alder

(continues)

(continued)

reaction. Woodward had become fascinated with the Diels-Alder reaction even before he entered college, proposed a mechanism for it in 1942 (and again in 1959), and used it in some of his subsequent syntheses.

Woodward's syntheses were as unique and characteristic as a score by Mozart. Examples of his virtuosity included creating several chiral centers with correct relative configurations in a single step as well as his "ring strategy." An example of the latter occurred in the synthesis of colchicine in which he employed a stable isothiazole ring as a rigid template only to open and destroy it toward the end. Here are parts of Woodward's "eulogy" to his noble isothiazole ring:

> *Our investigation now entered a phase that was tinged with melancholy. Our isothiazole ring had served admirably in every anticipated capacity and some others as well . . . It had mobilized its special directive and reactive capacities dutifully, and not once obtruded a willful and diverting reactivity of its own. Now it must discharge but one more responsibility—to permit itself gracefully to be dismantled . . . And perform this final act of grace it did.*

Robert Burns ("R.B.") Woodward, winner of the 1965 Nobel Prize in chemistry (Harvard University Archives)

Had Woodward not died at a relatively young age, he would certainly have shared the Nobel Prize with Hoffmann and Fukui. Moreover, a good argument could be made for sharing in a *third* Nobel Prize in chemistry for his work on ferrocene (see chapter 6).

gasoline components having high octane ratings. Mobil patented its MTG (methanol-to-gasoline) process and commercialized it in New Zealand in 1985. This is a very critical connection between methanol, available from methane using Fischer-Tropsch chemistry and newer chemistries, and gasoline.

The LCD (Liquid Crystal Display) Is Born

In 1888, Austrian botanist Friedrich Reinitzer (1857–1927) was synthesizing esters of cholesterol when he discovered a very curious phenomenon. Investigating the melting point of cholesterol benzoate, he discovered that at 293°F (145°C) it did not really melt but turned "milky" and eventually melted (became clear) at 354°F (179°C). Further study by German physicist Otto Lehmann (1855–1922) convinced him that they had discovered a fourth state of matter and he coined the term "liquid crystal." Molecules forming liquid crystals are generally long and rodlike in shape. The nematic phase of liquid crystalline materials consists of layers of rodlike molecules oriented in the same direction in each layer but with the ability to move past each other—more ordered than a liquid and less ordered than a crystalline solid.

In 1962, chemist Richard Williams (1927–   ) at RCA David Sarnoff Laboratories discovered that if a liquid crystal was placed between two glass slides coated with transparent, electrically conducting materials, a small electrical current could change the material reversibly from cloudy to clear. In 1968, his RCA colleague George H. Heilmeier (1936–   ), an electrical engineer, fabricated the first LCD (liquid crystal display). The first heat-stable liquid crystal was MBBA (p-methoxybenzylidene-p-n-butylaniline). LCDs require much less power than conventional displays and were used starting in the 1970s in calculators and wristwatches, and today they are employed in flat-screen TVs.

Conclusion

The 1960s witnessed the development of sensitive analytical instruments and their integration with computers. In turn, these new instruments would allow scientists to provide more sensitive and accurate data in support of the environmental and ecological studies that would blossom during the 1970s. Computer calculation of chemical properties would become much more reliable during the 1970s allowing "computational experiments" of considerable credibility. The chemical studies of DNA during the 1960s and cracking of the genetic code would presage the biotechnology revolution that began during the next decade. The application of liquid crystals to LCDs would help to enable the coming age of handheld calculators, digital wristwatches, and flat-screen TVs.

Further Reading

American Chemical Society. "It's Elemental: The Periodic Table." *Chemical & Engineering News (Special Issue)* 81 (September 8, 2003). In addition to articles on elements 103 through 105, particularly recommended is the article on noble gases by Neil Bartlett.
———. "Fighting Malaria." *Chemical & Engineering News* 83 (October 24, 2005): 69–82. This article describes the history and latest advances in preventing and treating malaria.
Ball, Philip. *Elegant Solutions: Ten Beautiful Experiments in Chemistry.* Cambridge: Royal Society of Chemistry, 2005. This highly readable book includes essays on heavy artificial elements (see chapter 5) and on noble gas compounds (see chapter 8).

Benfey, Otto Theodore, and Peter J. Morris, ed. *Robert Burns Woodward: Architect and Artist in the World of Molecules.* Philadelphia: Chemical Heritage Foundation, 2001. This large pictorial work includes numerous insightful essays by collaborators of Woodward.

Carson, Rachel. *Silent Spring.* Boston: Houghton Mifflin Co., 1962. First described to a popular readership the ecological dangers posed by DDT.

Christie, Karl O. "A Renaissance in Noble Gas Chemistry." *Angewandte Chemie International Edition* 40 (2001): 1,419–21. This review article describes the latest advances in noble gas chemistry including the synthesis of HArF.

Eisner, Thomas. *For Love of Insects.* Cambridge, Mass.: The Belknap Press of Harvard University Press, 2003. This highly readable book discusses a broad range of insect chemistry.

El-Sayed, Ashraf M. *The Pherobase: Database of Insect Pheromones and Semiochemicals.* 2006. Available online. URL: www.pherobase.com/guide. htm. Accessed February 16, 2006. This is a database of pheromones and semiochemicals of over 7,000 species.

Gray, Harry B. "Molecular Orbital Theory for Transition Metal Complexes." *Journal of Chemical Education* 41 (1964): 2–12. Appropriate for teachers and students who wish to understand bonding in transition-metal compounds.

Hoffmann, Roald. "A Claim on the Development of the Frontier Orbital Explanation of Electrocyclic Reactions." *Accounts of Chemical Research* 43 (2004): 6,586–90. Considers the role of Elias J. Corey at Harvard in the development of the theory of concerted electrocyclic reactions.

Laszlo, Pierre, and Gary J. Schrobilgen. "One or Several Pioneers? The Discovery of Noble-Gas Compounds." *Angewandte Chemie International Edition* 27 (1988): 479–89. This is a discussion of the history of discovery of xenon and other noble gas compounds.

Ridley, Matt. *Francis Crick: Discoverer of the Genetic Code.* New York: Atlas Books/HarperCollins, 2006. This is a brief biography emphasizing the major discoveries and human traits of Francis Crick.

Scott, Robert A., A. Grant Mauk, and Harry B. Gray. "Experimental Approach to Studying Biological Electron Transfer." *Journal of Chemical Education* 62 (1985): 932. This article is written for teachers and students who wish to understand electron-transfer in biological systems.

Sherman, John D. "Synthetic Zeolites and Other Microporous Oxide Molecular Sieves," *Proceedings of the National Academy of Sciences* 96 (1999): 3,471–3,478. This is a discussion of current developments in the design of these important and novel catalysts.

Thomas, Lewis. *The Lives of a Cell.* New York: Viking Press, 1974. Consists of brief, very enjoyable essays about the relationships between individuals and societies including an essay titled "A Fear of Pheromones."

United States Food and Drug Administration (U.S. FDA), *Food and Drug Administration Policy Statement for the Development of New Stereoisomeric Drugs* (May 1, 1992; last updated July 6, 2005). Available online. URL: www.fda.gov/cder/guidance/stereo.htm. Accessed February 12, 2006. Provides guidelines for testing and separation of chiral drugs.

8

1971–1980:
Chemical Breakthroughs in Medicine, Biotechnology, and Materials Science

The Age of a New Materials Science and Biotechnology Begins

Chemistry can, with considerable justification, consider itself the "central science," and the new decade abundantly supported this claim. A revolution in *materials science* and electronics began with the discovery that *doping* the organic polymer polyacetylene produces an *organic metal* with electrical conductivity approaching that of copper. The structural chemistry of nucleic acids and proteins, originating in the 1950s, contributed to the synthesis of a fully functioning gene and to rapid techniques of DNA sequencing. This knowledge, combined with the discovery of DNA *ligase* in 1967 and *restriction endonucleases* in 1970, led to the first molecule of *recombinant DNA* and the subsequent revolution in genetic engineering and biotechnology that followed almost immediately. The development of 2-D NMR combined with advances in computational techniques provided chemists and biologists with detailed three-dimensional structures of large molecules in solution, not limited now to solid-state X-ray crystallography. NMR spectroscopy would give birth during the decade to magnetic resonance imaging (MRI), a vital tool for examining soft tissue in modern hospitals and clinics. The development of catalysts for selective syntheses of single enantiomers of drugs would add efficiency, economy, and safety to the pharmaceutical industry. The mechanism of the analgesic aspirin, a true "wonder drug," would at last be clarified. New realms explored chemically would include the surface of Mars and "black smokers" on the floors of the Earth's oceans.

Seaborgium (Element 106) and Bohrium (Element 107)

In 1971, Glenn Seaborg rejoined his old Berkeley group now directed by Albert Ghiorso, after serving as chair of the Atomic Energy Commission. In early 1974, the Joint Institute for Nuclear Research in Dubna claimed synthesis of element 106. Four months later, the Ghiorso group bombarded ^{249}Cf with ^{18}O and reported a few atoms of element 106 with atomic mass 263 and $t_{1/2}$ of 0.9 seconds. The Berkeley results were confirmed in 1993. In 1997 IUPAC agreed to name element 106 seaborgium (Sg) after the famous American chemist who discovered plutonium and the actinide series. This was the first time an element would be named for a living scientist. The most stable isotope of seaborgium is ^{266}Sg, $t_{1/2}$ = 26 seconds. Today, fast isolation techniques allow limited chemical studies of nuclei having half-lives less than 10 seconds. Much to his satisfaction, Seaborg learned that "his" element resembles its Group 6 "siblings" tungsten (W) and molybdenum (Mo) although there remain subtle chemical differences. Seaborg suffered a stroke in late 1998 and died in February 1999.

The earliest theory of nuclear structure was the "liquid drop" theory, developed around 1940. It pictured the nucleus as a structureless drop of liquid in which repulsions between positive charges are opposed by a kind

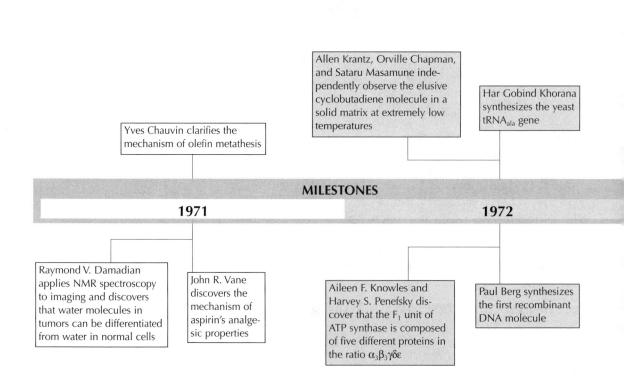

Allen Krantz, Orville Chapman, and Sataru Masamune independently observe the elusive cyclobutadiene molecule in a solid matrix at extremely low temperatures

Har Gobind Khorana synthesizes the yeast tRNA$_{ala}$ gene

Yves Chauvin clarifies the mechanism of olefin metathesis

MILESTONES

1971

1972

Raymond V. Damadian applies NMR spectroscopy to imaging and discovers that water molecules in tumors can be differentiated from water in normal cells

John R. Vane discovers the mechanism of aspirin's analgesic properties

Aileen F. Knowles and Harvey S. Penefsky discover that the F_1 unit of ATP synthase is composed of five different proteins in the ratio $\alpha_3\beta_3\gamma\delta\epsilon$

Paul Berg synthesizes the first recombinant DNA molecule

of surface tension holding it together. One prediction was that the limit of stability is reached at atomic number 106 and that the nucleus of element 107 should be particularly unstable. The early theory was replaced in the 1950s by a quantum theory of nuclear structure, developed independently by Maria Goeppert-Mayer (1906–72) in Chicago and J. Hans D. Jensen (1907–73) in Heidelberg. It is well known that the most stable nuclei have even numbers of protons and even numbers of neutrons. The quantum theory predicted "magic" nuclear quantum numbers: number of protons (Z) or neutrons (N) = 2, 8, 20, 28, 50, 82, 126, . . . , much like the "magic" chemistry numbers 2, 8, and 18. Nuclides in which both protons and neutrons satisfy magic numbers, are termed "doubly magic" and are especially stable. Examples include ^{40}Ca (20 protons; 20 neutrons), ^{48}Ca (20 protons; 28 neutrons), and ^{208}Pb (82 protons; 126 neutrons). There are some other predictions for "magic numbers." For example, special stability is predicted for the nucleus having Z = 114 and N = 184 (perhaps part of the so-called island of stability). Instead of imagining element 107

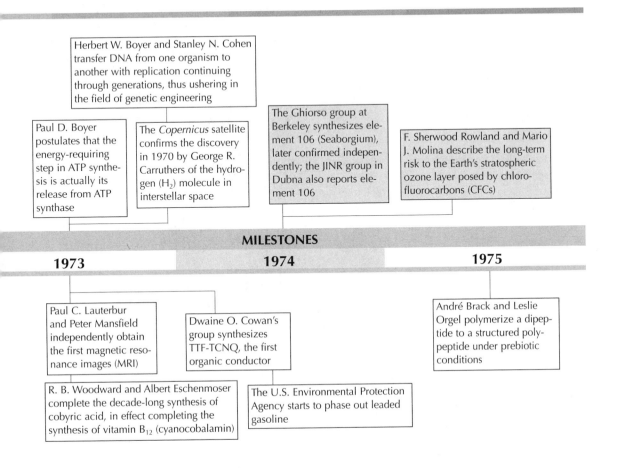

Herbert W. Boyer and Stanley N. Cohen transfer DNA from one organism to another with replication continuing through generations, thus ushering in the field of genetic engineering

Paul D. Boyer postulates that the energy-requiring step in ATP synthesis is actually its release from ATP synthase

The *Copernicus* satellite confirms the discovery in 1970 by George R. Carruthers of the hydrogen (H_2) molecule in interstellar space

The Ghiorso group at Berkeley synthesizes element 106 (Seaborgium), later confirmed independently; the JINR group in Dubna also reports element 106

F. Sherwood Rowland and Mario J. Molina describe the long-term risk to the Earth's stratospheric ozone layer posed by chlorofluorocarbons (CFCs)

MILESTONES

1973   **1974**   **1975**

Paul C. Lauterbur and Peter Mansfield independently obtain the first magnetic resonance images (MRI)

Dwaine O. Cowan's group synthesizes TTF-TCNQ, the first organic conductor

André Brack and Leslie Orgel polymerize a dipeptide to a structured polypeptide under prebiotic conditions

R. B. Woodward and Albert Eschenmoser complete the decade-long synthesis of cobyric acid, in effect completing the synthesis of vitamin B_{12} (cyanocobalamin)

The U.S. Environmental Protection Agency starts to phase out leaded gasoline

as "the end of the road," it was newly envisioned as the first superheavy element. Goeppert-Mayer and Jensen shared the 1963 Nobel Prize in physics with Eugene Wigner (1902–95). In 1976 the Russian group discovered a new technique called *cold fusion* or "soft fusion" (see chapters 9 and 10) and successfully synthesized element 107, confirmed by the Darmstadt group in 1981. In 1997 it was officially named bohrium (Bh), after Niels Bohr. Its most stable isotope, ^{267}Bh, has $t_{1/2}$ = 17 seconds.

Two-Dimensional NMR: Structures of Large Molecules in Solution

X-ray crystal diffraction is a powerful technique for determining detailed structures of large, complex molecules, but it is not applicable to solutions where most chemistry occurs. In studying a protein, for example, it is desirable to observe the continuous variations in structure with changes in pH, temperature, denaturation, or binding with substrates. Starting in the 1970s, nuclear magnetic resonance (NMR) spectroscopy became the only technique capable of providing detailed structural information on very large, complex molecules in solution. It is a challenging task because

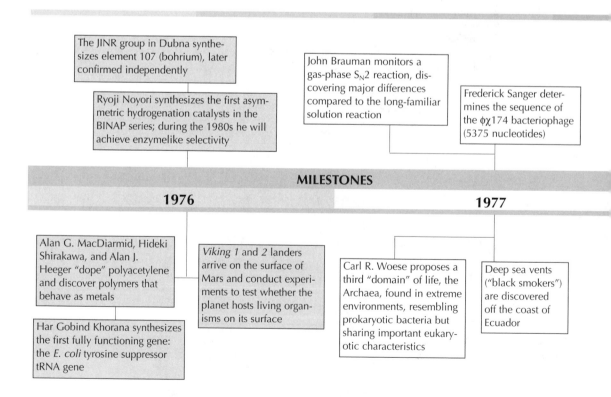

The JINR group in Dubna synthesizes element 107 (bohrium), later confirmed independently

Ryoji Noyori synthesizes the first asymmetric hydrogenation catalysts in the BINAP series; during the 1980s he will achieve enzymelike selectivity

John Brauman monitors a gas-phase S_N2 reaction, discovering major differences compared to the long-familiar solution reaction

Frederick Sanger determines the sequence of the φχ174 bacteriophage (5375 nucleotides)

MILESTONES

1976

1977

Alan G. MacDiarmid, Hideki Shirakawa, and Alan J. Heeger "dope" polyacetylene and discover polymers that behave as metals

Har Gobind Khorana synthesizes the first fully functioning gene: the *E. coli* tyrosine suppressor tRNA gene

Viking 1 and *2* landers arrive on the surface of Mars and conduct experiments to test whether the planet hosts living organisms on its surface

Carl R. Woese proposes a third "domain" of life, the Archaea, found in extreme environments, resembling prokaryotic bacteria but sharing important eukaryotic characteristics

Deep sea vents ("black smokers") are discovered off the coast of Ecuador

proteins have hundreds of different protons, very similar in chemical shift, with complex coupling patterns.

The coupling constants (denoted by J) between different ^{1}H nuclei separated by two or three bonds, such as the ^{3}J between the methyl and methylene groups in ethanol (see page 195), arise through the intervening chemical bonds. If ^{1}H nuclei in a molecule are separated by four or more bonds, this coupling is usually weak or absent. If two hydrogen atoms are attached to carbon atoms connected by a single bond (H$_A$-C-C-H$_B$), the torsional angle, the projection between the C-H$_A$ and C-H$_B$ bonds, fits the Karplus equation, developed by Martin Karplus (1930–   ). If the molecule is folded so that other hydrogen atoms are very close in space, the distance between them can be measured using the Nuclear Overhauser Effect (NOE): "Saturating" one proton nucleus (H$_B$) causes enhanced NMR absorption of another (spatially close) proton (H$_Y$). The magnitude of the NOE between two ^{1}H nuclei is inversely proportional to the sixth power of the distance between them (1/r^6). By "marching through" a complex molecule in solution, using the Karplus equation and NOE, chemists in the 1960s could "assemble" a time-averaged, three-dimensional structure for a fairly complex molecule in solution.

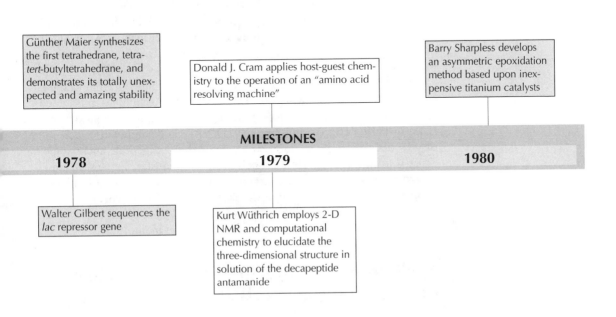

Günther Maier synthesizes the first tetrahedrane, tetra-*tert*-butyltetrahedrane, and demonstrates its totally unexpected and amazing stability

Donald J. Cram applies host-guest chemistry to the operation of an "amino acid resolving machine"

Barry Sharpless develops an asymmetric epoxidation method based upon inexpensive titanium catalysts

MILESTONES

1978   **1979**   **1980**

Walter Gilbert sequences the *lac* repressor gene

Kurt Wüthrich employs 2-D NMR and computational chemistry to elucidate the three-dimensional structure in solution of the decapeptide antamanide

The Fourier transform (FT NMR) technique, developed by Richard R. Ernst during the 1960s, was also applicable to the development of two-dimensional NMR. While FT NMR employs a single radiofrequency pulse, collects time-domain data, and transforms it to frequencies, 2D NMR employed two pulses. In later years, 3D and 4D techniques, employing a variety of pulse sequences, have transformed NMR into a method whose power was undreamed of in its "childhood." In 2D ^{1}H-NMR, a method called "COSY" (or correlation spectroscopy) plots the same scale of ^{1}H chemical shifts on both x- and y-axes with the third dimension (z-axis) reflecting peak heights. The classical ("1D") NMR spectrum is seen on the diagonal of the 2D spectrum making a 45-degree angle with the x- and y-axes. There are also "off-diagonal" peaks symmetrically disposed about the diagonal that directly indicate which ^{1}H nuclei are coupled to each other. A similar 2D experiment produces a "NOESY" spectrum indicating which hydrogen nuclei are related by NOE effects, and therefore spatially close.

Another key factor driving the revolution in NMR spectroscopy was the development of high-field superconducting magnets. The original instruments introduced in the early 1960s, the 60 MHz and 100 MHz NMR instruments, required magnetic fields of 1.41 tesla (T) (14,100 gauss [G]) and 2.35 T (23,500 G) for ^{1}H-NMR respectively. The following decades witnessed introduction of superconducting magnets, which employ liquid helium at 4.2 K (-452°F or -269°C) to cool their wire coils and make them superconducting: 400 MHz (94,000 G) in 1975, 500 Mz (117,000 G) in 1979, 600 MHz in 1986, 750 MHz in 1993, 800 MHz in 1997, and 900 MHz (210,000 G) in 2000. The 500 MHz instrument, for example, magnifies the difference in ^{1}H chemical shifts by a factor of 8.3 (500 MHz/60 MHz), vastly increasing the ability to resolve an exceedingly complex spectrum.

Ernst's colleague at the ETH, Kurt Wüthrich (1938–   ), employed the new high-field FT NMR spectrometers with 2D techniques and added computational chemistry to determine structures of large biological molecules. In 1979, he successfully applied 2D NMR and computational chemistry to determine the solution structure of the decapeptide antamanide. Ernst was awarded the 1991 Nobel Prize in chemistry. For his groundbreaking work in solving the structures of large biological molecules in solution, Kurt Wüthrich shared the 2002 Nobel Prize in chemistry with John B. Fenn and Koichi Tanaka, who successfully applied mass spectrometry (see chapter 9) to studies of structures of large biomolecules.

Applications of NMR to Solids and to Magnetic Resonance Imaging (MRI)

NMR samples normally consist of homogeneous liquid solutions in tubes that are rapidly spun so as to keep as homogeneous a field as possible in the sample. The NMR peaks typically obtained from a solid sample are so broad as to be nearly useless. However, during the 1960s E. Raymond Andrew (1921–2001) at the University of Wales and Irving T. Lowe (1929–) at the University of Pittsburgh, using NMR theory, independently realized that an NMR sample spun rapidly at an angle of precisely 54.74 degrees with respect to the applied magnetic field should produce fairly thin resonance-absorption lines. This "magic-angle" spinning technique became the first practical way to analyze solid samples. In the early 1970s, John S. Waugh (1929–), at MIT, and his student Alexander Pines (1945–, later at Berkeley), and Peter Mansfield (1933–), independently at Nottingham in the United Kingdom, developed a solid-state NMR technique based upon cross-polarization: polarization from ^1H nuclei passed on to ^{13}C nuclei.

Mansfield's studies of the solid state led him to examine the possibility of using NMR for imaging of samples including human tissues. At the State University of New York at Stony Brook (SUNY Stony Brook), Paul C. Lauterbur (1929–2007) realized that instead of the uniform magnetic field needed for chemical samples in NMR tubes, different magnetic fields (gradients) in the NMR probe could provide an actual image. In 1973, he published a seminal paper that reported ^1H-NMR imaging of two capillary tubes filled with H_2O mounted in an NMR tube filled with D_2O. In that same year, Mansfield, using similar techniques, published an image of a stack of slides. Interest in applying NMR to the study of human tissue had begun during the 1960s. A 1971 publication by Raymond V. Damadian (1936–), SUNY Downstate Medical Center in Brooklyn, demonstrated differences in the rates of tumbling of H_2O molecules in tumors and in normal tissues. These early experiments in magnetic resonance imaging (MRI) would lead to the MRI machines widely employed in hospitals today. The 2003 Nobel Prize in physiology or medicine was shared by Paul C. Lauterbur, a chemist, and Sir Peter Mansfield, a physicist, primarily for making MRI a practical imaging technology.

A Bridge between Organic and Inorganic Chemistries

In the early 1970s, Roald Hoffmann developed a very useful model based upon frontier MO theory, hybridization and symmetry: "isolobal fragments" (ML_n). Two fragments are said to be *isolobal* if their frontier orbitals are equal in number, have the same symmetry and lobal properties, and are very similar in energy. One very simple example is the comparison between the CH_3 and $Mn(CO)_5$ radicals (see the figure on page 272). Methyl radical is "built" from one 2s and three 2p orbitals on carbon hybridized to four sp^3 orbitals, one of which is singly occupied. In $Mn(CO)_5$, manganese ($4s^2 5d^5$) employs its single 4s orbital, three 4p

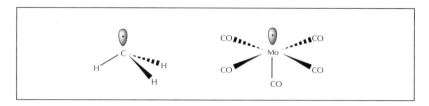

Two isolobal fragments

orbitals, and *two* of its five 3d orbitals to form six d^2sp^3 hybrids pointed to the corners of an octahedron. Combination with five CO ligands, each contributing two electrons, leads to $Mn(CO)_5$, with 17 valence-shell (frontier MO) electrons, leaving one unpaired electron in a single d^2sp^3 orbital, similar to the sp^3 orbital in CH_3.

Just as two methyl radicals combine to form ethane ($H_3C\text{-}CH_3$), two $Mn(CO)_5$ radicals form the Mn-Mn single bond in $Mn_2(CO)_{10}$ (see chapter 7). When $Mn_2(CO)_{10}$ is chemically reduced, the anion $Mn(CO)_5^-$ reacts with CH_3I to form the stable "mixed" compound $CH_3\text{-}Mn(CO)_5$ analogous to reaction of CH_3^- with CH_3I to form ethane. The $:CH_2$ fragment is a carbene and is isolobal with $Fe(CO)_4$. The corresponding dimer $H_2C=CH_2$ is well known, although $(CO)_4Fe=Fe(CO)_4$ is not very stable and has been observed only at very low temperature. "Mixed" compounds, such as $H_2C=Fe(CO)_4$, are metallocarbenes (see chapter 7) known to play vital roles in olefin metathesis (see the later section in this chapter).

"Organic Metals"

Organic materials (polyethylene, Styrofoam, wood) are almost always insulators (poor carriers of electric current). Conductivities of insulators typically range from 10^{-22} to 10^{-14} ohm^{-1}cm^{-1}. Good conductors of electricity, such as copper, have conductivities in the range 10^5 to 10^6 ohm^{-1}cm^{-1}. Semiconductors range from 10^{-9} to 10^3 ohm^{-1}cm^{-1}. Although diamond is an insulator, its allotrope graphite conducts electricity and the shiny appearance of graphite (pencil "lead") hints at this metallic property. Graphite has a virtually infinite two-dimensional array of conjugated C=C bonds in each layer as well as weak interactions between the π-electron clouds of successive layers. The result is a small energy-band gap between the valence band of filled (bonding) MOs and the conduction band of vacant (antibonding) MOs. This allows easy promotion of electrons from the valence to the conduction band and charge mobility. Insulators have large band gaps.

In 1973, Dwaine O. Cowan (1935–) and collaborators at Johns Hopkins University combined two organic molecules, tetrathiafulvalene (TTF) and tetracyanoquinomethane (TCNQ), in a 1:1 solid complex and discovered the first organic conductor. TTF has a fairly low ionization potential (IP) and loses an electron readily, while TCNQ has a fairly high electron affinity (EA) and can gain an electron readily. Solid TTF-TCNQ consists of alternating "stacks" of TTF and TCNQ that allow mobility of electrons through the material with accompanying conductivity.

The big breakthrough came after some fortuitous accidents and coincidences. Hideki Shirakawa (1936–) began studies of the polymerization of acetylene (H-C≡C-H) using Ziegler-Natta catalysts at Tokyo Institute of Technology in 1966. Acetylene had first been polymerized in the presence of copper salts at the end of the 19th century by Paul Sabatier to form a disordered, cross-linked substance called "cuprene." The new polyacetylene [$(CH=CH)_n$ or simply $(CH)_n$] samples were typically brown powders. In 1975, a foreign student working in Shirikawa's laboratory misread his directions and added a molar (mol), rather than a millimolar (mmol), quantity of catalyst to the polymerization reaction and obtained a "glittery, silvery film" instead of the usual powder. At about this time, physicist Alan J. Heeger (1936–) stimulated the interest of his University of Pennsylvania chemistry colleague Alan G. MacDiarmid (1927–2007) in the conductivity of a shiny film of sulfur nitride polymer [$(SN)_x$]. Visiting Tokyo in 1975 MacDiarmid met Shirakawa and was shown the silvery $(CH)_n$ film. He invited Shirakawa to spend a year at Penn. In November 1976, Shirikawa attempted to measure the changes in conductivity when Br_2, which readily adds to C=C bonds, is added slowly to the $(CH)_n$ film. Upon the first small addition, the conductivity jumped perhaps 10 millionfold, destroying the apparatus. Thus was discovered chemical doping of *trans*-polyacetylene to form conductors, some as good as copper metal. Such conducting polymers have the properties of metals with the mechanical and processing properties of plastics.

The extensive linear conjugation in polyacetylene produces valence and conduction bands separated by a moderate gap, making it a semiconductor. The polymer can lose or gain electrons relatively easily. When "doped" with a small amount of I_2, for example, polyacetylene loses electrons and reduces iodine to I_3^-. The extended polymer network carries mobile positive charges ("holes") and is called a "p-type" conductor. Substances that readily donate electrons to polyacetylene create a negative network of mobile electrons in n-type conductors. There are other ways to "dope" polyacetylene and related families of conducting polymers. Their use in light-emitting diodes (LEDs), starting around 1990, is just one of a growing list of applications. Hideki Shirakawa, Alan G. MacDiarmid, and Alan J. Heeger shared the 2000 Nobel Prize in chemistry.

Olefin Metathesis: Custom Design of Industrial Chemical Feedstocks

The magical-looking olefin metathesis reaction (see chapter 7) has become a mainstay in the petroleum industry and a powerful addition to the synthetic organic chemistry "toolbox." For example, the 1964 discovery at Phillips Petroleum of the interconversion of ethylene ($CH_2=CH_2$) and 2-butene ($CH_3CH=CHCH_3$) into propylene ($CH_3CH=CH_2$), using $Mo(CO)_6$ on alumina, laid the basis for the modern Phillips triolefin process.

Initially, the most obvious mechanism for olefin metathesis was a kind of molecular "square dance" in which two different olefin molecules join to form a cyclobutane ring and then "change partners" to form two new olefin molecules. While this thermal reaction is "Woodward-Hoffmann" forbidden, transition metals were initially perceived to allow "violations" of these rules. However, no cyclobutanes were detected in olefin metathesis reactions, nor did cyclobutanes produce olefins when placed into metathesis reaction mixtures. The breakthrough came in 1971 when Yves Chauvin (1930–), at the French Petroleum Institute, made the conceptual link between the Phillips Petroleum reaction discovered in 1964 and metallocarbenes isolated in the same year by Ernest Otto Fischer (see chapter 7). Other important discoveries were made by Michael F. Lappert (1928–) at Sussex, Charles P. Casey (1942–) at Wisconsin, and especially Thomas J. Katz (1936–) at Columbia. The mechanism involves formation of a metallocyclobutane (see the accompanying figure), from reaction of a metallocarbene ("$M=CR'_2$") with an olefin ($R_2C=CR_2$), that splits into a new olefin ($R'_2C=CR_2$) and a new metallocarbene ("$M=CR_2$").

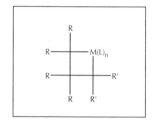

Olefin metathesis intermediate

The mechanistic studies on olefin metathesis were joined in the 1970s by Robert H. Grubbs (1942–), who moved from Michigan State to Caltech in 1978, and Richard R. Schrock (1945–), who joined the MIT faculty in 1975 following three years at DuPont. They developed metallocarbene catalysts that are now widely used in industry. Schrock made the first such catalysts in 1990, employing tungsten and molybdenum, and Grubbs made improved catalysts based on ruthenium in 1992. In 2005, Yves Chauvin, Robert H. Grubbs, and Richard R. Schrock shared the Nobel Prize in chemistry for their contributions to olefin metathesis.

Surprising Reactivities in the Gas Phase

If methanol (CH_3OH) is added to a solution of a toluene Grignard reagent, such as $C_6H_5CH_2MgBr$, it promptly "kills" the Grignard reagent and forms toluene ($C_6H_5CH_3$). In effect, the following reaction occurs:

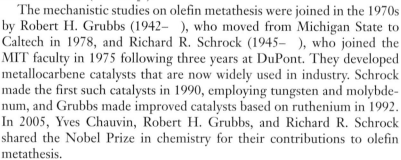

$$C_6H_5CH_2^- \text{ (soln)} + CH_3OH \text{ (soln)} \rightarrow C_6H_5CH_3 \text{ (soln)} + CH_3O^- \text{ (soln)}$$

Strong Base   Strong Acid   Weak Acid   Weak Base

The classical textbook explanation is deceptively simple: Methanol is a stronger acid because oxygen is more electronegative than carbon and better holds a negative charge.

Starting in the 1960s, a technique called ion cyclotron resonance (ICR) mass spectrometry, developed by John Brauman (1937–) at Stanford University, facilitated measurement of the products formed from gas-phase reactions between molecules and ions. Jesse L. Beauchamp (1942–), at Caltech, was an early investigator of this new gas-phase chemistry. In contrast to the solution-phase chemistry, in the gas phase toluene is a stronger acid than methanol:

$$CH_3O^- \text{ (gas)} + C_6H_5CH_3 \text{ (gas)} \rightarrow CH_3OH \text{ (gas)} + C_6H_5CH_2^- \text{ (gas)}$$

Strong Base   Strong Acid   Weak Acid   Weak Base

Is there something strange or more complex about the new gas-phase chemistry? The answer is "no." To the contrary, gas-phase chemistry is much simpler to understand than the solution chemistry that has been the foundation of decades (indeed centuries) of chemical laboratory practice. The "classical textbook explanation" above considers the two acids and two bases only and mentions nothing of the solvent that surrounds them. In the gas phase there really are no solvent molecules and the acidity of any HA derives from the sum of the energies of just three processes:

$HA \rightarrow H\cdot + A\cdot$ E_1 = Bond Dissociation Energy for H-A

$H\cdot \rightarrow H^+ + e^-$ E_2 = Ionization Potential (IP) of the H atom

$A\cdot + e^- \rightarrow A^-$ E_3 = Electron Affinity (EA) of the A atom or group

Net (Gas-Phase) Reaction: $HA \rightarrow H^+ + A^-$; Net Energy = $E_1 + E_2 + E_3$

Since the IP (a positive energy) of the H atom is common to the calculations for both methanol and toluene it can be neglected. The gas-phase electron affinity (EA, a negative energy for most radicals) of $CH_3O\cdot$ is about 10 kcal/mol more negative (more favorable) than the value for $C_6H_5CH_2\cdot$. That is fully consistent with the greater electronegativity of oxygen compared to carbon. However, the bond dissociation energy (a positive energy) of the CH_3O-H bond is 15 kcal/mol higher (more positive; stronger bond) than that for the $C_6H_5CH_2$-H bond since the $C_6H_5CH_2$ radical is resonance stabilized and easier to form. The net difference is 5 kcal/mol, making toluene more acidic (in the gas phase). In solution, however, polar solvent molecules stabilize the small CH_3O^- ion more than the bulky $C_6H_5CH_2^-$ ion and the "expected" order is observed. Methanol is a stronger acid than methane (CH_4) in both gas phase and solution. The CH_3-H bond dissociation energy is virtually equal to that of CH_3O-H and conventional electronegativity factors are decisive, with solvation being comparable for the small CH_3O^- and CH_3^- ions.

The reaction coordinate for a typical (solution-phase) S_N2 reaction is depicted in chapter 4: CH_3Cl and OH^- react in a single step forming a transient activated complex that instantaneously transforms to the CH_3OH and Cl^- products. In 1977, John Brauman discovered that reactions of this type behave very differently in the gas phase, without a solvent to stabilize reactants, transition state, and products. First, CH_3Cl and OH^- combine to form a fairly stable "loose" ion-dipole complex (HO^-–CH_3Cl). The slow step actually involves the reorientation inside the complex to a structure resembling the activated complex. This "falls into" another fairly stable "loose" ion-dipole complex ($HOCH_3$–Cl^-) which slowly forms the products CH_3OH and Cl^-. The mechanism is very different from the solution mechanism and the limiting factor in the slow step is entropy and not the energy of activation.

Although these examples of gas-phase chemistry might appear to be esoteric, the ability to separate *intrinsic* reactivities of molecules and ions from the influences of solvents is fundamental to understanding chemistry. It may also be relevant for chemistry in interstellar space.

High-Energy Organic Molecules: Caught in Frozen Matrices and Some Surprises

Strained organic molecules continued to hold the attention of chemists who enjoy testing the limits of bonding (see chapter 7). Elementary levels of theory, such as Hückel MO theory (see chapter 4), predict that planar trimethylenemethane (see the structure below) has two unpaired electrons and is a ground-state triplet. Unlike molecular oxygen, which is a stable ground-state triplet, carbon-centered diradicals are exceedingly reactive. In 1966, Paul Dowd (1936–96) at Harvard generated trimethylenemethane photochemically from and observed it via EPR at -300°F (-185°C) in a dilute frozen solvent matrix. A solid matrix limits movement, preventing the reactive diradical from dimerizing. If all electrons in trimethylenemethane were paired (singlet diradical), there would be no EPR signal. The EPR spectrum observed by Dowd clearly signaled the triplet predicted by very simple Hückel MO theory.

Molecular nitrogen (N_2) lacks a dipole moment and therefore does not absorb infrared radiation. Frozen nitrogen provides a suitable solid matrix for observing the IR spectra of exceedingly reactive intermediates. Similarly, argon has no bonds, no bond vibrations, and no IR spectrum. In 1973, Orville L. Chapman (1932–2004) at Iowa State generated the transient 1,2-benzyne (see chapter 6) in a solid argon matrix at 8 K (-445°F or -265°C) and recorded its IR spectrum. The spectrum was

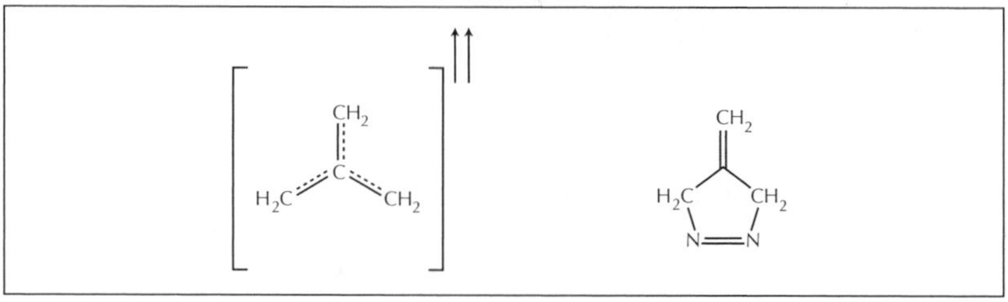

Triplet trimethylenemethane; precursor to trimethylenemethane

fully consistent with the figure on page 276, which pairs the electrons on carbons 1 and 2 forming a singlet (no free electron spins) with a very short C_1-C_2 distance. If any susceptible compound is also present in the matrix, warming the mixture to only 50 K (-370°F or -223°C) causes immediate reaction of benzyne. During 1972–73, the research groups of Chapman, Allen Krantz (1940–   ), at SUNY Stony Brook, and Sataru Masamune (1928–   ), at Alberta, each generated the elusive 1,3-cyclobutadiene in low-temperature matrices and observed it by IR and UV.

As noted in chapter 7, the tetrahedrane molecule appeared to be unattainable following the failed efforts of some outstanding chemists, one or two of whom were fooled initially and thought they had succeeded. The strain energy in tetrahedrane, 130 kcal/mol, is about 32.5 kcal/mol per carbon or 21.7 kcal/mol per C-C bond, while that in cyclopropane is only 9.3 kcal/mol per carbon or per C-C bond. Cleavage of a single C-C bond in tetrahedrane releases strain energy almost equal to the strength of that bond. Bond cleavage should occur very easily and the diradical created should instantly rearrange to the more stable isomer, cyclobutadiene, itself short-lived. The best possibility for observing tetrahedrane appeared to be in an inert solid matrix close to 0 K. However, in 1978 the worldwide chemical community was amazed to learn that Günther Maier, at Justus Liebig University in Giessen, made tetra-*tert*-butyltetrahedrane (see the figure, middle right), actually distilled it, and found it to be stable in air with a melting point of 275°F (135°C). Heating this compound isomerizes it to its cyclobutadiene isomer (see the figure, bottom right). Maier attributes the amazing stability of tetra-*tert*-butyltetrahedrane to a "corset effect": the four bulky *tert*-butyl substituents are as far apart as possible in this molecule and cleavage of one C-C bond must force them closer together.

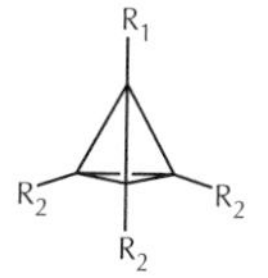

One of the beautiful aspects of organic chemistry is that carbon forms strong bonds with so many different atoms (electropositive and electronegative) that molecules may be "fine-tuned" by varying attached substituents. During the 1970s, theory suggested that electropositive substituents might stabilize the tetrahedrane structure. In 1989, Maier made a second tetrahedrane using the bulky electropositive trimethylsilyl group (see the structures), and found it to be even more stable than his first tetrahedrane, exhibiting a melting point of 354°F (179°C). Six years later, eight tetrahedranes were known. In 2002, the Giessen research group and researchers from the University of Tsukuba in Japan made a third derivative with four trimethylsilyl groups (see the structures). It has a melting point 396°F (202°C) with no decomposition below 572°F (300°C). While the first two tetrahedranes describe isomerize upon heating to their more stable cyclobutadiene isomers, this last tetrahedrane is more stable than its cyclobutadiene isomer, decomposing to $(CH_3)_3Si$-$C{\equiv}C$-$Si(CH_3)_3$ above 572°F (300°C). Other tetrahedranes synthesized successfully are also depicted here.

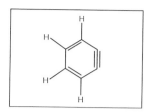

1,2-Benzyne

R_1

R_2 R_2

R_2

a. $R_1 = R_2 = C(CH_3)_3$
b. $R_1 = Si(CH_3)_3 ; R_2 = C(CH_3)_3$
c. $R_1 = R_2 = Si(CH_3)_3$
d. $R_1 = CH_3 ; R_2 = Si(CH_3)_3$
e. $R_1 = H ; R_2 = Si(CH_3)_3$

Stable tetrahedranes

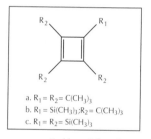

a. $R_1 = R_2 = C(CH_3)_3$
b. $R_1 = Si(CH_3)_3 ; R_2 = C(CH_3)_3$
c. $R_1 = R_2 = Si(CH_3)_3$

Stable cyclobutadienes

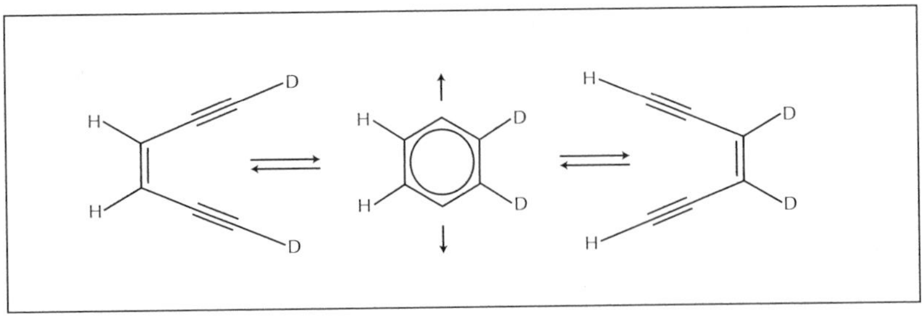

Labeled hexaenediyne; labeled 1,4-Benzyne, labeled hexaenediyne

The tetrahedrane story is reminiscent of the history of xenon chemistry. Failed attempts to react xenon in the early 1930s set a psychological barrier finally shattered by Neil Bartlett in 1962, opening the way for syntheses of other rare gas compounds. Failed efforts in the 1950s and 1960s and the formidable strain energy of tetrahedrane set a psychological barrier to isolating tetrahedranes, shattered by Günther Maier in 1978. There are now over a dozen stable tetrahedranes including a wondrous molecule, synthesized in Tsukuba, containing two such units connected by a single bond.

At Caltech Robert G. Bergman (1942–) investigated 1,4-benzyne, an even less stable isomer of 1,2-benzyne. Synthesizing the deuterated compound (shown above), he heated it and observed it rearrange. A fairly simple combination of kinetic measurements and energy estimates indicated that 1,4-benzyne (see the structure; a singlet having the two electrons paired) is a true chemical intermediate. This pure research study would have totally unexpected applications to cancer treatment in future decades (see chapter 9).

Supramolecular Chemistry: Molecular Hosts and Their Guests

Certain metal ions, such as copper and vanadium, catalyze auto-oxidation leading to breakdown of petroleum products as well as rubber. In 1967, Charles J. Pedersen (1904–89), at DuPont, was investigating new compounds to deactivate such metals and made a fortuitous discovery. Combining two small molecules, catechol ($C_6H_6O_2$) and the ether $O(CH_2CH_2Cl)_2$ in the presence of sodium hydroxide (NaOH) provides the 18-membered ring compound represented below, which Pedersen named dibenzo-18-crown-6. It is well to recall how difficult it is to make large-ring (macrocyclic) compounds (see chapter 3). Pedersen had mixed two simple compounds and out "popped" an 18-membered ring in good yield. Although this compound is insoluble in methanol, Pedersen discovered that small amounts of Na^+ in methanol greatly increase its solubility. He realized that Na^+ forms a methanol-soluble complex by sitting in the hole in the center of the molecule: the first example of a neutral ligand complexing an alkali metal ion. Pedersen realized that complexation by Na⁺ actually promotes organization of the growing molecule as it wraps itself around the ion and closes to form the 18-membered ring. Synthesis of a large family of *crown ethers* followed this initial discovery with vacancies custom-made for cations of different sizes.

Crown ethers found application in a new technique called phase-transfer catalysis. If one wishes to react NaCN with $C_6H_5CH_2Br$, there is a problem because the first compound is water soluble and the second soluble only in nonpolar solvents. However, placing an aqueous solution containing NaCN in direct contact with an organic solution of the other reactant with a small amount of crown ether causes rapid reaction. The organic-soluble crown ether complexes Na⁺ to form an organic-soluble complex. CN⁻ crosses into the organic layer to preserve electroneutrality and, in the nonpolar medium, this anion becomes highly reactive and rapidly forms organic-soluble product. When the reaction is complete, the organic product is in the organic layer and NaBr is in the aqueous layer.

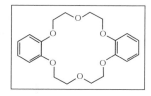

A crown ether

At the University of Strasbourg in France, Jean-Marie Lehn (1939–) followed Pedersen's work with keen interest. Lehn was aware that the cyclic peptide drug valinomycin controls transport of K⁺ through the cell membranes of bacteria. Lehn and his colleagues designed classes of compounds with various vacancies to hold cations of different sizes. The synthesis of a wide-ranging series of compounds termed *cryptands*, after "crypt" (see the figure, bottom right), began in 1969 and has continued for decades since. The Lehn group also pioneered selective complexation of anions, either in suitably-designed cryptands or cryptands that included a cation to pair with the anion. Lehn coined the term *supramolecular chemistry* to characterize the emerging new field.

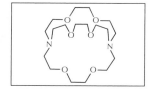

A cryptand

At UCLA, Donald J. Cram (1919–2001) was intrigued by the idea of chiral crown ethers as hosts that selectively bind smaller chiral guest molecules (like a right hand in a right glove). One of the most intriguing molecules the Cram group made during the 1970s is the chiral crown ether depicted below (this is the *R,R*-enantiomer). Chirality in this molecule derives from its propellerlike structure originating from steric repulsions between the nonbonded, twisted naphthalene neighbors. The *R,R*-enantiomer has specific affinity for the uncommon D-amino acids while its *S,S*-enantiomer binds the common L-amino acids. In 1979, Cram disclosed his "amino-acid resolving machine" that employed both the *R,R*- and its *S,S*-enantiomer to continuously resolve racemic amino acids.

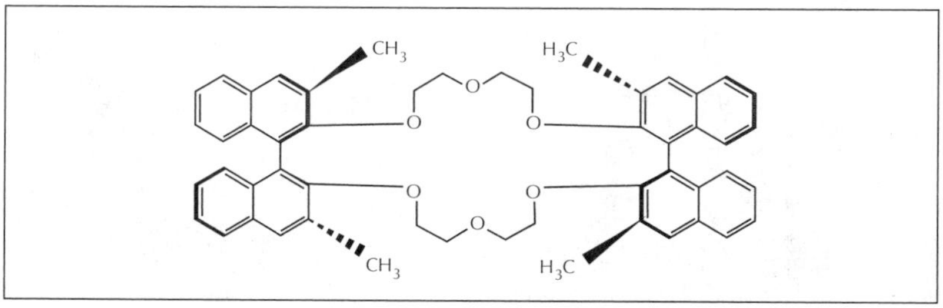

A chiral (propellerlike) crown ether

He achieved levels up to 90 percent "ee" (ee = enantiomeric excess, i.e., 90 percent ee equates to 95 percent D + 5 percent L in one chamber and 95 percent L + 5 percent D in the other). The achievements of Charles J. Pedersen, Jean-Marie Lehn, and Donald J. Cram were recognized by their receipt of the 1987 Nobel Prize in chemistry. In 1991, Cram's group synthesized the incredibly reactive cyclobutadiene molecule (see the previous section) in the center of an inert host. The complex is stable at room temperature for indefinite periods.

Conquering Vitamin B_{12}

The structure of vitamin B_{12} was solved by Dorothy Hodgkin in 1956 (cyanocobalamin, see chapter 6) using X-ray crystallography and the actual biological coenzyme was solved in 1961. Prior chemical investigations had shed little light on the structure of vitamin B_{12}. Other challenges included the first known carbon metal bond (Co-C) in a biological molecule and the presence of nine chiral centers in the corrin ring system alone and a total of 14 chiral centers in cyanocobalamin. R. B. Woodward, at Harvard, began synthesis of the A and D rings of the corrin system in 1960–61. At the ETH in Zurich, Albert Eschenmoser had been investigating synthetic approaches to corrins since 1959. Communications between the two groups evolved in 1965 to collaboration. Much like generals assaulting a formidable fortified foe, Woodward attacked the Western half of the molecule (the A and D rings of corrin) and Eschenmoser the Eastern half (the B and C rings). In 1973, their combined efforts achieved the synthesis of cobyric acid. Since Wilhelm Friedrich and Konrad Bernhauer (1900–75), in Stuttgart had, in 1960,

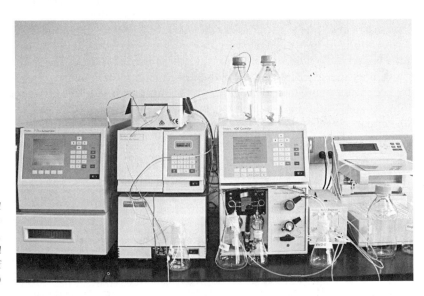

High-performance liquid chromatograph (HPLC) equipped with solvent pump, injector, analytical column, and detectors (Stevens Institute of Technology)

converted cobyric acid (obtained from natural vitamin B_{12}) to vitamin B_{12}, synthesis of cobyric acid was equivalent to total synthesis of vitamin B_{12}. In one of the final steps en route to cobyric acid, Woodward's group employed a Waters Associates high-performance liquid chromatograph (HPLC, see the photograph), a still-novel technique, to purify an intermediate. More than 100 talented scientists worked as a transatlantic supergroup to complete the synthesis. Among the bonuses achieved during the 12-year quest, a failed reaction led to the Woodward-Hoffmann rules described in the previous chapter. Woodward formally completed total synthesis of cyanocobalamin in 1976.

New Synthetic Routes to Pure Enantiomers

The thalidomide tragedy, described in chapter 7, started to focus the pharmaceutical industry on synthesis of single enantiomers rather than racemic mixtures. Even if there are no antagonistic or undesirable side effects from the other enantiomer, a racemic mixture may waste 50 percent of the mass of a drug. Optically pure compounds such as vitamin B_{12}, morphine, and L-dopa are available naturally. In some cases (e.g., vitamin B_{12}), the natural source is really the only practical source. For simpler compounds like L-dopa, chemical synthesis is very practical but resolution of enantiomers may double the production cost.

Catalytic hydrogenation is one of the core techniques of organic synthesis. Until the synthesis of the Wilkinson catalyst, $RhCl(PPh_3)_3$ (where Ph = phenyl or C_6H_5), in 1965, catalytic hydrogenation employed heterogeneous conditions requiring vigorous conditions. The Wilkinson catalyst, employed in homogeneous solutions under mild conditions, captured the imagination of synthetic chemists seeking enantiomerically pure products. One of the first to explore this possibility was William S. Knowles (1917–) at Monsanto Corporation. A suitable prochiral olefin could, in principle, be hydrogenated by a chiral Wilkinson-type catalyst to form a large excess of one enantiomer over the other. Exclusive formation of the desired enantiomer corresponds to an *enantiomeric excess* (ee) of 100 percent (100 percent desired enantiomer; 0 percent other enantiomer). If the reaction is totally unselective (50 percent of each enantiomer) the ee is 0 percent. If 95 percent of the desired enantiomer is formed with 5 percent of the other enantiomer, ee is 90 percent. One way to make a chiral Wilkinson-type catalyst is to employ an optically pure chiral ligand in place of the achiral PPh_3. After initial studies of other chiral phosphine ligands, Knowles chose "CAMP" (see the structure below) to form the optically pure catalyst $Rh(CAMP)_2(C_8H_{12})$. The geometry around phosphorus in phosphines $(:PR_3)$ such as CAMP is a trigonal pyramid due to the electron lone pair on phosphorus. If a phosphine has three different attached groups $(:PR_aR_bR_c)$, it is chiral. While similarly substituted amines $(:NR_aR_bR_c)$ rapidly invert and racemize at room temperature, Kurt Mislow (1923–), at Princeton, and Leopold Horner (1911–2005), at Mainz, had

Phosphine ligand with asymmetric phosphorus

Phosphine ligand with chiral propellerlike twist

isolated optically pure phosphines and demonstrated that chiral phosphines such as "CAMP" invert so slowly at ambient temperature that they maintain optical purity. At Monsanto, the Knowles group achieved an ee of 88 percent in the synthesis of L-dopa through catalytic hydrogenation. In 1971, Henri B. Kagan (1930–), University of Paris South, achieved 83 percent ee with the chiral ligand "DIOP" that acts as a chelator (two binding groups). This led the Monsanto group to ligands that are chelators comprised of two chiral phosphine units. Monsanto achieved values around 95 percent ee, selectivity approaching that of enzymes.

Ryoji Noyori (1938–), born in Kobe, Japan, received his first real exposure to asymmetric synthesis working with Hitosi Nozaki at Kyoto. Also intrigued by the Wilkinson catalyst, Nozaki achieved the first asymmetric hydrogenation with a well-defined catalyst. However, the ee was low. At Nagoya University, Noyori synthesized the BINAP catalyst (e.g., R-BINAP, see the structure) in 1976 and used it to make a Wilkinson-type BINAP-Rh complex. As in Cram's chiral crown ether, there are no chiral atoms in the BINAP-Rh complex and chirality originates in its stable, propellerlike conformation that minimizes steric repulsion. During the 1980s, Noyori achieved ee up to 100 percent using BINAP-Rh.

Barry Sharpless (1941–) began his academic career at MIT in 1970, spent the years 1977–80 at Stanford, returned to MIT in 1980, and joined the Scripps Research Institute in 1990. He also focused on prochiral olefins. The olefin linkage has the ability to be "hidden" (or "protected chemically") during a multistep synthesis and reappear upon (chemical) command for further reaction. H. C. Brown's hydroboration reaction (see chapter 6) was also well-suited to asymmetric syntheses based on olefin chemistry. Sharpless's work focused upon reactions that added oxygen to the olefin linkage. In 1980 the Sharpless group discovered the titanium-catalyzed reaction that today bears his name. It is illustrated for the pleasant-smelling terpene geraniol (see below). Reaction of geraniol with the catalyst $Ti(O-i-Pr)_4$ [i-Pr = $-CH(CH_3)_2$] and (+)-diethyl tartrate [(+)-DET] yields a pure epoxide enantiomer. The reaction is regiospecific because it reacts with only one of the two distinct double bonds in geraniol. It is also enantiospecific since only one enantiomer is formed. The chiral influence on the titanium catalyst is (+)-diethyl tartrate. One can only imagine the soul of Louis Pasteur rejoicing in the current use of the fruits of his original 1848 resolution of tartaric acid. For their breakthroughs in asymmetric synthesis William S. Knowles, Ryoji Noyori, and Barry Sharpless shared the 2001 Nobel Prize in chemistry.

Sharpless asymmetric epoxidation of geraniol

How Does Aspirin Work?

Prostaglandins, first isolated by Ulf von Euler in 1935 (see chapter 4), are incredibly active "messenger molecules" that influence inflammation, fever, pain, induction of labor, blood pressure, and blood clotting. In 1945, von Euler met young Sune K. Bergström (1916–2004) at a conference at the Karolinska Institute in Stockholm. He stimulated Bergström's interest in identifying prostaglandin structures and "passed the baton" by giving him a prewar sheep gland extract containing these mysterious, potent substances. Bergström moved from Karolinska to Lund in 1947 but returned in 1958 to join his collaborator Ragnar Ryhage, who built one the world's earliest GC/MS instruments. By 1962, Bergström and Ryhage had identified the structures of six prostaglandins (see the figure below). Others would follow in the 1960s and, by the end of the decade, E. J. Corey at Harvard synthesized some prostaglandins. Bengt I. Samuelsson (1934–) was a medical student at Karolinska

Cascade of biosynthesis of prostaglandins from arachidonic acid and the role of aspirin (acetylsalicylic acid) in blocking biosynthesis and easing inflammation

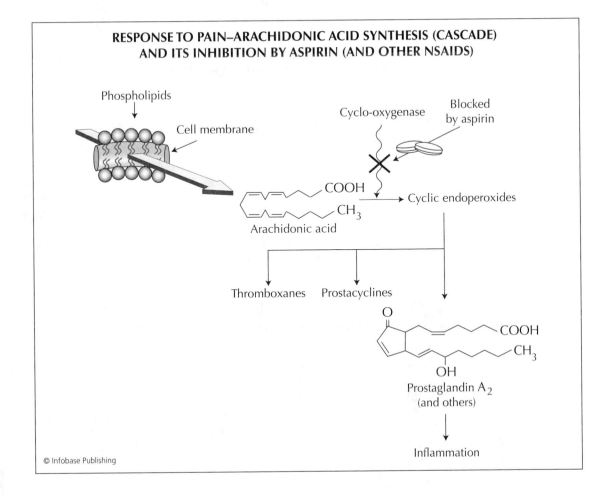

RESPONSE TO PAIN–ARACHIDONIC ACID SYNTHESIS (CASCADE) AND ITS INHIBITION BY ASPIRIN (AND OTHER NSAIDS)

Phospholipids

Cell membrane

Cyclo-oxygenase

Blocked by aspirin

COOH

CH₃

Arachidonic acid

Cyclic endoperoxides

Thromboxanes   Prostacyclines

Prostaglandin A₂ (and others)

Inflammation

© Infobase Publishing

while performing research on prostaglandin structures with Bergström. He moved to Stockholm in 1967 but returned to Karolinska a few years later. At Karolinska, Samuelsson discovered cyclic endoperoxides that are intermediates between prostaglandins and arachidonic acid found in cell membranes (see the figure).

John R. Vane (1927–2004) began an 18-year career at the Royal College of Surgeons in London in 1955, leaving to join the Wellcome Foundation in 1973. During the late 1960s, he developed the cascade superfusion bioassay technique in which the artery of an animal (e.g., a dog or rabbit) is pumped for blood (perhaps 10–15 mL per minute) and the blood is then used to perfuse chambers containing up to six samples of isolated smooth muscle before returning to a large vein of the living animal. The contraction of the muscle furnishes the biological response. Rat stomach, rat colon, and chicken rectum muscle strips were found to be particularly sensitive to prostaglandins. Administration of aspirin reduced prostaglandin levels and, in 1971, Vane discovered that in cell-free solutions aspirin inhibits the conversion of arachidonic acid to prostaglandins due to its inhibition of an enzyme. The figure depicts the accepted mechanism for the inhibition of prostaglandin biosynthesis by aspirin. An enzyme called cyclooxygenase (COX) catalyzes addition of O_2 to arachidonic acid to form cyclic endoperoxides which are enzymatically transformed into prostaglandins and other related classes. Inhibiting COX inhibits inflammation, fever, and pain. Sune K. Bergström, Bengt I. Samuelsson, and John R. Vane shared the 1982 Nobel Prize in physiology or medicine. Ibuprofen, introduced in 1969, is twice as effective as aspirin in reducing pain. It is understood these days that both aspirin and ibuprofen block a channel in COX that normally "docks" arachidonic acid. It is also known that there are actually two cyclooxygenases: COX-2, associated with inflammation and pain, and COX-1, responsible for a variety of functions including protecting stomach linings. Aspirin inhibits both COX-1 and COX-2, hence the side effects of stomach irritation accompanying prolonged use. Some modern analgesics have been designed to bind with COX-2 but not COX-1.

Designing New Drugs: Structure-Activity Relationships and Molecular Modeling

Although the science of rational drug design, based upon the antimetabolite concept, was born in the 1940s, some very important breakthroughs were made just prior to the start of the 20th century. Charles E. Overton (1865–1933) found that the anesthetic effects of chemicals such as ether and chloroform are rapidly induced *and* rapidly reversed. He assumed that the effects were physical rather than chemical in nature and investigated solubility as a determinant. Testing many animals and plants, Overton discovered that (within limits) the greater the *lipophilicity* (solubility in natural fats and oils) the more potent the anesthetic. The best correlations involved oil-water partitioning coefficients: the distribution of concentrations of drug "D" between the two layers in direct contact ($[D]_{oil}/[D]_{water}$). Overton presented his findings in 1899, the year that Hans Horst Meyer (1853–1939), in Marburg, independently reached similar conclusions.

During 1962–64, Corwin Hansch (1918–) at Pomona College developed the concept of the QSAR (Quantitative Structure Activity Relationship) and its application to drug design. In so doing, he combined linear free energy (LFE) relationships of the type developed by Louis Hammett in the 1930s (see chapter 4), modified by Robert Taft and others two decades later (see chapter 6), and added to it a measure of lipophilicity. Hansch defined lipophilicity by the partition constant (P) of drug D between 1-octanol and water ($P = [D]_{1\text{-octanol}}/[D]_{water}$), where 1-octanol is considered to reasonably mimic the polarity of membrane lipids. Combining Overton's data on the molar concentration of a given chemical that stopped the movement of tadpoles (C), with his own P values for each of the 51 chemicals tested by Overton, Hansch discovered the excellent correlation:

$$\log (1/C) = 0.94 \log P + 0.87; \; n = 51, \; r = 0.971$$

Plots of logarithm versus logarithm ("log/log" plots) examine huge differences in effect ($\log 1 = 0.00$; $\log 10 = 1.00$; $\log 100 = 2.00$; $\log 200 = 2.30$; $\log 10,000 = 4.00$) and easily obscure smaller but significant variations. Nonetheless, the very high correlation coefficient (r, a value of 1.00 would be perfect linear correlation) for a sizable number of test chemicals (n = 51) demonstrated genuine statistical significance. Note that the more effective the narcotic, the lower the concentration (C) required to render tadpoles motionless. Low C values equate to high values of 1/C and log (1/C). The positive slope (0.94) indicates that the greater the drug lipophilicity (P), the greater the narcotic effect.

Just as Hammett developed individual electronic substituent constants (σ_X) relative to hydrogen ($\sigma_H = 0$) (see chapter 4), Hansch developed a hydrophobicity parameter π_X, based on $\log P$, for each substituent relative to hydrogen. Just as σ could be used to predict changes in reactivities for a related series of molecules, π could be employed to predict changes in partition coefficients. Hansch understood that even "simple" biological effects (e.g., binding of a molecule by a membrane or an enzyme, catalytic breakdown by an enzyme) depends upon lipophilicity as well as the electronic nature of the substituents and some measure of steric effects. Although Robert Taft pioneered the steric parameter (E_s) of a given substituent, Hansch employed the molar refractivity (MR_X), another measure of substituent size.

Hansch applied his QSAR approach to hydrolysis of esters of structure ($X\text{-}C_6H_4O_2CCH_2NH\text{-}COC_6H_4\text{-}Y$) by the enzyme papain. The cor-

"Polywater:" Science Nearly Imitates Fiction

In his 1963 novel *Cat's Cradle,* author Kurt Vonnegut conjures up a new form of water, "ice-nine," sought by generals wishing to turn mud solid to speed their troops to battle. The problem is solved by an isolated, scientific genius who makes a tiny quantity of the dangerous substance, innocently starting the count-down to the end of all life on Earth. Since "ice-nine" is more stable than water, any water it touches (puddles, lakes, reservoirs, oceans, rain) becomes "ice-nine" and all liquid water vanishes from the planet.

In 1962, in an isolated laboratory in Kostroma, Russia, Nikolai N. Fedyakin made a surprising discovery. He found that water sealed in extremely thin glass capillary tubes, stored for a few days, spontaneously formed a new column of water, denser and more viscous than the remaining column of water in the capillary. Not long after Fedyakin reported this result, Boris V. Deryagin (1902–94), at the Soviet Academy of Sciences in Moscow, took over the project. Deryagin was a senior scientist whose work commanded worldwide respect. He performed careful experiments in a chamber in which pressure, temperature, and water saturation were controlled. Deryagin placed open, freshly drawn, ultraclean quartz capillary tubes in the chamber. He discovered that "modified water" could not form in tubes with inside diameters greater than 100 microns (0.004 inches). Its viscosity was 15 times that of water, its density (1.4 g/cm^3) was 40 percent higher than that of water, its boiling range (480°F [250°C] to 572°F [300°C]) and melting range (-22°F [-30°C] to -76°F [-60°C]) differed greatly from those of water. Scientists outside of the Soviet Union first learned of these results in 1965 at an IUPAC conference in Moscow, and much more widely at a conference in Nottingham in 1966. There was an explosion in research as scientists throughout the world duplicated Deryagin's apparatus and formed what was soon known as "anomalous water." From two Russian papers in 1962, research publications grew rapidly, reaching a peak in 1970, with 115 papers in the United States alone. Although there were reservations from the very beginning, many excellent and renowned scientists began to study "anomalous water," some funded by the military.

In 1969, Ellis R. Lippincott (1920–74), at the University of Maryland College Park, performed the first infrared spectroscopic study of "anomalous water," discovered significant differences from the spectra of water, and hypothesized a polymeric form of water he called polywater. Frank J. Donahoe (1922–), at Wilkes College, warned that if water could spontaneously change to polywater, then "I regard this polymer as

relation observed for 25 different esters differing only in substituents X and/or Y was:

$$\log (1/K_m) = 1.03\ \pi + 0.57\ \sigma + 0.61\ MR + 3.80;$$
$$n = 25;\ r = 0.907$$

K_m is the Michaelis-Menten constant (see page 59, where it is referred to simply as "K"): a measure of the enzyme's affinity for binding substrate (a low K_m, or high log [$1/K_m$], equates to high binding affinity). For the range of substrates investigated, binding affinity increases with the hydrophobicities (π) and sizes (MR) of substituents X and/or Y as well as their electron-withdrawing (positive σ) power. One might infer that papain's active site is a large hydrophobic pocket with some mild electron-donating character.

Of course, the obvious goal is to apply QSAR to designing new drugs that work for whole animals. This is a much more complex situation than

the *most dangerous material on earth.*" At the American Chemical Society National Meeting in September 1969, polywater (pro and con) was a major discussion topic and received coverage (including plenty of hype) in national and international news media.

As noted in chapter 7, computational chemistry was just coming into its own during the late 1960s. Larger molecules (and networks of small molecules) required ever rougher approximations to be feasible for quantum chemical computations: If computer calculation of H_2O takes 30 minutes, $(H_2O)_2$ takes about 8 hours and $(H_2O)_4$ about 125 hours using comparable methods. A distinguished Princeton theoretician, Leland C. Allen (1926–) and his graduate student Peter A. Kollman (1944–2001), later famous for studies of proteins, calculated the structure and properties of polymeric water. They relied on claims that the experimentalists were working with a pure substance. Allen and Kollman were limited to computations of only moderate sophistication. Their study, published in 1970, predicted a structure similar to graphite (regular "ice" is similar to diamond). Their calculated energies for polywater and liquid water were quite similar. This begged a question that many chemists had raised earlier: If "anomalous water" or polywater forms so readily (and is comparable in energy to liquid water), why had it not been seen before and, for that matter,

why had not substantial amounts of Earth's water (or all of it) been converted to polywater eons ago?

While there were doubts from the beginning about "anomalous water" or polywater, based upon thermodynamics, experimental studies began to fully dismantle the hypothesis. Most notably, Denis L. Rousseau (1940–), using extremely sophisticated and sensitive techniques at Bell Laboratories, demonstrated that polywater prepared according to Deryagin's technique had significant ionic impurities and even traces of organic matter. At a conference devoted to polywater at Lehigh University in June 1970, Lippincott reported that certain impurities had to be present to reproduce the IR spectra of polywater. Allen recalculated polywater and found that it was much less stable than regular water. By 1971 consensus in the scientific community had tipped decisively against "anomalous water" and polywater. Some now called the impure brew "polycrap." There was certainly embarrassment in the scientific community as the polywater affair assumed some characteristics that Irving Langmuir had defined in 1953 as "pathological science." It was a temporary setback for computational chemistry. However, the issue was fully resolved five years after it had become truly accessible to the scientific community. In 1973, Deryagin fully accepted the findings.

simple hydrolysis of a substrate by a pure enzyme. Such studies usually involve more parameters in addition to σ, π, and MR, as well as a large number of test compounds. In 1979, Hansch successfully applied QSAR to analysis of a series of the antimalarials, depicted right, in which substituents X and Y were varied. It becomes a fairly straightforward exercise to synthesize new compounds having X and/or Y substituents whose π, MR, and σ constants suggest that they *may* be more potent. Successful results for real animals or humans are never guaranteed.

Rapid advances in the analyses of protein structures using X-ray crystallography and high-field 2D NMR, combined with major advances in computer hardware, software, and graphics led to a new field called "molecular modeling" in the 1970s. One of the goals of molecular modeling is fitting biologically active molecules in binding sites on proteins

A family of substituted antimalarials

and determining the specificities and energetics of such "docking." The hope is the design of new biologically active molecules by computer. Such calculations were far removed from the realm of rigorous quantum mechanics and became the provenance of molecular mechanics and greatly simplified semiempirical MO calculations. Protein-substrate binding is largely determined by weak van der Waals and related forces that are impossible or exceedingly difficult to model using such simplified methods.

While no new drugs were "predicted from scratch" by computer during the 1970s, the new ways of calculating the shapes of substrates and binding sites and the dynamics of binding (increasingly depicted by computer-generated animations) greatly influenced the way scientists analyzed biological activity. Instead of substrate molecules being "balls-and-sticks," they became three-dimensional shapes with outer contours defined by overall electron density and regions of electron "excess" and "deficiency" seeking complementary sites on biological receptors. The pharmaceutical industry (as well as the flavor and fragrance industries) immediately began to add computational chemists to their research staffs. Structures and shapes of substrates and receptors determined by X-ray and NMR became starting points for computational study as well as independent checks of accuracy. In some circumstances, the shape and nature of a receptor would nicely rationalize the parameters obtained by QSAR studies. Still, in the late 1960s and early 1970s, the limits on computational chemistry made the reliability of some studies of larger, more complex systems questionable. This point is exemplified in the sidebar discussion of "polywater."

Atoms and Molecules in Space

The study of extraterrestrial chemistry began with the spectroscope in the latter half of the 19th century. Until 1951 the science was based entirely on optical spectroscopy: the emission of light from hot bodies (e.g., Sun, stars) and the absorption of light by the solar atmosphere and Earth's atmosphere (Fraunhofer lines) (see chapter 1). The visible spectrum ranges from 700 nm (red) to 400 nm (blue) and the ultraviolet (UV) ranges from 10–400 nm. Atmospheric ozone absorbs 99 percent of UV wavelengths shorter (higher energy) than 320 nm. UV emission or absorption of extraterrestrial wavelengths shorter than 320 nm can only be detected outside of Earth's atmosphere. The total solar eclipse of 1869 provided a clear view of the solar corona and the emission lines of a new element, helium, were discovered on the Sun some 25 years before the element was found on Earth. During 1937–41, the absorption of starlight at visible wavelengths equaling those observed in the laboratory for CH (4,300 Å or 430.0 nm), CH^+ (4,232 Å or 423.2 nm) and CN (a series of lines) was reported. During the 1960s, the relative intensities of the CN lines led to determination of a background interstellar temperature of 2.7 K (-454.9°F or -270.5°C) in excellent agreement with the 1965 findings by Arno Penzias (1933–) and Robert W. Wilson (1936–), at Bell Laboratories, using a different technique. Penzias and Wilson discovered the background microwave radiation that infuses the universe, a remnant of the big bang of 15 billion years ago. They shared the 1978 Nobel Prize in physics with Pyotr Kapitsa (1894–1984).

Radar technology developed during World War II that led to NMR spectroscopy also produced the radio telescope. In 1951, Edward Purcell, the codiscoverer of nuclear magnetic resonance, and Harold I. Ewen (1922–) pioneered radioastronomy when they detected the microwave emissions from interstellar hydrogen atoms (H) at a frequency of 1,420 MHz (~21 cm wavelength). Unlike UV and visible absorption, which measure electronic transitions comparable to the strengths of chemical bonds (~100 kcal/mol), the energy of 21 cm microwave radiation is only about 0.00014 kcal/mol. An electron has two values for spin (+1/2 and -1/2, represented by ↑ and ↓) and the hydrogen nucleus, a proton, has two values for spin (+1/2 and -1/2, represented by ↑ and ↓). The hydrogen atom (↑↑) state is 0.00014 kcal/mol higher in energy than its (↑↓) state and relaxation to the low-energy state emits 1,420 MHz microwaves. Starting in 1963, radioastronomers discovered hydroxyl (OH) radical, followed by water (H_2O), ammonia (NH_3), formaldehyde (H_2CO), hydrogen cyanide (HCN), and cyanoacetylene (HC_3N). By 1977, 42 interstellar molecules had been reported. Almost 30 years later the number exceeds 130, with cyanopentaacetylene ($HC_{11}N$) the largest molecule. It must be noted that the frequencies of molecules moving at high speeds relative to the observer must be corrected for Doppler shifts (e.g., redshift if moving away).

An interesting problem that perplexed astrophysicists and chemists was the hunt for homodiatomic molecules such as molecular hydrogen (H_2). Hydrogen comprises about 90 percent of the universe, helium roughly the remaining 10 percent with all other elements at levels of 0.01 percent and less. As noted in chapter 3, only vibrations which change dipole moments of molecules are infrared active. For a molecule such as H_2, bond vibration cannot change the dipole moment from zero and the molecule has no IR spectrum. For similar reasons, there is also no microwave spectrum for a homodiatomic molecule. While H_2 does have an electronic absorption spectrum, it is derived from a very-high-energy transition (σ MO → σ* MO) found in the far UV (FUV) region not observable from Earth. The enormous abundance of free hydrogen atoms (their n =3 → n=2 [656.0 nm] emission provides the red glow of galaxies) suggested a similar abundance of hydrogen molecules since collision of two hydrogen atoms should yield H_2. However, a third body is usually required to facilitate collision and to remove excess energy. Direct observation of H_2 in space awaited the launch of an Aerobee-150 rocket equipped with an FUV spectrometer (100-140 nm) in March 1970. Naval Research Laboratory physicist George R. Carruthers (1939–) observed absorption of H_2 bands by a dark space-dust cloud in the path of the star ξ *Persei*, confirmed by the *Copernicus* satellite in 1973. The matter in the space dust furnishes the third body required for reaction, hence the finding of H_2 in such clouds. Carruthers, an African American, invented the FUV camera-spectrograph carried to the Moon on *Apollo 16* in 1972. Hydrogen (H_2) is the most abundant molecule in space. The second most abundant molecule, carbon monoxide (CO), was discovered in 1970 at levels one 10-thousandth those of H_2. William Klemperer (1927–   ) at Harvard has noted that the reaction:

$$CO + 3\ H_2 \rightarrow CH_4 + H_2O$$

is overwhelmingly favored in simple thermodynamics calculations. However, the observations that interstellar concentrations of CH_4 and H_2O are only, respectively, $<10^{-6}$ and $<10^{-4}$ that of CO make it evident that the universe is incredibly far from chemical equilibrium. Of course the extraordinarily low temperature and pressure of the universe indicates that it is far removed from standard temperature and pressure (STP) although this fact changes none of Klemperer's points.

The concentration of atmospheric molecules at sea level on Earth is about 10^{19} per cubic centimeter. In the interstellar gas, concentrations are about 1 molecule per cubic centimeter. Under these ultravacuum conditions there are few collisions to produce H_2 and the rate of its decomposition by high-energy radiation is much greater. Virtually all hydrogen in interstellar gas is atomic hydrogen. In contrast, space dust acts as a catalytic surface for the $2H \rightarrow H_2$ reaction, as noted above, and blocks out some radiation. Dark dust clouds, like the one observed by Carruthers, are incubators and repositories for H_2. The search for interstellar molecular nitrogen (N_2) was far more challenging than that for H_2. The same spectroscopic limitations are present but the element nitrogen is orders of magnitude less abundant than hydrogen. Interstellar N_2 was finally observed with certainty in 2004.

The molecular ion H_3^+ is the most abundant polyatomic ion in the universe. First discovered in the laboratory by J. J. Thomson in 1911, it is usually the most abundant ion in hydrogen plasmas due to the stability of this species having its hydrogen atoms at the corners of an equilateral triangle. In 1973, Klemperer and Eric Herbst, as well as W. G. Watson, predicted the dramatic effects of this ion on interstellar chemistry. The spectral bands suitable for characterizing H_3^+ in space were discovered in the laboratory by Takeshi Oka in 1980, and the ion was finally found in interstellar space by Oka and Thomas R. Geballe in 1996. It is formed when cosmic rays ionize molecular hydrogen to H_2^+ and this collides with another H_2 molecule to form H_3^+ and H. One of the most fascinating findings attributed to H_3^+ is the enrichment of deuterium-containing compounds (e.g., D_2CO, ND_3, CD_3OH) in the cold cores of dark interstellar clouds. It is postulated that in such environs, molecules such as CO that are usually primarily responsible for destruction of H_3^+ are condensed onto particles. The predominant disappearance pathway for

H_3^+ then becomes reactive with HD to produce H_2D^+ and H_2 (note the same reaction of H_3^+ with H_2 regenerates H_3^+). Defying normal intuition, the consequences of this chemistry suggest that the relative abundance of related isotopic species in these environs is $H_3^+ < H_2D^+ < D_2H^+ \ll D_3^+$, totally the reverse of the natural isotopic abundances. These species can react with other molecules to produce the enrichment noted for deuterated species.

Crash-Landing of the Murchison Meteorite: The Miller Experiment Revisited

The half-life ($t_{1/2}$) of carbon 14 is about 5,730 years, useful for objects younger than 50,000 years. Geological timescales are on the order of hundreds of millions to billions of years. Isotopes commonly employed for geologic dating include potassium 40 ($^{40}K \rightarrow {}^{40}Ar$, $t_{1/2}$ = 1.25 billion years), rubidium 87 ($^{87}Rb \rightarrow {}^{87}Sr$, $t_{1/2}$ = 48.8 billion years), uranium 235 ($^{235}U \rightarrow {}^{207}Pb$, $t_{1/2}$ = 0.704 billion years) and uranium 238 ($^{238}U \rightarrow {}^{206}Pb$, $t_{1/2}$ = 4.47 billion years). In minerals (e.g., K-feldspar) where both potassium and rubidium are abundant, the two decays furnish independent confirmations of each other. The age of the Earth is about 4.6 billion years. The first prokaryotic organisms (e.g., bacteria) appeared between 3.6 and 3.7 billion years ago, only 200–300 million years after the Earth's molten crust solidified, a remarkably brief period geologically speaking.

Stanley Miller's 1953 prebiotic chemistry experiment had a great impact upon the scientific community. It provided experimental support for the Oparin-Haldane-Urey theory that Earth's atmosphere was, at one time, reducing and that such conditions could create important biological molecules. The high yield of amino acids suggested to chemists and biologists how readily they formed. A 1961 prebiotic-type experiment by Spanish-born Juan Oró (1923–2004), at the University of Houston, employed an aqueous solution of HCN and ammonia (NH_3) to produce the nucleotide base adenine in quantity along with amino acids. The formula ($C_5H_5N_5$) and structure of adenine are readily viewed as simple combination of five HCN molecules.

In the decades following Miller's experiment, many scientists replicated it, varied reactants, conditions, and energy sources, and have successfully produced amino acids and other important precursors. The energy sources in Miller's experiment (electric arcs and boiling water) were far too high to be realistic for the prebiotic Earth but were employed to make reactions occur in days rather than months or years. Following decades of research, it is now understood that the great volcanic activity of the early planet would produce far more CO_2, CO, and N_2 than NH_3, and CH_4, Miller's precursors. Moreover, with no O_2 and therefore no ozone (O_3) in the atmosphere, intense UV radiation would decompose H_2O to form radicals that destroy NH_3 and convert CH_4 to CO_2 and

H_2. The H_2 would diffuse out of Earth's atmosphere. Even in these less reducing atmospheres (e.g., CO and CO_2 instead of CH_4, N_2 instead of NH_3), Miller-type experiments yield amino acids, nucleic acid bases, and simple sugars. However, such syntheses do not occur in the presence of molecular oxygen (O_2) and the principle holds: prebiotic synthesis requires a reducing atmosphere and is not possible in Earth's current oxidizing atmosphere.

On September 28, 1969, a large meteorite crashed into Murchison, Australia. The Murchison meteorite was one of the relatively rare meteorites classified as carbonaceous chondrites that are fairly rich in organic matter (2–5 percent). The meteorite was collected rapidly and parts sent to various laboratories for sophisticated analyses. The most striking discovery (at the time) was reported in 1970 by Cyril Ponnamperuma (1923–1994) and collaborators at the University of Maryland, College Park. They found a number of protein- and nonprotein amino acids. The question was whether the amino acids were nonterrestrial in their origin. The presence of nonprotein amino acids was consistent with extraterrestrial origin rather than earthly contamination. The Maryland researchers used capillary column GC/MS to determine that amino acids were racemic (50:50 D and L enantiomers) rather than solely L as they are in all proteins. It is worth noting that typical GC columns of the period could not separate amino acid enantiomers. The nonvolatile amino acids were reacted with an optically pure alcohol so that each pair of enantiomers was converted to a pair of amino acid ester *diastereomers* separable on the capillary column. These findings, with appropriate controls, supported an extraterrestrial origin for the amino acids and suggested that these (and potentially other) critical biological building blocks might be made in interstellar space. Analyses of the Murchison meteorite have continued as methods have become more discriminating and sensitive. By 2000 over 70 different amino acids, a wealth of other molecules, and some totally unanticipated, highly challenging findings were reported (see chapter 10).

The next question was how small building-block molecules polymerize to form proteins, nucleic acids, and polysaccharides. Such polymerizations require condensation reactions that release water molecules. This is illustrated by the reaction:

$$\text{n Amino Acids (AA)} \overset{\longleftarrow}{\longrightarrow} (\text{AA})_n \text{ (a peptide)} + (\text{n} - 1) \, H_2O$$

The reaction is reversible and in a dilute "prebiotic broth," the reaction vastly favors free amino acids due to the overwhelming concentration of water molecules. The need to eliminate water suggested conditions in volcanoes, hot sand remaining after evaporation of prebiotic broth, concentration in cold conditions that freeze out pure ice from aqueous solutions, and condensations on clays and other minerals. Another possibility is self-organization of structures in aqueous environments that exclude water. Micelles (see chapter 2) have hydrophobic interiors that could be sites for reactions that eliminate water. In 1975, André Brack (1938–) and Leslie Orgel, at the University of California, San Diego, polymerized a dipeptide (made from a hydrophilic plus a hydrophobic amino acid) into polypeptides under reasonable prebiotic conditions. In the presence of salt, the polypeptides formed an ordered β-sheet with hydrophilic amino acid residues on the exterior and hydrophobic residues on the interior. During the 1960s, Sidney W. Fox (1912–98), at the University of Miami, caused a stir by heating amino acids together, quenching the melt in water and observing "proto-cells" (some seen to be "dividing"). Although this observation was quickly understood to have little, if any, relevance to living cells, it did provide a demonstration of the ease in forming structures that could sequester organic molecules in an aqueous medium.

The discovery of exciting prebiotic molecules in space (HCN, readily converted to adenine; cyanoacetylene, producing cytosine under "Miller-like" conditions) and extraterrestrial amino acids on meteorites gave impetus to the search for extraterrestrial life (see the next section). However, scientists would soon discover new "rather unearthly" environments on Earth. In 1977 the first deep-sea hot spring (geothermal vent) was discovered at a depth of 1.6 miles (2.5 kilometers) off the coast of Ecuador. In 1979 the submersible "Alvin" explored a high-temperature, geothermal vent in the East Pacific Ocean. The temperature at the opening was about 716°F (380°C). Black emissions poured from this "black smoker." The pressure at this depth is about 250 bars (250 × atmospheric pressure). While the boiling point of water at 1 atmosphere is 212°F (100°C), the enormous pressures at the depth of these vents maintain water in a superheated state. (The critical temperature T_c of water is 705°F [374°C], i.e., above this temperature no pressure can force it to be liquid; however, as the steam emerges from a ca. 750°F vent, it immediately cools below its T_c and liquefies). What are the physical properties of superheated (subcritical) water? One of the most interesting is the dielectric constant (ε). The extremely high value for water (ε = 78.4 at 77°F or 25°C) allows it to be a great solvent for ionic salts such as NaCl and a poor solvent for nonpolar substances like benzene. At 410°F (210°C), the dielectric constant of water (ε = 33) is similar to that of methyl alcohol. At 572°F (300°C), the solubility of benzene in water is an amazing 23 percent by weight.

The gases emerging from the geothermal vents are of volcanic origin and are rich in hydrogen sulfide (H_2S). There is a rich ecology based on "lawns" of sulfur-metabolizing "bacteria," giant (6-foot or 2-m) tube worms (see the photograph) whose metabolism is based on sulfur as well as giant clams and mussels. The tube worms have no mouth, gut, or anus, no digestive system of their own, and live in a tight symbiotic relationship with sulfur-metabolizing bacteria. In 1977, Carl R. Woese (1928–), University of Illinois, discovered that very simple organisms resembling bacteria and living in extreme environments have ribosomal

RNA very different from the bacteria. He proposed a new domain called the Archaea for these living creatures distinct from the "true bacteria," termed eubacteria, and the eukaryotes (animals, plants, fungi, and protozoans, such as the paramecium). Current theory has them evolving from

Tube worms feeding at a hydrothermal vent (NOAA/ Department of Commerce, National Undersea Research Program Collection)

eukaryotes after the evolutionary split from prokaryotes. Archaea include *Euryarcheota* (methanogens, halophiles, and thermoacidophiles) and *Crenarchaeota*. Methanogens live in the bottoms of swamps, rumens of cows, and guts of termites, and convert H_2 and CO_2 into methane (CH_4). Thermoacidophiles are the found near deep sea vents and the thermal springs in Yellowstone Park. Halophiles live in the Great Salt Lake and in the Dead Sea. Members of the *Crenarchaeota* include organisms that survive at 250°F (121°C), typical autoclave temperature. It appears that one does not have to leave the Earth to find alienlike creatures with exotic biochemistries.

NASA's Viking Mission: Two Laboratories on the Surface of Mars

Mars, Earth's nearest planetary neighbor, has fascinated since ancient times. The Italian astronomer Giovanni V. Schiaparelli (1835–1910) observed Mars from Milan and drew pictures of *"canali"* ("canals") in 1877. Harvard-educated astronomer Percival Lowell (1855–1916) moved to Flagstaff, Arizona and, in 1894, began many years of Mars observations.

Earth follows a nearly circular path around the sun completing a cycle in one year. The 23.5° tilt of Earth's axis is responsible for the four seasons. Mars has an axis tilted to a very similar degree to that of Earth. The seasonal contrasts on Mars are enhanced because its orbit departs from circular and it is closer to the Sun during part of the Martian year. Lowell observed significant seasonal color changes on Mars and shrinking and expansion of its polar "ice caps." He imagined construction of the above-mentioned *"canali"* by an advanced civilization. H. G. Wells published his novel *The War of the Worlds* in 1898 and Lowell published a book titled *Mars as the Abode of Life* in 1908.

Better observations from Earth and from the *Mariner 4, 6,* and *7* space probes in the late 1960s found no canals and demonstrated that the "ice caps" were made of frozen CO_2, not water. On August 20, 1975, and September 9, 1975, *Viking 1* and *Viking 2* were launched toward Mars, achieving orbit on June 19, 1976, and August 8, 1976, respectively. Each mission carried two laboratories, an orbiter and a lander (see the photograph). The landers, fully sterilized on Earth, floated to the Martian surface about one month after reaching orbit. The first landed at a site in the northern hemisphere, measuring temperatures near 7°F (- 14°C) at midday to -107°F (-77°C) at predawn. *Viking 2* landed 930 miles to the north, on the opposite side of the planet. It measured fairly constant temperatures around -184°F (-120°C; lower than the solidification temperature of CO_2.) Each lander carried a TV camera, a pyrolysis-gas chromatograph/mass spectrometer (GC/MS) and apparatus for three simple chemical-biochemical experiments. The TVs sent images to

Earth showing the reddish surface and pink-hued atmosphere. Nothing visible crawled or walked past the cameras. The GC/MS detected no organic matter in the Martian soil at part-per-billion (ppb) levels. The surface of Mars has nearly 20 percent oxides of iron.

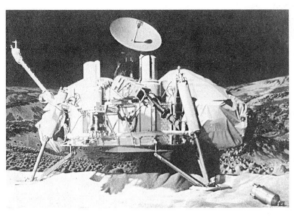

Viking lander for Mars mission launched in summer 1975 for the purpose of conducting biological and chemical analyses and tests on Martian soil

The experiments designed to detect microorganisms in the Martian soil were: 1) Labeled-Release (LR) experiment to detect catabolism (breakdown of nutrients), 2) Pyrolytic-Release (PR) experiment to detect anabolism (synthesis of complex organic molecules from CO_2 and CO, both found in the thin Martian atmosphere), and 3) Gas-Exchange (GEX) experiment in which a known mixture of gases is placed into the experimental chamber containing soil samples and nutrients to see if gases disappear or are added to the mixture. Experiments 1 and 3 used aqueous solutions and assumed water is necessary for life. The PR experiment involved no water. The LR experiment used a broth of ^{14}C-labelled nutrients, including the amino acid glycine, to test if $^{14}CO_2$ is released. Martian soil produced an initial burst of radioactive gas upon addition of nutrient solution. Soil samples preheated to kill microorganisms did not show this effect. But evolution of gas did not increase during the 10-day experiment as expected for biological growth. The PR experiment was illuminated with a bright arc lamp since anabolism requires energy. Soil samples were incubated with $^{14}CO_2$ and ^{14}CO for 5 days. These radioactive gases were then flushed out and the soil heated to vaporize any new newly synthesized radioactive organic substances. Minute quantities of organic matter were detected in 7 of 9 trials. However, some of these positive trials were from soil samples preheated to kill all microorganisms. In the GEX experiment, a nutrient solution was added to the reaction chamber but not to soil in the chamber. A burst of O_2 appeared and then subsided; small amounts of CO_2 were formed. One week later, nutrient was added to the soil in the chamber; some CO_2 (but no O_2) appeared, then subsided.

Each of the experiments posed ambiguities in their results. However, the general consensus of the scientific community is that the surface of Mars contains very strong chemical oxidants, such as peroxides and species that generate hydroxyl radicals (OH), or perhaps iron in a highly reactive oxidation state (e.g., Fe(VI) as in K_2FeO_4, which is stable under very dry conditions). The surface of Mars is said to be "self-sterilizing" due to its extreme dryness, exposure to high-intensity UV radiation and the presence of powerful oxidants. In 2003, studies of soils in Chile's Atacoma Desert, 50 times more arid than Death Valley, found them to be virtually devoid of any life, incapable of sustaining bacterial growth and yet capable of reproducing some of Viking's results. Still, the ambiguities in Viking's results led a few respected scientists to argue in favor of positive indications of life. Very recent results appear to establish that Mars did have significant quantities of running water at earlier stages in its history. Thus, current and future studies may concentrate on evidence for life having existed during the earlier history of Mars as well as on searches for life below the hostile Martian surface.

An interesting question that future explorations to Mars and other extraterrestrial bodies may have to answer is: What is meant by the term "living" as opposed to "nonliving?" In discussing the "Molecular Logic of Living Organisms," Albert L. Lehninger defines the identifying characteristics as follows:

1. A living organism is highly complex and organized.
2. Each component of a living organism has a specific function; individual molecules (lipids, proteins, nucleic acids, saccharides) have specific functions.
3. Living organisms extract energy from the environment, use it for locomotion and other mechanical functions and transform it to maintain their own complexity.
4. Living organisms self-replicate.

An interesting question is, How many of these criteria are satisfied by viruses? The virus particle, which may be crystallized like any salt to provide an X-ray diffraction pattern, might well satisfy at least three of these criteria. However, it is totally dependent upon a living cell for self-replication.

The Molecular Machine That Stores Energy as ATP

David Keilin discovered the structures of cytochromes a, b, and c in 1925 (see chapter 3). By 1939, Vladimir Belitzer, Herman Kalckar, and Severa Ochoa had demonstrated that electron transfer from the Krebs cycle through the cytochromes to oxygen is coupled with ATP formation. In 1941, Fritz Lipmann postulated that the conversion of ADP to ATP is the actual energy-storage pathway inside prokaryotic and eukaryotic organisms. Living organisms do not use heat transfer (from "combustion") as a source of energy because their temperatures are essentially uniform throughout. In eukaryotic cells most of the stored energy derives from electron transfer in the mitochondria during respiration. Similar processes occur in the chloroplasts of green plant cells during photosynthesis.

As a graduate student in Cambridge during the 1940s, Peter Mitchell (1920–92) met Keilin and was much influenced by him. He accepted a faculty position at Edinburgh University in 1955 and stayed until illness forced him to resign in 1963. During two years of recuperation, he obtained financing and supervised the transformation of the Glynn Mansion in Cornwall to the Glynn Research Laboratory where he continued his earlier studies on electron transport and bioenergetics. In the early 1960s, Mitchell advanced his chemiosmotic theory of energy coupling. Mitchell demonstrated that, coupled to electron transfer, there is active proton transport from the inside to the outside of the *mitochondrion's* inner membrane. The H^+ concentration on the outside is much higher than in the inner matrix; this proton gradient incurs a potential difference like that between electrodes. If mitochondria are incubated in phosphate buffer without added ADP, their uptake (reduction) of O_2 is very slow. Upon addition of ADP, there is rapid uptake and coupled formation of ATP. Addition of various organic acids, such as 2,4-dinitrophenol (DNP), decouples O_2 reduction from ATP formation. Inside the matrix, DNP is found in its deprotonated form (call it "A^-"), which can cross the inner mitochondrial membrane. On the outer side of the membrane, the concentration of protons is higher as noted, "HA" is formed and migrates through the membrane back to the matrix. Continued addition of O_2 pumps H^+ through the inner membrane even as DNP carries it back. The H^+ gradient disappears with no new storage of energy in ATP. Peter Mitchell received the 1978 Nobel Prize in chemistry.

Electron micrographs, obtained by Efraim Racker (1913–91) in 1960 at the Public Health Research Institute in New York City, showed mushroomlike structures having their "caps" protruding from the inner membranes of mitochondria. These are the ATP synthase complexes. In 1961 Racker isolated the F_1 particles from these structures and demonstrated their activity as an ATPase (i.e., catalyzing ATP → ADP + P_i). Although Racker moved on to Cornell in 1966, his colleagues at the Institute continued studies of bioenergetics and, in 1972, Aileen F. Knowles (1942–) and Harvey S. Penefsky separated five different peptide chains from F_1: α, β, γ, δ, and ε. They are found in the ratio 3:3:1:1:1 corresponding to a formula $\alpha_3\beta_3\gamma\delta\varepsilon$. In 1973, Paul D. Boyer came to a very surprising conclusion about energy storage in ATP. The key step was not, as expected, the formation of the high-energy pyrophosphate bond. Thermodynamically, this reaction between ADP and inorganic phosphate (P_i) is very endergonic (positive free energy) and unfavorable:

$$ADP + P_i \leftarrow ATP + H_2O$$

Boyer concluded that binding of ATP to ATP synthase is considerably tighter than the binding of ADP and this extra stabilization effectively lowers the energy of bound ATP relative to bound ADP allowing its formation in equilibrium with ADP:

$$ADP/Enzyme + P_i \rightleftharpoons ATP/Enzyme + H_2O$$

(weak binding)   (strong binding)

In 1978, John E. Walker (1941–) at Cambridge commenced his structural studies of ATP synthase combining determination of the amino acid sequences in the subunits with detailed X-ray crystallographic structures. The F_1 "mushroom cap," in the mitochondrial matrix, is the location of the sites that catalyze ADP to ATP conversion. The γ peptide chain connects F_1 to the F_o "mushroom stalk," embedded in the mitochondrial inner membrane, that also includes the δ and ε chains. The stalk is the site of proton pumping coupled with electron-transfer that provides the energy for ATP formation. When Racker originally separated F_1 from F_o, lacking the proton energy pump F_1 simply catalyzed the reverse reaction (ATP $\rightarrow$ ADP + P_i). The three β units, which alternate with the three α units on F_1, each function as ADP/ATP binding sites with the following sequence at each site: a) bind ADP + P_i; b) tighten binding, then conversion to ATP; c) loosen binding of ATP, then release it. The three β units change cooperatively so that each is sequentially in a, b, then c with about 50–100 complete cycles per second. The thermodynamics of the ATP synthase "machine" remains today a subject of active debate.

In 1997, Paul D. Boyer, John E. Walker, and Jens C. Skou (1918–) shared the Nobel Prize in chemistry. Skou, at Aarhus University in Denmark, discovered during the 1950s and '60s the mechanism whereby energy derived from ATP is used to pump Na^+ and K^+ ions across cell membranes. Inside cells there is high K^+ concentration and low Na^+ concentration while the reverse is true in extracellular fluids. Energy is required to keep each of these intra- and extracellular gradients from disappearing. The key enzyme involved in this process, Na^+/K^+-ATPase was finally isolated in chemically stable form from cell membranes in 1980.

The Beginnings of Genetic Engineering

Phages are viruses that infect bacteria. Bacteria defend themselves by restricting the growth of phages using restriction enzymes. In 1970, Hamilton O. Smith (1931–) and Daniel Nathan (1928–99) at Johns Hopkins University successfully isolated the first cleavage-site-specific restriction endonuclease. These enzymes cleave duplex (but not single-stranded) DNA within the chain (see figure on page 300) at specific sites and there are now more than 200 known restriction enzymes each with unique specificities. The example shown is *Eco*R1, isolated from *E. coli* and specific for the sequence GAATTC. Smith, Daniel, and Werner Abner (1929–), who studied DNA exchange at the University of Basel, shared the 1978 Nobel Prize in physiology or medicine for their studies of site-specific restriction endonucleases. DNA ligases were known since 1967 and employed by H. Gobind Khorana in his chemical syntheses of genes (see chapter 7). Two different DNA duplexes, one "original" and one "foreign," with "sticky ends" formed by a restriction enzyme such as *Eco*R1, can be "glued together" using a DNA ligase to form recombinant DNA. In 1972, Paul Berg (1926–), at Stanford University, employed *Eco*R1 to make a scission in the circular Simian ("monkey") Virus (SV40)

DNA. He used the same restriction enzyme to cut a circular plasmid (λdv gal) that included three *E. coli* genes for metabolizing the sugar galactose. Further customizing the ends of the two (now-linear) DNA duplexes to make them sticky and mutually compatible, Berg and his collaborators used a DNA ligase to unite these two different duplexes into a single cyclic SV40-λdv gal molecule: the first artificial recombinant DNA. In 1973, Herbert W. Boyer (1936–), at the University of California at San Francisco, and Stanley N. Cohen (1935–), at Stanford, conducted the first experiment in which DNA from one organism was added into the DNA in another organism and replicated through subsequent generations. This was the birth of genetic engineering. In 1976, Herbert Boyer would cofound Genentech, Inc., one of the first biotechnology companies.

Growing concern over potential dangers of genetic engineering led scientists to call a special and unprecedented conference in February 1975 at the Asilomar Conference Center in Pacific Grove, Calif. The

The formation of recombinant DNA requires specific scission of a sequence of double-stranded DNA with formation of complementary "sticky ends" that may then be chemically combined.

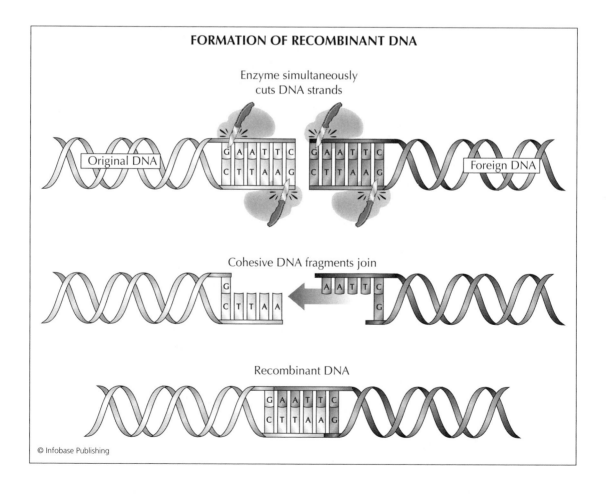

FORMATION OF RECOMBINANT DNA

Enzyme simultaneously cuts DNA strands

Original DNA

Foreign DNA

Cohesive DNA fragments join

Recombinant DNA

© Infobase Publishing

Paul Berg, Walter Gilbert, and Frederick Sanger, who shared the 1980 Nobel Prize in chemistry for studies of recombinant DNA (Berg) as well as sequencing DNA (Gilbert and Sanger). Sanger is the only person to have been awarded two Nobel Prizes in chemistry. (Paul Berg and Stanford University, Walter Gilbert, and Frederick Sanger)

Asilomar Conference developed voluntary restrictions on certain types of research, for example the insertion of cancer genes into the DNA of *E. coli*, the ubiquitous bacteria in the human digestive tract. In 1976, the NIH enacted formal rules and guidelines.

More control over the nature of recombinant DNA was achieved through rapid new techniques in DNA sequencing developed by Frederick Sanger in Cambridge and Walter Gilbert (1932–) at Harvard. They both rely upon initial cleavage of DNA into smaller, overlapping fragments by restriction endonucleases. These fragments are then further sequenced. The Gilbert technique is more chemical in nature and used for specialized cases, while the Sanger technique is totally enzymatic and more general. In 1977, Sanger's group published the complete base sequence for $\phi\chi174$ bacteriophage (5,375 nucleotides). The first long DNA sequence determined using Gilbert's method was that of the *lac* repressor gene (1,080 base pairs) in 1978. Ironically, the choice of this gene was dictated by the fact that the sequence of the corresponding protein (360 amino acid residues) was published so that, using the genetic code, there would be an independent check on the sequence. As events transpired, Gilbert's DNA sequence for the *lac* repressor gene demonstrated that there were a couple of small errors in the corresponding protein sequence. It started to become clear that it is easier to sequence long linear DNA than the coded proteins because the chemistries of the peptide fragments are so diverse. The Sanger DNA sequencing method would eventually be used to completely sequence the human genome (3 billion base pairs) in 2001. Paul Berg, Frederick Sanger, and Walter Gilbert shared the 1980 Nobel Prize in chemistry (the second such award for Sanger).

Cleaning Up Automobile Emissions

By the 1960s, automobiles were huge contributors of lead, carbon monoxide, unburned hydrocarbons, and oxides of nitrogen (NO_x) to the troposphere. The 1970 Clean Air Act set new standards for automobile emissions that led to the widespread introduction of catalytic converters in new cars. In 1973 the U.S. EPA enacted regulations that would start to phase out leaded gasoline. Since catalytic converters are poisoned by lead, the EPA required that at least one grade of unleaded gasoline be available at all stations.

The first generation of catalytic converters oxidized deadly carbon monoxide (CO) and unburned hydrocarbons such as octanes (C_8H_{18}) to carbon dioxide (and water). Oxides of nitrogen (NO_x) contribute to the acid rain problem and also are very major contributors to smog. All high-temperature combustion reactions produce NO_x. In 1980, the first three-way catalytic converters were introduced in California. They include a catalyst for oxidation of CO and hydrocarbons to CO_2, a catalyst for reduction of NO_x to N_2, and an oxygen sensor to vary the fuel-to-air mixing ratio for maximum efficiency. The catalysts are coated on a beehive of ceramic (clay) material resistant to hot exhaust gases. A

Schematic diagram of a catalytic converter in an automobile that reduces oxides of nitrogen (NO_x) to nitrogen (N_2) and oxidizes unburned hydrocarbons and carbon monoxide (CO) to carbon dioxide (CO_2)

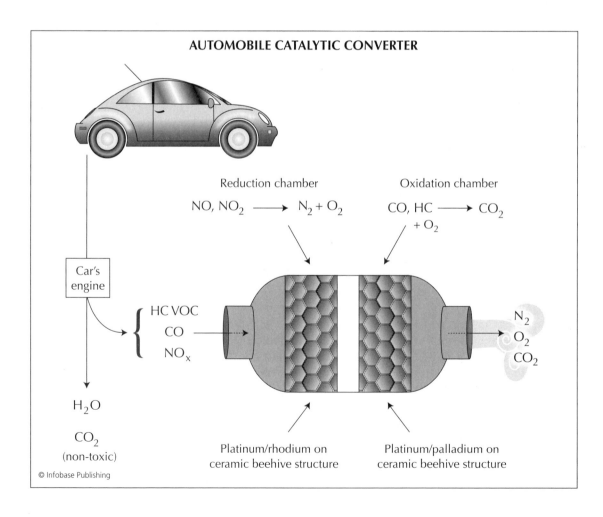

AUTOMOBILE CATALYTIC CONVERTER

Reduction chamber

$NO, NO_2 \longrightarrow N_2 + O_2$

Oxidation chamber

$CO, HC \longrightarrow CO_2$
$+ O_2$

Car's engine

HC VOC
CO
NO_x

N_2
O_2
CO_2

H_2O

CO_2
(non-toxic)

Platinum/rhodium on ceramic beehive structure

Platinum/palladium on ceramic beehive structure

schematic diagram of a three-way catalytic converter is depicted in the figure on page 302.

While catalytic converters and conversion to unleaded gasoline have had dramatic effects in reducing airborne lead, particulates, and smog, they do not reduce emission of CO_2. Carbon dioxide is a final product from combustion of all carbon-containing compounds. It has been known for decades that CO_2 is a "greenhouse gas." That is to say, it is transparent to the longer UV and visible wavelengths that reach the Earth's surface. Most of this light is absorbed at the surface and reflected back into the atmosphere as infrared radiation (sensed as heat). Carbon dioxide is an effective absorber of infrared (IR) radiation, trapping it and warming the biosphere. The effect is much the same as a greenhouse (or the interior of a car), where glass admits visible and longer wavelength UV light but absorbs reflected IR light creating an indoor temperature appreciably higher than outdoors. Until the industrial revolution, anthropogenic emissions of CO_2 were almost negligible. They started to increase drastically and increased more than tenfold during the 20th century. Water vapor is also a major greenhouse gas as are methane, nitrous oxide, ozone, SF_6, chlorofluorocarbons (CFCs), and hydrofluorocarbons (HFCs). The threat from global warming (global climate change) was certainly a concern during the 1970s but by the end of the 20th century it became the primary environmental problem as evidence mounted that the biosphere is warming, with enormous potential consequences.

An Unimagined but Very Real Threat to the Earth's Stratospheric Ozone

James E. Lovelock is a talented and restless person. With a Ph.D. in medicine (1948) and a D.Sci. in biophysics (1959) he has moved in and out of instrumentation design, analytical chemistry, and environmental science at a variety of institutions since the 1950s. He is the inventor of the electron capture detector (ECD) for gas chromatography, sensitive and selective for molecules carrying electronegative groups such as Cl and F, and he contributed to the technology of the miniature GC/MS on the Mars Viking landers. The ECD enabled trace analysis of environmental PCBs that helped stimulate Rachel Carson's 1962 book *Silent Spring* (see chapter 7). The U.S. EPA banned PCB manufacture in 1979. Lovelock is also the father of Gaia theory, which he formulated around 1965. A simple statement of Gaia theory is: "Earth is a self-regulating system able to keep its climate and chemical composition comfortable for the organisms that inhabit it." In Greek mythology, Gaea (or Gaia) is the goddess of the planet Earth. In 1971, Lovelock took a scientific cruise from England to Antarctica on the RV *Shackleton* and conducted chemical analyses to test his Gaia theory. On this cruise, his sensitive GC/ECD detected the chlorofluorocarbon (CFC) CCl_3F in every air sample collected. This was a cause for concern because CCl_3F was a manmade chemical of only recent vintage and already ubiquitous in Earth's atmosphere. More worrisome was Lovelock's approximate calculation suggesting that virtually all of the CCl_3F ever made remained in the geosphere. It appeared to have no major chemical or physical "sink."

The CFCs CF_4 and CCl_2F_2 were invented by Thomas C. Midgley, Jr. (1889–1944), an engineer/chemist at General Motors, during the years 1928–30. Refrigerators had been introduced toward the end of the 19th century, adding convenience and reducing the risk of bacterial contamination of food. In order to be a useful refrigerant a gas should have a boiling point (bp) not too much lower than ambient temperature (~77°F or 25°C), so that it may be compressed to a liquid under mild pressure. Following the compression stage, expansion and evaporation produce cooling. The coolants in early refrigerators, ammonia (NH_3, bp -29°F or -34°C), sulfur dioxide (bp 14°F or -10°C), and methyl chloride (CH_3Cl, bp -11°F or -24°C) are all very toxic as well as corrosive or flammable. Countless injuries and even deaths in the home and workplace resulted from malfunctions or accidents involving these gases. At a public demonstration, Midgley famously inhaled a lungful of CCl_2F_2 (bp -22°F or -30°C) and exhaled it over a burning candle, promptly extinguishing the flame. In the following decades a family of nontoxic, nonflammable CFCs, including CCl_2F_2 (CFC-12), CCl_3F (CFC-11), and $CCl_2F-CClF_2$ (CFC-113), were manufactured on a massive scale for refrigerators, freezers, and air conditioners and as propellants for aerosol cans containing deodorants, hair sprays, shaving creams, household cleaners, whipped cream, and numerous other products. Much like the fire-protective asbestos, CFCs seemed to have no downside.

F. Sherwood Rowland (1927–) was a varsity basketball player at Ohio Wesleyan College. Shortly after he arrived at the University of Chicago in 1948 he met his future Ph.D. adviser, Willard F. Libby, who had recently discovered carbon 14 dating and would win the 1960 Nobel Prize in chemistry. Professor Libby exclaimed to the young Rowland: "I see you made all A's in undergraduate school. We're here to find out if you are any damn good!" In spite of (or because of) playing for the Chicago varsity basketball *and* baseball teams, Rowland wrote an excellent thesis in nuclear chemistry and started a successful career. In 1964, he joined the chemistry department at the University of California at Irvine and in 1972 attended a lecture in which James Lovelock disclosed his findings on the ubiquitous atmospheric contaminant CCl_3F. Rowland's background in kinetics and atmospheric transport interested him in the question of the atmospheric fate of CCl_3F and other CFCs. In 1973, Rowland was joined on the CFC project by graduate student Mario J. Molina (1943–), born in Mexico City and educated at the National Autonomous University.

CCl_3F and other CFCs are nonpolar compounds and, unlike HCl, are not washed from the atmosphere by rain. Unlike compounds such as methane and benzene that have C-H bonds, CFCs are inert to the extremely reactive hydroxyl (OH) radical. It is this very inertness that makes CFCs nontoxic. The colorless CFCs do not absorb visible light nor do they absorb the UV light that freely passes through stratospheric ozone (400 nm to 320 nm wavelength, termed UVA) or the tiny fraction of damaging UVB (320 nm to 290 nm) radiation that makes it to the Earth's surface. Thus, from the planet's surface up through most of the stratosphere, there is no significant chemical or photochemical decomposition pathway for the CFCs. As the stratosphere thins and ozone levels drop, higher-energy UV light becomes accessible and CCl_3F, which absorbs UV light of wavelengths <220 nm, can decompose to form Cl and CCl_2F radicals. Rowland and Molina performed laboratory experiments and kinetic modeling studies that predicted that the atmospheric lifetime of CCl_3F is 40–55 years and that of CCl_2F_2 75–100 years. They predicted that the most likely target of the Cl radical is stratospheric ozone. They were also aware of the dangers posed to stratospheric ozone by nitrogen oxides (NO_x), published by Paul Crutzen in 1970 (see chapter 7). Rowland and Molina discovered a mechanism in which Cl radical plays the same catalytic role as NO plays in destroying atmospheric ozone:

$$Cl + O_3 \rightarrow ClO + O_2$$

$$ClO + O \rightarrow Cl + O_2$$

Net: $O_3 + O \rightarrow 2\ O_2$

Molina would accept a faculty position at Irvine, move to the Jet Propulsion Laboratory in Pasadena, and then resume his academic career at MIT where he now resides.

The 1974 paper Rowland and Molina published in *Nature*, titled "Stratospheric sink for chlorofluoromethanes: chlorine atom-catalyzed destruction of ozone," was truly frightening. Stratospheric ozone protects against most of the DNA-damaging high-energy UV light. It was also not clear what effect enhanced high-energy UV radiation would have on the sea plankton near the base of the ocean food chain. All of the models predicted that an immediate (and impossible) halt to all CFC emissions would not stop a continuing increase in their stratospheric concentrations (and a decrease in stratospheric ozone) for some decades into the future. The response to this environmental emergency was swift if cautious. In the late 1970s, the United States, Canada, Sweden, and Norway placed controls on CFC-11 and CFC-12 in aerosol sprays. The EPA banned the manufacture of CFC-based aerosols in 1978. The average levels of CCl_3F in the Northern Hemisphere continued to increase: from 70 ppt_v (parts-per-trillion in volume) in 1971 to 170 ppt_v in 1979 to 250 ppt_v in 1987.

For more than 80 years atmospheric ozone has been measured from the ground using a Dobson UV spectrometer, invented by Gordon M. B. Dobson (1889–1976), that measures UV absorbance through a vertical ozone column simultaneously at two wavelengths (>90 percent of atmospheric ozone is in the stratosphere). One of these is in the UVA region (e.g., 332.4 nm) where ozone does not absorb and the other in the UVB region (e.g., 311.4 nm) where ozone has some absorption. Total ozone measurements are given in Dobson Units (DU). One (1) DU unit is equivalent to compressing all the O_3 in an atmospheric column into a layer of pure gas 0.01 mm thick at standard temperature and pressure. Normal atmospheric ozone levels (300–500 DU) would correspond to pure ozone equivalent to the thickness of two pennies. During the 1960s, typical ozone data at Holly Bay in Antarctica were around 300–320 DU. By 1984, the comparable data were below 200 DU. By the 1980s, the *Nimbus-7* satellite had obtained about 100,000 daily ozone measurements and confirmed ground observations. On October 12, 1993 (springtime at the South Pole), a value of 91 DU was recorded. The accompanying figure compares atmospheric ozone levels in Dobson units in March 1979 and March 1994 (darker areas represent *lower* O_3 levels). March is a maximum period for ozone levels in the Northern Hemisphere. The reduction in ozone levels during this 15-year period is remarkable. In March 1979, most of Greenland had ozone levels corresponding to >450 DU. By March 1994, these had decreased to 300– 400 DU. In 1987, the Montreal Protocols planned

During the 15-year period from 1979 through 1994, the stratospheric levels of ozone declined. Darker regions in these two plots represent lower levels of stratospheric ozone. The decline of stratospheric ozone, due to chlorofluorocarbons (CFCs) in large part, is readily seen in the northward movement of ozone-poor regions in the stratosphere.

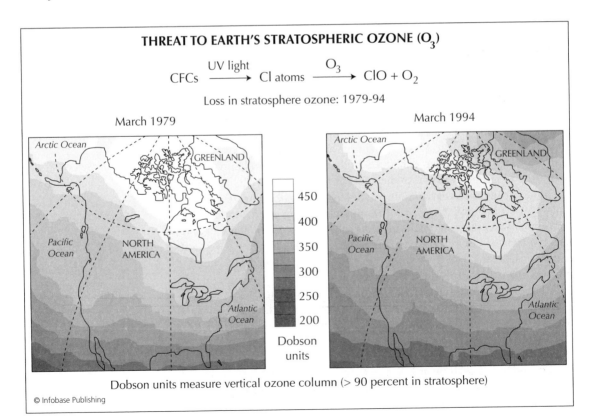

THREAT TO EARTH'S STRATOSPHERIC OZONE (O_3)

$$CFCs \xrightarrow{\text{UV light}} Cl \text{ atoms} \xrightarrow{O_3} ClO + O_2$$

Loss in stratosphere ozone: 1979-94

Dobson units measure vertical ozone column (> 90 percent in stratosphere)

a 50 percent cutback among industrial nations in CFC production and use, with total elimination by 2001. Not long afterward, total elimination was scheduled for 1996 including related chemicals as well as "halons" (e.g., $CBrF_3$) in fire extinguishers. The replacement propellants have included hydrofluorocarbons (HFCs), which contain C-H bonds susceptible to attack by OH and lack the C-Cl and C-Br bonds so susceptible to UV photochemistry. There are reasons for some optimism. By 1995, measurements indicated that atmospheric concentrations of CFC-11 had leveled off while those of CFC-12 were increasing at only half the rate of a few years earlier. Nonetheless, the concern and warnings about sun exposure, so different from the first half of the 20th century, are reminders of the depletion of the ozone layer by CFCs. F. Sherwood Rowland, Mario J. Molina, and Paul Crutzen would share the 1995 Nobel Prize in chemistry for their studies of atmospheric ozone, discoveries having an immense impact on human health and the future environment of this planet.

Thomas W. Midgley, Jr., not only invented the CFCs but also tetraethyl lead, a substance that improves the performance of gasoline. History has not treated him kindly. One popular author, writing about the "regrettable Ohio inventor," opined that "Midgley was an engineer by training, and the world would no doubt have been a safer place if he had stayed so" and not developed an interest in chemistry. As is often the case, hindsight is 20/20. While Mr. Midgley solved a serious gasoline problem with tetraethyl lead, and energetically promoted the use of this known toxic substance, he certainly did not make the business decisions to mass produce it or, for that matter, to package food in lead-lined cans, to market leaded paints, or plumb drinking water through lead pipes. His invention of CFCs for refrigeration appeared to offer unmitigated benefits just as asbestos and DDT did in their early decades of use.

Conclusion

The 1970s witnessed the widespread impact of chemistry on diverse fields of science and technology. During the 1980s, perhaps the key words are "smaller" and "faster." The discovery of a third allotrope of carbon (fullerenes or buckyballs) and the related bucky tubes may perhaps be considered to be the beginning of nanotechnology, the design of molecular-scale machines. The new timescales of the 1980s will be in the femtosecond (10^{15} s) range, on the same order as the lifetimes of transition states. And speaking of small, the tiny nitric oxide (NO) molecule, heretofore regarded only as an air pollutant (an important one) will have its dramatic biological roles revealed. While DNA had occupied center stage since 1944, RNAs may actually be the more interesting molecules. Studies of DNA, RNA, and other huge biological molecules will be enabled by mass spectrometry, an application that would have provoked laughter or scorn in earlier decades.

Scientist of the Decade: Roald Hoffmann (1937–)

Roald Hoffmann was born in Zloczow, Poland. On September 1, 1939, Germany invaded Poland signaling the start of World War II. The course of his next decade is best articulated by Professor Hoffmann (excerpted from the biography he provided to the Nobel Prize committee):

> In 1939 the war began. Our part of Poland was under Russian occupation from 1939–1941. Then in 1941 darkness descended, and the annihilation of Polish Jewry began. We went to a ghetto, then a labor camp. My father smuggled my mother and me out of the camp in early 1943, and for the remainder of the war we were hidden by a good Ukrainian in the attic of a school house in a nearby village. My father remained behind in the camp. He organized a breakout attempt which was discovered. Hillel Safran was killed by the Nazis and their helpers in June 1943. Most of the rest of my family suffered a similar fate. My mother and I, and a handful of relatives, survived. We were freed by the Red Army in June 1944. At the end of 1944 we moved to Przemysi and then to Krakow, where I finally went to school. My mother remarried, and Paul Hoffmann was a kind and gentle father to me until his death, two months prior to the Nobel Prize announcement.
>
> In 1946 we left Poland for Czechoslovakia. From there we moved to a displaced persons' camp, Bindermichl, near Linz, in Austria. In 1947 we went to another camp in Wasseralfingen bei Aalen in Germany, then to München. On Washington's Birthday 1949 we came to the United States.

After attending Stuyvesant High School in New York City, then Columbia University, Hoffmann moved to Harvard where he earned his Ph.D. in theoretical chemistry. Hoffmann was then elected a Junior Fellow at Harvard and, as related in the discussion of R. B. Woodward (see chapter 7), began the collaboration that would lead to publication, in 1965, of the Woodward-Hoffmann Rules. He would share the 1981 Nobel Prize in chemistry with Kenichi Fukui (R. B. Woodward died in 1979).

Hoffmann's integration of molecular orbital theory and symmetry have influenced the way chemists think of molecules, their spectroscopic properties and reactions and the properties of solid-state structures since the mid-1960s. But he has also been an example and a role model for young scientists. While distinguished university

Further Reading

Ball, Phillip. *Elegant Solutions: Ten Beautiful Experiments in Chemistry*, 160–74. Cambridge: The Royal Society of Chemistry, 2005. This is an excellent discussion of the synthesis of vitamin B_{12}.

Bornstein, Max P., Scott A., and Louis I. Allamandola. "Molecules from Space." *Scientific American* 281 (July 1999): 41–49. This article considers the possible extraterrestrial origin of some fairly sizable carbon-containing molecules.

Djerassi, Carl, and Roald Hoffmann. *Oxygen*. Weinheim: Wiley-VCH, 2001. This is a two-act play examining a hypothetical retro Nobel Prize for the discovery of oxygen.

Roald Hoffmann, corecipient with Kenichi Fukui of the 1981 Nobel Prize in chemistry (Roald Hoffmann)

faculty often avoid teaching freshman chemistry, Hoffmann taught the course on many occasions at Cornell and he presented a 26-lecture series, *The World of Chemistry,* that was first broadcast in 1990 on public television. During his undergraduate days at Columbia, Hoffmann developed a love for poetry and almost three decades later published a book of poems, *The Metamict State* (1987), followed by *Gaps and Verses* (1990), and *Memory Effects* (1999). In 1993, the book *Chemistry Imagined: Reflections on Science* was coauthored with artist Vivian Torrence who illustrated Hoffmann's essays with imaginative artwork. His 1995 book *The Same and Not The Same* reached a wide audience and illustrated the underlying dualities in chemistry. *Old Wine New Flasks,* coauthored in 1997 with Shira Leibowitz Schmidt, explored the interface between religion and science. *Oxygen,* a play imagining a retro Nobel Prize for the discovery of oxygen and its role in combustion, was coauthored with the renowned chemist/novelist Carl Djerassi and published and performed in 2001. The play sets a meeting at the Royal Swedish Court in the 18th century between Joseph Priestley, Antoine Lavoisier, and Carl Wilhelm Scheele and uses this event to reflect upon the motivations for doing science, relationships between men and women, and other themes of modern interest. Roald Hoffmann, a unifier of the so-called Two Cultures, is currently Frank H. Rhodes Professor of Humane Letters at Cornell University.

Georgia State University. "Rubidium/Strontium Dating of Meteorites." Available online. URL: http://hyperphysics.phy-astr.gsu.edu/hbase/nuclear/meteorrbsr. Accessed February 12, 2006. This Web site provides useful background material for understanding geological dating using radioisotopes.

Franks, Felix. *Polywater.* Cambridge: The MIT Press, 1981. This book is a brief, highly accessible history of the polywater controversy that started very tentatively in 1962, ended decisively in 1973, and was a topic of worldwide interest between 1966 and 1971.

Gabella, Thomas, and Takeshi Oka. "A Key Molecular Ion in the Universe and in the Laboratory." *Science* 312 (2006): 1,610–1,614. This brief article summarizes the discussions in a January 2006 conference devoted to H_3^+.

Hazen, Robert M. *Genesis: The Scientific Quest for Life's Origins.* Washington, D.C.: Joseph Henry Press, 2005. Available online. URL: www.nap.edu/catalog/10753.html. Accessed February 12, 2006. This book is a highly readable and informative, if somewhat idiosyncratic, discussion of current views about the chemical origins of life.

Hoffmann, Roald, and Vivian Torrence. *Chemistry Imagined: Reflections on Science.* Washington and London: Smithsonian Institution Press, 1993. This book matches the images of artist Torrence to conceptual descriptions of chemistry by Nobel laureate Hoffmann.

———. *The Same and Not The Same.* New York: Columbia University Press, 1995. This popular book describes the dualities at the core of chemistry.

Langmuir, Irving (transcribed and edited by Robert N. Hall). "Pathological Science." *Physics Today* 42 (October 1989): 44 (originally presented on December 18, 1953). Available online. URL: http://www.cs.princeton.edu/~Ken/Langmuir/langmuir.htm. Accessed February 12, 2006. This essay includes Langmuir's famous criteria for assessing "pathological science."

Margulis, Lynn, and Carl Sagan. *What Is Life?* London: Weidenfeld and Nicholson, 1995. This is a popular book that defines fundamental characteristics of living organisms as criteria in the search for extraterrestrial organisms.

Molina, Mario J., and F. Sherwood Rowland. "Stratospheric Sink for Chlorofluoromethanes: Chlorine-Atom Catalyzed Destruction of Ozone." *Nature* 249 (1974): 810–112. This is the article that first predicted destruction of the ozone layer by chlorofluorocarbons (CFCs).

National Research Council. *The Search for Life's Origins: Progress and Future Directions in Planetary Biology and Chemical Evolution.* Washington, D.C.: National Academy Press, 1990. Available online. URL: www.nap.edu/books/0309042461/. Accessed February 12, 2006. This report was assembled by the Space Research Committee of the NRC to assess future directions in the search for extraterrestrial life.

Rouhi, A. Maureen. "Olefin Metathesis: Big-Deal Reaction." *Chemical & Engineering News* 80 (December 23, 2002): 29–33; "Olefin Metathesis: The Early Days." *Chemical & Engineering News* 80 (December 23, 2002): 34–38. These two brief articles explain the complex history of the discovery of the olefin metathesis reaction as well as its applications.

University of Cologne. *Cologne Database for Molecular Spectroscopy (CDMS),* managed by the University of Cologne, Cologne, Germany. Available online. URL: www.ph1.uni-koeln.de/vorhersagen/. Accessed February 12, 2006. This is a database (in English) for molecules discovered in interstellar space.

9

1981–1990:
Powerful Instruments Advance Materials Science and Biochemistry

Nanotechnology, High-Temperature Superconductors, and Analyses of Huge Molecules

The 1980s would witness the major impact of instrumentation on all aspects of chemical science, but especially on materials science, biochemistry, and the newly emerging fields of nanotechnology, structural biology and proteomics. The first "high-temperature" superconductors were synthesized, offering promise of more energy with less fuel and waste. Until 1985, the only isolated solid *allotropes* of carbon were graphite and diamond. The discovery of a third allotrope, C_{60}, would help launch nanotechnology, further boosted by the discovery of nanotubes by the end of the decade. The *scanning tunneling microscope (STM)* would permit analysis of atoms and molecules on the surfaces of materials. The related *atomic force microscope (AFM)* would permit testing of forces on individual molecules and manipulation of individual metal atoms. The decade would also witness the birth of femtochemistry and the experimental observation of reaction transition states. The development of methods of mass spectrometry based upon *fast atom bombardment (FAB)*, *matrix-assisted laser desorption ionization (MALDI)*, and *electrospray ionization (ESI)* would permit scientists to analyze proteins and other huge polymeric molecules in the gas-phase, feats almost unthinkable a few years earlier. High-field NMR spectroscopy, coupled with new synthetic methods, especially asymmetric catalysis, would enable synthesis of amazing natural products such as optically pure palytoxin (64 chiral centers). X-ray crystallography will advance beyond the structures of individual complex, high-molecular-weight biomolecules and will enable studies of the structures and mechanisms of complexes containing many protein molecules and other cofactors.

A somber development during the 1980s was the discovery of acquired immune deficiency syndrome (AIDS) which is transmitted by the human immunodeficiency virus (HIV). Now, more than two decades later, AIDS has killed more than 20 million people, and tens of millions more are infected. The first AIDS treatment drug, AZT, was approved in 1987. In 1989, the crystallographic structure of HIV-1 protease was determined, lending hope for the development of protease inhibitors as effective AIDs treatments. In 1990, the Human Genome Project commenced, with promise for understanding human origins, diversity, variation, and susceptibility to disease at the most fundamental level.

Hassium (Element 108) and Meitnerium (Element 109)

The transuranium elements up to 106 were synthesized by accelerating neutrons or very light nuclei into other actinides including costly, unstable artificial elements such as californium (98). In 1973, Yuri Oganessian (1933–) and Alexander G. Demin in Dubna developed the concept of "soft fusion" or "cold fusion" (not to be confused with the unrelated "cold fusion" debacle of 1989) which they successfully

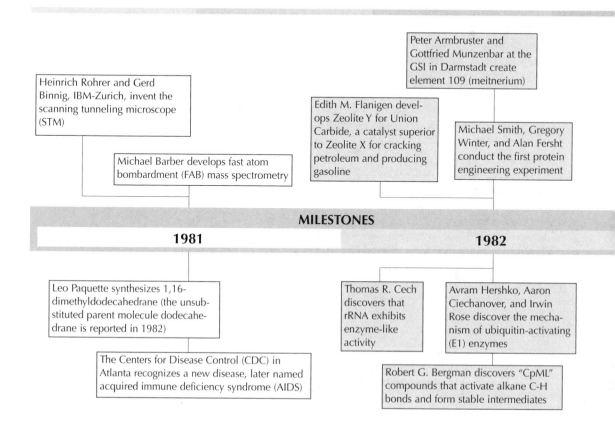

Heinrich Rohrer and Gerd Binnig, IBM-Zurich, invent the scanning tunneling microscope (STM)

Michael Barber develops fast atom bombardment (FAB) mass spectrometry

Edith M. Flanigen develops Zeolite Y for Union Carbide, a catalyst superior to Zeolite X for cracking petroleum and producing gasoline

Peter Armbruster and Gottfried Munzenbar at the GSI in Darmstadt create element 109 (meitnerium)

Michael Smith, Gregory Winter, and Alan Fersht conduct the first protein engineering experiment

MILESTONES

1981

1982

Leo Paquette synthesizes 1,16-dimethyldodecahedrane (the unsubstituted parent molecule dodecahedrane is reported in 1982)

The Centers for Disease Control (CDC) in Atlanta recognizes a new disease, later named acquired immune deficiency syndrome (AIDS)

Thomas R. Cech discovers that rRNA exhibits enzyme-like activity

Avram Hershko, Aaron Ciechanover, and Irwin Rose discover the mechanism of ubiquitin-activating (E1) enzymes

Robert G. Bergman discovers "CpML" compounds that activate alkane C-H bonds and form stable intermediates

applied in 1976 to the synthesis of the superheavy element bohrium (107) (see chapter 8). This discovery was confirmed by the Darmstadt group in 1981. The concept involved bombarding a target of thin layers of lead or bismuth with ions of intermediate mass (ca. 40–70). The nucleus of lead 208 is "doubly magic" (see chapter 8). The bismuth 209 nucleus also holds 126 neutrons, a "magic number," the same as ^{208}Pb. Bombardment of such "super-stable" nuclei with ions having enormous velocities and energies (40-50 MeV) produces energetic (excited) states of the new nuclei that typically eject ("evaporate") four or five neutrons. In "cold fusion" the collisions are much "cooler," on the order of 10-15 MeV and typically ejecting only one neutron upon formation. The new nuclei are more likely to survive than if they were formed "hot." One disadvantage of this technique is that the superheavy elements synthesized in this manner tend to be relatively "neutron-poor" (reflecting low the N/Z ratios in the ion "bullets" in the 40-70 atomic mass range) and not as intrinsically stable as more neutron-rich isotopes.

In 1982, Peter Armbruster (1931–), Gottfried Munzenbar, and their colleagues at the GSI in Darmstadt in Germany applied the "cold

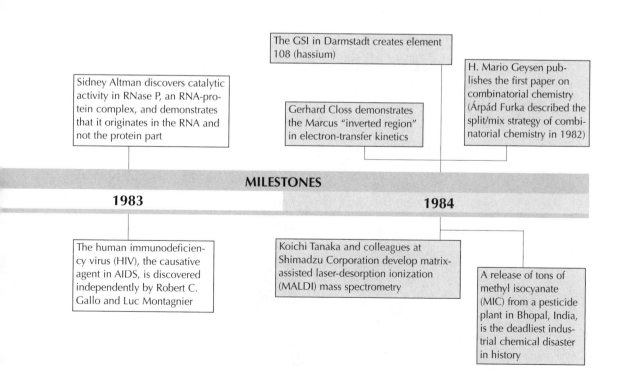

The GSI in Darmstadt creates element 108 (hassium)

H. Mario Geysen publishes the first paper on combinatorial chemistry (Árpád Furka described the split/mix strategy of combinatorial chemistry in 1982)

Sidney Altman discovers catalytic activity in RNase P, an RNA-protein complex, and demonstrates that it originates in the RNA and not the protein part

Gerhard Closs demonstrates the Marcus "inverted region" in electron-transfer kinetics

MILESTONES

1983

1984

The human immunodeficiency virus (HIV), the causative agent in AIDS, is discovered independently by Robert C. Gallo and Luc Montagnier

Koichi Tanaka and colleagues at Shimadzu Corporation develop matrix-assisted laser-desorption ionization (MALDI) mass spectrometry

A release of tons of methyl isocyanate (MIC) from a pesticide plant in Bhopal, India, is the deadliest industrial chemical disaster in history

fusion" technique and accelerated ^{58}Fe ions into ^{209}Bi. Following one week of bombardment, they obtained a single atom of element 109 with atomic mass 266, confirmed by four simultaneous independent techniques. The new element was later named meitnerium (Mt) after Lise Meitner, a codiscoverer of nuclear fission. Its very short half-life ($t_{1/2}$ ~ 1.7 milliseconds) precludes exploration of its chemistry, although ^{276}Mt, an intermediate in the decay of roentgenium (111, discovered in 1994), has $t_{1/2} = 0.72$ seconds.

Element 108 was synthesized by the Darmstadt team in 1984 by bombarding ^{208}Pb with ^{58}Fe ions to create an element of mass 265. The element was later named hassium (Hs) after the state of Hessen, which includes the city of Darmstadt. The most stable isotope of hassium is ^{270}Hs, $t_{1/2}$ 21 seconds. Extremely skilled online chemical investigations of this short-lived, ultrarare substance demonstrated the formation and some properties of HsO_4, bearing similarity to its Group 8 relative OsO_4.

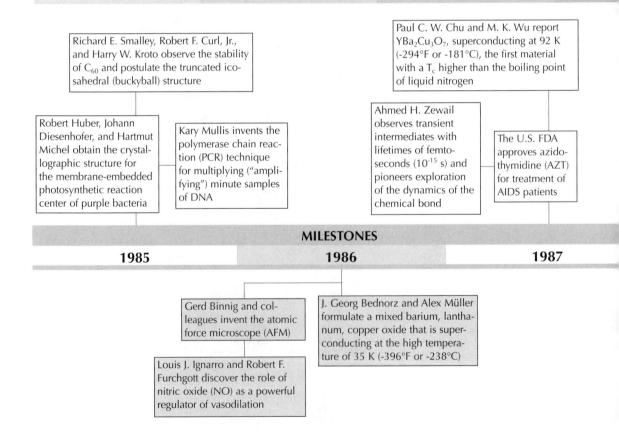

Richard E. Smalley, Robert F. Curl, Jr., and Harry W. Kroto observe the stability of C_{60} and postulate the truncated icosahedral (buckyball) structure

Paul C. W. Chu and M. K. Wu report $YBa_2Cu_3O_7$, superconducting at 92 K (-294°F or -181°C), the first material with a T_c higher than the boiling point of liquid nitrogen

Robert Huber, Johann Diesenhofer, and Hartmut Michel obtain the crystallographic structure for the membrane-embedded photosynthetic reaction center of purple bacteria

Kary Mullis invents the polymerase chain reaction (PCR) technique for multiplying ("amplifying") minute samples of DNA

Ahmed H. Zewail observes transient intermediates with lifetimes of femtoseconds (10^{-15} s) and pioneers exploration of the dynamics of the chemical bond

The U.S. FDA approves azidothymidine (AZT) for treatment of AIDS patients

MILESTONES

1985   **1986**   **1987**

Gerd Binnig and colleagues invent the atomic force microscope (AFM)

J. Georg Bednorz and Alex Müller formulate a mixed barium, lanthanum, copper oxide that is superconducting at the high temperature of 35 K (-396°F or -238°C)

Louis J. Ignarro and Robert F. Furchgott discover the role of nitric oxide (NO) as a powerful regulator of vasodilation

The Scanning Tunneling Microscope (STM): Images of Individual Atoms on Surfaces

"Tunneling" is one of many illogical-seeming realities predicted by quantum theory. If one imagines an individual atom, the nucleus is surrounded by an electron cloud where there is high probability for finding the atom's electrons. Outside of the cloud the electron probability is very small and decreases exponentially with distance from the atom (the "probability tail"). Still, there is a finite but exceedingly small probability of finding an electron at some distance outside the atom. If two atoms (e.g., of gold) are separated by a distance of 10 Å for example, to "pull" an electron from an atom to a distance of 5 Å from each nucleus should require considerable energy (an energy barrier). However, the very, very minute probability of atom A's electron being near atom B and the reverse, in effect exchanging atoms, corresponds to these electrons passing through a barrier without extra energy, that

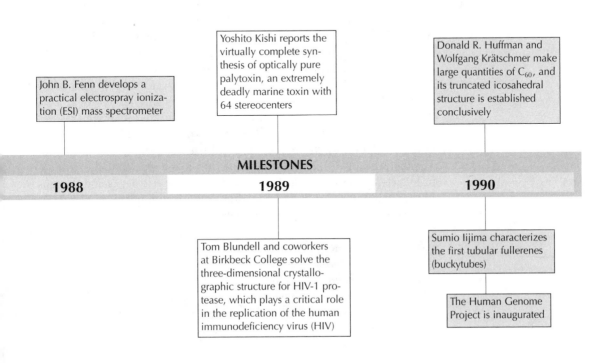

John B. Fenn develops a practical electrospray ionization (ESI) mass spectrometer

Yoshito Kishi reports the virtually complete synthesis of optically pure palytoxin, an extremely deadly marine toxin with 64 stereocenters

Donald R. Huffman and Wolfgang Krätschmer make large quantities of C_{60}, and its truncated icosahedral structure is established conclusively

MILESTONES

1988   **1989**   **1990**

Tom Blundell and coworkers at Birkbeck College solve the three-dimensional crystallographic structure for HIV-1 protease, which plays a critical role in the replication of the human immunodeficiency virus (HIV)

Sumio Iijima characterizes the first tubular fullerenes (buckytubes)

The Human Genome Project is inaugurated

is overlapping the tiny tails of their probability curves and tunneling. Other very small bits of matter, e.g., hydrogen atoms and protons, are also known to tunnel. The emission of α-particles from a radioactive nucleus such as uranium is a manifestation of tunneling. This is readily understood by considering the enormous energies required to accelerate and fuse positively-charged α-particles with positive nuclei. An α-particle leaving the nucleus (α-decay) would have to cross this same incredibly huge energy barrier but without a cyclotron's acceleration. Quantum mechanical tunneling is how the α-particle escapes the atom while avoiding the energy barrier.

In 1981, two German physicists working at the IBM Zurich Research Laboratory, Heinrich Rohrer (1933–) and Gerd Binnig (1947–), applied these principles to the design and construction of the scanning tunneling microscope (STM). The principle is shown schematically in Part A of the figure on page 317. A wire of an unreactive, refractory metal such as platinum (often platinum/iridium alloy) or tungsten is cut so that it comes to a tip consisting of a few atoms or even one atom. The tip moves very closely (less than 10 Å = 1 × 10^{-7} cm or 4 × 10^{-8} in) across the surface of a material. A cantilever maintains a constant electrical (tunneling) current as the needle tip skims along the surface following the electronic contours of the atoms and molecules.

In 1986, Binnig and coworkers published a paper describing a modified version of the STM, the atomic force microscope (AFM). The AFM measures force applied to the surface and enables the movement of individual atoms while not breaking any chemical bonding rules. One of the iconic images of modern physics is that presented in Part B of the figure. It is a presentation of the "quantum corral" formed by moving 48 iron atoms into a circle one-by-one using the AFM. It is an amazing image! The atoms in the circle do not appear as spheres but rather as cones tapering toward the STM probe tip. This is, in fact, a visual validation of the Heisenberg uncertainty principle (see chapter 3), since the probe tip and the tunneling it induces actually strongly influence (change) what it measures. The concentric peaks and troughs of the "quantum corral" are consistent with standing waves like those predicted by a simple quantum calculation called "the particle in a circle."

Gerd Binnig and Heinrich Rohrer shared the 1986 Nobel Prize in physics with Ernst Ruska (1906–88). Ruska invented the electron microscope, which was based upon focusing cathode rays, and built the first powerful instrument (12,000X magnification) in Berlin in 1933. Starting in the 1950s it has become a standard research and teaching instrument, particularly in the fields of biology and materials science.

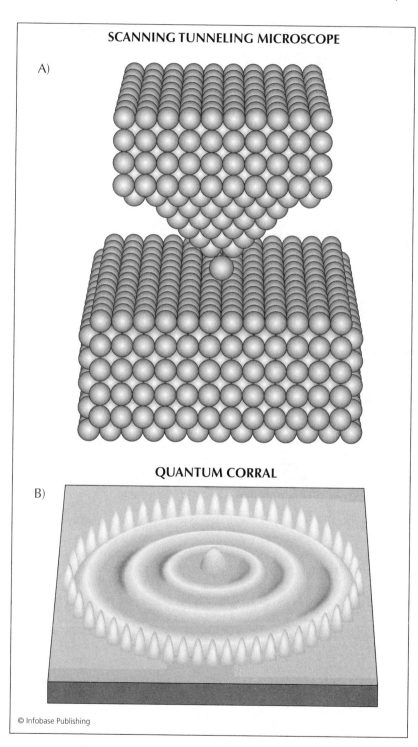

SCANNING TUNNELING MICROSCOPE

A)

QUANTUM CORRAL

B)

© Infobase Publishing

A) Schematic diagram of the scanning tunneling microscope (STM) in which a tip of atomic dimensions glides across an atomic surface but does not touch it. Electrons are exchanged between the surface and the probe tip by quantum mechanical tunneling. B) The "quantum corral" was made by moving 48 iron atoms into a circle.

Confirming the Marcus "Inversion Region" for Electron Transfer

Electron transfer is the most fundamental process in chemistry. Starting in 1956, Rudolph Marcus analyzed the rate and energy relationships in electron transfer and in 1960 he published a revolutionary conclusion (see chapter 6). It is logical that for a series of closely related reactions (including electron transfer), the more energetically favorable (more exothermic) the reaction, the faster it should occur. That is in accord with the vast history of chemical observations. However, in 1960 Marcus predicted the existence of an "inverted region" in which rates might actually decrease as a series of reactions became extremely exothermic. In 1984, some 25 years after this startling prediction was made, Gerhard L. Closs (1928–92) at the University of Chicago confirmed it using the molecular system depicted below: a rigid cholesterol "spacer" separating a biphenyl substituent, the electron donor, from an electron acceptor substituent ("X"). Closs pumped an electron into the biphenyl substituent and monitored its rapid disappearance. Although eight related molecules were employed, three are used here to illustrate Closs's results. In one molecule, the acceptor group X has an affinity for an electron just slightly (~ 0.1 eV) greater than that of the biphenyl. The electron transfer rate constant is relatively low (~ 10^6/sec). In a second molecule, the acceptor group X has an affinity for an electron that is much greater (by ~ 1.2 eV) than biphenyl. The rate of electron transfer from the biphenyl substituent in this molecule is ~ 10^9/sec, one thousand times faster than in the first molecule, as expected. In the third molecule depicted below, substituent X has an affinity for an electron that is extremely high: fully 2.4 eV (55 kcal/mol; more than half the strength of an H-O bond in H_2O) greater than that of biphenyl. One might expect another thousandfold increase in the electron transfer rate of this molecule compared to its predecessor. Instead, the rate is only ~ 10^8/sec, one-tenth the rate of its predecessor. This powerful

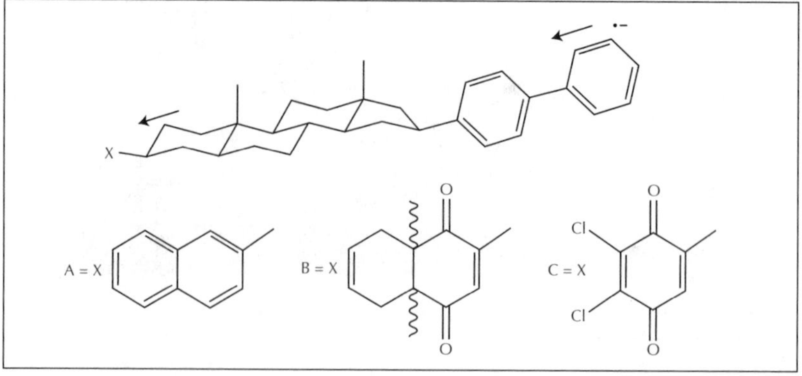

Marcus's study of intramolecular electron transfer

confirmation of Marcus Theory helped to validate its application to a wide range of chemical and biochemical processes. Marcus received the 1992 Nobel Prize in chemistry.

"High-Temperature" Superconductors

During the first decade of the 20th century, the Dutch physicist Heike Kamerlingh Onnes established a cryogenics (low-temperature) laboratory in Leiden where, in 1908, he was the first to make liquid helium (4.2 K; see chapter 4). By expansion of liquid helium he even achieved a temperature of 1.5 K. These extreme temperatures were measured by a helium-gas thermometer: 145 mm pressure at 273 K (32°F or 0°C; 3 mm at 4.25 K (-452°F or -269°C). It would take two more decades to achieve 0.1 K (see chapter 4). The Leiden laboratory attracted world-famous physicists who visited and conducted experiments at temperatures never before experienced on the planet.

In 1911, Kamerlingh Onnes cooled a thread of pure mercury (1/20 mm or 0.002 inch diameter) in a capillary tube and found a smooth decrease in resistance as the temperature was lowered. At 4.2 K, he observed an abrupt decrease in resistivity from about 1/500 that at 273 K to $1/10^6$ that at 273 K; it reduced to about $1/10^9$ at 1.5 K. Resistance had virtually disappeared and solid mercury became a superconductor at these incredibly low temperatures. Similar superconductivity transitions were observed by Kamerlingh Onnes for tin (3.8 K) and lead (6 K). The thermal motions of the atoms, associated with defects in conducting electricity, drastically decrease below the superconducting temperature (T_c). Heike Kamerlingh Onnes won the 1913 Nobel Prize in physics. The modern theory of superconductivity was developed in 1957 by three physicists at the University of Illinois, John Bardeen (1908–91), Leon N. Cooper (1930–), and John Robert Schrieffer (1931–). They shared the 1972 Nobel Prize in physics (Bardeen also shared the 1956 Nobel Prize in physics for invention of the transistor; he is the only double Nobel laureate in physics).

Practical superconductivity is a holy grail of physics and engineering. The resistance that electrical currents normally encounter adds to the waste of heat in conducting electricity. Superconducting circuits could, in principle, make much more efficient use of fuels consumed to make electricity. However, to achieve temperatures near absolute zero requires huge energy inputs and quantities of an expensive substance (helium). Until the 1980s, this appeared to be an intractable problem. In 1982, J. Georg Bednorz (1950–) joined the research group of K. Alex Müller (1927–) at IBM Zurich Research Laboratories. Bednorz, with a background in crystallography, had his appetite whetted a few years earlier when he discovered that chemical reduction (to remove some oxygen atoms) from the *ceramic* $SrTiO_3$, having a perskovite ($CaTiO_3$)-type structure, made it superconducting at 0.3 K. In the 60

A) La$_2$CuO$_4$ is one example of a superconducting ceramic material. B) Another ceramic material, YBa$_2$Cu$_3$O$_7$, becomes a superconductor (~zero resistance) at 92 K—an extremely high temperature for superconductivity. C) A ceramic behaving as a superconductor at liquid nitrogen temperature (-321°F; -196°C; 77 K) produces its own magnetic field and can "levitate" a magnet.

years since Kamerlingh Onnes's discovery, explorations of new materials slowly raised the superconductivity temperature to 23.3 K (-417.8°F or -249.9°C), obtained for Nb$_3$Ge in 1973. Studies by Müller led the IBM Zurich scientists to discover, in early 1986, that a mixed oxide containing barium, lanthanum and copper exhibits a superconducting temperature (T$_c$) of 35 K, a 50 percent increase over the previous record. Bednorz and Müller had discovered an entirely new class of superconductors and opened a new range of temperatures. Paul C. W. Chu (1941–   ), at the University of Houston, soon demonstrated that the T$_c$ of this substance increased to over 50 K (-369.8°F or -223.2°C) under very high pressure. Part A of the figure below depicts the structure of one of these new ceramics, La$_2$CuO$_4$. Research activity in this area exploded during the remainder of 1986 and early 1987. In February 1987, Paul Chu and his former student Mau-Kuen ("MK") Wu, at the University of Alabama

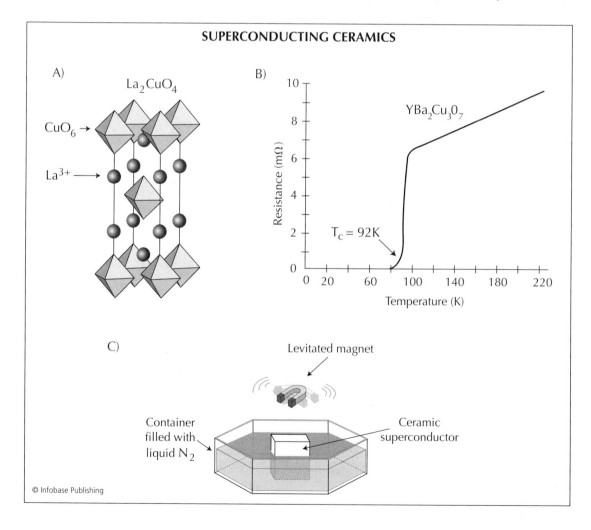

SUPERCONDUCTING CERAMICS

A) La$_2$CuO$_4$

CuO$_6$ →

La^{3+} →

B) YBa$_2$Cu$_3$O$_7$

Resistance (mΩ)

T$_c$ = 92K

Temperature (K)

C)

Levitated magnet

Container filled with liquid N$_2$

Ceramic superconductor

at Huntsville, discovered that replacement of lanthanum in the IBM ceramic by yttrium produced a dramatic effect and they observed a T_c of 92 K (-294°F or -181.1°C) for $YBa_2Cu_3O_7$ (the "1:2:3 Superconductor" depicted in Part B of the figure). This was a major advance because it was the first material whose T_c is higher than the boiling point of nitrogen (77 K, -321°F or -196°C). Nitrogen is the most abundant gas in the atmosphere and cooling to 92 K is much less energy-intensive than cooling to lower temperatures. Superconductivity is induced by cooling the ceramic in liquid nitrogen—the induced magnetic current "levitates" magnets (Part C of the accompanying figure).

The growing excitement was clear to the entire world when, on March 18, 1987, the American Physical Society hosted a meeting at the New York City Hilton hotel on superconductivity. Physicists talked, argued, snacked, and socialized throughout the night and early morning hours; the meeting has been called the "Woodstock of Physics." Today, the record T_c stands at 138 K (-211°F or -135°C) for a thallium-doped mercuric cuprate. It increases by another 30 K at a pressure of 300,000 atmospheres. J. Georg Bednorz and K. Alex Müller shared the 1987 Nobel Prize in physics one year after their IBM Zurich colleagues Heinrich Rohrer and Curt Binnig shared the 1986 Nobel Prize in physics with Ernst Ruska.

"Seeing" Activated Complexes on the Femtosecond (fs) Timescale

During the first half of the 20th century chemists gained the ability to shorten the timescale of chemical reactions they could monitor from seconds, using chemical kinetics (see chapters 2-4), to milliseconds (10^{-3} s) using stopped-flow techniques (see chapter 5) to microseconds (10^{-6} s) using flash photolysis and relaxation techniques (see chapters 5-7). With the introduction of the laser during the 1960s, *nanosecond* (10^{-9} s) and *picosecond* (10^{-12} s) timescales became accessible. Peter M. Rentzepis (1934–) and colleagues at Bell Laboratories published the first papers on picosecond spectroscopy in 1967. Starting around 1987, Egyptian-born Ahmed H. Zewail (1946– , see the profile in chapter 10), Caltech, employed techniques that would bring this timescale down to the *femtosecond* (10^{-15} s) scale. Part A of the figure on page 322 depicts Zewail's "arrow of time" tracing the evolution of accessible timescales over 150 years. Part B of this figure illustrates the femtosecond-scale experiment schematically.

Two femtosecond (fs) laser pulses, a pump pulse and a probe pulse, are initiated from a single laser source. The probe pulse is delayed, introducing a time lag, by a longer optical path that may be varied. The technology of fs pulses rests on principles of laser optics. Several modes (wavelengths) of laser light are emitted together coherently.

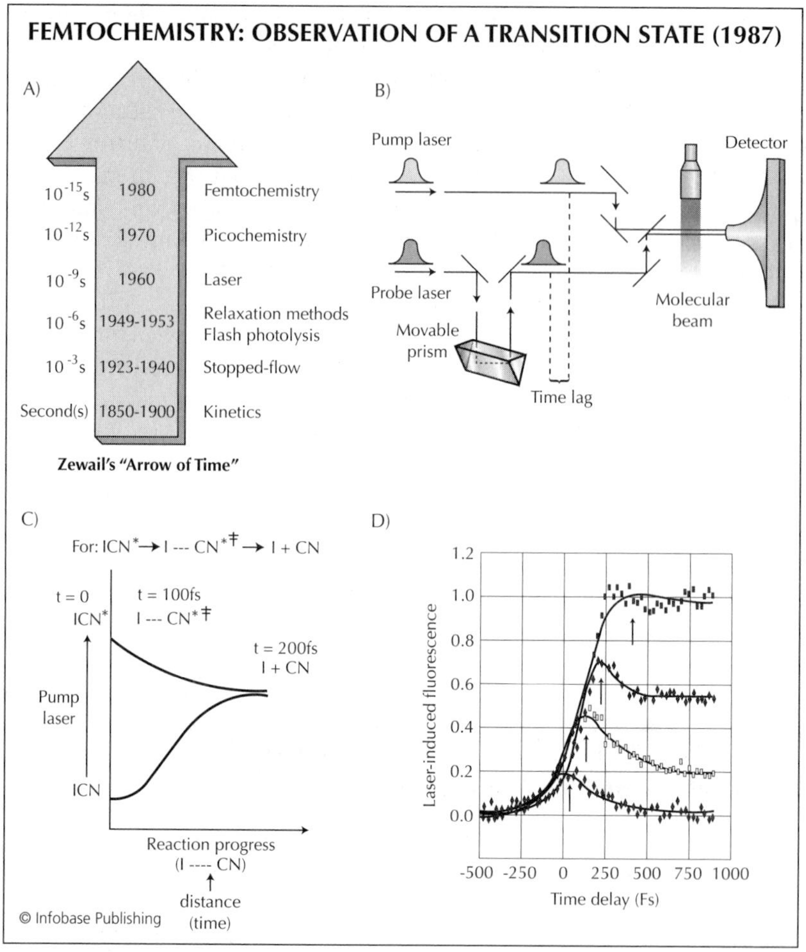

FEMTOCHEMISTRY: OBSERVATION OF A TRANSITION STATE (1987)

A)

10^{-15}s	1980	Femtochemistry
10^{-12}s	1970	Picochemistry
10^{-9}s	1960	Laser
10^{-6}s	1949-1953	Relaxation methods Flash photolysis
10^{-3}s	1923-1940	Stopped-flow
Second(s)	1850-1900	Kinetics

Zewail's "Arrow of Time"

B)

Pump laser

Detector

Probe laser

Movable prism

Molecular beam

Time lag

C)

For: $ICN^* \rightarrow I \text{ --- } CN^{*\ddagger} \rightarrow I + CN$

t = 0   t = 100fs
ICN*   I --- CN*‡

t = 200fs
I + CN

Pump laser

ICN

Reaction progress
(I ---- CN)

distance
(time)

© Infobase Publishing

D)

Laser-induced fluorescence

1.2
1.0
0.8
0.6
0.4
0.2
0.0

-500 -250 0 250 500 750 1000
Time delay (Fs)

A) Ahmed H. Zewail's "arrow of time" depicting the evolution in the timescale of chemical reactions accessible to measurement over the course of roughly 130 years. B) Schematic diagram illustrating how femtosecond reactions are monitored. C) A reaction coordinate diagram illustrating the discrete formation of the [I–CN] activated complex on the femtosecond timescale. D) Data for the determination of the lifetime of an activated complex.

When these wavelengths superimpose in phase they are said to be "mode-locked" and behave as a wave packet or "pulse." The pump and probe pulses are focused into a chamber containing gaseous molecules for study. The pump pulse excites a change (e.g., chemical reaction) while absorption of the probe pulse monitors the course of structural change as time passes on the fs scale. Zewail has likened the process to the effects of a strobe light that furnishes stop-action pictures of a fast process.

Femtosecond spectroscopy occurs near the limit of quantum physics. The Heisenberg uncertainty principle states that the product of the uncertainty in position (Δx) and the uncertainty in momentum (Δp) of an object must be nonzero and greater than the quantity $h/4\pi$ ($\sim 10^{-34}$ joule-second), where h is Planck's constant:

$$\Delta x \ \Delta p > h/4\pi$$

This nonzero product means that there are fundamental physical limits to accuracy that have nothing to do with how sophisticated the equipment is or how perfectly the experiment is performed. At the atomic scale, the very act of measuring alters slightly the object being measured. If the speed of a car is clocked using a radar gun, the radar beams will not alter the speed of the car in any meaningful way. However, on the atomic and subatomic scale, any such measurement (using photons or electrons for example) will alter to some extent the position and velocity of the object being measured.

Momentum is mass times velocity. Typical velocities of atomic motions are on the order of 1 km/s (2,400 mph). To traverse a distance of 1 Å (10^{-10} m) at this velocity takes a time period of 100 fs. Movements on the order of 1 Å characterize the conversion of reactants into activated complexes (at the transition state) and thus fs timescales are on the order of lifetimes of transition states, the ultimate limit of chemistry and biology. Taken *together* these magnitudes (Å and fs) are close to the limits but do not violate the uncertainty principle. Part C of the figure depicts Zewail's results for laser-induced decomposition of ICN to I + CN. The transition state is reached at about 100 fs and the product obtained by 200 fs. Zewail has applied fs kinetics using laser-induced fluorescence (Part D in the figure) and electron diffraction on the fs scale. Much as Linus Pauling explored the nature of the chemical bond, so did Zewail pioneer the dynamics of the chemical bond. Atoms could be localized in space and time and observed. The application of fs-scale spectroscopy to biological problems has proved to be very valuable. For example, the absorption of visible light by rhodopsin (see chapter 4) was long assumed to precede *cis-trans* isomerization. Zewail demonstrated that simultaneous light absorption by and isomerization of a retinal analogue suggest they are concerted in this system.

Carbon's Genius: C$_{60}$, Buckyballs, and Buckytubes

Argon comprises almost one percent of the air we breathe, yet it remained hidden for 120 years after the separation of oxygen from air by Carl Wilhelm Scheele in 1771–72. Henry Cavendish isolated a tiny bubble of argon in 1785 after sparking all of the nitrogen in a sample of air with added oxygen. But he lacked instrumentation and theory to probe and understand the bubble. Similarly, as familiar as the two carbon allotropes graphite and diamond are, the 1980s witnessed discovery of a third stable solid allotrope "simply" awaiting solvent extraction from certain carbon residues. Of course the discovery was not simple and required construction of new instrumentation, performance of incisive experiments, and the perception and intuition of gifted scientists.

The history of this discovery begins with the construction of the supersonic beam laser spectroscopy apparatus by Richard E. Smalley

(1943–2005) and his research group at Rice University. Smalley was interested in small gas-phase clusters of atoms that might provide insight into the properties of bulk crystalline materials. It is easy to understand this interest by posing a simple question: "How many atoms of gold does it take to form gold metal?" The answer is certainly not 1 or 2 or 10. Is it 50, 100, 1,000, or 10,000? Smalley was particularly interested in clusters formed from silicon, gallium arsenide (GaAs) and other substances used to fabricate computer chips.

Carbon vapor studies during the Manhattan Project demonstrated the existence of C_{15} species and early theoretical studies indicated that species up to C_{20} or so were likely to be straight chains and rings of carbon atoms. Carbon is unique in that other elements are known to exist as individual atoms or diatomics above 1,000 K (2,320°F or 1,270°C). The Rice apparatus employed 5-nanosecond bursts from a 532 nm laser to "blast" clusters from the solid surface of the material in question. The clusters are thrust by pressurized puffs of helium gas toward an "integration cup" that allows varying times for equilibration before entering a supersonic nozzle. The nozzle causes rapid expansion into a vacuum and cooling to near 0 K before the clusters are analyzed by detectors including a time-of-flight (TOF) mass spectrometer.

In 1984, Andrew Kaldor (1944–) at Exxon Research employed a "clone," designed and built at Rice, of the Smalley apparatus to investigate the nature of carbon deposits that form on catalysts. The mass spectrum obtained from this experiment is now world famous. It includes individual mass-to-charge (m/e) peaks of 12, 24, 36, 48 . . . corresponding to chains and rings up to 25 carbons, each differing by one carbon. A near-absence of peaks between 25 carbons (m/e 300) and 35 carbons (m/e 420) is followed by a series of peaks starting around 40 carbons, differing by units of 2 carbons, to well over 100 carbons. The largest (most abundant) peak corresponded to C_{60} (m/e 720) and was about 20 percent larger than any other peaks in that even-carbon series.

Robert F. Curl, Jr. (1933–), Smalley's faculty colleague at Rice, had a background in microwave spectroscopy and concomitant interest in radio-astronomy and space chemistry. Curl and Harold W. Kroto (1939–), University of Sussex, shared research interests in spectroscopy and astronomy and had met and corresponded earlier. When Kroto attended a conference in Austin in spring 1984, Curl invited him to visit Houston to meet Smalley and view the new instrument. The three scientists discussed potential use of the apparatus to generate and study carbon clusters. At Sussex, Kroto had investigated microwave spectra of the linear HC_5N, HC_7N, and HC_9N molecules and established their identity with interstellar molecules detected by radiotelescopes. Kroto and Curl shared a view that the mysterious diffuse interstellar bands (DIBs) that absorb UV, visible, and IR light, known since the 1930s, arise from chains of carbon atoms. In late August 2005, Kroto was informed that the carbon experiment would be performed in short order and within a few days he was in Houston.

The laser beam was aimed at a slowly rotating low-density graphite disk. The mass spectral data were fully consistent with the Exxon data. However, by varying the conditions and lifetimes of the fresh clusters, the researchers found conditions in which C_{60} was 50 times more abundant than the other clusters surrounding it. There was also a sizable but smaller "shadow" cluster at C_{70} and Kroto enjoyed referring to C_{60} and C_{70} as "the Lone Ranger and Tonto" or "Don Quixote and Sancho Panza." The special stability of C_{60} (and C_{70}) was now abundantly clear. What was the structure of C_{60} and why was it so stable? It certainly could have been a ring but one would also expect *abundant* . . . C_{56}, C_{58}, C_{62}, C_{64} . . . rings contrary to experiment. If it was a sheet of tiled carbon hexagons (as in "graphene," a single sheet of graphite), there would be "dangling bonds" (free valences) at the edges and C_{60} would have been too reactive to survive the experimental conditions. The molecule had to wrap around itself so as to leave no "dangling bonds." Working with paper cutouts (much as Pauling did when he postulated the *alpha*-helix nearly 40 years earlier), Smalley arrived at a truncated icosahedron (as in the figure on page 326): see any soccer ball to observe a structure of the same symmetry. While the structure might be thought of as "aesthetically obvious," it was unproven. Circumstantial evidence in support would appear almost immediately but the definitive work awaited isolation of milligram and greater quantities five years hence. Kroto dubbed the spherical C_{60} structure buckminsterfullerene after the American architect-engineer-inventor R. Buckminster Fuller (1895–1983), who designed the geodesic dome at the American exhibit in Montreal Expo 67. C_{60} is often referred to as *buckyball* and the general class of compounds as *fullerenes*. They have vacancies in their interiors. Kroto would soon return to Sussex and continue work on C_{60}. One of the early experiments in Houston involved soaking the graphite disk in a solution of $LaCl_3$, allowing it to dry and then conducting the pulsed-laser experiment. The observation of a stable $C_{60}La^+$ ion in the mass spectrum (*not* $C_{60}La_2^+$, $C_{60}La_3^+$, *etc.*) was fully consistent with the formation of an endohedral complex: one lanthanum atom fully enclosed in the buckyball cage (see the figure). The fact that the next largest possible buckyball cage is C_{70}, the ubiquitous "Sancho Panza," was another piece of early circumstantial evidence supporting the polyhedral structures.

Once focused on the icosahedral hypothesis for the structure of C_{60}, Smalley, Curl and Kroto learned that in 1970 Eiji Osawa (1936–   ), at Hokkaido University, had explicitly postulated the existence of icosahedral C_{60} and its aromatic stability (it has about 12,500 Kekulé resonance structures). Russian researchers published Hückel MO calculations on this symmetric molecule in 1973 and demonstrated its large HOMO-LUMO gap, so typical of a stable aromatic molecule. The distinguished organic chemist Orville L. Chapman had even obtained National Science Foundation support to explore its rational synthesis. No rational, step-

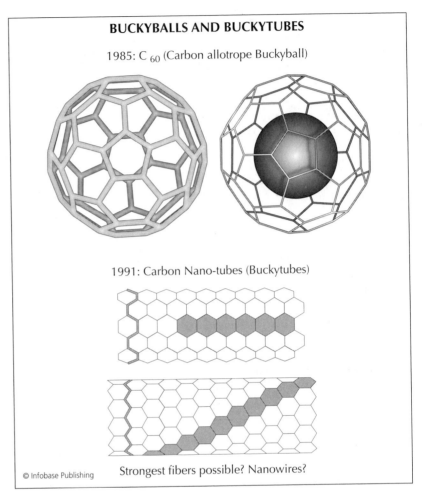

BUCKYBALLS AND BUCKYTUBES

1985: C_{60} (Carbon allotrope Buckyball)

1991: Carbon Nano-tubes (Buckytubes)

© Infobase Publishing

Strongest fibers possible? Nanowires?

The third allotrope of carbon: C_{60}, the major member of a class of pure carbon compounds called fullerenes (top); two different types of carbon nanotubes, substances having great potential in materials and in nanotechnology

wise synthesis of C_{60} has been achieved even into the 21st century. The team also discovered that mathematician Leonhard Euler (1707–83) had proven that hexagonal tiling requires not less than 12 pentagonal tiles to close up and leave no free vertices or edges. Since Hückel MO calculations and chemical experience indicate that fused five-membered conjugated rings have circuits of $4n$ π-electrons (rather than $4n + 2$), such units are unstable. Thus, the smallest stable "fullerene" must have $12 \times 5 = 60$ carbon atoms.

There remained considerable debate over whether the circumstantial evidence really supported the amazing icosahedral structure for C_{60} until 1990, when milligram and higher quantities of C_{60} were isolated and subjected to spectroscopic study. Wolfgang Krätschmer (1937–   ) and Donald R. Huffman (1935–   ), astrophysicists at the Max Planck Institute in Heidelberg and the University of Arizona, had collaborated since 1982 on a method to simulate the creation of carbon clouds in space. One technique was to run a spark through a small gap between two graphite rods in a helium atmosphere. Later, the carbon residue was analyzed by infrared spectroscopy and four strong IR absorption bands reported. Kroto realized that this is precisely what was expected for the highly symmetric C_{60}. His student extracted carbon residue, made by the Krätschmer-Huffman technique with benzene, obtained a red solution but was delayed in obtaining really solid confirmation of the presence of C_{60}. The next day, Kroto received a manuscript to review from *Nature* disclosing the isolation and characterization of significant quantities of C_{60}, coauthored by Krätschmer, Huffman, and their students. In his tongue-in-cheek British style Kroto recollects: "I considered committing suicide, but decided to go for lunch instead." With exhilaration for having been proven correct, and disappointment in being scooped, he recommended immediate acceptance of the paper. Kroto's group did have the honor of obtaining the first NMR (natural abundance-^{13}C that is, there are no ^{1}H) spectra of both C_{60} and C_{70}. His colleague Roger Taylor (1935–) chromatographically resolved the red extract into a magenta solution (C_{60}) and a red solution (C_{70}). The ^{13}C-NMR spectrum of C_{60} must be the most "boring and exciting" one ever recorded. Downfield from a huge singlet for the solvent benzene was a tiny singlet for C_{60}: exactly as one would predict for an aromatic molecule containing 60 identical carbon atoms. The ^{13}C-NMR spectrum of C_{70} exhibited the four singlet peaks expected for this somewhat less-symmetrical molecule which contains four distinct types of carbon atom.

In 1990, Sumio Iijima (1939–), working at NEC Laboratories in Japan, reported isolation and characterization of tubes derived from rolling up of graphene sheets with pentagonal faces and capping on one end. Thus, were born *buckytubes* (see the figure), with conductivity properties reminiscent of metal wires. Literally thousands of papers and patents on buckyballs and buckytubes now appear each year. Richard E. Smalley, Robert F. Curl, Jr., and Harry W. Kroto shared the 1996 Nobel Prize in chemistry. The three Nobel laureates were effusive in sharing credit with their students, James Heath, Sean O'Brien, and T. Lee, who performed the experiments. In his Nobel lecture, Smalley paid homage to his true hero of fullerene chemistry:

> *Carbon has wired within it, as part of its birthright ever since the beginning of this universe, the genius for spontaneously assembling into fullerenes.*

Here is a footnote to the C_{60} story: In some old theaters there exist in old projectors their used graphite rods. When these rods are ground up and extracted with hot toluene (benzene is carcinogenic; both solvents are toxic and highly flammable), a red solution is obtained. Guess which carbon compounds it contains?

Activating Unactivated Carbon-Hydrogen Bonds

Alkanes are abundant components of petroleum but normally react only under the most vigorous conditions (combustion; free radicals such as Cl and HO). If their C-H bonds could be activated under mild conditions, especially if this could be done catalytically, then it would be feasible to convert alkanes from mere fuel to fine chemicals that might be used and recycled. This is particularly desirable for methane (CH_4), a by-product of anaerobic bacteria and a potential source of methanol (CH_3OH). Nature routinely activates C-H bonds on saturated 4-coordinate carbon when enzymes called oxygenases employ cytochrome-P450 to catalyze conversions to alcohols:

$$P\text{-}450$$
$$R\text{-}H + O_2 + 2\ e^- + 2\ H^+ \rightarrow R\text{-}O\text{-}H + H_2O$$

The discovery in 1961 that Vaska's compound, $IrCl(CO)(PPh_3)_2$, reacts with H_2 to form a stable complex suggested to chemists the possibility that similar oxidative-addition reactions could activate C-H bonds (see chapter 7). In 1969, Alexander E. Shilov discovered transition-metal-catalyzed exchange of CH_4 with deuterium from D_2O, demonstrating the activation of the strong C-H bond in methane. In 1982, Robert G. Bergman and colleagues at Caltech employed molecules of the "CpML"-type (Cp = $C_5H_5^-$ or cyclopentadienide; M = Ir or Rh; L = ligands) to initiate oxidative addition reactions on unactivated alkane C-H bonds and form stable complexes such as the one represented below, formed from cyclohexane. Once isolated, the activated alkane can react with "external reagents" to form other compounds. For example, Bergman converted this compound under gentle conditions to bromocyclohexane. Thus, an unreactive alkane had been activated to form a functionalized compound (an alkyl bromide) capable of an enormous range of further chemistry. Related studies were soon published by William D. Jones (1953–) at the University of Rochester and W. A. Graham. Other researchers such as Robert H. Crabtree (1948–) and Masato Tanaka demonstrated that transition metal activation of alkanes could insert CO as well as form alkenes. Patricia L. Watson (1949–), at DuPont, demonstrated that metals that form d$^\circ$-complexes and cannot engage in oxidative addition can nonetheless activate C-H bonds on unreactive molecules such as methane:

$$Cp^*_2LuCH_3 + {}^{13}CH_4 \leftrightarrows Cp^*_2Lu^{13}CH_3 + CH_4$$

$$[Cp^* \text{ is } (CCH_3)_5^-;\ Cp = C_5H_5^- \text{ or } (CH)_5^-]$$

Just as the stable Vaska compound cannot function as a catalyst, so too did the stability of the Bergman complex described here preclude its use in a catalytic sense. However, Wilkinson's catalyst (see chapter 7) is labile and discoveries of various catalytic activators of C-H bonds followed in short order.

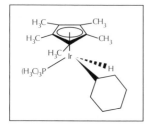

Bergman's stable C-H insertion intermediate

Triumphs in the Synthesis of Unnatural and Natural Products

The beauty of the five platonic solids attracted the admiration of organic chemists seeking elegant molecules with unusual properties. The regular icosahedron has 20 faces, all triangles, and would require that each carbon vertex forms five bonds at a very unstable geometry and is not a realistic goal for organic chemists. An octahedron with carbon occupying its six vertices is also unrealistic. It is true that in carboranes and boron hydride anions these electronic-deficient species have carbon and boron coordinated to more than four neighbors. Cubane (see chapter 7) was synthesized in 1964, and the first tetrahedrane was reported in 1978 (see chapter 8) although the parent molecule tetrahedrane, $(CH)_4$, remains unknown.

The remaining member of the class, dodecahedrane (see chapter 7), finally yielded to the synthetic efforts of Leo Paquette (1934–   ), Ohio State University, in 1981–82, following failed attempts by other talented chemists. Dodecahedrane, $(CH)_{20}$, has 12 fused pentagonal faces and is strained due to this feature and its 20 eclipsed C-H bonds. However, the real difficulty in the synthesis of this molecule having icosahedral symmetry is entropy: the challenge of organizing 20 carbon atoms into a precise dodecahedron instead of thousands of other potential arrangements. The synthesis of triquinacene (see the structure below) by R. B. Woodward's group in 1964 offered a potential pathway. This $(CH)_{10}$ is a pre-organized "hemisphere" of the "spheroid" dodecahedrane. "All" that was needed was seemingly straightforward dimerization through the three C=C bonds in each of two molecules of triquinacene. While the thermal reaction was soon understood to be thermally forbidden by the Woodward-Hoffmann rules, this dimerization is photochemically allowed. However, no success was achieved by this approach since other, less-ordered, compounds are formed. Paquette then connected two triquinacene molecules by a single bond to form clamlike "bivalvane" molecules. Even this approach failed. However, in a beautiful series of reactions that maintained twofold symmetry throughout, Paquette made a dimethyl derivative in 1981 and finally the parent molecule dodecahedrane $[(CH)_{20}]$ in 1982.

Both dodecahedrane, $(CH)_{20}$, and buckminsterfullerene, C_{60}, appear to "thwart" entropy by folding 20 atoms and 60 atoms, respectively, into spheroid molecules of icosahedral symmetry. Unlike C_{60}, dodecahedrane

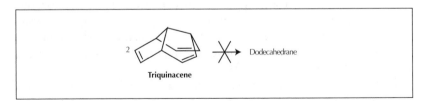

2   ⟶   Dodecahedrane

Triquinacene

Triquinacene

has not been found in nature and has only been made through a complex, but rational series of laboratory reactions. Even if it did occur naturally, as the tetrahedrally symmetric adamantane does (see chapter 7), lacking a chromophore to absorb UV or visible light, it would be very hard to spot among a complex mixture. It is also less volatile than adamantane. As noted earlier, the magenta-colored C_{60} has eluded rational stepwise synthesis. The secret of its natural synthesis appears to be the formation of incredibly strongly bonded two-dimensional sheets from carbon vapor, some of which by chance form the twelve 5-membered rings that curl them into a ball, satisfying valences on all 60 carbons and removing any residual reactivity.

An ongoing debate about C_{60} is whether or not "curiosity-driven" (pure science) investigation of the space chemistry of carbon led to the modern buckytube industry, itself a cornerstone of the nanotechnology revolution. A more obvious example of the unexpected impact of pure science on medicine and technology is furnished by the series of "enediyne" anticancer drugs discovered during the 1980s. When he was investigating the possible intermediacy of "1,4-benzyne" in the rearrangement of deuterium-labeled enediynes during the early 1970s (see chapter 8), Robert G. Bergman was probing very fundamental chemical theory. It is difficult to imagine that he envisioned any practical application beyond adding to chemical knowledge. Yet in the mid-1980s, a series of natural products containing the enediyne unit were found to have potent anticancer activity. Thanks to Bergman's research, the role of the enediyne unit in these anticancer agents was almost self-evident. As true intermediates, 1,4-benzynes react as radicals and attack DNA. Based upon considerable structural, computational, and mechanistic chemistry, the mechanism of one of these compounds, calicheamicin (see the figure on page 331, top), isolated in 1987, is envisioned as follows. The molecule is said by K. C. Nicolaou (1946–), Scripps Research Institute, to consist of: a) a warhead, b) a delivery system, and c) a trigger. The delivery system, a "sugar" (an oligosaccharide) that is a component of calicheamicin docks it into the minor groove of double-helical DNA at TCCT sites. The trisulfide linkage in the molecule is enzymatically cleaved (the trigger) to form an intermediate which undergoes Bergman cyclization to a "1,4-benzyne" (the warhead). The separation between reacting C=C terminal carbons in the enediyne formed by cleavage of the trisulfide linkage (3.16 Å) is smaller than that in calicheamicin (3.35 Å) allowing immediate rearrangement to the 1,4-benzyne derivative. Once formed, the 1,4-benzyne diradical removes hydrogen atoms from two deoxyribose C5 carbons destroying each of two DNA strands in the rapidly multiplying cancerous cells. In 1992, Nicolaou synthesized calicheamicin γ^{1}_{1}. Samuel J. Danishefsky (1936–), at Yale University and then Columbia University, synthesized this molecule in 1994.

Perhaps no molecule synthesized during the 1980s better reflects the fruits of asymmetric catalysis and new carbon-carbon bond-form-

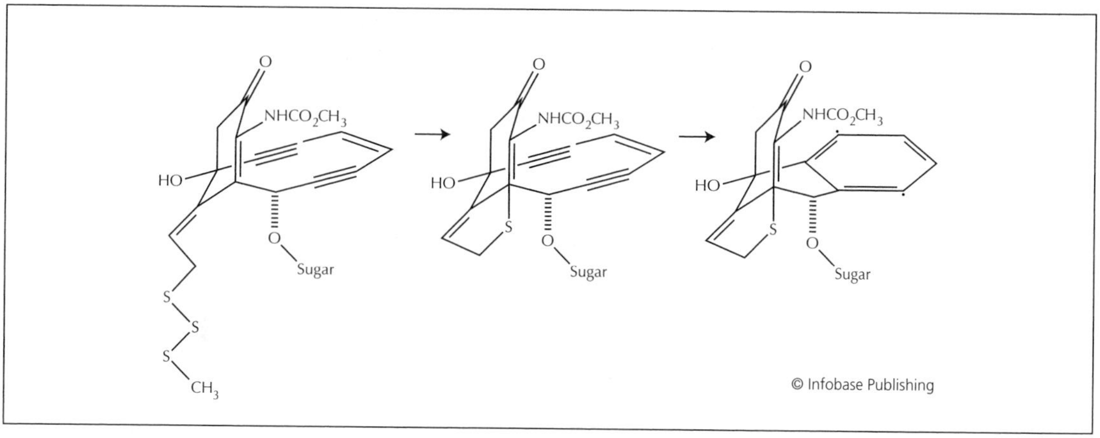

© Infobase Publishing

ing reactions better than palytoxin (see the structure below). Palytoxin is an incredibly toxic chemical derived from certain corals and other marine animals (lethal dose killing 50 percent of test animals, LD_{50} = 1.5 ng toxin/kg rat). Vitamin B_{12} (cyanocobalamin), the amazing "moon shot" completed in 1973 by R. B. Woodward, Albert Eschenmoser, and a hundred coworkers has 14 chiral ("stereogenic") centers. Woodward and Eschenmoser prepared the racemate, not the optically pure natural enantiomer. In 1989, only 16 years later, Yoshito Kishi (1937–   ), a former Woodward student, and his group at Harvard reported the virtual synthesis of optically pure (fully active) palytoxin. They had deduced its complete structure in 1982 but rational total synthesis was the only pathway to absolute verification. Palytoxin has 64 stereogenic centers as well as 7 C=C bonds that could be Z or E (*cis* or *trans*) and thus 2^{71} or 2.3 ×

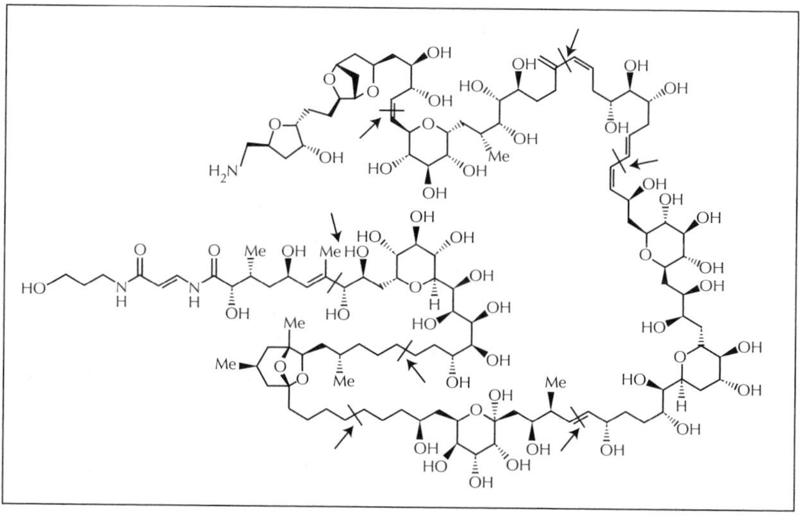

Activation of the anticancer compound calicheamicin to a diradical

"Palytoxin" and the fragments employed to assemble it

10^{21} possible stereoisomers. Kishi assembled palytoxin from eight preassembled units (see dashed lines in its structure). The amazing advance in synthesis from racemic vitamin B_{12} to optically pure palytoxin reflects the following late-20th century advances:

- the use of new carbon-carbon coupling reactions, some developed by Kishi, as well as older coupling reactions such as the Wittig reaction (see chapter 6)
- the revolution in asymmetric synthesis (see chapter 8)
- the advances in high-field 2-D NMR (see chapter 8) that permitted accurate analysis of minute quantities of each intermediate.

The toxicity of palytoxin, determined by experiments and molecular modeling, originates in its disabling of the sodium/potassium cell membrane pump (see chapter 8).

Dendrimers: From Exotic Curiosities to More Than 100 Patents a Year

In 1978, Fritz Vögtle (1939–   ), at the University of Bonn, published the first paper describing a new type of highly branched molecular species. Molecules such as the one depicted below could be formed starting with a core and then moving successively through carefully controlled staged reactions to generate a first tier, a second tier, a third tier, and beyond, increasing exponentially the number of branches and reaction sites. During this period Donald A. Tomalia (1938–   ) at Dow Chemical Company also discovered routes to these exotic molecules which Dow termed *dendrimers* (from the Greek *dendra* for "tree"). Tomalia and his colleagues soon developed and patented efficient syntheses for other dedrimer molecules but little application was initially found for these chemical curiosities.

Dendrimers (sometimes called "arbor," "cascade," or "starburst" molecules) share some characteristics with polymers but also manifest critical differences. Whereas linear polymers like polystyrene are polydisperse (have a range of molecular weights and character), dendrimers, synthesized in a stepwise manner, are monodisperse (have uniform molecular mass). Unlike polymers, their growth becomes at some stage self-limiting as the molecule folds into itself. Unlike linear polymers, which present countless rapidly interconverting shapes, dendrimers are nearly spherical in shape with diameters typically between 2 and 10 nm.

During the 1980s, dendrimers were regarded mostly as curiosities. In the 1990s they became of interest in the context of nanotechnology. In addition, the size and near-spherical shape of dendrimers and their ability to simultaneously "host" many small molecules has given them a role as drug-delivery agents carrying high "payloads." The number of functional groups on the exterior surface of a dendrimer molecule offers a Velcro-like array of reactive sites suitable for many potential physical and chemical applications (e.g., 6 reaction tiers produce 2^6 or 64 reaction sites). The initial synthetic strategy for the synthesis of dendrimers, including the one depicted here, was to start from the core and move outward. This approach is termed divergent synthesis. In 1990, Jean M. J. Fréchet (1944–), then at Cornell, pioneered convergent syntheses of dendrimers (i.e., from the outside in). This approach allows assembling of differently functionalized "wedges" attached to the inner core and offers the opportunity to place diverse groups on the exterior surfaces. Starting in the 1990s, interest in the potential applications of dendrimers increased rapidly and presently over 100 patents per year are granted for new dendrimers and their applications.

Nitric Oxide (NO): A Simple but Powerful Physiological Regulator

Nitric oxide (NO) was first isolated by Reverend Joseph Priestley and demonstrated in 1774 to immediately consume oxygen on contact. He

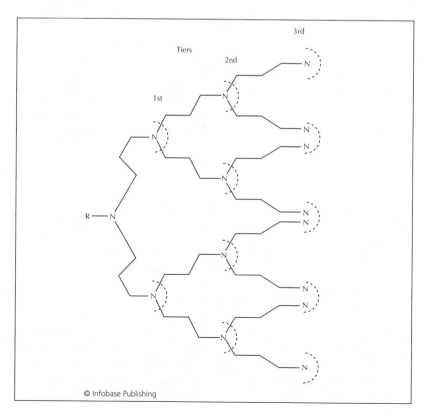

Building plan for a dendritic molecule

The Bhopal Disaster

Major chemical accidents during manufacture, storage, or shipping have certainly occurred in the past and remain concerns today as government and industry strive to even further improve both safety and security. On December 6, 1917, a ship loaded with tons of benzene, guncotton, picric acid, and TNT, awaiting transatlantic crossing to the war in Europe, collided with another ship as it moved toward the Port of Halifax, Canada. The initial fire and explosion attracted onlookers and the second explosion killed 1,900 immediately with a final death toll over 2,000 with some 9,000 injuries. On April 17, 1947, a cargo ship loaded with ammonium nitrate (NH_4NO_3) fertilizer was moored at Texas City, a town of 16,000 residents near Galveston, Texas. A fire broke out aboard ship and the explosion and fire that followed set off another massive fire at the Monsanto plant in the town. The death toll ultimately ran to more than 600.

On December 3, 1984, the worst industrial disaster in history began in Bhopal, India. It involved the accidental release of tons of methyl isocyanate (MIC) and the death in short order of over 2,000 people with hundreds, possibly thousands more in succeeding months and years. The U.S. EPA Web site indicates a final death toll of about 3,800 with adverse and serious health effects for about 170,000 people. Other reputable sources attribute thousands more deaths to the Bhopal incident and its aftermath.

In 1969, Union Carbide had established a plant to produce the pesticide sevin (carbaryl) in Bhopal. One of the chemical intermediates in the synthesis was methyl isocyanate (CH_3NCO), a highly reactive, volatile, and toxic compound. On the day in question there was an inappropriate addition of water to the tank holding MIC. Reaction was rapid, producing CO_2 gas and releasing MIC under pressure. Scrubbing tanks that could have neutralized MIC were not operational and the compound was released into the atmosphere. The terrible results of this tragedy were both short- and long-term. There remain a number of unsolved aspects. In 1989, courts awarded the Indian government $470 million to deal with the aftermath of the Bhopal disaster.

It is certainly difficult to find any redeeming aspect to this story. However, it did lead the Chemical Manufacturers Association (CMA) to adopt, in 1988, its Responsible Care program. The first step was the voluntary Community Awareness & Emergency Response program. While chemical companies have demonstrated commitment to these values, today there is renewed concern over protecting chemical plants from terrorists.

was delighted that mice were no longer needed to test the "goodness of air." NO is a short-lived molecule with a half-life of seconds in O_2. In 1970, Paul Crutzen discovered the potential role of stratospheric NO in destroying ozone (see chapter 7). Known for decades "merely" as an air pollutant, in 1986 this tiny molecule was discovered to be a potent regulator of the cardiovascular system.

For many years Robert F. Furchgott (1916–), at the SUNY Health Science Center in Brooklyn, had investigated the effects of chemicals on relaxation of smooth muscle in vascular tissues. Relaxation of blood vessels enhances blood flow. In 1980 he demonstrated that cells from the innermost layer (the endothelium) in blood vessels produce a chemical factor necessary to relax the smooth muscles in vascular tissues. Furchgott termed it the "endothelium dependent relaxing factor" or EDRF.

It was well known in the late 19th century that ingestion of nitroglycerine eases chest pains caused by angina. Alfred Nobel, who stabilized nitroglycerine with clay to make dynamite, was treated with nitroglycerine to ease his angina. During the late 1970s Ferid Murad (1936–   ), University of Texas Medical School in Houston, discovered that in some smooth muscles nitroglycerine activates guanylyl cyclase. This enzyme converts guanosine triphosphate (GTP) to cyclic guanosinemonophosphate (cGMP). Increased cGMP levels increase muscle relaxation. In 1981, Furchgott discovered that EDRF also stimulates the production of guanylyl cyclase in vascular smooth muscle leading to increased cGMP levels and enhanced relaxation.

Louis J. Ignarro (1941–   ), UCLA School of Medicine, was stimulated by Murad's discovery of the relationship between nitroglycerine, the formation of cGMP, and vascular muscle relaxation. He investigated the ability of nitroglycerine and other organic nitrates, nitrite esters such as isoamyl nitrite, and nitroprusside [$(CN)_5$Fe-NO] to release nitric oxide and demonstrated that they all did so in aqueous solutions. In 1979, Ignarro demonstrated that gaseous NO itself relaxes calf bovine arteries. At a 1986 conference at the Mayo Clinic, Ignarro and Furchgott independently concluded that Furchgott's EDRF was in fact nitric oxide (NO). The discovery that a simple diatomic gas molecule is a potent biological regulator was unprecedented and amazed the research community. Subsequently, the source of intracellular NO was identified as the amino acid arginine, oxidized by O_2 in the presence of various nitric oxide synthases (NOS). Robert F. Furchgott, Louis J. Ignarro, and Ferid Murad shared the 1998 Nobel Prize in physiology or medicine.

While guanylyl cyclase increases membrane levels of the vasodilator cGMP, a phosphodiesterase enzyme breaks down cGMP. In 1985, the Pfizer Corporation sought a drug that could mimic cGMP and block the activity of phosphodiesterase while not inhibiting cGMP's role as a vasodilator. Such a drug would offer potential to lower blood pressure and reduce angina. Pfizer employed molecular modeling in rational drug design and synthesized hundreds of molecules that mimic the structure of cGMP. This led to the discovery of sildenafil (Viagra), fully licensed in 1998 and marketed to men of the baby-boomer generation seeking to extend their youthful years.

Combinatorial Chemistry: Thousands of Candidate Drugs in a Few Easy Steps

There are many different ways to search for new and effective pharmaceuticals. Typically a "lead" compound is found in nature following extraction (e.g., from tree bark or bacteria) and purification. A "library" of related compounds may then be created one-by-one through chemical modification of the lead compound, careful purification, and testing.

Study of the mechanism of action, QSAR, and molecular modeling (see chapter 8) are all systematic methods for design of individual promising candidates followed by laborious synthesis, purification, and testing.

As so often happens in science, there is some debate about the primacy of the discovery of combinatorial chemistry. After all, it is almost certain that Carl Wilhelm Scheele was the first to discover oxygen (ca. 1771–72) but the discovery was made independently in 1774 by Joseph Priestley who published first. Similarly, Árpád Furka (1931–   ), at the Eötvös Lóránd University in Budapest, first described the concept that would later be called *combinatorial chemistry* in a document notarized in May 1982. A Ph.D. thesis by his student on this topic was completed in 1987 and presented at conferences in Prague and Budapest in 1988 (a year before the fall of the Berlin Wall and the end of the cold war). His work first appeared in a refereed journal in 1991. In 1984, H. Mario Geysen (1944–   ) at Glaxo Wellcome in North Carolina published research that employed combinatorial chemistry. In that year, Richard A. Houghton (1946–   ) started the nonprofit Torrey Pines Institute for Molecular Studies and developed the "tea bag" method of combinatorial chemistry.

What is clear is that all of these early combinatorial experiments had their basis in the solid-phase peptide synthesis developed in 1964 by Bruce Merrifield (see chapter 7). The Furka "split-mix" technique is outlined in the figure on page 337. For the sake of brevity, only 3 different components (X, Y, and Z) are depicted and only trimers (3 steps) are depicted so that the "library" has 3^3 entries (combinations). In practice, Furka was initially interested in peptide synthesis. If all 20 common amino acids are employed to make a library of pentapeptides, then the number of entries is 20^5 or 3.2 million. For a decapeptide, the library would have 1.02×10^{13} entries. The use of solid-phase beads serves two purposes:

- As in Merrifield's original design, it permits ease of use, rapid clean-up, high-yields and "one-pot" synthesis

- In using beads, it is very easy to add a large excess of reagents so that the less-reactive amino acids and peptides ultimately react as fully as the more reactive amino acids and peptides providing, in principle, equal "weighting" for all combinations.

The first step is to take the three different building blocks (X, Y, and Z) and, in three separate tubes, chemically attach each to the polymeric

(Opposite page) *An early example of combinatorial chemistry methodology: Furka's split/mix bead separation technique. Contrary to chemical orthodoxy, this clever technique actually has chemists mixing (rather than always separating) substances. The very simple example shown might be a way of forming a "library" of 27 tripeptides. The one having desired activity could bind with a substrate that fluoresces when it binds allowing one to remove the fluorescing beads and determine the structure of the active tripeptide.*

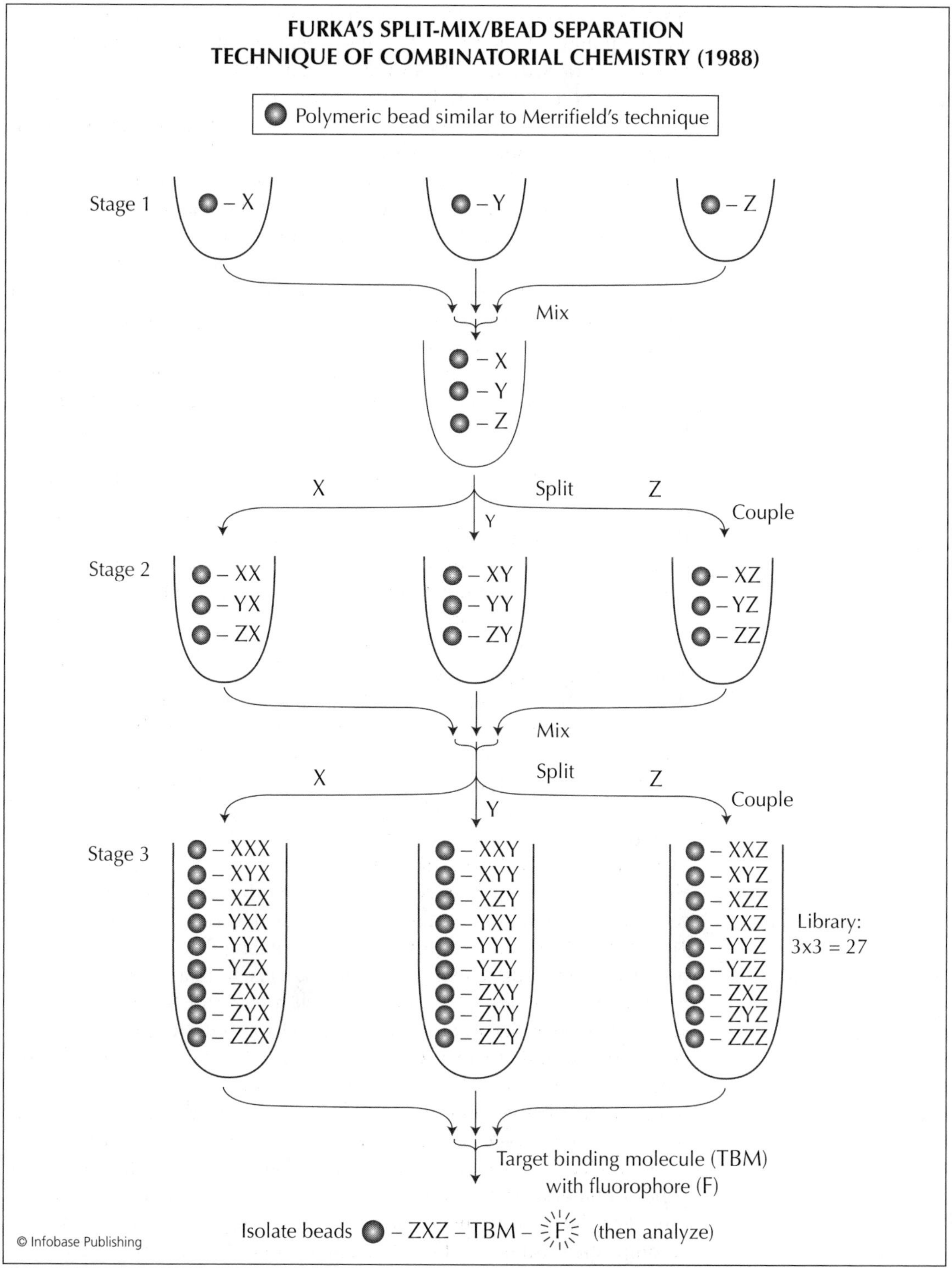

FURKA'S SPLIT-MIX/BEAD SEPARATION
TECHNIQUE OF COMBINATORIAL CHEMISTRY (1988)

Polymeric bead similar to Merrifield's technique

Stage 1 ● – X   ● – Y   ● – Z

Mix

● – X
● – Y
● – Z

X   Split   Z
Y   Couple

Stage 2

● – XX   ● – XY   ● – XZ
● – YX   ● – YY   ● – YZ
● – ZX   ● – ZY   ● – ZZ

Mix

X   Split   Z
Y   Couple

Stage 3

● – XXX   ● – XXY   ● – XXZ
● – XYX   ● – XYY   ● – XYZ
● – XZX   ● – XZY   ● – XZZ
● – YXX   ● – YXY   ● – YXZ
● – YYX   ● – YYY   ● – YYZ
● – YZX   ● – YZY   ● – YZZ
● – ZXX   ● – ZXY   ● – ZXZ
● – ZYX   ● – ZYY   ● – ZYZ
● – ZZX   ● – ZZY   ● – ZZZ

Library:
3x3 = 27

Target binding molecule (TBM)
with fluorophore (F)

Isolate beads ● – ZXZ – TBM – ☼F☼ (then analyze)

resin beads (Stage 1). The next step is the truly unconventional one: equal amounts of the three different labeled beads are mixed. This flies in the face of orthodox chemistry; normally chemists separate mixtures into pure components rather than create mixtures from pure components. The mixture is then split into three identical fractions and, in Stage 2, one fraction reacts with X, another with Y, and another with Z to generate three different and unique species in each of the three tubes (9 combinations total). One more round of "mix-and-split" generates three tubes containing 9 different and unique tripeptides each and these are again mixed to make one tube containing all 27 combinations. These steps have accomplished the synthesis of every possible combination in equal amounts. How does one find which tripeptide (there may be more than one) has the desirable property—perhaps selective binding for a substrate? There are countless possibilities but one might imagine a substrate molecule with a chromophore (light-absorbing group) attached to it that fluoresces only when it is bound to a tripeptide. If binding turns out to be selective, then only a small fraction of the beads will fluoresce, these can be separated, and the tripeptide sequence attached to them chemically analyzed. Thus, the truly unique aspects to the approach depicted in the figure are the use of beads with "split/mix" to insure equal amounts of all possible combinations and some sort of signal to indicate which beads have active combinations attached to them. While great excitement met the earliest applications of combinatorial chemistry, today it is one more method in the chemical toolbox. It has also been extended to fields well beyond pharmaceutical chemistry. Peter G. Schultz (1956–) developed microcombinatorial techniques applicable to many fields while at Berkeley and continues this work at Scripps Research Institute and as the director of the Novartis Institute for Functional Genomics.

Another approach to combinatorial chemistry is termed "parallel synthesis." Very simply exemplified, one might imagine a potential "library" of antimalarials related to the structure depicted on page 337. Synthesis of 10 molecules each with methyl ($X = CH_3$) at the same position on one ring and 10 different Y substituents on the other can start a library. If 7 other x substituents are synthesized and each in turn reacted to add to the 10 different Y substituents, then a library totaling 80 candidates has been produced. One might imagine taking 20 closely related molecules and conducting 50 separate reactions on each to create 1,000 different molecules. If 40 new separate reactions are performed on these 1,000 molecules, this would create a total "library" of 40,000 potential candidates. The compounds in each of the 40,000 individual test tubes or reaction wells are fully known and catalogued in advance of testing. If a particular protein or membrane of interest binds to 12 of these "library entries," for example, these candidates may be further studied for the "molecular logic" of binding to find a best candidate or perhaps a well designed new candidate. Such an immense program of parallel syntheses and assays is accomplished using robotics. The application of either of these combinatorial approaches helps to explain some of the explosive growth in the CAS Registry of known compounds described in the introduction to this book.

"Wings for Molecular Elephants" and the Beginnings of Proteomics

Nuclear magnetic resonance (NMR) spectrometers continued to evolve during the 1980s as larger superconducting magnets and more complex pulse sequences (2-D, 3-D, 4-D) made it a formidable technique for determining the structures of huge biomolecules in solution. The accompanying photograph shows an 800 MHz NMR spectrometer. A major breakthrough in the 1980s was the application of mass spectrometry to analysis of "molecular elephants" such as proteins, a process unimaginable a decade earlier.

From its early beginnings in J. J. Thomson's laboratory (see chapter 1) and Aston's discovery of the two isotopes of neon (see chapter 2) through its development as a laboratory tool starting in the 1940s, mass spectrometry was reserved for small molecules having some degree of volatility. In the early 1920s, physicist Arthur J. Dempster (1886–1950), at the University of Chicago, developed the classical magnetic-sector, electron-impact (EI) instruments that would dominate mass spectrometry for many decades. In the EI mode, molecules must be volatilized before they are ionized by high-energy electrons and analyzed for the

800 MHz nuclear magnetic resonance (NMR) spectrometer (University of Illinois-Chicago, Center for Structural Biology)

mass-to-charge (m/e) ratios of "parent" and "daughter" ions. Mass resolution is specified by $m/\Delta m$, meaning that an instrument having a resolution of 1,000 mass units can differentiate between m/e values of 100.1 and 100.2. High-resolution instruments, which focus both mass and velocity, give m/e values accurate to five decimal places or more. This allows accurate determinations of molecular formulas comparable to classical elemental analysis. For example, the precise molecular masses of $C_{12}H_{10}N_2$ (182.08440) and $C_{13}H_{10}O$ (182.07317) differ in the second decimal place and are accurately determined by high-resolution MS. Another later development was chemical ionization (CI) mass spectrometry. In EI mass spectrometry molecules collide with high-energy electron beams (70 eV electrons; typical C-C bonds are only ~ 4 eV in strength). Fragmentation of the molecular ("parent") ion (M^+) into many smaller "daughter" ions offers the advantage of a complex fragmentation pattern (numerous m/e peaks of characteristic intensities) and a virtual "molecular fingerprint." Highly energetic parent ions often decompose so rapidly that they never reach the detector, thus losing information on molecular mass and confounding interpretation. This can be mitigated using a lower-energy electron beam (e.g., 15 eV) for EI. In CI, a reagent gas (often CH_4) is added in thousandfold excess. The unstable reagent ions formed under high vacuum (CH_5^+) collide with the gas molecules to be analyzed in a much "softer" manner: typically protonating them to form MH^+, the "pseudomolecular ion," with much less fragmentation and with near-certainty of the molecular weight M (actually M+1).

The 1970s and 1980s would witness "democratization" of mass spectrometry. The large magnetic sector instruments of the 1960s were replaced by less expensive and smaller time-of-flight (TOF) mass spectrometers (ions "racing" in a straight line to detectors—lightest arriving first), quadrupole mass spectrometers (specific ions tuned in resonance arriving at detectors), and ion trap mass spectrometers. Throughout the 1980s and beyond, benchtop GC/MS instrumentations became available for under $100,000, an amazingly low price for such capability.

The breakthroughs in mass spectral analysis of huge (nonvolatile) biomolecules began in earnest in the 1980s although there were earlier progenitors. Clearly, any attempt to volatilize a protein, DNA, or polysaccharide molecule by heating it (even in high vacuum) will fail since they decompose rather than volatilize. In 1981, Michael Barber (1934–91), in Manchester, England, developed a technique called fast atom bombardment (FAB). It involved hitting the surface of a solution containing large molecules with a high kinetic energy stream of atoms (frequently xenon) such that these large molecules were propelled into the gas phase and ionized. The FAB technique is still in use. In 1984, Koichi Tanaka (1959–   ), working at Shimadzu Corporation in Kyoto, Japan, with a group analyzing laser desorption of surfaces, made an accidental but critical discovery. He found that a matrix consisting of glycerin and ultrafine metallic particles (UFMP) was very efficient in absorbing UV laser light and transferring the energy to huge molecules (and associated ions) in the matrix. These became charged gas-phase species that lose attached matrix molecules to the vacuum prior to entering a TOF mass spectrometer (see the figure below). The process discovered by Tanaka and his colleagues is called matrix-assisted laser desorption/ionization (MALDI). By late 1987, Shimadzu Corporation reported analyses of substances with mass numbers as high as 72,000. MALDI-TOF mass spectrometry rapidly became one of two principle modern techniques for analyzing biomolecules such as proteins. The MALDI matrix usually contains an

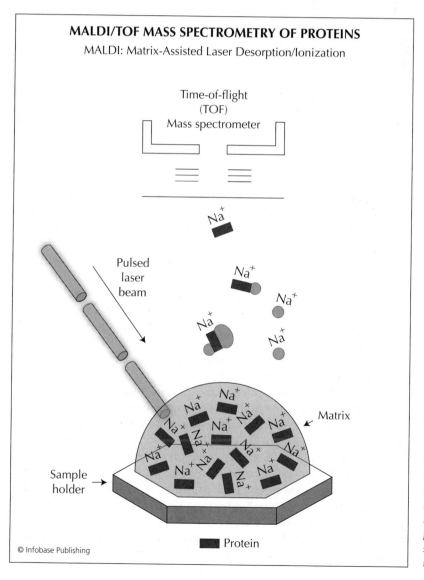

MALDI/TOF MASS SPECTROMETRY OF PROTEINS
MALDI: Matrix-Assisted Laser Desorption/Ionization

Time-of-flight (TOF) Mass spectrometer

Pulsed laser beam

Matrix

Sample holder

Protein

© Infobase Publishing

Schematic representation of MALDI (matrix-assisted laser desorption ionization) in conjunction with mass spectrometry. A protein salt is mixed into a matrix that is subjected to pulsed laser beams. Small volumes of matrix-bound proteins are aerosolized and stripped of matrix molecules under high vacuum.

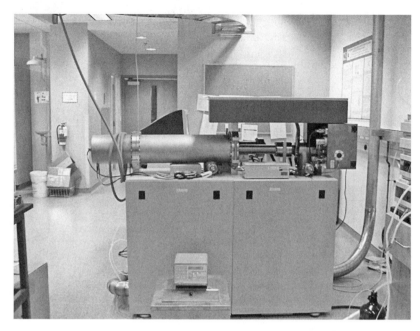

organic acid. Most ions produced in MALDI are singly charged so that the m/e values directly reflect molecular mass. The accompanying photograph shows a MALDI-TOF mass spectrometer.

The other great breakthrough in mass spectrometry during the 1980s was the development of electrospray ionization (ESI) by John B. Fenn (1917–   ) at Yale University. This technique was actually first explored by Malcolm Dole (1903–90), at Northwestern University, in 1968 for analysis of polymers such as polystyrene and its oligomers. Fenn was pointed toward Dole's work by Sandy Lipsky and Csaba Horvath at Yale Medical School, scientists who played early roles in pioneering GC/MS and HPLC (see chapter 7). Fenn made the technique into a practical one for analyzing peptides and proteins around 1988. Solutions containing huge molecules move through an electrically charged capillary tube entering a vacuum chamber en route to a mass spectrometer such as a TOF or quadrupole system. The electrostatic-charged exit of the capillary tube can produce charges on the macromolecule of interest. A mildly acidic solution of a protein molecule may also form a poly-protonated ion (there are numerous basic sites on a typical protein). If a protein of mass 120,000 has 20 protons attached to it, its actual m/e is only 6,000. Once formed the suspended microdroplets in the electrospray are stripped of solvent in the vacuum chamber forming huge multiply charged ions that are accelerated by ion-focusing lenses and separated according to their m/e ratios. Some of the early work involved analysis of the cyclic peptide cyclosporine: a single dominant m/e 1,203 peak corresponded to its molecular mass (1,184) plus H_3O^+. The cyclic peptide gramicidin S (the first peptide ever sequenced, see chapter 5), had its dominant ion at a mass close to half the molecular weight indicating that it was diprotonated. Fenn referred to the process of creating multiply charged gas-phase ions of huge biomolecules as "Ionic Wings for Molecular Elephants." ESI became a natural "partner" for high performance liquid chromatography (HPLC) as well as for another protein separation technique called capillary electrophoresis (CE). The MALDI and ESI techniques have become major contributors to protein sequencing. John B. Fenn and Koichi Tanaka shared the 2002 Nobel Prize in chemistry, for their development of mass spectrometric methods, with Kurt Wüthrich (see chapter 8) for his application of NMR to the studies of large biomolecules.

The development of these powerful mass spectrometry techniques in the late 1980s led to the development of a new field called proteomics in the 1990s. While many people are familiar with the term *genomics* (sequencing the genomes of various species and types of proteins encoded), fewer are aware of proteomics. An exceedingly simple definition is that proteomics involves the comparison of the levels of the full complement of proteins in the "well" and "diseased" states of an organism. This entails understanding the functions of these proteins and the interrelationships between hundreds if not thousands of proteins. It is a field that ties together detailed chemical analysis, molecular biology, and a new field called bioinformatics.

A brief outline of the analysis of proteins using mass spectrometry is provided below. It is well to remember that the Edman degradation, starting at the C-end of proteins (see chapter 6), also remains an important technique today. Typically, a complex protein extract is spotted in the middle of the left side of a polyacrylomide gel electrophoresis plate that has varied acidity from top (acidic) to bottom (alkaline) with the middle being neutral. The plate is connected to electrodes and the proteins migrate based upon their *charges* in either direction in a vertical line on the left-hand side of the plate. The second dimension involves mixing with an anionic detergent with migration left-to-right depending on molecular mass (highest mass migrates most slowly). The result is a two-dimensional array of (mostly) separated individual proteins. Individual gel spots may be located and scraped and the individual proteins digested by enzymes (e.g., trypsin) of known specificities for peptide linkages, the technique developed decades earlier by Frederick Sanger (see chapter 6). The mixture of peptides formed can be spotted on a plate and analyzed by MALDI. The m/e values of the various singly charged peptides, as well as information on their natural isotopic distribution, can be employed to provide overlaps of fragments and sequences as Sanger had done earlier. Alternatively, protein fragments may be separated by HPLC or capillary electrophoresis and analyzed using ESI. Any peptides that elude analysis by these techniques may be subjected to tandem mass spectrometry (MS/MS). In MS/MS, individual ions generated by MALDI are sent one-by-one into a second MS that produces EI fragmentation that may lead to complete structural solution. A proteomics study would compare the results from a 2-D gel study of the proteins of a healthy individual with that of a diseased individual.

How Regulatory Proteins Are "Marked for Destruction"

Proteins in living organisms are in dynamic equilibrium: constant synthesis and degradation. This protein "turnover" was first documented by Rudolph Schoenheimer (see chapter 6) in his book *The Dynamical State of Bodily Constituents*, published in 1942, the year after he died. The presence of Harold Urey at Columbia made that university an early center for metabolism research using isotopic labeling. Schoenheimer received ^{15}N, a nonradioactive isotope, from his colleague Urey, and employed mass spectrometry to monitor the turnover of ^{15}N-labelled proteins. Protein and peptide degradation to amino acids occurs in the gastrointestinal tract and is catalyzed by enzymes such as pepsin (stomach) and trypsin (small intestine). As catalysts, enzymes increase reaction rates but do not affect equilibria. These *extracellular* reactions are exergonic (favorable free energy change), due simply to the high concentration of water that favors hydrolysis of the peptide linkage. In 1953, Melvin V. Simpson (1921–), then at Tufts College of Medicine, discovered that the rapid metabolic breakdown of *intracellular* regulatory proteins actually requires energy in the form of ATP.

In 1976, Aaron Ciechanover (1947–), a young M.D. fresh from military service in Israel, recommenced studies with Avram Hershko (1937–), a biochemist at the Technion in Haifa. They were interested in the intracellular degradation of abnormal hemoglobin, an example of an energy dependent (ATP-requiring) proteolysis. They discovered an ATP-dependent proteolytic factor that could be separated into two inactive fractions: APF-I and APF-II. That was contrary to the accepted concept of catalysis by a single protease. In 1980, APF-1 was demonstrated to be identical to ubiquitin, a 76-residue amino acid protein found in 1975 by Gideon Goldstein (1937–), NYU School of Medicine and Sloan-Kettering, to be "ubiquitous" in eukaryotic cells. By 1980, Hershko and Ciechanover were collaborating with Irwin Rose (1926–), then at the Fox Chase Cancer Center, on the APF studies. A key breakthrough occurred in 1982 when the mechanism and role of the ubiquitin-activating (E1) enzymes was discovered.

Rapid breakdown of regulatory proteins inside the cell is quite logical. Once they are synthesized and accomplish their delicate regulatory roles, rapid breakdown is required in order to shut them off. The energy (ATP) requirement is not associated with the breakdown of these proteins, a thermodynamically favorable process inside the cell. Energy is required for the formation of covalent bonds between ubiquitin and proteins "marked for destruction." In effect, ubiquitin "tags" the intracellular protein for catalytic destruction by a huge complex called the 26S proteosome that acts as a protease. "S" refers to the ultracentrifuge sedimentation coefficient that is discussed further in chapter 10. A complex of three different enzymes (E1, E2, and E3) comprises the "tagging" mechanism. Ubiquitin (or a peptide chain composed of ubiquitins) forms a high-energy thioester (-CO-S–) linkage at its carboxylate-end with a cysteine (SH-containing) linkage on the E1 (Ub-activating) enzymes. ATP is required much as it is in the formation of acetyl CoA, another thioester (see chapter 5). E2 and E3 enzymes work in concert to recognize and transfer ubiquitin to the protein marked for destruction. What marks a protein for destruction? In 1986, Alexander J. Vershavsky (1946–), a Russian-born biochemist at MIT, reported that the lifetimes of intracellular proteins are determined by the identities of the amino acids on their N-termini (the "N-degron"). For example, the half-lives of proteins with serine as the N-degron are relatively long (>20 minutes) while those with the aspartic acid N-degron have half-lives around 3 minutes.

The ubiquitin-mediated degradation of intracellular proteins is a universal phenomenon in eukaryotic cells that is fundamental to the regulation of various cell processes. In 2004, Aaron Ciechanover, Avram Hershko, and Irwin Rose shared the Nobel Prize in chemistry for their discovery of this pathway.

Total Structure and Function of a Complete Photosynthesis Reaction Center

In 1957, John C. Kendrew determined a low-resolution X-ray crystallographic structure for the protein myoglobin. In 1960, Max Perutz achieved a low-resolution structure for hemoglobin. By the late 1970s, many other proteins had been solved crystallographically and at higher resolution but there remained a widespread belief that proteins embedded in membranes could not be crystallized. In 1985, a complete crystallographic structure was obtained for the photosynthetic reaction center embedded in the purple cell membranes of the photosynthetic bacteria *Rhodopseudomonas viridis*. This reaction center consists of four protein subunits (H [heavy], M [medium], L [light], and a cytochrome) bound with 14 cofactors including chlorophylls, the closely related pheophytin molecules, quinones, carotenoids, and nonheme iron. The photosynthetic center is about 130 Å (13 nm) in length and its elliptical cross section has diameters of 70 Å (7 nm) and 30 Å (3 nm). The function of this center is to capture light energy and harness it to pump electrons across the cell membrane. A decade later, such a structure would likely be classified as a biological nanomachine.

The stunning feat of purifying this protein complex, obtaining X-ray crystallographic data, and solving the three-dimensional structure was accomplished by three German scientists working together at the Max Planck Institute for Biochemistry during the early 1980s. Robert Huber (1937–) was a chemist by training who moved steadily into crystallography and then protein crystallography and the crystallography of antibodies. Johann Diesenhofer (1943–) was trained in physics and moved into solid state physics prior to joining Huber's group in 1971. Hartmut Michel (1948–) was a biologist who studied the membranes of bacteria and joined Huber's group in the early 1980s. He was the first to obtain crystalline membrane protein samples suitable for X-ray analysis. The structural studies of this team of scientists established the function of the photosynthetic reaction center. The complete structure was completed in 1985 with improvement to atomic (e.g., 2.3 Å) resolution in 1987. It is a measure of the impact of this work that Huber, Diesenhofer, and Michel shared the 1988 Nobel Prize in chemistry only three years after their first solution for the structure of this amazing protein complex.

Catalytic RNA ("Ribozymes") and Conjectures about a Prebiotic "RNA World"

The regular, rigid tubular structure of the DNA double helix was a key factor in its rapid solution by Watson and Crick over a half century ago. In contrast, the single-stranded RNA molecules have freedom to adopt winding, irregular shapes and pose more challenging structural problems. RNA serves a variety of roles in the transcription of the genetic code to form proteins on ribosomes: messenger RNA (mRNA), ribosomal RNA (rRNA), and transfer RNA (tRNA).

Starting in the late 1970s, Thomas R. Cech (1947–) and coworkers at the University of Colorado began a study of the rRNA gene in the ciliated protozoan *Tetrahymena*. The gene is located on a smaller DNA molecule free of chromosomal protein and is thus relatively easy to isolate. It actually codes for an rRNA segment that is longer than the final rRNA. In this precursor rRNA there are intervening segments (IVS), or introns, that are cut out while the remaining exons, segments having genetic information, are spliced to form active mRNA. Cech discovered that the cutting and splicing of precursor mRNA is catalyzed, not by a conventional enzyme (i.e., a protein), but by the precursor mRNA itself. His research group scrupulously analyzed the precursor mRNA for protein impurities that might be the source of its rapid breakdown but, to their surprise and growing enthusiasm, found none. Cech and his coworkers were forced to conclude that precursor mRNA catalyzes its own cutting and splicing. The idea that an RNA molecule could behave as an enzyme (termed a *ribozyme*) was revolutionary and was resisted by many enzymologists on very fundamental grounds. Rigorously speaking, a catalyst accelerates a chemical reaction without being consumed (or changed) during the course of the reaction. Individual catalyst units typically "turn over" hundreds, thousands, or many more substrate molecules. In the case of the precursor mRNA, the molecule itself emerged from the reaction changed, that is excised from the original precursor with no remaining cut/splice activity. Cech, however, isolated the small segment of the mRNA precursor containing the IVS and demonstrated that it alone showed catalytic activity for other precursor mRNA molecules.

Sidney Altman (1939–   ) of Yale University, was, during this period, performing an unrelated study of precursor tRNAs and discovered a very specific reaction that cleaves the 5'-leader segment from these precursors to produce the final tRNAs. Altman and his colleagues isolated a noncovalent RNA-protein complex they named RNase P ("P" for "precursor") responsible for this catalytic behavior. These enzymes are found in all living cells. An individual RNase P has the ability to cleave leader segments from the 5'-end of the full family of precursor-tRNAs. Typically, Mg^{2+} and the nucleotide guanosine (G) are required for activity; the G being added to the new 5' end of the tRNA. It was relatively easy for Altman's group to separate the RNA part (some 400 nucleotides) from the protein and they were able to demonstrate that all of the enzymatic activity rests with RNA. The protein component increased the activity of the RNA component by a factor of 10-20, significant but very small in magnitude.

In contrast to proteins, which include 20 different amino acids and a "toolbox" of chemical functions, polarities, acidic and basic ionization constants, RNA has but four nucleotides and seemingly not a very promising catalytic chemistry. Solving the chemical mechanisms of ribozyme catalysis required X-ray crystallographic and NMR-based solution structures before realistic hypotheses could be advanced. Such studies started during the late 1980s and continue today. In the face of the initial skepticism in the enzymology community, Altman cited another RNA-protein complex, the ribosome, on which proteins are synthesized catalytically. During the 1990s, high-resolution studies of the ribosome began and, in 2000, two papers appearing in the journal *Science* reporting atomic-scale resolution (2.4 Å) crystallographic structures for the large ribosomal unit of a specific species of bacteria (see chapter 10). The study disclosed that the active sites for protein synthesis in ribosomes are localized in the RNA component, not the protein component. This strongly supports the "ribozyme" hypothesis. Thomas R. Cech and Sidney Altman shared the 1989 Nobel Prize in chemistry.

The discovery that some RNA molecules act as enzymes even as they function as repositories for information excited scientists investigating the origins of life (see chapters 6 and 8). One still-relevant question is a classic "chicken or egg" paradox: Which came first, nucleic acids or proteins? Protein synthesis requires DNA and RNA while DNA synthesis requires proteins (enzymes). Carl R. Woese (1967), Francis Crick (1968), and Leslie Orgel (1968) independently postulated that life, based upon RNA, might have predated DNA/protein-based life. The information content and potential for self-replication of RNA through base pairing fit one set of criteria while the ability of single-stranded RNA to adopt folded conformations suggested to them potential enzyme-like activity. The discovery of ribozymes, by Cech and Altman, supported the concept of an "RNA world" suggested by Walter Gilbert in 1986, not yet requiring the genetic code, at the cusp between nonliving and living matter over 3.7 billion years ago. There remain many tantalizing hints about this possibility as well as limitations (e.g., extremely low yields and limited stability of ribose under prebiotic conditions). A decade later "ribozyme engineering" somewhat broadened the possibilities in an "RNA World," while hypothesis of an even more elementary PNA (peptide nucleic acid) family (see chapter 10) suggests a very different scenario.

PCR: A "Printing Press" for Genes

Kary B. Mullis (1944–   ) was born and raised in rural North Carolina where he developed interests in chemistry and rockets among other country pastimes. He obtained his B.S. in chemistry at Georgia Tech and a Ph.D. in biochemistry at Berkeley. In 1979, he joined the fledgling biotechnology company Cetus Corporation. It was at Cetus that Mullis invented the *polymerase chain reaction* (*PCR*) technique that allows the amplification of picograms (10^{-12} g) of a specific DNA, roughly 100,000 molecules, to micrograms (10^{-6} g) or about 100 billion molecules, in a few hours. PCR is commonly used to amplify human DNA, for example, to prove guilt or innocence in a crime. But it can also be applied to multiply the genetic material from a frozen woolly mammoth for sequencing and comparison with modern elephants. Michael Crichton and Stephen Spielberg popularized PCR in the novel and movie *Jurassic Park* in which minuscule amounts of DNA in dinosaur blood extracted from Jurassic mosquitoes trapped in amber are multiplied with results wonderful and terrible. There is also a direct connection of the PCR technique with the "extremophiles" discovered little more than a decade earlier in the hot springs of Yellowstone National Park (see chapter 8). PCR requires enzymes that are highly active and stable at very high temperatures and the "extremozymes" seem to have arrived "made to order."

While considering a technique that could rapidly determine the identity of DNA termini, Mullis reasoned his way to a method that could readily replicate DNA. DNA polymerase is present in every living cell. It adds new nucleotides to a growing strand of DNA only in the 5'→3' direction: a free 3' hydroxyl at the end of a growing DNA chain reacts with a new 5'-mononucleoside triphosphate, eliminates $P_2O_7^{4+}$, and adds one more unit to the growing chain. The original DNA coding strand is synthesized continuously while its complementary (template) strand must be synthesized in fragments. In order for DNA polymerase to function, there must be at least a short section of oligonucleotide already in place to act as a "primer."

The PCR process was first published by Mullis in 1985. It uses a mixture of the DNA to be duplicated, heat-stable polymerase, Mg^{2+} required by the polymerase, the four 2'-deoxyribonucleoside triphosphate building blocks (A,T,C,G), and the oligonucleotide primers (about 20 nucleotides long). There are three main steps in the process:

1. Denaturation of duplex DNA to two molecules of single-stranded DNA. This typically requires a temperature around 203°F (95°C) to break all hydrogen bonds between the two strands in the DNA double helix.
2. Annealing of the short oligonucleotide primers onto the corresponding ends of the coding and template strands of the original DNA. A temperature of about 131°F (55°C) is required to allow the short oligonucleotide and the DNA strand to form, break, and reform hydrogen bonds so as to create the optimal ("annealed") hydrogen-bonded structure.
3. Extension of each growing chain by (heat-stable) DNA polymerase at about 158°F (70°C).

If one was to employ a normal polymerase, fresh enzyme would be needed after the annealing step in each cycle because the high temperatures in the first two steps would denature it. Shortly after developing his concept, it was apparently Mullis who realized that an "extremozyme" was the answer to this problem. Thermophilic "bacteria" were first isolated from hot springs in Yellowstone National Park in 1969 and named *Thermus aquaticus*. Their heat stable DNA polymerase (Taq polymerase) was isolated in 1976 and this was the enzyme Mullis suggested for PCR. Its maximum activity is found in the amazing temperature range of 167–176°F (75–80°C) and it has a half-life of 1.6 hours at 203°F (95°C). Some DNA polymerases actually have the ability to correct a random error in synthesis by cleaving the newest added nucleotide if it is incorrect. These DNA polymerases are said to possess 3'→5' exonuclease activity. Taq polymerase lacks this activity and averages one error per 10,000-50,000 base pairs. Vent polymerase, from another thermophile, has 3'→5' exonuclease activity, causes an order of magnitude fewer errors, and has a half-life of 7 hours at 203°F (95°C). "Taq" still remains the industry standard and in 1989 *Science* named Taq polymerase its first "Molecule of the Year."

Each full PCR cycle doubles DNA content. While 30 cycles can be accomplished in hours and produce, in principle, 10^9 copies, in practice 10^6–10^8 are achieved since the process is not 100 percent efficient. For perspective, it is useful to recall that, in 1455, Johannes Gutenberg printed the very first book using movable type. Relieving monks of the drudgery of handwritten manuscripts and making books widely available, the printing press revolutionized human culture. PCR has already had enormous impact in criminal trials as well as in research laboratories and may well usher in another revolution of comparable impact.

Following years of litigation, Cetus sold all of its PCR intellectual property to Roche pharmaceuticals in 1992 for $300 million and settled with Kary Mullis for $10,000. In 1993 he shared the Nobel Prize in chemistry with Michael Smith of the University of British Columbia for the development of site-directed mutagenesis.

Site-Directed Mutagenesis: Substituting Individual Amino Acids in Proteins

Michael Smith (1932–2000) was born and educated in England but went to Vancouver in 1956 to work in the laboratory of H. Gobind Khorana on synthetic methods for nucleic acids and oligonucleotides. In 1966, he arrived at the University of British Columbia where he would remain for the remainder of his career. "Combinatorial" thinking led Smith to consider what size *oligonucleotides* are required for "unique recognition" of every possible sequence in a complete genome. The formula is simple:

$$4^N \geq 2 \times (\text{Number of Base Pairs})$$

where N = "uniqueness number" = shortest possible oligonucleotide length

For a virus whose genome consists of 4.6×10^4 base pairs, N = 9; therefore, nonanucleotides cover all possible genomic sequences. For *E. coli* (4.1×10^6 base pairs), N = 12 and for humans (3.3×10^9 base pairs), N = 17. Smith was interested in using synthetic oligonucleotides to bind to specific genes as a means for isolation of these genes. In his studies of binding between various oligonucleotides he began to investigate the binding of two otherwise complementary nucleotides in which one base had been changed. These studies led him to develop the powerful site-directed mutagenesis technique.

As noted in chapter 8, plasmids are small circular duplex DNA molecules found outside of the chromosomal material in bacteria. There may be 20 different plasmids in a bacterium like *E. coli*, each containing a small number of genes. These are easily transferred from one bacterium to another and act as "vectors" of genetic material. DNA from other organisms is readily spliced into plasmids and when transferred into *E. coli*, these bacteria produce proteins coded for by the new gene. Smith developed a technique in which he chemically synthesized oligonucleotides (15–20 nucleotides in length), complementary to the gene in question on the plasmid *but* having a single base substitution (a "point mutation") in the middle. The oligonucleotide fragment acts as a primer and, with DNA polymerase, Mg^{2+}, and the four different deoxyribonucleosides, a mutated complement will be formed. Denaturation provides two single-stranded cyclic DNAs: one original ("wild-type") and one mutated. These will produce a 1:1 mixture of the two different plasmids. Alternatively, there are means to selectively degrade the "wild-type" DNA and leave the mutated DNA. The mutant plasmids are transferred into bacteria such as *E. coli* and expressed in the synthesis of mutant proteins whose activities are investigated.

The ability to introduce a point mutation in a gene allows the synthesis of specific proteins with rational replacement of amino acids. In 1982, Smith collaborated with Gregory Winter (1951–) and Alan R. Fersht (1943–) at Cambridge in the very first protein engineering experiment: the design of a mutant form of the enzyme tyrosyl tRNA synthetase. Another study demonstrated that specific replacement of tyrosine 198 in carboxypeptidase-A with phenylalanine, using site-directed mutagenesis, produces a mutant enzyme having the same activity as the "wild-type" enzyme. In this manner, the earlier hypothesis that Tyr-198 played an active catalytic role through its acidic OH group was disproved. In contrast, replacement of glutamate 165 by aspartate in triose phosphate isomerase drastically reduces its activity consistent with the accepted catalytic role of Glu-165 in the active site of the enzyme. For his development of oligonucleotide-based site-directed mutagenesis, Michael Smith shared the 1993 Nobel Prize in chemistry with Kary Mullis.

AIDS: A Worldwide Crisis and a Race to Find Effective Treatment

In 1981, the Centers for Disease Control in Atlanta notified the worldwide health community of a new disease that came to be called acquired immunology deficiency syndrome or AIDS. Two years later, Robert C. Gallo (1937–), at the National Cancer Institute (NCI), and Luc Montagnier (1932–), at the Pasteur Institute, independently discovered that AIDS is caused by a virus, dubbed the human immunodeficiency virus (HIV). They found that HIV is a retrovirus, the first one known to infect humans. Retroviruses were discovered during the first half of the 20th century by Peytan Rous (1879–1970), who received the 1966 Nobel Prize in physiology or medicine. A retrovirus carries RNA instead of DNA in its genome. HIV attacks lymphocytes called T-helper cells which normally confer resistance to disease. When the virus invades a host cell, a reverse transcriptase converts RNA to DNA in the cell's cytosol. Reverse transcriptases are essentially DNA polymerases that use RNA rather than DNA as a substrate in "replication." A duplex of the viral DNA is formed and is incorporated in the chromosomes. The genetically modified T-cells express a series of new proteins including HIV protease and various precursor proteins. HIV protease cleaves the precursor protein into smaller units that provide the full machinery for replication of HIV and infection and destruction of other T-helper cells. The discovery of reverse transcriptases and their function was accomplished by David Baltimore (1938–), Howard M. Temin (1934–94), and Renato

Scientist of the Decade: Richard E. Smalley (1943–2005)

Richard E. Smalley was born to a close-knit family in Akron, Ohio. His early interest in the beauty of nature (and art and music) was stimulated by his mother who loaned him her microscope, a gift from her husband, to examine the one-celled creatures in a nearby pond. Smalley's father sparked his interest in building things and taking them apart. The launching of the *Sputnik* satellite by the USSR in 1957 played a role in moving the future Nobel laureate toward a career in science. In summer 1961 "Rick" Smalley worked in the chemistry laboratory of Dr. Sara Jane Rhoads at the University of Wyoming. Dr. Rhoads, his mother's youngest sibling, was one of the first women to rise to the rank of full professor at an American research university. She received her Ph.D. with William von Eggers Doering at Columbia University and was therefore a "chemical granddaughter" of R. B. Woodward. Her nephew admired her intellect and called her the "Colossus of Rhoads." Smalley entered Hope College in Michigan as a chemistry major that fall, completing his degree at the University of Michigan. From 1965 to 1969 he worked in New Jersey in a laboratory owned by

Richard E. Smalley, who shared the 1996 Nobel Prize in chemistry for the discovery of C_{60} (buckminsterfullerene, or buckyball) (Richard Smalley and Brookhaven National Laboratory)

Dulbecco (1914–   ), who shared the 1975 Nobel Prize in physiology or medicine. The cellular origin of the modified genes was discovered by J. Michael Bishop (1936–   ) and Harold Varmus (1939–   ), who shared the 1989 Nobel Prize in physiology or medicine.

The pharmaceutical approach to AIDS treatment has focused primarily on two vulnerability points in the HIV cycle. The first is inhibition of reverse transcriptase so as to prevent synthesis of viral DNA. The first successful drug in this line of defense was AZT (azidothymidine), authorized for use in 1987. The second point of vulnerability is HIV protease, the enzyme that cleaves the newly formed precursor viral proteins to form the active proteins needed for its duplication. Protease inhibitors would be developed during the 1990s.

It is worthwhile to recall that during the late 1940s Gertrude Elion and George Hitchings at Burroughs Wellcome synthesized the first rationally

Shell Oil, investigating Ziegler-Natta polymerization, and marrying in 1968. Smalley left Shell to pursue graduate studies and completed his Ph.D. in 1973 with Elliot R. Bernstein (1941–) at Princeton. As a postdoctoral researcher at the University of Chicago, Smalley collaborated with Donald H. Levy (1939–) and Lennard Wharton on low-temperature spectroscopy studies that led to supersonic laser-beam spectroscopy. He joined the Rice University faculty in 1976, attracted in part by the laser studies of Robert F. Curl, Jr. The apparatus that Smalley built at Rice would eventually lead to discovery of C_{60} and other buckyballs, major contributions to the nascent field of nanotechnology. Smalley, Kroto, and Smalley shared the 1996 Nobel Prize in chemistry. Thereafter, Smalley devoted his research to buckytubes and started Carbon Nanotechnologies Inc. in Houston devoted to their synthesis and applications.

Rick Smalley was a major contributor to the public debates on energy and nanotechnology. He pushed world governments, especially that of the United States, to plan for the doubling of world population and the disappearance of petroleum by 2050. He was a champion of renewable energy, particularly solar power and its economical distribution worldwide. In 1986, K. Eric Drexler (1955–), then a research associate at the MIT Artificial Intelligence Laboratory, published a stimulating article envisioning nano-assemblers ("nanobots") that could someday be programmed to assemble virtually anything on the nanoscale, given suitable instructions. The scary aspect was the possibility that such nanoassemblers might be capable of assembling other nanoassemblers, thus becoming self-replicating. Smalley and Drexler engaged in a number of spirited discussions in print over the "nanobot" scenario. Smalley specifically postulated limits on nanobot-directed assembly that he called the "fat fingers" and the "sticky fingers" problems. The "fat fingers" limitation questioned whether a nanoscale assembler could really pick up, sort, and accurately place individual nanoscale objects. The "sticky fingers" limitation focused on the knowledge that individual atoms and molecules influence nearest, next-nearest, and even more distant neighboring atoms and molecules, so that replacement or insertion of a "nanopart" should have unpredictable effects on its surroundings, both for the object and its assembler.

Richard E. Smalley died on October 28, 2005, at the age of 62 following a long battle with cancer. He is survived by his wife and two sons.

designed anticancer drugs based upon the new antimetabolite paradigm. Diaminopurine, thioguanine, and 6-mercaptopurine mimic DNA bases and inhibit DNA synthesis, which occurs more rapidly in cancerous cells than in normal cells. This approach was widely adopted and, in 1964, Jerome P. Horwitz (1919–), at the Michigan Cancer Foundation, synthesized azidothymidine (AZT) as an anticancer candidate drug. It was not effective against cancer and not patented. During the early 1980s, the small number of known AIDS cases elicited a weak response from federal and industrial research laboratories. However, Samuel Broder (1945–), at the NCI, persisted and set up a drug-screening program to search for anti-AIDS drugs and some 50 companies sent candidates for testing. Burroughs Wellcome had an active research program focused on antiherpes drugs that inhibit DNA polymerase. In 1985, a candidate drug submitted to the NCI by this company was found to be effective

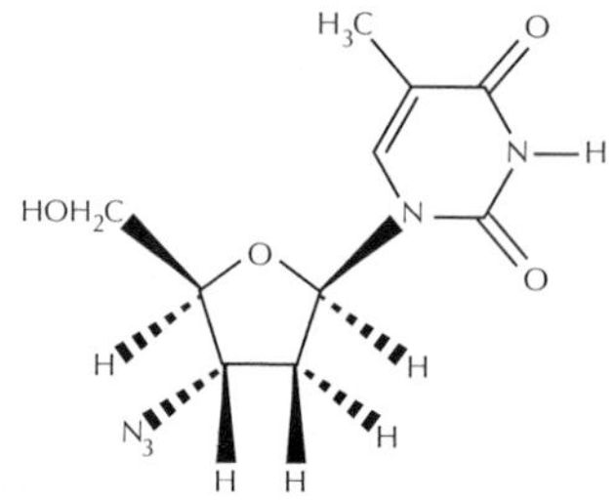

The anti-HIV drug (+)-AZT

against HIV: (+)-AZT (see the figure above). Although AZT was not seen as a cure for AIDS and while its side effects are severe, political activism, especially by the gay community, was successful in obtaining approval by the FDA in 1987 for its use in the treatment of AIDS patients. HIV develops resistance to AZT during prolonged treatment. In combination with other drugs that inhibit this mutation, AZT is still useful in anti-HIV "drug cocktails" although newer related reverse transcriptase inhibitors have followed and become part of anti-HIV treatments during the 1990s.

As AIDS research continued, the focus shifted to study of HIV protease. The crystallographic structure of HIV-1 was determined by Tom Blundell (1942–   ) and coworkers at Birkbeck College in London in 1989. Blundell had studied under Dorothy Hodgkin, the Nobel laureate who solved the structures of penicillin, insulin, and vitamin B_{12}. Study of the active site of HIV-1 protease combined with molecular modeling enabled the design of the family of protease inhibitors, the new anti-HIV drugs of the 1990s and beyond.

Conclusion

The emergence of Japan, China, India, and other Asian nations as regions of chemical innovation and invention will be very striking during the 1990s. The human genome will be solved by J. Craig Venter and the NIH years before the initial predictions. Computational chemistry will become much more accessible and powerful due to advances in theory and increased computer power. Indeed, there will be studies in which computation is considered to be equivalent to experiment. Computers will model protein folding and design new candidate drugs. This need is urgent due to the rapid buildup of immunity by bacteria to antibiotics as well as the threat that the AIDS virus and other deadly viruses may evolve faster than new drugs are developed. "Green Chemistry" will emerge with the promise of much more efficient use of matter with less pollution. Nanotechnology will offer the promise of design and manufacture at the molecular level. Studies of "self-organization" will not only provide a means toward assembling nanomachines, but also will shed light on the nature and origins of life. The ability to modify and produce functional DNA will bring the human race to ask the most fundamental questions about living organisms. As the 20th century comes to an end, chemistry will be so deeply a part of the methodology in different sciences and technology that at times it will seem to simply merge with other sciences.

Further Reading

Baggott, Jim. "Chemistry in a New Light." In *The New Chemistry*, edited by Nina Hall, 43–54. Cambridge: Cambridge University Press (2000). This chapter describes how lasers can be employed to selectively break chemical bonds as well as to monitor femtochemistry.

Ball, Philip. *Elegant Solutions: Ten Beautiful Experiments in Chemistry*, chapter 10. Cambridge: The Royal Society of Chemistry, 2005. This chapter describes the research that led to the exploration of C_{60} (buckyball) and related chemical species.

Baskin, J. Spencer, and Ahmed H. Zewail. "Freezing Atoms in Motion: Principles of Femtochemistry and Demonstration of Laser Stroboscopy." *Journal of Chemical Education* 78 (2001): 737–51. This article has the goal of making femtosecond spectroscopy accessible to teachers and students.

Baum, Rudy. "Point-Counterpoint—Nanotechnology: Drexler and Smalley Make the Case For and Against 'Molecular Assemblers.'" *Chemical & Engineering News* 81 (December 1, 2003): 37–42. This is a very brief debate about the feasibility of "molecular assemblers," sometimes called "nanobots."

Drexler, K. Eric. "Machine-Phase Nanotechnology." *Scientific American* 285 (September 2001): 74–75. This very brief article describes the potential for creation of "molecular self-assemblers."

Halford, Bethany. "Dendrimers Branch Out." *Chemical & Engineering News* 83 (June 13, 2005): 30–36. This is a brief discussion of the applications, including pharmaceutical, of dendrimer molecules.

Heyes, Stephen J. "Structures of Simple Inorganic Solids." Oxford University. Available online. URL: www.chem.ox.ac.uk/icl/heyes/structure_of_solids/Lecture4/Lec4.html. Accessed February 12, 2006. This Oxford University lecture includes a superb discussion of superconducting ceramics and is actually the final lecture in a series of four.

Henry, Celia M. "Drug Delivery." *Chemical & Engineering News* 80 (August 26, 2002): 39–47. This is a presentation of new means, often based on nanotechnology, for effective and selective drug delivery.

Nicolaou, K. C., and W.-M. Dai. "Chemistry and Biology of Enediyne Anticancer Antibiotics." *Angewandte Chemie International Edition* 30 (1991): 1387–1416. This is a review of the structural, mechanistic and medicinal properties of this recently discovered, novel class of anticancer compounds.

———, and Eric J. Sorensen. *Classics in Total Synthesis*. Weinheim: Wiley-VCH, 1996. This is a critical review of some classic total syntheses of complex organic molecules.

———, Dionisius Vourloumis, Nicolas Winssinger, and Phil S. Baran. "The Art and Science of Total Synthesis at the Dawn of the Twenty-First Century." *Angewandte Chemie International Edition* 39 (2000): 44–122. This is an annotated collection of some of the great, classic total syntheses of the late-20th century.

Smalley, Richard E. "Of Chemistry, Love and Nanobots." *Scientific American* 285 (September 2001): 76–77. Nobel Laureate Smalley describes some of the fundamental limitations in the possibilities for creating "molecular assemblers" or "nanobots."

SUPERCONDUCTORS.ORG (Joe Eck). "Type 2 Superconductors." Available online. URL: http://superconductors.org/Type2.htm. Accessed February 12, 2006. This site shows structures for various superconductors and includes a current list of T_c values.

Ward, Peter. *Life As We Do Not Know It.* New York: Viking Penguin, 2005. This book describes the NASA search for extraterrestrial life and related prebiotic experiments.

The Wellcome Trust. "Two-Dimensional Polyacrylamide Gel Electrophoresis." Available online. URL: www.wellcome.ac.uk/en/genome/technologies/hg17b013.html. Accessed February 12, 2006. This site provides an introduction to modern molecular biology operations applied in genomics and proteomics.

Zewail. Ahmed H. "Chemistry at the Uncertainty Limit." *Angewandte Chemie International Edition* 40 (2001): 4,371–75. This is a nonmathematical presentation of the relationship between femtosecond (10^{-15} s) spectroscopy [and even attosecond (10^{-18} s) spectroscopy] with the Heisenberg uncertainty principle.

10

1991–2000:
Understanding and Designing
Supermolecular Systems

Synthesis, Analysis, and Computational Studies of Large Molecules and Supermolecular Complexes

The scientific journey toward the anticipated *"island of stability"* for super-heavy elements will continue and yield a relatively stable isotope for element 114, providing support for that concept. Further exploration of the periodic table will provide the first stable argon compound. Computational chemistry will take a leap forward as *density function theory* (*DFT*) permits very sophisticated calculations, thought previously to be impossible, on very large molecules. The powerful synthetic and analytical techniques developed during the most recent decades will provide chemists with the ability to study large and complex molecules. This will include construction of molecule-size motors and motor parts as a new field, nanotechnology, offers the promise of a trillion-dollar business in the early 21st century. Biochemistry, molecular biology, and structural biology will merge as sophisticated techniques in X-ray crystallography, NMR, mass spectrometry, recombinant DNA technology, and computational chemistry offer powerful techniques to probe nature. Membrane channel proteins for water as well as ions and proteins that assist the folding of newly created or damaged proteins will be discovered and their structures solved. The atomic-scale resolution of the structure of a *ribosome* will provide insights into the operation of one of nature's sophisticated nanomachines and provides another proof of the catalytic role of RNA. The *Hubble Space Telescope* will provide the first data on the chemical composition of an extrasolar planet. The decade will end with the announcement of the completion of the sequence of 90 percent of the humane genome with virtual completion (99 percent) only three years later.

Testing the Periodic Table Near the "Island of Stability"

During the period 1991–2000 (and shortly afterward), elements 110-112, 114, 116, and 118 were reported. The initial claim for 116 and 118 was retracted in 2001. A more reliable observation of 116 was published in 2001. Elements 113 and 115 were reported in 2004 along with the possible observation of 118. These ambiguities arise from the considerable difficulty in performing and interpreting these experiments. Elements 110 and 111 have been fully validated and assigned official names. Element 112 is likely to be accorded this status in the near future. There is currently consensus favoring elements 113-116, while the evidence for 118 became much more solid in 2006.

The superheavy elements are leading to deeper understanding of nuclear chemistry and the periodic table much as the lanthanides did at the start of the 20th century and the actinides did in mid-century. The favored +3 oxidation states of the lanthanides have electronic configurations $4f^1$, $4f^2$, $4f^3$ . . . $4f^{12}$, $4f^{13}$, $4f^{14}$ for the 14 consecutive lanthanides Ce^{+3} through Lu^{+3} respectively. These rare earths are chemically similar (and hard to separate) because their 4f orbitals exert little influence on reactivity. When Glenn T. Seaborg synthesized americium (95) and curium (96) in 1944, he discovered that, like the lanthanides, they readily form +3 oxidation states and fill 5f orbitals. In 1944, he proposed a new transi-

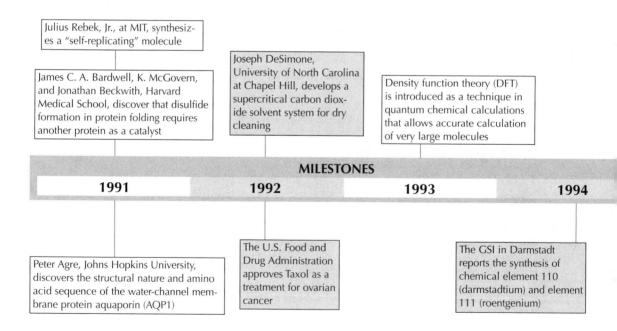

Julius Rebek, Jr., at MIT, synthesizes a "self-replicating" molecule

James C. A. Bardwell, K. McGovern, and Jonathan Beckwith, Harvard Medical School, discover that disulfide formation in protein folding requires another protein as a catalyst

Joseph DeSimone, University of North Carolina at Chapel Hill, develops a supercritical carbon dioxide solvent system for dry cleaning

Density function theory (DFT) is introduced as a technique in quantum chemical calculations that allows accurate calculation of very large molecules

MILESTONES

1991 **1992** **1993** **1994**

Peter Agre, Johns Hopkins University, discovers the structural nature and amino acid sequence of the water-channel membrane protein aquaporin (AQP1)

The U.S. Food and Drug Administration approves Taxol as a treatment for ovarian cancer

The GSI in Darmstadt reports the synthesis of chemical element 110 (darmstadtium) and element 111 (roentgenium)

tion series, the actinides (89-102, but "chemically speaking," thorium, 90 to 103, see chapter 7), even though only 7 of 14 actinides were actually known at the time. The model worked amazingly well. When elements 103-105 were synthesized during the 1960s, 103 (lawrencium) was found to be most stable in the +3 oxidation state typical of actinides beyond uranium while elements 104 and 105 (rutherfordium and dubnium) resembled the d-block transition metals hafnium and tantalum respectively. Seaborg was honored by naming element 106 after him as well as by inauguration of the Glenn T. Seaborg Institute (GTSI) at Lawrence Livermore National Laboratory, cofounded by Darleane C. Hoffman (1926–), its first director.

As comforting as these agreements with expectation are, there are many potential complications. There are complex corrections for relativity that affect inner s and p atomic orbitals differently than outer d and f orbitals and these grow more significant in the heavy and superheavy elements. When relativistic effects are included, the inner s and p orbitals contract somewhat and better shield electrons. Consequently, the outer d and f orbitals expand a bit. These relativistic corrections lend extra stability

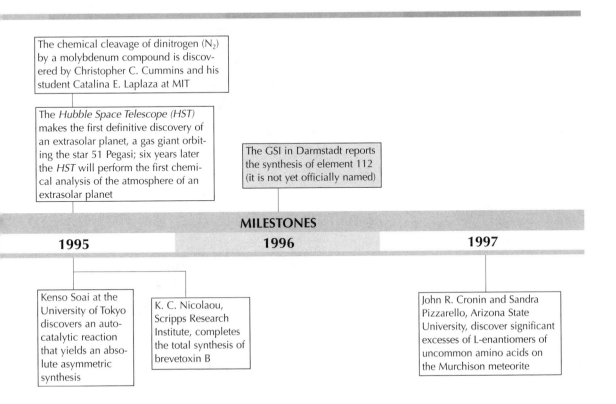

The chemical cleavage of dinitrogen (N_2) by a molybdenum compound is discovered by Christopher C. Cummins and his student Catalina E. Laplaza at MIT

The *Hubble Space Telescope (HST)* makes the first definitive discovery of an extrasolar planet, a gas giant orbiting the star 51 Pegasi; six years later the *HST* will perform the first chemical analysis of the atmosphere of an extrasolar planet

The GSI in Darmstadt reports the synthesis of element 112 (it is not yet officially named)

MILESTONES

1995   **1996**   **1997**

Kenso Soai at the University of Tokyo discovers an autocatalytic reaction that yields an absolute asymmetric synthesis

K. C. Nicolaou, Scripps Research Institute, completes the total synthesis of brevetoxin B

John R. Cronin and Sandra Pizzarello, Arizona State University, discover significant excesses of L-enantiomers of uncommon amino acids on the Murchison meteorite

to s and p orbitals and reduce the stabilities of outer d and f orbitals, causing some reversals in the expected ordering of orbital energies. This is one reason why the chemistry of the superheavy elements is of continuing interest. While an earlier definition classified superheavy elements as those with atomic number Z greater than 106, a more modern definition starts them at Z = 104 based upon comparison of experimental and calculated half-lives.

Quantum calculations suggested that the nuclei of elements with even numbers of protons and neutrons are stable and particularly so when certain "magic numbers" are met (see chapter 9). An "island of stability" was predicted in the vicinity of the element having Z = 114 and N = 184. Such elements are of interest both from the standpoint of nuclear physics and chemistry. The chemistries of individual atoms with nuclear half-lives under 10 seconds, sometimes as brief as 1 second, can be studied immediately following their creation, atom-by-atom, in accelerators using online chemical techniques.

The syntheses of transuranium elements have passed through three distinct stages of evolution. Starting in the 1940s, relatively stable, neutron-rich metals such as uranium and plutonium were bombarded

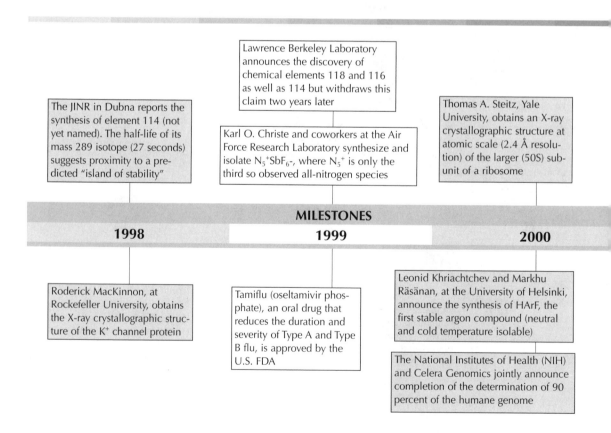

The JINR in Dubna reports the synthesis of element 114 (not yet named). The half-life of its mass 289 isotope (27 seconds) suggests proximity to a predicted "island of stability"

Lawrence Berkeley Laboratory announces the discovery of chemical elements 118 and 116 as well as 114 but withdraws this claim two years later

Karl O. Christe and coworkers at the Air Force Research Laboratory synthesize and isolate $N_5^+SbF_6^-$, where N_5^+ is only the third so observed all-nitrogen species

Thomas A. Steitz, Yale University, obtains an X-ray crystallographic structure at atomic scale (2.4 Å resolution) of the larger (50S) subunit of a ribosome

MILESTONES

1998   **1999**   **2000**

Roderick MacKinnon, at Rockefeller University, obtains the X-ray crystallographic structure of the K^+ channel protein

Tamiflu (oseltamivir phosphate), an oral drug that reduces the duration and severity of Type A and Type B flu, is approved by the U.S. FDA

Leonid Khriachtchev and Markhu Räsänan, at the University of Helsinki, announce the synthesis of HArF, the first stable argon compound (neutral and cold temperature isolable)

The National Institutes of Health (NIH) and Celera Genomics jointly announce completion of the determination of 90 percent of the humane genome

by neutrons or light particles such as helium nuclei (α-particles). The limitation of this approach is that many of the target elements are short-lived, artificial elements generally available in minute quantities and at enormous expense. During the 1970s, the Russian JINR group in Dubna developed the "soft fusion" or "cold fusion" technique that employs Pb-208 or Bi-209 targets bombarded by neutron-poor isotopes of the medium-heavy nuclei (mass 40-70) at the lowest possible energy, 10-15 MeV. The extremely stable lead or bismuth nuclei produce new atoms in "cooler" states that are less prone to disintegrate than the "hot" states produced in earlier experiments. This proved to be an effective technique for synthesizing elements 107-112. However, since the neutron-to-proton (N/Z) ratios in nuclear projectiles such as ^{48}Ca, ^{58}Fe, ^{62}Ni, and ^{70}Zn are low the nuclei of the heavy elements formed by their fusions with ^{208}Pb or ^{209}Bi have N/Z ratios toward the low end of each new isotopic series. These isotopes are usually less stable than those with higher N/Z ratios.

In order to make isotopes of new elements having high N/Z ratios, there has been more recent interest in "hot fusion" reactions involving nuclei such as ^{238}U, ^{244}Pu, ^{248}Cm, and ^{254}Es as targets and light ions such as ^{18}O, ^{22}Ne, and ^{26}Mg as projectiles. Ion beams are accelerated to 10 percent of the speed of light where energies are on the order of 40-50 MeV. Although the collision is "hot" (releasing 4 or 5 neutrons), the intrinsic stabilities of the final product (high N/Z) nuclei offer entry to longer lived superheavy elements amenable to chemical study. One synthesis employed a ^{248}Cm target and a ^{26}Mg projectile, simultaneously creating ^{269}Hs ($t_{1/2}$ 10 s) and ^{270}Hs ($t_{1/2}$ 2-7 s). Curium 248 has a long half-life (340,000 years). Typical ion beams provide some 10^{12} projectiles per second. The exceedingly minute probability of one nucleus colliding with and fusing with another (nuclei are 1/10,000 the diameter of atoms and their positive charges repel each other) make yields (cross sections) almost unimaginably low: a few atoms per minute to a few atoms per day. New atoms are generally characterized by their unique α-particle decay series. Since lifetimes of the most stable known superheavy atoms are on the order of seconds, chemistry must be done online one atom at a time. Chemical investigations of single atoms require concepts very different from the usual thermodynamic considerations. In thermodynamics, trillions of atoms (or molecules) are in equilibrium with trillions of atoms (or molecules) in a different physical state or chemical species. When working with a single atom, it is either in state "A" or state "B" and probabilities rather than populations must be employed. The concept of half-life is also changed accordingly.

In late 1994, the GSI in Darmstadt conducted a "cold fusion" experiment and bombarded ^{208}Pb with a beam of ^{62}Ni ions to produce the 269 isotope ($t_{1/2}$ 170 μs) of element 110, following expulsion of 1 neutron. The GSI also produced $^{271}110$ ($t_{1/2}$ 56 ms) by substituting ^{64}Ni for ^{62}Ni. Only a few weeks later, in December 1994, the GSI reported element $^{272}111$

($t_{1/2}$ 1.6 ms) following collision of a ^{64}Ni beam with ^{209}Bi. Both discoveries were published in 1995. The Ghiorso group at Berkeley reported ^{267}110 in 1995 and the Dubna group reported ^{273}110 in 1996. However, there were no independent confirmations of the Berkeley and Dubna findings. In early 1996, the GSI once again used "cold fusion," firing ^{70}Zn projectiles into a ^{208}Pb target, and obtained ^{277}112, with a half-life of 0.7 ms. Not long afterward, a Joint Working Party (JWP) was formed comprised of representatives from the International Union of Pure and Applied Chemistry (IUPAC) and the International Union of Pure and Applied Physics (IUPAP), to judge whether the discoveries could be officially confirmed and to assign priority. In 2003, the JWP officially validated elements 110 and 111, assigned priority for both to the GSI and accepted the names darmstadtium (Ds) for 110 and roentgenium (Rg), after the discoverer of X-rays, for 111. Although 112 has not yet been added to the JWP "confirmed" list, it is expected to join it soon with priority assigned to the GSI. Although commonly called "element 112," its provisional name is the systematic, but awkward ununbium (Uub, pronounced "oon-oon-bium," corresponding to "1-1-2"). None of the confirmed isotopes of Ds, Rg, or Uub are long-lived enough for chemical study at present.

Roentgenium is intriguing because the most sophisticated calculations including relativistic effects suggest that its electron configuration is $6d^9 7s^2$, in contrast to gold (Au) which occupies the space above Rg in the periodic table but is $6d^{10} 7s^1$. Rg might behave more like other d-block transition metals rather than gold. Element 112 (Uub) is thought to be $6d^{10} 7s^2$ making it analogous to mercury ($5d^{10} 6s^2$). However, relativistic corrections suggest extra stabilization for the 7s orbital leading to speculation that Uub might resemble the rare gas radon or perhaps resemble both radon and mercury. The JINR group reported $t_{1/2}$ of 5 minutes for ^{283}Uub. This has not been confirmed and a later international study, that included JINR, suggested that ^{283}Uub may have a half-life of 4 seconds, which would permit chemical investigation.

In 1998, Yuri Oganessian and his research group in Dubna obtained isotopes from Lawrence Berkeley National Laboratory and accelerated a ^{48}Ca beam into a ^{244}Pu target in a "hot fusion" experiment. Calcium 48, with Z = 20 and N = 28, is "doubly magic" and ^{244}Pu is the most neutron-rich plutonium isotope. The JINR observed two isotopes of element 114 (ununquadrium or Uuq): ^{289}Uuq, $t_{1/2}$ = 27 s and ^{288}Uuq, $t_{1/2}$ = 2 s. The striking stability of ^{289}Uuq hints at approach to an "island of stability," although there are increasing doubts as to whether extremely long-lived nuclei are in the immediate neighborhood. This isotope will certainly lend itself to interesting chemical investigations. The work is well regarded, if not yet fully confirmed by the JWP. In June 1999 the Lawrence Berkeley group claimed synthesis of element 118 (via "cold fusion" of ^{86}Kr and ^{208}Pb), its decay to another new element (116), and subsequent decay to element 114. This claim was retracted by the Berkeley group in July 2001 and a key scientist suspected of fabricating data was fired.

In 2000, the Dubna group bombarded ^{248}Cm with ^{48}Ca and published, in 2001, the synthesis of element 116 (ununhexium, Uuh), $t_{1/2}$ ca. 50 ms. This synthesis has not yet been officially confirmed by the JWP.

In February 2004, the Dubna and Berkeley groups announced their collaborative discovery of elements 113 (ununtrium or Uut) and 115 (ununpentium or Uup). Using *hot fusion* the researchers fired ^{48}Ca at a ^{243}Am target with formation of both ^{287}Uup (expulsion of 4 neutrons) and ^{288}Uup (expulsion of 3 neutrons). The lifetimes of these two nuclei were tens of milliseconds and they each ejected an α-particle to form ^{283}Uut and ^{284}Uut respectively with half-lives of tens of milliseconds. The results, published in a respected journal, are not yet confirmed by the JWP. The researchers also very tentatively noted the observation of one possible decay event from element 118 and, in 2006, corroborating evidence was obtained in the United States and in Russia.

In a review published in 2006, GSI nuclear chemist Matthias Schädel noted that until the early 1980s scientists expected "an 'island of stability' centered at $Z = 114$ and $N = 184$ which was surrounded by a 'sea of instability.'" He declared that current studies

> ... *emphasize the importance of the $N = 162$ neutron shell, ... we know that the sea of instability has drained and that sandbanks and rocky footpaths connect the region of shell-stabilized spherical nuclei to our known world ... recent theoretical results indicate that the atomic numbers 126 and, more likely, 120 are also closed shells; with possibly even more pronounced shell stabilization than for element 114.*

Quantum Chemical Studies of Very Large Molecules

With increasing access to mainframe computers, the 1960s witnessed the development of computational quantum chemistry. Any atom or molecule with more than one electron cannot be solved exactly by the Schrödinger wave function equation. Larger systems require ever rougher approximations in order to be feasible for calculation. John A. Pople shared the 1998 Nobel Prize in chemistry for his contributions to all-electron (*ab initio*) computations that began in the 1960s. Since computational time using these methods increases with the fourth power of the number of orbitals ($[n]^4$), even the enormous advances in computing power during the 1980s and early 1990s could not move the limits of *ab initio* calculations beyond fairly modest-sized systems (e.g., 20 carbon atoms). For this reason the early *ab initio* calculations of polywater had to be very limited in sophistication and they provided incorrect answers (see chapter 8).

Walter Kohn shared the 1998 Nobel Prize in chemistry with John A. Pople for introducing density function theory (DFT). His initial work with Pierre C. Hohenberg (1934–   ) in 1964 and Lu J. Sham (1938–   ) in 1965 established that the electron density of a molecule can provide the energy and numerous important properties of the molecule at the *ab initio* level. In DFT computational time increases much more slowly with the size of the system. Starting in the 1970s, DFT was employed in solid state chemistry in applications that did not require great accuracy. In the late 1980s and early 1990s, theoretical chemists including Robert G. Parr (1921–   ) and Axel D. Becke (1953–   ) introduced modifications that made DFT computations accurate enough for molecular calculations. The first papers employing these techniques began to appear in 1993. By the end of 2000, the annual papers numbered in the thousands. It is no longer unusual to see very large molecules such as a large buckytube calculated at a respectable all-electron level. The accompanying figure

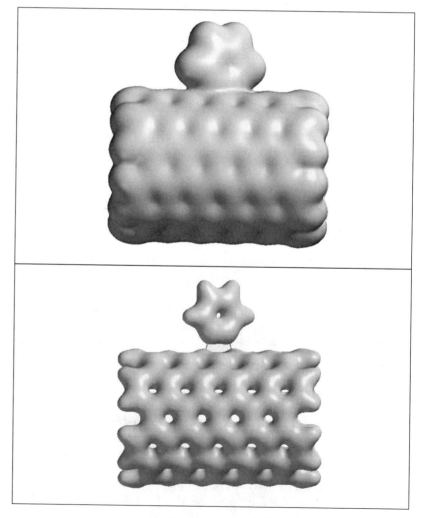

A) Electron density contour, calculated using density function theory (DFT), of the activated complex formed by Diels-Alder reaction of 1,2-benzyne (C_6H_4) with a 132-carbon buckytube capped at each end with 12 hydrogen atoms ($C_{132}H_{24}$); B) bond density contour of the same activated complex described in Part A (Richard P. Johnson and Iain Mackie)

depicts the electron density contour (top) and the bond density contour (bottom) of the potential Diels-Alder reaction of the extremely reactive intermediate 1,2-benzyne with a 132-carbon buckytube capped at each end by 12 hydrogens ($C_{132}H_{24}$). In the late 1980s accurate quantum chemical calculations on a molecule of such large size seemed as inconceivable as obtaining mass spectra for proteins and nucleic acids seemed in the late 1970s (see "Wings for Molecular Elephants" in chapter 9). While DFT theory was the conceptual breakthrough that made such computations feasible, the huge advances in computing power and software have also contributed to this revolution. In addition, graphic interfaces allow a novice to easily draw on a computer screen a molecule for computation and then view the structure, vibrations, electron density, and regions of reactivity after completion of the calculation.

The First Stable Argon Compound

When Neil Bartlett formed a compound between xenon and PtF_6 in 1962, he broke a psychological barrier. A number of other xenon compounds were synthesized in short order as was KrF_2 and probably a radon compound. The next lightest member of the series, argon, resisted attempts to make a stable compound for almost four more decades. There are still no argon compounds isolable at ambient conditions.

Leonid Khriachtchev, Markku Räsänen (1949–), and their colleagues at the University of Helsinki synthesized argon fluorohydride (HArF) in 2000. They formed a solid matrix of HF in argon at 7.5 K (-447°F or -266°C). Photolysis of the matrix in the vacuum ultraviolet (127-160 nm) dissociates HF into H and F atoms. These form a new species demonstrated by IR spectroscopy and computation to be HArF. The calculations indicated resonance of the type:

$$\text{H-Ar-F} \leftrightarrow \text{H-Ar}^+ \text{ F}^-$$

The HArF molecule decomposes upon heating at 27 K (-411°F or -246°C). It appears that small amounts of oxygen-containing impurities in the matrix initiate decomposition. It is possible that without these impurities HArF could survive at higher temperatures. A substance that decomposes at -411°F (-246°C) does not fit conventional notions of stability. It is also predicted, using high-levels molecular orbital calculations, to be 5.87 eV (135 kcal/mol) *less* stable than Ar and HF. But HArF still requires an activation energy in excess of 0.35 eV (8.1 kcal/mol) to decompose. It is thus a real molecule with vibrations of its H-Ar and Ar-F bonds.

New Nitrogen Chemistry

Molecular nitrogen (N_2, or dinitrogen) is the most abundant component of the atmosphere. Its extremely strong N≡N bond is very resistant to chemical reaction. In nature, only certain anaerobic bacteria and leguminous plants have mastered the reduction of nitrogen to ammonia ("fixing nitrogen"). The nitrogenase systems required were only first isolated from cells and studied in the 1960s. Artificial nitrogen fixation, using high temperature and pressure, was pioneered by Fritz Haber in 1908 (see chapter 1) and won him the 1918 Nobel Prize in chemistry.

In 1995, Christopher C. Cummins (1966–) and his student Catalina E. Laplaza at MIT discovered that a molybdenum(III) compound of formula $Mo(NRAr)_3$ (R is an alkyl group and Ar an aromatic group, not argon) could decompose the extremely stable N_2 molecule under relatively mild conditions. The system converts N_2 to two nitrido (N^{3-}) ligands which can, in turn, be converted to ammonia (NH_3) and other useful nitrogen compounds.

As abundant as nitrogen is, until 1999 there were but two stable all-nitrogen units: the gaseous molecule N_2 and the azide ion (N_3^-). In that year, Karl O. Christe (1936–) and colleagues reported the synthesis of $N_5^+AsF_6^-$, a salt that is "marginally stable" at 72°F (22°C) but can be stored indefinitely at dry ice temperature (-108°F or -78°C). The salt is a violent detonator, explodes on contact with water, and ignites foam rubber. The fact that N_5^+ is isolable is attributable in part to its very stable, unreactive counterion AsF_6^-. It is one member of a class commonly termed *"weakly coordinating anions"* (WCA) or "superweak anions." Such anions tend to be large and spread their negative charge over a large surface area. They are considered to be "soft bases" in the hard and soft acid base (HSAB) theory developed by Ralph G. Pearson (1919–) at Northwestern University during the 1960s. WCAs have played an important role in the observations of reactive carbocations paired with SbF_6^- in SbF_5 solution by George Olah and in Neil Bartlett's epical formation of $XeF^+PtF_5^-$ (see chapter 7 and above). Some of these anions are so stable as to tolerate coexistence with phenomenally reactive cations. The closed carborane anion $CHB_{11}Cl_{11}^-$ is so stable that its solid conjugate acid $H[CHB_{11}Cl_{11}]$ is a million times stronger than concentrated sulfuric acid. The $CB_{11}H_6Cl_6^-$ anion is the only one known to form a stable salt with protonated buckyball ($C_{60}H^+$). The WCAs are also found in the ionic liquids described later in this chapter.

The *Hubble Space Telescope*

The development of the spectroscope in the mid-19th century allowed chemists to explore emissions of visible light by extraterrestrial objects such as stars as well as absorption (Fraunhofer lines) by the Earth's atmosphere and that of the Sun. Helium was discovered during the total solar eclipse of 1868 by its emission. Other elements were discovered in the solar atmosphere by matching of their Fraunhofer lines. Between 1937 and 1941 visible emissions were assigned for three interstellar molecules: CH (430.0 nm), CH^+ (423.2 nm), and CN (a series of lines). There were very limited opportunities to observe ultraviolet spectra (<400 nm) from space because stratospheric ozone absorbs most of the UVB light (320–

290 nm) and all UV light of wavelength shorter than 290 nm. The birth of radioastronomy in 1951 provided a means for monitoring microwave emissions from interstellar molecules and vastly increased the knowledge of space chemistry. The absence of UV spectra still left a large gap that could be explored briefly by small sensors on rockets or space satellites. Although H_2 is the most abundant molecule in space, it eluded observation until its detection in March 1970, in a dark space cloud by a far ultraviolet (FUV, 100-140 nm) spectrometer aboard a rocket. This observation was confirmed in 1973 by the *Copernicus* satellite.

The *Hubble Space Telescope (HST)* was launched by the National Aeronautics and Space Administration (NASA) in April 1990. Outside of the Earth's atmosphere it obtains undistorted visual images and collects UV and IR spectral data at high resolution and sensitivity. Among its original instruments were the Faint Object Spectrograph (FOS), which detected light from the UV (115 nm) through the IR (800 nm), and the Goddard High-Resolution Spectrograph (GHRS), which detected UV light in the ranges 105-170 nm and 115-320 nm. The GHRS was removed in 1997 and replaced by the Space Telescope Imaging Spectrometer (STIS). This instrument measured UV, visible, and IR wavelengths. The Near Infrared Camera and Multi-Object Spectrometer (NICMOS) was also installed in the *HST* in 1997. It measures IR radiation in the 800-2,500 nm range and was maintained at -321°F (-196°C), to reduce background IR radiation, by a 230-pound block of solid nitrogen that was replaced by a cryocooler in 2002. The FOS was removed in 2002 and the STIS shut down in 2004.

By any measure the *Hubble* mission has been a huge success. In 1992, the *HST* detected the UV emission of the element boron in an ancient star, HD 140283, 100 light years distant in the Constellation Libra. The star is estimated to be about 15 billion years old and one of the first stars in the Milky Way. Beryllium had earlier been detected in this star by ground telescope. The observations suggest that beryllium and boron may have formed in the first moments of this star's creation. In 1996, observation of Comet Hyakutake (1996B2) by *HST* provided data on the H/OH photochemistry of water in its coma (comet atmosphere). In 2001 Comet C/1999S4 (Linear) "blew its top" as it melted away near the Sun but released few volatiles such as methane (CH_4) and methanol (CH_3OH). This suggested that the comet was formed in a warmer region in contrast to other comets such as Hale-Bopp that are thought to be formed in colder regions.

The search for planets outside of the solar system was one of the major goals of the *HST.* In 1995, the *Hubble* STIS provided the first definitive evidence for an extrasolar planet, a gas planet similar to Jupiter orbiting the star 51 *Pegasi.* A decade later there are over 170 known extrasolar planets. In 1999, the planet HD 209458b, a gas planet slightly larger but less dense than Jupiter, was discovered orbiting a star 150 light-years from Earth in the Constellation Pegasus. It was the first extrasolar plant observed to partially eclipse its star in a transit. In 2001, STIS made the first discovery of the atmosphere of an extrasolar planet. It found sodium in the lower atmosphere (the planet is very close to its star and has a surface temperature of 1,800°F or 980°C). In 2003, the *HST* STIS detected hydrogen in the upper atmosphere and signs that the planet is losing mass. In late 2003, *HST* discovered that the planet also blows off oxygen and carbon. Planet HD 209458b is now commonly called *Osiris* in honor of the Egyptian god who was slain and cut into 14 pieces scattered over the Earth to prevent his return.

"There's Plenty of Room at the Bottom": Nanotechnology

Richard P. Feynman (1918–88), winner of the 1965 Nobel Prize in physics, presented a now-famous talk, titled "There's Plenty of Room at the Bottom," at an American Physical Society meeting on December 29, 1959. In challenging scientists to explore miniaturization to its fundamental limits he said:

> But I am not afraid to consider the final question as to whether, ultimately . . . in the great future . . . we can arrange the atoms the way we want, the very atoms, all the way down! What would happen if we could arrange the atoms one by one the way we want them (within reason, of course; you can't put them so that they are chemically unstable, for example).

What a prediction! Some 25 years later IBM scientists invented the scanning tunneling microscope (STM) and the atomic force microscope (AFM). The AFM was able to move 48 iron atoms, one-by-one, into a circle (page 317). The discovery of buckyball (C_{60}) and buckytubes during the 1980s furnished the basis for a significant fraction of today's emerging *nanotechnology* revolution. The development of supramolecular (host-guest) chemistry during the late 1960s and 1970s provided scaffolding for the assembly of potential "nanomotor" parts. The development of high-field NMR and mass spectrometric techniques for high-molecular-weight molecules played an important role as did crystallographic investigations of Nature's own nanomotors. Although Feynman's original suggestion implied manipulation of atoms and molecules to form objects such as the 48-atom "quantum corral" by a "top-down" approach, today most attention is devoted to the "bottom-up" approach (molecular recognition and self-organization) that has been Nature's way on Earth for nearly 4 billion years. The term *nanotechnology* has itself become extremely broad. The polymeric material Gore-Tex was invented in 1969 by Robert W. Gore (1937–   ), W. L. Gore & Associates. It is a thin porous membrane bound to nylon or polyester fabrics that helps to waterproof them. It is an expanded polytetrafluoroethylene (PTFE) containing 9 billion pores per square inch. The pores are large enough to pass molecules of water vapor but exclude microscale droplets of water and might be considered a "nanofabric" today.

Although it is tempting to view molecules as mechanical motor parts, it is important to remember that quantum effects are significant at this scale. The spherical buckyball (C_{60}) molecule was envisioned initially as a potential "nano-ball bearing," having similar uses in nanomotors as ball bearings have in regular motors. Closer study of C_{60} soon demonstrated that van der Waals forces make buckyball sticky, a kind of molecular Velcro, the opposite of the desired property. Molecules are in constant random Brownian motion in a "thermal bath" whose energy is not much lower than the energies that bind and move the molecular motors themselves.

During the 1990s, J. Fraser Stoddart (1942–), at the University of Birmingham in England (1990–97) and then UCLA (starting 1997), developed a design for a molecular switching device. The system, shown in the figure below, is based upon a catenate, two interlocked molecular rings that are not covalently bonded to each other (see the molecule in the center of the figure which corresponds to representation [A^0]). When catenates were first explored three decades earlier, they were merely curiosities and nobody seriously offered a practical use for

Stoddart's nano-switch design, in which a catenate molecule is able to move between two positions of equal energy controlled by oxidizing or reducing conditions. Such bifunctional switches can serve as parts of nanomachines or nanocomputers.

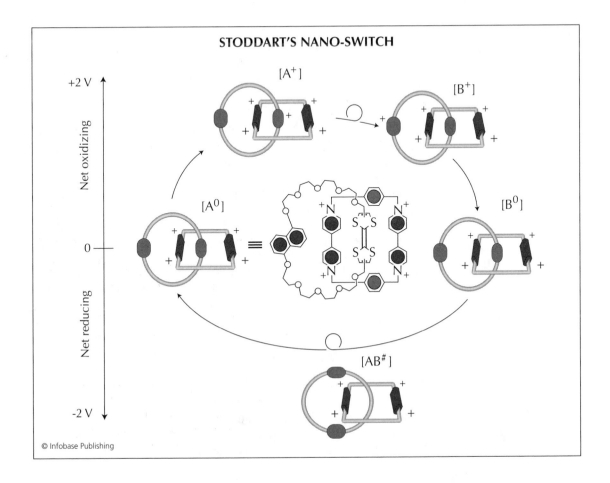

STODDART'S NANO-SWITCH

© Infobase Publishing

them. But scientific curiosity often produces unanticipated technological breakthroughs.

In 1960, Edel Wasserman (1932–   ), at Bell Laboratories, explored the novel questions posed by catenanes. Is the catenane truly a new molecule or is it two separate molecules that just happen to be linked to each other? Entropy makes catenane formation exceedingly challenging. Rings with vacancies wide enough to accommodate another ring as a link have to be quite large (on the order of 30 carbons). Entropy makes it very difficult to synthesize such large rings. During the 1920s, Leopold Ruzicka was surprised when he discovered a natural compound with a 17-membered ring. To make catenanes one ring must allow a long extended chain to thread its cavity before the latter closes ends to form the other interlocked ring. This is also highly improbable (high negative entropy). With considerable skill, Wasserman synthesized a 0.2 percent yield of a catenane comprised of two 34-membered rings. He also posed similar questions for another esoteric and then unknown species called "rotaxanes," in which a dumb-bell-shaped molecule has a ring encircling its "bar" too small to slide over the "masses" at either end. During the 1960s Arthur Lüttringhaus (1906–92), Gottfried Schill (1930–   ), and others developed a variety of clever techniques to synthesize catenanes and rotaxanes in very low or modest yields. The supermolecular host-guest chemistry developed by Pederson, Cram, Lehn, and others during the 1970s led to high-yield syntheses of catenanes such as those in Stoddart's nanoswitch.

Stoddart exploited host-guest chemistry to guide the formation of the catenane in 70 percent yield. It moves between two states, $[A^0]$ and $[B^0]$, using controlled reduction-oxidation (REDOX) chemistry. The ring containing the four positively charged nitrogens ($CPBQT^{4+}$) is attracted strongly to the side of the other interlinked ring (a crown ether) containing the tetrathiafulvalene (TTF) unit with four sulfur atoms. The $CPQT^{4+}$ ring has a much weaker attraction to the other side of the crown ether ring that has a naphthalene unit. That is why the normal structure of this catenane is $[A^0]$. When two equivalents of an oxidizing agent $[Fe(ClO_4)_3]$ is added, TTF loses two electrons, becomes positively charged, is repelled by $CPBQT^{4+}$, and moves to the position outside while naphthalene occupies the hole in $CPBQT^{4+}$ (structure $[B^0]$). Addition of two equivalents of a reducing agent (ascorbic acid = vitamin C) converts $[B^0]$ back to $[A^0]$. The same controlled interconversion can be accomplished by using an electric circuit. The individual catenane molecule is effectively a controllable switch ($[A^0]/[B^0]$ = On/Off) or an addressable binary element (0/1) in a nanocomputer.

Charles M. Lieber (1959–   ), at Harvard, is designing connections (nanowires) between nanodevices. Buckytubes are potential nanowires and are being investigated in a number of laboratories. Buckytubes are not produced in a uniform size and this limits their utility since a mixture typically contains good electrical conductors as well as semiconductors. Lieber's group employs other approaches toward obtaining uniform

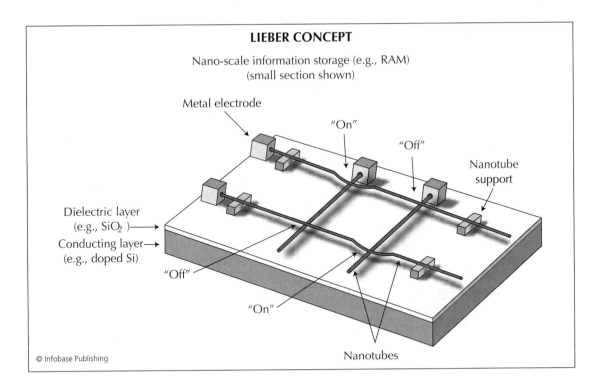

LIEBER CONCEPT

Nano-scale information storage (e.g., RAM)
(small section shown)

Metal electrode

"On"

"Off"

Nanotube support

Dielectric layer (e.g., SiO$_2$)

Conducting layer (e.g., doped Si)

"Off"

"On"

Nanotubes

© Infobase Publishing

Lieber's concept of a nano-information storage system based on crossing of nanowires at addressable sites

nanowires for application in an array. Such an array is shown above. Nanowires are crisscrossed in a two-dimensional (x-y) array. Charging a specific x_m nanowire and a specific y_n nanowire creates an addressable site at location $x_m y_n$. A large array of such addressable sites may be used as a computer. Stoddart and his coworkers have exploited monolayers formed by DMPA anions (a negatively charged "head" attached to two 16-carbon nonpolar "tails") to bind switches such as his $[A^0]/[B^0]$ system in an orderly two-dimensional array resembling a Langmuir film. Lieber notes that while miniaturization on the microscale (10^{-6} m) is done "top-down," photolithography on a silicon microchip, at the nanoscale the approach will be "bottom-up" by molecular recognition and association. He speculates that: "One day your computer may be built in a beaker."

When Irving Langmuir discovered that soaps such as sodium stearate $[CH_3(CH_2)_{16}CO_2^-Na^+]$ form monolayers on water with their nonpolar hydrocarbon tails aligned like a "lawn" growing from the water surface (page 60), he was exploring nanotechnology even though that term was unknown 90 years ago. In 1983, David L. Allara (1937–) at Bell Laboratories discovered that long-chain organic molecules ending in a disulfide (R-S-S-R) linkage form strong stable attachments to gold (as well as silver and copper). In 1989, George M. Whitesides (1939–), at Harvard, discovered that long-chain thiols (R-SH) form stable, strong thiolate attachments to gold surfaces (R-S-Au). He used this approach to form Langmuir-like films on gold surfaces (for example, gold film on a silicon chip) with chemical functionality on the surface of the "lawn." One example is a molecule such as HS-$(CH_2)_{15}$-COOH. While the polar (or ionic) heads of molecules comprising Langmuir films are solvated by water, the sulfur ends of Whitesides's thiols are chemically bonded to gold surfaces. The functional group at the other end (e.g., COOH) is free to engage in strong association (hydrogen bonding, ionic bonding) or chemical reactions. This allows "customizing" of chemical surfaces for countless potential applications.

Lithography is undergoing its own nanotechnology revolution. Chad A. Mirkin (1963–   ), at Northwestern University, is one of the pioneers of a technique called "dip-pen lithography." In this process an atomic force microscope (AFM) lays down a pattern in a monolayer on a gold surface. Appropriately designed R-S-Au surfaces, such as Au-S-$(CH_2)_{15}$-COOH as noted above, may selectively attract, but not covalently bond, molecules reflecting a designed pattern. The newly bound molecules react with each other and are then released from the monolayer. Such a process mimics a stamping machine or a printing press that turns out multiple copies.

While nanotechnology is a recent human discovery, Nature has been at it for nearly 4 billion years in systems described earlier in the present book. The ubiquitous conversion of ADP to ATP for storage of metabolic energy occurs through a biological nanomotor called ATP synthase. Another example is the membrane-embedded photosynthesis reaction center of purple bacteria. The ribosome is a highly structured machine that constructs proteins from amino acids from a "blueprint" and its detailed, atomic-level structure is described later in this chapter.

One of Nature's other motors, this one a microsized motor with recognizable nanoscale components, is the flagellum (see the photograph), the whiplike reversible propeller found on numerous types of bacteria as well as on sperm. The controlled rotation of the flagellum (clockwise or counterclockwise as needed) is one marvel of this motor. During the 1990s researchers synthesized nanoscale rotors that could be started and stopped at will. Most turn both clockwise and counterclockwise unselectively, limiting their utility.

One approach to unidirectional rotors (clockwise or counterclockwise but not both) is the use of chiral molecules of appropriate design. A propeller mounted to an airplane engine is chiral and rotation in one direction pulls air smoothly over the wings. Steric repulsions between large, nonbonded groups create propellerlike twists in organic molecules. Ben L. Feringa (1951–   ), at the University of Groningen, has synthesized the crowded chiral molecule drawn on page 373. The specific enantiomer

Photograph of a microorganism propelled by flagella (Pathology Teaching Image Collection, Queen Mary's School of Medicine and Dentistry)

shown (*P, P*) rotates clockwise only in the presence of ultraviolet light and mild heat. Its enantiomer (*M, M*) rotates counterclockwise under the same conditions (*P* and *M* refer to nomenclature for helical-twist molecules and is related to the *R, S*-nomenclature introduced in chapter 6).

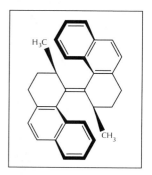

Feringa's chiral rotor molecule

The flagellum has been an object of the "intelligent design" argument advocated in recent years as an alternative to evolution, the scientific framework universally accepted by the scientific community. The flagellum is viewed by advocates of "intelligent design" as a structure of "irreducible complexity." This means that the flagellum can only function as a fully assembled complex unit and thus evolutionary "transition" structures, lacking necessary parts, cannot function and could not exist. Therefore, the argument goes, the flagellum is found only fully formed in organisms that were created fully formed. Scientific evidence suggests that evolutionary precursors (intermediate stages) to flagella did exist (and exist today) and simply serve different functions. For example, a subset of flagella proteins is well organized into the functional part of the type-III secretory system (TTSS) that allow bacteria to inject toxins into their host organism. At an even more elementary level, Steven A. Benner (1954–), at the University of Florida, has noted that protein molecules, such as enzymes that are very close on the evolutionary tree, often serve very different metabolic functions even as their chemistry is quite similar.

One of the most striking nanomachines reported is the "nanocar" that Kevin F. Kelly, James M. Tour (1959–), and colleagues at Rice University started work on in the late 1990s and published in 2005. It is synthesized using fairly straightforward organic chemistry ending with four buckyball (C_{60}) wheels attached simultaneously through chemical reaction with linear axles on the molecular chassis. The horizontal dimensions of the nanocar are about 3.3 nm width by 2.1 nm length. The nanocar is a single molecule of formula $C_{430}H_{274}O_{12}$, fully characterized by NMR and MALDI-TOF mass spectrometry. As noted previously, buckyball is "sticky" and adheres sufficiently well so that STM shows that it remains motionless on a gold surface up to about 340°F (170°C). Above that temperature the nanocar rolls slowly but not randomly. Above 570°F (300°C), the tires fall off and above 660°F (350°C) the nanocar decomposes. An STM tip placed in front of the nanocar gently pulls it forward as the buckyball tires rotate and provide traction and direction on the gold surface. The figure below provides a computer-drawn picture of the nanocar and its STM-guided trek on a gold surface. For the sake of comparison the size of a red blood cell is 20,000 nm; staphylococcus, 2,000 nm; Ebola virus, 200 nm; and Rhinovirus, 30 nm.

Quantum dots are nanocrystals whose light absorption and emission varies with the size of the crystal rather than its composition. This surprising property was discovered quite accidentally by Louis E. Brus (1943–) working at Bell Laboratories in 1983. Brus was working with colloidal solutions of semiconductor particles and discovered that the specific and

Computer picture of the Rice University "nanocar" and its roll guided by the probe of a scanning tunneling microscope (STM) (The Richard Smalley Institute for Nanotechnology, Rice University)

discrete wavelength of absorption and emission increased over days. He reasoned that the cause was crystal growth and that its origin was due to "quantum confinement" in the three-dimensional nanoscale crystals. Today the most common quantum dots consist of a few hundred atoms comprising cadmium selenide (CdSe) with a coating of organic surfactant. Particle size is controlled by the techniques employed to make the quantum dots. Applications of quantum dots include using them to tag proteins or specific biological sites with these colored particles and may lead to future "bar coding" with selected librairies of quantum dots.

Organic Synthesis: Challenging Natural Products and New Frontiers

The search for biologically active compounds (natural and synthetic) continued to be a significant inspiration for organic synthesis. Asymmetric catalysis, new synthetic reactions, and advances in separation techniques (HPLC) and analytical techniques (NMR and mass spectrometry) support these advances. In 1995, Kyriacos Costa (K.C.) Nicolaou (1946–) at Scripps Research Institute reported the total synthesis of brevetoxin B (see the figure on page 375). This toxic substance is produced by algae in red tide and is very deadly to fish. It binds to sodium channels in membranes of muscle and nerve cells producing an excessive influx of Na⁺.

Brevetoxin B has 23 chiral centers as well as 11 *trans*-fused rings. While it has far fewer chiral centers than palytoxin (page 331), the

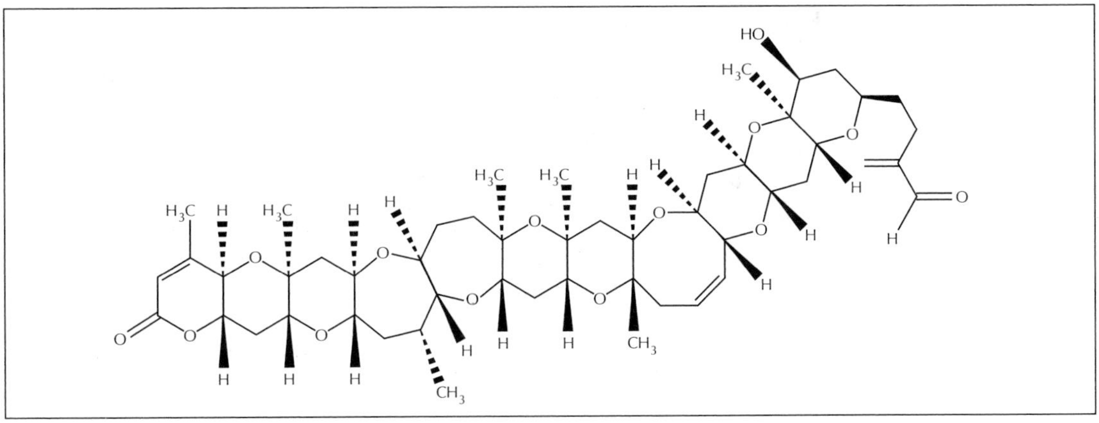

Brevetoxin B

combination of chiral centers and *trans*-fused rings presented an extraordinary challenge that required 12 years to solve. Brevetoxin B also "threw a curve" to the Nicolaou research group. Far into the synthesis, a reaction anticipated to work well essentially failed. Seeing this seeming dead end as an opportunity, they developed an entirely new approach to the transformation in question that is now of wide use to the chemical community. The total synthesis started with 2-deoxyribose, required 83 steps, and resulted in 0.043 percent yield of brevetoxin B. While the yield seems extremely low, it actually represents an average 91 percent yield for each step. Unlike automated syntheses of proteins and nucleic acids that employ solid support (polymeric beads) and provide nearly 100 percent yield at each step of a repetitive procedure, each step in the synthesis of brevetoxin B requires unique chemistry, purification, and full spectroscopic characterization. Why spend 12 years synthesizing brevetoxin B? Aside from the scientific challenge and the unanticipated advances in technique, synthesis allows for investigations of nonnatural derivatives to better investigate the mechanism of action and possible means for prevention or treatment.

In addition to natural products and their derivatives, organic chemists have continued to synthesize and study some markedly unnatural products. One area of interest is the synthesis of organic *ferromagnets*. A ferromagnet is a substance that has been permanently magnetized. The magnetic properties of iron and iron compounds are due to unpaired spins in 3d-orbitals and are generally understood using ligand-field theory as described in chapter 6. The possibilities of making organic magnets and magnetic memory devices are stimulating the investigation of organic molecules and polymers having many unpaired (parallel-spin) electrons ("polyradicals"). The first stable organic diradical was synthesized in 1915 by Walter Schlenk (1879–1942) in

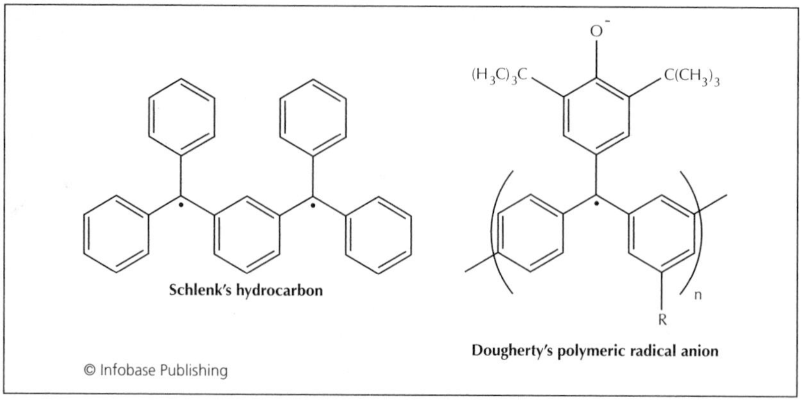

Schlenk's hydrocarbon and Dougherty's polymeric radical anion

Berlin. Schlenk, inspired by Moses Gomberg's discovery of triphenyl-methyl radical in 1900 (see chapter 1), extended this work to larger related radicals and eventually to Schlenk's hydrocarbon (see above). This type of molecule is now commonly referred to as a non-Kekulé molecule because it has no reasonable structure that pairs all electrons as they are nicely paired in the Kekulé structure of benzene. A closer look at this molecule reveals a design motif in organic ferromagnets. The radical centers at left and right (each of which resembles the classical triphenylmethyl radical) are connected through a "ferromagnetic coupler." The coupler in Schlenk's hydrocarbon is the middle benzene ring whose *meta* linkage (rather than *ortho* or *para*) is only compatible with a non-Kekulé structure. Today a number of research groups are investigating extended organic ferromagnets by building oligomers and polymers with many unpaired electrons. One example is the polymeric radical anion synthesized by Dennis A. Dougherty (1952–   ) at Caltech that employs the design in Schlenk's hydrocarbon and literally extends it.

Organic chemists typically synthesize complex molecules by forming covalent bonds in a highly directed and irreversible way. However, there is a great deal of interest in copying the manner in which Nature assembles complex structures. The key is often the use of many bonds of low strength (e.g., hydrogen bonds), which may form reversibly so as to "anneal" en route to the most stable structure. The amide linkage is particularly amenable and it plays critical roles in self-organization of proteins as well as nucleic acids. Molecular recognition can be the key to building complex structures "from the bottom up." This is the general route considered practical for assembling nanostructures. An example is the creation, by the Whitesides group, of the "rosette" structure (see figure page 377) formed by the combination of three molecules each of the two types circled. This aggregate of six molecules is a finite array, but virtually infinite one-, two-, and three-dimensional arrays may be

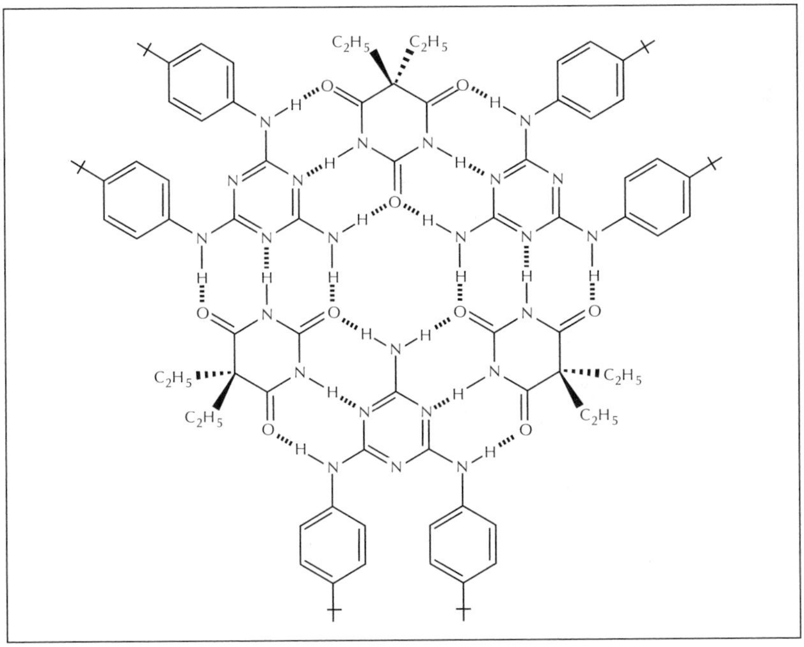

Whiteside's rosette structure

formed through hydrogen bonding and represent contributions to a field referred to as "crystal engineering." Peter J. Stang (1941–), at the University of Utah, has employed dative bonds (e.g., N→Pt) to simply mix 20 molecules of a pyramidal tripod molecule in solution with 30 molecules of a linear molecule to form virtually 100 percent of $C_{2900}H_{2300}N_{60}P_{120}S_{60}O_{200}F_{180}Pt_{60}$, a nanometer-scale dodecahedron molecule, in 10 minutes, despite a large negative entropy for this chemical process.

Molecular recognition and self-organization are not only of interest in building materials, nanostructures, and nanomotors from the bottom up. These processes are also critical in self-replicating systems such as DNA and also in a postulated pre-DNA and pre-protein "RNA world." In 1991, Julius Rebek, Jr. (1944–), then at MIT and now at Scripps Research Institute, designed a self-replicating molecule. Its component parts are demonstrated in Rebek's self-duplicating system composed of template molecule **T** that attracts and aligns two component molecules, an amine and an activated ester. In order to be self-replicating, the system must be autocatalytic: the product template molecule (**T**) must catalyze its own formation by bringing together the reactants which spontaneously react to form more **T** which then dissociates from the original template **T**. This new **T** then also connects with a new amine and activated ester molecules to form a new cycle and so on. Although some news reports hyped this discovery as creation of a "living" molecule, Rebek made it clear that it was merely a model for self-replication process.

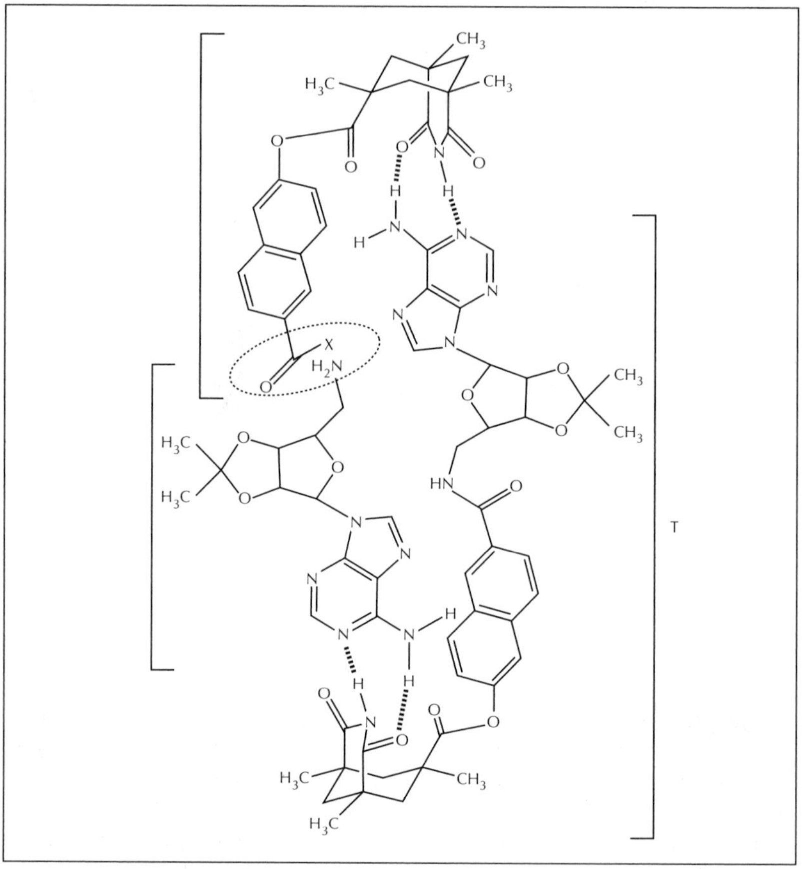

Rebek's self-replicating molecule

Is the Universe Biased (Toward L-Amino Acids and D-Sugars)?

Stanley Miller's prebiotic chemistry experiment in 1953 supported the hypothesis that small biologically significant molecules, such as amino acids, were synthesized from very simple molecules in the reducing atmosphere of the Earth some 4 billion years ago. Another theory suggests that such molecules may have been synthesized in interstellar space and gradually deposited on Earth over hundreds of millions of years. This theory gained some strength as radioastronomy grew and identified well over 100 interstellar molecules with the largest known to date comprised of 13 atoms.

Another interesting question concerns the origin of chirality ("handedness") on Earth: Why are the alpha-amino acids that compose proteins on Earth all L (not D) in absolute configuration (see the figure on page 379) while glucose and related saccharides are all D (not L)? Why are not the amino acids D and the saccharides L? A protein molecule composed entirely of L-amino acids is more stable than one composed of a mixture of L- and D-amino acids. However, a right-handed alpha-helix of L-amino acids has identical stability to a left-handed alpha-helix of D-amino acids. Did homochirality (all L-amino acids/D-saccharides) arise after living organisms emerged or did it predate life?

When a simple chemical reaction converts achiral reactants into chiral products, those products should be racemic (consist of equal quantities of enantiomers). The application of tiny quantities of optically pure asymmetric catalysts to such reactions revolutionized synthetic chemistry and provided enantiomeric excesses (ee) close to 100 percent, nearly equaling the specificities of enzymes, the "champions" of all chiral catalysts. A closer look at the conversion of achiral reactants into chiral products without addition of optically pure chiral catalysts brings up an interesting but readily understandable point. Statistically one can expect in any given reaction run of this type a miniscule excess of one enantiomer over the other. This can be illustrated by perfectly flipping a perfect coin. The probability of flipping a coin 1,000 times and obtaining precisely 500 heads and 500 tails in a given run is actually quite low. One run might yield 507 heads and 493 tails. The next run might yield 489 heads and 511 tails. Over hundreds of runs, the average will be 500 heads and 500 tails. Similarly, hundreds of runs of chemical reactions converting achiral to chiral products will produce an overall 50:50 ratio of enantiomers. However, if a given reaction run could somehow drastically amplify a miniscule statistical excess of one enantiomer then the possibility exists that it could produce a large enantiomeric excess. A process that starts with perfectly achiral reactants and spontaneously produces enantiomeric excess (small or large) is termed "absolute asymmetric synthesis." In 1995, Kenso Soai (1950–), University of Tokyo, achieved this using an autocatalytic reaction. Autocatalytic reactions have been known for decades. If reactants A and B form product C and product C catalyzes the A and B reaction, the reaction is termed "autocatalytic":

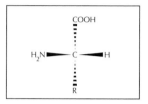

L-amino acid structure

Autocatalysis: A + B   →   C

reactants   catalysis by C   product

Where reactants A and B are achiral and the catalyst is an enantiomer formed in miniscule excess (e.g., [(+)-C]), it may spontaneously produce a large enantiomeric excess of (+)-C. Donna G. Blackmond, at Imperial College in London, worked out general mechanistic details of such asymmetric autocatalysis and predicted conditions for optimizing the spontaneous creation of homochirality from a minute excess of one enantiomer. She successfully demonstrated it for a prebiotic-type system. A rather amazing (and accidental) result was obtained by Daniel A. Singleton at Texas A&M University. Exploring asymmetric autocatalysis, he anticipated that half of his successful reaction runs would give an excess of the (+)-enantiomer while the other half would provide an excess of the (-)-enantiomer since the influences are purely random. Much to his amazement, every run produced a significant excess of the *same* enantiomer. The source was pinpointed as an impurity present at parts-per-trillion levels. Such dramatic impact by an ultratrace, almost undetectable impurity suggests a possible origin for homochirality on this planet. As one writer put it: "Like an apocryphal butterfly that flapped its wings and caused a hurricane halfway across the world, a faint trace of impurities in a prebiotic catalytic reaction could have induced the left-handed nature of all biological molecules."

Initial analysis of the Murchison meteorite that crashed in Australia in 1969 appeared at the time to answer two important questions. Careful study of the common amino acids found on the meteorite indicated that they were racemic (equal L and D). This established their extraterrestrial origin since the amino acids on Earth are L. In addition, it supported the intuitive notion that in space, in the absence of life, there is no intrinsic bias toward L- or D-amino acids. The findings from the Murchison meteorite lent support to the hypothesis of "seeding" the Earth with amino acids.

In recent years, more sophisticated studies of α-amino acids suggested very slight excesses (2 percent) of the L-amino acids but earthly contamination remained a concern for these low levels. However, in 1997, John R. Cronin (1937–) and Sandra Pizzarello (1933–), at Arizona State University, reported unambiguous evidence that α-methylisoleucine (below, left), isolated from the Murchison meteorite, had a 7 percent excess of the L-enantiomer over the D-enantiomer. The related α-methylalloisoleucine had an even greater excess of L over D (9 percent). Both of these amino acids have α-methyl groups in place of the α-hydrogen atoms characteristic of the common amino acids and have never been found in terrestrial matter. The enantiomeric excesses (L over D) far exceed any experimental uncertainties. The result is at odds with the expectation that interstellar synthesis of amino acids should give a pure racemic mixture (1:1 L/D). It suggests a possible "bias" in the universe toward L-amino acids. Common α-amino acids contain an α-hydrogen with very weakly acidic properties that could allow these compounds to racemize extremely slowly in the presence of any water bound in the meteorite. In contrast, α-methyl amino acids lack this acidic α-hydrogen and resist any racemization. It is possible that both types of amino acid were formed simultaneously but those in the α-hydrogen series, while enriched initially in L, racemized slowly while those in the α-methyl series did not. Alternatively, they might have been formed at different times and by different processes.

In order to evolve a homochiral world, three general steps have been recognized:

- Mirror symmetry-breaking: favoring of one enantiomer over the other
- Enrichment of one dominant enantiomer
- Transmission of chirality from the dominant enantiomer to induce homochirality in another substance

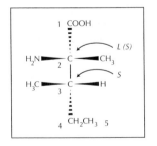

L-α-methylisoleucine

The first step remains the biggest mystery. It may have been a "statistical fluke" on Earth but this is now a less-than-satisfactory explanation given a seeming bias in the universe. Another possibility may be circularly polarized light from stars which could, in principle, favor formation of one enantiomer over the other. Physicists discovered 50 years ago that there is asymmetry in the weak nuclear force possibly giving some intrinsic bias in matter favoring one enantiomer over the other. At present these remain speculations.

The second and third steps are somewhat easier to understand and there are experimental precedents. R. Graham Cooks (1941–), Purdue University, demonstrated that the amino acid serine (R = CH_2OH) exhibits the unique ability to form in the gas phase a "magic cluster" of eight molecules, Ser_8. This is quite reminiscent of the "magic carbon cluster" that led to the discovery of buckyball, C_{60}. In a mixture of both serine enantiomers, the homochiral $(L-Ser)_8$ cluster dominates if the L-enantiomer is in small excess. This offers a specific mechanism for selection of a single enantiomer. The $(L-Ser)_8$ cluster reacts with other amino acids to replace individual L-Ser molecules. Particularly striking is the difference in the gas-phase reactions of the $(L-Ser)_8$ cluster with L-threonine [R = $CH(OH)CH_3$], a close relative of L-serine, and D-threonine. For L-threonine, 8 different clusters are derived by substitution of, in turn, 1 L-serine [i.e. $(L-Ser)_7(L-Thr)_1$], 2, 3, all the way to 8 [$(L-Thr)_8$]. The clusters in which 3, 4, 5, and 6 L-serines are replaced [e.g., $(L-Ser)_3(L-Thr)_5$] are the major products. Reactions of $(L-Ser)_8$ with D-threonine form 3 different clusters with displacement of 1 and 2 serines [e.g., $(L-Ser)_6(D-Thr)_2$] dominating. Similar differentiation between enantiomers is seen with L-cysteine (R = CH_2SH). The conclusion is that the $(L-Ser)_8$ cluster can transmit its homochirality to L-threonine. In this way, one might imagine formation of all 19 common L-amino acids and how, in principle, D-saccharides, rather than L, could be associated with L-amino acids.

Membrane Transport Proteins

In 2003, Roderick MacKinnon (1956–), Rockefeller University and Howard Hughes Medical Institute, and Peter Agre (1949–), Johns Hopkins University School of Medicine, shared the Nobel Prize in chemistry for the discoveries, respectively, of proteins that conduct ions such as K^+, Na^+, Ca^{2+}, and Cl^- across cell membranes, and transport water across cell membranes. All living organisms are composed of cells, all cells have membranes, and transport of ions as well as water across these membranes is universal. The independent studies of MacKinnon and Agre, which began in the late 1980s, were triumphs combining protein engineering, biophysics, and structural biochemistry.

The general features of cell membrane structure have been known since Evert Gorter (1881–1954) and his student F. Grendel first postulated the bilayer structure in 1925. James F. Danielli (1911–84) and Hugh Davson (1909–96) firmly established it in 1935. In 1972, S. Jonathan Singer (1924–) and Garth L. Nicolson (1943–), in San Diego, introduced the fluid mosaic model. It retains the lipid bilayer while postulating that globular membrane proteins float in the lipid bilayer. Lipids comprising such membranes, about 40 Å thick, are amphiphilic forming a bilayer composed of their long nonpolar "tails" and polar (or ionic) "heads" exposed to the extracellular aqueous matrix on one side of the membrane and the intracellular (cytoplasmic side) on the other. The interiors of these membranes are nonpolar and inhospitable to ions. Ion channel research began in the 1950s with the theory that the giant squid axon undergoes changes that influence the transport of K^+ and Na^+ ions across its membrane. In 1955, studies using radioactive ^{42}K demonstrated that when K^+ ions flow in one direction, flow in the other direction is inhibited, suggesting a channel narrow enough to accommodate only a single file of ions. Research during the following 20 years demonstrated that the proteins that comprise Na^+ channels and K^+ channels are mutually exclusive, leading to the concept of a "selectivity filter." Ion flows are gated (turned off and on) by various stimuli. One of the most remarkable aspects of the K^+ channels, investigated by MacKinnon and others, is that they conduct ions incredibly rapidly (10^7-10^8 ions per second, almost as rapidly as ions collide with membrane) and yet are totally selective for K^+ over Na^+. This is remarkable since the radius of the Na^+ ions (0.95 Å) is significantly less than that of K^+ (1.33 Å) and thus a channel large enough to permit K^+ to flow through could also conduct Na^+.

In the late 1980s, the K^+ channel protein gene of the common fruit fly was cloned and its sequence revealed the amino acid sequence of the channel protein. The interesting question that emerged was which sequences of amino acids correspond to the pore, the selectivity filter, and the gate. In 1991, MacKinnon and colleagues discovered that the K^+ ion channel is actually a tetramer: four repetitions of the chain arranged in a cylinder. A particularly striking aspect is the fact that there is a highly conserved sequence of amino acids in this protein that is almost identical in humans, mice, fruit flies, plants, worms, bacteria, and archaea: Thr-Met-Thr-Thr-Val-Gly-Tyr-Gly (in humans). What that means is that this section of the protein is so perfectly optimized that it has remained virtually unchanged for over 3 billion years.

In collaboration with crystallographers, MacKinnon obtained an X-ray crystallographic structure at 3.2 Å resolution in 1998, with 2.0 Å resolution achieved in 2001. The details indicate that the conserved sequence is part of a loop that can be either external to the pore or extend into the pore to form the selectivity filter. This structure helps explain an interesting evolutionary anomaly. Charybdotoxin, a small protein in scorpion venom, inhibits the K^+ channel in skeleton muscle cells. MacKinnon discovered that it also inhibits the fruit fly K^+ channel protein and even the K^+ channel in *E. coli* bacteria. He posed the rhetorical question:

"This surprised us from an evolutionary standpoint, because why should a scorpion want to inhibit a bacterial K^+ channel!" The answer is that the venom binds to the external loop that includes the virtually perfect amino acid sequence that evolution has conserved.

When the pore loop reaches into the membrane it forms the filter that selects for K^+. Crystallographic studies of the K^+ channel protein provided visual understanding of its function. In the center there is a cavity 10 Å in diameter, large enough to hold a K^+ ion fully solvated by water molecules. The helical peptide chains that comprise the protein are oriented so that their negatively charged carboxylate ($-CO_2^-$) tails surround the K^+ ion. The pore leading to this cavity is narrow enough to allow passage of only one K^+ ion at a time. The structure of the pore channel filter, reinforced by the conserved amino acid sequence, has the carbonyl oxygen atoms in the protein chain ($-\mathbf{CO}-NH-$) lining the pore channel to mimic water solvation down the channel. The result is to create a low-energy pathway for K^+ in which it "feels" solvated by water through the pore/filter and into the cavity. The Na^+ ion, in contrast, is too small to "feel" solvated in the channel and lacks a low-energy route through the K^+ membrane channel protein.

In contrast to the structure of the K^+ channel, the Cl^- channel maintains a large cavity but the ion is surrounded by the positive amino ends ($-NH_3^+$) of peptide chains. The pore channel/filter places amide nitrogen atoms ($-CO-\mathbf{N}H-$) rather than carbonyl oxygen atoms in contact with Cl^-. The result is to create a low-energy pathway for an anion rather than for a cation through the Cl^- membrane channel protein. MacKinnon's group and others are currently involved in studies of the structure and function of the gating mechanism that opens and closes the channel at the intracellular end.

In 1988, Peter Agre and his research group discovered proteins, called aquaporins, which conduct water molecules across membranes and are found in all living organisms. While all cell membranes permit some small degree of water diffusion, some cells are specialized for significant water transport across their membranes. Aquaporins filter out protons and pass neutral water from the extracellular to the intracellular environment. They are particularly important as components of red blood cells, salivary glands, and renal tubules in kidneys. While the existence of water channel proteins was long suspected, actually finding them was quite difficult. Water comprises about 70 percent by weight of living organisms. To mark (label) specific sites of absorption is quite difficult. Agre, a hematologist, was studying blood Rh group antigens and accidentally isolated a protein of 28,000 daltons (atomic mass units, u) from red blood cells. The newly discovered protein was very abundant, some 200,000 molecules per red blood cell. Agre equated this to discovering a previously unknown and unmapped city having a population of 200,000.

In 1991, Agre's research group established that the new protein was a transmembrane protein and cloned the c-DNA (complementary strand

of DNA) from a red blood cell library and discovered the 269-amino
acid protein, initially called "aquaporin" but soon officially called AQP1,
the first water-channel protein. Its sequence suggested six layer-span-
ning domains including three extracellular loops (A, C, E) and two
intracellular loops (B, D) where A is close to the N (amino) end and E
is close to the C (carboxylate) end. Although there are four cysteine (R
= CH_2SH) amino acid residues, only one (Cys-189, present in loop E)
is reactive with added mercury, thus inhibiting water transport function. When site-directed mutagenesis is employed to substitute serine
(R = CH_2OH) for Cys-189, there is full permeability to water and no
inhibition by mercury. Similarly, replacement of alanine-73 (loop B) by
cysteine produces a mutant AQP1 that can be inhibited by mercury. It
seemed clear that loops B and E, although distant from each other in
linear sequence, are spatially close in AQP1. Both loop B and loop E
include a "signature motif": Asp-Pro-Ala. The model advanced by Agre
had the six membrane-spanning sections of a single AQP1 molecule fold
in such a way as to form a narrow channel formed by overlap of the two
Asp-Pro-Ala segments to form a circle. There are actually four AQP1
molecules (subunits) comprising the channel protein complex, each add-

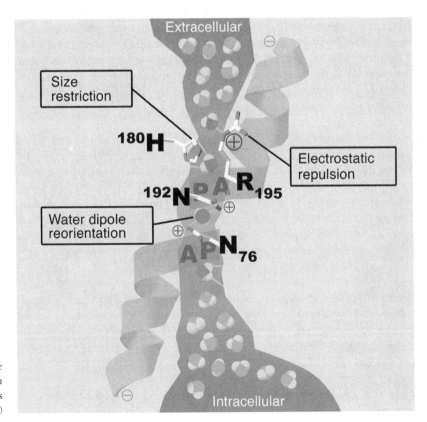

*Schematic diagram of the
narrow water channel in
aquaporin (AQP1) that repels
protons* (Dr. Peter Agre)

ing a ring formed by the two Asp-Pro-Ala units to form a channel. As Agre notes, the overall structure is reminiscent of an hourglass (see the figure on page 384). There is no active driving force—AQP1 is simply a conduit for carrying water.

The amazing ability of AQP1 to "strip" protons from H_3O^+ solutions and protect the interior cytoplasm of the cell from acidification is another evolutionary marvel in this protein. The structure of AQP1 explains this feature. Starting from the extracellular end, solvated H_3O^+ molecules enter a "vestibule" before moving toward the tightest "pinch" in the narrow channel. At this entrance sit protonated arginine and half-protonated histidine amino acid residues. These positively charged amino acids electrostatically repel protons which are reflected backward through the remaining water molecules so they cannot enter the channel (see the accompanying figure). A slightly different interpretation has H_2O molecules "flipping" their orientation at this point, disturbing the one-molecule thick "proton wire" that passes through the AQP1 "hourglass" and filtering out protons in this manner. AQP1 proteins are found in human kidneys. The closely related AQP2 is found in renal collecting ducts. AQP6, closely related genetically to AQP2, is not a good water conductor but conducts NO_3^- ions. AQP0 is located in the fiber cells of the eye lens, AQP4 is found in the brain, and AQP5 is found in salivary glands. There are also aquaglyceroporins AQP7 and AQP9 that transport glycerol. AQP7 is found in fat cells (adipocytes) where triglycerides are broken down during fasting and glycerol migrates through the cell membranes. In the fasted state glycerol is carried to liver cells (hepatocytes) and transported through the cell membranes by AQP9.

Protein Folding: Chaperoned and Unchaperoned

One of the most important and challenging problems in modern biochemistry is to discover how proteins fold into their three-dimensional (tertiary) structures. It is clear that proteins fold spontaneously in artificial environments outside of living systems (in vitro) as well as within living systems (in vivo). Studies that began in the late 1980s suggest that protein folding in vivo is also assisted by other proteins. All proteins are synthesized in linear sequence on ribosomes but they are only fully active in specific tertiary structures. What happens when newly synthesized protein molecules leave the ribosome? In an extended conformation they might simply clump together and damage the cell. During the 1990s evidence began to accumulate that some diseases, such as Alzheimer's and Parkinson's, are associated with errors in protein folding. Artificial proteins, created by site-directed mutagenesis or by solid-phase synthesis, have considerable potential as pharmaceutical agents. The ability to predict their folding is critical to success.

During the late 1920s Vincent du Vigneaud established the presence of disulfide (-S-S–) linkages in proteins. He discovered that insulin is gently reduced by glutathione to form thiol (-SH) units but when gently reoxidized to reform its disulfide linkages, the protein is inactive. Du Vigneaud realized that incorrect disulfide linkages were formed. The complete amino acid sequence (primary structure) of insulin was determined by Frederick Sanger in 1955. The protein consists of an A chain (21 amino acid residues) and a B chain (30 amino acids), with two interchain disulfide linkages and one intrachain disulfide linkage. The mystery of how the A and B chains correctly combine in insulin's biosynthesis was solved by Donald F. Steiner (1930–), University of Chicago, in 1967. He discovered that initially a "pro-hormone" he termed proinsulin is produced. Proinsulin is a single 86-amino acid chain in which a 35-amino acid section, called peptide-C, links the A and B chains. It is the single chain that facilitates folding that forms the correct disulfide linkages prior to enzymatic excision of peptide-C to form active insulin.

In 1961, Christian Anfinsen discovered that denaturation and reduction of ribonuclease A (124 amino acid residues) *in vitro* is fully reversible by removing the denaturing agent using dialysis and allowing the enzyme to reoxidize in air. It is a single chain with four disulfide linkages connecting the following cysteine residue pairs (#1 = amino end; #124 = carboxylate end): #26 and #84; #40 and #95; #58 and #110; and #65 and #72. This study and his investigations during the 1960s and 1970s indicated that the tertiary structure of a protein is inherently determined by its amino acid sequence. This conclusion was powerfully confirmed by Merrifield's automated total synthesis of ribonuclease, amino acid by amino acid, with full activity. Subsequent research showed that some proteins spontaneously refold to fully active structures in vitro while many others do not. The fact that folding is normally complete in seconds, minutes, or hours and not billions of years suggests specific pathways and intermediates rather than a random search. In vivo proteins normally fold into their active conformations and do so even much more rapidly than in vitro, suggesting that assistance occurs in living organisms.

While the peptide linkage in a protein is rigid and planar, there is free rotation about the alpha-carbon N-C and C-CO bonds. These torsional angles were termed φ and ψ respectively by Gopalasamudram Narayana Iyer (G.N.) Ramachandran (1922–2001), at Madras University, who developed a map for plotting the energies of conformations (secondary structures) of peptides and proteins. A protein 100 amino acids long has 50 φ and 50 ψ angles. As noted in chapter 6, completely free rotation of all angles to test all possible conformations of such a protein, at the rate of 1 billion per second, is estimated to require about 10 billion years: more than twice the age of the Earth ("Rosenthal's paradox"). As structural data on proteins began to accumulate, attempts were made to predict tertiary structures based on amino acid sequences (primary structures). Walter Kauzmann's 1959 prediction that hydrophobic amino acids seek the interior while hydrophilic amino acids seek the exterior of proteins was followed by systematic assignments of structural tendencies (e.g., "helix makers" and "helix breakers") by Harold A. Scheraga (1921–) at Cornell and many others. The emergence of powerful computational techniques based upon molecular mechanics and molecular dynamics advanced this field starting in the 1970s but even in the early 21st century computation of the pathway to a best tertiary structure remains an exceedingly complex task.

The study of protein folding in vivo is made more complex because it is assisted by two distinct classes of proteins. Both classes are ubiquitous and highly conserved in all living organisms (*archaebacteria, prokaryotes, eukaryotes*). One class consists of enzymes that include PDIs (protein disulfide isomerases) and PPIs (peptidyl prolyl isomerases). Isomerization of disulfide linkages and peptidyl proline isomerization are slow steps in protein folding. In 1991, James C. A. Bardwell, K. McGovern, and Jonathan R. Beckwith (1935–) at Harvard Medical School demonstrated that formation of disulfide linkages in *E. coli* proteins requires the presence of another protein, termed DsbA (Dsb = "disulfide bond") that oxidizes thiol (-SH) linkages. In turn, reduced DsbA must first be oxidized by another protein (DsbB) which is connected through an electron transport chain to O_2. In 2004, Beckwith, Hiroshi Kadokura, and their colleagues caught disulfide isomerization "in the act" when they isolated a mixed compound from mutant bacteria in which DsbA is actually bound to an extended protein molecule by a shared disulfide linkage.

The PPIs are a diverse class of enzymes first reported by Kurt Lang, Franz Schmid, and Gunter Fischer in 1987. Proline is the only cyclic common amino acid (the α-side chain R forms a 5-membered ring including the α-nitrogen). In a protein chain, proline residues induce hairpin turns. It is also unique in that *cis* and *trans* peptide linkages involving the proline nitrogen are about equal in energy while other peptide linkages are considerably more stable as *trans*. Shifting from *cis* to *trans* in the proline peptide linkage or vice versa is like pressing a light switch (on or off) and induces a large folding change in the protein. PPIs catalyze this *cis-trans* isomerization by lowering the rotational barrier of the normally stiff peptide (N-CO) linkage.

The second class of proteins that assist protein folding is termed *chaperonins* or *chaperone proteins*. They were discovered independently by Arthur L. Horwich (1951–), Yale School of Medicine, and Franz-Ulrich Hartl, Max Planck Institute of Biochemistry, who then collaborated and coauthored a paper in 1989. Actually, the history of chaperonins began about 20 years earlier with the discovery that fruit fly larvae exposed to heat produced "heat shock proteins" (Hsps). In 1980, Hsps were found in other organisms. Their amino acid sequences were found to be highly conserved in diverse organisms (e.g., yeasts and humans). Horwich and Hartl isolated Hsp60 from yeast and they and other researchers in the 1990s recognized the chaperone functions of Hsps and other stress proteins.

There remains today considerable debate about how chaperone proteins work. Perhaps the most widely studied chaperonin is GroEL60, closely related to Hsp60, and isolated from the cytoplasm of *E. coli* bacteria. GroEL is a barrel-shaped dimer, consisting of 7 units each (14 units total) of a 60 KDa protein, arranged like two stacked donuts. The interior of the empty barrel is lined with nonpolar amino acid residues that attract the hydrophobic sections of an unfolded (or partially folded) protein chain which sticks to the surface of one "donut" unit of the dimer. This unit then binds with ATP (actually 7 ATPs) as well as with a co-chaperonin called GroES, a unit that consists of 7 identical 10 KDa proteins and is shaped like a lid. Binding of GroES and ATP to GroEL sequesters the protein inside the barrel. In addition, the binding provides energy that causes a conformational change in GroEL. In the GroEL-GroES-ATP

What Is the Molecular Mass of a Protein?

The concept of molecular mass is generally a pretty straightforward one. To obtain the relative molecular mass of methane (CH_4) one need only consult the periodic table and add the atomic masses of carbon (12.011 u) and four hydrogen atoms (4×1.0079 u) to obtain 16.043 u. One mole of methane has a mass of 16.043 grams. Since 1.07 percent of naturally occurring carbon is actually ^{13}C (the natural abundance of ^3H is only 0.0115 percent), roughly 1 molecule per 100 CH_4 molecules is actually $^{13}CH_4$ with a molecular mass of 17.0 u instead of the 16.0 u mass of the remaining 99 molecules. Since it is exceedingly challenging to separate $^{12}CH_4$ and $^{13}CH_4$ and there is generally no reason to do so this has little interest except in mass spectrometry where two mass-to-charge (m/z) peaks, one at m/z 16.0 and one at m/z 17.0 in a ratio of 99:1, are expected for CH_4^+. (Actually, CH_3^+ and CH_5^+ are the major ions and each also exhibits the characteristic 99:1 isotope ratio). For a molecule such as C_{60} (buckyball), there are 60 independent ways of having a single carbon 13 in the molecule and the probability (relative abundance) of such an ion (m/z 721) is about 60×1 percent or 60 percent of the m/z 720 peak. That means for every 100 $^{12}C_{60}$ molecules there are about 60 $^{12}C_{59}{}^{13}C_1$ molecules. Although there are 1,770 different ways to obtain $^{12}C_{58}{}^{13}C_2$,

the probability for each one is 1 percent of 1 percent [$(0.01)^2 \times 100$] or 0.01 percent. The m/z 722 peak will be about 17 percent as abundant as the m/z 720 peak. The abundances continue to drop rapidly for m/z 723, 724, etc.

For a molecule of formula C_{120} the m/z 1,441 peak, corresponding to $^{12}C_{119}{}^{13}C_1$, should be 20 percent more abundant than m/z 1,440 peak which corresponds to $^{12}C_{120}$. Should the molecular mass be considered to be 1,441, corresponding to the most abundant molecule, or should it be 1,440, corresponding to the molecule composed entirely of the common ^{12}C isotope? Of course, if one wants to simply pour one mole of C_{60} powder, it contains 1 percent ^{13}C distributed statistically. Thus, 60×12.011 or 720.66 grams are required. One does not need a molecule as exotic as C_{60} or C_{120} to confront this issue. Naturally occurring chlorine includes 75.78 percent ^{35}Cl (34.97 u) and 24.22 percent ^{37}Cl (36.97 u). For the common solvent carbon tetrachloride (CCl_4) an interesting distribution occurs. There is only one way to obtain $C^{35}Cl_4$ (molecular mass 152) and its fraction can be calculated as $(0.7578)^4$ or 0.330. There is only one way to obtain $C^{37}Cl_4$ (molecular mass 160) and its fraction is $(0.2422)^4$ or 0.003. There are four equivalent ways of obtaining $C^{35}Cl_3{}^{37}Cl_1$ (molecular mass 154) and the fraction is $4 \times (0.7578)^3 \times$

complex, the exposed interior wall becomes hydrophilic (mimicking the external aqueous environment) and releases the protein chain which may begin to fold. Enzymatic hydrolysis of ATP to ADP furnishes the energy to release GroES and ADP into solution. The protein chain is then released to the solution. The next cycle involves binding with the other "donut" GroEL monomer. By sequestering individual protein molecules into the centers of these chaperones, clumping together of protein molecules and other potential defects are avoided. There remains considerable debate over whether complete folding (in one or a sequence of encapsulation-releases) occurs inside the barrel or whether the barrel simply sequesters unfolded protein chains, keeping them from clustering, diffuses from the source and releases them under dilute conditions where they fold without clustering. The increase in expression of chaperone

(0.2424) or 0.422. Similar considerations provide a fraction for $C^{35}Cl_2{}^{37}Cl_2$ (molecular mass 156) of 0.202 and for $C^{35}Cl_1{}^{37}Cl_3$ (molecular mass 158) a fraction of 0.043. The molecule of molecular mass 152, composed entirely of the lightest, most abundant nuclei (^{35}Cl), accounts for only 33.0 percent of the CCl_4 molecules. The most abundant molecules are those containing three ^{35}Cl and one ^{37}Cl, accounting for 42.2 percent. How should one report the molecular mass when a mass spectrometer can cleanly separate and identify all five isotopic CCl_4 species? Once again, a simple molecular mass determination using the ideal gas law would give the average molecular mass value $(12.011 + 4[35.45] = 153.81)$ and one mole of carbon tetrachloride weighs 153.81 grams.

Huge molecules such as proteins and nucleic acids include a range of molecular masses due to the statistical issues so evident in the preceding discussion. For example, the molecular mass of one specific protein having 69 amino acid residues is $C_{398}H_{618}N_{100}O_{132}S_3$. Taking atomic weights directly from a periodic table provides a molecular mass of 9,011.2 which is, in fact, an *average* molecular mass since it reflects the natural distribution of C, H, N, O, and S isotopes. One mole of this protein weighs 9,011.2 grams and an accurate osmotic pressure experiment will reflect this value. Mass spectral techniques, based on MALDI and electrospray, with the improved TOF (time-of-flight) instruments developed during

the 1990s, can resolve high molecular proteins of very similar m/z. These techniques directly measure m/z, not molecular mass. A huge protein analyzed using electrospray/TOF may have an m/z of 360,000 mass units/40 charges or 9,000. It is also possible to have singly charged species where m/z gives molecular mass directly. For the 69-residue amino acid protein under discussion, the most abundant mass is 9,011 daltons (Da) (15.9 percent), followed closely by mass 9,012 (15.0 percent), mass 9,010 (14.4 percent), 9,013 (12.4 percent), 9,009 (10.6 percent), 9,014 (9.1 percent), and others. Different "mixes" of atoms in other proteins (e.g., no sulfurs) give other distributions.

A commonly employed convention is to characterize the molecular mass of the protein by using the lightest isotopes. This is reasonable because for lighter atoms, such as C, H, O, N, S, and P, the stable isotopes of lowest atomic mass are also the most abundant isotopes. For the 69-amino acid protein of formula $C_{398}H_{618}N_{100}O_{132}S_3$, the lowest molecular mass is derived from the combined masses of the lightest nuclides of each element and equals 9,006.4 or 9,006 Da (9.006 KDa). This species is calculated to account for only 0.5 percent of the distribution noted above. Experimentally, it becomes an issue of sensitivity to accurately determine the first (lowest mass) peak in the series of isotopic peaks: the lowest monoisotopic molecular mass.

proteins under various conditions of stress (not just heat) protects the organism against clumping of denatured proteins. Chaperone proteins are not considered to be catalysts since their roles are to sequester proteins from other proteins and allow them to fold as they normally would with no involvement of a catalytic site. By many definitions they can be considered nanomachines.

In 1993, Stephen B. H. Kent (1945–) and collaborators used automated peptide synthesis to construct all-D-amino acid superoxide dismutase. As expected it folded so as to be the mirror image of the native (all-L) enzyme. This D-protein is equally effective as the native protein in catalyzing the disappearance of superoxide (O_2^-), a toxic species, because superoxide is achiral. The potential advantage of this approach is that D-proteins should not be destroyed by natural proteases nor should they elicit immune responses.

The Atomic-Scale Structure of a Ribosome

John C. Kendrew determined the first atomic-scale (2Å resolution) crystallographic structure of a protein, myoglobin (molecular mass 16,900 Da or 16.9 KDa) in 1959 and Max Perutz followed shortly afterward with atomic scale resolution of the tetrameric protein hemoglobin (64,500 Da). The first crystallographic structure for an enzyme, lysozyme (13,900 Da), was determined by David Phillips in 1965. The crystallographic analysis of the structure of the supermolecular photosynthetic reaction center of purple photosynthetic bacteria in 1985 led to a Nobel Prize in chemistry for Robert Huber, Johann Diesenhofer, and Hartmut Michel. The reaction center, a complete "nanomachine" embedded in the cell membrane of purple photosynthetic bacteria, consists of 4 protein subunits and 14 cofactors.

The structural biology of large complexes such as ribosomes (diameter ca. 21 nm or 210 Å) is complicated not only by their size but also by difficulties in crystallizing them. Progress was made in this area, particularly during the 1990s by a technique called cryo-electron microscopy (cryo-EM). Two scientists who have been recognized for playing a major role in this field are Joachim Frank, presently at the State University of New York at Albany, and David J. DeRosier (1939–), presently at Brandeis University. The technique requires embedding the particles for study in a glassy matrix typically at liquid nitrogen temperature (-321°F or -196°C), acquiring numerous cryo-EM images at different orientations, and then using them to computationally reconstruct a 3-D picture. This avoids the requirement of crystals suitable for X-ray crystallography although the resolution may be on the order of 8-10 Å. While this is not the atomic resolution achievable by X-ray crystallography, cryo-EM can provide more detail on the dynamics of such particles including rather dramatic movement within the ribosome. X-ray crystallography and cryo-electron microscopy are complementary.

The race toward high-resolution crystallography of the ribosome became very dramatic at the end of the 20th century and start of the 21st century. In 1999, Harry F. Noller (1939–   ) and coworkers at the University of California at Santa Cruz conducted an X-ray crystallographic study of intact bacterial ribosomes at the Advanced Light Source (ALS) Center at Lawrence Berkeley Laboratory. They achieved a resolution of 7.8 Å. In 2000, Thomas A. Steitz (1940–   ) and collaborators at Yale University and the Howard Hughes Medical Institute determined the X-ray crystallographic structure at atomic scale (2.4 Å resolution) of the large (50S) ribosomal unit from *Haloarcula marismortui*. The ribosome is a cell organelle visible by optical microscopy (there are about 15,000 ribosomes in an *E. coli* cell). Typical composition is about 65 percent RNA and 35 percent protein. The mass of a complete prokaryotic ribosome is about 2.6 million daltons (2.6 Megadaltons). The ribosome can be separated using an ultracentrifuge (chapter 3) into a large (50S) subunit and a small (30S) subunit. S refers to the Svedberg, the unit of the sedimentation coefficient (s) according to the Svedberg equation:

$$\text{Sedimentation Rate} = s\omega^2 x$$

where ω is the angular velocity (radians per second) of the centrifuge and x is the distance of the visible boundary of the protein layer in the centrifuge cell from the center of rotation in cm. The sedimentation coefficient s is directly proportional to the molecular weight of the protein and varies with the volume of the protein and the density of the solution. When s = 1 S (1 Svedberg), it corresponds to a value of 1×10^{-13} seconds. If the value of s = 30 S, it means that under the same solvent-temperature conditions, a given colloidal particle or large molecule will sediment thirty times more rapidly than an S = 1 colloid. The 50S ribosome subunit sediments 1.67 times more rapidly than the smaller 30S subunit under the same solvent and temperature conditions.

The large (50S) ribosomal subunit is where protein synthesis, catalyzed formation of peptide bonds, takes place. In light of the discoveries by Thomas Cech and Sidney Altman of ribozymes, RNA molecules that behave as enzymes, the question of catalysis of protein synthesis by RNA or proteins in the ribosome was a major one. The 30S ribosomal subunit is where transfer RNAs bind with ribosomal RNA codons. The 50S ribosomal subunit can be further separated into a 23S secondary subunit and a smaller 5S secondary subunit that are normally held together by protein molecules. The 23S subunit includes 3045 nucleotides and 31 proteins. There are six discrete RNA domains in the S23 unit particle. The 5S unit effectively adds a seventh domain. The proteins permeate the exterior of the RNA of S23, but are located over 18 Å distant from the active site of catalytic protein bond formation. The structures of complexes of the S23 subunit with two inactive substrate molecules suggest mechanistic similarities to the enzyme chymotrypsin. The S23 structure indicates that an adenine base at the active site plays a role analogous to that of histidine-

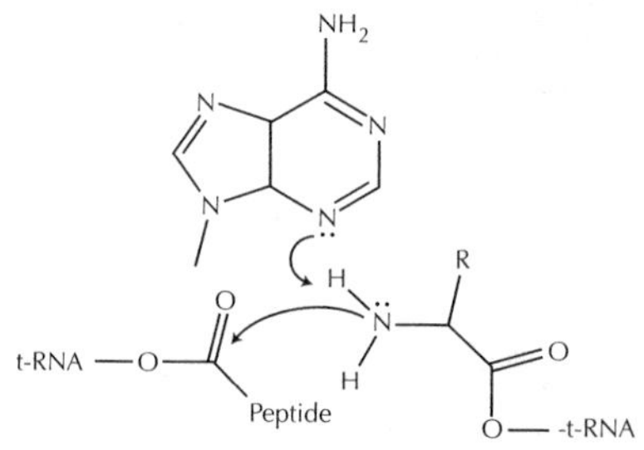

The mechanistic role of a rRNA base in protein synthesis

57 in chymotrypsin. In summary, the ribosome behaves as a ribozyme in the synthesis of proteins.

In 2001, Noller's team and the ALS Center achieved an X-ray crystallographic structure of the ribosome at 5.5 Å resolution. In 2005, the Santa Cruz team in collaboration with researchers at the Free University of Berlin (Germany) achieved a crystallographic structure on a complete ribosome of 3.5 Å. These are really amazing results for a complex structure on the order of 200 Å in each dimension. Combination of such high-resolution images with the dynamic images from the lower-resolution cryo-EM approach should in the coming years provide enormous insight into the workings of the protein factory present in the cells of all organisms on Earth.

If There Was an "RNA World," What Preceded It?

The excitement over the discovery in 1944 that DNA is the genetic material, the discovery of its structure in 1953, and how the genetic code functions focused most of the initial attention on this molecule. Starting in the 1960s, there began a growing realization that while rigid, double-stranded DNA is an archival library, the far more flexible RNA family of molecules (mRNA, rRNA, and tRNA) serves a wider variety of functions and may be the key to a primordial "RNA world." This hypothesis was strengthened by the discovery of ribozymes, catalytic RNA, during the 1980s and the atomic-scale structure of the ribosome and understanding of the catalytic role of rRNA starting in the late 1990s.

The logical problem in imagining a prebiotic DNA/protein world is determining which came first: the genetic library to specify proteins or the enzymes that catalyze the formation of DNA? "RNA world" appears to solve some of this dilemma since RNA is both informational and catalytic. However, RNA is very reactive and does not appear to be capable of synthesis and survival under prebiotic conditions.

There is simply no firm fossil evidence identifying primordial biochemistry. In the evolution of flowering plants, the fossil record is rather clear that flowers having radial symmetry (like daffodils) predate those with a plane of symmetry such as orchids. *Archaeopteryx* is widely accepted as fossil evidence for a transition between dinosaurs and birds. There are also numerous examples of primitive organisms such as the Archaea and the rare *Coelacanth* fish, organisms that diverged early and are still living. There are no corresponding biochemical (pre-protein, pre-nucleic acid) fossils, transition models, or living molecules.

In the absence of such data, scientists can only speculate and test speculation against experiment. Robin D. Knight and Laura F. Landweber, Princeton University, describe one such hypothesis: PNAs or peptide nucleic acids (see the structure below). The molecule has a polymeric backbone, based on N-(2-aminoethyl)-glycine (AEG), which has five single bonds separating each "peptide" linkage. In polypeptides and proteins there are two single bonds that intervene between each peptide linkage. This chain serves the function of the ribose phosphate polymeric backbone in RNA. Attached to each nonpeptide nitrogen is an N-acetic acid derivative (N-AA) for each base (purine or pyrimidine), providing the informational component. Prebiotic-type syntheses of AEG, its polymer and N-AAs have been demonstrated although support is not yet conclusive for this pathway nor for the ability of PNA to demonstrate both catalytic and informational utility. The PNA hypothesis implies that the genetic code arose from some more primitive early "cross talk" between future nucleotides and amino acids. The study of aptamers (next sidebar) seems to support this view.

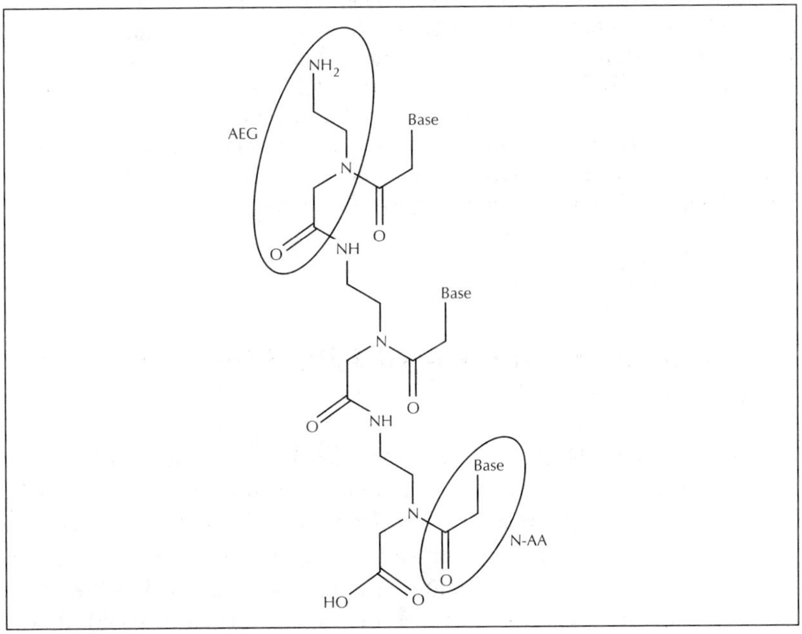

Postulated structure of a peptide nucleic acid (PNA)

Aptamers as Substitutes for Antibodies in Research

The use of animal antibodies to detect antigens is highly effective but it involves the use of animals, complex separations, and has a variety of limitations. Starting around 1990 a new method for detection and separation of substances, including amino acids, proteins, and pharmaceuticals, was developed based on synthetic nucleic acids termed aptomers (*aptos* = "to fit"). Aptomers are DNA or RNA molecules that bind with high specificity to certain molecules. Their application depends upon many principles described earlier in this book: chromatography, combinatorial chemistry, and the polymerase chain reaction (PCR) technique.

The formation of aptamers rests upon a technique termed SELEX (systematic evolution of ligands by exponential enrichment). It involves the synthesis of a DNA molecule with constant sections at both ends and a randomly variable segment of nucleotides in the middle. A variable segment as short as 10 nucleotides has a combinatorial library of 4^{10} or about 10^6 different sequences; a variable sequence of 30 nucleotides generates a combinatorial library of 4^{30} or about 10^{18} different sequences. The DNA mixture so synthesized is then enzymatically transcribed to a combinatorial RNA library. This mixture is applied to a chromatography column in which the substance of interest (e.g., amino acid, protein, drug) is bound. RNA molecules in the combinatorial library that do not bind with the target compound are simply washed out of the column.

The few selected RNA molecules are then eluted by a solution containing the molecule of interest. Active RNA aptamers are used as templates for enzymatic synthesis of the corresponding DNA. The resulting samples of DNA are then amplified using PCR and sequenced so that the specific synthetic DNA or RNA aptamer may be obtained in high yield.

In their discussion (previous section), Knight and Landweber note the surprising, if logical, relationship of aptamers for specific amino acids and the codons at their amino acid binding sites. The aptamers have an abundance, well beyond statistical, of the codon specific for that amino acid. It is not fully clear why such specificity should work so well since transcription does not involve binding an amino acid directly to a codon. Although the codon in mRNA binds the anticodon in the tRNA molecule carrying the specific amino acid in question, the mechanism for coupling of a specific tRNA molecule with its amino acid is more complex. That key step is catalyzed by aminoacyl tRNA synthetases that bring the corresponding tRNA and amino acid molecules together. In some cases, this involves recognition by the synthetase of the specific anticodon on tRNA but it usually involves other structural factors. The experimental observations using SELEX that RNA codons strongly influence favorable binding of the amino acids they encode suggests a possible course for earlier stages in the evolution of the genetic code.

A Chemical Taxonomy of Life: Genomics and Proteomics

Carolus Linnaeus (1707–78) published his book *Species Plantarum* in 1753 and started the science of taxonomy of plants as well as animals. Linnaean taxonomy, which remains the basis of modern classification, relies upon structure (morphology) and function. The close relationship between horses and zebras is quite clear to any observer. On the other hand, a new observer (a scientist from another planet?) would almost certainly initially conclude that a dolphin is more similar to a shark than to a horse. It would take closer observation and more detailed study to learn that dolphins, like horses, are warm-blooded, suckle their young, and do not lay eggs.

There are much more subtle differences between closely related animals or plants. The figure below is a modern cladogram demonstrating genetic relationships between six species of clams, supplied by Robert C. Vrijenhoek (1946–). These genetic relationships are derived through comparison of the DNA sequences pertaining to mitochondrial oxidase I in the six species. Prior to this chemically based taxonomy, classification was based upon the structure (morphology) of the clamshells. The four species derived from genus *Calyptogena* are not as closely related as their shells seemed to indicate. Indeed, *Calyptogena kilmeri* is more closely related to *Ectenagena extenta* and also *Vesicomya gigas* than to the other three species also classified as *Calyptogena*.

The systematic study of whole DNA sequences is termed genomics and, although in its infancy, will have revolutionary impacts on evolutionary biology, anthropology, and human health. An example is furnished by the study of the DNA in mitochondria, the energy-producing organelles in cells, thought to have been separate, very primitive organisms in the early life history of the Earth. Their DNA molecules are much smaller and simpler in sequence than DNA in the nuclear zone of prokaryotes or in chromosomes. Mitochondrial DNA is not reproduced sexually and is

Chemical taxonomy of clams based on DNA sequences, in contrast to taxonomy based on morphology (shell structure; information supplied by Dr. Robert Vrijenhoek). Calyptogena elongata is morphologically similar to Calyptogena kilmeri, but its DNA is actually closer to that of a clam, Vesicomya gigas, of a different genus.

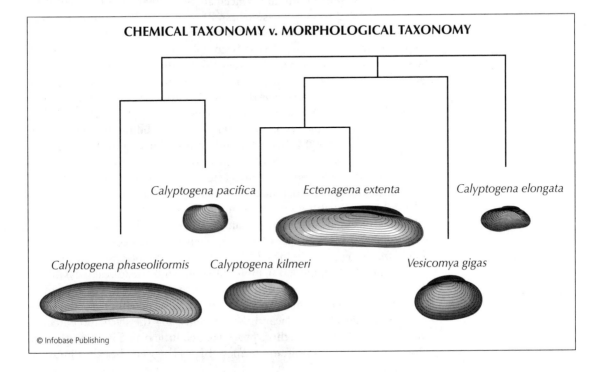

CHEMICAL TAXONOMY v. MORPHOLOGICAL TAXONOMY

Calyptogena pacifica

Ectenagena extenta

Calyptogena elongata

Calyptogena phaseoliformis

Calyptogena kilmeri

Vesicomya gigas

© Infobase Publishing

passed through generations maternally. Mitochondrial DNA sequencing of living populations of humans during the 1980s has established that *Homo sapiens* is at least 200,000 years old and originated in Africa. There is general agreement that migration from Africa began 60,000 to 85,000 years ago although there are disagreements about specific migration paths and timing after that period.

In 1990, the National Institutes of Health (NIH) began the Human Genome Project, effectively the "moon shot of biochemistry." The project, a worldwide collaboration, involved very systematic degradation of DNA from a wide selection of human volunteers whose identities remain anonymous. The minuscule quantities of DNA fragments obtained were enhanced by orders of magnitude using the polymerase chain reaction (PCR, see chapter 9). During the mid-1990s, J. Craig Venter (1946–), a geneticist who joined the NIH in 1984 but then formed the Institute for Genomics Research (TIGR) in 1992, developed an independent approach that he was certain would complete the project much more rapidly than the NIH approach. His "whole genome shotgun" method was based upon degradation of DNA to produce random fragments and computer reconstruction of the sequences. In 1995 TIGR and researchers at the University of California at Berkeley announced the complete sequence for the genome of a bacterium: the first completed genome of an organism. Venter formed Celera Genomics in 1998 and reported the complete genome of the fruit fly in 2000. Celera and the NIH began to collaborate and jointly announced in June 2000 the sequence of 90 percent of the 2.9 billion base pairs (50 million to 300 million for each chromosome) in human DNA and published the findings in 2001. In 2003, the NIH announced virtual completion (over 99 percent of the base pairs) of the sequence. The total cost for the NIH effort is estimated at $2.7 billion (1991 dollars). One surprise from the Human Genome Project was the discovery that the human genome includes about 30,000 genes. The number was previously assumed to be as high as 200,000. The genome of a rat includes about 30,000 genes (2.75 billion base pairs), that of the fruit fly 13,600 genes (180 million base pairs), and the bacterium *E. coli* 3,200 genes (4.7 million base pairs).

Comparative analyses of amino acid sequences of proteins began in the 1960s and quickly demonstrated evolutionary relationships between related proteins within an organism and between homologous proteins of different organisms. Myoglobin and hemoglobin are so similar in function and sequence that they likely evolved from a common ancestor. The same is true for the proteolytic enzymes chymotrypsin and trypsin. The alpha-chain in human hemoglobin (141 amino acid residues) differs from that of an elephant by 18 percent of its residues, 30 percent from an ostrich, 33 percent from a crocodile, and roughly equally from the goldfish (48 percent), the coelacanth (49 percent), and the shark (50 percent), suggesting that these last three have changed little over 350 million years. Today a computer program termed BLAST (Basic Local Alignment

Search Tool) is available on the World Wide Web to compare sequences between different nucleotides or proteins in order to search for homologies. Such studies also support research into the very nature of protein evolution. It appears that amino acids present at critical folding sites and at the active sites of enzymes are more conserved than less "consequential" enzymes. It is also clear that, under evolutionary pressure, groups of amino acids on different parts of a protein chain forming a critical unit, such as a reactive site, probably coevolve. This exciting approach toward understanding the evolution of life at the molecular scale will provide exciting insights well into the 21st century.

"Green Chemistry"

During the 1990s there was a revolutionary movement to a new type of chemistry collectively determined "green chemistry", meaning environmentally friendly chemistry. On its Web site, the U.S. Environmental Protection Agency lists 12 Principles of Green Chemistry:

1. Prevent waste
2. Design safer chemicals and products
3. Design less-hazardous chemical syntheses
4. Use renewable feedstocks (often from agricultural products)
5. Use catalysis, not stoichiometric reagents (catalysts are used in small amounts and re-used many times; stoichiometric reagents are used once)
6. Avoid chemical derivatives (blocking or protecting groups, once removed, may generate waste)
7. Maximize atom economy (design processes so as not to "waste" atoms)
8. Use safer solvents and reaction conditions
9. Increase energy efficiency (run reactions at ambient temperature and pressure)
10. Design chemicals and products to degrade after use
11. Analyze in real time to prevent pollution (monitoring to insure maximum efficiency)
12. Minimize the potential for accidents

One example of the use of renewable feedstocks is the extraction of a precursor of the anticancer compound paclitaxel (Taxol) from the needles of English yew shrubs. Taxol was originally discovered in the bark of Pacific yew trees, but in quantities so small that large amounts of bark would have to be stripped, killing trees the replacements for which require 200 years to grow and mature. A published 40-step chemical synthesis of taxol was also not practical commercially. The needles of the English yew shrub are rapidly renewable. Bristol-Meyers Squibb, partnering with the National Cancer Institute in 1991, developed a semisynthetic process based upon the paclitaxel precursor and put it into production in 1995. In the late 1990s, the company applied biotechnology to develop an inexpensive process for direct production of paclitaxel. Cell clusters from needles of the Chinese yew tree are started in petri dishes, cultured in fermenters that produce paclitaxel, which is then purified by chromatography and crystallization. The process uses renewable resources, is biologically benign, eliminates many steps, and cuts down on the need for solvents and reagents.

A second example is the use of a renewable feedstock, lactic acid, to make a biodegradable plastic. The first such polymer, polylactic acid, was actually made in 1932 by Wallace Carothers at DuPont. Dextrose [D-(+)-glucose], obtained from corn, sugar beets, or other crops, is readily fermented to lactic acid. In some instances, both L-(+)-lactic acid and the less common D-(-)-lactic acid are obtained. Lactic acid ($C_3H_6O_3$) is readily dimerized with loss of two molecules of water to form "lactide" ($C_6H_8O_4$). Lactide may be polymerized to polylactic acid under mild conditions. Since lactide may be formed as the L,L, the D,D or the *meso* (D,L = L,D) compound, polylactic acid may be pure L, pure D, 1:1 L and D (the racemate), or other mixtures. Just as isotactic polypropylene, formed by Ziegler-Natta polymerization (see chapter 6), is comprised of polymer chains that are all-*R* or all-*S* and is highly ordered, crystalline polylactic acid polymers includes pure D or pure S chains. Polylactic acid is thermoplastic, meaning that it may be molded by heat into a permanent shape. It is biodegradable and particularly well suited for application as disposable meal utensils, food packaging, or compost bags.

There are numerous other innovations that distinguish the development of green chemistry. Olefin metathesis, recognized with the 2005 Nobel Prize in chemistry, is regarded as a "green reaction." It employs catalysts and, in the best processes, redistributes but does not waste carbon atoms. There are continuing efforts to remove chlorine from chemical processes, as solvents and oxidizers, due to toxicity and persistence in the environment. There is renewed interest in water as a solvent for the manufacture of organic substances. That would, at first, appear to be a contradiction in terms since so many organic substances have low water solubilities. Moreover, many organometallic catalysts react and/or lose activity in water. Yet there are active studies of homogeneous catalysis in water. Ironically, the hydrophobic ("water-fearing") nature of many organic molecules can be used to advantage. For example, the Diels-Alder reaction is typically a reaction between two hydrophobic molecules. In many instances there are two potential products: a more extended molecule and a more compact molecule. In water, the more compact hydrophobic molecule is favored since it minimizes surface interaction with water.

During the 1990s, two truly novel "green" approaches to industrial solvents began to mature. One of these involves the use of ionic liquids and the other supercritical carbon dioxide. The term "ionic liquids" almost suggests an oxymoron (internal inconsistency). One normally thinks of ionic substances, such as sodium chloride (NaCl) or calcium carbonate (CaCO₃), as very-high-melting solids. However, substances composed of larger cations and anions exhibit diminished electrostatic attractions and lower melting points. In 1914, the Latvian-born German chemist Paul Walden (1863–1958) was the first to characterize a room-temperature ionic liquid: ethylammonium nitrate ($C_2H_5NH_3^+NO_3^-$, mp 54°F or 12°C). But interest in this and other ionic liquids would languish for almost 70 years. Two decades earlier, Walden had made the fundamental discovery of the stereochemistry ("Walden inversion") of the substitution reaction later termed S_N2 by Ingold and Hughes in the 1930s.

The modern era of ionic liquids began during the 1980s with the formulation of binary liquid systems, combining for example 1-ethyl-3-methylimidazolium ("emim") chloride with aluminum chloride ($AlCl_3$) to form low-melting systems such as (emim)Cl-AlCl₃ [better represented with $(emim)Al_2Cl_7^-$, shown below, right, rather than $(emim)AlCl_4^-$]. In contrast to a simple salt like ethylammonium nitrate, there are different formulations for (enim)Cl-AlCl₃ that vary with the mole ratios of AlCl₃ to emim and produce mixtures of ionic species. The "green" aspect of ionic liquids is that they have insignificant vapor pressures (or at least exceedingly minute vapor pressures). Industrial-scale reactions in ionic liquids produce no (or at least virtually no) fugitive emissions of solvent vapor. The ability to continuously vary mole fraction provides a wide range of "designer solvents." Rather than simply being beneficial as the result of their negligible vapor pressure, ionic liquids possess novel solvent properties that facilitate some chemical reactions. They have been used as solvents for catalytic cracking of polyethylene to light alkanes and for low-temperature, highly selective Diels-Alder reactions to name two of hundreds if not thousands of applications.

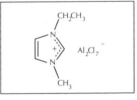

Ionic liquid: emim-Al₂Cl₇

Chapter 8 briefly introduced the concept of *supercritical fluids* in the context of undersea thermal vents. The supercritical point for water occurs at a temperature of 705°F (374°C) and a pressure of 222.3 bar (atmosphere). Above this temperature, no pressure can condense water to its liquid state. For carbon dioxide (CO_2), the critical temperature (88.0°F or 31.1°C) and critical pressure (73.8 bar) are much lower. Above the supercritical point, CO_2 behaves as a liquidlike gas: liquidlike densities, gaslike viscosities. The solubility properties of supercritical CO_2 are "tunable" by varying temperature and/or pressure. Density and dielectric constant increase with increasing pressure and decreasing temperature. Water and ionic substances are insoluble in supercritical CO_2. The ability of supercritical CO_2 to dissolve and extract relatively non-polar substances has been known for decades. The range may be extended by adding polar solvents such as methanol or acetone. The addition of surfactants helps to disperse microscopic particles to form colloidal suspensions. Carbon dioxide is nonflammable, nontoxic, and inexpensive.

The first major industrial application of supercritical CO_2 was in the extraction of caffeine (96–98 percent efficiency) from coffee beans.

This was previously done using methylene chloride (CH_2Cl_2) which also removes some flavor and aroma components from the beans. Methylene chloride is toxic and even trace quantities in the extracted beans are undesirable. While carbon dioxide is a greenhouse gas, no new CO_2 needs to be created in order to employ it as a solvent. NASA, noting that 95 percent of the Martian atmosphere is CO_2, is even contemplating recovery of fuels such as magnesium from the Martian surface using supercritical CO_2.

Although many chemists and engineers have investigated and applied supercritical fluids as solvents, the studies of Joseph M. DeSimone (1964–) at the University of North Carolina at Chapel Hill are of particular note. He employs supercritical CO_2 as a solvent for certain polymerization reactions. As noted above, supercritical CO_2 is a poor

Scientist of the Decade: Ahmed H. Zewail (1946–)

Ahmed H. Zewail, winner of the 1999 Nobel Prize in chemistry for his work on femtosecond kinetics (Caltech Public Relations Office)

Ahmed H. Zewail was born in the city of Damanhur in northern Egypt, located close to and almost equidistant from the Mediterranean port city of Alexandria and the town of Rosetta. The Library and Museum of Alexandria, the greatest library of antiquity, was built starting in the third century b.c.e. with a "daughter" library built around 235 b.c.e. The library lasted centuries until it was destroyed in civil wars in the late third century c.e. with the "daughter" library destroyed by Christians in 391. Rosetta is the location of the discovery in 1799 of the Rosetta Stone, the piece of black basalt that held the key to understanding ancient Egyptian hieroglyphics. Zewail was raised in the city of Disuq. His father was a government official and a businessman and his mother devoted herself to her son and three daughters. His intellectual gifts were recognized early and the family placed a sign on the door to his study room: "Dr. Ahmed", in the warm and familiar style that Egyptians often use to refer to distinguished professional colleagues.

The young "Dr. Ahmed" was passionate about reading and enjoyed music, some sports, and backgammon. His early interest in things scien-

solvent for polar and ionic substances. It finds use as a solvent for polymerization of fluoropolymers related to polytetrafluoroethylene (Teflon) as well as silicone-based polymers. Chlorofluorocarbons (CFCs), once used as solvents for the preparation of fluoropolymers, were found in the 1970s to contribute to destruction of the stratospheric ozone layer (see chapter 8) and were phased out. Supercritical CO_2 finds application in synthesis of dispersion polymers. The monomer methylmethacrylate is soluble in supercritical CO_2 but the growing polymethylmethacrylate (PMMA) chains are insoluble. Addition of a small quantity of surfactant suspends colloid-size particles that continue to polymerize. Many other applications of supercritical CO_2 are in process or can be envisioned. With added surfactant, it is often employed in the dry-cleaning industry in place of the probable human carcinogen perchloroethylene ("perc" or

tific and mechanical had him assemble an apparatus of several test tubes and a small oil burner to decompose wood into flammable gas and a liquid. He was accepted for study in science at Alexandria University. Visiting the campus with a favorite uncle, Zewail noted: "I had tears in my eyes as I felt the greatness of the university and the sacredness of its atmosphere." He graduated with a bachelor of science "Distinction with First Class Honor" and was given a lifetime appointment at Alexandria University, initially as *Moeid* (demonstrator) with the expectation of his pursuing research toward a master's degree and then a Ph.D. and a professorship at the university. After he completed a master's project on spectroscopy, two of his mentors at Alexandria encouraged him to pursue a Ph.D. in the United States. This period followed the 1967 Six-Day War between Israel and its Arab neighbors including Egypt. Relations between Egypt and the United States, Israel's closest ally, were strained and there was considerable mutual distrust. However, Zewail obtained full academic support as a graduate student from the University of Pennsylvania, met the challenges posed by a different language and culture, and was educated in chemistry and in physics. His thesis work was virtually completed in 1973, the year of the Yom Kippur War. With an eye toward his eventual return to Alexandria University, Zewail went to Berkeley as a postdoctoral associate with Charles Harris. With Professor Harris, Zewail learned much about lasers and started investigating picosecond (10^{-12} s) spectroscopy. By 1976 he had a number of attractive offers of faculty positions and joined Caltech. His breakthrough studies in femtosecond (10^{-15} s) spectroscopy appeared in 1987. He would win the 1999 Nobel Prize in chemistry for femtosecond studies of the transition states of reactions, a feat long thought to be impossible. Zewail was the third Egyptian to win a Nobel Prize. Anwar el-Sadat, president of Egypt, and Menachem Begin, prime minister of Israel, shared the 1978 Nobel Peace Prize, and Naguib Mahfouz won the 1988 Nobel Prize in literature.

Zewail's interests stretch well beyond science and include dedication to improving the plight of the poor worldwide. He has received well over 100 major awards, the elementary school he attended bears his name as does a road to Rosetta, and he has been awarded the Grand Collar of the Nile, Egypt's highest distinction. His image was engraved upon two Egyptian postage stamps. Zewail is currently Linus Pauling Professor of Chemistry and Professor of Physics at Caltech.

tetrachloroethylene, C_2Cl_4). Dissolved impurities such as "grease" are readily separated from supercritical CO_2 by depressurizing the solvent and thus reducing its density.

Conclusion

At the end of the 20th century chemists were working with very large molecules, their complexes, and even working systems that mimic the feedback loops that characterize processes such as metabolism. These studies have been enabled by a combination of synthetic techniques and instrumental analysis, especially mass spectrometry (MALDI-TOF), high field NMR, scanning tunneling microscopy (STM), cryo-electron microscopy, and X-ray crystallography. The application of density function theory (DFT) to quantum chemical computation, combined with exponential advances in computing power (hardware, software, and graphic interfaces), allows accurate computations of large molecules unimaginable a few years earlier. Biological complexes, such as the ribosome, are being studied spatially and temporally and the conclusions will clarify much about how living systems function. The 1990s can really be considered the first decade of nanotechnology research *and* application. The design of materials and machines at the molecular level augurs huge impacts on the 21st century economy. During the 1990s the *Hubble Space Telescope* provided the first evidence of an atmosphere on an extrasolar planet. Space probes have also provided tantalizing hints of potential abodes of life in Earth's own solar system. The possibility of finding extraterrestrial life, at least at a very elementary level, during the 21st century seems very real. Discovery of even the most elementary extraterrestrial organisms would have the most profound imaginable impact upon chemistry and the life sciences. The world is expected to exhaust its petroleum reserves at mid-century and clearly must solve its energy problem by then. It is hoped that progress toward reversing global climate change and fully implementing "green manufacturing" will have occurred well before that time.

Further Reading

Bada, Jeffrey L. "Extraterrestrial Handedness?" *Science* 275 (1997): 942–43. This is a brief commentary on the discovery of an excess of L-amino acids on the Murchison meteorite.

Bag, Braja Gopal, and Günter von Kiedrowski. "Templates, Autocatalysis and Molecular Replication." *Pure & Applied Chemistry* 68 (1996): 2,145–52. This accessible article provides principles of molecular self-replication and describes investigations in the field.

Baneyx, François. "Molecular Chaperones and Foldases," University of Washington. Available online. URL: http://faculty.washington.edu/baneyx/res/Chaperones.html. Accessed April 4, 2006. This site describes protein chaperones as well as folding enzymes.

Ban, Nenad, Poul Nissen, Jeffrey Hansen, Peter B. Moore, and Thomas A. Steitz. "The Complete Atomic Structure of the Large Ribosomal Subunit at 2.4 Å Resolution." *Science* 289 (2000): 905–20. This is the first of two consecutive articles on the X-ray structure of the ribosome.

Baskin, J. Spencer, and Ahmed H. Zewail. "Freezing Atoms in Motion: Principles of Femtochemistry and Demonstration of Laser Stroboscopy." *Journal of Chemical Education* 78 (2001): 737–51. This is a challenging but accessible introduction to the techniques and promise of femto-chemistry.

BI Biointelligence Laboratory. "Molecular Motors," Seoul National University. Available online. URL: http://bi.snu.ac.kr/Courses/g-ai04/motors-1.ppt#3. Accessed April 3, 2006. This is a pictorial tour of nano-machines, both manmade and biological.

Blackmond, Donna G. "Asymmetric Autocatalysis and its Implications for the Origin of Homochirality." *Proceedings of the National Academy of Sciences* 101 (2004): 5,732–36. This review describes the kinetics of auto-catalysis and possible mechanisms for spontaneous resolution of mixtures having a miniscule excess of one enantiomer.

Borman, Stu. "Scientists Refine Understanding of Protein Folding and Design." *Chemical & Engineering News* 74 (May 26, 1996): 29–35. This is a very accessible, well-illustrated discussion of mechanisms of protein folding.

Bowden, Ned B., Marcus Weck, Insung S. Choi, and George M. Whitesides. "Molecule-Mimetic Chemistry and Mesoscale Self-Assembly." *Accounts of Chemical Research* 34 (2001): 231–38. This brief review explores progress in the self-assembly of nanodevices.

Cronin, John R., and Sandra Pizzarello. "Enantiomeric Excesses in Meteoric Amino Acids," *Science* 275 (1997): 951–55. This is the first truly definitive report of an excess of uncommon L-amino acids on the Murchison meteorite.

Drexler, K. Eric. "Machine-Phase Nanotechnology." *Scientific American* 285 (September 2001): 74–75. The author describes the potential for self-assembling assemblers ("nanobots") and the risks they might pose.

Earle, Martyn J., and Kenneth R. Seddon. "Ionic liquids. Green solvents for the future." *Pure and Applied Chemistry* 72 (2000): 1,391–98. This is a very brief and accessible review of ionic liquids.

Horwich, Arthur, "Horwich Laboratory Web Site," Yale University. Available online: URL: http://info.med.yale.edu/genetics/horwich/. Accessed April 3, 2006. This site describes a mechanism for protein folding by the GroEL/GroES chaperone system.

Iwamura, Hiizu. "Approaches from Superhigh-Spin Molecules to Organic Ferromagnets." *Pure & Applied Chemistry* 65 (1993): 57–64. This is a very accessible brief review describing principles in the design of organic ferromagnets and providing a survey of molecules investigated for related applications.

Jones, John E., III. *Tammy Kitzmiller, et al. (Plaintiffs) v. Dover Area School District, et al. (Defendants), Case No. 04cv2688, In the United States District Court for the Middle District of Pennsylvania (2005).* Available online. URL: http://msnbcmedia.msn.com/i/msnbc/sections/news/051220_kitzmiller_342.pdf. Accessed March 18, 2006. This is the full written opinion of U.S. District Court Judge John E. Jones, III, on the "intelligent design" suit involving the School Board of Dover, Pennsylvania, argued during 2005–06.

Kirschner, Marc W., and John C. Gerhart. *The Plausibility of Life: Resolving Darwin's Dilemma.* New Haven, Conn.: Yale University Press, 2005. This book provides highly accessible coverage of the most recent discoveries in evolutionary biochemistry and biology.

Knight, Robin D., and Laura F. Landweber. "The Early Evolution of the Genetic Code." *Cell* 101 (2000): 569–72. This very accessible paper describes the requirements of a prebiotic, "pre-RNA world" and potential protein nucleic acid (PNA) molecules.

Krossing, Ingo, and Ines Raabe. "Noncoordinating Anions: Fact or Fiction? A Survey of Likely Candidates." *Angewandte Chemie International Edition* 43 (2004): 2,066–90. This is an in-depth review of weakly coordinating anions (WCAs) and the cations whose isolation they enable.

Lieber, Charles M. "The Incredible Shrinking Circuit." *Scientific American* 285 (September, 2001): 58–64. This is an accessible article describing how arrays of molecules are connected to produce nanochips, nanocomputers, and other nanoelectronic devices.

National Aeronautics and Space Administration (NASA). "The Hubble Space Telescope." Available online. URL: http://hubble.nasa.gov/index.php. Accessed March 12, 2006. This is NASA's complete guide to the history, mission, structure, and results obtained by the *Hubble Space Telescope (HST).*

Nissen, Poul, Jeffrey Hansen, Nenad Ban, Peter B. Moore, and Thomas A. Steitz. *Science* 289 (2000): 920–30. This is the second of two consecutive articles on the X-ray structure of the ribosome and focuses on the mechanism of its ribozyme activity.

Oganessian, Yuri Ts., Vladimir K. Utyonkov, and Kenton J. Moody. "Voyage to Superheavy Island." *Scientific American* 282 (January 2000): 63–67. This is a highly accessible discussion of the synthesis of superheavy elements using both "cold fusion" and "hot fusion" techniques.

Pizzarello, Sandra. "The Chemistry of Life's Origin: A Carbonaceous Meteorite Perspective." *Accounts of Chemical Research* 39 (2006): 231–37. This brief review article discusses the possible origins of homochirality on Earth.

"The Proper Study of Mankind." *The Economist* 377 (December 24, 2005): 10 pp, following p. 74.

Saibil, Helen, "Molecular Chaperone Group School of Crystallography," Available online. URL: http://people.cryst.bbk.ac.uk/~ubcg16z/chaperone.html. Accessed April 3, 2006. This Web site has animations of chaperone proteins and a directory of other related sites.

Schädel, Matthias. "Chemistry of Superheavy Elements." *Angewandte Chemie International Edition* 45 (2006): 368–401. This is a review article accessible to most scientists and, to some extent, a more general readership and is the source for most of the discussion of superheavy elements in this chapter.

Shirai, Yauhiro, Andrew J. Osgood, Yuming Zhao, Kevin F. Kelly, and James M. Tour. "Directional Control in Thermally Driven Single-Molecule Nanocars." *Nanoletters* 5 (2005): 2,330–34. This is the original journal publication of the "nanocar" describing its chemical synthesis and its directed motion, including a Web address for viewing animations.

Smalley, Richard E. "Of Chemistry, Love and Nanobots." *Scientific American* 285 (September 2001): 76–77. The author describes fundamental limitations in the construction and use of nanoassemblers or "nanobots."

Stoddart, J. Fraser (Guest Editor). *Accounts of Chemical Research (Special Issue on Molecular Machines)* 34 (June 2001). Eleven technical articles, amply illustrated, provide a view of the range of molecular machines and components designed at the end of the 20th century.

Terry, Thomas M. "H⁺ Pump." University of Connecticut. Available online. URL: http://www.sp.uconn.edu/~terry/images/anim/ATPmito.html. Accessed February 16, 2006. This site contains animations of the proton pump powering ATP synthase.

United States Environmental Protection Agency, "Green Chemistry." Available online. URL: www.epa.gov/greenchemistry/principles.html. Accessed February 25, 2006. This is part of the U.S. EPA's comprehensive site devoted to green chemistry.

Wang, Hong Yun, and George Oster. "ATP Synthase," University of California at Berkeley. Available online. URL: http://www.cnr.berkeley.edu/~hongwang/Project/ATP_synthase. Accessed April 4, 2006. This Web site has excellent animations of ATP synthase.

Whitesides, George M., and J. Christopher Love. "The Art of Building Small." *Scientific American* 285 (September 2001): 38–47. This is a very accessible overview of various processes in nanofabrication.

———. "The Once and Future Nanomachine." *Scientific American* 285 (September 2001): 78–83. This account describes nature's own nanomachines.

Young, Jennifer L., and Joseph M. DeSimone. "Frontiers in Green Chemistry Utilizing Carbon Dioxide for Polymer Synthesis and Applications." *Pure and Applied Chemistry* 72 (2000): 1,357–63. This is a brief review of the use of supercritical carbon dioxide in the synthesis of polymers.

Zewail, Ahmed H. *Voyage Through Time: Walks of Life to the Nobel Prize.* Singapore: World Scientific Pub. Co. Pte. Ltd. By arrangement with The American University of Cairo Press, 2002. This is the autobiography of Ahmed H. Zewail, from a small city in Egypt to the Nobel Prize in chemistry.

11

The Early Twenty-first Century:
A Chemistry Odyssey

Introduction

How could a person, writing in the year 1900, have predicted the course of 20th century science, including chemistry? The first three decades would witness solutions to most aspects of atomic structure and usher in the mysterious quantum mechanics, whose predictions were so different from our perceptions of reality. The Second World War would inaugurate the Atomic Age with a weapon of hitherto unimaginable destructiveness but, with the development of radar, would pave the pathway to nuclear magnetic resonance (NMR) spectroscopy and three decades later magnetic resonance imaging (MRI). The computer would revolutionize science and, starting in the 1980s, would become an appliance in most American homes.

In 1903, the Wright Brothers accomplished the first brief powered flight. By the end of the century men had landed on the Moon, Martian soil was directly sampled for signs of life, and the atmosphere of a planet from another solar system had been analyzed. Motion pictures began in the late 19th century. By the end of the 20th century "molecular movies" approaching a speed of a million-billion (10^{15}) frames per second were in process. At the start of the 20th century some very famous chemists and physicists did not fully accept the reality of atoms and molecules. By the end of the century, the motions of individual molecular machines were observed by scanning tunneling microscopes. Mendel's discoveries concerning heredity were just being incorporated into mainstream biology around 1900. By the end of the century, a working gene had been chemically synthesized from simple compounds, chemical methods were applied to make recombinant DNA, a sheep had been cloned, and the human genome deciphered.

Predictions of chemical breakthroughs in the 21st chemistry must be made with a great deal of humility. Who, after all, could have imagined the Internet and e-commerce in 1900? 1960? 1970? 1980?

New Superheavy Elements and Their Chemistries

The 21st century is likely to see new superheavy elements that will provide insight on their nuclear stability and chemical reactivity. It is likely that means for studying online chemistry of freshly produced elements will become much shorter than the current 1-10–second "window." Definitive evidence for element 118 was obtained by the Dubna laboratory in 2006, and confirmed by Lawrence Livermore National Laboratory. The isotope obtained ($^{294}118$) is the heaviest known element and the three nuclei created had a lifetime of 0.9 milliseconds. There remains a great deal of fascinating chemistry to be performed on elements 108–114 and higher elements to see how well they fit into the periodic table and the extent to which relativistic corrections influence their chemistries (the lifetime of ^{270}Hs was recently found to be 30 seconds). The isotope of the unknown element 126 having 184 neutrons (^{310}Ubh) is considered to be "doubly magic" and predicted to be very stable. Gulzari L. Malli (1938–), at Simon Fraser University, recently employed quantum chemical calculations to predict that this element will have occupied 5g orbitals (no elements having occupied ground-state g-orbitals are presently known) and may form a stable diatomic molecule with fluorine.

Chemical Bonding and Theory

When F. Albert Cotton discovered the quadruple bond between transition metals in 1964, he altered the "terrain" on which chemical bonding is explored. In 2005, Philip P. Power (1953–), at the University of California at Davis, published compelling evidence for the first quintuple bond connecting two transition metals. (A sextuple bond is considered to be the highest possible.) All five d-orbitals are engaged in the bonding between two chromium atoms in a compound of formula ArCrCrAr, where Ar is a sterically crowded aromatic ring. Although the dark red crystals are air-sensitive, the compound is stable up to almost 400°F (200°C).

Femtochemistry should continue to open reactions, mechanisms, intermediates, and transition states to scrutiny unimaginable today. Ahmed H. Zewail is one among an elite group of scientists pioneering ultrafast electron diffraction, which could provide detailed structures of transition states. In 2004, scientists at the Canadian National Research Council (CNRC), in collaboration with Japanese and other Canadian colleagues, applied femtosecond laser pulses to deduce the shape of the highest occupied molecular orbital (HOMO) of the nitrogen molecule. The continuing advances in quantum theory and its application, as well as advances in hardware and software, offer the very real possibility of calculating fully the reaction dynamics for any imaginable chemical reaction and calibrating the results with femtosecond (even hundreds of *attoseconds*, 10^{-18} s) stroboscopic pictures. In 2005, CNRC scientists in collaboration with scientists at Sandia National Laboratories and the University of Southern California employed femtosecond spectroscopy and quantum calculations to provide a "molecule's-eye" picture of its own decomposition. The weakly bound molecule ON-NO (nitric oxide dimer) forms a very loosely bound Rydberg state (the two NO units are bound by only very weak van der Waals–type attractions) within 150 femtoseconds after it absorbs a UV pulse. This excited-state species then dissociates about 600 femtoseconds later to produce two NO molecules.

Materials and Nanotechnology

The combinatorial approach so useful in drug investigations is finding application in the search for new materials based, for the most part, on inorganic chemistry. This would allow rapid simultaneous synthesis and screening of hundreds if not thousands of new candidate materials. The challenges of this approach include the fact that the properties of materials depend upon the size of the sample and upon the means of fabrication. Physical and chemical testing is also challenging. One common approach is to add thin layers of each of the components in various thicknesses upon each other, then raise the temperature to allow free diffusion and mixing. One of the earliest investigations was published in 1995. Using combinations of six elements ("Bi-Pb-Cu-Ca-Sr-O composition space"), a tiny library of 16 compositions was generated and examined for superconductivity. In this limited test case, the anticipated superconductors did emerge from the combinatorial library.

Nanotechnology is in its infancy, but it will define what is and what is not feasible during the 21st century. Certainly nanomachines are feasible: Nature has evolved them over the course of billions of years. Fundamental issues in nanotechnology include the relevance of quantum behavior and the organization and movement of nanomachines in the "thermal bath" surrounding them. The bottom-up approach used by nature relies upon molecular recognition and a variety of weak forces (hydrogen bonding, pi-stacking, and van der Waals forces) that will surely be imitated.

Medicinal Chemistry

The solution of the human genome is only the beginning of a new and powerful approach toward understanding and protecting human health during the 21st century. The sequence should provide clues to why some humans are more susceptible to diseases like cancer and others less so. It may allow for individualized medicine based upon an individual's specific genome. It should also place gene therapy on a rational basis. A recent example of an application of gene therapy is provided by a French research group treating severe combined immune deficiency (SCID). This is the genetic disease of the "boy in the bubble." Treatment involved removal of the boy's genetically defective bone marrow cells and exposure of these cells to a normal gene (normal DNA) inserted into a "vector," a retrovirus (HIV is also a retrovirus). The retrovirus invaded the boy's bone marrow cells, coded for normal DNA capable of creating an immune system. The bone marrow cells were then returned to the patient. The results from such gene therapies have been mixed and the U.S. Food and Drug Administration (FDA) has not yet approved any gene therapy regime.

The function of DNA is to code for the proteins that provide most of the structural integrity of living systems as well as enzymes, transport systems, antibodies, and other vital functional molecules. In 2001, Roger D. Kornberg (1947–), Stanford University, obtained an X-ray structure at 2.8 Å resolution of yeast RNA polymerase II, a protein of 12 subunits and molecular weight 550,000. This is the enzyme that transcribes the duplex DNA sequence to synthesize messenger-RNA in the nucleus prior to its transport from the nucleus to the ribosome. He also published the crystallographic structure of a complex between RNA polymerase II and DNA, essentially capturing transcription "in the act." This triumph of structural chemistry provided enormous insight into the transcription of eukaryotes, a process much more complex than that in prokaryotes. For this work, Roger Kornberg received the 2006 Nobel Prize in chemistry. His father, Arthur Kornberg, had shared the 1959 Nobel Prize in physiology or medicine for isolating DNA polymerase I, which contributed to the understanding of DNA biosynthesis (replication). The Kornbergs are the sixth father and son to win individual Nobel Prizes. Ronald Breslow, Columbia University, has noted that "even when genes play a major role, we must not ignore the function of proteins in regulating the expression of genes." The field of proteomics, which compares the relationships between the 30,000 or so proteins in healthy and diseased humans, will certainly be an important field during the 21st century. Increasingly peptides, proteins, and antibodies will find application as pharmaceutical agents with high specificities. In turn, such proteins are typically regulated by smaller molecules (ligands). Stuart L. Schreiber (1956–), at Harvard, envisions a small "activator" and a small "deactivator" molecule designed for each protein and predicts completion possibly well before 2050. The fortuitous discovery of taxol in the bark of the yew tree during the 1960s led to the discovery of an entirely new mechanism for inhibiting the growth of cancer cells: stabilization of microtubules formed during cell division to the extent that cell division is thwarted. Samuel J. Danishefsky (1936–) and his group at Sloan-Kettering are studying another class of compounds, the epothilones, structurally dissimilar from taxol, that stabilize microtubules.

Certainly one of the most serious threats to human health during the 21st century is the rapid development of resistance by bacteria to antibiotics. This has been exacerbated by careless use and overprescription of commercial antibiotics. If bacteria, the most abundant organisms on Earth, triumph in this race, the last half of the 20th century may seem to be merely a brief respite from epidemics such as plague and flu. The isolation by Selman A. Waxman of streptomycin from soil bacteria in 1944 was the start of decades of discoveries of new compounds from various species of soil bacteria collectively termed *Actinomycetes*. In the early 21st century fundamental questions about the evolution of various *Actinomycetes* may lead to new, more effective antibiotics. How did these *Actinomycetes* evolve? Are antibacterials such as streptomycin merely accidents of nature, secondary metabolites that are almost natural "afterthoughts," or did they arise as responses to competitive pressures with other Gram-positive bacteria? The observation that *Saccharaopolyspora erythrea*, soil bacteria that produce erythromycin, devote 60,000 DNA bases and 21 proteins to the synthesis of this antibiotic argues that it serves a fundamental role in the evolution and survival of this species. The various species of *Actinomycetes* actually synthesize mixtures of antibacterials that behave synergistically. Just as bacteria have evolved β-lactamases as countermeasures to β-lactam antibiotics, such as penicillin, produced by other bacteria, so have soil bacteria produced counter-countermeasures. For example, several *Streptomyces* species produce clavulanic acid, a β-lactam that inhibits β-lactamases, along with their own β-lactam antibiotic (e.g., cephamycin C). The biological evidence suggests that clavulanic acid biosynthesis was a later evolutionary adaptation to resistance conferred by β-lactamases. Understanding the role of mixtures in these bacterial antibacterial "cocktails" may allow the researchers to enhance the effectiveness of antibiotics.

Rather than simply being a spectator trying to understand and exploit the warfare between bacteria, scientists will attempt to tilt the field in favor of human health. The antibiotic vancomycin, also obtained from *Actinomycetes*, is often referred to as "an antibiotic of last resort" but is encountering increasingly resistant strains of deadly bacteria such as *Staphylococcus aureus*. Christopher T. Walsh (1944–   ), at Harvard Medical School, recently discovered the molecular basis for the development of vancomycin resistance: The most common mutation changes an amino acid crucial in the construction of the bacterial cell wall from D-alanine to D-lactate. In turn, this decreases vancomycin's ability to bind this mutant precursor and interfere with cell-wall construction. In 2004, Dale L. Boger (1953–   ) and associates at Scripps Research Institute designed and synthesized a very slightly modified vancomycin capable of strongly binding to the mutant precursor as well as to the native (wild-type) precursor. It is also worth noting that in 2000 the U.S. FDA approved the use of a synthetic substance named Linezolid as a new treatment for Gram-positive bacteria resistant to drugs including vancomycin. Linezolid is the first approved member of a new class of antibiotics called oxazolidinones.

In the early 21st century there is grave concern over the possibility of a flu pandemic as widespread and dangerous as the flu pandemic that followed World War I. Bird flu, similar to the flu that "crossed over" into a contagious human flu, recently appeared in Southeast Asia and has, by 2006, been discovered throughout Asia, the Middle East, and Europe. More than 200 humans have died from infection by diseased (domesticated) birds. The flu has not yet evolved into one capable of passing the infection between humans, but the concern is that it is only a matter of time before this happens. Antibiotics did not exist in 1918 to treat the secondary bacterial infections that are associated with flu. The situation is very different today although there is also grave concern over growing antibacterial resistance to drugs. While sophisticated early warning systems exist today and sophisticated epidemiology, preventative medicine, and vaccine manufacturing processes are in place, worldwide travel and trade greatly enhance the risk of rapid spread of a flu epidemic.

Chemists have contributed to the arsenal that could be employed to counter such a pandemic. The synthesis and design of new antibiotics to counter drug-resistant bacteria has already been described. In 1999 the U.S. FDA approved the use of the oral drug Tamiflu (oseltamivir phosphate), developed by Gilead Sciences and brought to market by Hoffmann-LaRoche. Tamiflu is a neuroaminidase inhibitor. Neuroaminidase is an enzyme exposed on the surface of both Type A and Type B flu viruses. This enzyme allows the virus to invade other cells. Tamiflu binds with neuroaminidase and thus inhibits cell-to-cell migration. While Tamiflu neither prevents nor cures flu, it reduces its duration and severity. Hopefully, even more effective antiflu drugs will be developed during the early 21st century.

Another important aspect of 21st-century pharmaceutical chemistry is drug delivery. Typically drugs require a balance of properties in order to pass through membranes. A new area of investigation involves a method called protein transduction. Certain proteins (e.g., the TAT protein from HIV and the VP22 protein from herpes simplex) pass readily through membranes. Such proteins are being investigated for their abilities to transport drugs through membranes.

One of the ultimate challenges in all of science is the complete understanding of the human brain and the mysteries of memory and self-consciousness. A recent article in *Chemical & Engineering News* expressed the complexity of this problem:

> *With its 100 billion or so neurons—each one a living electrochemical wonder that connects via cell-to-cell synapses with tens, hundreds or sometimes many thousands of other neurons—the brain's cellular architecture itself offers a gargantuan number of possible states for storing and processing information.*

The challenge will involve chemists, biochemists, neuroscientists, computer scientists, physiologists, and psychologists and will surely benefit from medical ethicists and philosophers. Hopefully the early part of the century will witness the discovery of methods to prevent, cure or at least greatly mitigate Alzheimer's disease.

Space Exploration and the Origins of Life

The results of 21st century space exploration are truly impossible to imagine. The Wright brothers flew for 28 seconds in 1903 and less than a century later there were tangible plans to establish a permanent base on the Moon in preparation for a manned landing on Mars. It was only in 1995 that the first extrasolar planet was identified definitively. As of January 2006, 153 extrasolar planetary systems have been identified including a total of at least

176 planets. Will any of these harbor life or at least provide hints of what prebiotic Earth looked like? There is now ample evidence that Mars had flowing water at one time and still has periodic water flows on its surface. Close examination over an extended period may uncover fossil evidence for primitive forms of life as we know it or perhaps discover living organisms below its surface. In July 2005 NASA's *Cassini* spacecraft on its third pass near Enceladus, a 300-mile-wide moon orbiting Jupiter, approached within 110 miles of the surface and flew through a plume of water vapor and ice crystals. *Cassini* also detected methane and carbon dioxide. Normally such tiny moons are incredibly cold barren "rocks." The presence of the plume suggests that liquid water may be close to the surface, with a source of heat with more complex organic molecules below the surface. Organic matter, water, and energy are considered minimum ingredients for sustaining life. Enceladus has been added to the small family of known extraterrestrial objects that are candidates for the search for life. Chemical questions will include whether the minimal chemical requirements for life are the same in other parts of the solar system and in other solar systems. If they are, another question will be whether life is protein/nucleic acid based and, if so, whether the L-amino acid/D-sugar "paradigm" is universal. While there is really no firm basis on which to predict the discovery of extraterrestrial life, at least in a primitive form, during the 21st century, such a discovery appears increasingly plausible and likely with every passing year. It does appear likely that scientists will synthesize living matter from nonliving matter during the 21st century. This will not come as a cultural shock but initially as a "soft crossing" of a "fuzzy boundary."

In 2006, the first discovery of a molecular anion (C_6H^-; H-C≡C-C≡C-C≡C:$^-$) in space was reported by researchers at the Harvard-Smithsonian Center for Astrophysics studying the Taurus Molecular Cloud. They extended earlier radioastronomy observations of "mystery" spectral bands by Okayama University scientists through comparison of these bands with the microwave of C_6H^- ions generated in the laboratory. This exciting discovery opens an entirely new area for investigating molecules in space. The only confirmed anion reported previously was the atomic ion H^-, reported in the solar spectrum by Robert Wildt in 1940. Generally, anions hold their extra electron weakly, and it is commonly assumed that they will be lost owing to absorption of radiation in space. Many simple hydrocarbon anions are effectively evanescent metastable "ghosts." They have negative ionization energies and, if formed in the laboratory, spontaneously lose the extra electron. For example, the ionization energy of ethyl anion ($CH_3CH_2:^-$) is -0.26 electron volts (eV). $H:^-$ holds its electron but its ionization energy is only 0.75 eV (~18 kcal/mol), slightly more than one-sixth the strength of the H-H bond in H_2. The sheer abundance of hydrogen in space allows a minute steady-state concentration of $H:^-$. The ionization energy of the vinyl anion ($C_2H_3^-$; H_2C≡$CH:^-$) is 0.67 eV and that of the acetylide ion (C_2H^-; H-C≡C:$^-$) is 2.96 eV. The ionization energy of C_6H^- is 3.80 eV, nearly 90 percent the strength of the H-H bond in H_2. Since the closely related anions

C_8H^- (3.96 eV) and C_4H^- (3.56 eV) also have high ionization energies, there is clear interest in searching for these and other related species in interstellar molecular clouds as well. Although reports of the isocyanato anion (NCO^-) on interstellar ice grains remain unconfirmed, its high ionization energy (3.61 eV) makes it a reasonable target for further study.

Studies of the evolutionary tree will continue at the molecular level as the marriage between chemistry, biology, and bioinformatics clarifies relationships between organisms. In 2006 a group of 375-million-year-old fish fossils, four to nine feet in length and dubbed *Tiktaalik roseae*, were discovered in the Canadian Arctic. Their swiveling necks, forward fins, and other skeletal features clearly indicated a transitional creature between fish and four-legged land animals, much as *Archaeopteryx* is a well-accepted transitional creature between dinosaurs and birds. Modern genomic evidence will almost certainly provide chemical evidence for more modern transitional organisms. Although 100-million-year-old DNA may never be found, the possibility of reconstructing "dino-DNA" from reasonable evolutionary information and using cloning techniques cannot be dismissed as a possibility in the 21st century.

Future of Fuel and Energy

Present estimates suggest that the world will exhaust its petroleum reserves by the middle of the 21st century if not sooner. Even as the 21st century began, reduced refinery capacity, natural disasters such as Hurricane Katrina in the Gulf Coast, and shaky geopolitics in the Middle East, Africa, South America, and Eurasia, along with the growth of demand in Asia, notably China and India, are creating a crisis in petroleum prices and supply. Ronald Breslow has stated that:

> It will become increasingly clear that it is a crime against the future to take petroleum and burn it. Not just because of global warming, but because we are burning away materials that are tremendously valuable for other uses.

The catalytic activation of C-H bonds in methane and other alkanes can convert waste gas and fuel into chemical intermediates for materials, medicines, and other valuable applications. Literally centuries worth of coal remains to be deep-mined or strip-mined. Coal mining remains an environmentally costly process at present, the emissions tend to add to pollution, and coal combustion produces more atmospheric CO_2 per BTU than petroleum combustion, thus exacerbating global warming. Coal gasification technologies have been present since Fischer and Tropsch technology began in the 1920s.

Another vast potential source of hydrocarbon fuel is in complexes called methane hydrates that are buried in cold, high-pressure conditions in the ocean and in the Arctic. Methane hydrates are hydrogen-bonded cages of water molecules surrounding methane molecules. They are examples of supermolecular complexes called clathrates. One U.S. Geological Survey

(USGS) scientist estimated the United States has as much as 317×10^{15} (317 quadrillion) cubic feet of methane stored in this form in the United States. This could be well over one thousand times the estimated natural gas reserves in the United States. The USGS estimates on the order of 60×10^{18} cubic feet of methane are potentially available worldwide. However huge these reserves are, they are very difficult to "harvest" and not yet practical. There is also concern that as global warming continues, some small fraction of these huge methane hydrate reserves will release the gas, thereby further contributing to global warming.

The use of ethanol and methanol as fuels is once again receiving considerable attention. As liquids, they are easier and safer to transport than gases. Ethanol is renewable. Planting vast tracts of land to grow plants whose biomass can be fermented to ethanol may eventually raise serious ethical questions as fuel competes with food for acreage. The energy source for "fixing" CO_2 in plants is ultimately sunlight. Methanol has long been available from coal using Fischer-Tropsch technology, more recently using zeolites as catalysts, and can also be produced using transition-metal catalyzed C-H activation of methane. Nobel laureate George A. Olah is a strong proponent of methanol as both liquid fuel and in fuel cells. He and his colleagues have pioneered chemistry that could, on a massive scale, reduce carbon dioxide back to methanol.

Combustion of hydrogen (H_2) produces water and no greenhouse gases or pollutants. The source of hydrogen gas is water itself. On a per-weight basis, hydrogen has about three times the energy content of gasoline. However, cryogenic liquefied H_2 has energy content per volume of only 8 megajoules per liter (8 MJ/L) compared with 32 MJ/L for (liquid) gasoline. The United States Department of Energy (DOE) is calling for hydrogen-storage systems with an energy content of 5.4 MJ/L by 2010 (6 weight percent of hydrogen or 45 kg of hydrogen per cubic meter). While applications of high-pressure gaseous hydrogen or cryogenic liquid storage are being explored, the greatest promise seems to be in solid-state storage. Solid metallic hydrides offer potential: Lithium amide ($LiNH_2$) is capable of storing and releasing 11.5 percent hydrogen. Other storage techniques, including some based on nanotubes, are of active and future interest.

Certainly increased use of solar power and wind power has the potential to play an important role in the energy portfolio of the 21st century. Trapping the Sun's energy is both a physical and engineering problem (passive heating of water and of living areas) as well as a chemical challenge in the development of fuel cells and other means for storing solar energy chemically. Once again, nature has furnished model systems that trap solar energy and convert it to chemical energy. Since there are at present no practical means to trap and recycle CO_2, a by-product of combustion of all organic materials (petroleum, coal, methanol, and ethanol), all such energy use contributes to the global warming problem. At the start of the 21st century there is renewed interest in nuclear fission power (nuclear fusion still looks like a distant prospect). The Chernobyl disaster, the Three Mile Island accident, and the continuing difficulty in cleaning the Hanford, Washington, site are also stark reminders of the dangers. However, nuclear power does not contribute greenhouse gases and, if truly safe and secure means can be found to store spent fuels, many environmentally concerned and knowledgeable experts favor reconsideration of nuclear power.

Conclusion

Science in general and chemistry in particular must, by the very nature of the scientific method, take a reductionist view of nature. One abiding fear held by some is that reducing nature to physical laws and chemical equations might remove its mystery. I believe that such fears are unfounded. As we discover many of nature's most profound secrets, our sense of wonder, awe, and beauty only increases. What we cannot duplicate is the unique history of the 15 billion years or so that have passed in the timescale of the universe and the 4.5 billion years that have passed on Earth. A somewhat different fear is that the truly momentous, paradigm-shifting discoveries have already been made and all that remains is to clean up the corners of the attic, so to speak, and to refine and apply these momentous discoveries. Although every generation seems to raise this question anew, a provocative book titled *The End of Science* raises specific issues in support of this position, while another, titled *What Remains to Be Discovered*, indirectly refutes it. Both are worthwhile for a reader who is willing to do some extra homework and think critically.

Further Reading

Amato, Ivan. "New Chemical Lows in Brain Surveillance." *Chemical & Engineering News* 84 (February 20, 2006): 12–17. This is a brief survey of the future role of electrochemistry in probing the brain.

American Chemical Society. "A Look at Drugs That Changed Our World." *Chemical & Engineering News (Special Issue)* 83 (June 20, 2005). This issue provides an overview of modern pharmaceutical chemistry and specific details on 46 drugs that have had a major impact upon human health.

American Chemical Society. "Element 118 Detected, with Confidence." *Chemical & Engineering News* 84 (October 23, 2006): 11. This is a brief article announcing definitive evidence for element 118.

Baum, Rudy M. "Chemistry's Golden Age." *Chemical & Engineering News* 76 (January 12, 1998): 143–151. This is an interview with a number of prominent chemists on the future of chemistry to the year 2023 as part of the 75th Anniversary Special Issue.

Borman, Stu. "Protein Factory Reveals Its Secrets." *Chemical & Engineering News* 85 (February 19, 2007): 13–16. This is an accessible discussion of the structural biology of the ribosome at the atomic level.

Challis, Gregory L., and David A. Hopwood. "Synergy and Contingency as Driving Forces for the Evolution of Multiple Secondary Metabolite Production of *Streptomyces* Species." *Proceedings of the National Academy of Sciences* 100, Suppl. 2 (2003): 14555–61. This research article provides a highly accessible background toward understanding how various species of *Actinomycetes* soil bacteria may have evolved antibiotics.

Crames, Patrick, David A. Bushnell, and Roger D. Kornberg. "Structural Basis of Transcription: RNA Polymerase II at 2-8 Å Resolution," *Science* 292 (2001): 1,863–1,876. This is the first reported structure of a yeast RNA polymerase by the winner of the 2006 Nobel Prize in chemistry.

Henry, Celia M. "The Next Pharmaceutical Century." *Chemical & Engineering News* 78 (October 23, 2000): 85–95. This is a very brief survey of developments in pharmaceuticals at the end of the 20th century with projection into the next century.

Horgan, John. *The End of Science: Facing the Limits of Knowledge in the Twilight of the Scientific Age.* Boston: Addison-Wesley, 1996. This is a provocative examination of the author's hypothesis that almost all of the truly momentous discoveries in science (relativity, quantum theory, evolution) have already been made.

Jacoby, Mitch. "Filling Up with Hydrogen." *Chemical & Engineering News* 83 (August 22, 2005): 42–47. This brief update on present and future techniques for hydrogen storage has an accompanying point-counterpoint debate titled "Competing Visions of a Hydrogen Economy" on pages 30–35 of the same issue.

Kahn, Jennifer. "Nano's Big Future." *National Geographic* 209 (June 2006): 98–119. This is a very accessible, highly pictorial peak at nanotechnology's present and future.

Keinan, Ehud, and Israel Schechter, eds. *Chemistry for the 21st Century.* Weinheim: Wiley-VCH, 2001. This book consists of 15 chapters authored by experts in diverse fields examining the state of the art in their fields at the start of the 21st century.

Maddox, John. *What Remains to Be Discovered.* New York: The Free Press, 1998. This book discusses great discoveries in science anticipated during the 21st century and beyond.

Olah, George A., Alain Goeppert, and G. K. Surya Prakash. *Beyond Oil and Gas.* New York: John Wiley & Sons, 2006. This is a very accessible book describing the use of methanol in combustion fuels and fuel cells and the possibility of recycling carbon dioxide to make methanol thus reducing the greenhouse gas emission problem.

Ritter, Steve R. "'Quintuple Bond' Makes Its Debut." *Chemical & Engineering News* 83 (September 26, 2005): 9. This is a very brief review of the article describing the first example of a quintuple bond.

Rouvray, Dennis H., and R. Bruce King. *The Periodic Table: Into the 21st Century.* Baldock (Hertfordshire): Research Studies Press, 2004. This book describes the forms and utilities of periodic tables from the 1800s onward into the 21st century.

Schneemeyer, L. F., and R. B. van Dover. "The Combinatorial Approach to Materials Discovery." In *Chemistry for the 21st Century*, 151–74. Edited by Ehud Keinan and Israel Schechter. Weinheim: Wiley-VCH, 2001. This brief review introduces the principles and limitations to the application of combinatorial chemistry to the study of new materials.

Tullo, Alexander H. "Methane on Ice." *Chemical & Engineering News* 83 (August 22, 2005): 16–17. This brief article describes the nature and occurrence of methane hydrate crystals and the prospects of their use as a future source of fuel.

The Periodic Table

A Quick Orientation to the Modern Periodic Table

The consecutive numbering in the periodic table starting with $Z = 1$ (hydrogen), and $Z = 2$ (helium) through 118 (Uuo, ununoctium, pronounced "oon-oon-octium") corresponds to the atomic numbers, the number of protons in the nucleus, of the elements. "Z," from the German *zu zahlen* ("to count") is commonly used to denote atomic number. Under the symbols for the elements are the relative atomic masses which are based upon taking the mass of the carbon 12 isotope as precisely 12.0000. . . . These masses are actually weighted averages of the specific naturally occurring isotopes (see below). While the term *atomic weight* is commonly used, it is incorrect since weight is actually force (= mass × acceleration; on Earth this acceleration is g [32 ft/s^2 or 9.8 m/s^2]). Although relative atomic masses, which are dimensionless, were classically referred to in amu (atomic mass units), today "u" is the accepted term. The most unambiguous unit employed to describe atomic mass, molecular mass, and the mass of complexes such as protein complexes, is the dalton (Da), defined as precisely 1/12 the mass of the carbon 12 isotope. Currently (2007), there are 111 elements ($Z = 1$ to 111) that have been officially recognized and named by the International Union of Pure and Applied Chemistry (IUPAC), with the expectation that $Z = 112$ (Uub), reported in 1996 by the GSI in Darmstadt, Germany, will follow soon (chapter 10). In 1998 the JINR in Dubna reported element 114 (Uuq). The isotope ^{289}Uuq is reported to have a half-life of 27 seconds (chapter 10). Element 118 (Uuo) and its disintegration to element 116 (Uuh) were reported by Lawrence Berkeley Laboratory in 1999, but had to be officially retracted in 2001. The JINR reported creation and observation of Uuh in 2000 (chapter 10). The JINR disclosed the creation of elements 115 (Uup) and 113 (Uut) in February 2004; the study has been published in a widely respected, refereed journal although not yet officially confirmed by other laboratories (chapter 10). In that study, there was a very tentative observation suggesting creation of a single atom of Uuo. There is no claim for element 117. Thus, the world's scientific community officially recognizes elements through $Z = 111$ and will probably soon officially recognize $Z = 112$. There is general acceptance of the observations of elements with $Z = 113–116$ and, in 2006, confidence in the detection of three nuclei of Uuo (element 118).

It is clear that the search for the superheavy elements is pressing nuclear physics to its current limits as, typically, only one or a few atoms are created and these have lifetimes on the millisecond (or shorter) timescale. For example, a single atom of element 112 (^{277}Uub) was made artificially in Germany in 1996 with a reported half-life of 0.0007 seconds. However, if the 27-second half-life for ^{289}Uuq is officially accepted, it may prove to be the most compelling evidence yet for the long-anticipated "island of stability" predicted for superheavy elements in this mass range (chapter 10).

Students are commonly told that there are 92 naturally occurring elements. Actually, things are a bit more complicated. It *is* true that element 92, uranium (U), is the element with the highest atomic number (92) to occur naturally in any significant quantity. However, two lighter elements [$Z = 43$, technetium (Tc); $Z = 61$, promethium (Pm)], surprisingly, have unstable nuclei and do not occur naturally. The first two transuranium elements [$Z = 93$, neptunium (Np); and $Z = 94$, plutonium (Pu)] are found in ultraminute quantities in uranium ores. Indeed, elements 43 and 61 as well as the transuranium elements are short-lived radioactive species produced artificially. One might perhaps more properly speak of 90 "naturally occurring elements" although the ultraminute traces of Np and Pu that occur naturally could return the figure to 92.

A Closer Look at the Atomic Weights of Natural and Artificial Elements

The atomic weights listed in the periodic table are relative numbers (^{12}C = 12.0000 . . .) based upon the weighted average of naturally occurring isotopes (e.g., the atomic mass of chlorine is 35.45 reflecting the roughly 3:1 ratio of ^{35}Cl to ^{37}Cl). The isotope ^{35}Cl has 17 protons (atomic number = 17) and 18 neutrons in its nucleus; ^{37}Cl has 17 protons and 20 neutrons. A more precise analysis combines the relative abundances and precise relative masses of the two stable nuclides of chlorine (^{35}Cl: 75.78 percent; 34.968853. ^{37}Cl: 24.22 percent; 36.965903) as follows: Relative Atomic Mass of Chlorine: 0.7578 (34.968853) + 0.2422 (36.965903) = 35.45 It is noteworthy that on rare occasions, IUPAC may introduce a very slight modification to the atomic mass provided for an element in the periodic table. The relative masses of the nuclides are known to great accuracy (often eight decimal places or more). However, relative abundances may change very slightly depending upon the set of minerals chosen.

There is another interesting aspect to this discussion. The relative (^{12}C) masses of the neutron (1.008665 u), proton (1.007276 u), and electron (0.000549 u) have been accurately determined. The element hydrogen (atomic mass 1.00794 ± 0.00007 u) comprises 99.9885 percent protium (^{1}H, 1.007825 u) and 0.0115 percent deuterium (^{2}H, 2.014102 u). The atomic mass of protium equals the simple sum of the mass of one proton and one electron as one would expect. The atomic mass of deuterium (2.014102) is, however, very slightly less than the sum (2.016490 u) of one proton plus one neutron plus one electron. The tiny discrepancy (0.002388 u) arises from the nuclear binding energy of the deuterium nucleus which can be evaluated by Einstein's famous mass-energy equivalence equation ($E = mc^2$). The energy equivalent to exactly 1 atomic mass unit (u) is 932 MeV (million electron volts). The nuclear binding energy in deuterium, corresponding to the loss of 0.002388 u, is 2.22 MeV. In protium, there is no such binding energy. The ionization potential of protium, the energy required to remove the one electron from this atom, is 13.6 eV. This means that when a free electron and a proton combine, 13.6 eV is released. It is clear that this chemical energy is on the order of one-millionth of the nuclear binding energies and has no significant impact on atomic mass. The mass of the helium-4 nucleus (4.002603 u) is 0.030377 u (28.3 MeV) lighter than its constituent protons, neutrons, and electrons. The relative mass of ^{35}Cl (34.968853 u) is less than 35 even though the relative masses of each of its 17 protons and 18 neutrons is greater than one. The discrepancy between the experimental and the calculated relative atomic mass for the chlorine 35 nuclide (35.288995 u) is 0.320142 u (298 MeV). For uranium 238 (92 protons and 146 neutrons), the mass of the nuclide (238.050788 u) is almost 2 u less than that calculated (240.439562) by summing of protons, neutrons, and electrons due to the nuclear binding energy. The near cancellation of added mass by nuclear binding energy allows the blissfully simple addition of protons and neutrons to obtain atomic mass.

There are, of course, no natural abundances for the artificial (synthetic) elements since they do not occur naturally. IUPAC recommends the use of the relative atomic weight of the most stable isotope for these artificial elements. For element 111, roentgenium (Rg), there are four reported isotopes (lifetimes in parentheses): 272 (1.6 milliseconds), 274 (6.4 milliseconds), 279 (170 milliseconds), and 280 (3.6 seconds). According to IUPAC practice the atomic mass of Rg should be 280, but this depends upon how widely the evidence for ^{280}Rg is accepted. Hence one atomic weight may be found in one table and a different atomic weight in another.

PERIODIC TABLE OF THE ELEMENTS

1 IA																		18 VIIIA
1 H 1.00794	2 IIA											13 IIIA	14 IVA	15 VA	16 VIA	17 VIIA	2 He 4.0026
3 Li 6.941	4 Be 9.0122											5 B 10.81	6 C 12.011	7 N 14.0067	8 O 15.9994	9 F 18.9984	10 Ne 20.1798
11 Na 22.9898	12 Mg 24.3051	3 IIIB	4 IVB	5 VB	6 VIB	7 VIIB	8 VIIIB	9 VIIIB	10 VIIIB	11 IB	12 IIB	13 Al 26.9815	14 Si 28.0855	15 P 30.9738	16 S 32.067	17 Cl 35.4528	18 Ar 39.948
19 K 39.0938	20 Ca 40.078	21 Sc 44.9559	22 Ti 47.867	23 V 50.9415	24 Cr 51.9962	25 Mn 54.938	26 Fe 55.845	27 Co 58.9332	28 Ni 58.6934	29 Cu 63.546	30 Zn 65.409	31 Ga 69.723	32 Ge 72.61	33 As 74.9216	34 Se 78.96	35 Br 79.904	36 Kr 83.798
37 Rb 85.4678	38 Sr 87.62	39 Y 88.906	40 Zr 91.224	41 Nb 92.9064	42 Mo 95.94	43 Tc (98)	44 Ru 101.07	45 Rh 102.9055	46 Pd 106.42	47 Ag 107.8682	48 Cd 112.412	49 In 114.818	50 Sn 118.711	51 Sb 121.760	52 Te 127.60	53 I 126.9045	54 Xe 131.29
55 Cs 132.9054	56 Ba 137.328	57-70 ☆	72 Hf 178.49	73 Ta 180.948	74 W 183.84	75 Re 186.207	76 Os 190.23	77 Ir 192.217	78 Pt 195.08	79 Au 196.9655	80 Hg 200.59	81 Tl 204.3833	82 Pb 207.2	83 Bi 208.9804	84 Po (209)	85 At (210)	86 Rn (222)
87 Fr (223)	88 Ra (226)	89-102 ★	104 Rf (261)	105 Db (262)	106 Sg (266)	107 Bh (262)	108 Hs (263)	109 Mt (268)	110 Ds (271)	111 Rg (272)	112 Uub (277)	113 Uut (284)	114 Uuq (285)	115 Uup (288)	116 Uuh (292)		118 Uuo (294)

Atomic number

3 Li 6.941 — Symbol / Atomic weight

☆ Lanthanoids

57 La 138.9055	58 Ce 140.115	59 Pr 140.908	60 Nd 144.24	61 Pm (145)	62 Sm 150.36	63 Eu 151.966	64 Gd 157.25	65 Tb 158.9253	66 Dy 162.500	67 Ho 164.9303	68 Er 167.26	69 Tm 168.9342	70 Yb 173.04

★ Actinoids

89 Ac (227)	90 Th 232.0381	91 Pa 231.036	92 U 238.0289	93 Np 237	94 Pu (244)	95 Am 243	96 Cm (247)	97 Bk (247)	98 Cf (251)	99 Es (252)	100 Fm (257)	101 Md (258)	102 No (259)

Numbers in parentheses are atomic mass numbers of most stable isotopes

THE CHEMICAL ELEMENTS

(g) none (c) metallics

element	symbol	a.n.	element	symbol	a.n.	element	symbol	a.n.
aluminum	Al	13	lead	Pb	82	scandium	Sc	21
bohrium	Bh	107	lutetium	Lu	71	seaborgium	Sg	106
cadmium	Cd	48	manganese	Mn	25	silver	Ag***	47
chromium	Cr	24	meitnerium	Mt	109	tantalum	Ta	73
cobalt	Co	27	mercury	Hg	80	technetium	Tc	43
copper	Cu***	29	molybdenum	Mo	42	thallium	Tl	81
darmstadium	Ds	110	nickel	Ni	28	titanium	Ti	22
dubnium	Db	105	niobium	Nb	41	tin	Sn	50
gallium	Ga	31	osmium	Os****	76	tungsten	W	74
gold	Au***	79	palladium	Pd****	46	ununbium	Uub	112
hafnium	Hf	72	platinum	Pt****	78	ununtrium	Uut	113
hassium	Hs	108	rhenium	Re	75	ununquadium	Uuq	114
indium	In	49	rhodium	Rh****	45	vanadium	V	23
iridium	Ir****	77	roentgenium	Rg	111	yttrium	Y	39
iron	Fe	26	ruthenium	Ru****	44	zinc	Zn	30
lawrencium	Lr	103	rutherfordium	Rf	104	zirconium	Zr	40

(g) alkali metal (c) metallics

element	symbol	a.n.	element	symbol	a.n.
cesium	Cs	55	potassium	K	19
francium	Fr	87	rubidium	Rb	37
lithium	Li	3	sodium	Na	11

(g) alkaline earth metal (c) metallics

element	symbol	a.n.	element	symbol	a.n.
barium	Ba	56	magnesium	Mg	12
beryllium	Be	4	radium	Ra	88
calcium	Ca	20	strontium	Sr	38

(g) chalcogen (c) nonmetallics

element	symbol	a.n.	element	symbol	a.n.
oxygen	O	8	sulfur	S	16
polonium	Po	84	tellurium	Te	52
selenium	Se	34	ununhexium	Uuh	116

(g) none (c) semimetallics

element	symbol	a.n.
boron	B	5
germanium	Ge	32
silicon	Si	14

(g) noble (c) nonmetallics gases

element	symbol	a.n.
argon	Ar	18
helium	He	2
krypton	Kr	36
neon	Ne	10
radon	Rn	86
xenon	Xe	54
unoctocium	Uuo	118

(g) none (c) nonmetallics

element	symbol	a.n.
carbon	C	6
hydrogen	H	1

(g) lanthanoid (c) metallics

element	symbol	a.n.
cerium	Ce	58
dysprosium	Dy	66
erbium	Er	68
europium	Eu	63
gadolinium	Gd	64
holmium	Ho	67
lanthanum	La	57
neodymium	Nd	60
praseodymium	Pr	59
promethium	Pm	61
samarium	Sm	62
terbium	Tb	65
thulium	Tm	69
ytterbium	Yb	70

(g) halogens (c) nonmetallics

element	symbol	a.n.	element	symbol	a.n.
astatine	At*	85	fluorine	F	9
bromine	Br	35	iodine	I	53
chlorine	Cl	17			

(g) pnictogen (c) metallics

element	symbol	a.n.	element	symbol	a.n.
arsenic	As*	33	nitrogen	N**	7
antimony	Sb*	51	phosphorus	P**	15
bismuth	Bi	83	ununpentium	Uup	115

(g) actinoid (c) metallics

element	symbol	a.n.
actinium	Ac	89
americium	Am	95
berkelium	Bk	97
californium	Cf	98
curium	Cm	96
einsteinium	Es	99
fermium	Fm	100
mendelevium	Md	101
neptunium	Np	93
nobelium	No	102
plutonium	Pu	94
protactinium	Pa	91
thorium	Th	90
uranium	U	92

a.n. = atomic number
(g) = group
(c) = classification

* = semimetallics (c)
** = nonmetallics (c)
*** = coinage metal (g)
**** = precious metal (g)

Nobel Prize Winners

in Chemistry: 1901–2000

The Nobel Foundation maintains a Web site (http://nobelprize.org) that provides full information including biographies and Nobel Prize lectures for all laureates in all fields so recognized. The list of winners of the Nobel Prize in chemistry is obtained using the address: http://nobelprize.org/nobel_prizes/chemistry/laureates/. The brief descriptions of the specific awards are directly quoted from this site.

1901

Jacobus Henricus van't Hoff (1852–1911), Netherlands. "In recognition of the extraordinary services he has rendered by the discovery of the laws of chemical dynamics and osmotic pressure in solutions."

1902

Hermann Emil Fischer (1852–1919), Germany. "In recognition of the extraordinary services he has rendered by his work on sugar and purine syntheses."

1903

Svante Arrhenius (1859–1927), Sweden. "In recognition of the extraordinary services he has rendered to the advancement of chemistry by his electrolytic theory of dissociation."

1904

Sir William Ramsay (1852–1916), United Kingdom. "In recognition of his services in the discovery of the inert gaseous elements in air, and his determination of their place in the periodic table."

1905

Johann Friedrich Wilhelm Adolph von Baeyer (1835–1917), Germany. "In recognition of his services in the advancement of organic chemistry and the chemical industry, through his work on organic dyes and hydroaromatic compounds."

1906

Henri Moissan (1852–1907), France. "In recognition of the great services rendered by him in his investigation and isolation of the element fluorine, and for the adoption in the service of science of the electric furnace called after him."

1907

Eduard Buchner (1860–1917), Germany. "For his biochemical researches and his discovery of cell-free fermentation."

1908

Ernest Rutherford (1871–1937), United Kingdom and New Zealand. "For his investigation into the disintegration of the elements, and the chemistry of radioactive substances."

1909

Wilhelm Ostwald (1853–1932), Germany. "In recognition of his work on catalysis and for his investigations into the fundamental principles governing chemical equilibria and rates of reaction."

1910

Otto Wallach (1847–1931), Germany. "In recognition of his services to organic chemistry and the chemical industry by his pioneer work in the field of alicyclic compounds."

1911

Marie Curie (1867–1934), France. "In recognition of her services to the advancement of chemistry by the discovery of the elements radium and polonium, by the isolation of radium and the study of the nature and compounds of this remarkable element."

1912

Victor Grignard (1871–1935), France. "For the discovery of the so-called Grignard reagent, which in recent years has greatly advanced the progress of organic chemistry." Paul Sabatier (1854–1941), France. "For his method of hydrogenating organic compounds in the presence of finely disintegrated metals whereby the progress of organic chemistry has been greatly advanced in recent years."

1913

Alfred Werner (1866–1919), Switzerland. "In recognition of his work on the linkage of atoms in molecules by which he has thrown new light on earlier investigations and opened up new fields of research."

1914

Theodore William Richards (1868–1928), United States. "In recognition of his accurate determinations of the atomic weights of a large number of chemical elements."

1915

Richard Willstätter (1872–1942), Germany. "For his researches on plant pigments, especially chlorophyll."

1916

The prize money was allocated to the Special Fund of this Prize section.

1917

The prize money was allocated to the Special Fund of this Prize section.

1918

Fritz Haber (1868–1934), Germany. "For the synthesis of ammonia from its elements."

1919

The prize money was allocated to the Special Fund of this Prize section.

1920

Walther Hermann Nernst (1864–1941), Germany. "In recognition of his work in thermochemistry."

1921

Frederick Soddy (1877–1956), United Kingdom. "For his contribution to our knowledge of the chemistry of radioactive substances, and his investigations into the origin and nature of isotopes."

1922

Francis William Aston (1877–1945), United Kingdom. "For his discovery, by means of his mass spectrograph, of isotopes, in a large number of non-radioactive elements, and for his enunciation of the whole-number rule."

1923

Fritz Pregl (1869–1930), Austria. "For his invention of the method of micro-analysis of organic substances."

1924

The prize money was allocated to the Special Fund of this Prize section.

1925

Richard Adolph Zsigmondy (1865–1929), Germany. "For his demonstration of the heterogeneous nature of colloid solutions and for the methods he used, which have since become fundamental in colloid chemistry."

1926

The (Theodor) Svedberg (1884–1971), Sweden. "For his work on disperse systems."

1927

Heinrich Otto Wieland (1877–1957), Germany. "For his investigations of the constitution of the bile acids and related substances."

1928

Adolph Otto Reinhold Windaus (1876–1959), Germany. "For his services rendered through his research into the constitution of the sterols and their connection with the vitamins."

1929

Arthur Harden (1865–1940), United Kingdom, and Hans Karl August Simon von Euler-Chelpin (1873–1964), Sweden. "For their investigations on the fermentation of sugar and fermentative enzymes."

1930

Hans Fischer (1881–1945), Germany. "For his researches into the constitution of haemin and chlorophyll and especially for the synthesis of haemin."

1931

Carl Bosch (1874–1940), Germany, and Friedrich Bergius (1884–1949), Germany. "In recognition of their contributions to the invention and development of chemical high pressure methods."

1932

Irving Langmuir (1881–1957), United States. "For his discoveries and inventions in surface chemistry."

1933

The prize money was 1/3 allocated to the Main Fund and with 2/3 to the Special Fund of this prize section.

1934

Harold Clayton Urey (1893–1981), United States. "For his discovery of heavy hydrogen."

1935

Frédéric Joliot (1900–58), France, and Irène Joliot-Curie (1897–1956), France. "In recognition of their syntheses of new radioactive elements."

1936

Petrus (Peter) Josephus Wilhelmus Debye (1884–1966), Netherlands. "For his contributions to our knowledge of molecular structure through his investigations in dipole moments and on the diffraction of X-rays and electrons in gases."

1937

Walter Norman Haworth (1883–1950), United Kingdom. "For his investigations on carbohydrates and vitamin C." Paul Karrer (1889–1971), Switzerland. "For his investigations on carotenoids, flavins and vitamins A and B_2."

1938

Richard Kuhn (1900–67), Germany. "For his work on carotenoids and vitamins."

1939

Adolf Friedrich Johann Butenandt (1903–95), Germany. "For his work on sex hormones." Leopold Ruzicka (1887–1976), Switzerland. "For his work on polymethylenes and higher terpenes."

1940

The prize money was with 1/3 allocated to the Main Fund and with 2/3 to the Special Fund of this prize section.

1941

The prize money was with 1/3 allocated to the Main Fund and with 2/3 to the Special Fund of this prize section.

1942

The prize money was with 1/3 allocated to the Main Fund and with 2/3 to the Special Fund of this prize section.

1943

George de Hevesy (1885–1966), Hungary. "For his work on the use of isotopes as tracers in the study of chemical processes."

1944

Otto Hahn (1879–1968), Germany. "For his discovery of the fission of heavy nuclei."

1945

Artturi Ilmari Virtanen (1895–1973), Finland. "For his research and inventions in agricultural and nutrition chemistry, especially for his fodder preservation method."

1946

James Batcheller Sumner (1887–1955), United States. "For his discovery that enzymes can be crystallized." John Howard Northrop (1891–1987), United States, and Wendell Meredith Stanley (1904–71), United States. "For their preparation of enzymes and virus proteins in pure form."

1947

Sir Robert Robinson (1886–1975), United Kingdom. "For his investigations on plant products of biological importance, especially the alkaloids."

1948

Arne Wilhelm Kaurin Tiselius (1902–71), Sweden. "For his research on electrophoresis and adsorption analysis, especially for his discoveries concerning the complex nature of the serum proteins."

1949

William Francis Giauque (1895–1982), United States. "For his contributions in the field of chemical thermodynamics, particularly concerning the behavior of substances at extremely low temperatures."

1950

Otto Paul Hermann Diels (1876–1954), Germany, and Kurt Alder (1902–58), Germany. "For their discovery and development of the diene synthesis."

1951

Edwin Mattison McMillan (1907–91), United States, and Glenn Theodore Seaborg (1912–99), United States. "For their discoveries in the chemistry of the transuranium elements."

1952

Archer John Porter Martin (1910–2002), United Kingdom, and Richard Laurence Millington Synge (1914–94), United Kingdom. "For their invention of partition chromatography."

1953

Hermann Staudinger (1881–1965), Federal Republic of Germany. "For his discoveries in the field of macromolecular chemistry."

1954

Linus Carl Pauling (1901–94), United States. "For his research into the nature of the chemical bond and its application to the elucidation of the structure of complex substances."

1955

Vincent du Vigneaud (1901–78), United States. "For his work on biochemically important sulfur compounds, especially for the first synthesis of a polypeptide hormone."

1956

Sir Cyril Norman Hinshelwood (1897–1967), United Kingdom, and Nikolay Nikolaevich Semenov (1896–1986), Union of Soviet Socialist Republics. "For their researches into the mechanism of chemical reactions."

1957

Lord (Alexander R.) Todd (1907–97), United Kingdom. "For his work on nucleotides and nucleotide coenzymes."

1958

Frederick Sanger (1918–   ), United Kingdom. "For his work on the structure of proteins, especially that of insulin."

1959

Jaroslav Heyrovsky (1890–1967), Czechoslovakia. "For his development of the polarographic methods of analysis."

1960

Willard Frank Libby (1908–1980), United States. "For his method to use carbon-14 for age determination in archaeology, geology, geophysics, and other branches of science."

1961

Melvin Calvin (1911–97), United States. "For his research on the carbon dioxide assimilation in plants."

1962

Max Ferdinand Perutz (1914–2002), United Kingdom, and John Cowdery Kendrew (1917–97), United Kingdom. "For their studies of the structures of globular proteins."

1963

Karl Ziegler (1898–1973), Federal Republic of Germany, and Giulio Natta (1903–79), Italy. "For their discoveries in the field of chemistry and technology of high polymers."

1964

Dorothy Crowfoot Hodgkin (1910–94), United Kingdom. "For her determinations by X-ray techniques of the structures of important biochemical substances."

1965

Robert Burns Woodward (1917–79), United States. "For his outstanding achievements in the art of organic synthesis."

1966

Robert S. Mulliken (1896–1986), United States. "For his fundamental work concerning chemical bonds and the electronic structure of molecules by the molecular orbital method."

1967

Manfred Eigen (1927–   ), Federal Republic of Germany, Ronald George Wreyford Norrish (1897–1978), United Kingdom, and George Porter (1920–2002), United Kingdom. "For their studies of extremely fast chemical reactions, effected by disturbing the equilibrium by means of very short pulses of energy."

1968

Lars Onsager (1903–76), United States. "For the discovery of the reciprocal relations bearing his name, which are fundamental for the thermodynamics of irreversible processes."

1969

Derek H. R. Barton (1918–98), United Kingdom, and Odd Hassel (1897–1981), Norway. "For their contributions to the development of the concept of conformation and its application in chemistry."

1970

Luis Leloir (1906–87), Argentina. "For his discovery of sugar nucleotides and their role in the biosynthesis of carbohydrates."

1971

Gerhard Herzberg (1904–99), Canada. "For his contributions to the knowledge of electronic structure and geometry of molecules, particularly free radicals."

1972

Christian B. Anfinsen (1916–95), United States. "For his work on ribonuclease, especially concerning the connection between the amino acid sequence and the biologically active conformation." Stanford Moore (1913–82), United States, and William H. Stein (1911–80), United States. "For their contribution to the understanding of the connection between chemical structure and catalytic activity of the active center of the ribonuclease molecule."

1973

Ernst Otto Fischer (1918–   ), Federal Republic of Germany, and Geoffrey Wilkinson (1921–96), United Kingdom. "For their pioneering work, performed independently, on the chemistry of the organometallic, so-called sandwich compounds."

1974

Paul J. Flory (1910–85), United States. "For his fundamental achievements, both theoretical and experimental, in the physical chemistry of macromolecules."

1975

John Warcup Cornforth (1917–   ), Australia and United Kingdom. "For his work in the stereochemistry of enzyme-catalyzed reactions." Vladimir Prelog (1906–98), Switzerland. "For his research into the stereochemistry of organic molecules and reactions."

1976

William N. Lipscomb (1919–   ), United States. "For his studies on the structure of boranes illuminating problems of chemical bonding."

1977

Ilya Prigogine (1917–2003), Belgium. "For his contributions to non-equilibrium thermodynamics, particularly the theory of dissipative structures."

1978

Peter D. Mitchell (1920–92), United Kingdom. "For his contribution to the understanding of biological energy transfer through the formulation of the chemiosmotic theory."

1979

Herbert C. Brown (1912–2004), United States, and Georg Wittig (1897–1987), Federal Republic of Germany. "For their development of the use of boron- and phosphorus-containing compounds, respectively, into important reagents in organic synthesis."

1980

Paul Berg (1926–   ), United States. "For his fundamental studies of the biochemistry of nucleic acids, with particular regard to recombinant-DNA." Walter Gilbert (1932–   ), United States, and Frederick Sanger (1918–   ), United Kingdom. "For their contributions concerning the determination of base sequences in nucleic acids."

1981

Kenichi Fukui (1918–98), Japan, and Roald Hoffmann (1937–   ), United States. "For their theories, developed independently, concerning the courses of chemical reactions."

1982

Aaron Klug (1926–   ), United Kingdom. "For his development of crystallographic electron microscopy and his structural elucidation of biologically important nucleic acid-protein complexes."

1983

Henry Taube (1915–2005), United States. "For his work on the mechanisms of electron transfer reactions, especially in metal complexes."

1984

Robert Bruce Merrifield (1921–2006), United States. "For his development of methodology for chemical synthesis on a solid matrix."

1985

Herbert A. Hauptman (1917–), United States, and Jerome Karle (1918–), United States. "For their outstanding achievements in the development of direct methods for the determination of crystal structures."

1986

Dudley R. Herschbach (1932–), United States, Yuan T. Lee (1936–), United States, and John C. Polanyi (1929–), Canada. "For their contributions concerning the dynamics of chemical elementary processes."

1987

Donald J. Cram (1919–2001), United States, Jean-Marie Lehn (1939–), France, and Charles J. Pedersen (1904–89), United States. "For their development and use of molecules with structure-specific interactions of high selectivity."

1988

Johann Deisenhofer (1943–), Federal Republic of Germany, Robert Huber (1937–), Federal Republic of Germany, and Hartmut Michel (1948–), Federal Republic of Germany. "For the determination of the three-dimensional structure of a photosynthetic reaction center."

1989

Sidney Altman (1939–), Canada and United States, and Thomas R. Cech (1947–), United States. "For their discovery of catalytic properties of RNA."

1990

Elias James Corey (1928–), United States. "For his development of the theory and methodology of organic synthesis."

1991

Richard R. Ernst (1933–), Switzerland. "For his contributions to the development of the methodology of high resolution nuclear magnetic resonance (NMR) spectroscopy."

1992

Rudolph A. Marcus (1923–), United States. "For his contributions to the theory of electron transfer reactions in chemical systems."

1993

Kary B. Mullis (1944–), United States. "For his invention of the polymerase chain reaction (PCR) method." Michael Smith (1932–2000), Canada. "For his fundamental contributions to the establishment of oligonucleotide-based, site-directed mutagenesis and its development for protein studies."

1994

George A. Olah (1927–), United States. "For his contribution to carbocation chemistry."

1995

Paul J. Crutzen (1933–), Netherlands, Mario J. Molina (1943–), United States, and F. Sherwood Rowland (1927–), United States. "For their work in atmospheric chemistry, particularly concerning the formation and decomposition of ozone."

1996

Robert F. Curl, Jr. (1933–), United States, Sir Harold W. Kroto (1939–), United Kingdom, and Richard E. Smalley (1943–2005), United States. "For their discovery of fullerenes."

1997

Paul D. Boyer (1918–), United States, and John E. Walker (1941–), United Kingdom. "For their elucidation of the enzymatic mechanism underlying the synthesis of adenosine triphosphate (ATP)." Jens C. Skou (1918), Denmark. "For the first discovery of an ion-transporting enzyme, Na^+, K^+-ATPase."

1998

Walter Kohn (1923–), United States. "For his development of the density-functional theory." John A. Pople (1925–2004), United Kingdom. "For his development of computational methods in quantum chemistry."

1999

Ahmed H. Zewail (1946–), Egypt and United States. "For his studies of the transition states of chemical reactions using femtosecond spectroscopy."

2000

Alan J. Heeger (1936–   ), United States, Alan G. MacDiarmid (1927–2007), United States and New Zealand, and Hideki Shirakawa (1936–   ), Japan. "For the discovery and development of conductive polymers."

# Glossary

absolute zero the lowest possible temperature (0 K = -459.7°F = -273.2°C)

achiral not chiral

acid a substance behaving as proton donor or electron pair acceptor

actinide one of 14 radioactive metallic elements including thorium (90) through lawrencium (103) corresponding to filling of 5f atomic orbitals

activated complex transient structure at the transition state of a reaction

adiabatic no heat exchanged

alkali classical term for a base

alkali metal member of the IA family (e.g., Na) in the periodic table

alkaline earth metal member of the IIA family (e.g., Ca) in the periodic table

alkaloid a naturally occurring cyclic or polycyclic organic compound containing nitrogen

allotrope a specific chemical form of an element (e.g., charcoal versus diamond)

alpha [α] particle ("ray") radiation particle composed of helium nuclei

amino acid building block of proteins

amphiphilic a molecule that has a hydrophobic end and a hydrophilic end

angstrom (Å) atomic level measure of distance (10^{-10} m; 10^{-8} cm; 3.9×10^{-9} in)

anion negatively charged ion

antibody a large Y-shaped protein that complexes with foreign substances in immune responses

aromaticity special stability associated with benzene and other related $4n + 2$ rings

atactic without specific order in polymerizations forming new chiral centers

atom the smallest unit of an element

atomic force microscope (AFM) instrument for testing stresses at atomic scale

atomic mass total mass of all subatomic particles (relative to ^{12}C = 12.0000 . . .); commonly obtained by adding the number of protons and neutrons

atomic mass unit (amu or u) one u is precisely one-twelfth the mass of ^{12}C

atomic weight generally used interchangeably with the more proper atomic mass

attosecond 10^{-18} second

Avogadro's number (N) 6.022×10^{23}; the number of ^{12}C atoms in one mole (12.0000 . . . grams) of carbon 12

Balmer series the lines from the visible spectrum of atomic hydrogen

base a substance behaving as a proton acceptor or an electron pair donor

beta [β] particle ("ray") an electron released from the nucleus of a radioactive substance

Bohr model solar-system model of the atom: electrons in specific orbits around the nucleus

bond dissociation energy the energy required to break the bond between two atoms

Brønsted acid a substance that donates protons

Brønsted base a substance that accepts protons

Brownian motion random movement in suspensions caused by collisions with molecules

buckyball informal name for C_{60}; sometimes used for related molecules such as C_{70}

buckytube informal name for elongated structures resembling buckyball

Cahn-Ingold-Prelog (CIP) rules nomenclature specifying absolute configurations of enantiomers (R and S) and other stereoisomers (E and Z)

calorie unit of energy required to heat 1 gram of water by 1°C (food "calories" are actually each equivalent to 1,000 calories or 1 kilocalorie)

canal rays stream of positively charged particles produced by high voltage in an evacuated tube with a perforated cathode; they move in the direction opposite to that of the cathode rays

carbene short-lived dicoordinate carbon intermediates (CH_2 is the simplest)

carbocation positively charged carbon intermediates that are usually carbenium ions (e.g., CH_3^+) or carbonium ions (e.g. CH_5^+)

carbocyclic referring to rings composed of carbons

carbon 14 the radioactive isotope of carbon used in radiocarbon dating

carcinogen substance or mixture having the property of causing cancer

catalyst an agent that increases the rate of a chemical reaction without being consumed

cathode ray   stream of electrons produced by high voltage in an evacuated tube

cation   a positively charged ion

centigrade (°C)   metric scale of temperature; relationship to Fahrenheit: $°F = 9/5(°C) + 32$

ceramic   a solid inorganic material generally with a high melting point

chain reaction   a reaction in which a short-lived intermediate starts a reaction sequence which regenerates the intermediate at the end so that it can initiate another sequence

chaperonin (or **chaperone protein**)   a protein complex that assists the proper folding of protein chains

chelate   a metal complex formed with ligands having more than one coordinating group

chiral   "handedness" in an object or molecule; such an object or molecule cannot be superimposed on its mirror image

chiral center   an atom in a molecule that produces chirality by virtue of its substituents

chromatography   general term for methods that use a stationary phase in contact with a mobile phase in order to separate mixtures into individual substances

cloud chamber   a closed system that uses condensed vapor to track radiation

cold (or soft) fusion   in the synthesis of transuranium elements this involves low energy collisions of very heavy and moderately heavy nuclei at the lowest possible energy

colloid   particles of a substance or material larger than typical solutes but small enough to remain in suspension

combinatorial chemistry   a series of techniques for creating large libraries of related substances

combining volumes law   only specific relative volumes of gases combine to form compounds

concerted reaction   bonds are broken and formed simultaneously

conductivity   the ability of a substance or mixture to conduct electricity

configuration   pertains to the absolute or relative positions in space of atoms in a molecule

conformation   a structure determined by rotation around single bonds (usually)

conformational analysis   understanding a molecule's chemistry based on its conformation

conjugated   alternating unsaturated linkages (e.g., two double bonds separated by a single bond)

conservation of matter law   in a chemical reaction the mass of the reactants equals the mass of the products

conservation of orbital symmetry   in concerted reactions maintaining the symmetry of orbitals during the transformation is associated with a low energy of activation

coordinate covalent bond   see dative bond

coordination compound   formed between a transition metal and ligands

coordination number   the number of adjacent atoms bonded to the atom in question

covalent bond   a chemical bond formed by sharing electrons between atoms

critical micelle concentration   point at which a micelle is formed from free molecules in solution

crown ether   cyclic molecule containing many oxygen atoms that may coordinate a cation

cryptate   a molecule that can capture and hold a small molecule or ion in its cavity

cyclotron   an instrument for accelerating nuclei or subatomic particles into a target nucleus

cytochrome   member of a class of heme-containing electron transfer compounds

dative bond   a covalent bond in which one atom supplies two electrons

definite proportions law   a chemical compound has a characteristic and specific proportion of its constituent elements

degenerate   (orbitals) two or more orbitals (atomic or molecular) of equal energy

denaturation   induced change in the structure of a protein from its native structure

dendrimer   a polymeric molecule formed by consecutive stages of branching

density function theory (DFT)   a computational method in quantum theory that derives all properties from the electron density and drastically reduces computation time

dextrorotatory (*d* or [+])   clockwise rotation of plane polarized light

deoxyribonucleic acid (DNA)   the substance that stores genetic information

deoxyribonucleic acid (DNA) ligase   an enzyme that joins segments of DNA

deuterium   the isotope of hydrogen of atomic mass 2 (^{2}H)

dialysis   a method for separating colloidal species such as proteins from smaller solutes such as ionic salts

diamagnetic   characteristic of a substance with no unpaired electrons that is repelled by a magnetic field

diastereomer   a stereoisomer that is not an enantiomer

diffraction   breaking a ray of light into dark and light bands or colors of the spectrum due to interference of parts of the beam when the ray passes through a narrow slit

dimer   a unit formed by combing two single units (monomers)

dipole   the separation of opposite charges in a molecule

dipole moment   the degree of charge separation in a molecule

diradical   a chemical species having two unshared electrons

doping   addition of a small impurity to a material to enhance a property such as electrical conductivity

doublet   the spin state of a free radical with one unshared electron

eighteen electron rule   a guideline that indicates that transition metal complexes are especially stable if they involve the metal with a total of 18 valence electrons

electrolysis   decomposition induced by electrical current

electrolyte   a substance that allows a solution to conduct an electric current

electron   negatively charged particle outside the nucleus of an atom that has a mass roughly 1/2,000 that of a proton or a neutron

electron affinity (EA)   the energy associated with adding an electron to a chemical species

electron volt (eV)   a measure of energy (equivalent to 23.1 kcal/mol)

electronegativity   a measure of the affinity of an atom for electrons including its resistance to losing electrons

electrophile   a chemical species that has a high affinity for electrons

electrospray ionization (ESI)   a means for forming high-molecular-weight ions in the gas phase as an interface to a mass spectrometer

element   the simplest chemical substance

enantiomer   a molecule or ion non-superimposable with its mirror image

enantiomeric excess (ee)   a percent given by $100(\chi_R - \chi_S)/(\chi_R + \chi_S)$, where χ_R and χ_S are the mole fractions of the R and S enantiomers, if R is in excess

endergonic   a net increase of free energy in a process

endothermic   a net increase in enthalpy in a process

enthalpy   a thermodynamic quantity defined by $H = E + PV$; in a process with no change in volume, the change in enthalpy equals the heat absorbed or released in the process

entropy   a thermodynamic quantity measuring the number of states of equal probability in a system; higher entropy corresponds to less order

enzyme   a natural catalyst that is almost always a protein

equilibrium   a state of no net change; in chemistry generally corresponding to the point where forward and reverse processes occur at equal rates

exergonic   a net decrease of free energy in a process

exothermic   a net decrease in enthalpy in a process

Fahrenheit (°F)   English temperature scale; relationship to centigrade: $°C = 5/9(°F - 32)$

fast atom bombardment (FAB)   a means for blasting large molecules into the gas phase prior to their introduction into a mass spectrometer

femtosecond 10^{-15} second

fermentation   metabolic decomposition of natural substances (e.g., carbohydrates) in the absence of oxygen

ferromagnet   a substance that has been permanently magnetized

formal charge   a convention in which the number of valence electrons in an atom is compared to the number assigned to that atom (one electron per bond; two electrons per lone pair) in a molecule. The formal charge of N in NH_4^+ is +1.

Fourier transform   a mathematical technique that breaks a complex curve into a sum of simple sine and cosine curves

Fraunhofer lines   dark lines that arise due to absorption of sunlight by components of the atmospheres of the Earth or the Sun

free radical   a substance, usually a short-lived intermediate, having an unshared electron

frontier orbital   highest energy occupied or lowest energy unoccupied orbital

fullerene   general description of a molecule related to buckyball (C_{60})

gamma [γ] ray   very high energy radiation from radioactive objects

Gibbs free energy   given by $G = H - TS$; a measure of the spontaneity of a chemical process

glycolysis   the anaerobic stage of the breakdown of a saccharide such as glucose

Gram-negative bacteria   species with low polysaccharide content in the cell wall that give a pink stain in the Gram dye test

Gram-positive bacteria   species with high polysaccharide content in the cell wall that give a purple stain in the Gram dye test

greenhouse effect   caused by gases (e.g., CO_2) that are transparent to ultraviolet light from the Sun but absorb infrared radiation (heat) reflected by the Earth

half-life   the period of time for a substance disappearing via first-order reaction (such as radioactive decay) to reduce to half of its original concentration

highest occupied molecular orbital (HOMO)   the highest energy orbital containing electrons

hormone   a biological substance secreted at one site producing a biological effect at a remote site in the same organism

hot fusion   a technique in which a neutron-rich medium-sized nucleus is fired at a neutron-rich heavy nucleus to form a neutron-rich, stabilized superheavy element

Hund's rules   the order and nature of filling atomic or molecular orbitals

hybridization   linear combination of atomic orbitals to optimize bonding geometries

hydrocarbon   a molecule consisting of carbon and hydrogen only

hydrogen bond   a relatively weak, yet significant attraction in which a hydrogen atom is shared between two electronegative atoms such as oxygen and nitrogen

hydrophilic   manifesting a high affinity for water

hydrophobic   manifesting a low affinity for water

in vitro   in glass, that is, in an artificial laboratory environment

in vivo   in a living organism

inert gas   elements in Group 8A, such as neon, also referred to as noble or rare gases

infrared spectrum   absorption of infrared radiation versus wavelength corresponding to excitation of bond vibrations and rotations

ion   a charged atom that either lacks some electrons or has excess electrons

ionic bond   formed between atoms in which one has transferred its electron(s) to the other

ionization potential (IP)   energy required to pull an electron from an atom, molecule, or ion

island of stability   an anticipated range of atomic numbers and atomic weights of stable superheavy elements

isobaric   constant pressure

isomer   a molecule having the same formula as another molecule but a different arrangement of atoms

isomerization   a chemical conversion of one isomer to another

isotactic   in a polymerization forming chiral centers, all new centers have the same absolute configuration

isothermal   no change in temperature

isotope   the same element but differing in atomic mass (number of neutrons)

Jahn-Teller effect   an energy-lowering distortion from symmetric molecular geometry

Kelvin (K)   the scale of absolute temperature where °C = K - 273.2

kinetics   studies of the rates of reactions and how they pertain to reaction mechanisms

lanthanide   one of 14 metals starting with cerium (58) and ending with lutetium (71) which correspond to filling 4f atomic orbitals

Le Chatelier's principle   a system at equilibrium will respond to a change so as to restore equilibrium

lead compound   a newly discovered drug molecule in which a new structural feature is introduced that can be tested with subsequent related molecules

leaving group   an atom or group of atoms displaced in a chemical reaction

levorotatory (*l* ot [-]   counterclockwise rotation of plane-polarized light

Lewis acid   an electron pair acceptor

Lewis base   an electron pair donor

Lewis (Lewis-Langmuir) dot structure   a simple representation of atoms emphasizing the number of valence electrons and the octet rule

ligand   an ion or molecule that coordinates to a metal ion to form a complex

ligand field theory   combined molecular orbital and crystal field theory to account for the geometry, bonding, and properties of transition metal complexes

ligase   see deoxyribonucleic acid ligase

lipid   water insoluble natural compounds including fats such as triglycerides, steroids, and terpenes

lipophile   a substance having high affinity for lipids, fats, and oils

lowest unoccupied molecular orbital (LUMO)   lowest energy vacant molecular orbital

Lyman series   the lines from the ultraviolet spectrum of the hydrogen atom

macrocyclic   a large ring system (perhaps 12-membered and higher)

macromolecular   consisting of very large molecules, usually polymeric in nature

MALDI (matrix-assisted laser desorption ionization)   a method for introducing huge molecules in their ionic form into the gas phase prior to mass spectrometry

materials science   the study of polymers, ceramics, and related matter that may be fabricated to form objects or serve other useful purposes

micelle   amphiphilic molecules (perhaps hundreds) combined to form colloidal particles commonly in water with hydrophilic exteriors and hydrophobic interiors

micron   (micrometer; μm) 10^{-6} meter (3.94×10^{-5} in)

microsecond 10^{-6} second

mitochondrion   cell organelle that produces energy

mole   chemical unit corresponding to the atomic or molecular weight in grams and also corresponding equivalently to Avogadro's number of units (atoms or molecules)

molecule   smallest unit of a chemical compound

molecular orbital (MO) theory   based upon linear combination of atomic orbitals

monolayer   a surface that is one molecule thick

monomer   the basic building block of a polymer

multiple proportions law   for two or more binary compounds of the same elements, the ratio of an element in one compound to the other is a simple whole number

nanometer   (nm) 10^{-9} meter (3.94×10^{-8} in; 10 A)

nanosecond 10^{-9} second

nanotechnology   pertains to the design of functional units of nanometer dimensions

neutron   neutral subatomic particle in the nucleus, roughly equal to the mass of the proton

noble gas   see inert gas

nuclear fission   neutron-induced splitting of an unstable nucleus

nuclear fusion   joining of very light nuclei induced by enormous energy

nuclear magnetic resonance (NMR)   a spectroscopic method based upon absorption of radiofrequency radiation by specific nuclei in molecules in a high magnetic field

nucleic acid   an oligomer or polymer of nucleotides forming DNA or RNA

nucleophile   a chemical species that has high affinity for a nucleus; in practice high affinity for a region of partial electron depletion

nucleotide   the building block of nucleic acids

nucleus   the dense, miniscule center of an atom containing protons, neutrons, and more than 99.9 percent of the mass of matter

octet rule   the tendency for main group elements to complete a valence shell of eight electrons

oligonucleotide   a molecule built from many nucleotide units

orbital   the spatial distribution of an electron of allowed energy value

organic metal   an organic substance with the conductivity and other properties of a metal

oxidation   loss of electrons; roughly equivalent in some instances to reaction with oxygen or loss of hydrogen

oxidation state   a positive or negative whole number assigned to an element in a molecule or ion that may correspond to its formal charge

paramagnetic   describes a substance with unpaired electrons that is attracted to a magnetic field

Paschen series   the lines from the infrared spectrum of the hydrogen atom

Pauli exclusion principle   rule that states that no two electrons in an atom can have the same values for all four quantum numbers (n, l, m, and s)

PCR (polymerase chain reaction)   a technique for amplifying trace samples of DNA

peptide   a molecule composed of amino acids but generally smaller than a protein

periodic table   the organization of the chemical elements by atomic number and family

pH   a measure of acidity ($pH = - \log_{10} [H^+$ concentration])

pheromone   a chemical released by an organism producing a change in behavior in another organism of the same or different species

picosecond (ps) 10^{-12} second

polar (polarity)   a measure of unequal sharing of electrons in covalent bonds

polymer   a giant molecule composed of numerous units called monomers

primary structure   (protein) the amino acid sequence of a protein molecule

prochiral   refers to an achiral atomic center that becomes chiral upon reaction

prostaglandin   "secondary messenger" molecules that induce dramatic physiological changes from trace quantities

protein   a macromolecule comprised of amino acid building blocks

protium   the lightest, most abundant isotope of hydrogen (^1H)

proton   positively charged subatomic particle in the nucleus, roughly equal in mass to the neutron

quantum dot   a crystal of a semiconductor of nanometer dimension whose color reflects the number of its component atoms

quantum numbers   allowed values for n, l, m, and s

quarternary structure   (protein) the spatial organization of more than one protein chain in a protein complex

racemate (racemic mixture modification)   equimolar mixture of enantiomers

radical   old expression for a unit of atoms that remains together in chemical reactions

radioactive   describing substances having unstable nuclei that emit radiation as they disintegrate

rare earth   see lanthanide

rare gas   see inert gas

reaction mechanism   a step-by-step description at the molecular level of a chemical change

reaction surface   a plot in three dimensions of the energy of a chemical reaction as a function of changes in molecular geometry and structure

recombinant DNA   a new deoxyribonucleic acid formed from two or more distinct DNA molecules

REDOX   shorthand for oxidation-reduction

reduction   gaining of electrons; roughly equivalent in some cases to loss of oxygen or addition of hydrogen

resonance   a theory in which molecules having many equivalent valence bond structures are stabilized

respiration   metabolism involving oxygen and oxidation

restriction endonuclease   an enzyme that can cut DNA at specific sites

ribonucleic acid (RNA)   a nucleic acid having a variety of functions in living organisms

ribosome   cell organelle in which protein synthesis occurs

ribozyme   RNA that exhibits enzyme activity

ring strain   a destabilizing increase in energy caused by very small (or very large) bond angles in certain molecular ring systems

scanning tunneling microscope (STM)   a technique for mapping atoms on a surface

secondary structure   (protein) the conformational motif (e.g., α-helix) of a protein chain

singlet the spin state of a chemical species in which all electrons are paired and there is no net spin

spectroscope optical instrument for studying the emission spectra of chemical elements

steady state assumption the rate of reaction to form an unstable chemical intermediate is virtually equal to its rate of disappearance; therefore its concentration is negligible

stereochemistry the study of the three-dimensional structures of molecules

stereogenic center see chiral center

stereoisomer an isomer differing only in the arrangement of atoms in space

steric effect usually repulsive effect caused by crowding of atoms or groups of atoms

steroid natural substances with a system of four carbocyclic rings typified by cholesterol

stoichiometry pertaining to the precise ratios of substances reacting with each other

strain any effect that raises the energy of a molecule through unusual bond angles, repulsive and unavoidable steric effects, or other unusual structural features

sulfa drugs family of antibiotics developed during the 1930s derived from aromatic sulfonamides

superconductor a material that loses all resistivity (usually near 0 K)

supercritical fluid (SCF) a state in which a liquid is at a high enough temperature such that no pressure can condense it to a liquid

supramolecular chemistry based upon noncovalent complexes between two or more molecules

syndiotactic in polymerization forming chiral centers, an alternation between S and R configurations at the new chiral centers

terpene a natural hydrocarbon composed of two or more isoprene (C_5H_8) units

tertiary structure (protein) refers to the three-dimensional folding of a protein chain

thermodynamics study of the free energies, enthalpies, and entropies of chemical species

TOF (time of flight) a type of mass spectrometer that separates low mass ions from high mass ions by the time they require to migrate down a straight path

transactinides elements beyond lawrencium (103)

transition metals elements in the B families of the periodic table filling 3d, 4d, 5d, and even 6d orbitals

transition state a maximum on a two-dimensional reaction coordinate or the saddle point on a three-dimensional reaction point corresponding to an activated complex

transuranium element   element higher in atomic number than uranium (92)

triplet   the spin state of a chemical species having two unpaired electrons of parallel spin

tritium   the heaviest isotope of hydrogen (^{3}H)

tunneling   a quantum mechanics phenomenon whereby an atomic or subatomic particle passes between two states separated by an energy barrier without climbing the barrier

ultracentrifuge   apparatus that can attain forces that are hundreds of thousands of times the force of gravity in order to separate macromolecules and various colloidal particles

ultramicroscope   an apparatus capable of viewing Brownian motion

ultraviolet-visible spectrum   absorption of ultraviolet or visible radiation versus wavelength corresponding to excitation of electrons

unit cell   the fundamental repeating unit (like that in a wallpaper pattern) in a crystal

unsaturation   each double bond or ring corresponds to a unit of unsaturation and a triple bond corresponds to two such units

valence   the capacity of an element to combine with other elements, which can be equated to the number of hydrogen atoms it can combine with

valence bond (VB) theory   structures and stabilities of molecules are related to stable Lewis structures and, where relevant, relevant resonance contributors

valence shell electron pair repulsion (VSEPR) theory   electron pairs (bonding and nonbonding) around a central atom are arranged to achieve maximum mutual separation

van der Waals forces   weak attraction between molecules originating in the mutual correlation of the motions of their electrons

viscosity   the internal resistance of a liquid caused by molecular attractions

vitamin   organic substances present in small quantities in food required to sustain health

weakly coordinating anion (WCA)   a species that resists losing an electron to a highly reactive cation and acts as if it is totally unassociated with that cation

Werner complex   coordination compound formed between a transition metal ion and ligands

Woodward-Hoffmann rules   see conservation of orbital symmetry

X-rays   highly penetrating electromagnetic radiation produced through bombardment of a target (usually heavy metals) with high energy electrons in a vacuum tube

X-ray crystallography   a diffraction technique employed to study the distances between atoms or ions in crystalline materials

zeolite   a mineral typically composed of silicon, aluminum, oxygen, and metals that is characterized by the presence of uniform pores of molecular scale

Further Resources

Books and Other Reading

American Chemical Society. Washington, D.C. *Chemistry. 125 Years American Chemical Society*, 2001. A booklet focusing on chemistry as science and a career in the 20th century.

———. Washington, D.C. *Luminaries of the Chemical Sciences*, 2002. Illustrated biographical sketches of 54 famous 20th century chemists.

———. Washington, D.C. *The Pharmaceutical Century. Ten Decades of Drug Discovery*, 2000. A thick booklet examining advances in biochemistry, medicinal chemistry, and the development of new drugs during each decade of the 20th century.

Ball, Philip, *Elegant Solutions. Ten Beautiful Experiments in Chemistry*. Cambridge: The Royal Society of Chemistry, 2005. Ten highly accessible chapters each covering an important discovery (or related discoveries) in chemistry.

Berson, Jerome A., *Chemical Creativity. Ideas from the Work of Woodward, Hückel, Meerwein, and Others*. Weinheim: Wiley-VCH, 1999. This is a work about ideas as much as about selected historical discoveries in organic chemistry.

Bowden, Mary Ellen, *Chemical Achievers. The Human Face of the Chemical Sciences*. Philadelphia: Chemical Heritage Foundation, 1997. Biographical sketches of over 80 prominent chemists, many from the chemical industry during the 20th century.

———, Amy Beth Crow, and Tracy Sullivan, *Pharmaceutical Achievers. The Human Face of Pharmaceutical Research*. Philadelphia: Chemical Heritage Press, 2003. Advances during the 20th century in identification, purification, and synthesis of diverse drugs and vitamins, with nearly 90 pictorial biographical sketches.

Breslow, Ronald, *Chemistry Today and Tomorrow: The Central, Useful, and Creative Science*. Washington, D.C. and Sudbury, MA: American Chemical Society and Jones and Bartlett, 1997. Presentation of what chemistry is, what chemists do, and how the field and its practitioners affect the society.

Brock, William H., *The Norton History of Chemistry.* New York and London: W. W. Norton & Co., 1993. This book provides coverage from ancient times through the 1980s with particular strengths in organic chemistry.

Chemical & Engineering News, 75th Anniversary Special Issue, Vol. 76: January 12, 1998. This issue summarizes 75 years of research and industrial progress and recognizes 75 top contributors to the chemical enterprise between 1923 and 1998.

————. *It's Elemental: The Periodic Table. Celebrating C&EN's 80th Anniversary Special Issue,* Vol. 81: September 8, 2003. Each element listed in atomic number order has its history and properties described by experts.

————. *Special Issue: Top Pharmaceuticals from Aspirin to Viagra and More.* Vol. 83: June 20, 2005. This issue profiles nearly 50 modern drugs (or classes of drugs) that impact modern society.

Chemical Heritage. The newsmagazine of the Chemical Heritage Foundation, 315 Chestnut Street, Philadelphia, PA 19106. Information available online. URL: www.chemheritage.org. Accessed on February 14, 2006. This magazine is published four times per year and includes accessible articles on chemistry of the 20th century and earlier.

ChemMatters, a magazine for high school students and teachers published four times per year by the American Chemical Society, Washington, D.C. Information available online. URL: www.chemistry.org. Accessed on February 14, 2006.

Emsley, John. *Molecules at an Exhibition: Portraits of Intriguing Materials in Everyday Life.* New York: Oxford University Press, 1998. The "hidden lives" of some "everyday" molecules.

Greenberg, Arthur. *From Alchemy to Chemistry in Picture and Story.* Hoboken: John Wiley & Sons, 2007. An expanded pictorial tour through the history of chemistry to modern times including nanotechnology and femtochemistry.

Hall, Nina. *The New Chemistry.* Cambridge: Cambridge University Press, 2000. This is an extremely useful and accessible book organized in seventeen chapters and reviewing research during the final three decades of the 20th century.

Hargittai, István. *Candid Science: Conversations with Famous Chemists.* London: Imperial College Press, 2000. Interviews of world-famous chemists by a well-regarded structural chemist.

Hoffmann, Roald, and Vivian Torrence. *Chemistry Imagined. Reflections on Science.* Washington, D.C.: Smithsonian Institution Press, 1993. A collaboration between Nobel laureate Hoffmann and artist Torrence visualizing chemical concepts.

Hoffmann, Roald. *The Same and Not the Same.* New York: Columbia University Press, 1995. A book for a general readership examining dualities in chemistry.

Ihde, Aaron J. *The Development of Modern Chemistry.* New York: Harper & Row, 1964. This book is a classic, somewhat stronger in organic chemistry, but covers only slightly past the mid-20th century.

Journal of Chemical Education. Published by American Chemical Society, Washington, D.C. Information available online. URL: http://jchemed. chem.wis.edu. Accessed on February 14, 2006. This is a monthly journal of interest to high school and college-level teachers and students.

Keinan, Ehud, and Israel Schneider, eds. *Chemistry for the 21st Century.* Weinheim: Wiley-VCH, 2001. This book is comprised of a series of essays, suited for scientists, on areas of research anticipated to be important during the 21st century.

Lagowski, Joseph J., ed. *Chemistry: Foundations and Applications.* New York: Macmillan Reference USA, 2004. This is a four-volume reference set that includes 509 articles arranged alphabetically.

Laidler, Keith J. *The World of Physical Chemistry.* Oxford: Oxford University Press, 1993. This is a very accessible book that provides good coverage in the 20th century.

Partington, James R. *A History of Chemistry.* Vol. 4: London: MacMillan Ltd., 1964. This fourth and final volume of the definitive work on chemical history emphasizes physical chemistry, is devoted mostly to the 19th century, and covers the first half of the 20th century.

Rayner-Canham, Marelene, and Geoffrey Rayner-Canham. *Women in Chemistry: Their Changing Roles from Alchemical Times to the Mid-Twentieth Century.* Washington, D.C. and Philadelphia: American Chemical Society and the Chemical Heritage Foundation, 1998. Biographical sketches classified according to chemical specialization.

Reinhardt, Carsten, ed. *Chemical Sciences in the 20th Century.* Weinheim: Wiley-VCH, 2000. This book has chemists as its primary audience and includes essays that are crosscutting in their chronological integration and interdisciplinary nature.

Sacks, Oliver. *Uncle Tungsten: Memories of a Chemical Boyhood.* New York: Alfred A. Knopf, 2001. Autobiographical memoir by the famous neurologist about his life-long love affair with the chemical elements.

Scerri, Eric R. *The Periodic Table: Its Story and its Significance.* New York: Oxford University Press, 2007. This is an excellent and accessible book by a respected historian and philosopher of chemistry.

Seeman, Jeffrey I. *Profiles, Pathways and Dreams Series.* Washington, D.C.: American Chemical Society, 1991–2000. This series includes about 20 autobiographical memoires of 20th century chemists.

Stanitski, Conrad L., Lucy Pryde Eubanks, Catherine H. Middlecamp, and Norbert J. Pienta, *Chemistry in Context: Applying Chemistry to Society* (An American Chemical Society Project), 4th ed. Boston: McGraw-Hill, 2003. This book includes twelve chapters on topics of current societal interest and connects them with fundamental chemistry.

Tarbell, Dean Stanley, and Ann Tracy Tarbell, *Essays on the History of Organic Chemistry in the United States, 1875–1955.* Nashville: Folio Publishers, 1986. Coverage of a period during which the United States replaced Germany as the world center of organic chemistry.

Web Sites

American Chemical Society, 1155 Sixteenth St. NW, Washington, D.C. 20036. Information available online. URL: www.chemistry.org. Accessed on February 14, 2006. The largest chemical society in the world with many educational resources online.

Chemical Abstracts Service, Columbus, Ohio. Available online. URL: www.cas.org. Accessed on February 15, 2006. This site provides guidance on the use of *Chemical Abstracts* and furnishes historical data on the number of abstracts, papers and compounds including the most current figures.

Chemical Heritage Foundation, 315 Chestnut Street, Philadelphia, Pa. 19106. Available online. URL: www.chemheritage.org. Accessed on February 14, 2006. This organization is open for visitors, scholars, and class trips and includes museum pieces and other exhibits of the history of chemistry.

Chemical Heritage Foundation, Philadelphia. Available online. URL: www.chemheritage.org/exhibits/ex-oral-results-all.asp. Accessed on February 15, 2006. Oral interview series of over 250 famous chemists starting in 1979.

Chemical Institute of Canada, 550-130 Slater St., Ottawa ON K1P 6E2, Canada. Available online. URL: www.chemeng.ca. Accessed on February 14, 2006. A site combining chemists, chemical engineers, and chemical technicians in Canada and a rich educational resource.

National Historical Chemical Landmarks. Available online. URL: www.chemistry.org/landmarks. Accessed on February 14, 2006. There are now over 50 historical chemical landmarks that may be visited. This Web site provides details useful for class and vacation trips.

National Science Teachers Association, 1840 Wilson Blvd., Alexandria, VA 22201. Available online. URL: www.nsta.org. Accessed on February 14, 2006. Educational resources include a huge list of science education Web sites.

Nobel Foundation, The Official site of the Nobel Foundation. Available online. URL: http://nobelprize.org/nobel_prizes/chemistry/laureates/ (for Nobel Prizes in chemistry). Accessed on February 15, 2006. This extraordinarily valuable resource includes biographies and all Nobel Prize lectures as well as references to the printed versions of this material.

Royal Society of Chemistry, Milton Road, Cambridge CB4 0WF, United Kingdom. Available online. URL: www.rsc.org. Accessed on February 14, 2006. Educational resources may be accessed online.

▶▶ Index